25/24

C Hale Sipe

THE INDIAN CHIEFS
OF PENNSYLVANIA

———————— OR ————————

A Story of the Part Played by the American Indian in the History of Pennsylvania, Based Primarily on the Pennsylvania Archives and Colonial Records, and Built Around the Outstanding Chiefs

By

C. HALE SIPE, A.B.

of the Pittsburgh and Butler Bars,
Member of the Historical Society of Pennsylvania,
Historical Society of Western Pennsylvania;
Author of "Mount Vernon and the Washington Family",
and "A History of Butler County".

With Introduction by
DR. GEORGE P. DONEHOO

Former Secretary of the Pennsylvania Historical Commission and
State Librarian; Collaborator of the "Handbook of American Indians",
and Author of "Pennsylvania—A History".

WENNAWOODS PUBLISHING
Lewisburg, Pennsylvania
1999

Originally published 1927, Butler, PA
Reprinted 1994, 1995, Lewisburg. PA
First paperback printing 1997, Lewisburg, PA
Second paperback printing 1998, Lewisburg, PA
Third paperback printing 1999, Lewisburg, PA
© Copyright Wennawoods Publishing

Please direct all correspondence and book orders to:
WENNAWOODS PUBLISHING
RR 2 BOX 529C - GOODMAN ROAD
LEWISBURG, PENNSYLVANIA 17837
(800) 796-1702
www.wennawoods.com

Library of Congress Catalog Card Number 95-75966
ISBN: 1-889037-00-1 (cloth)
ISBN: 1-889037-08-7 (paper)

Other Books Published by
WENNAWOODS PUBLISHING
Indian Wars of Pennsylvania (1927)
by C. Hale Sipe
Indian Villages and Place Names in Pennsylvania (1928)
by George P. Donehoo
The Wilderness trail, Volumes 1 & 2 (1911)
by Charles A Hanns
Early History of Western Pennsylvania (1846)
by I. D. Rupp
Conrad Weiser, Friend of Colonist & Mohawk (1945)
by Paul A. W. Wallace
Loundon's Indian Narratives, Volume 1 & 2 bound as one (1888)
by Archbald Loundon
Sargent Book
Early Western Journals (1748-1765)
by Reuben Gold Thwaites

Printed in the United States of America

WHERE HAVE THEY GONE?

Are you like me interested in the Indian history of our state? Where did they live? Where did they come from? How long were they here? What did they do? Where did they go? We knew there were many other people like us who were asking those same questions without any idea of where to go for the answers.

We always knew the prominent place that Pennsylvania played in early American history, but little did we know the importance the American Indian played in shaping both Pennsylvania and American history.   With those thoughts in mind, we searched for legitimate sources to answer questions about the part the American Indian played in Pennsylvania history, given the little attention historians have traditionally granted them.   Their existence is fact and knowledge of their history is critical to understanding the comprehensive history of our country.

In our search for the roots of those lonely Indian braves, unbelievably, we found that no state is richer in Indian names or Indian history than Pennsylvania. And within or near its boundaries, most of the early history of our nation was formed. With Pennsylvania as keystone of the colonies and gateway to the west, it is indeed appropriate to call the Indian history of Pennsylvania the Indian history of the Eastern Frontier. Little did we know that the answers to our questions were buried deep within the hallowed halls of our Pennsylvania research libraries in the form of three long forgotten books: "The Indian Chiefs of Pennsylvania," "The Indian Wars of Pennsylvania," and "A History of the Indian Villages and Place Names in Pennsylvania." Books that were originally published over 70 years ago, forgotten by generations, and revived by us to give the American Indian his rightful place in our history.

So this year as you read classic Pennsylvania Indian history, remember that lonesome Indian brave, before his campfire on a cold and windy night, high a top a lonely river ridge giving thanks to his god. Remember, this was his land. It is indeed hallowed ground! He still lives here in spirit We will help you remember him forever. To his memory these books are dedicated!

Ron Wenning
Wennawoods Publishing 1998

To the Memory of his Sainted Mother,
from Whom he in Inherited a Love
for the History of Pennsylvania,
this Book is Reverently
Dedicated by
The Author

INTRODUCTION

By Dr. George P. Donehoo,
Former State Librarian of Pennsylvania

The early Indian history of Pennsylvania is, in many respects, of more interest and importance in the development of Anglo-Saxon civilization and settlement on the continent, than that of any other section of the United States.

The real importance of this period in the history of Pennsylvania is little realized by students of history, because it has been given but scant attention by historical writers who have dealt with the larger field of the United States.

To a very large extent, the entire Indian "problem" of the Colonies was worked out within the boundaries of Pennsylvania, or by Pennsylvanians outside of these boundaries. The Indian Councils held in New York, Maryland, Virginia, and later in Ohio, were, to a marked degree, dominated by Pennsylvania influence. The most influential Indian diplomats and chiefs, such as Canassatego, Tanacharison, Scarouady, Shikellamy and Peter Chartier, were directly connected with the policy of the Provincial Council, and the influence of such men as William Penn, Richard Peters, Conrad Weiser, George Croghan in the field of Indian Affairs, was almost unbounded. It may be safely said that the entire "Indian problem" of the Colonies, at the most critical period in American history, had to be solved by Pennsylvanians. With the exception of Sir William Johnson, of New York, all of the men who were prominent during this period were Pennsylvanians. It would be possible to carry this influence far beyond the limits of this period in the work and influence of such men as Daniel Boone, Sam Huston, George R. Clark and many others.

From the outbreak of the French and Indian War, in 1755, during the long years of Border Wars and the American Revolution, to the Treaty of Greenville, made by General Anthony Wayne, the "Indian problem" was practically in the hands of Pennsylvanians. The physical reason for this was because Pennsylvania was the Gateway to Ohio, Indiana and the West, as well as to Kentucky and the South. The Ohio river, having its headwaters in Pennsylvania, was the great trail to the Mississippi and to the French possessions in Louisiana. The vast territory through which this great stream flowed was more easily reached from Pennsylvania than from any of the other Colonies, and, notwithstanding the claims of New England historians, this great stream became the highway over which the Pennsylvania influence and not that of New England, reached to the uttermost limits of the Continent, founding new settlements and then moulding the institutions wherever it went.

A knowledge of this early Indian period in the history of Pennsylvania is essential to a right understanding of the history of Ohio, Indiana, Kentucky, Texas, as well as to a comprehensive understanding of the history of the Nation. Nearly all of the early expeditions into the Indian country beyond the Ohio, as well as nearly all of the first companies of settlers in Ohio, Indiana and far distant Texas, were made up of Pennsylvanians. The expeditions of Colonel William Crawford, General Arthur St. Clair, General George R. Clark, General Anthony Wayne and many others of lesser fame were made up chiefly, if not entirely, of Pennsylvanians.

The migration of the Lenape, or Delaware, from the Atlantic to the Susquehanna and then to the Ohio, taking with it the warlike and powerful Shawnee, had a far reaching influence in the development of civilization of the Continent. These two dominant tribes carried after them the great train of Indian traders from Pennsylvania, who roamed as far northward as Detroit and as far westward as the Mississippi. The presence of these traders in the territory claimed by France was the underlying cause of the French and Indian War, which was the first in the series of events resulting in the birth of the United States. With all of these events which were taking place, the migration of the Indians, the Indian trade, the rivalry between France and Great Britain, the building of the French forts, and then the long fight for possession of the Continent, Pennsylvania was directly related.

The period of Border Wars in Pennsylvania is one of the most thrilling and bloody chapters in American history. Pennsylvania suffered more than did any of the other Colonies during this long period stretching from 1755 to 1795. The massacre at Penn's Creek, 1755, marks its actual commencement and the Treaty at Greenville, in 1795, marks its ending. During this period of forty years, Pennsylvania was engaged in an unbroken war with the Indians, and during that time the soil of the Province and then of the State was literally drenched with blood. Years after a new Nation had been born, and after peace had come to the settlements east of the Alleghenies, the settlers on the Ohio were still fighting to hold what they possessed, and it was not until General Anthony Wayne finally conquered the Indians, that peace came to the harried frontiers of Pennsylvania.

The author of this introductory note has long been a student of this vital and romantic period of Pennsylvania history. For many years he has made the period of Indian occupation and the conflict of the Indian with the white man a special field of investigation. He feels that the work, so well done by Mr. Sipe, is a most valuable contribution to the written history of this period. When Mr. Sipe had written a part of his history of "The Indian Chiefs of Pennsylvania", he wrote to the author of this introduction saying that if its publication in book form would in any way interfere with anything which he had in mind, he would stop work. The author replied to this very gracious letter, urging Mr. Sipe to go on with his work and to publish it. After having read the entire manuscript which Mr. Sipe has prepared with infinite care, the writer is glad that he has such a worthy fellow-worker in the field of Indian history of Pennsylvania. His methods have been truly scientific and scholarly, and, as a result the book is accurate and reveals an immense amount of careful research for all of the material used.

The book is a real contribution to the vitally important and thrillingly romantic period of the history of Pennsylvania.

GEORGE P. DONEHOO.

Principal Sources Utilized in the Preparation of this Work

Archives of Pennsylvania.

Colonial Records of Pennsylvania.

Egle's History of Pennsylvania.

Gordon's History of Pennsylvania.

Day's Historical Collections.

Frontier Forts of Pennsylvania.

Pennypacker's Pennsylvania, the Keystone.

Loudon's Indian Narratives.

Rupp's County Histories.

Magazines of the Historical Society of Pennsylvania.

Egle's Notes and Queries.

Miner's History of Wyoming.

Jenkin's Pennsylvania, Colonial and Federal.

Lossing's Field Book of the Revolution.

On the Frontier with Colonel Antes.

Meginness' Otzinachson.

Linn's Annals of Buffalo Valley.

Hassler's Old Westmoreland.

Fisher's Making of Pennsylvania.

McClure's Old Time Notes.

Parkman's Works.

Jones' Juniata Valley.

Hanna's Wilderness Trail.

March's History of Pennsylvania.

Smith's History of Armstrong County.

Veech's Monongahela of Old.

McKnight's Pioneer History of Northwestern Pennsylvania.

Conover's Journal of the Military Expedition of Major-General Sullivan against the Six Nations of New York in 1779.

Craig's The Olden Time.

Darlington's Fort Pitt and Letters from the Frontier.

Darlington's Christopher Gist's Journals.

Hodge's Handbook of American Indians.

Hulbert's Historic Highways of America.

Rupp's Early History of Western Pennsylvania and the West.

Thwaites' Early Western Travels.

Thwaites' Documentary History of Lord Dunmore's War.

Walton's Conrad Weiser and the Indian Policy of Colonial Pennsylvania.

Withers' Chronicles of Border Warfare.

Craig's History of Pittsburgh.

Cort's Henry Bouquet.

Keith's Chronicles of Pennsylvania.

Boucher's History of Westmoreland County.

Albert's History of Westmoreland County.

Donehoo's Pennsylvania—A History.

DeSchweinitz's Life of David Zeisberger.

Espenshade's Pennsylvania Place Names.

Heckewelder's Works.

Mann's Life of Henry Melchior Muhlenberg.

Father Lambing's Works.

Butterfield's Washington-Irvine Correspondence.

Washington's Journal.

Celeron's Journal.

Colden's History of the Five Nations.

Volwiler's George Croghan.

Johnson's Swedish Settlements on the Delaware.

Loskiel's History of the Mission of the United Brethren Among the Indians of North America.

Patterson's History of the Backwoods.

Doddridge's Settlement and Indian Wars of Virginia and Pennsylvania.

Godcharles' Daily Stories of Pennsylvania.

Sawvel's Logan, the Mingo.

And Others.

CONTENTS

CHAPTER I.

A View of the Indian Tribes Inhabiting Pennsylvania

WHEN the historic curtain first rises on the region embraced within the bounds of Pennsylvania, we find its remote and awful solitudes inhabited by a number of Indian tribes which it is the purpose of the first two chapters of this book briefly to describe. Here, along the streams and in the mountain valleys of our state, they had lived for generations lives full of romance, of love, of rivalry, of hatred, of tragedy. They roamed the hills and vales; they pursued the deer amid the forests; they paddled their bark canoes along the streams; they built their council-fires on the shore; they warred; they worshipped the Master of Life, and from their dusky bosoms went up many a pure prayer to the Great Spirit. Thus, in the vast solitudes of nature, they had lived from remote ages, never dreaming that from afar would come a stronger race which would plant amid the wilderness the hamlet and the town, and cause cities to rise where the forest waved over the Red Man's home.

Go where we may, in Pennsylvania, we are put in remembrance of the great race that roamed the hills and vales of our state. Their council-fires have long since gone out on the shores of our rivers; they themselves have gone to the "Happy Hunting Ground"; but their names will linger on the mountains and streams of Pennsylvania to the end of time.

> *"Ye say they have all pass'd away,*
> *That noble race and brave,—*
> *That their light canoes have vanish'd*
> *From off the crested wave;*
> *That 'mid the forest where they roam'd*
> *There rings no hunter's shout:*
> *But their name is on your waters;*
> *Ye may not wash it out.*

"Ye say their cone-like cabins,
 That cluster'd o'er the vale,
Have disappear'd as wither'd leaves
 Before the autumn gale;
But their memory liveth on your hills,
 Their baptism on your shore,
Your everlasting rivers speak
 Their dialect of yore."

THE DELAWARES OR LENAPE

At the dawn of the historic period of Pennsylvania, we find the basin of the Delaware River inhabited by an Indian tribe called the Delawares, or Lenape. The English called them Delawares from the fact that, upon their arrival in this region, they found the council-fires of this tribe on the banks of the Delaware River. The French called them Loups, "wolves", a term probably first applied to the Mohicans, a kindred tribe, on the Hudson River in New York. However, in their own language, they were called Lenape, or Lenni-Lenape, meaning "real men", or "original men".

The Lenape belonged to the great Algonquin family—by far the greatest Indian family in North America, measured by the extent of territory occupied. This family surrounded on all sides the Iroquoian family, of which we shall hereafter speak, and extended from Labrador westward through Canada to the Rocky Mountains and southward to South Carolina. It also extended westward through the Mississippi Valley to the Rocky Mountains. The most important tribes of this family were the Mohican, Massachuset, Miami, Sac and Fox, Ojibwa, Blackfoot, Illinois, Shawnee, and Lenape; and among the great personages of the Algonquins were King Philip, Pocahontas, Pontiac, Tecumseh, and Tamenend, the last of whom made the historic treaty with William Penn described in Chapter V.

Traditional History of the Lenape

The early traditional history of the Lenape is contained in their national legend, the Walum Olum. According to this sacred tribal history, the Lenape, in long ages past, lived in the vast region west of the Mississippi. For some reason not known, they left their western home, and, after many years of wandering east-

ward, reached the Namaesi Sipu, or Mississippi, where they fell
in with the Mengwe, or Iroquois, who had likewise emigrated from
the distant West in search of a new home, and had arrived at this
river at a point somewhat higher up. The spies sent forward by
the Lenape for the purpose of reconnoitering, had discovered, before the arrival of the main body, that the region east of the
Mississippi was inhabited by a powerful nation called the
Talligewi, or Alligewi, whose domain reached eastward to the
Allegheny Mountains, which together with the beautiful Allegheny
River, are named for this ancient race. The Alligewi had many
large towns on the rivers of the Mississippi and Ohio valleys, and
had built innumerable mounds, fortifications and intrenchments,
hundreds of which still remain, and are called the works of the
"Mound Builders". Says Schoolcraft: "The banks of the Allegheny were, in ancient times, occupied by an important tribe, now
unknown, who preceded the Delawares and Iroquois. They were
called Alleghans (Alligewi) by Colden." It is related that the
Alligewi were tall and stout, and that there were giants among
them.

When the Lenape arrived at the Mississippi, they sent a message to the Alligewi requesting that they be permitted to settle
among them. This request was refused, but the Lenape obtained
permission to pass through the territory of the Alligewi and seek
a settlement farther to the eastward. They accordingly began to
cross the Mississippi; but the Alligewi, seeing that their numbers
were vastly greater than they had supposed, made a furious attack
upon those who had crossed, and threatened the whole tribe with
destruction, if they dared to persist in crossing to the eastern side
of the river.

Angered by the treachery of the Alligewi and not being prepared for conflict, the Lenape consulted together as to whether
they should make a trial of strength, and were convinced that the
enemy were too powerful for them. Then the Mengwe, who had
hitherto been spectators from a distance, offered to join the Lenape,
on condition that, after conquering the Alligewi, they should be
entitled to share in the fruits of the conquest.

Having united their forces, the Lenape and the Mengwe declared war against the Alligewi, and started on their onward
march eastward across the continent, gradually driving out the
Alligewi, who fled down the Mississippi Valley never to return.
This conquest lasted many years, during which the Lenape lost
great numbers of their best warriors, while the Mengwe would

always lag back in the rear leaving them to bear the brunt of battle. At the end, the conquerors divided the possessions of the defeated race; the Mengwe taking the country in the vicinity of the Great Lakes and their tributary streams, and the Lenape taking the land to the south. There has been much conjecture as to who the ancient Alligewi were, some historians believing them to have been the "Mound Builders," but most modern authorities believe them to have been identical with the Cherokees.

For a long period, possibly many centuries, according to the Walum Olum, the Mengwe and Lenape resided peacefully in this country, and increased rapidly in population. Some of their hunters and warriors crossed the Allegheny Mountains, and, arriving at the streams flowing eastward, followed them to the Susquehanna River, and this stream to the ocean. Other enterprising pathfinders penetrated the wilderness to the Delaware River, and exploring still eastward, arrived at the Hudson. Some of these explorers returned to their nation and reported the discoveries they had made, describing the country as abounding in game and the streams as having an abundance of water-fowl and fish, with no enemy to be dreaded.

The Lenape considered these discoveries as fortunate for them, and believed the newly found region to be the country destined for them by the Great Spirit as their permanent abode. Consequently they began to migrate thither, settling on the four great rivers,—the Susquehanna, the Potomac, the Delaware, and the Hudson. The Walum Olum states, however, that not all of the Lenape reached the eastern part of the United States, many of them having remained behind to assist a great body of their people who had not crossed the Mississippi, but had retreated into the interior of the country on the other side, on being informed of the treacherous attack of the Alligewi upon those who had attempted to cross this stream. It is further stated that another part of the Lenape remained near the eastern bank of the Mississippi.

According to this traditional history, therefore, the Lenape nation finally became divided into three separate bodies; the part that had not crossed the Mississippi; the part that remained near the eastern bank of the Mississippi; and the part that settled on the four great eastern rivers above named.

That branch of the Delawares which settled in the eastern part of the country divided into three divisions, or clans,—the Munsee, (later corrupted to Monsey), the Unami, and the Unalachtigo. These were called the Wolf, the Turtle, and the Turkey clans respectively, from their respective animal types of totems. With these creatures which they had adopted as their symbols, they believed themselves connected by a mystic and powerful tie.

The Munsee (Wolf Clan), at the dawn of the historic period, were living in the mountain country, from about the mouth of the Lehigh River northward into New York and New Jersey, embracing the territory between the Blue or Kittatinny Mountains and the sources of the Susquehanna and Delaware rivers. A part of the tribe, also, dwelt on the Susquehanna, and still another part had a village and peach orchard near Nazareth in Northampton County, in the triangle between the Delaware and Lehigh. However, their chief village was Minisink, in Sussex County, New Jersey. The Munsee were the most warlike of the Delawares; they took a prominent part in the Indian wars of Colonial Pennsylvania. Being defrauded out of their lands by the notorious "Walking Purchase" of 1737, which obliged them to move, first to the Susquehanna and then to the Ohio, they became the bitter enemies of the white man, and drenched the frontier settlements with the blood of the pioneers. The Munsee have frequently been considered a separate tribe, inasmuch as they differed greatly from the other clans of the Lenape, and spoke a different dialect.

The Unami (Turtle Clan), "down river people", at the opening of the historic period dwelt on both sides of the Delaware from the mouth of the Lehigh to the line dividing the states of Pennsylvania and Delaware. Their chief village was Shackamaxon, which was probably the capital of the Lenape nation, and it stood on about the site of Germantown, a suburb of Philadelphia. The principal chief of the Unami was the "King" of the united Lenape nation, by immemorial custom presiding at all the councils of the tribe.

The Unalachtigo (Turkey Clan) "people living near the sea," at the opening of the historic period, occupied the land on the lower reach of the Delaware River and Delaware Bay. Their villages were on both sides of the river; and their chief village, or capital of the clan, was Chikoki, on the site of Burlington, New Jersey.

From these three clans, or tribes, comprising the great body of the Delawares, have sprung many others, who, for their own convenience, chose distant parts in which to settle. Among these were the Mahicans, or Mohicans, who by intermarriage became a detached body, and crossing the Hudson River, dwelt in eastern New York and western Connecticut; and the Nanticokes, who had proceeded to the South, and settled in Maryland and Virginia.

It is to be noted, too, that the Delawares, by reason of priority of political rank and of occupying the central home territory from which the kindred tribes had diverged, were assigned special dignity and authority. It is said that forty tribes looked up to them with respect, and that, in the great councils of the Algonquins, they took first place as "grandfathers" of the race, while others were called by them "children", "grandchildren", and "nephews". It is not certain that this precedence of the Delawares had any importance within the period of white settlement, but it no doubt had in the far dim past. And it seems true that the Algonquin tribes refrained from war with one another.

THE IROQUOIS FORM A GREAT CONFEDERATION AND SUBJUGATE THE LENAPE

It will be remembered that, when the Lenape, or Delawares, and the Mengwe, or Iroquois, divided the country of the Alligewi between them, the Mengwe took the part in the vicinity of the Great Lakes and their tributary streams, north of the part taken by the Lenape. The Mengwe later proceeded farther and settled below the Great Lakes and along the St. Lawrence River, so that when the Lenape had moved to the eastern part of the United States, the Mengwe became their northern neighbors. The Mengwe now became jealous of the growing power of the Lenape, and finally assumed dominion over them.

To the Moravian Missionary, Rev. John Heckewelder, who had lived among the Delawares for more than thirty years, they related how this dominion came about. The great chiefs of the Delawares stated to Heckewelder that the Mengwe clandestinely sought to start quarrels between the Lenape and distant tribes, hoping thus to break the might of the Lenape. Each nation had a particular mark on its war clubs, different from that of any other nation. So the Mengwe, having stolen into the Cherokee country and secretly murdered a Cherokee and left beside the victim a war club, such as the Lenape used, the Cherokees naturally concluded that the Lenape committed the murder, and fell suddenly upon them, and a long and bloody war ensued between the two nations. The treachery of the Mengwe having been at length discovered, the Lenape resolved upon the extermination of this deceitful tribe. War was declared against the Mengwe, and carried on with vigor, when the Mengwe, finding that they were no match for the powerful Lenape and their kindred tribes, resolved upon uniting their clans into a confederacy.   Up until this time, each tribe of the Mengwe had acted independently of the others, and they had not been inclined to come under any supreme authority.   Accordingly, about the year 1570, the Mengwe formed the great confederacy of their five kindred tribes, the Mohawks, the Oneidas, the Onondagas, the Cayugas, and the Senecas, known as the Five (later Six) Nations.

Thus the Delawares claimed that the Iroquois Confederacy was formed for the purpose of preventing the extermination of the Mengwe by the Lenape.   Other authorities say that the purpose was to end inter-tribal feud and war among the Mengwe, themselves; to enable the allied tribes to make mutual offense and defense, and to advance their general welfare.   Thannawage, it is claimed, was the aged Mohawk chief who first proposed the alliance.   Other authorities say that Dekanawida, the Iroquois statesman, prophet and lawgiver, planned and formed the historic confederation; and that he was assisted in this work by his disciple and co-adjutor, Hiawatha, whose name has been immortalized by the poet, Longfellow, in his charming poem.   It is to be noted, however, that, while in "Hiawatha", Longfellow gave the English language one of its finest poems; yet, due to his adopting the error of Schoolcraft in applying to Hiawatha the myths and legends relating to the Chippewa deity, Manabozho, this poem does not contain a single fact or fiction relating to the great chieftain of the Iroquois.

The following chiefs, also, assisted in forming the confederacy: Toganawita, representing the Onondagas; Togahayon, representing the Cayugas; and Ganiatario and Satagaruyes, representing the Senecas.   This confederacy is known in history as the Five Nations, until the Tuscaroras, a tribe having been expelled from North Carolina and Virginia in 1712 or 1713, and having sought an asylum among the Iroquois of Pennsylvania and New York, were formally admitted to the alliance in 1722, after which time the confederacy is known as the Six Nations.   The French gave the Indians of the confederacy the name of Iroquois, while the Delawares continued to call them Mengwe, later corrupted to Mingo. The Mohicans and the Dutch called them Maquas, while Powhatan called them Massawomekes.

But, to resume the story which the Delawares told Heckewelder.   They said that, after the forming of the confederacy, very bloody wars were carried on between the Iroquois and themselves in which they were generally successful, and while these wars were in progress, the French landed in Canada and combined against the Iroquois, inasmuch as the Five Nations were not willing that these Europeans should establish themselves in that country. At last the Mengwe, or Iroquois, seeing themselves between two fires, and not seeing any prospect of conquering the Lenape by arms, resorted to a stratagem to secure dominion over them.

The plan was to persuade the Lenape to abstain from the use of arms, and to assume the station of mediators and umpires among their warlike neighbors. In the language of the Indians, the Lenape were to be made "women". As explaining the significance of this expression, the Delawares said that wars among the Indians in those days were never brought to an end, but by the interference of the weaker sex. It was not considered becoming for a warrior to ask for peace. He must fight to the end. "With these dispositions, war would never have ceased among Indians, until the extermination of one or the other party, if the tender and compassionate sex had not come forward, and by their moving speeches, persuaded the enraged combatants to bury their hatchets, and make peace. On these occasions they were very eloquent . . . They would describe the sorrows of widowed wives, and, above all, of bereaved mothers. The pangs of child-birth, they had willingly suffered. They had carefully reared their sons to manhood. Then how cruel it was to see these promising youths fall victims to the rage of war,—to see them slaughtered on the field, or burned at the stake. The thought of such scenes made them curse their own existence and shudder at the thought of bearing children." Speeches like these generally had the desired effect, and the women, by the honorable function of peace-makers, held a very dignified position. Therefore, it would be a magnanimous and honorable act for a powerful nation like the Lenape to assume that station by which they would be the means of saving the Indian race from extinction.

Such, according to Heckewelder, were the arguments used by the artful Iroquois to ensnare the Lenape. Unfortunately the Delawares listened to the voice of their enemies, and consented to become the "woman nation" among the Indians. With elaborate ceremonies, they were installed in their new function. Eloquent speeches were made, accompanied with belts of wampum. The place of the ceremony of "taking the hatchet out of the hand of the Lenape" and of placing them in the situation of "the woman" was at Nordman's Kill, about four miles south of Albany, New York.

The year of the alleged occurrence is unknown, but it is said to have been somewhere between 1609 and 1620. Both the Delawares and the Mohicans told Heckewelder that the Dutch were present at this ceremony and had no inconsiderable part in the intrigue, the Mohicans explaining that it was fear that caused the Dutch of New York to conspire with the Mengwe against the Lenape. It appears that, at the place where the Dutch were then making their settlement, great bodies of warriors would pass and repass, interrupting their undertakings; so that they thought it well to have an alliance with the Iroquois. Furthermore, the Delawares told Heckewelder that, when the English took New York from the Dutch, they stepped into the same alliance with the Iroquois that their predecessors had made.

The Iroquois denied that such an intrigue as related above ever took place. They alleged, on the other hand, that they had conquered the Lenape in battle and had thus compelled them to become "women",—to submit to the greatest humiliation a spirited and warlike nation can suffer. Many historians believe that the Delawares imposed upon the venerable Rev. Heckewelder by inventing a cunning tale in explanation of the humiliation under which they were smarting. Also, President William Henry Harrison, in his "Aborigines of the Ohio Valley", gives the story of the Delawares little credence. He says that the Delawares were too sagacious a race to fall into such a snare as they allege the Iroquois laid for them. Rev. Heckewelder, the staunch friend of the Delawares, calls attention to the fact that, while the Iroquois claim they conquered the Delawares by force of arms and not by stratagem, yet the Iroquois have no tradition among them of the particulars of the conquest.

So much for the story which the Delawares told Heckewelder. Many authorities state, however, that the time of the subjugation of the Delawares was much later than the date given Heckewelder. Some have stated that the Delawares were not made tributaries of the Iroquois until after the coming of William Penn; but the celebrated Delaware chief, King Beaver, told Conrad Weiser at Aughwick on September 4, 1754, that the subjugation took place before Penn's arrival. At the first extended conference between the Pennsylvania Authorities and the Indians, of which a record has been preserved, held at Philadelphia on July 6, 1694, the Delaware chief, Hithquoquean, or Idquoquequoan, advised the Colonial Authorities that he and his associate chiefs had shortly before this time received a message from the Onondagas and Senecas containing the following statement: "You Delaware Indians do nothing but stay at home and boil your pots, and are like women; while we Onondagas and Senecas go ahead and fight the enemy." We, therefore, conclude that it cannot be stated with exactness, just when the subjugation of the Delawares took place; and, inasmuch as there is no record of any conquest after the time of Penn's arrival, it may be that the subjugation took place through fear and intimidation rather than by war.

Whatever may be the facts as to how the Iroquois reduced the Delawares to a state of vassalage—whether by artifice, intimidation, or warfare—the fact remains that about the year 1720, this powerful northern confederacy assumed active dominion over them, forbidding them to make war or sales of lands,—a condition that existed until the time of the French and Indian War. During the summer of 1755, the Delawares declared that they were no longer subjects of the Six Nations, and, at Tioga, in the year 1756, their great chieftain, Teedyuscung, extorted from the chiefs of the Iroquois an acknowledgment of Delaware independence. However, from time to time, after 1756, the Iroquois persisted in claiming the Delawares were their vassals, until shortly before the treaty of Greenville, Darke County, Ohio, in August, 1795, when they formally declared the Delaware nation to be no longer "women", but MEN. This was the famous treaty between the United States Government, represented by General Anthony Wayne, who had defeated the western tribes at the battle of the Fallen Timbers, on August 20 of the preceding year, and the Shawnees, Delawares, Wyandots, Ottawas, Potawattomies, Miamis and smaller tribes, by the terms of which treaty about two-thirds of the present state of Ohio was ceded to the United States. As will be seen later, the subjection of the Delawares to the Six Nations greatly complicated negotiations on the part of the colony of Pennsylvania for the purchase of the lands of the Delawares, inasmuch as the Iroquois' seat of government was in the colony of New York.

WESTWARD MIGRATION OF THE DELAWARES

As early as 1724, Delawares of the Turtle and Turkey clans began, by permission of the Six Nations, to migrate from the region near the Forks of the Susquehanna to the valleys of the Allegheny and Ohio, coming chiefly from the country to the east and southeast of Shamokin (Sunbury). They proceeded up the east side of the West Branch of the Susquehanna as far as Lock

Haven, where they crossed this stream, and ascended the valley of Bald Eagle Creek to a point near where Milesburg, Center County, now stands. From there, they went in a westerly direction along Marsh Creek, over or near Indian Grave Hill, near Snowshoe and Moshanon, Center County, crossing Moshanon Creek; and from there through Morris, Graham, Bradford, and Lawrence townships, Clearfield County, reaching the West Branch of the Susquehanna again at Chinklaclamoose, on the site of the present town of Clearfield, Clearfield County. From this point, they ascended the West Branch of the Susquehanna for a few miles; thence up Anderson's Creek, crossing the divide between this stream and the Mahoning, in Brady Township, Clearfield County; thence down the Mahoning Valley through Punxsutawney, Jefferson County, to a point on the Allegheny River, about ten miles below the mouth of the Mahoning, where they built their first town in the course of their westward migration, which they called Kittanning, —a town famous in the Indian annals of Pennsylvania. Other Delaware towns were soon established in the Allegheny Valley and other places in the western part of the state to which the migration continued until the outbreak of the French and Indian War. The "Walking Purchase" of 1737 caused the westward migration of the Delawares of the Wolf clan. Thus it is seen that the Delawares retraced their steps across Pennsylvania.

DOMAIN OF THE IROQUOIS

When the historic period of Pennsylvania begins, we find the domain of the Five Nations extending from the borders of Vermont to Lake Erie, and from Lake Ontario to the headwaters of the Delaware, Susquehanna, and Allegheny. This territory they called their "long house". The Senecas, who lived on the headwaters of the Allegheny, and many of whose settlements were in Pennsylvania, guarded the western door of the house, the Mohawks, the eastern, and the Cayugas, the southern, or that which opened on the Susquehanna.

The principal village and capital of these "Romans of America", as DeWitt Clinton called them, was called Onondaga, later Onondaga Castle, and was situated from before 1654 to 1681, on Indian Hill, in the present town of Pompey, near Onondaga Lake, in central New York. In 1677 it contained 140 cabins. Afterward it was removed to Butternut Creek, where the castle was burned in 1696, in the war between the Five Nations and the

French. In 1720, it was again removed to Onondaga Creek, a few miles south of Lake Onondaga.

The Smithsonian Institution, in its "Handbook of American Indians", says the following of the Iroquois: "Around the Great Council Fire of the League of the Iroquois at Onondaga, with punctilious observance of the parliamentary proprieties recognized in Indian diplomacy and statescraft, and with a decorum that would add grace to many legislative assemblies of the white man, the federal senators of the Iroquois tribes devised plans, formulated policies, and defined principles of government and political action, which not only strengthened their state and promoted their common welfare, but also deeply affected the contemporary history of the whites in North America. To this body of half-clad federal chieftains were repeatedly made overtures of peace and friendship by two of the most powerful kingdoms of Europe, whose statesmen often awaited with apprehension the decisions of this senate of North American Savages." And Colden in his "History of the Five Nations", says: "The Five Nations are a poor and, generally called barbarious people; and yet a bright and noble genius shines through these black clouds. None of the greatest Roman heroes discovered a greater love to their country, or a greater contempt of death, than these people called barbarians have done, when liberty came in competition . . . . They carried their arms as far southward as Carolina, to the northward of New England, and as far west as the River Mississippi, over a vast country, which extends twelve hundred miles in length, and about six hundred miles in breadth; where they entirely destroyed many nations, of whom there are now no accounts remaining among the English."

So great was the scourge of the Iroquois that, during the closing decades of the seventeenth century and the first two decades of the eighteenth century, the region south of Lake Erie on both sides of the upper Ohio and Allegheny contained practically no Indian population; and the Iroquois looked upon this vast territory as their great hunting ground.

Speaking of the warfare of the Iroquois, DeWitt Clinton said:

"They reduced war to a science, and all their movements were directed by system and policy. They never attacked a hostile country until they had sent out spies to explore and designate its vulnerable points, and when they encamped, they observed the greatest circumspection to guard against spies. Whatever superiority of force they might have, they never neglected the use of stratagem, employing all the crafty wiles of the Carthagenians."

The unwritten law of this great confederation had a power unequaled by any statutes ever recorded in the statute books of the white man.   Professor W. W. Clayton, in his excellent work, "The History of Onondaga County, New York," in which county the central seat of the Five Nations was located, gives an instance of the power of this unwritten law.   Says Professor Clayton:

"A young man of the Cayugas came to the Onondagas and claimed their hospitality.   He lived among them two years, attaching himself to a Mr. Webster who lived for many years among the Onondagas and had a woman of that tribe for a wife. He appeared contented and happy, always foremost in the chase, most active in the dance, and loudest in the song.   Mantinoah was his name.   One morning he said to his friend, 'I have a vow to perform.   My nation and my friends know that Mantinoah will be true.   My friend, I wish you to go with me.'   Webster consented. After a pleasant journey of a few days, enlivened with fishing and hunting, they came in the afternoon to a place that Mantinoah said was near his village, and where he wished to invoke the Great Spirit.   After a repast and after a pipe had been smoked, Mantinoah said: 'Two winters have gone since, in my village, in the fury of anger, I slew my bosom friend and adopted brother.   The chief declared me guilty of my brother's blood, and I must die. My execution was deferred for two full years, during which time I was condemned to banishment.   I vowed to return.   It was then I sought your nation (the Onondagas); it was thus I won your friendship; the nearest in blood to him I slew, according to our customs, is the avenger.   The time expires when the sun sinks behind the topmost boughs of the trees.   I am ready.   My friend, we have had may a cheerful sport together; our joys have been many; our griefs have been few; look not sad now.   When you return to the Onondagas, tell them that Mantinoah died like a true brave of the Cayugas; tell them that he trembled not at the approach of death, like the coward pale face, nor shed tears like a woman.   My friend, take my belt, my knife, my hunting pouch, my horn, my rifle, as tokens of my friendship.   Soon the avenger will come; the Great Spirit calls; Mantinoah fears not death; farewell.   Vainly Mr. Webster urged him to escape.   A short period of silence, and a yell is heard.   Mantinoah responds.   The avenger appears and takes the hand of his former friend, now his victim.   Mutual salutations follow, with expressions of regret made by the executioner, but none by the doomed.   The tomahawk gleams in the air, not a muscle moves nor does the cheek of

Mantinoah blanch; folding his arms on his breast he received the blow. As if by magic, a host appears; the song of death is sung, and the solemn dance or death march is performed. Webster is invited to the village, where he is hospitably entertained, and when ready to return, is accompanied by a party of Cayugas to his home. Thus powerful was the unwritten law of the Iroquois."

The government of the Iroquois gave to the orator, who by his eloquence could sway his hearers, a vast influence; and we find that many men of note appeared among them since they came in contact with the whites, who were well qualified to conduct their negotiations and reflected as much renown on their nation as their bravest warriors. DeWitt Clinton says of the speech of the great Iroquois chief, Garangula, to the French General, De la Barre: "I believe it impossible to find in all the affusions of English or modern oratory a speech more appropriate or convincing. Under the veil of respectful profession, it conveys the most biting irony, and while it abounds with rich and splendid imagery, it contains the most solid reasoning. I place it in the same rank with the celebrated speech of Logan."

In concluding this sketch of the Iroquois Confederation, we add that, for many years after the historic curtain first rises on the domain of Pennsylvania, the Iroquois carried on a relentless warfare with the Catawbas of the South. The Susquehanna River was the highway followed by their war parties on their way to and return from the territory of the Catawbas.

CHAPTER II

A View of the Indian Tribes Inhabiting Pennsylvania

(Continued)

THE SUSQUEHANNAS, MINQUAS, OR CONESTOGAS

THE Susquehannas is the general term applied to the Indians living on both sides of the Susquehanna River and its tributaries, in Pennsylvania, at the beginning of the historic period. Racially and linguistically, they were of Iroquoian stock, but were never taken into the league of the Iroquois, except as subjects. These related tribes were known by various names. Captain John Smith, the Virginia pioneer, who met them while exploring Chesapeake Bay and its tributaries in 1608, called them the "Susquehannocks." The French called them the Andastes, while the Dutch and Swedes called them Minquas. In the latter days of their history as a tribe, they were called the Conestogas.

To Captain John Smith belongs the distinction of being the first white man to see the Indians of Pennsylvania, though he never set foot on Pennsylvania soil; and the Indians, meeting him and his companions, beheld for the first time the race that was coming to drive them from their streams and hunting grounds. These Indians were the Susquehannas. Smith's meeting with them came about in the following manner:

On the 24th day of July, 1608, Smith left Jamestown, Virginia, on a voyage of discovery. He sailed in an open barge of only several tons burden, and had with him only twelve companions. His party entered Chesapeake Bay and the Susquehanna River almost to the Pennsylvania line, returning to Jamestown on the 7th day of September. He states that, in crossing the bay, his party encountered seven or eight canoes full of Iroquois, whom he called Massawomeks, and that, after a parley, they presented the Virginians with venison, bears' flesh, and some bows and arrows, and informed them that they had just been at war with the Tockwoghs, who lived nearby. They exhibited "greene wounds", which they explained to Smith they had received in battle with the Tockwoghs. They left Smith's party in the evening, promising to return in the morning, but never reappeared.

Smith then determined to visit the Tockwoghs, which he did, finding them living near the head of the bay, on the Tockwogh or Sassafras River, in Maryland. He says that he found the Tockwoghs possessed of many hatchets, knives and pieces of brass, which, they explained, they had received from the Susquehannas, a mighty people living farther to the north on the Susquehanna River, and mortal enemies of the Massawomeks, or Iroquois. Smith prevailed with his interpreter to take with him another interpreter from the Tockwoghs, to visit the towns of the Susquehannas, and to persuade them to pay Smith's party a visit. The two interpreters then conveyed Smith's invitation to the Susquehannas, finding their chiefs in one of their principal towns, in what is now Lancaster County, Pennsylvania.

Smith's party remained with the friendly Tockwoghs on the shores of the Sassafras for three or four days, awaiting the return of the two messengers, whom he had sent to the Susquehannas. At the end of that time, in response to Smith's invitation, sixty of the Susquehannas came, and presented themselves before his party. Smith gives the following interesting description of these Indians:

"Such great and well proportioned men are seldom seen, for they seemed like giants to the English, yea, and to their neighbors, yet seemed of an honest and simple disposition. They were with much ado restrained from adoring us as gods. These are the strangest people of all these countries, both in language and attire; for their language it may well become their proportions, sounding from them as a voice in the vault. Their attire is the skins of bears and wolves; some have cossacks made of bears' heads and skins, that a man's head goes through the skin's neck, and the ears of the bear fastened to his shoulders, the nose and teeth hanging down his breast, another bear's face split behind him, and at the end of the nose hung a paw, the half sleeves coming to the elbows were the necks of bears, and the arms through the mouth with paws hanging at their noses. One had the head of a wolfe hanging in a chain for a jewel, his tobacco pipe three quarters of a yard long, prettily carved with a bird, a deer, or some such device at the great end, sufficient to beat out one's brans; with bows, arrows, and clubs, suitable to their greatness. Five of their chief Werowances came aboard us and crossed the bay in the barge. The picture of the greatest of them is signified in the map. The calf of whose leg was three-quarters of a yard about, and all the rest of his limbs so answerable to that proportion that he seemed the goodliest man we ever beheld. His hair, the one side was long, the other shorn close with a ridge over his crown like a cock's comb. His arrows were five quarters long, headed with the splinters of a white christall-like stone, in form of a heart, an inch broad, an inch and a half or more long. These he wore in a wolf's skin at his back for his quiver, his bow in the one hand and his club in the other, as is described."

Smith goes on to say that these Susquehannas were scarce known to Powhatan, the great Virginia chief, but that they were a powerful tribe living in palisaded towns to defend them from the Massawomeks, or Iroquois, and having six hundred warriors. During the ceremonies connected with the visit of this band of Susquehannas, Smith says that they first sang "a most fearful song," and then, "with a most strange, furious action and a hellish voice began an oration." When the oration was ended, they decorated Smith with a chain of large white beads, and laid presents of skins and arrows at his feet, meanwhile stroking their hands about his neck. They told him about their enemies, the Iroquois, who, they said, lived beyond the mountains far to the north and received their hatchets and other weapons from the French in Canada. They implored Smith to remain with them as their protector, which, of course, he could not do. "We left them at Tockwogh," he says, "sorrowing for our departure."

Smith's account of the large stature of the Susquehannas has been corroborated by subsequent discoveries, when burying grounds of this tribe, in Lancaster County, were opened and very large human skeletons found.

The Susquehannas, in the latter part of the seventeenth century, carried on war with the "River Indians", as the Delawares, or Lenape then living along the Delaware River, were called. The Susquehannas were friendly with both the Swedes and the Dutch, and shortly after the Swedes arrived on the Delaware in 1638, they sold part of their lands to them. The Swedes equipped these Indians with guns, and trained their warriors in European tactics. When the Hurons were being worsted by the Iroquois in 1647, the Susquehannas offered the friendly Hurons military assistance, "backed by 1300 warriors in a single palisaded town, who had been trained by Swedish soldiers." They were also friendly with the colony of Maryland in the early days of its history, selling part of their lands to the Marylanders, and receiving military supplies from them.

The French explorer, Champlain, says that, in 1615, the Carantouannais, as he calls the Susquehannas, had many villages on the upper part of the Susquehanna, and that their town, Carantouan, alone, could muster more than eight hundred warriors. The exact location of Carantouan has been a matter of much conjecture, but the weight of authority places it on or near the top of Spanish Hill, in Athens Township, Bradford County, Pennsylvania, and within sight of the town of Waverly, New York.

Carantouan has a firm place in the history of Pennsylvania on account of its connection with the Frenchman, Estienne Brule, the first white man, so far as is known, to set foot on Pennsylvania soil, and to behold its Indians on their native heath. The student of history will recall that, in 1615, the French explorer, Champlain, in order to learn more about the region embraced in what is now New York State, joined a war party of Hurons against the Iroquois; and, in August of that year, he and the Hurons proposed to attack a strong town of the Onondaga tribe of the Five Nations, located most likely near the town of Fenner, in Madison County, not far from Lake Oneida, New York. When Champlain was at the village of Cahiague, near the lower end of Lake Simcoe, making preparations for his advance against the Iroquois town, he learned from the Hurons that there was a certain nation of their allies dwelling three days journey beyond the Onondagas; who desired to assist the Hurons in this expedition with five hundred of their warriors. These allies were none other than that portion of the Susquehannas, living along the Susquehanna River, near the boundary between the states of Pennsylvania and New York. Accordingly, Champlain sent his interpreter, Estienne Brule, with twelve Huron companions, to visit Carantouan, the chief town of the Susquehannas in that region, for the purpose of hastening the coming of the five hundred warriors.

Brule and his five hundred allies from Carantouan arrived before the Onondaga fortress too late to be of any assistance to Champlain, who had already made two attacks upon the town, had been wounded twice by the Onondagas, and, despairing of the arrival of the promised assistance of five hundred warriors, had already retreated toward Canada several days before the arrival of Brule and his Indians. Brule then returned with his five hundred warriors to the town of Carantouan.

Brule spent the autumn and winter of 1615 and 1616 in a

tour of exploration into the very heart of Pennsylvania, visiting the various clans of the Susquehannas and, some authorities say, the Eries. He followed the Susquehanna River to its mouth, and returned to Carantouan. This intrepid Frenchman thus gained, by actual observation, a knowledge of a large section of the state and of its primitive inhabitants almost one hundred years before any other white man set foot within the same region.

Another town of the Susquehannas was the one, later called Gahontoto, at the mouth of Wyalusing Creek, Bradford County. The Moravian missionaries, Bishop Commerhoff and David Zeisberger, visited the site of this town in the summer of 1750. Says Bishop Cammerhoff:

"On proceeding, we came to a place called Gahontoto by the Indians. It is said to be the site of an ancient Indian city, where a peculiar nation lived. The inhabitants were neither Delawares nor Aquanoschioni, (Iroquois) but had a language of their own, and were called Te-ho-ti-tach-se. We could still notice a few traces of this place in the old ruined corn-fields near. The Five Nations went to war against them, and finally completely extirpated them. The Cayugas for a time held a number captive, but the nation and the language are now exterminated and extinct. The Cayuga told us that these things had taken place before the Indians had any guns, and still went to war with bows and arrows."

Another of the towns of the Susquehannas is believed to have been at the mouth of Sugar Creek, in Bradford County, above the present town of Towanda. Still another of their towns, this one fortified, was near the mouth of Octorara Creek, on the east side of the Susquehanna River, in Maryland, about ten miles south of the line between Pennsylvania and Maryland. One of their forts was in Manor Township, Lancaster County, near the Susquehanna River, between Turkey Hill and Blue Rock. Another was on Wolf Run, near Muncy, Lycoming County. The location of their principal fort was long a matter of dispute, and, at one time, actual warfare, between the heirs of Lord Baltimore and the heirs of William Penn, for the reason that the southern boundary of Penn's colony was supposed to be marked by it. The weight of authority seems to place its location on the west side of the Susquehanna River, in York County, Pennsylvania, opposite Washington Borough.

The Iroquois, the mortal enemies of the Susquehannas, attacked them at one of their principal towns, in either York or Lancaster County, Pennsylvania, in 1663, sending down the Susquehanna River, in April of that year, an expedition of eight hundred Onondagas, Cayugas, and Senacas. On their arrival, they found the town defended on one side by the river and on the other by tree trunks; it was flanked by two bastions, constructed after the European method, and had also several pieces of artillery. The Iroquois decided not to make an assault, but to attempt to outwit the Susquehannas by a ruse. Twenty-five Iroquois were admitted into the fort, but these were seized, placed on high scaffolds, and burned to death in sight of their comrades. The humiliated Iroquois now returned to their home in New York.

After this defeat of the Iroquois, the war was carried on by small parties, and now and then a Susquehanna was captured and carried to the villages of the Iroquois, and tortured to death. In 1669, the Susquehannas defeated the Cayugas, and offered peace; but their ambassador was put to death, and the war went on. At this time, the Susquehannas had a great chief named Hochitqgete, or Barefoot; and the medicine men of the Iroquois assured the warriors of the confederacy that, if they would make another attack on the Susquehannas, their efforts would be rewarded by the capture of Barefoot and his execution at the stake. So, in the summer of 1672, a band of forty Cayugas descended the Susquehanna in canoes, and twenty Senecas marched overland to attack the enemy in the fields; but a band of sixty Susquehanna boys, none over sixteen, routed the Senecas, killing one and capturing another. The band of youthful warriors then pressed on against the Cayugas, and defeated them, killing eight and wounding fifteen or sixteen more, but losing half of their own gallant band. At this time, it is said, the Susquehannas were so reduced by war and pestilence that their fighting force consisted of only three hundred warriors.

Finally in 1675, according to the Jesuit Relation and Colden in his "History of the Five Nations", the Susquehannas fell before the arms of the Iroquois; but the details of the defeat are sadly lacking. It seems that the Iroquois, about this time, had driven them down upon the tribes of the South who were then allies of the English, and that this involved them in war with Maryland and Virginia. Finding themselves surrounded by enemies on all sides, a portion of the Susquehannas left the land of their forefathers and the beautiful river bearing their name, and took up their abode in the western part of Maryland, near the Piscataways.

In the summer of 1675, a white man was murdered by some Indians, most probably Senecas, on the Virginia side of the Potomac; whereupon, a party of Virginia militia killed fourteen of the Susquehannocks and Doeg Indians in retaliation. Shortly afterwards several other whites were murdered on both sides of the Potomac. The colony of Virginia then organized several companies, led by Colonel John Washington, great-grandfather of George Washington, to co-operate with a Maryland force of two hundred and fifty troops, led by Major Thomas Truman. The Susquehannocks claimed that they were entirely innocent of any of these murders and sent four of their chiefs as an embassy to Major Truman, who were knocked on the head by his soldiers. This so enraged the Susquehannocks that a long border warfare ensued which was kept up until they became lost to history.

Another portion of the Susquehannocks remained near their old home at Conestoga, Lancaster County, where they were later joined by a third portion which had been taken by the Iroquois to the Oneida country in New York, and there retained until they lost their language, when they were permitted to join their brethren at Conestoga. Here William Penn and his son, William, visited the Conestogas during his last stay in his province in 1701. Here, also, the Conestogas lived until the descendants of this remnant of a once powerful tribe were killed in December, 1763, by a band of Scotch-Irish settlers from Donegal and Paxtang,—the last melancholy chapter in the history of the Susquehannas, or Conestogas. Conestoga, for generations the central seat of this tribe in the lower Susquehanna region, was about four miles southwest of Millersville, Lancaster County. A monument marks the site of this historic Indian town. It was erected in 1924 by the Lancaster County Historical Society and the Pennsylvania Historical Commission.

THE SHAWNEES

The Shawnees, too, occupied parts of Pennsylvania during the historic period. The name means "Southerners". They were a branch of the Algonquin family, and are believed to have lived in the Ohio Valley in remote ages, and to have built many of the mounds and earthworks found there. Some have attempted to identify them with the Eries of the early Jesuits, the Massawomecks of Smith, and the Andaste, but without success. The traditional history of the Lenape, the Walum Olum, connects them, the Lenape, and Nanticokes as one people, the separation having taken place after the Alligewi, (Cherokees) were driven from the Ohio Valley by the Lenape and the Mengwe (Iroquois) on their onward march eastward across the continent. Then the Shaw-

nees went south.   Their real history begins in 1669-70, when they
were living in two bodies a great distance apart,—one body being
in South Carolina and the other in the Cumberland basin in Tennessee.   Between these two bodies were the then friendly Cherokees, who claimed the land vacated by the Shawnees when the
latter subsequently migrated to the North.   The Shawnees living
in South Carolina were called Savannahs by the early settlers.

On account, probably, of dissatisfaction with the early settlers,
the Shawnees of South Carolina began a general movement to the
north in 1690, and continued it at intervals for thirty years.   The
first reference to this tribe to be found in the Provincial records of
Pennsylvania is probably a deposition made before the Provincial
Council, December 19, 1693, by Polycarpus Rose.   In this deposition there is a reference to "strange Indians" called "Shallna-
rooners".   These strange Indians appear to have made a temporary stop in Chester County in migrating possibly from Maryland
to the Forks of the Delaware or to Pequea Creek.   Many authorities believe these "strange Indians" mentioned in the affidavit of
Polycarpus Rose to have been Shawnees.   This is conjecture.

But, leaving the realm of conjecture and entering the realm
of historical truth, we find that the first Shawnees to enter Pennsylvania were a party who settled on the Delaware at Pechoquealin
near the Water Gap, in the summer of 1694, or shortly thereafter.
These came from the Shawnee villages on the lower Ohio.   Arnold
Viele, a Dutch trader, from Albany, New York, spent the winter
of 1692-1693 with the Shawnees on the lower Ohio, returning in
the summer of 1694, and bringing with him a number of this tribe
who settled at Pechoquealin.   Pechoquealin was a regional name
whose center seems to have been the mouth of Shawnee Run in
Lower Smithfield Township, Monroe County, and which included
the surrounding territory on both sides of the Delaware, above the
Delaware Water Gap.   Viele was probably the first white man to
explore the region between the valleys of the Susquehanna and the
Ohio.

About four years later, or in 1697 or 1698, about seventy
families of Shawnees came from Cecil County, Maryland, and
settled on the Susquehanna River, near the Conestoga Indians, in
Lancaster County.   Probably at about the same time others
migrated to the Ohio Valley.   At the mouth of Pequea Creek,
Lancaster County, the seventy families come from Maryland, built
their village, also called Pequea.   Their chief was Wapatha, or
Opessah.   They secured permission from the Colonial Govern-

ment to reside near the Conestogas, and the latter became security for their good behavior, under the authority of the Iroquois Confederation. By invitation of the Delawares, a party of seven hundred Shawnees came soon after and settled with the Munsee Clan on the Delaware River, the main body taking up their abode at the mouth of the Lehigh, near Easton, while others went as far south as the mouth of the Schuylkill. Those who had settled on the Delaware afterwards removed to the Wyoming Valley near the present town of Plymouth, Luzerne County, on a broad plain still called Shawnee Flats. This band under Kakowatcheky removed from Pechoquealin to the Wyoming Valley in 1728; and it is probable that they were joined there by those who had settled at Pequea, which was abandoned about 1730.

The Shawnees also had a village on the flats at the mouth of Fishing Creek, near Bloomsburg, and another at Catawissa,—both being in Columbia County. They had other villages in the eastern part of the state on the Swatara, Paxtang, Susquehanna, and Delaware. Several villages were scattered along the west side of the Susquehanna, between the mouth of Yellow Breeches Creek and the Conodoguinet, in Cumberland County. Another of their villages, called Chenastry, was at the mouth of Chillisquaque Creek on the east side of the West Branch of the Susquehanna, in Northumberland County.

The Shawnees from Tennessee migrated to the Ohio Valley, finally collecting along the north bank of the Ohio in Pennsylvania as far north as the mouth of the Monongahela, about the year 1730. Sauconk and Logstown were villages on the Ohio which they established possibly as early as that time. The former was at the mouth of the Beaver, and the latter on the north bank of the Ohio, about eighteen miles below Pittsburgh.

Another clan of Shawnees, called the Sewickleys, Asswikales, Shaweygila, and Hathawekela, came from South Carolina prior to 1730 by way of Old Town, Maryland and Bedford, Pa., and settled in different parts of Southwestern Pennsylvania. Their principal village called Sewickley Town was at the junction of this creek and the Youghiogheny River, in Westmoreland County. They were probably the first Shawnees to settle in Western Pennsylvania.

The Shawnees of the eastern part of Pennsylvania eventually went to the Ohio and Allegheny Valleys. In the report of the Albany congress of 1754, it is found that some of the tribe had moved from the eastern part of the state to the Ohio about thirty years previously; and, in 1734, another Shawnee band consisting of about forty families and described as living on the Allegheny, refused to return to the Susquehanna at the solicitation of the Delawares and Iroquois. During their westward migration, they established villages on the Juniata and Conemaugh. About the year 1755 or 1756, practically all the Shawnees abandoned the Susquehanna and other parts of eastern Pennsylvania, and joined their brethren on the Ohio, where they became allies of the French in the French and Indian War. It should be remembered that, in the early records, the term "Ohio Valley" means both the Ohio and Allegheny valleys. In those times, the present Allegheny River was considered as simply a continuation of the Ohio River.

Wanderings of the Shawnees

There is something mysterious in the wanderings of the Shawnees. As we have seen, their home, in remote times, was in the Ohio Valley; then we later hear of them in the South; and still later they came to Pennsylvania. There is good evidence, however, tending to show that that body of the Shawnees which entered Lancaster County, Pennsylvania, in 1697 or 1698, came originally from as far west as the region of Fort St. Louis, near the town of Utica, LaSalle County, Illinois, leaving that place in 1683 and being accompanied in their wanderings to Maryland by Martin Chartier, a French Canadian, who had spent some eight or nine years among them. At any rate, this band reached Maryland near the mouth of the Susquehanna in 1692, and such is the story they told. They gradually moved up the Susquehanna to Lancaster County, as we have seen, where Chartier became a trader at their village of Pequea, on the east side of the Susquehanna near the mouth of Pequea Creek, and only a few miles from Conestoga, which was on the north side of Conestoga Creek.

The Shawnees who settled at Paxtang, on or near the site of Harrisburg, most likely came from Pequea. Before 1727, many of this tribe from Paxtang and Pequea had settled on the west side of the Susquehanna River at what is now New Cumberland, near the the mouth of Yellow Breeches Creek and as far north as the mouth of the Conodoguinet. These dwellers on the west side of the Susquehanna, about the year 1727, crossed the mountains to the valleys of the Ohio and Allegheny. Some, however, had gone to Big Island (Lock Haven) before going to the Ohio region.

Opessah, the chief of the Shawnees on the lower Susquehanna, did not remove to the Ohio or Allegheny Valley. He remained at Pequea until 1711, when he abandoned both his chieftainship and his tribe, and sought a home among the Delawares of Sassoonan's clan. It is not clear why he abandoned his people. There is a traditionary account that he left because he became enamoured of a Delaware squaw, who refused to leave her own people. Later, in 1722, he removed to what was called Opessah's town on the Potomac, now Old Town, Maryland.

Neither the Pennsylvania Archives nor the Colonial Records show the name of the chief of those Shawnees who settled at Pechoqueálin until 1728, when their head man was Kakowatchey. Some of Kakowatchey's clan removed directly to the Ohio before 1732, but a majority seem to have gone only as far as the Wyoming Valley in Luzerne County, where, as we have seen, they took up their abode on the west side of the North Branch of the Susquehanna at a place subsequently known as Shawnee Flats, just below the site of the present town of Plymouth. Their town at this place was called Skehandowana (Iroquois for "Great Flats"), and it remained a town of considerable importance until 1743. Some time after April of that year, Kakowatchey himself, with a number of his followers removed from Skehandowana and settled at Logstown on the Ohio.

After Kakowatchey left Wyoming, Paxinosa became chief of the Shawnees who still remained at that place. He said that he was born "at Ohio", and possibly he was one of the company of Shawnees who accompanied Arnold Viele to the Pechoquealin territory.

A number of the Shawnees at Chenastry, on the West Branch of the Susquehanna, near the mouth of Chillisquaque Creek, went to the valleys of the Ohio and Allegheny prior to the autumn of 1727 to hunt, and no doubt some of them made their permanent homes or took up their abode in this western region, during or prior to the summer of 1727.

But some of the Shawnees went directly from Maryland to the Ohio and Allegheny. Two chiefs of the Potomac Shawnees, Opaketchwa and Opakeita, by name, came from the Ohio Valley to Philadelphia in September, 1732, after they had abandoned their town on the north branch of the Potomac. Governor Gordon asked them why they had gone "so far back into the woods as Allegheny", and they replied that "formerly they had lived at 'Patawmack' [Potomac], where their king died; that, having lost him, they knew not what to do; that they then took their wives and children and went over the mountains (to Allegheny) to live."

THE TUSCARORAS

Another Indian tribe inhabiting portions of Pennsylvania within the historic period was the Tuscaroras. They were of the Iroquoian linguistic group. It will be recalled that this tribe, after being expelled from North Carolina and Virginia, sought an asylum with the Five Nations, and was later, in 1722, admitted formally as an addition to the Iroquois Confederacy, making the Six Nations. The Tuscaroras had suffered greatly in wars with the people of North Carolina and Virginia, before they were expelled in 1712. Their women were debauched by the whites, and both men and women were kidnapped and sold into slavery. Some were brought as far north as Pennsylvania, and sold as slaves. Moreover, the colonists of North Carolina, like the Puritans of New England, did not recognize in the Indian any right to the soil; and so the lands of the Tuscaroras were appropriated without any thought of purchase. They had suffered these and similar wrongs for many years, and, as early as 1710, sent a petition to the Government of Pennsylvania reciting their wrongs and stating that they desired to remove to a more just and friendly government. Governor Charles Gookin and the Provincial Council of Pennsylvania dispatched two commissioners to meet the embassy which brought the petition, at Conestoga, Lancaster County, on June 8, 1710, where they found not only the Tuscarora embassy, but Civility and four other Conestoga chiefs, as well as Opessah, head chief of the Shawnees.

In the presence of these officials, the Tuscarora ambassadors delivered their proposals, which were attested by eight belts of wampum. This petition was a very lucid and condensed statement of the wrongs suffered by the Tuscaroras in their southern home. By the first belt, the aged women and mothers of the tribe besought the friendship of the Christian people and the Indians and Government of Pennsylvania, so that they might bring wood and water without danger. By the second, the children, born and unborn, implored that they might be permitted to play without danger of slavery. By the third, the young men sought the privilege of leaving their towns to pursue the game in the forest for the sustenance of the aged, without fear of death or slavery. By the fourth, the old men sought the privilege of spending their declining days in peace. By the fifth, the entire Tuscarora nation sought a firm and lasting peace with all the blessings attached thereto. By the sixth, the chiefs and sachems sought the establishment of lasting peace with the Government and Indians of Pennsylvania, so that they would be relieved from "those fearful apprehensions which they have these several years felt." By the seventh, the Tuscaroras implored a "cessation from murdering and taking them", so that they might not be in terror upon every rustling of the leaves of the forest by the winds. By the eighth, the entire Tuscarora tribe, being hitherto strangers to the colony of Pennsylvania, implored that the sons of "Brother Onas" might take them by the hand and lead them, so that they might lift up their heads in the wilderness without fear of slavery or death.

This petition, it is seen, was couched in the metaphorical language of the Indian; but its plain meaning proves it to be a statement of a tribe at bay, who, on account of the large numbers of their people killed, kidnapped, or sold into slavery by the settlers of North Carolina, were endeavoring to defend their offspring, friends, and kindred, and were seeking a more friendly dwelling place in the North, within the domain of the just government of Penn, the apostle.

The Provincial Council of Pennsylvania advised the Tuscarora ambassadors that, before they could consent to the Tuscaroras taking up their abode within the bounds of Penn's Province, they should first be required to produce a certificate from the colonial authorities of North Carolina as to their good behavior in that colony. This, of course, the Tuscaroras were unable to do. Then, the Conestoga chiefs, by the advice of their council, determined to send the wampum belts, or petition, of the Tuscaroras to the Five Nations of New York. This was done, and it was the reception of these belts, setting forth the pitiful message of the Tuscaroras, that moved the Five Nations to take steps to shield and protect the Tuscaroras, and eventually receive them, in 1722, as an additional member of the Iroquois Confederation.

In their migration northward, the Tuscaroras did not all leave their ancient southern homes at once. Some sought an asylum among other southern tribes, and lost their identity. However, the major portion came north, and many of them resided for a number of years in Pennsylvania, before going to New York, the seat of the Five Nations. In fact, the Tuscaroras were ninety years in making their exodus from their North Carolina home to more friendly dwelling places in the North.

One body of the Tuscaroras, on their way north, tarried in the Juniata Valley in Juniata County, Pennsylvania, for many years, giving their name to the Tuscarora Mountain. There is evidence of their having been there as late as 1755. Another band settled about two miles west of Tamaqua, in Schuylkill County, where they planted an orchard and lived for a number of years. Also, in May, 1766, a band of Tuscaroras halted at the Moravian mission at Friedensheutten, on the Susquehanna in Wyoming County, and remained there several weeks. Some remained at the mission, and these had planted their crops in 1766, at the mouth of Tuscarora Creek, Wyoming County.

In a word, the residence places of the Tuscaroras in Pennsylvania during their migration to New York, were those localities where their name has been preserved ever since, such as: Tuscarora Mountain dividing Franklin and Perry counties from Huntingdon and Juniata; Tuscarora Path Valley (now Path Valley) in the western part of Franklin County at the eastern base of Tuscarora Mountain; Tuscarora Creek running through the valley between Tuscarora and Shade mountains, which valley forms the greater part of Juniata County; and also the stream called Tuscarora Creek running down through the southeastern part of Bradford County and joining the North Branch of the Susquehanna in the northwestern part of Wyoming County. The Tuscarora Path marks the route followed by the Tuscaroras during their migration to New York and of their subsequent journeyings to and fro between New York and Pennsylvania on the north and Virginia and North Carolina on the south.

THE CONOY, GANAWESE, OR PISCATAWAY

The Conoy, also called the Ganawese and the Piscataway, inhabited parts of Pennsylvania during the historic period. They were an Algonquin tribe, closely related to the Delawares, whom they called "grandfathers", and from whose ancestral stem they no doubt sprang. Heckewelder, an authority on the history of the Delawares and kindred tribes, believed them to be identical with the Kanawha, for whom the chief river of West Virginia is named; and it seems that the names, Conoy and Ganawese, are simply different forms of the name Kanawha, though it is difficult to explain the application of the same name to the Piscataway tribe of Maryland, except on the theory that this tribe once lived on the Kanawha.

As stated formerly, the Conestogas, when defeated by the Iroquois in 1675, invaded the territory of the Piscataways in western Maryland. This, it is believed, caused the northward migra-

tion of the Piscataways. At any rate, they shortly thereafter retired slowly up the Potomac, some entering Pennsylvania about
1698 or 1699, and the rest a few years later. The Iroquois assigned them lands at Conejoholo, also called Connejaghera and Dekanoagah, on the east side of the Susquehanna at the present town of
Washington Borough, Lancaster County. Later they removed
higher up the Susquehanna to what was called Conoy Town, at the
mouth of Conoy Creek, in Lancaster County. Still later they
gradually made their way up the Susquehanna, stopping at Harrisburg, Shamokin (Sunbury), Catawissa, and Wyoming; and in
1765, were living in southern New York. After their arrival in
Pennsylvania, they were generally called Conoy. During their
residence in Pennsylvania, their villages, especially those on the
the lower Susquehanna, were stopping places for war parties of the
Iroquois on their way to and return from attacks upon the
Catawbas in the South; and this fact made considerable trouble for
the Colonial Authorities as well as the Conoy.

THE NANTICOKES

The Nanticokes, also, dwelt within the bounds of Pennsylvania during the historic period. These were an Algonquin tribe,
formerly living on the Nanticoke River on the eastern shore of
Maryland, where Captain John Smith, in 1608, located their principal village called Nanticoke. They were of the same parent
stem as the Delawares. The tenth verse of the fifth song of the
Walum Olum, the sacred tribal history of the Lenape, contains the
statement that "the Nanticokes and the Shawnees went to the
Southlands." It is not clear, however, where the separation of the
Nanticokes from the Lenape took place, but Heckewelder states
that they separated from the Lenape after these had reached the
eastern part of the United States, and that the Nanticokes then
went southward in search of hunting and trapping grounds, they
being great hunters and trappers.

A short time after the settlement of Maryland, they had difficulties with the settlers of that colony. They were formally declared enemies in 1642, and the strife was not ended until a treaty
entered into in 1678. A renewal of hostilities was threatened in
1687, but happily prevented, and peace was once more reaffirmed.
In 1698, and from that time forward as long as they remained
within the bounds of Lord Baltimore's colony, reservations were
set aside for them. At this early day they began a gradual migra-

tion northward, though a small part remained in Maryland. The migration to the North covered many years. On their way they stopped for a time on the Susquehanna as guests of the Conoy; later at the mouth of the Juniata; and still later, in 1748, the greater part of this tribe went up the Susquehanna, halting at various points and finally settling, during the French and Indian War, under the protection of the Iroquois, at Chenango, Chugnut, and Owego, on the east branch of the Susquehanna in southern New York. For a number of years, their principal seat in Pennsylvania was on the east bank of the Susquehanna below the mouth of the Lackawanna, not far from Pittston, Luzerne County.

Many marvelous stories were told concerning this tribe. One was that they were said to have been the inventors of a poisonous substance by which they could destroy a whole settlement at once. They were also accused of being skilled in the art of witchcraft, and, on this account they were greatly feared by the neighboring tribes. Heckewelder states that he knew Indians who firmly believed that the Nanticokes had men among them who, if they wished, could destroy a whole army by merely blowing their breath toward them.

They had the singular custom of removing the bones of their dead from place to place during their migrations, and this they would do even in cases where the dead had not been buried long enough to be reduced to a skeleton. In cases where the dead had not been buried long, they would scrape the flesh from the bones, reinter it, and then take the skeleton with them. Heckewelder relates that between the years 1750 and 1760 he saw several bands of Nanticokes go through the Moravian town of Bethlehem, Pennsylvania, on their migration northward, loaded with the bones of their relatives and friends.

THE TUTELO

The Tutelo were a Siouan tribe, related to the Sioux, of Dakota of the far Northwest. For some time before their entering Pennsylvania soon after 1722, they had been living in North Carolina and Virginia. They were first mentioned by Captain John Smith, of Virginia, in 1609, as occupying the upper waters of the James and Rappahannock, and were described by him as being very barbarous. Their first seat in Pennsylvania was at Shamokin (Sunbury) where they resided under Iroquois protection. At this place, the Rev. David Brainerd found them in 1745. Later they moved up the Susquehanna to Skogari. In 1771, the Tutelo were settled on the east side of Cayuga inlet about three miles from the south end of the lake of that name in New York. How this tribe became so widely separated from the western Sioux still remains unknown.

The Conoy, the Nanticoke, and the Tutelo were not large tribes. In 1763, according to Sir William Johnson, the three tribes numbered about one thousand souls.

As has been stated, the Shawnees, the Conoy, and the Nanticokes, belonged to the Algonquin parent stem; the Tutelo to the Siouan; and the Tuscarora to the Iroquoian. These three groups were widely separated. It is thus seen that, at the time when the English, the Germans, and the Scotch-Irish, and other European races were coming to Pennsylvania, as widely separated races of North American Indians were coming from the South to make their homes in its wilderness and along its streams. Of these incoming tribes, the one to figure most prominently in the history of Pennsylvania was the Shawnee. Following Braddock's defeat, July 9th, 1755, Pennsylvania suffered the bloodiest Indian invasion in American history,—the invasion of the Shawnees and Delawares, brought about in part, by the fact that the Shawnees yielded to French influence.

THE ERIES, WENRO, BLACK MINQUAAS, AND AKANSEA

The Eries, also known as the Erieehronons, were populous sedentary tribe of Iroquoian stock, which, in the seventeenth century, inhabited that part of Pennsylvania extending from Lake Erie to the Allegheny River, possibly as far south as the Ohio River, and eastward to the lands of the Susquehannas. They are also known as the Cat Nation, from the abundance of wild cats and panthers in their territory. Recorded history gives only glimpses of them; but it appears that they had many towns and villages, and that their town, Rique, had, in 1654, between 3,000 and 4,000 combatants, exclusive of women and children.

In the Jesuit Relation of 1653, it is stated that the Eries were forced to proceed farther inland in order to escape their enemies dwelling west of them. Who these enemies were is not positively known. Finally, about 1655 or 1656, they were conquered by the Iroquois. The conquerors entered their palisaded town of Rique, and there "wrought such carnage among the women and children that the blood was knee-deep in places." However, this victory at Rique was dearly bought by the Iroquois, who were compelled to remain in the country of the Eries two months to care for the wounded and bury the dead. The Erie power now being broken, the people were either destroyed, dispersed, or led into captivity. Six hundred Eries, who had surrendered at one time, were taken to the Iroquois country and adopted. There is a tradition that, some years after the defeat of the Eries, a band of their descendants cames from the West, ascended the Allegheny River, and attacked the Senecas, and were slain to a man.

The Wenro, a tribe of Iroquoin stock, also known as the Ahouenrochrhonons, are mentioned in the Jesuit Relation as having dwelt some time prior to 1639, "beyond the Erie", or Cat Nation; and it is probable that their habitat was on the upper territory of the Allegheny, and, part of it at least, within the bounds of the State of Pennsylvania. This tribe, too, fell before the arms of the Iroquois. A notation on Captain John Smith's map of his explorations, says that they traded with the whites on the Delaware River.

They seem to have been allied with the Black Minquaas, which later, according to Herrmann's map of 1670, are placed in the region west of the Allegheny Mountains, and on the Ohio, or "Black Minquaas River". The Jesuit Relation states that both the Wenro and the Black Minquaas traded with the people on the upper Delaware, some going by way of the West Branch of the Susquehanna, down to Sunbury (Shamokin), up to Wyoming, and then across to the Delaware River, near the Water Gap; and others reaching the Delaware by way of the Conemaugh, Juniata, and Susquehanna. The Black Minquaas were so called because "they carried a black badge on their breast." About all that is known of the fate of this tribe is the legend on Herrmann's map, which reads: "A very great river called Black Minquaas River—where formerly those Black Minquaas came over the Susquehanna, as far as the Delaware to trade; but the Sasquhana and the Sinnicus Indians went over and destroyed that very great nation."

A Siouan tribe, the Akansea, in remote times, occupied the upper Ohio Valley, according to many historians, and were driven out by the Iroquois. This stream was called the "River of the Akansea", because this tribe lived upon its shores. When or how long this river valley was their habitat, is not known.

No other rivers in Pennsylvania, or on the continent, have seen more changes in the races of Indians living in their valleys than have the Ohio and the Allegheny,—the dwelling place of the

Alligewi; the Delawares, or Lenape, in the course of their migration eastward; the Akansea; the Shawnees; the Black Minquaas; the Wenro; the Senecas; then once more the Shawnees and Delawares in their march toward the setting sun before the great tide of white immigration. What battles and conquests, all untold, took place in the valleys of these historic streams before the white man set foot upon their shores! Who would not seek to draw aside the curtain, which, it seems, must forever hide this unrecorded history from our view?

We have seen that the French explorer, Brule, and the Dutch explorer, Viele, entered Pennsylvania at the very dawn of the historic period. Perhaps to these should be added the French explorer, LaSalle. It is a moot question, however, among historians whether this gallant Frenchman ever entered the limits of Pennsylvania, though Parkman lends the weight of his great name to the contention that he explored the Allegheny Valley.

Having given this survey of the Indian tribes who inhabited Pennsylvania, we shall now take up the biographies of their outstanding chiefs.* In the course of our narrative will appear many things that reflect no honor on the whites—the anointed children of education and civilization. But it is our duty to record the wrongs committed upon the untutored Red Man, as well as the wrongs committed by him. History must not hide the truth. Furthermore, the author has no prejudice against any of the European races who came in contact with the Indians of Pennsylvania. His ancestors came to the Province in 1693, and the blood of nearly all these races flows in his veins—English, German, Irish, Scotch, Scotch-Irish, and French.

---

* See the chapter, "The Red Neighbours" in Charles P. Keith's "Chronicles of Pennsylvania" for a concise and well written account of the aborigines of Pennsylvania.

CHAPTER III

Mattahorn and Naaman

THIS chapter is devoted to the two outstanding Delaware chiefs before the arrival of William Penn. Playing a part in the history of the lower Delaware, during its occupancy by the Swedes and the Dutch, the few recorded facts concerning these worthy representatives of the aborigines of Pennsylvania, are as a voice from the distant past.

MATTAHORN

Mattahorn claims our remembrance as one of the few Delaware chiefs distinguishable by name before the arrival of William Penn. We first meet him in April, 1633, when he and several other chiefs sold the land on which Philadelphia stands to Arent Corssen, the Dutch agent, commander of Fort Nassau, on the east bank of the Delaware River, near Gloucester, New Jersey. At that time the Dutch of Manhattan were endeavoring to establish an Indian trade on the South, or Delaware River.

We next meet Mattahorn when the Swedes came to the Delaware. Late in the autumn of 1637, two ships left Sweden carrying a small band of resolute emigrants purposing to establish a Swedish colony in the New World under the patronage of Queen Christina, the daughter of Sweden's most famous king, Gustavus Adolphus, the "Lion of the North". These ships, commanded by Peter Minuit, who had been the Dutch Company's director at Manhattan from 1626 to 1632, arrived on the west bank of the Delaware River in the middle of March, 1638. Charmed by the beauty of the region, the Swedes gave the name of Paradisudden (Paradise Point) to a particularly beautiful spot where they landed temporarily. Passing on up the river, their ships arrived at the Minquas Kill of the Dutch (White Clay and Christina creeks), which enters the Delaware from the west. The ships then sailed up the Minquas Kill some distance, and cast anchor at a place where some Indians had pitched their wigwams.

Peter Minuit then fired a salute of two guns and went ashore with some of his men to reconnoiter and establish connection with the Indians. They also went some distance into the country.

Minuit then returned to his ship. The roar of his cannon had the desired effect; several Indian chiefs made their appearance, and Minuit at once arranged a conference with them for the sale of land. The leader of these chiefs was Mattahorn. Possibly Minuit from his acquaintance with the Dutch trade on the Delaware River during his administration at Manhattan, had some previous knowledge of this chieftain. Minuit and the chiefs had no difficulty in coming to an agreement. He explained to the Indians that he wanted ground on which to build a "house", and other ground on which to plant. For the former he offered a "kettle and other articles", and for the latter, half of the tobacco raised upon it. On the same, or following day, Mattahorn and five other chiefs went aboard one of the ships of the Swedes and sold as much "of the land on all parts and places of the river, up the river, and on both sides, as Minuit requested."

The merchandise specified in the deeds being given to them, the chiefs traced their totem marks on the documents, and Peter Minuit, Mans Kling, and others signed their names below. The extent of this purchase embraced the territory lying below the Minquas Kill to Duck Creek, a distance of forty miles and up the river to the Schuylkill, a distance of twenty-seven miles along the bank of the Delaware, in both cases stretching an indefinite distance to the westward. The purchase being concluded, Minuit with his officers and soldiers went ashore. A pole was then erected with the Coat of Arms of Sweden upon it; "and with the report of cannon, followed by other solemn ceremonies, the land was called New Sweden." This was the first Swedish colony in America.

Mattahorn's next appearance on the stage of history is in 1641 when a third nation, the English, becomes definitely connected with the history of the Delaware. English merchants and planters of New Haven, finding that their colony was poorly situated for trade with the Indians, looked for other places where they could settle and establish trading posts; and some of the principal merchants who had sent ships to the Delaware for some years, and had observed that this territory was sparsely settled and that the Swedish and Dutch forts and trading stations did not control the river, determined, in the autumn of 1640, to extend their activities systematically to the Delaware region. Accordingly, the "Delaware Company" was formed for the purpose of colonizing and trading on the Delaware; and two agents, Lamberton and Turner, with a number of assistants, were sent "to view and purchase part of the Delaware", in the spring of 1641. They were instructed to

buy lands from the Indians not yet occupied by any Christian
nation. Turner and Lamberton sailed up the Delaware River in
April, 1641, held several conferences with Mattahorn on its shores,
and on April 19th, purchased from this chieftain certain lands on
the Schuylkill, possibly within the limits of Philadelphia.

Mattahorn's name appears, in 1645, in the annals of the
Swedes on the Delaware, the only year in which Indian troubles
threatened the Swedish colony. The cause of this trouble was the
fact that the Dutch at Manhattan adopted a course of "extermination" of the Indians on the lower reaches of the Hudson, and during the years 1644 and 1645, had killed sixteen hundred of the
natives at Manhattan and in its neighborhood. They slaughtered
all ages and both sexes; and the word of these shocking and unpar-
donable cruelties spread along the Atlantic Ocean, causing the
Indians of the Delaware to feel bitter towards all newcomers. In
the spring of 1644, a Swedish woman and her husband, an Englishman, were killed not far from the site of Chester, Pennsylvania,—
the first white blood shed in Pennsylvania by the Indians. Governor John Printz of the Swedish colony then assembled his people
for the defense of Chester; but the Indian chiefs of that region
came to him disowning the act and desiring peace. He then made
a treaty of peace with them, distributing presents and restoring
friendly relations. During this year there was a great Indian
council held, which has been described by Rev. John Campanius,
over which Mattahorn presided and in which the destruction of
the Swedes was considered. Mattahorn is said to have presented
the question for the consideration of the council; but the decision
was that the Swedes should not be molested. The warriors said
that the Swedes should be considered "good friends", and that the
Indians had "no complaint to make of them."

Once more, this time in April, 1648, we meet Mattahorn, when
he and the Delaware chief, Sinquees, declared to the Dutch at Fort
Nassau that they and others had sold to Corssen, the Dutch agent,
in 1633, "the Schuylkill and adjoining lands."

The last time we meet Mattahorn in recorded history is when
he appeared, on July 9th, 1651, before a commission presided over
by the Dutch Director-General, Peter Stuyvesant, who was then
at the mouth of the Schuylkill. Mattahorn was then questioned
as to the purchase of lands by the Swedes from him in 1638, and
made the following reply: "That when Minuit came to the
country with a ship, he lay before the Minquaas Kill, where he,
the Sachem, then had a house and lived; that Minuit then pre-

sented him with a kettle and other trifles, requesting of him as much land as Minuit could set a house on, and a plantation included between 6 trees, which he, the Sachem, sold him, and Minuit promised him half the tobacco that would grow on the plantation, although it was never given to him. He declared further that neither the Swedes nor any other nation had bought the lands of them as right owners except the patch on which Fort Christina stood, and that all the other houses of the Swedes, built at Tinnecongh, Hingeesingh on the Schuylkill, and at other places were set up there against the will and consent of the Indians, and that neither they, nor any other natives had received anything therefor." On this day, (July 9, 1651), Mattahorn, Pemicka, Ackehon and Sinquees conveyed to Peter Stuyvesant a certain tract named Tamenconch, lying on the west shore of the Delaware, beginning at the west point of the Minquas Kill, extending unto Carasse, "and as far landward as our right extends, to-wit: to the bounds and limits of the Minquas [Susquehanna country]."

It is thus seen that this conveyance to the Dutch included a part, at least, of the lands which the Indians had conveyed to the Swedes in the spring of 1638; but it must be understood that the Indian ownership of the land was very vague and undefined. It was seldom that definite limits were established, and often several chiefs would lay claim to the same land, claiming jurisdiction over any region where they had established their hunting ground, by force or otherwise. Mattahorn assured Stuyvesant that he and his fellow sachems "were great chiefs and proprietors of the lands, both by ownership and consent and appointment of Minquas [Susquehanna] and River Indians." As has already been seen, the term "River Indians" was applied to the Delawares on the river of that name. This conveyance was signed by four Minquas or Susquehanna chiefs as witnesses thereto. It would thus seem that the Delawares on the lower part of the Delaware River were at that time subject to the authority of the Susquehannas. About twenty-five years after this conveyance was made, the Susquehannas were defeated by the Iroquois and the power of their nation forever destroyed. Consequently their sovereignty over the Indians on the Delaware River passed to the Five Nations.

Mattahorn being, in 1633, a chief of such importance as to sell lands of his tribe, was no doubt an elderly man when he made his exit from the stage of history, in 1651.

NAAMAN

Another outstanding Delaware chief, who figured in the history of the lower Delaware before the arrival of William Penn, was Naaman, whose name is preserved in Naaman's Creek, near the Delaware line. About all that is known of him is the fact that he was present on June 17th, 1654, at a great council of the Delawares at Printz Hall, at Tinicum, held for the purpose of renewing the ancient bond of friendship that existed between the Delawares and the Swedes. At this council Naaman praised the virtues of the Swedes. Campanius Holm thus describes this occasion:

"The 17th June, 1654, was gathered together at Printz Hall at Tinicum, ten of the sachemans of the Indian chiefs, and there at that time was spoken to them in the behalf of the great Queen of Sweedland for to renew the old league of friendship that was betwixt them, and that the Sweeds had bought and purchased land of them. They complained that the Sweeds they should have brought in with them much evil, because so many of them since are dead and expired. Then there was given unto them considerable presents and parted amongst them. When they had received the presents they went out, and had a conference amongst them a pretty while, and came in again, and then spoke one of the chiefs, by name Noaman [Naaman], rebuked the rest, and that they had spoken evil of the Sweeds and done them harm, and that they should do so no more, for they were good people. Look, said he, pointing upon the presents, what they have brought us, and they desire our friendship, and then he stroked himself three times down his arm, which was an especial token of friendship. Afterwards he thanked for the presents they had received, which he did in all their behalfs, and said that there should hereafter be observed and kept a more strict friendship amongst them than there hath been hitherto. That, as they had been in Governoeur Printz his time, one body and one heart, (beating and knocking upon his breast), they should henceforward be as one head. For a token waving with both his hands, and made as if he would tye a strong knot; and then he made this comparison, that as the callibash is of growth round without any crack, also they from henceforth hereafter as one body without any separation, and if they heard or understood that any one would do them or any of theirs any harm, we should give them timely notice thereof, and likewise if they heard any mischief plotting against the Christians, they would give them notice thereof, if it was at midnight. And then answer was made unto them, that that would be a true and lasting friendship, if every one would consent to it. Then the great guns were fired, which pleased them exceedingly well, saying, 'Pu-hu-hu! mo ki-rick pickon.' That is, 'Hear! now believe! The great guns are fired.' And then they were treated with wine and brandy. Then stood up another of the Indians and spoke, and admonished all in general that they should keep the league and friendship with the Christians that was made, and in no manner or way violate the same, and do them no manner of injury, not to their hogs or their cattle, and if any one should be found guilty thereof, they should be severely punished, others to an example. They advised that we should settle some Sweeds upon Passaiunck, where then there lived a power of Indians for to observe if they did any mischief, they should be confirmed, the copies of the agreements were then punctually read unto them. But the originals were at Stockholm, and when their names (were read) that had signed, they seemed when they heard it rejoiced, but when anyone's name was read that was dead, they hung their heads down and seemed to be sorrowful. And then there was set upon the floor in the great hall two great kettles, and a great many other vessels with sappan, that is, mush, made of Indian corn or Indian wheat, as groweth there in abundance. But the sachemans they sate by themselves, but the common sort of Indians they fed heartily, and were satisfied. The above mentioned treaty and friendship that then was made betwixt the Sweeds and the Indians, hath been ever since kept and observed, and that the Sweeds have not been by them molested."

In closing this sketch of the two outstanding Delaware chiefs before the arrival of Penn, we call attention to the fact that one of the most notable features in the history of the Swedes on the Delaware, with whom both Mattahorn and Naaman came into intimate contact, is the fact that the Swedes had no war either with the Lenape or Delawares, or their more dangerous neighbors, the Minquas, or Susquehannas. The Swedes even assisted the Susquehannas in their struggle against the might of the Iroquois, furnishing them arms for their warriors after the manner of European soldiers. They were on especially friendly terms with the Delawares, and sought to convert them to the Christian faith.

The principles upon which New Sweden was founded and its benevolent intentions towards the Indians are thus set forth in the letter granting the privileges to the colonists, signed by Chancellor

Axel Oxenstierna of Sweden, dated January 24th, 1640, and directed to the Commandant and inhabitants of Fort Christina, in New Sweden:

"As regards religion, we are willing to permit that, besides the Augsburg Confession, the exercise of the pretended reformed religion may be established and observed in that country, in such manner, however, that those who profess the one or the other religion live in peace, abstaining from every useless dispute, from all scandal and all abuse. The patrons of this colony shall be obliged to support, at all times, as many ministers and schoolmasters as the number of inhabitants shall seem to require, *and to choose, moreover, for this purpose, persons who have at heart the conversion of the pagan inhabitants to Christianity.*"

Carrying out these principles, we find Reverend John Campanius, the Swedish Lutheran clergyman, who accompanied Governor John Printz to New Sweden in 1643, active as a missionary among the Delawares and translating Martin Luther's Catechism into the Delaware tongue,—the first book to be translated into the language of the North American Indians. The petition, "Give us this day our daily bread," Campanius translated, "Give us this day a plentiful supply of venison and corn." Reverend Campanius was the first missionary of the Christian religion to labor among the Indians of Pennsylvania; and the Swedish Lutheran church at Tinicum, which he dedicated on September 4, 1646, and of which he was pastor, "was the first regularly dedicated church building within the limits of Pennsylvania."

If we examine the history of New Sweden from its founding, in 1638, to its overthrow by the Dutch, in 1655, we find many excellencies that stand out in strong contrast with the early history of her neighboring colonies. She had an instructed citizenship. With her, liberty of conscience was a historical fact, and not a mockery, or a myth, as with the "Pilgrim Fathers" of New England. She laid down the principles of liberty of conscience and education of the people, as the foundation of her political structure, before William Penn was born; and she steadfastly adhered to these principles to the end of her separate and independent existence, giving them an impetus that contributed very largely to their adoption as the most cherished and sacred principles in the structure of our American Commonwealth. These "Pilgrim Fathers", who landed on the shores of the Delaware and made the first settlements in Pennsylvania, had far more to do with molding American history than the Pilgrims of New England. "America," says Woodrow Wilson, "did not come out of New England."

Throughout New Sweden's entire history, that other outstanding fact, which has been alluded to, appears,—the preservation of friendly relations with the Indians, in contrast with the
bloody pages in the history of other colonies. Indeed, the just and
kindly treatment of the Delawares by the Swedish colonists had
much to do in causing the friendly reception which these children
of the forest gave William Penn at a later day when, with open
heart and open hand, they welcomed him to the shores of this
Western World.

A Picture of the Delawares in the Day of Mattahorn and Naaman

On July 28th, 1639, Adriaen van der Donck and others signed
a document describing the Delawares and their manners and customs as they were in the days of Mattahorn and Naaman and when
they first met the Europeans on the Delaware River. This description gives one of the most complete pictures of the Pennsylvania
Indians of this early period, and is as follows:

"The natives are generally well limbed, slender around the
waist, broad shouldered; all having black hair and brown eyes;
they are very nible and swift of pace, well adapted to travel on
foot and to carry heavy burdens; they are dirty and slovenly in
their habits; make light of all sorts of hardships, being by nature
and from youth upwards accustomed thereto. They resemble the
Brazilians in color, or are as tawny as those called Gipsies. Generally, the men have very little or no beard, some even pluck it
out; they use very few words, which they previously well consider.
Naturally they are quite modest, without guile, and inexperienced,
but in their way haughty enough, ready and quick witted to comprehend or learn, be it good or bad, whatever they are most inclined to. As soldiers they are far from being honorable, but perfid-
ious and accomplish all their designs by treachery; they also use
many stratagems to deceive their enemies and execute by night
almost all their plans that are in any way hazardous. The thirst
for revenge seems innate in them; they are very pertinacious in
self defence, when they cannot escape, which, under other circumstances, they like to do; they make little of death, when it is inevitable, and despise all tortures that can be inflicted on them at the
stake, exhibiting no faintheartedness, but generally singing until
they are dead.

"They also know right well how to cure wounds and hurts, or

inveterate sores and injuries, by means of herbs and roots indigen-
ous to the country, and which are known to them. The clothing
as well of men as of women consists of a piece of duffels, or of deer-
skin, leather, or elk hide around the body, to cover their nakedness.
Some have a bearskin of which they make doublets; others again,
coats of the skins of raccoons, wild cats, wolves, dogs, squirrels,
beavers and the like; and they even have made themselves some
of turkey's feathers; now they make use for the most part of duffels
cloth which they obtain in trade from the Christians; they make
their stockings and shoes of deerskins or elk hides, some even have
shoes of corn husks whereof they also make sacks. Their money
consists of white and black wampum which they themselves manu-
facture; their measure and value is the hand of fathom, and if it
be corn that is to be measured, 'tis done by the denotas which are
bags of their own making. Their ornaments consist of scoring
their bodies, or painting them of various colors, sometimes entirely
black, when they are in mourning; but mostly the face. They
twine both white and black wampum around their heads; formerly
they were not wont to cover these, but now they are beginning to
wear bonnets or caps, which they purchase from the Christians;
they wear wampum in the ears, around the neck and around the
waist, and thus in their way are mighty fine. They have also long
deers-hair which is dyed red, whereof they make ringlets to encircle
the head; and other fine hair of the same color, which hangs around
the neck in braids, whereof they are very vain. They frequently
smear their skin and hair with all sorts of grease. Almost all of
them can swim; they themselves construct the boats they use,
which are of two sorts; some of entire trees excavated with fire,
axes and adzes; the Christians call these canoes; others, again,
called also canoes, are made of bark, and in these they can move
very rapidly.

"Traces, and nothing more, of the institution of marriage can
be perceived among them. The man and woman unite together
without any special ceremony, except that the former, by agreement previously made with the latter, presents her with some wampum or cloth, which he frequently takes back on separating, if this
occur any ways soon. Both men and women are excessively un-
chaste and lacivious, without the least particle of shame; and that
is the reason that the men so frequently change their wives and the
women their husbands. They have, usually, but one wife; sometimes even two or three, but this mostly obtains among the chiefs.
They have also among them different ranks of people, such as

noble and ignoble. The men are generally lazy and will not work until they become old and of no consideration; then they make spoons, and wooden bowls, traps, nets, and various other such trifles; in other respects, they do nothing but hunt, fish and go to war.

"The women must perform the remainder of the labor, such as planting corn, cutting and hauling fire wood, cooking, attending to the children, and whatever else has to be done. Their dwellings are constructed of hickory poles set in the ground and bent bow fashion, like arches, and then covered with bark which they peel in quantities for that purpose. Some, but principally the chiefs; houses, have, inside, portraits and pictures somewhat rudely carved. When fishing or hunting, they lie under the blue sky, or little better. They do not remain long in one place, but remove several times a year and repair, according to the season, to wherever food appears to them, beforehand, best and easiest to be obtained.

"They are divided into various tribes and languages. Each tribe usually dwells together, and there is one among them who is chief; but he does not possess much power or distinction except in their dances and in time of war. Some have scarcely any knowledge of God; others very little. Nevertheless they relate very strange fables of the Deity. In general they have a great dread of the Devil, who gives them wonderful trouble; some converse freely on the subject and allow themselves to be strangely imposed upon by him; but their devils they say, will not have anything to do with the Dutch. Scarcely a word is heard here of any ghost or such like. Offerings are sometimes made to them, but with little ceremony. They believe also, in an Immortality of the soul; have likewise, some knowledge of the Sun, Moon, and Stars, many of which they even know how to name; they are passable judges of the weather. There is scarcely any law or justice among them, except sometimes in war matters, and then very little. The next of kin is the avenger; the youngest are the most daring, who mostly do as they like. Their weapons used to be a war club and the bow and arrow, which they know how to use with wonderful skill. Now, those residing near, or trading considerably with the Christians, make use of firelocks and hatchets, which they obtain in barter. They are excessively fond of guns; spare no expense on them, and are so expert with them that, in this respect they excel many Christians.

"Their fare, or food, is poor and gross, for they drink water, having no other beverage; they eat the flesh of all sorts of game that the country supplies, even badgers, dogs, eagles, and similar trash, which Christians in no way regard; these they cook and use uncleaned and undressed. Moreover, all sorts of fish likewise, snakes, frogs, and such like, which they usually cook with the offals and entrails. They know, also, how to preserve fish and meat for the winter in order then to cook them with Indian meal. They make their bread, but of very indifferent quality, of maize, which they also cook whole, or broken in wooden mortars. The women likewise perform this labor and make a pap or porridge, called by some Sapsis, by others, Duundare, which is their daily food. They mix this, also, thoroughly with little beans, of different colors, raised by themselves; this is esteemed by them rather as a dainty, than as a daily dish."

CHAPTER IV.

Tamanend

TAMANEND, (Tammany, etc.) was the head chief of the Unami or Turtle Clan of Delawares from before 1683 until 1697 and, perhaps later. He is referred to in the Colonial Records of Pennsylvania as "King" of the Delawares. As was seen in Chapter I, the head chief of the Turtle Clan always presided at the councils of the three clans composing the Delaware Nation. Tamanend lived and hunted along the Neshaminy Creek in what is now Bucks County. His name signifies "the affable". The town of Tamanend, in Schuylkill County, is named for this noted chieftain.

Tamanend is thus described by the Moravian missionary, Rev. John Heckewelder, who, as was stated in the first chapter of this book, was the staunch friend of the Delawares, and had lived among them in all the intimacy of friends and companions for more than thirty years:

"The name of Tamanend is held in the highest veneration by all the Indians. Of all the chiefs and great men which the Lenape nation ever had, he stands foremost on the list. But, although many fabulous stories are circulated about him among the whites, but little of his real history is known. The misfortunes which have befallen some of the most beloved and esteemed personages among the Indians since the Europeans came among them, prevent the survivors from indulging in the pleasure of recalling to mind the memory of their virtues. No white man who regards their feeling, will introduce such subjects in conversation with them. All we know, therefore, of Tamanend is that he was an ancient Delaware chief who never had an equal. He was, in the highest degree, endowed with wisdom, virtue, prudence, charity, affability, meekness, hospitality; in short with every good and noble qualification that a human being may possess. He was supposed to have had intercourse with the great and good Spirit; for he was a stranger to everything that is bad. The fame of this great man extended even among the whites, who fabricated numerous legends concerning him, which I never heard, however, from the mouth of an Indian, and, therefore, believe to be fabulous. In the Revolutionary War, his enthusiastic admirers dubbed him a saint and he was established under the name of Saint Tammany, the Patron Saint of America. His name was inserted in some calendars and his festival celebrated on the first day of May in every year."

Heckewelder then describes the celebrations in honor of Saint Tammany. They were conducted along Indian lines, and included the smoking of the calumet and Indian dances in the open air. "Tammany Societies" in the early part of our history as a nation, were organized in several American cities.

William Penn Purchases Land From Tamanend

William Penn did not set foot upon the soil of his Province until the 29th day of October, 1682; but, after maturing his plans for the new colony during the summer of 1681, he appointed his cousin, William Markham, to be his deputy governor. Markham left England in the spring of 1682, and arrived at New York about the middle of June of that year. He then proceeded to Upland, or Chester, Pennsylvania, and, no doubt, presented his credentials to the justices and announced to them and the settlers that once more a change of government had been decreed.

William Penn decided to follow the advice of the Bishop of London and the example of the Swedes, and purchase from the Indians inhabiting his Province whatever lands, within the bounds of the same, might from time to time, become occupied by his colonists. The first Indian deed of record was a purchase of lands in Bucks County, made by Deputy Governor Markham for William Penn, dated the 15th day of July, 1682; and though Tamanend was not of the grantors therein, we mention it in this connection on account of its historical importance. The native grantors were fourteen Delaware chiefs or "sachemakers", bearing the following names: Idquahon, Ieanottowe, Idquoquequon, Sahoppe for himself and Okonikon, Merkekowon, Orecton for Nannacussey, Shaurwawghon, Swanpisse, Nahoosey, Tomakhickon, Westkekitt and Tohawsis.

Markham paid the Indians for this purchase: 350 fathoms of wampum, 20 fathoms of "stroudwaters", 20 white blankets, 20 guns, 20 coats, 40 shirts, 40 pairs of stockings, 40 hose, 40 axes, 2 barrels of powder, 60 fathoms of "duffields", 20 kettles, 200 bars of lead, 200 knives, 200 small glasses, 12 pairs of shoes, 40 copper boxes, 40 tobacco tongs, 2 small barrels of pipes; 40 pairs of scissors, 40 combs, 20 pounds of red lead, 100 awls, two handfuls of fish hooks, two handfuls of needles, 40 pounds of shot, 10 bundles of beads, 10 small saws, 12 drawing knives, 2 ankers of tobacco, 2 ankers of rum, 2 ankers of cider, 2 ankers of beer, and 300 guilders in money,—a formidable list, indeed, and all very acceptable to the Indians.

However, on June 23rd, 1683, William Penn, at a meeting with Tamanend and a number of other Delaware chiefs at Shakamaxon, within the limits of Philadelphia, purchased four different tracts of land from the Indians. The first deed was from Tamanend, who made "his mark" to the same, being a snake coiled. This deed conveyed all of Tamanend's lands "lying betwixt the Pemmapecka [Pennypack] and Nessaminehs [Neshaminy] Creeks, and all along Nessaminehs Creek." The consideration was "so many guns, shoes, stockings, looking glasses, blankets, and other goods as the said William Penn shall please to give."

On the same date, (June 23, 1683), William Penn purchased a second tract of land from Tamanend, the deed being signed by Tamanend and Metamequan. It conveyed all the grantors' lands "lying betwixt and about Pemmapecka and Nessaminehs Creeks, and all along Nessaminehs Creek." The consideration was "so much wampum and other goods as he, the said William Penn, shall be pleased to give unto us." However, there is a receipt attached to this deed for the following articles: 5 pairs of stockings, 20 bars of lead, 10 tobacco boxes, 6 coats, 2 guns, 8 shirts, 2 kettles, 12 awls, 5 hats, 25 pounds of powder, 1 peck of pipes, 38 yards of "duffields", 16 knives, 100 needles, 10 glasses, 5 caps, 15 combs, 5 hoes, 9 gimlets, 20 fish hooks, 10 tobacco tongs, 10 pairs of scissors, 7 half-gills, 6 axes, 2 blankets, 4 handfuls of bells, 4 yards of "stroudswaters" and 20 handfuls of wampum.

Also, on the 5th day of July, 1697, "King Taminy [Tamanend], and Weheeland, my Brother and Weheequeckhon alias Andrew, who is to be king after my death, Yaqueekhon alias Nicholas, and Quenameckquid alias Charles, my Sons", granted to William Penn, who was then in England, all the lands "between the Creek called Pemmapeck [Pennypack] and the Creek called Neshaminy, in the said province extending in length from the River Delaware so far as a horse can travel in two summer dayes, and to carry its breadth according as the several courses of the said two Creeks will admit, and when the said Creeks do so branch that the main branches or bodies thereof cannot be discovered, then the Tract of Land hereby granted, shall stretch forth upon a direct course on each side and so carry on the full breadth to the extent of the length thereof."

It is to be noted that in the list of articles which Penn gave in exchange for the various tracts of land purchased from Tamanend and his associate chiefs, no brandy or other strong liquor appeared. It will be recalled that in Markham's purchase in Bucks County on the 15th of July, 1682, he gave the contracting sachems, rum, cider and beer as part of the purchase price. Penn, however, was more scrupulous than his deputy governor, doubtless having realized more strongly than Markham, the injury done the Indians by liquor. Indeed, in the "Great Law" which Penn drew up shortly after his arrival, there was a provision for punishing any person by fine of five pounds who should "presume to sell or exchange any rum or brandy or any strong liquors at any time to any Indian, within this province." Later the Indians found their appetite for strong liquor to be so strong that they agreed, if the colonists would sell them liquor, to submit to punishment by the civil magistrates "the same as white persons."

Penn's Treaty with Tamanend

Penn's memorable treaty with Tamanend and other Delaware chiefs, under the great elm at Shakamaxon, within the limits of Philadelphia, is full of romantic interest. Unarmed, clad in his sombre Quaker garb, he addressed the Indians assembled there, uttering the following words, which will be admired throughout the ages: "We meet on the broad pathway of good faith and good-will; no advantage shall be taken on either side, but all shall be openness and love. We are the same as if one man's body was to be divided into two parts; we are of one flesh and one blood." The reply of Tamanend, is equally noble: "We will live in love with William Penn and his children as long as the creeks and rivers run, and while the sun, moon, and stars endure."

No authentic record has been preserved of the "Great Treaty", made familiar by Benjamin West's painting and Voltaire's allusion to it "as the only treaty never sworn to and never broken;" and there has been a lack of agreement among historians as to the time when it took place. Many authorities claim that the time was in the November days, shortly after Penn arrived in his Province. "Under the shelter of the forest," says Bancroft, "now leafless by the frosts of autumn, Penn proclaimed to the men of the Algonquin race, from both banks of the Delaware, from the borders of the Schuylkill, and, it may have been, even from the Susquehanna, the same simple message of peace and love which George Fox had professed before Cromwell, and Mary Fisher had borne to the Grand Turk."

Other authorities, in recent times, fix the time of the treaty as on the 23rd day of June, 1683, when Penn, as has been seen, purchased the four tracts of land from Tamanend and his associates; in other words, that the purchase of land and the "Great Treaty" took place at the same time and at the same place. Moreover, a study of West's painting of the treaty scene shows the trees to be in full foliage, thus not suggesting a late autumn or winter day, as contended by Bancroft, but rather a day in the leafy month of June. Even if we should not grant the purchase of the four tracts of land from Tamanend and others on the 23rd of June, 1683, the distinction of being the "Great Treaty", it was most certainly *a treaty* of great importance and entitled to a prominent place in the Indian history of Pennsylvania and the Nation.

Says Jenkins, in his "Pennsylvania, Colonial and Federal": "In the years following 1683, far down into the next century, the Indians preserved the tradition of an agreement of peace made with Penn, and it was many times recalled in the meetings held with him and his successors. Some of these allusions are very definite. In 1715, for example, an important delegation of the Lenape chiefs came to Philadelphia to visit the Governor. Sassoonan— afterward called Allummapees, and for many years the principal chief of his people—was at the head, and Opessah, a Shawnee chief, accompanied him. There was 'great ceremony', says the Council record, over the 'opening of the calumet'. Rattles were shaken, and songs were chanted. Then Sassoonan spoke, offering the calumet to Governor Gookin, who in his speech spoke of 'that firm Peace that was settled between William Penn, the founder and chief governor of this country, at his first coming into it', to which Sassoonan replied that they had come 'to renew the former bond of friendship; that William Penn had at his first coming made a clear and open road all the way to the Indians, and they desired the same might be kept open and that all obstructions might be removed', etc. In 1720, Governor Keith, writing to the Iroquois chiefs of New York, said: 'When Governor Penn first settled this country he made it his first care to cultivate a strict alliance and friendship with all the Indians, and condescended so far as to purchase his lands from them.' And in March, 1722, the Colonial Authorities, sending a message to the Senecas, said: 'William Penn made a firm peace and league with the Indians in these parts near forty years ago, which league has often been repeated and never broken.' "   In fact, the "Great Treaty" was never broken until the Penn's Creek Massacre of October 16, 1755.

Unhappily, then, historians are not able to agree in stating the exact date of the "Great Treaty" under the historic elm on the banks of the Delaware,—a treaty that occupies a high and glorious place in the Indian history and traditions of Pennsylvania and the Nation.   Though the historian labors in vain to establish the date, the *fact* of the treaty remains as inspiring to us of the present day as it was to the historians, painters, and poets of the past.

On August 16th, 1683, William Penn wrote a long letter to the Free Society of Traders, in which he describes a council that he had with the Indians,—possibly the "Great Treaty":

"I have had occasion to be in council with them (the Indians) upon treaties for land, and to adjust the terms of trade.   Their order is thus: The King sits in the middle of an half moon, and hath his council, the old and wise, on each hand; behind them or at a little distance, sit the younger fry in the same figure.   . . . When the purchase was agreed, great promises passed between us of kindness and good neighborhood, and that the Indians and English must live in love as long as the sun and moon give light; which done, another made a speech to the Indians in the name of all the Sachamakers or Kings, first to tell them what was done; next to charge and command them to love the Christians, and particularly live in peace with me, and the people under my Government; that many Governors had been on the River, but that no Governor had come himself to live and stay here before; and having now such an one that treated them well, they should never do him or his any wrong.   At every sentence of which they shouted and said Amen in their way."

Last Days of Tamanend

Tamanend's last appearance in recorded history was when he, his brother and sons, conveyed the lands to William Penn on July 5th, 1697.   But three years prior thereto, or on July 6th, 1694, he appeared at a council at Philadelphia, a number of other Delaware chiefs accompanying the venerable sachem.   At this council, he thus expressed his friendly feelings for the colonists, in a speech addressed to Lieutenant-Governor Markham: "We and the Christians of this river [Delaware] have always had a free roadway to one another, and although sometimes a tree has fallen across the road, yet we have still removed it again, and kept the path clean; and we design to continue the old friendship that has been between us and you."

Tamanend died before July, 1701, but the date of his death is not known. All that is mortal of this great and good chieftain reposes in the soil of the beautiful valley of the Neshaminy,—the region which he and his associate chiefs conveyed to "Miquon", or "Brother Onas", as the Indians affectionately called William Penn. His grave is believed to be in "Tammany Burial Ground", near Chalfonte, Bucks County.

CHAPTER V.

Opessah and His Son, Loyparcowah

OPESSAH

S we have seen, in Chapter II, Opessah, or Wopaththa, was the chief of the band of Shawnees, consisting of seventy families, who came from Cecil County, Maryland, and settled at Pequea, Lancaster County, Pennsylvania, about the year 1697 or 1698. No doubt his name was pronounced "Opeththa", as the Shawnee language did not contain the sibilant.

William Penn's Treaty with Opessah and Other Indians of the Susquehanna Region

William Penn returned to Pennsylvania in December, 1699, after an absence of fifteen years; and he remained in his Province until the autumn of 1701, when he left finally, arriving in England about the middle of December of that year. During his second sojourn in Pennsylvania, he made his home in his commodious Manor House, at Pennsbury, in Falls Township, Bucks County, about twenty miles from Philadelphia. The erection of the mansion had been started during his absence and was completed by him after his return. Here he received many visits from different Indian chiefs, a room in the mansion having been set apart for Indian conferences.

During Penn's second sojourn in his Province, he endeavored to obtain additional legislation placing restrictions on the intercourse with the Indians, in order to protect them from the arts of the whites and the ravages of the rum traffic. He also endeavored to have the natives instructed in the doctrines of Christianity. In order to improve the temporal condition of the natives, he held frequent conferences at his manor house with various sachems; and frequently visited them in their forest homes, participating in their festivals. When they visited him at Pennsbury, it is said that he joined with them in their sports and games, ate hominy, venison, and roasted acorns with them, and matched them in strength and agility. It is recorded that nineteen Indian treaties were concluded and conferences held at Pennsbury.

After the close of King William's war, the governor of New York made a treaty of peace with the Five Nations; and at William Penn's suggestion it was extended to the other English colonies. On April 23rd, 1701, Penn entered into "Articles of Agreement", or a treaty, at Philadelphia, with the Susquehannas, Minquas, or Conestogas, the Shawnees, the Ganawese, Conoys, or Piscataways, the latter then dwelling on the northern bank of the Potomac, and the Five Nations. In this treaty the Susquehannas were represented by Connodaghtoh, their "king", and three chiefs of the same; the Shawnees were represented by Opessah, or Wopaththa, their "King", and two other chiefs; the Conoys, Ganawese, or Piscataways, were represented by four of their chiefs; and the Five Nations were represented by Ahoakassongh, "brother to the emperor or great king of the Onondagas."

We are now ready to state the provisions of the treaty. After first reciting the good understanding that had prevailed between William Penn and his lieutenants, on the one hand, and the various Indian nations inhabiting his Province, on the other hand, since his first arrival in Pennsylvania, and expressing that there should be forever a firm and lasting peace between Penn and his successors and the various Indian chiefs of his Province, the treaty provided as follows:

First. That the said "kings and chiefs" and the various Indians under their authority should, at no time, hurt, injure or defraud any inhabitants of the Colony of Penn; and that Penn and his successors should not suffer any injury to be done the Indians by any of his colonists.

Second. That the Indians should, at all times, behave themselves in a sober manner according to the laws of the Colony where they lived near or among the Christian Inhabitants thereof; and that they should have the full and free privileges and immunities of the laws of the Colony of Penn in the same manner as the whites, and acknowledge the authority of the crown of England in the Province.

Third. That none of the Indians should, at any time, aid, assist or abet any other nation, whether of Indians or others, that would at any time not be in amity with the king of England.

Fourth. That, if at any time, the Indians should hear from evil-minded persons or sowers of sedition any unkind reports of the English, representing that the English had evil designs against the Indians, in such case the Indians should send notice thereof to Penn or his successors, and not give credence to such reports until fully satisfied concerning the truth of the same. Penn agreed that he and his successors should at all times act in the same manner toward the Indians.

Fifth. That the Indians should not suffer any strange nations of Indians to settle on the farther side of the Susquehanna or about the Potomac, except those that were already seated there, nor bring any other Indians into any part of the Province without the permission of Penn or his successors.

Sixth. Penn, for the purpose of correcting abuses that were too frequently connected with the fur trade with the Indians, agreed on the part of himself and his successors, that no one should be permitted to trade with the Indians without first securing a license under the Governor's hand and seal; and the Indians agreed, on their part, not to permit any person whatsoever to buy or sell, or have any trade with them, without first having a license so to do.

Seventh. The Indians agreed not to sell or dispose of any of their skins or furs to any person whatsoever outside of the Province; and Penn bound himself and his successors to furnish the Indians with all kinds of necessary goods for their use, at reasonable rates.

Eighth. The Conoys, Ganawese, or Piscataways, should have leave of Penn and his successors to settle on any part of the Potomac River within the bounds of Penn's Province. (At this time, the vexed question as to the boundary line between Pennsylvania and Maryland was unsettled).

Ninth. The Susquehannas, or Conestogas, as a part of these articles of agreement, absolutely ratified and confirmed the sale of lands lying near and about the Susquehanna, formerly conveyed to William Penn, by deed of Governor Dongan of New York, and later confirmed by the deed of the Conestogas, dated the 13th day of September, in the year 1700, to both of which conveyances reference will be made in Chapter VI. The Susquehannas also agreed to be, at all times, ready further to confirm and make good the said sale, according to the tenor of the same, and that they would be answerable to Penn and his successors for the good behavior of the Conoys or Ganawese, and for their performing of their several agreements which were a part of this treaty.

Tenth.   In the last item of the agreement, Penn promised, for himself and his successors, that they would, at all times, show themselves true friends and brothers to all of the Indians by assisting them with the best of their "advices, directions and counsel", and would, in all things just and reasonable, befriend them; and the chiefs promised, for themselves and their successors, to behave themselves according to the tenor of the agreement, and to submit to the laws of the Province in the same manner as "the English and other Chrstians therein do."   The agreement was then concluded by the exchange of skins and furs, on the part of the Indians, and goods and merchandise, on the part of Penn.

At about the time of making this historic treaty of peace with the Indians on the Susquehanna, William Penn had journied into the interior of his Province, and conferred with the Conestogas at Conestoga, their principal town, in Lancaster County, the Conestogas being responsible for the good behavior of the Shawnees in their vicinity, as was pointed out in Chapter II.   Penn wrote to James Logan, in June, 1701, of his visit to the Conestoga region, as follows: "We were entertained right nobly at the Indian King's palace at Conestoga."   At that time, Penn intended the founding of a "great city" in the Conestoga region, on the Susquehanna.

At the time of this treaty, most of the Conoy were living on the north bank of the Potomac, though some had already entered Pennsylvania as early as 1698 or 1699, as stated in Chapter II. Some years after the treaty, or in the summer of 1705, the Delaware chief, Manangy, living on the Schuylkill, interviewed Governor John Evans, at Philadelphia, explaining that the Conoy, "settled in this Province near the head of the Potomac, being now reduced by sickness to a small number, and desirous to quit their present habitation where they settled about five years ago with the Proprietor's consent, the Conestoga Indians then becoming guarantees of a treaty of friendship, made between them, and showing a belt of wampum they had sent to the Schuylkill Indians to engage their friendship and consent that they might settle amongst them near Tulpehocken, request of the Governor that they may be permitted to settle in the said place."   The Governor then permitted the Conoy to settle in the valley of the Tulpehocken, Manangy and his band on the Schuylkill guaranteeing their good behavior.

Governor Evans Holds Councils with Opessah

On the sixth and seventh of June, 1706, a council was held at Philadelphia between Governor John Evans and "the chiefs of the Conestogas, Shawnees, and Ganawese, or Conoys", concerning public affairs relating to these tribes. Indian Harry, of the Conestogas, was the interpreter. In the minutes of the council, the Colonial Records do not specifically state that Opessah was present, but, being the head of the Shawnees at Pequea, there is no doubt that he attended the council. This council opened with Secretary James Logan's account of his journey to the Conestogas and Conoy during the preceding October and the treaty which was then held with the Conoy at their town (Connejaghera, Conejoholo, Dekanoagah) near the site of Washington Borough, Lancaster County, by the terms of which treaty, the Conoy were assured that they would be safe in Penn's Province. The Conoy explained to James Logan, at the time of his visit, that they had had much trouble with the Virginians, and, considering it not safe to dwell in their old abode on the Potomac, had come within the bounds of Pennsylvania, where they hoped to dwell in peace.

During this council at Philadelphia, Andaggy-Junguagh, chief of the Conestogas, laid before Governor Evans a very large belt of wampum, which he said was a pledge of peace formerly delivered by the Onondagas to the Nanticokes when the Onondagas had subjugated this tribe. He explained that the Nanticokes, being lately under some apprehension of danger from the Five Nations, some of them had, in the spring of 1706, come to the region of the Conestogas, and had brought this belt with them, as well as another belt, which, the chief explained, he left at his village in Lancaster County. He further advised the Governor that the Five Nations, of whom the Onondagas, as has been seen, were a member, were presently expected to send deputies to receive the tribute of the Nanticokes; that he had brought this belt to Philadelphia in order that the Colonial Authorities might be able to show it to any of the Five Nations, who might come to Philadelphia, as evidence to them that peace had been made. The Provincial Council, after considering the matter, concluded to keep the belt according to the proposal of the Conestogas; and the Conestogas promised to retain the other belt at their chief town, to be shown to the Five Nations, if any of their deputies should come to Conestoga.

The remaining time of the council was taken up by explaining to the chiefs of these three nations the laws which had been recently enacted regulating the intercourse between the Province and these Indians. Evans explained to the chiefs that a law had recently been enacted providing that no person should trade with them but such as should first have a license from the Governor under his hand and seal. The chiefs requested the Governor that only two traders be licensed, but Evans explained that the fewer the number of traders the more likely it would be that the Indians would be imposed upon. They then desired of the Governor that he would not permit the traders to go beyond their towns and meet the Indians returning from hunting, explaining that it had been the traders' custom to meet the Indians returning from their hunt, when they were loaded with furs and peltries, make them drunk, and get all of the fruits of their hunt before they returned to their wives and families. The Governor agreed to this proposal and told the chiefs that their people should have no dealings with the traders, except at their own villages, and that he would instruct the traders not to go any farther into the Susquehanna region than the principal Indian towns, and to do no trading whatever, except in those places. Liberal presents were then given the chiefs, and the council adjourned.

At a meeting of the Provincial Council on the 31st of August, 1706, it was decided that Governor Evans should visit Conestoga and the region round about it, for the purpose of further strengthening the bond of friendship between the Indians and the Colony. The Governor accordingly journeyed to this region early in September, where he was well received by the Conestogas, Shawnees and Conoys; but his visit was the cause of much scandal on account of his actions while there.

The French, as early as 1707, had their emissaries among the Conestogas under the guise of traders, miners or colonists, in an effort to draw them away from their allegiance to the English. Likewise, the colony of Maryland was pushing her pioneers over the boundary, in an effort to forestall the claims of William Penn by actual settlement.

In the month of June, 1707, Governor Evans, accompanied by Colonel John French, William Tonge, and several other Friends, and four servants, made a journey among the Susquehanna Indians, upon receiving a message from the Conestogas that the Nanticokes, who now had been tributaries of the Five Nations for twenty-seven years, intended journeying to the Onondagas in New York. He visited the following places: Pequea, Dekonoagah, Conestoga, and Paxtang, near Harrisburg.

At Pequea, the Governor and his party were received by the Shawnees with a discharge of firearms, and a conference was held, on June 30th, with Opessah, in which the chief told the Governor that he and his people were "happy to live in a country at peace, and not as in those parts where we formerly lived, for, then, upon returning from hunting, we found our town surprised, and our women and children taken prisoners by our enemies." While the Governor was at Pequea, several Shawnees from the South came to settle there, and were permitted to do so by Opessah, with the Governor's consent.

At Dekonoagah, the Governor was present at a meeting of the Shawnees, Conoys, and Nanticokes from seven of the surrounding towns. After having satisfied himself that the Nanticokes were a well meaning people, the Governor guaranteed them the protection of the Colony of Pennsylvania.

The Governor, having received information at Pequea that a Frenchman, named Nicole, was holding forth among the Indians at Paxtang, about whom he had received many complaints, and having advised the chief at Paxtang of his intention to seize this French trader, captured Nicole, after much difficulty, and, having mounted him on a horse with his legs tied, conveyed him through Tulpehocken and Manatawney, to Philadelphia, and lodged him in jail.

In Chapter II, a detailed account was given of the conference at Conestoga, on June 8th, 1710, between the two commissioners of Governor Evans (John French and Henry Worley) and Opessah, Civility, and the Tuscarora commissioners, to which conference reference is made at this point.

Opessah continued as chief of the Shawnees on the lower Susquehanna, with his principal seat at Pequea, until 1711. Then he voluntarily abandoned both his chieftainship and his tribe, and made his home among the Delawares to the northward, whose chief was Sassoonan, or Allummappees. Three principal chiefs of the Conestogas appeared before Governor Charles Gookin and the Provincial Council, at Philadelphia, on October first, 1714, and advised them that Opessah, "the late King of their neighbors and friends, the Shawnees," had left his people about three years previously, and, though often urged to return, refused to do so. The Shawnees at Pequea then elected a new king, named Cakundawanna, who accompanied the delegation of Conestoga chiefs and was presented to the Council. On June 14, 1715, Opessah, with Sassoonan, chief of the Delawares, attended the conference with Governor Gookin, mentioned in Chapter IV.

It is probable that Opessah sought an asylum among the Delawares through fear that the Five Nations or the English would hold him responsible for the murder of Francis de la Tore and several other white bond-servants of the trader, John Hans Steelman, by some young Shawnees, in 1710.   Another account, this one traditionary, ascribes his desertion to the fact that he fell in love with a Delaware squaw who refused to leave her people.

A few years later, (1722) Opessah settled at Old (Shawnee) Town, on the Potomac, in Maryland, a town frequently called Opessah's Town by the Marylanders, as late as 1725. It is probable that he was the chief referred to by the Potomac Shawnee chiefs from the Ohio, Opakethwa and Opakeita, when they told Governor Gordon, upon their visit to Philadelphia, in September, 1732, that "formerly they lived at Patowmack, where their king died; that, having lost him, they knew not what to do; that they took their wives and children and went over the mountains, [to the Ohio and Allegheny valleys] to live."

LOYPARCOWAH

Loyparcowah was a son of Opessah.   His name appears several places in the Colonial Records in the following form: "Loyparcowah, Opessah's Son."   The Shawnee chief, Neucheconneh, "Deputy King", seems to have acted as vice-regent during the young manhood of this heir of the famous Shawnee chief, who came with his people to Pequea, Lancaster County, in 1697, or thereabouts.

Loyparcowah was one of the Shawnees who left the Susquehanna Valley and crossed the mountains to the valley of the Allegheny. The year in which he did this is not known, but it is likely that he was among those of his tribe who went west from Paxtang and New Cumberland about 1727—the first Shawnees to follow the Delawares to the valleys of the Ohio and Allegheny.

Loyparcowah Opposes Rum Traffic

Reference has been made to the fact that the Shawnees were highly displeased on account of the constant supply of rum brought to them by the traders in violation of the laws of the Colony. Their wise men recognized that it was the curse of the Red Man, causing his physical, mental, and moral deterioration. Protests were made by the leaders of this tribe time and again to the effect that the Colony failed to enforce the laws against the rum traffic. In fact, one of the main reasons why the Shawnees migrated to the western part of Pennsylvania was their desire to escape the ruinous effects of strong liquor. But the trader with his rum followed them into the forests of their western homes.

Then the Shawnee on the Conemaugh, Kiskiminetas, and Allegheny took steps, in 1738, to restrain this pernicious traffic. On March 20th of that year, three of their chiefs in this region, namely: "Loyporcowah (Opessah's Son), Newcheconneh (Deputy King), and Coycacolenne, or Coracolenne (Chief Counsellor)", wrote a letter to Thomas Penn and James Logan, Secretary of the Provincial Council, in which they acknowledged the receipt of a present from Penn and Logan of powder, lead, and tobacco, delivered to them by the trader, George Miranda; in which they say they have a good understanding with the French, the Five Nations, the Ottawas, and all the French Indians; that the tract of land reserved for them by the Proprietory Government on the west side of the Susquehanna does not suit them at present; and that they desire to remain in the region of the Allegheny and Kiskiminetas, make a strong town there, and keep their warriors from making war upon other nations at a distance. They then add:

"After we heard your letter read, and all our people being gathered together, we held a council together, to leave off drinking for the space of four years. . . . There was not many of our traders at home at the time of our council, but our friends, Peter Chartier and George Miranda; but the proposal of stopping the rum and all strong liquors was made to the rest in the winter, and they were all willing. As soon as it was concluded of, all the rum that was in the towns was staved and spilled, belonging both to Indians and white people, which in quantity consisted of about forty gallons, that was thrown in the street; and we have appointed four men to stave all the rum or strong liquors that is brought to the towns hereafter, either by Indians or white men, during the four years." A pledge signed by ninety-eight Shawnees and the two traders above named accompanied this letter, agreeing that all rum should be destroyed, and four men appointed in every town to see that no strong liquor should be brought into the Shawnee towns for the term of four years.

Previous to this action on the part of Loyparcowah and other chiefs of the Shawnees, the Delawares at Kittanning made complaints concerning the rum traffic. In 1732, the trader, Edmund Cartlidge, wrote the Governor from Kittanning that the chiefs there made reflections on the Government for permitting such large quantities of rum to be carried to the Allegheny and sold to the Indians at that place, contrary to law. Also, in 1733, the Shawnee chiefs in the Allegheny region wrote the Governor requesting that he send them an order permitting them "to break in pieces all kegs of rum so brought yearly and monthly by some new upstart of a trader without a license, who comes amongst us and brings nothing but rum, no powder, nor lead, nor clothing, but takes away with him those skins which the old licensed traders, who bring us everything necessary, ought to have in return for their goods sold us some years since." Also in 1734, the Shawnee chiefs at Allegheny wrote the Governor and requested that none of the licensed traders be allowed to bring them more than thirty gallons of rum twice in a year, except Peter Chartier, who "trades further than ye rest."

Loyparcowah later descended the Allegheny and Ohio, probably remaining for some time at Chartier's Old Town, on or near the site of Tarentum, Allegheny County, and at Logstown, near the site of Economy, in the same county. In 1752, we find him at the Lower Shawnee Town, at mouth of the Scioto. On February 8th, of this year, he joined with three other Shawnee chiefs of the Lower Shawnee Town, in a letter to Governor James Hamilton of Pennsylvania, informing the Governor that "all the nations settled on this River Ohio and on this side of the Lakes are in friendship and live as one people; but the French trouble us much; they threaten to cut us off, and have killed thirty of our brothers, the Twightwees (Miamis); and we now acquaint you that we intend to strike the French."

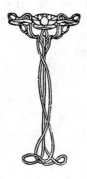

CHAPTER VI.

Oretyagh, Ocowellos and Captain Civility

ORETYAGH

RETYAGH claims our remembrance as one of the chiefs of the Conestogas to come into touch with William Penn. He attended the council at Philadelphia, on July 6th, 1694, mentioned at the close of Chapter IV. This is his first appearance in recorded history.

Oretyagh Sells Susquehanna Land to William Penn

Oretyagh next appears as one of the grantors of lands on the Susquehanna to William Penn, the history of which transaction is as follows:

By deed, dated September 10th, 1683, the Conestoga chief, Kekelappan, granted to Penn "that half of all my lands betwixt Susquehanna and Delaware, which lieth on ye Susquehanna side." In this same deed he promises to sell Penn in the following spring, upon his return from hunting, the other half of his lands. Also, on October 18th, 1683, the Conestoga chieftain, Machaloha, who claimed to exercise authority over the Indians "on the Delaware River, Chesepeake Bay and up to ye falls of ye Susquehanna River", conveyed to Penn his right in his land.

With reference to the deeds of Kekelappan and Machaloha, Penn seems to have thought it advisable to get the consent of the Five Nations to his possession of the lands in the interior of the country in the region of the Susquehanna. He had no doubt learned of the defeat of the Susquehannas at their fort, in either Lancaster or York County, at the hands of the Five Nations, or Irquois, in 1675. Accordingly, he sent two agents to confer with the Irquois chiefs in New York, in the summer of 1683, with reference to these lands; and in July of that year, he wrote acting Governor Brockholls of New York, commending to his favor these agents sent to treat with the Iroquois "about some Susquehanna land on ye back of us, where I intend a colony forthwith."

On August 25th, 1683, a new Governor, Thomas Dongan, reached New York, displacing Brockholls. He remained Governor of the colony until August, 1688. Immediately upon his arrival, he heard of the negotiations of Penn's agents; and both he and the Albany justices feared that Penn would plant a strong settlement on the Susquehanna, and thus get the profitable fur trade of the Five Nations of New York. The Susquehanna River afforded a splendid highway from the central part of the Five Nations' territory right to the settlement which Dongan feared Penn would found on the lower part of that river. Dongan called "an extraordinary meeting" of the justices on September 7th. When they assembled, they had with them several chiefs of the Iroquois, among them being two Cayugas and "a Susquehanna." The justices closely questioned the chiefs concerning the "situation of the Susquehanna River" as to its geographical and trade relations with the settlements of the colony of New York, especially that of Albany. The chiefs replied that it was "one day's journey" from the Mohawk castles to the lake where the Susquehanna rises; that it was one and one-half days' journey overland from Oneida "to the kill which falls into the Susquehanna River", and one day from there to the river itself; that it was but a half day's journey overland and one day by water from Onondaga to the Susquehanna River; that it was but one and one-half days' journey by land and water from Cayuga to the Susquehanna River; and that it was three days' journey overland and two by water from the "four castles" of the Senecas to the Susquehanna River, and then only five days' journey by water to the Susquehanna castles. The chiefs explained that all this journey was "very easy, they conveying their packs in canoes."

It was but natural that the chiefs should inquire as to the reason for such detailed questioning. They inquired why the justices wanted all this information and pointedly asked whether the white men were coming to the Susquehanna. The justices asked them in turn how that would suit them, and the chiefs frankly replied "very well"; that it would be much easier and nearer for trade than Albany offered, "insomuch as they must bring everything thither on their backs." This candid statement of the chiefs was very alarming to the justices, and they immediately wrote Dongan urging that he find "an expedient for preventing" Penn's acquisition of a Susquehanna Indian title. On September 18th, Dongan advised the justices that he considered it "very convenient and necessary to putt a stopp to all proceedings in Mr. Penn's affairs with the Indians until his bounds and limits be adjusted"; and he instructed them "to suffer no manner of proceedings in that business" until they should receive further advice from him.

The justices, therefore, prevailed with the chiefs to advise the agents of Penn that they had no right to sell the Susquehanna lands, having promised them to "Corlaer"—the generic name for the New York governors—on some previous occasion, and to decline to proceed with the negotiations. Then Dongan, in order to get the matter in his own hands, procured from some of the sachems a deed of the lands to himself. Then he wrote Penn, on the 10th of October, advising him of the purchase, and again, on the 22nd of October, saying that it had been further confirmed by the Iroquois, but that he and Penn would not "fall out" over the matter.

Thus the matter stood until the 13th day of January, 1696, on which date Dongan executed a lease and release to William Penn of "all that tract of land lying upon, on both sides, the river commonly called or known by the name of Susquehanna River, and the lands adjacent, beginning at the mountains or head of the said river, and running as far as and into the bay of Chesapeake." The territory conveyed is further described as being the same "which the said Thomas Dongan lately purchased of or had given him by the Sinneca Susquehanna Indians."

This deed gave Penn whatever title to the Susquehanna Dongan had procured in 1683 from the Iroquois as over lords of the Susquehanna clans. But, in order to get indisputable title to these Susquehanna lands, Penn, after he returned to his Province early in December, 1699, from his fifteen years absence in England, made and concluded, on the 13th day of September, 1700, a treaty with Oretyagh, or Widaagh, and Andaggy-Junkquagh, "Kings or Sachems of the Susquehannagh Indians, and of the river under that name, and lands lying on both sides thereof", by the terms of which these chiefs granted to him all the rights they possessed on the Susquehanna, and ratified and confirmed unto him "ye bargain and sale of ye said lands, made unto Col. Thomas Dongan, now Earl Limerick, and formerly Governor of New York." This sale was further confirmed in the "Articles of Agreement" which Penn concluded with the Susquehanna or Conestoga Indians, at Philadelphia, on April 23, 1701, which agreement was related in Chapter V.

Oretyagh Bids Farewell to William Penn

Shortly before embarking for England, in the autumn of 1701, William Penn assembled a large company of the Delawares at his manor house at Pennsbury to review and confirm the covenants of peace and good will, which he had formerly made with them. The meeting was held in the great hall of the manor house. The sachems assured him that they had never broken a covenant "made with their hearts and not with their heads." After the business of the conference had been transacted, Penn made them many presents of coats and other articles, and then the Indians retired into the courtyard of the mansion to complete their ceremonies.

Likewise, Oretyagh, with a number of the sachems of the Conestogas and Shawnees, came to Philadelphia shortly before Penn's final departure for England, to take leave of their beloved "Brother Onas." At this conference, which was held on October 7th, 1701, Penn informed the chiefs that it was likely the last interview that he would ever have with them; that he had ever loved and been kind to them and ever would continue so to be, not through political designs or for a selfish interest, but out of real affection. He desired them, in his absence to cultivate friendship with those whom he would leave in authority, so that the bond of friendship already formed might grow the stronger throughout the passing years. He also informed them that the Assembly was at that time enacting a law, according to their desire, to prevent their being abused by the selling of rum among them, with which Oretyagh, in the name of the rest, expressed great satisfaction, and desired that the law might speedily and effectually be put into execution. Oretyagh said that his people had long suffered from the ravages of the rum traffic, and that he now hoped for redress, believing that they would have no reason for complaint of this matter in the future.

Penn early saw the degradation which the Indians' unquenchable thirst for strong drink wrought among them, and he did all in his power to remedy this matter. He said that it made his heart sick to note the deterioration of character and the degradation which the strong liquor and vices of the white man wrought among the Indians during his short stay in the Province.

Finally, at this leavetaking, Penn requested the Indians that, if any of his colonists should ever transgress the law and agreement, which he and his governor had entered into with them, they should at once inform the government of his Province, so that the offenders might be prosecuted. This they promised to observe faithfully, and that, if any rum were brought among them, they would not buy it, but send the person who brought it back with it again. Then, informing the chiefs that he had charged the members of his Council that they should, in all respects, be kind and just to the Indians in every manner as he had been, and making them presents, he bade them adieu never to meet them again.

Well would it have been for the Colony of Pennsylvania, if Penn's successors had always emulated his example in dealing with the Indians—if his successors had been imbued with his kindly spirit, and had treated the natives with justice. He died on the 30th of July, 1718, at Ruscombe, near Tywford, in Buckinghamshire, England, at the age of seventy-four; and when his great heart was cold and still in death, the Red Man of the Pennsylvania forests lost his truest friend. During Penn's life there were no serious troubles between his colony and the Indian, and no actual warfare, as we shall see, for some years thereafter; but, less than a generation after this great apostle of the rights of man was gathered to his fathers, the Delawares, who had welcomed him so kindly, and the Shawnees, rose in revolt, after a long series of wrongs, and spread terror, devastation, and death throughout the Pennsylvania settlements.

Says Dr. George P. Donehoo: "The memory of William Penn lingered in the wigwams of the Susquehanna and the Ohio until the last red man of this generation had passed away; and then the tradition of him was handed down to the generations which followed until today, when it still lingers, like a peaceful benediction, among the Delaware and Shawnee on the sweeping plains of Oklahoma."

Oretyagh made a later protest against the abuses of the rum traffic by the Pennsylvania traders. In May, 1704, according to the Colonial Records: "Oretyagh, the chief now of Conestoga, requested him [Nicole Godin, a trader] to complain to the Governor [John Evans] of the great quantities of rum continually brought to their town, insomuch that they (the Conestogas) are ruined by it, having nothing left, but have laid out all, even their clothes for rum, and may now, when threatened with war, be surprised by their enemies, when besides themselves with drink, and so utterly be destroyed." With this protest against the detestable traffic, which, even at this early day, was bringing ruin upon the Pennsylvania Indians, we close this sketch of Oretyagh, the friend of William Penn.

OCOWELLOS

Perhaps the first reference to the Shawnee chief, Ocowellos, is in the account of the conference which Governor William Keith of Pennsylvania held with the Shawnees, Conestogas, Conoy, and other Indians at Conestoga, in July, 1717, at which time and place he asked them to explain their connection with an attack made by the Senecas upon the Catawbas, then under the protection of Virginia. The Shawnee chief advised the Governor that six Shawnees had accompanied the war party of Senecas who made the attack, but that these six were from a Shawnee settlement much higher up the Susquehanna. At any rate, Ocowellos is referred to as "King of the Upper Shawnees" in the minutes of a council held at Philadelphia, May 20th, 1723, when an address from him to the Provincial Council was read in which he mentioned past visits to the Governor of Canada, and another which he then contemplated making. Most authorities believe that his seat was then near the mouth of Chillisquaque Creek, on the east bank of the West Branch of the Susquehanna, in Northumberland County.

Ocowellos removed from the Susquehanna to the valley of the Conemaugh prior to 1731, possibly several years earlier. On October 29th, 1731, Jonas Davenport, an Indian trader, made an affidavit for the Provincial Council, in which he said: "On Connumach [Conemaugh] Creek, there are three Shawnee towns; 45 families; 200 men; Chief Okowela [Ocowellos], suspected to be a favorer of the French interest."

The three Conemaugh towns, over which Ocowellos ruled in 1731 and later, can not be definitely located. They were probably the following: Keckenpaulin's Old Town, at the mouth of the Loyalhanna, in Westmoreland County; Black Legs Town, at the mouth of Black Legs Creek, in Indiana County; and Conemaugh Old Town on the site of Johnstown, Cambria County.

From the few glimpses of Ocowellos that we get in the Colonial Records, it is seen that he was one of the Shawnee chiefs who early yielded to French influence.

CAPTAIN CIVILITY

Captain Civility, or Civility, was a chief of the Conestogas, descendants of the ancient Susquehannas. As "Chief of the Conestogas", he is mentioned in the Colonial Records from 1710 to 1736. He was present at the conference at Conestoga, June 8th, 1710, between the Pennsylvania commissioners, John French and Henry Worley, and the deputies of the Tuscaroras, when this tribe sought permission to settle within the bounds of Penn's Colony, an account of which conference was given in Chapter II.

He seems to have had varying degrees of authority. For instance, in the minutes of the conference at Conestoga, above referred to, he is mentioned as "the Senneques' [Conestogas'] King", and on July 23rd, 1712, as a "War Captain and Chief"; in June, 1713, he is mentioned as "the young Indian called Civility, now one of their [the Conestogas] chiefs; in June, 1715, he and Satayoght, or Satayriote, are called "the chiefs of the Conestogas"; while, July 30th, 1716, Satayriote is called chief, and Civility the "Captain", of the Conestogas. In June, 1718, he attended a conference at Philadelphia, in the minutes of which he is called "the present chief or captain of the Conestogas."

In this conference, Civility informed Governor Keith that the Conestogas had chosen, Oneshanayan, to be their new king. He also attended a conference at Philadelphia, in July, 1720, and soon thereafter seems to have become the ruling chief of the Conestogas; though in the minutes of a conference held at Conestoga, May 26th, 1728, between Governor Gordon and the Conestogas, Shawnees, and Conoy, (which will be described in Chapter VIII) he, Tawenna, Ganyataronga, and Tanniatchiaro are mentioned as "chiefs of the Conestogoe Indians." In October, 1728, he wrote Governor Gordon acquainting him with the fact that several of the Delawares, Shawnees, and Conoy had come to Conestoga and brought many skins with them as a present for the Governor; "that they purposed to fulfill their promise of coming to Philadelphia this fall, but that the death of his, Civility's, child had so much afflicted him that he could not come with them, and therefore they had all resolved to defer their visit until spring, at which time they would surely come to the Governor of Philadelphia."

In 1729, he wrote Governor Gordon concerning the killing and capture of nine Shawnees near the Potomac by the "Southern Indians" [Catawbas]; and, on May 26th of that year, he was the chief speaker of the Conestogas at a conference held at Philadelphia between Governor Gordon and the Conestogas, Shawnees, and Conoy, in which he complained very bitterly of the baneful effects of the carrying of so much rum to the Indians. The last mention of Civility, in the Colonial Records, is in the minutes of a conference held at Philadelphia, on October 14th, 1736, between Thomas Penn and eighteen Iroquois chiefs, whose speaker informed Penn and the Provincial Council; "That if Civility at Connestogoe should attempt to make a sale of any lands to us, or any of our neighbors, they must let us know that he hath no power to do so, and if he does any thing of the kind, they, the Indians, will utterly disown him."

Troubles Between the Northern and
the Southern Indians

But Civility claims our remembrance chiefly on account of his conferences with the Colonial Authorities during the troubles between the Northern and the Southern Indians in the years following the migration of the Tuscaroras from Carolina and Virginia to the territory of the Five Nations in New York. As was pointed out in Chapter II, they began this migration in 1712 or 1713, and were formally admitted, in 1722, as a constituent part of the Iroquois Confederation. However, while the Tuscaroras were still living in their southern home, they were the bitter enemies of the Catawbas, and their hatred did not abate upon their removing to New York.

Almost every summer after 1713, roving bands of the Tuscaroras and other members of the Five Nations, followed the mountain valleys through Pennsylvania to the South, on their way to attack the Catawbas and Cherokees; and many Conestogas joined these war parties. Some destruction was done by these bands within the Province of Pennsylvania, but presently the Colonial Authorities adopted the method of having the farmers, whose crops were injured, place their bill in the hands of the nearest justice of the peace, who would, in turn, forward it to the Provincial Council; and, at the next conference with the Indians, the Council would deduct the amount of the bill from the present given to the Indians at that conference. This method made Pennsylvania practically free from ravages wrought by these bands. The colony of Virginia, however, did not fare so well, and both lives and property were destroyed by these bands of warriors from the North.

These war parties of the Iroquois frequently made Conestoga their stopping place on their way to and return from the territory of the Catawbas and Cherokees, and many a captive Catawba and Cherokee was tortured to death at Conestoga. Finally a treaty of peace was made between the Conestogas and Catawbas, on August 31st, 1715, but this did not put a stop to the expeditions of the Iroquois against the Southern Indians.

In June, 1717, Governor William Keith received a message from Civility and several other chiefs of the Conestoga region, desiring him to visit them without delay to consult about affairs of great importance. The Governor, accordingly, journeyed to Conestoga, in July, where he met the chiefs of the Conestogas, Delawares, Shawnees, and Conoys, and inquired of them the cause of their alarm. He ascertained that about two months previously a young Delaware, son of a chief, had been killed on one of the branches of the Potomac by a party of Virginians accompanied by some Indians. These latter were no doubt Catawbas, who, at that time, were at peace with Virginia. At this meeting at Conestoga, Governor Keith brought to the attention of the Indians that many complaints had been made by the inhabitants of Virginia concerning the destruction caused by the war parties of the Iroquois against the Catawbas; and he reminded them of the fact that, although divided into different colonies, the English were one people; that to injure or make war upon one body of them was to make war upon all, and that the Indians, therefore, must never molest or trouble any of the English colonists, nor make war upon any Indians who were in friendship with, or under the protection of, the English.

At this conference, Keith stressed the fact that recently a band of Senecas had attacked some Catawbas near Fort Christian, in the colony of Virginia, killing six and capturing a woman; and he called upon the Indians of the Conestoga region to explain their connection with this insult to Virginia. The Shawnee chief told the Governor that six young men of this tribe had accompanied the party of Senecas who made the attack upon the Catawbas, but explained that none of the six were present at the time and place of this conference, "their settlements being much higher up the Susquehanna River." The chief further stated that the six Shawnees declared, upon their return, that they had nothing to do with the attack upon the Catawbas.

Governor Keith closed the conference with the following stipulations, quoted from the minutes of the conference:

"1st. That he expected their strict observance of all former contracts of friendship made between them and the Government of Pennsylvania.

"2dly. That they must never molest or disturb any of the English Governments, nor make war upon any Indians whatsoever who are in friendship with and under the protection of the English.

"3dly. That, in all cases of suspicion or danger, they must advise and consult with this Government before they undertook or determined any thing.

"4thly. That, if through accident any mischief of any sort should happen to be done by the Indians to the English, or by the English to them, then both parties should meet with hearty intention of good will to obtain an acknowledgment of the mistake, as well as to give or receive reasonable satisfaction.

"5thly. That, upon these terms and conditions, the Governor did, in the name of their great and good friend, William Penn, take them and their people under the same protection, and in the same friendship with this Government, as William Penn himself had formerly done, or could do now if he was here present.

"And the Governor hereupon did promise, on his part, to encourage them in peace, and to nourish and support them like a true friend and brother.

"To all which the several chiefs and their great men presently assented, it being agreed, that, in testimony thereof, they should rise up and take the Governor by the hand, which accordingly they did with all possible marks of friendship in their countenance and behaviour."

But the trouble between them did not end with the foregoing conference at Conestoga. In 1719, great difficulties arose concerning the hunting grounds of the Northern and the Southern Indians. The Iroquois sent out many war parties, which stopped at Conestoga on their way south, and were joined by many of the Conestogas. These raids into the Shenandoah Valley brought many white settlers of Virginia and the Carolinas into hostility to the Iroquois; for these Colonies were then on friendly terms with the Catawbas and Cherokees, against whom the raids were directed. In fact, a general uprising of the settlers of Virginia and the Carolinas was imminent. The Iroquois conducted their warfare on the Southern Indians with great brutality, torturing many captives to death at Conestoga and villages on the Susquehanna.

On receiving a letter from Civility and other chiefs at Conestoga advising that some of their Indians had been killed by the Southern Indians, Governor Keith sent Colonel John French to Conestoga, where a council was held on June 28th, 1719, with Civility and Queen Canatowa of the Conestogas, "Wightomina, King of the Delawares, Sevana, King of the Shawnees", who succeeded Opessah at Pequea, and "Winninchack, King of the Canawages" [Conoys]. In the name of Governor Keith, Colonel French made the following demands of Civility and the other chiefs: That they should not receive the war parties of the Tuscaroras, or any other tribes of the Five Nations, if coming to their towns on their way to or return from the South; and that they would have to answer to the Colonial Authorities, if any prisoner were tortured by them. It appeared, however, that the warriors of the Five Nations, on their way southward, practically forced the young men of the Conestogas, Shawnees, and Conoy to accompany them. As the conquerors of these tribes, the Iroquois demanded their allegiance and help. The chiefs promised faithfully to obey the commands of Governor Keith, but the war went on.

James Logan, Secretary of the Provincial Council, on June 27, 1720, held a conference at Conestoga with Civility and chiefs of the Shawnees, Delawares, and Conoy, in an attempt to persuade these Indians from making raids into Virginia. Not long before, ten Iroquois and two Shawnees had been killed by the Southern Indians about one hundred and sixty miles from Conestoga. At this conference, Logan learned that the Pequea Shawnees could not be restrained from assisting the Iroquois, inasmuch as since the departure of Opessah, no one could control them. True, the Conestogas were answerable for the behavior of these Shawnees, but Civility advised Logan that he "had only the name without any authority, and could do nothing." Moreover, it was difficult for Logan to impress upon the minds of these Indians the fact that the English of Virginia and Maryland were not at war with the English of Pennsylvania. They could not see why the Indians in friendship with Pennsylvania should not go to war against the Virginians, just as the Iroquois went to war against the Indians of Virginia and the Carolinas.

At the close of the conference, Captain Civility told Logan privately that the Five Nations, especially the Cayugas, were much dissatisfied because of the large settlements the English were making on the Susquehanna, and that the Iroquois claimed a property right in those lands. As to the Iroquois' claim to a property right in the Susquehanna lands, Logan told Civility that the Indians well knew that the Iroquois had long before conveyed those lands to the Governor of New York, and that William Penn had purchased this right, as was pointed out in Chapter VI. Civility acknowledged this fact.

Realizing the awful consequences of a general war between the Iroquois and their allies, on the one side, and the Southern Indians on the other, involving the settlers of the South, Governor Keith, in the spring of 1721, visited Governor Spotswood of Virginia with whom he framed an agreement, by the terms of which the tribu-

tary Indians of Virginia would not, in the future, pass the Potomac
nor "the high ridge of mountains extending along the back of
Virginia; provided that the Indians to the northward of the Potomac and to the westward of those mountains" would observe the
same limits.

Governor Keith, accompanied by seventy armed horsemen,
visited Conestoga on July 5th, 1721, where he conferred, at
Civility's lodge, not only with the Conestogas but also with four
deputies of the Five Nations, who had recently arrived there, telling the spokesman of the Five Nations, Ghesoant, that, "whereas
the English from a very small beginning had now become a great
people in the Western World, far exceeding the number of all the
Indians, which increase was the fruit of peace among themselves,
the Indians continued to make war upon one another and were destroying one another, as if it was their purpose that none of them
should be left alive." He called attention to the suffering that
their wars caused to the women and children at home, and, in various ways, tried to mollify their warlike passions, but stated that,
if they were determined to continue warfare, they must, in journeying to and from the South, take another path lying farther to the
west, and not pass through the settled parts of the Province. The
result of the conference was the ratifying by the Conestogas and
Five Nations of the agreement arranged by Governor Keith and
Governor Spotswood as to the limits of the hunting grounds of the
Virginia and the Pennsylvania Indians. Keith closed the conference by giving Ghesoant a gold coronation medal of George, the
First, which he asked him to take as a token of friendship to the
greatest chief of the Five Nations, Kannygoodk. Thus, happily,
the immediate danger of a general Indian uprising was averted.

This was the most important Indian treaty ever held at
Conestoga. Later, troubles came on apace between the Iroquois
and the Southern Indians, but the Iroquois abandoned the Susquehanna route to the South, taking the Warrior's Path, which crossed
the Potomac at Old Town (Opessah's Town), and, still later, when
white settlers occupied the valley along Warrior Ridge, a trail
farther westward, crossing the counties of Westmoreland and Fayette.

While there was now a lull in the trouble between the Northern and the Southern Indians, the fears of the Province were further awakened by a quarrel between two brothers, John and
Edmund Cartilidge, and a Seneca Indian, near Conestoga, in
which the latter was cruelly murdered early in 1721. The Colon-

ial Authorities well knew the Indians' love for revenge, and they apprehended severe retaliation. A rigid inquiry was made into the matter, and an inquest was ordered to be held on the body, though the same had been buried for more than two months. The Cartilidge brothers were seized and put in jail in Philadelphia, awaiting trial under the laws of the Colony. Messengers were sent by the Colonial Authorities to the Five Nations, advising them that the Provincial Council deplored the incident, and, in order to prevent a repetition of such unfortunate occurrences, had prohibited the sale of rum and other strong drink to the Indians by re-enacting the former law on this matter, with additional penalties.

Treaty at Albany

In this sketch of Civility, we call attention to the Albany Treaty of 1722, definitely ending, for a time, the troubles between the Iroquois and the Catawbas, in which troubles he had a prominent part. The Iroquois, in the summer of 1722, invited Governor Keith to meet them with the Governors of Virginia, New York, and New England, in a great council at Albany, New York, in which all matters between the Indians and these colonies could be taken up. In extending the investigation, they explained that their king was an old man, and could not make a journey to Philadelphia. The council was accordingly held at Albany, on the 10th day of September, 1722, in which the Five Nations acknowledged that Penn's Governors had always observed the treaties that Penn had entered into with the Indians, surrendered all claim to their lands on the Susquehanna concerning which the Cayugas had made claim, and with great magnanimity pardoned the offense of the Cartilidge brothers in having murdered the Seneca Indian. Governor Keith had explained to them that the brothers were now out on bail awaiting trial. The reply of the great "king" of the Five Nations, pardoning the Cartilidge brothers, shows the better qualities of the Indians' nature. It is thus recorded in Volume III of the Colonial Records of Pennsylvania: "The great King of the Five Nations is sorry for the death of the Indian that was killed, for he was of his own flesh and blood; he believes the Governor [Keith] is also sorry; but, now that it is done, there is no help for it, and he desires that Cartilidge may not be put to death, nor that the Governor should be angry and spare him for some time, and put him to death afterwards; one life is enough to be lost; there should not two die."

At this treaty, Governor Spotswood, or Virginia, secured the assent of the Tuscaroras and other members of the Five Nations to a proposed boundary within the limits of which the Indians of Virginia should be safe, as follows: That the various tribes tributary to the colony of Virginia should not, without having a passport from the Governor, on any pretense whatsoever, cross to the northern side of the Potomac or to the west side of the Allegheny Mountains; in case they should do so without such passport, it should be lawful for the Indians to the northward to put such Southern Indians to death.   Also that the Five Nations and the Shawnees, should not, without having a passport, cross to the southern side of the Potomac River or to the eastward of the Allegheny Mountains; that, in case any of these Northern Indians should pass beyond these boundaries, they should be put to death or sold into slavery.

At the close of the treaty, "the speaker of the Five Nations holding up the Coronet, they [the Iroquois] gave six shouts, five for the Five Nations, and one for a Castle of the Tuscaroras, lately seated between Oneyde [Oneida] and Onondage [Onondaga]", indicating that the Tuscaroras were, at that time, an integral part of the Confederation of the Iroquois, thus making the Six Nations.

First Reference to the Ohio and Allegheny

In closing this sketch of Civility, we call attention to the fact that he attended a council held in Philadelphia on July 3rd to 5th, 1727, at which the Indians requested that "none of the traders be allowed to carry any rum to the remoter parts where James LeTorte trades, (that is Allegheny on the branches of the Ohio)."   This is the first mention in the Colonial Records of Pennsylvania of the region on the Ohio and Allegheny, and shows that, at this early date, the Indian traders from Conestoga had established trading posts in the valleys of the Ohio and Allegheny.   In the minutes of this conference, also, we find reference to "a fort" (no doubt trading house) which the French had already built in the valley of the Allegheny.   He also attended the conference held at Conestoga May 26th, 1728, between Governor Gordon and the chiefs of the Conestogas, Shawnees, Conoy, and Delawares, with reference to the Indian troubles of that year, as related in the chapter on Kakowatcheky (Chapter VIII).

CHAPTER VII.

Sassoonan or Allumapees

The Line of Succession From Tamanend

SASSOONAN, or Allumapees, was head chief of the Turtle Clan of Delawares from a date prior to June 14th, 1715, until his death in the autumn of 1747. By some very high authorities, it is claimed that he was a son of the great Tamanend and, as a little boy, was with his father at the "Great Treaty". These authorities make Sassoonan identical with "Weheequeckhon, alias Andrew", who as stated in Chapter IV, joined with his father, Tamanend, his two brothers, and his uncle, in conveying to William Penn, on the fifth day of July, 1697, certain lands between the Pennypack and Neshaminy creeks, and whom Tamanend describes in the deed, as, "my son who is to be king after my death."

As stated in Chapter IV, Tamanend died probably before 1701; for, at council held at Philadelphia on July 26th of that year, his name is not mentioned in the list of Delaware chiefs at that time. Who succeeded Tamanend in the kingship of the Turtle Clan of Delawares is not known, though some authorities think that Owechela was his successor, and identify him with Weheelan, Tamanend's brother, one of the grantors in the deed of July 5th, 1697, suggesting that he may have acted as vice-regent during the minority of Weheequeckhon, alias Andrew. Plausibility is given to the claim that Owechela succeeded Tamanend by the fact that a·chief named Owhala, or Ochale, (a name very similar to Owechela, if he was not actually this same chief) is called "King of the Delawares" in the Maryland Council Records of 1698 and 1700. Says Charles A. Hanna:

"Whether or not Owechela was the ruling chief of the Delawares from 1701 to 1709, the name of a new chief appears on the records of the latter year. This was Skalitchy, who with Owechela, Passakassy, and Sassoonan, attended the conference at Philadelphia in July, 1709."

The conference to which Mr. Hanna refers was held on the 26th of July, and, in the minutes thereof, Sassoonan's place of residence is set forth as being "at Peshtang [Paxtang] above Conestoga." But Skalitchy also attended a conference between the Indians and Governor Charles Gookin and the Provincial Council, held on May 19th, 1712, at the house of Edward Farmar, at White Marsh, in what is now Montgomery County, in which he took the most prominent part. Sassoonan, too, was present at the conference.

We pause in the narration of the successors to Tamanend's kingship to call attention to the fact that the conference at the house of Edward Farmar deserves our attention on account of the light it throws on the subjugation of the Delawares by the Five Nations. Governor Gookin and the Provincial Council had been summoned to Farmar's house to meet Skalitchy, Sassoonan and twelve other Delaware chiefs, who desired to confer with the Governor and Council before setting out on a journey to the Five Nations. At the conference, Skalitchy addressed the Governor as follows: "Many years ago, being made tributaries to the Mingoes, or Five Nations, and being now about to visit them, they [the Delaware chiefs] thought fit first to wait on the Governor and Council; to lay before them the collection they had made of their tribute to offer; and to have a conference with the Governor upon it."

They then spread out on the floor thirty-two belts of wampum having figures and designs wrought therein by their women, and a long pipe having a stone head and a cane shaft with feathers attached and arranged to resemble wings. They called this pipe the Calumet, and said that it had been given to them by the Five Nations at the time of their subjugation, to be kept and shown to other nations, among whom they might go, as a token of their subjection to the Iroquois. One of the wampum belts, they said, "was sent by one, who at the time of their agreement or submission, was an infant and orphan, the son of a considerable man amongst them." Skalitchy explained that twenty-four of these wampum belts were sent by women, because "the paying of tribute becomes none but women and children." Hanna suggests that the receipt by the Council of the Five Nations of so many tribute wampum belts from the women of the Delawares at this time and, no doubt, at times earlier and later, probably "did much to confirm the tradition among the Five Nations that the Delaware Indians were but a nation of women."

Skalitchy's name does not appear again in the Colonial Records until the conference held at Philadelphia on June 14th, 1715, which was the conference with Governor Gookin and the Provincial

Council mentioned in Chapter IV, in the minutes of which Sassoonan is reported as saying, among other things, "that their [the Delawares'] late king, Skalitchy, desired of them that they would take care to keep a perfect peace with ye English." Sassoonan was the head of the Delaware delegation at this conference, and his statement, just quoted, fixes the date af Skalitchy's death and Sassoonan's succession to the kingship of the Delawares as between the conference of May 19th, 1712, and the conference of June 14th, 1715.

As we have seen, there had been many conferences between the Colonial Authorities, on the one hand, and the Delawares, Shawnees, Conestogas, and Conoy on the other, during the intervening years; but the conference of June 14th, 1715, is entitled to more than passing notice, for the reason that Sassoonan referred particularly to the "Great Treaty", which Penn made with the Delawares in the early days of the history of the Province. The conference was simply for the purpose of renewing the ancient bond of friendship. In the minutes of this conference, we read the following:

"Then Sassoonan rose and spoke to the Governor and said that the calumet, the bond of peace, which they had carried to all the nations round, they had now brought hither; that it was a sure bond and seal of peace amongst them and between them and us, and desired, by holding up their hands, that the God of Heaven might be witness to it, and that there might be a firm peace between them and us forever. . . . . That they desired the peace that had been made should be so firm, that they and we should join hand in hand so firmly that nothing, even the greatest tree, should be able to divide them asunder."

The minutes of this council contain the statement that, "We [the Governor and Council] doubted not but they [the Indians] think themselves and their children, from generation to generation, obliged to keep inviolably those firm treaties of peace which had been made."

Sassoonan's Deed of Release

In the autumn of 1718, Sassoonan and several other chiefs of the Delawares came to Philadelphia, claiming that they had not been paid for their lands. Then, James Logan, secretary of the Provincial Council, produced to them, in the presence of the Council, a number of deeds, and convinced Sassoonan and his brother chiefs that they were mistaken in their contention. Accordingly, Sassoonan and six other chiefs executed a release on the 17th day of September, 1718, by the terms of which they acknowledged that their ancestors had conveyed to William Penn, in fee, all the land and had been paid for the same. By the same instrument these Indians released all the land "between the Delaware and the Susquehanna from Duck Creek [in Delaware] to the mountains [the South Mountain] on this side of Lechay [by the Lehigh River]."

At the time of executing this deed of release, Sassoonan was still living at Paxtang, and adjacent parts; but it is probable that shortly thereafter he took up his abode at Shamokin (Sunbury), which became his home for the remainder of his life. The Delawares, who, as pointed out in Chapter I, migrated from the vicinity of Shamokin to the Allegheny in 1724, were of Sassoonan's clan.

Sassoonan Clears Members of Turtle Clan From Blame for Murder of Thomas Wright

At a meeting of the Provincial Council, on September 27th, 1727, Secretary James Logan, advised the Council that, on the day before, he received a letter from John Wright, justice of the peace, giving an account of the murder of one, Thomas Wright, who was killed, on the eleventh day of that month, by some Indians at Snaketown, forty miles above Conestoga, possibly above the mouth of Swatara Creek, in Dauphin County. Enclosed with the letter were the depositions of John Wilkins, Esther Burt, and Mary Wright, and the inquisition held on the dead body.

The affair took place at the trading house of John Burt, an Indian trader at Snaketown. The unfortunate Thomas Wright and some Indians were drinking with Burt near the house, when a dispute arose between one of the Indians and Wright; whereupon, Burt urged Wright to knock the Indian down. Wright then laid hold of the Indian, and Burt struck him (the Indian) several blows with his fist. Wright and Burt then retired into the trading house, and the Indians followed. Wright endeavored to pacify them, but Burt called for his gun, and continued to provoke them more and more in a way too revolting and disgusting to be told in the language of decency. Wright fled to the hen-house to hide himself, whither the Indians pursued him, and the next morning he was found there dead. The inquisition on his body set forth that he came to his death by several blows on his head, neck, and temples.

The Colonial Authorities were much disturbed by this, the first murder of a white man by the Indians after William Penn first arrived in his Province, forty-five years before. They were of the opinion that John Burt was to blame for the unhappy incident, on account of his provoking the Indians to such a high degree. The record of the incident, as set forth in Volume III of the Colonial Records, states that although Burt was a licensed trader, yet "it was scarce possible to find a man in the whole Government more unfit for it." A warrant was issued for his arrest, but he escaped, and was next heard of at the Forks of the Ohio.

The Indians were Delawares of the Munsee or Wolf Clan as was ascertained in June, 1728, when Sassoonan, his nephew, Opekasset, and a number of other chiefs, including the great Shikellamy, the vice-gerent of the Six Nations, who had recently been sent to Shamokin (Sunbury) by the Six Nations to rule over the Shawnees and Delawares on the Susquehanna, met Governor Patrick Gordon at Philadelphia, where a great council was held on the 4th and 5th of that month. Sassoonan being asked by Governor Gordon about the death of Thomas Wright, replied: "That it [the murder] was not done by any of their people; that it was done by some of the Menysinck [Minisink] Indians; that the Menysincks live at the Forks of the Susquehannah, above Meehayomy [Wyoming], and that their king's name is Kindassowa." The "Forks of the Sasquehannah" may refer to the forks of the Tioga, or Chemung, and the Susquehanna near Athens, Bradford County; or it may refer to the junction of the Lackawanna and the Susquehanna in Luzerne County. At any rate, wherever the Indians lived that killed Thomas Wright, they never were brought to account.

Sassoonan and the Tulpyhocken Lands

At this same conference, (June 4th and 5th, 1728,) Sassoonan complained that the Palatines (immigrants from Germany) were settling on the lands in the valley of the Tulpyhocken, in Berks and Lebanon counties, which, as he claimed, had not been purchased from the Indians. These particular Palatines had first settled in the Schoharie Valley in New York, where they endured much suffering. When Governor William Keith, of Pennsylvania, attended the Albany conference in September, 1727, the hardships of these Palatines were related to him; whereupon his interest and sympathy were aroused, and he offered them a home in Pennsylvania. Then, in the autumn of 1727, about fifty families of these

Germans, under the leadership of the father of the famous Conrad Weiser, the Indian interpreter of the Colony of Pennsylvania, cut a road from the Schoharie Valley through the wilderness to the headwaters of the Susquehanna. They then descended this river to the mouth of Swatara Creek, in Dauphin County. Ascending this stream and crossing the divide between the Susquehanna and the Schuylkill, they entered the fertile and charming valley of the Tulpyhocken. They had scarcely erected their rude cabins and commenced to plant their little patches of corn in the clearings in the wilderness, when the Indians of the neighborhood informed them that this land had never been purchased by the Pennsylvania Government. The Indians were much surprised that these settlers should be permitted to take up their abode on unpurchased land. "Surely," said they, "if Brother Onos were living, such things would never happen."

At this conference, Sassoonan said that he could not have believed that these lands were settled upon, if he had not gone there and seen the settlements with his own eyes. In the minutes of the conference, we read: "He (Sassoonan) said he was grown old and was troubled to see the Christians settle on lands that the Indians had never been paid for; they had settled on his lands for which he had never received anything. That he is now an old man, and must soon die; that his children may wonder to see all their father's lands gone from them without his receiving anything for them; that the Christians now make their settlements very near them (the Indians); and they shall have no place of their own left to live on; that this may occasion a difference between their children and us, and he would willingly prevent any misunderstanding that may happen."

Governor Gordon suggested to Sassoonan that possibly the lands in dispute had been included in some of the other purchases; but Sassoonan and his brother chiefs replied that no lands had ever been sold northwest of the Blue Ridge, then called the Lehigh Hills. This conference did not succeed in settling the matter of these settlements in the Tulpyhocken Valley. The matter dragged along until 1732, when Sassoonan, Elalapis, Ohopamen, Pesqueetamen, Mayemoe, Partridge, and Tepakoasset, on behalf of themselves and all other Indians having a right in the lands, in consideration of 20 brass kettles, 20 fine guns, 50 tomahawks, 60 pairs of scissors, 24 looking glasses, 20 gallons of rum, and various other articles so acceptable to the Indians, conveyed unto John Penn, Thomas Penn, and Richard Penn, proprietors of the Province, all those lands "situate, lying and being on the River Schuylkill and the branches thereof, between the mountains called Lechaig (Lehigh) to the south, and the hills or mountains, called Keekachtanemin, on the north, and between the branches of the Delaware River on the east, and the waters falling into the Susquehanna River on the west,"—a grant which embraced the valley of the Tulpyhocken.

Sassoonan attended another conference at Philadelphia in the year 1728. This was a conference with Governor Gordon and the Provincial Council, on October 10th of that year, in which the old chief expressed his pleasure on the settlement of the troubles in that year with Kakowatcheky's Clan of Shawnees at Pechoquealin, an account of which is given in Chapter VIII. In the minutes of the conference of October 10th, are found these sentiments of Sassoonan: "He tells the Governor that he hopes all the differences between them and us will be buried deep and covered from sight; that, when our and their children, in after times, observe the great friendship that has been between us, it may rejoice and gladden their hearts. And he now hopes . . . . that their children may afterwards say: 'This is the place where our fathers and our brethren (meaning the Christians) ended and composed all their differences.'"

A Threatened Uprising

Sassoonan's name appears another time in the Colonial Records for the year 1728. In April of that year, James LeTort, a trader, who was then living in the Indian town of Chenastry, located on the West Branch of the Susquehanna, at the mouth of Chillisquaque Creek, not far above the present town of Sunbury, informed Governor Gordon that he had intended, in the autumn of 1727, taking a journey as far as the Miami Indians, who were then living on the Wabash River, to trade with them; but, on consulting with Madam Montour, then living at Chenastry, but who had lived among the Miamis and had a sister married to one of that nation, and also with Manawkyhickon, a celebrated chief of the Munsee Clan of Delawares in the region of Chenastry, he learned from these persons that the Delawares who were hunting on the Allegheny and Ohio, had been called home. Upon further inquiry he learned that Manawkyhickon was a near relative of Wequela, who had been hanged in New Jersey in 1727, and that Manawkyhickon, resenting the death of his relative had "sent a black belt to the Five Nations, and that the Five Nations sent the same to the Miamis with a message desiring to know if they would lift up their axes and join with them against the Christians; to which they agreed." LeTort advised that he inquired of Sassoonan whether he knew anything concerning the matters which had been brought to LeTort's attention by Madam Montour, and found Sassoonan entirely ignorant of them. The information which LeTort brought to the Colonial Authorities caused considerable uneasiness, and the Council ordered that presents be sent to Sassoonan, Madam Montour, and Manawkyhickon, and that messages be sent to them desiring them to report any new developments in regard to this rumor, which proved to be unfounded.

Governor Gordon Writes Sassoonan as to Robbing of Traders

Anthony Sadowsky, John Maddox, and John Fisher, traders on the Allegheny, made a complaint to Governor Gordon, on August 8th, 1730, stating that, in June, 1729, they had been robbed of one hundred pounds worth of goods, by the Indians on the Allegheny; and they asked that a demand for satisfaction be sent through "Allumappees [Sassoonan] at Shackachtan [Shamokin, now Sunbury] and Great Hill, at Allegheny." The Governor then wrote a letter concerning the matter to Sassoonan and Opekasset, at Shamokin, and Mechouquatchough, or Great Hill, at Kittanning. However, Maddox stated two years later that he was still without satisfaction for his stolen goods.

Sassoonan Kills Shackatawlin

At a meeting of the Provincial Council held in August, 1731, the frequent complaints made by the Indians on account of the large quantities of rum being carried to them by the traders, were taken up. The Council's attention was called to the fact that the pernicious liquor traffic had recently caused a very unhappy incident in the family of Sassoonan. In a fit of drunkenness, he had killed his nephew, (some authorities say his cousin) Shackatawlin, at their dwelling place at Shamokin, now Sunbury. Sassoonan's grief over the unhappy incident was so great that it almost cost him his life.

Asked at this conference whether he desired an entire stop put to the sending of rum to the Indians, Sassoonan replied, on August 13th, as follows:

"That the Indians do not desire that rum should be entirely

stopped and that none at all should be brought to them; they would have some but not much, and desire none may be brought but by sober good men, who will take a dram with them to refresh them and not so much as to hurt them.   The Governor knows there are ill people amongst the Christians as well as amongst them; that what mischief is done he believes is mostly owing to rum, and it should be prevented.

"He desires that no Christian should carry any rum to Shamokin where he lives, to sell; when they want any, they will send for it themselves; they would not be wholly deprived of it, but they would not have it brought by the Christians.

"He desires four men may be allowed to carry some rum to Allegheny, to refresh the Indians when they return from hunting, and that none else be permitted to carry any.   They also desire that some rum may be lodged at Tulpyhockin and Pextan, to be sold to them, that their women may not have too long a way to fetch it."

Sassoonan Requests Shawnees to Return to the Susquehanna Valley

Reference has been made in former chapters to the fact that the Shawnees began a migration from the Susquehanna Valley to the valleys of the Ohio and Allegheny as early as 1727.   A few years later, the Colonial Authorities of Pennsylvania took measures to induce the Allegheny Shawnees to return to a point nearer the Pennsylvania settlements, fearing that they would be drawn into an allegiance with the French, who, at that time, had their emissaries in the Allegheny Valley.   These efforts on the part of Pennsylvania will be more fully discussed in the chapters on Shikellamy.   But in order to show the part Sassoonan took in the efforts to induce the Shawnees to return, we point out that, at a conference held at Philadelphia, on October 15th, 1734, the Senaca chief, Hetaquantagechty, who accompanied Shikellamy and Conrad Weiser to this meeting, advised Governor Gordon and the Provincial Council: "That he has understood that when the Shawnees were desired to leave Allegheny, they sent a belt of wampum to the Delaware Indians, with a message intimating to them that, as they, the Shawnees, were to seek out a new country for themselves, they should be glad to have the Delawares with them.   That Sassoonan, the Delaware chief, had forbid any of his people to go with the Shawnees, and had desired that these last mentioned Indians should rather return to Susquehannah."   Hetaquantagechty said that he was afraid that, if the Shawnees went to the "French Country", the Delawares would follow them. Later developments proved the correctness of the Seneca chief's opinion.

A Friendly Visit

Sassoonan appeared at Philadelphia at a conference held with the Provincial Council on August 20th, 1736. Several other Delaware chiefs, a Cayuga chief and a Tuscarora chief, accompanied him. Sassoonan stated that "they were not come on any particular business, or to treat of anything of importance, but only to pay a friendly visit to their brethren, whose welfare they think themselves obliged to inquire after, as they and the Indians are one people. That when they came from home, they expected to have seen here their good friends, the Proprietor, the Governor, and the Council all together, but when they had come so far on their journey as George Boone's, they learned that one of their good friends, the Governor [Governor Patrick Gordon, who died in August, 1736,] was dead; this news made them sorrowful, but they are comforted in meeting their other friends, who, they hope, will still continue in their regards towards the Indians and their care and concern for preserving the same friendship that has hitherto subsisted between us and them."

Sassoonan was then asked whether or not the deputies of the Six Nations were on their way to Philadelphia to attend the treaty of September, 1736, an account of which treaty will be given in the chapter on Shikellamy (Chapter X). Sassoonan answered that "he knew nothing particularly of them, that he has been in expectation of seeing them for each of these three years past, but he understands they have been detained by nations that come to treat with them." These deputies finally arrived at Philadelphia on August 27th, 1736.

Nearing End of Old Regime

After William Penn returned to England, it was the custom for the old men of the Delawares to visit Philadelphia each autumn to "brighten the chain of friendship" by presenting the Governor and Provincial Council with skins and furs, and receiving presents in return. On such a mission Sassoonan, "with divers of their ancient men", conferred with Governor George Thomas and the Provincial Council, on October 3rd, 1738. Governor Thomas had arrived in the Province only a few months before. In the minutes of this conference, we find that Sassoonan said: "That, when he was at home at his own house, he heard his brother, the Governor, was arrived in this country, and thereupon he resolved to come to Philadelphia to visit him, and now he was glad to see him; that his brother, the Proprietor, told him he should come once a year to visit him." And, further, we read: "Then laying down four strings more of wampum, he [Sassoonan] said that there had always subsisted a perfect friendship and good understanding between the Indians and this Government, and it is his desire and hope that it will ever continue, and grow stronger and stronger, and that it will never be in the power of any to interrupt or break it. . . . . Then presenting three small bundles of deer skins in the hair, he said he had brought a few skins to the Governor; they were but a trifle and of little value, but he had no more, and desired the Governor's acceptance of them to make him gloves."

Still further we read in the minutes of this conference: "It is considered that the Old man (Sassoonan) being now become very weak, and the other Old people with him, as well as himself, poor and necessitous, the value of thirty pounds should be returned to them in Goods proper for them, which it was agreed should consist of Six Strowd Matchcoats, Twelve Dussells, Twelve Blankets, six hatts, Four shirts, Fifty Pounds of Powder and as much lead, a Dozen of knives, a Gross of Pipes with Tobacco, and also that they should be supplied with some necessary Provisions for their Journey home."

J. S. Walton, in his "Conrad Weiser and the Indian Policy of Colonial Pennsylvania", gives the following comment on this visit of the aged Sassoonan: "This was almost the last of the old regime in Indian affairs. A younger set of men were coming into power among the Delawares, and they were susceptible to the influence of the Shawnees."

Final Conferences of Sassoonan

On August 1st to 6th, 1740, Conrad Weiser served as interpreter at a conference held in the Friends' Meeting House, Philadelphia, between Governor Thomas and a party of eastern and western Delawares and a group of Iroquois. At this conference, Sassoonan represented the Delawares and Shikellamy the Iroquois. The Delawares from the Allegheny, under Captain Hill from Kittanning and Shannopin from Shannopin's Town, (on the east bank of the Allegheny within the present limits of Pittsburgh) fresh from French overtures, complained that the traders were charging them too much for goods, and that the whites were killing and driving away their game. "Your young men," said they, "have killed so many deer, beavers, bears, and game of all sorts that we can hardly find any for ourselves." They also desired that their guns and axes should be mended free. They were given presents to the value of one hundred fifty pounds, a more valuable gift than usually besowed upon the Delawares, and it is very likely that the giving of it aroused jealousy among the eastern Delawares. They were told that the Colony could not fix the price of traders' goods. As for the killing of game by the whites, they were told that this was done by unlicensed traders, and that, if the Indians would not patronize such, it would prevent their coming among the Indians and killing their game.

At this conference, Captain Hill and Shannopin told the Governor that about six years prior to that time, two children of the Delawares were taken prisoner and carried away by the Catawbas, and that they were advised that these children were still living among the Catawbas. These chiefs then asked the Governor to make inquiry of the Governor of Virginia concerning the captives; whereupon Governor Thomas promised to write the Governor of Virginia in the matter.

Sassoonan also attended the great conference or treaty with the Six Nations, at Philadelphia, in July, 1742, though he took little part in the proceedings. This treaty will be described in the Chapter on Shikellamy (Chapter X).

On February 4th, 1743, Sassoonan attended an important conference at Shamokin between Conrad Weiser and Shikellamy, as well as other chiefs of the Six Nations, Delawares, and Shawnees. Fresh troubles had recently broken out between the Catawbas and other Indians of Virginia, on the one hand, and the Iroquois and their tributary tribes on the other, which threatened the peace, not only of Pennsylvania and Virginia, but of all the English Colonies. The Iroquois were determined to chastize the Catawbas for recent injuries, and it was feared that they would involve Pennsylvania by demanding that the Colony should furnish provisions for their warriors passing through the Colony on their way to the country of the Catawbas.

Upon hearing of the fresh trouble between the Northern and the Southern Indians, Weiser was sent by Governor Thomas to meet the chiefs at Shamokin. It is not too much to say that the fate of the future nation was at stake when Weiser started for this conference. The Governor, upon receiving his report, sent him again to Shamokin, where, on April 9th, he held another conference with Shikeallamy, Sassoonan, and others, relative to the same matters taken up in the conference of February 4th. At the conference of April 9th, Sassoonan sent a message to Governor Thomas upholding him in his efforts to make peace between the Northern and the Southern Indians. He (Sassoonan) said that, as he "lives in the midway between the one and the other, and as both pass through the place of his residence, a state of war would be very disagreeable to him."

When the Governor and the Provincial Council received Weiser's report of his conference on a second trip to Shamokin, they resolved that he should at once go to the great council of the Six Nations at Onondaga, to deliver a generous present sent by Virginia, and arrange for the time and place of making a treaty. Weiser, then, in July, 1743, went to Onondaga accompanied by Shikellamy, and delivered the present of Virginia. After several days of ceremony and speech making, Weiser arranged for a treaty to take place at Lancaster, Pennsylvania, the following year between the Six Nations, Pennsylvania, Maryland, and Virginia. Weiser thus prevented a war between Virginia and the Six Nations, which would eventually have involved the other colonies.

Last Days of Sassoonan

Sassoonan was now nearing the end of his earthly career. He was visited at his home at Shamokin (Sunbury) by the Moravian Bishop Spangenberg, in May, 1745, as the Bishop and Conrad Weiser were on their way to the Great Council of the Six Nations, at Onondaga. Of this visit, Bishop Spangenberg wrote: "We also visited Allumapees, the hereditary king of the [Delaware] Indians. His sister's sons are either dead or worthless; hence it is not known on whom the kingdom will descend. He is very old, almost blind, and very poor; but withal has still power over and is beloved by his people; and he is a friend of the English." The sister's sons to whom Bishop Spangenberg refers were possibly Nettawatwees, or New Comer, who, among others, joined with Sassoonan, in 1718, in the deed of release to William Penn, and Kelappana, both of whom removed to Ohio, and were living at New Comer's Town at the time of the expedition of Colonel Bouquet, in 1764.

Again, on June 20th, 1747, Conrad Weiser wrote from his home near Womelsdorf, Berks County:

"Olumpies [Sassoonan] would have resigned his crown before now; but as he had the keeping of the public treasure (that is to say, the Council Bag), consisting of belts of wampum, for which he buys liquor, and has been drunk for these two or three years, almost constantly, and it is thought he won't die as long as there is a single wampum left in the bag, Sapapitten is the most fittest person to be his successor." Rum, the curse of the Red Man, was wearing the old chief's life away. About two months later, Weiser again wrote: "I understand Olumpies is dead, but I can not say I am sure of it." Finally, on October 15th, Weiser wrote: "Olumpies is dead. Lapaghpitton is allowed to be the fittest to succeed him, but he declines."

Thus, at Shamokin, on the banks of the beautiful Susquehanna, in the autumnal days of 1747, this aged chief, who had done so much to preserve the friendship that William Penn established with the Indians, yielded up his soul to the Great Spirit. Great changes in the relations between the Delawares and the Colony had taken place during the span of his life, and still greater changes were destined to come. In life's morning and noontide, he beheld the Delawares contented and happy in the bond of effection between them and "Onas"; yet, before the night had come, his dim eyes saw on the horizon the gathering clouds of the storm that, in the autumn of 1755, broke with fury upon the land of his birth.

We close this sketch of Sassoonan with the statement that, upon his death most of the Delawares moved to the Allegheny and the Ohio, living at Kittanning, Logstown, Sauconk, and Kuskuskies. As we have already seen, the town of Kittanning had been established by the Delawares possibly as early as 1724; and Logstown and Sauconk by the Shawnees possibly as early as 1730, the latter town being at the mouth of the Beaver. Kuskuskies, or Kuskuskie, was a regional name for a territory whose center was at or near the present site of New Castle, Lawrence County. Some authorities claim that the region extended westward into Butler county. This was a very important Indian settlement consisting of three or four towns of the Mingoes, or Iroquois, located along the Beaver, Mahoning, and Shenango Rivers, and Neshannock and Slippery Rock Creeks, and established some time prior to 1742.

CHAPTER VIII.

Kakowatcheky, Peter Chartier Kishacoquillas and Neucheconneh

KAKOWATCHEKY

KAKOWATCHEKY, chief of the Shawnees at Pechoquealin, near the Delaware Water Gap, is believed to have been the leader of the band of this tribe that accompanied Arnold Viele to Pechoquealin from the Shawnee villages on the lower Ohio, in 1794. At any rate, he was chief of the Pechoquealin as early as 1709; for, in the minutes of a meeting of the Provincial Council of New Jersey, on May 30th of this year, he is referred to as one of the sachems of the Shawhena (Shawnee) Indians then with the Maninsincks (Munsee, or Wolf Clan of Delawares).

Kakowatcheky's name does not appear in the Colonial Records of Pennsylvania until 1728, in connection with the following Indian troubles:

On May 6, 1728, Governor Gordon advised the Provincial Council that he had recently received a letter from John Wright, a trader, at Conestoga, stating that two Conestogas had been murdered by several of the Shawnees in that neighborhood, and that the Conestogas seemed to be preparing to declare war on the Shawnees, in retaliation. The Governor also advised the Council, at this time, that he had received a petition signed by a great number of the settlers in the back parts of Lancaster County, setting forth that they were under great apprehension of being attacked by the Indians, and that many families had left their homes through fear of an Indian uprising. Wright further informed the Governor, in his letter, that the Shawnees had brought the Shawnee murderers as far as Peter Chartier's house, at which place the party engaged in much drinking, and, through the connivance of Chartier, the two Shawnee murderers escaped. It is not surprising that Chartier let the murderers escape, as he himself was a half blood Shawnee. He was at that time trading at Pequea Creek. His action so incensed the Conestogas that they threatened to destroy all the Shawnees in that region.

Almost at the same time that the murder of the Conestogas

occurred, the settlers along the valley of the Schuylkill became much alarmed for their safety from another quarter. Kakowatcheky, who was the head of the Shawnees living at Pechoquealin, in what is now lower Smithfield Township, Monroe County, claimed that he had learned that the Flatheads, or Catawbas, from North Carolina, had entered Pennsylvania with the intention of striking the Indians along the Susquehanna; and he, accordingly, led eleven warriors to ascertain the truth of this rumor, who, when they came into the neighborhood of the Durham Iron Works, near Manatawny, in the northern part of Bucks County, their provisions failed, and they forced the settlers to give them food and drink. The settlers did not know these Indians, and believing the chief of the band to be a Spanish Indian, they were in great terror; families fled from their plantations and women and children suffered greatly from exposure, as the weather was raw and cold. There seems to be little doubt that Kakowatcheky was leading this band to Paxtang to assist the Shawnees of that place, who had been threatened by the Conestogas on account of the above mentioned murder of the two Conestogas.

A band of about twenty settlers took up arms and approached the invaders, sending two of their number to treat with the chief, who, instead of receiving them civilly, brandished his sword, and commanded his men to fire, which they did, and wounded two of the settlers. The settlers thereupon returned the fire, upon which the chief fell, but afterwards got up and ran into the woods, leaving his gun behind him. The identity of this Indian band was not known until May 20th, when two traders from Pechoquealin, John Smith and Nicholas Schonhoven, came to Governor Gordon and delivered to him a message from Kakowatcheky, explaining the unfortunate affair, sending his regrets, and asking the Governor for the return of the gun which he dropped when wounded. The Governor, then, accompanied by many citizens of Philadelphia, went to the troubled district, and personally pleaded with those settlers who had left their plantations to return. He found them so excited that they seemed ready to kill Indians of both sexes, but finally succeeded in pacifying them.

The Governor was about ready to return home when he received the melancholy news from Samuel Nut that an Indian man and two women were cruelly murdered, on May 20th, at Cucussea, then in Chester County, by John and Walter Winters, without any provocation whatever, and two Indian girls badly wounded; upon which a hue was immediately issued in an effort to apprehend the murderers. It appeared from investigation that, on the day of this murder, an Indian man, two women, and two girls, appeared at John Roberts' house, and that their neighbors noticing this, rallied to their defense, shot the man and one of the women, beat out the brains of the other woman, and wounded the girls, their excuse being that the Indian had put an arrow into his bow, and that they, having heard reports that some settlers had been killed by Indians, believed that the settlers might lawfully kill any Indian they could find.

The murderers were apprehended and placed in jail at Chester, for trial. A message was then sent to Sassoonan, Opekasset, and Manawkyhickon, acquainting them with the unhappy affair and requesting them to come to Conestoga, where a treaty would be held with Chief Civility and the other Indians at that place. The Provincial Council being apprehensive that this barbarous murder would stir up the Indians to take revenge on the settlers, a commission was appointed to get the inhabitants together and put them in a state to defend themselves. This commission consisted of John Pawling, Marcus Hulings, and Mordecai Lincoln, an ancestor of Abraham Lincoln, whose home was about ten miles south of the present town of Reading. Having sent Kakowatcheky the gun he had dropped, as well as the tomahawks dropped by his eleven warriors when they fled from the band of twenty settlers, as related above, together with a request that he warn the Indians under his authority to be more careful in the future, the Governor, accompanied by thirty residents of Philadelphia, met the Indians at a council at Conestoga on the 26th of May, where he conferred with Civility and other Conestoga, Shawnee, Conoy, and Delaware chiefs, made them many presents, and promised to punish the two murderers, if found guilty. John and Walter Winters were subsequently tried, found guilty, and hanged for the murder of the Indian man and two women.

Kakowatcheky Leaves Pechoquealin

As said in Chapter II, some of Kakowatcheky's clan left Pechoquealin before 1732, and went to the valley of the Ohio. Kakowatcheky himself, with the majority of his clan left Pechoquealin in the latter part of 1728, and went to the Wyoming Valley, settling on the Susquehanna, just below the town of Plymouth, Luzerne County. Here he was living in 1732, when some chiefs of the Six Nations on their way to attend a conference at Philadelphia, in August of that year, told him "that he should not look to Ohio, but turn his face to us." Evidently at that time, he contemplated joining his brethren on the Ohio and Allegheny.

Kakowatcheky at Treaty of 1739

The Colonial Authorities of Pennsylvania, realizing that the Shawnees were rapidly being won over by the French, induced Kakowatcheky, of Wyoming, Kishacoquillas of the Juniata, and Neucheconneh and Tamenebuck, of the Allegheny, and other Shawnee chiefs, whose settlements were scattered from Wyoming and Great Island (Lock Haven) to the Allegheny, to come to a conference, or treaty, at Philadelphia on July 27th to August 1st, 1739. At this conference the Conestoga and Shawnee agreement with William Penn, dated April 23rd, 1701, was brought to the attention of the chiefs; and they were told that the Colonial Authorities thought it proper to remind them of this solemn engagement which their ancestors had entered into with Penn, inasmuch as the said Authorities knew that the emissaries of the French were endeavoring to prevail upon the Shawnees to renounce their agreement with the Colony. In other words, the Governor and Provincial Council put the plain question of the Shawnees' loyalty to past agreements with Pennsylvania. The chiefs desired that their reply be postponed until the following day, explaining that "it was their custom to speak or transact business of importance only whilst the sun was rising, and not when it was declining." "In the morning, they showed that all past agreements had been kept by them quite as faithfully as by the white men. And since Pennsylvania had, about a year previously, promised to issue an order forbidding the sale of any more rum among them, they had sent one of their young men to the French, as an agent to induce them 'for all time, to put a stop to the sale of rum, brandy, and wine'." The result of the conference was that the Shawnees, with the full understanding that the rum traffic was to be stopped, promised not to join any other nation, and confirmed the old Conestoga and Shawnee agreement or treaty of April 23rd, 1701.

At this treaty, the Shawnee chief, Neucheconneh, repudiated the letter of March 20, 1738, which he, Loyparcowah, and Coycacolenne had sent the Governor advising him, among other things, that the Shawnees on the Kiskiminetas, Allegheny and Ohio had "a good understanding with the French." No doubt it was on account of this particular statement that Neucheconneh now repudiated the letter. He explained that it was written by "two white men", evidently the half-breed, Peter Chartier, and George Miranda, when all "were merry over a cup of good liquor."

Kakowatcheky Removes to the Ohio

Kakowatcheky did not obey the command that the representatives of the Six Nations gave him in August, 1732, "that he should not look to Ohio." He, with most of his clan, removed from Wyoming, in 1743, to Logstown, on the right bank of the Ohio, about eighteen miles below Pittsburgh. Possibly he founded Logstown, though some authorities claim, as pointed out in Chapter II, that this town was founded by Shawnees from Tennessee, possibly as early as 1730. Here he was living in the summer of 1744, when many Shawnees, under Peter Chartier, deserted to the French, which desertion will be described later in this chapter. However, Kakowatcheky remained true to the English, and was commended by the Colonial Authorities. On April 20th, 1747, he joined with Scarouady, Neucheconneh, Tanacharison and others, in writing a letter from "Aleggainey" to the Governor of Pennsylvania, in behalf of the Twightwees or Miamis of the Ohio Valley.

He was living at Logstown in the summer of 1748, when he, Neucheconneh, Tanacharison, Scarouady, and several other chiefs met in council and sent a message through the Delawares and Six Nations to the Colony of Pennsylvania, apologizing for the desertion of Peter Chartier and his band. Here, also, this aged sachem was met by George Croghan when the latter held a council with the Indians of Logstown on April 28th, 1748. Croghan had been sent by the Colony of Pennsylvania to advise the Ohio and Allegheny Indians that Conrad Weiser would come later in that year to make a treaty with them in behalf of the Colony, and to distribute generous presents. Weiser arrived at Logstown in September of that year as the head of what is generally called the first embassy ever sent by the Colony of Pennsylvania to the Indians of the Ohio and Allegheny, although it would be more nearly correct to say that Croghan's mission in the preceding April was the first. Weiser met Kakowatcheky at his conference in September, and his journal, under date of September 10th, contains the following reference to the sachem:

"This day I made a present to the old Shawnee chief, Kakowatcheky, of a strand, a blanket, a match-coat, a shirt, a pair of stockings, and a large twist of tobacco, and told him that the President and Council of Philadelphia remembered their love to him as to their old and true friend, and would clothe his body once more, and wished he might wear them out, so as to give them an opportunity to clothe him again.   There was a great many Indians present, two of which were the Big Hominy and the Pride, those that went off with Chartier, but protested his proceedings against our traders.   Kakowatcheky returned thanks, and some of the Six Nations did the same, and expressed their satisfaction to see a true man taken notice of, although he was now grown childish."

Kakowatcheky took no other part in Weiser's conferences at Logstown than that just mentioned.   In passing, we call attention to the fact that this embassy to the Shawnees, Senecas, and other Indians on the Ohio was eminently successful.   It left Pennsylvania in possession of the Indian trade from Logstown to the Mississippi and from the Ohio to the Great Lakes.   Moreover, its success was most gratifying to all the frontier settlers.   Not only Pennsylvania, but Maryland and Virginia were active in following up the advantage thus gained.   A number of Maryland and Virginia traders pushed into the Ohio region, and presently the Ohio Land Company, formed by leading men of Virginia and Maryland, among whom were George Washington's half-brothers, Lawrence and Augustine, sought to secure the Forks of the Ohio.

Last Days of Kakowatcheky

Once more, at Logstown on the Ohio, we meet this venerable chieftain, who, no doubt, was born in the valley of the beautiful river where he now is spending his latter years. On May 18th, 1751, George Croghan, the "King of the Traders", and Andrew Montour, visited Logstown bringing the Colony's present to the Ohio Indians, which they had promised on their former visit to this town in November, 1750. Croghan and Montour were welcomed by a great number of Delawares and Shawnees "in a very complacent manner in their way, by firing guns and hoisting the English colors." Among the sachems who welcomed them were the Seneca chief, Canayachrera, or Broken Kettle, who came to Logstown with a delegation from the Kuskuskies region, whose center was on or near the site of New Castle, Lawrence County.

On May 21st, Croghan visited the aged Kakowatcheky, writing in his journal under this date:

"I paid Kakowatcheky, the old Shawnee King, a visit, as he was rendered incapable of attending the Council by his great age, and let him know that his brother, the Governor of Pennsylvania, was glad to hear that he was still alive and retained his senses, and had ordered me to clothe him and to acquaint him that he had not forgot his strict attachment to the English interest. I gave him a strowd shirt, a match-coat, and a pair of stockings, for which he gave the Governor a great many thanks."

At this time, the English and the French were each doing everything possible to win the friendship and allegiance of the Indians of the Ohio and Allegheny. Each claimed the territory drained by these streams, the French basing their claim on the discoveries and explorations of La Salle and the heroic Jesuit missionaries,—true Knights of the Cross, to whom anyone who correctly writes the early history of the region between the Allegheny Mountains and the Mississippi must needs pay a high tribute of esteem. And at this conference at Logstown, Croghan met Joncaire, the French Indian agent, but succeeded in outwitting him in diplomacy, and the chiefs ordered the French from their lands, and reasserted their friendship for the English—a friendship which was broken four years later. The speaker of the Six Nations thus addressed Joncaire:

"How comes it that you have broken the general peace? Is it not three years since you, as well as our brother, the English, told us that there was a peace between the English and French, and how comes it that you have taken our brothers as your prisoners on our lands? Is it not our land (stamping on the ground, and putting his finger to Joncaire's nose)? What right has Onontio (the Governor of Canada) to our lands? I desire that you may go home directly off our lands, and tell Onontio to send us word immediately what was his reason for using our brothers so, or what he means by such proceedings that we may know what to do, for I can assure Onontio that we, the Six Nations, will not take such usage. You hear what I say, and that is the sentiments of all our Six Nations; tell it to Onontio that that is what the Six Nations said to you . . . . . . Our brothers [the English] are the people we will trade with and not you."

While there is no doubt about the loyalty of the Ohio Indians to the Pennsylvania Government at the time of Croghan's visit to Logstown (May, 1751); yet it is fair to assume that he exaggerated his translation of the speech which the Iroquois chief delivered to Joncaire, in that he alleged that the speaker told Joncaire that the Council of the Six Nations had determined to trade only with the English. The Onondaga Council had made no such decision.

For years it had endeavored to play an even game with the French and the English, preferring to be courted by both France and England.

While at Logstown, on the occasion just described, Croghan learned from Tanacharison and Scarouady that the Great Council of the Six Nations had agreed, since Celeron's expedition down the Allegheny and Ohio in the summer of 1749, that the English be permitted to build a trading house at the Forks of the Ohio; and, in open Council with Croghan, the chiefs at Logstown "requested that the Governor of Pennsylvania would immediately build a strong house [fort] . . . . . . for the protection of themselves and the English traders", where Pittsburgh now stands.

In June, 1752, Virginia and the Ohio Land Company made a treaty at Logstown with the Delawares, Shawnees, and Senecas of the Ohio Valley, by the terms of which Virginia secured permission to erect a few forts and make a few settlements west of the Allegheny Mountains. Colonel James Patton, one of the Virginia Commissioners at this treaty, makes the following reference to Kakowatcheky in his journal, under date of June 11th:

"The Commissioners, addressing themselves to the Shawnees, acquainted them that they understood that their chief, Kakowatcheky, who had been a good friend to the English, was lying bed-rid, and that, to show the regard they had for his past services, they took this opportunity to acknowledge it by presenting him with a suit of Indian clothing."

The year of Kakowatcheky's death is not known, but it was probably in 1755, as that is the last year in which his name appears in the Colonial Records. If he was the chief who led the Shawnees from the lower Ohio Valley to Pechoquealin, in 1694, his chieftainship must have extended over a period of sixty years.

PETER CHARTIER

Peter Chartier was the only son of Martin Chartier, who accompanied the Shawnees, under Opessah, to Pequea, Lancaster County, in 1697 or 1698, and his mother was a Shawnee squaw. The father was a Frenchman, who had lived among this band of Shawnees for many years prior to their entering Pennsylvania, and accompanied them in their wanderings. He set up a trading house at Pequea a few years after the Shawnees took up their abode there. At least, he traded at Pequea as early as 1707. Some years later, he removed his trading post to Dekanoagah, which we have seen was located on or near the present site of Washington Borough, Lancaster County. Here he died in 1718.

Peter Chartier is said to have followed his father's example by marrying a Shawnee squaw. In 1718, he secured a warrant for three hundred acres of land "where his father is settled, on Susquehanna river." For some years he traded with the Shawnees who had left Pequea and settled near the site of Washington Borough and at Paxtang. Later he traded with those members of this tribe who had settled on the west side of the Susquehanna, at the mouth of Shawnee (now Yellow Breeches) Creek, on the site of the present town of New Cumberland, Cumberland County. We have already seen how he, in 1728, aided in the escape of the Shawnees who had murdered the two Conestogas. Still later, he is said to have removed to the valley of the Conococheague. About 1730, he commenced trading with the Shawnees on the Conemaugh, and Kiskiminetas, and a little later, on the Allegheny.

Manor of Conodoguinet

On November 19th, 1731, Peter Chartier was informed by John Wright, Tobias Hendricks, and Samuel Blunston of the survey of the tract called the "Manor of Conodoguinet", a tract of land on the west side of the Susquehanna between Conodoguinet and Yellow Breeches creeks, set aside for the Shawnees, in an effort to induce those of that tribe who had gone to the Ohio and Allegheny, to return to the Susquehanna. Chartier conveyed this information to the Shawnees on the Ohio and Allegheny, but they refused to return.

Neucheconneh's Letter

Chartier was a witness to a letter which Neucheconneh and several other Shawnee chiefs on the Allegheny wrote Governor Gordon, in June, 1732, in response to a message which the Governor sent them in December of the preceding year. In their letter they explained why the Shawnees had removed from the Susquehanna. Said they:

"About nine years ago, the Five Nations told us at Shallyschohking, [Chillisquaque, a Shawnee town at the mouth of the creek of the same name in Northumberland County] we did not do well to settle there; for there was a great noise in the Great House [at Onondaga], and that in three years' time all should know what they [the Five Nations] had to say as far as there was any settlements or the sun set.

"About ye expiration of three years aforesaid, the Five Nations came and said, 'Our land is going to be taken from us. Come, brothers, assist us. Let us fall upon and fight with the English.' We answered them, 'No; we came here for peace, and have leave to settle here; and we are in league with them, and cannot break it.'

"About a year after, they, ye Five Nations, told the Delawares and us, 'Since you have not hearkened to us nor regarded what we have said, now we will put petticoats on you, and look upon you as women for the future, and not as men. Therefore, you Shawanese, look back toward Ohio, the place from whence you came; and return thitherward; for now we shall take pity on the English, and let them have all this land.'

"And further said, 'Now, since you are become women, I'll take Peahohquelloman [Pechoquealin], and put it on Meheahoming [Wyoming]; and I'll take Meheahoming and put it on Ohioh; and Ohioh I'll put on Woabach; [Wabash] and that shall be the warriors' road for the future.

"One reason of our leaving our former settlements and coming here is, several negro slaves used to run away and come amongst us; and we thought ye English would blame us for it.

"The Delaware Indians some time ago bid us depart, for they was dry, and wanted to drink ye land away. Whereupon, we told them, 'Since some of you are gone to Ohioh, we will go there also. We hope you will not drink that away, too."

At about the time of the above letter, the Shawnees in the Allegheny had received a report from John Kelly, a trader, that the Six Nations were ready to destroy them and drive out the French, if the English Governor would say the word. This report greatly agitated the Western Shawnees, and they would have declared war on the English traders at once, if Peter Chartier and some French agents had not persuaded them that the information was false.

Chartier Acts as Interpreter

On September 30th and October 5th, 1732, Opakethwa and Opakeita, two Shawnee chiefs from the Allegheny attended a conference at Philadelphia, with Thomas Penn, Governor Gordon and the Provincial Council, Peter Chartier, Edmund Cartilidge and John Wray being the interpreters. This is the conference, referred to in Chapter V, in which they explained that they had formerly lived on the Potomac, but their "king" having died, they knew not what to do, and "went over the mountains [meaning to the Allegheny] to live." The Proprietor urged them to return to lands which the Colony had set apart for them on the west side of the Susquehanna near Paxtang (Harrisburg), and they replied "that their young men had gone over the mountains to hunt where they might have more game, that when that was over they would return and see the land." They were also told that the traders might cease carrying goods as far as the Allegheny, and that the French could not supply them with as valuable goods, or at as cheap a price as the English traders could; "to which they answered that they were sensible of this, but they had horses of their own, and could bring their skins to the trader, or to this town (Philadelphia), if there were occasion." It was clear that the Shawnees who had gone to the Allegheny had no intention of returning nearer the English settlements.

With Chartier and the two chiefs, was Quassenung, son of the old Shawnee King, Kakowatcheky. On October 7th, Quassenung was taken ill with small-pox, and was nursed by Opakethwa, speaker for the Shawnees at the conference. In the minutes of the conference, we read: "Quassenung recovered from the small-pox, but Opakethwa, who tended him, was taken most violently with the same distemper, and dying on the 26th, was next day handsomely buried. Quassenung was seized with violent pains, and languished until the sixteenth of January. He then died, and was likewise the next day buried in a handsome manner."

Chartier's principal seat on the Allegheny was a town which he, and, no doubt, the Shawnee chief, Neucheconneh, founded about 1734, called Chartier's Town, or Chartier's Old Town, also Neucheconneh's Town, and located near the site of Tarentum, Allegheny County. Here he lived until his desertion to the French, in 1744. Other Shawnee villages west of the Alleghenies, at this time, besides those on the Juniata, Conemaugh, Kiskiminetas, and Allegheny, were Logstown and Sauconk on the Ohio, the latter being at the mouth of the Beaver; Asswikales, or "Sewickley Town", on the Youghiogheny, at the mouth of Big Sewickley Creek, in Westmoreland County; and "James Le Tort's Town", where Shelocta, Indiana County, now stands, the present town of Shelocta bearing the name of a Shawnee chief. The Shawnees at Asswikales are described in a letter of James Le Tort to Governor Gordon, October 29, 1731, as "about fifty families laterly from South Carolina to Potowmack, and from thence thither."

Murder of Sagohandechty

The Asswikales Shawnees, also called the Hathawekela, before coming to Pennsylvania, were known to the early settlers of South Carolina, as the Savannas. On September 10th, 1735, Hetquantagechty, a Seneca chief, and Shikellamy, the vice-gerent of the Six Nations, attended a meeting of the Provincial Council at Philadelphia, and gave the Council a report concerning the mission which the Six Nations had sent to the Ohio and Allegheny in a vain attempt to have the Shawnees of that place return to the Susquehanna. At this conference Hetaquantagechty informed the Council that a great chief of the Iroquois, named Sagohandechty, who lived on the Allegheny, probably at Kittanning, went with the other chiefs of the Six Nations in 1734 to prevail upon the Shawnees to return. Sagohandechty pressed the Shawnees so closely to return that they took a great dislike to him, and some months after the other chiefs had returned, the Shawnees cruelly murdered him. Hetquantagetchty said that this murder had been committed by the Asswikales, who then fled southward, and as he supposed had returned "to the place from whence they first came, which is below Carolina." Hetaquantagechty described them as "one tribe of those Shawnees who had never behaved themselves as they ought." The Asswikales were probably the first Shawnees to settle in Western Pennsylvania within historic times, coming by way of Old Town, Maryland, to Bedford, and then westward. Sewickley Creek, in Westmoreland County, Sewickley Town, at the mouth of that creek, and another placed called Sewickley Old Town, which some authorities locate on the Allegheny River some miles below Chartier's Old Town, were named for them.

Peter Chartier Deserts to the French

At a meeting of the Provincial Council held April 25, 1745, Governor Thomas laid before the Council a deposition made by James Cunningham, a servant of Peter Chartier, to the effect that Chartier had accepted a military commission under the French, and was going to Canada. Later, at a meeting of the Pennsylvania Assembly, held July 23, 1745, a petition from James Dinnen (Dunning) and Peter Tostee, two Indian traders from the Allegheny Valley, was presented and read, setting forth that, as Dunning and Tostee were returning up the Allegheny River, in canoes, on the 18th of April, 1745, from a trading trip, with a considerable quantity of furs and skins, "Peter Chartier, late an

Indian trader, with about 400 Shawne Indians, armed with guns, pistols, and cutlasses, suddenly took them prisoners, having, as he said, a captain's commission from the King of France; and plundered them of all their effects, to the value of sixteen hundred pounds; by which they are become entirely ruined, and utterly uncapable to pay their debts, or carry on any further trade."

The actual date of Charter's desertion is unknown, but it was likely some time during the summer of 1744.

Chartier and Chief Neucheconneh headed this band of Shawnees. They had fled from Chartier's Old Town, and started down the Allegheny and Ohio, when they met and robbed Dunning and Tostee. At Logstown, they made an unsuccessful attempt to have Kakowatcheky join them. They proceeded on down the Ohio to the mouth of the Scioto, at which place another Shawnee settlement had been made possibly a decade before, and known for many years afterwards as the Lower Shawnee Town. From the Lower Shawnee Town, Chartier and his Shawnees proceeded southward along the Catawba Trail, and established a town about twelve miles east of the site of the present town of Winchester, Kentucky. Their object was to be nearer the French settlements on the Mississippi.

Shortly after Chartier led his Shawnees from the Allegheny, there were many rumors that the Shawnees intended making raids upon the frontiers of Pennsylvania, Maryland, and Virginia. At a meeting of the Provincial Council at Philadelphia on December 17th, 1745, Governor Thomas laid before the board a letter he had just received from the Governor of New York advising him that Major Swartwoutz, a dweller in the Minisink region, had recently written the Governor that he (Swartwoutz) had received intelligence from two Indians at different times within a month to the effect that "the French and French Indians living at a town or fort on a branch of the River Mississippi have made a large house full of snow shoes, in order so soon as the snow shall fall, to attack Albany, Sopus, and the back parts of Jersey and Pennsylvania." Governor Thomas said that, although he was not apt to give credit to rumors of this kind, since they were often found false, yet, considering the fact that the French had recently plundered the inhabitants near Saratoga, New York, carrying off seventy as prisoners and burning their houses, barns and mills, and considering the further fact that Peter Chartier was now with the French, it was not improbable that something would be attempted upon the inhabitants of the back parts of Pennsylvania likewise. Hence the Governor dispatched a messenger with circular letters to the officers of the militia in Lancaster County, directing them to be on their guard and to make the best preparations they could for defense, at the same time cautioning them not to "do any injury to the Indians in amity with us, or to molest them in their hunting." He likewise sent directions to Conrad Weiser "to employ some of the Delaware Indians at Shamokin (Sunbury) as scouts to watch the enemy's motions, and to engage the whole body of Indians there to harrass them in their march, in case they should attempt anything against us, and afterwards to join our remote inhabitants for their mutual defense." However, Chartier and his Shawnees did no mischief in Pennsylvania, except the plundering of the traders, Dunning and Tostee.

Chartier's Shawnees Ask to Be Forgiven

Some time after the desertion of Peter Chartier, a number of his Shawnees returned, among whom were Neucheconneh and his band. In 1747, the Onondaga Council placed the Oneida chief, Scarouady, in charge of Shawnee affairs, with his central seat at Logstown. Shortly thereafter, Neucheconneh, with Kakowatcheky, at that time king of the Shawnees at Logstown, who had withstood the solicitations of Chartier, and whom the reader has followed in his migration from the eastern part of Pennsylvania to the Ohio Valley, applied submissively to Scarouady then living on the Ohio, to intercede for them with the Colonial Authorities of Pennsylvania. At a meeting on July 21st, 1748, at Lancaster, Pennsylvania, with the commissioners appointed by the Colony to hold a conference with the Six Nations, Twightwees, and other Indians, Conrad Weiser, having received the following apology of the Shawnees from Scarouady, who was too badly injured from a fall to attend the conference, delivered it to the commissioners, as follows:

"We, the Shawnees, have been misled, and have carried on a private correspondence with the French without letting you [the Delawares and Six Nations] or our brethren, the English, know of it. We traveled secretly through the bushes to Canada, and the French promised us great things, but we find ourselves deceived. We are sorry we had anything to do with them. We now find that we could not see, although the sun did shine. We earnestly desire that you would intercede with our brethren, the English, for us who are left at Ohio, that we may be permitted to be restored to the chain of friendship, and be looked upon as heretofore the same flesh with them." Scarouady reported to Weiser that the foregoing apology had first been addressed to the Six Nations and Delawares dwelling on the Ohio and Allegheny, by Neucheconneh, Kakowatcheky, Sonatziowannah, and Sequeheton, after these Shawnee chieftains had met in council.

Conrad Weiser was consulted as to the sincerity of the apology of the Shawnees. It does not appear what Weiser said on this occasion, but it is well known that he was always outspoken in his contempt for the Shawnees, and doubtless his influence shaped the course of the commissioners at Lancaster, who severely reprimanded the Shawnees for their conduct. Addressing the Six Nations, from the Ohio, the commissioners said through Weiser, the interpreter:

"Your intercession for the Shawnees puts us under difficulties. It is at least two years since the Governor of Pennsylvania wrote Kakowatcheky a letter, wherein he condescended out of regard to him and a few other Shawnees who preserved their fidelity, to offer those who broke the chain, a pardon, on their submission, on their return to the towns they had deserted, and on their coming down to Philadelphia to evidence in person the sincerity of their repentence. They should have immediately complied with, and they would have readily been admitted into favor, but as they did not, what can be said of them? . . . . Take this string of wampum and therewith chastize Neucheconneh and his party in such terms as will be a proper severity with them. . . . . Then tell the delinquent Shawnees that we will forget what is past, and expect a more punctual regard to their engagements hereafter. 'Tis but justice to distinguish the good from the bad; Kakowatcheky and his friends, who had virtue enough to resist the many fine promises made by the emissaries of the French, will ever be remembered with gratitude, and challenge our best services."

Then Taming Buck (Tamenebuck), one of the Shawnee chiefs, who had been in Chartier's band, and later returned, replied to the above reprimand as follows: "We, the Shawnees, sensible of our ungrateful returns for the many favors we have been all along receiving from our brethren, the English, ever since we first made the chain of friendship, came along the road with our eyes looking down to the earth, and have not taken them from thence until this morning, when you were pleased to chasitze us and then pardon us. We have been a foolish people, and acted wrong, though the sun shone bright, and showed us very clearly what was our duty. We are sorry for what we have done, and promise better behavior for the future. We produce to you a certificate of the renewal of our friendship in the year 1739, by the Proprietor and Governor. Be pleased to sign it afresh, that it may appear to the world we are now admitted into your friendship, and all former crimes are buried and entirely forgot."

The request of Taming Buck was rejected. The commissioners refused to sign the certificate, and the Shawnees were told that it was enough for them to know that they were forgiven on condition of future good behavior, and that when that condition was performed, it would be time enough for them to apply for such testimonials. It is not known whether Weiser advised this course or not, but it is certain that he could have prevented it, and induced the Colonial Authorities to make a valuable peace with the Shawnees now when they were so submissive and humble. Other tribes received presents at this Lancaster conference, but the Shawnees only had their guns mended. They went away in disgrace, brooding over such treatment.

Peter Chartier figured no more in Pennsylvania history after he deserted to the French in 1744. Two creeks in Pennsylvania bear his name—Chartier's Run, in Westmoreland County, emptying into the Allegheny not far from Chartier's Old Town (Tarentum), and Chartier's Creek, in Washington and Allegheny counties, emptying into the Ohio at McKees Rocks, once known as Chartiers, from the fact that he had a trading post near this place.

KISHACOQUILLAS

Kishacoquillas was one of the Shawnee chiefs who never waivered in friendship for the English. The first glimpse we get of him in the Colonial Records is in the year 1731, when he was living with his clan of twenty families at Ohesson,—later called Kishacoquillas' Town, located at the mouth of Kishacoquillas Creek, named for him, on the Juniata River, near Lewistown, Mifflin County. With Kakowatcheky, Neucheconneh, and Taming Buck, and other Shawnee chiefs, he attended the conference held at Philadelphia on July 27th to August 1st, 1739, which has been mentioned earlier in this chapter.

Kishacoquillas was well advanced in years when the first settlers entered the valley of the beautiful mountain stream bearing his name. With one of these, Arthur Buchanan, he was on especially friendly terms, and had his wigwam near Buchanan's cabin.

Some of Kishacoquillas' followers are said to have warned Buchanan and his sons of the expected attack on Fort Granville, near Lewistown, July 30th, 1756, enabling them and their families to escape to Carlisle.

He died in the summer of 1754. His sons notified Governor Morris of his death through John Shikellamy, son of the great vice-gerent of the Six Nations. As Kishacoquillas had always been a good friend of the Colony and well respected, the Governor sent a present to his sons, and a letter of condolence in which he said:

"I heartily condole with you on the loss of your aged father, and mingle my tears with yours, which, however. I would now have you wipe away with the handkerchiefs herewith sent. As a testimony of the love that the Proprietaries and this Government retain for the family of Kishacoquillas, you will be pleased to accept of the present which is delivered to John Shikellamy for your use. May the Great Spirit confer on you health and every other blessing. Continue your affection for the English and the good people of this Province, and you will always find them grateful."

NEUCHECONNEH

As pointed out in Chapter V, the Shawnee chief, Neucheconneh, very probably acted as vice-regent during the youth of Loyparcowah, the son of Opessah. As stated, also, in Chapter V, Neucheconneh joined with Loyparcowah and Coycacolenne, on March 20th, 1738, in sending a letter from the Allegheny to Thomas Penn and Secretary James Logan, advising of their desire to remain on the Allegheny, and of the steps they had taken against the rum traffic. He was no doubt then residing at Neucheconneh's Town, or Chartier's Old Town, on the Allegheny, near Tarentum, which, as we have seen, in the present chapter, he and Peter Chartier founded in 1734. In the present chapter, we have also seen that Neucheconneh joined with several other Shawnee chiefs on the Allegheny, in June, 1732, in a letter to Governor Gordon, explaining why the Shawnees had removed from the Susquehanna; that he, with Kakowatcheky, Kishacoquillas, and Tamenebuck, attended the conference at Philadelphia, on July 27th to August 1st, 1739, where he repudiated the letter of March 20th, 1738; that, in 1744, he, with Peter Chartier, left Chartier's Old Town, and deserted to the French; that he afterwards returned to Logstown; and that, in 1748, he asked the Colony that he be forgiven for his having, for a time, deserted to the French.

On May 1st, 1734, Neucheconneh and several other Shawnee chiefs dictated a letter to Governor Gordon and the Provincial

Council, regarding the character of the traders who came among them at Allegheny. This letter, which was probably written by Jonah Davenport, and which was witnessed by James Le Tort, Larey Lowrey, and Peter Chartier, was as follows:

"Edward Kenny, Jacob Pyatt, Timy. Fitzpatrick, Wm. Dewlap, and Jno. Kelly of Donegal, come trading with us without license; which is a hindrance to ye licensed Traders.

"Charles Poke and Thos. Hill are very pernicious; for they have abused us; and we gave them a fathom of white wampum, desiring them by that token to acquaint you how they had served us.

"And at a drinking bout, Henry Bayley, Oliver Wallis, and Jno. Young, took one of our old men, and after having tied him, abused him very much. Jas. Denning was among them, and abused us likewise. Such people, we think, are not proper to deal with us.

"Jno. Kelly of Paxtang has made a great disturbance by raising false reports among us; and Timy. Fitzpatrick, Thos. Moren, and Jno. Palmer quarrel often with us; therefore, we desire those four men may be kept particularly from us.

"Jonas Davenport, Laz. Lowrey, Jas. Le Tort, Fras. Stevens, Jas. Patterson, Ed. Cartilidge, we desire, may have license to come and trade with us; as also, Peter Cheartier, who we reckon one of us; and he is welcome to come as long as he pleases.

"Likewise, we beg at our Council, that no Trader above mentioned may be allowed to bring more than thirty gallons of rum, twice in a year, and no more; for by that means, we shall be capable of paying our debts and making our creditors easy; which we cannot do otherwise. And that every Trader may be obliged to bring his rum in ye cabin where he lives, directly, and not to hide any in ye woods; but for P. Cheartier to bring what quantity he pleases; for he trades further yn. ye rest. And that every Trader bring his license with him.

"And for our parts, if we see any other Traders than those we desire amongst us, we will stave their cags, [kegs] and seize their goods, likewise.

"We also beg, every Trader may be obliged to bring good powder.

"And, if we are indebted to any of those we desire may not be admitted to trade with us, if they will come without goods or rum, if we have it by us, we will pay them their due.

"We also hope no hired man will have liberty to bring any rum with him."

Other letters and messages of Neucheconneh were:

(1)   A letter from the Allegheny to Secretary James Logan, dated April 9th, 1738, advising that three Indians "of the nation called Maychepese, living near the French", had passed through the Shawnee Town (Chartier's Old Town) having three scalps of white persons killed by them in Virginia.   Says Neucheconneh: "We thought it proper to acquaint you by the first opportunity who they were that killed our brothers . . . . to prevent any suspicion; when inquiry is made, it will prevent enmity between us and our brothers."   He signed this letter, as "King" of the Allegheny Shawnees.

(2)   On April 9th, 1743, at a council at Shamokin (Sunbury), a message sent by him from the Allegheny, was delivered to Conrad Weiser for transmission to Governor Thomas, as follows:
"Brother, the Governor of Pennsylvania:

"I live upon this River of Ohio [Allegheny] harmless like a child.   I can do nothing.   I am but weak, and I don't so much as intend mischief.   I have nothing to say, and do; therefore, send these strings of wampum to Kakowatcheky, the chief man again. He will answer your message, as he is the older and greater man."

In explanation of this message, we state that, early in 1743, it was feared that the Shawnees on the Allegheny might attack the English traders.   Conrad Weiser was accordingly sent to Shamokin, where, on February 4th, he held a council with Shikellamy, Sassoonan and other chiefs of the Delawares, Shawnees, and Six Nations, which conference was mentioned in Chapter VII, and gave the Shawnee chief, Big Hominy, some belts of wampum to "send to the Great Island [Lock Haven], and Allegheny, in favor of the traders."   Weiser returned to Shamokin on April 9th, when Neucheconneh's answer was received, as above set forth.   Kakowatcheky was then at Wyoming, but, as is seen in the present chapter, he removed from that place to Logstown that same year, 1743.

(3)   On April 20th, 1747, he joined with Kakowatcheky, Tanacharison, Scarouady, Tamenebuck, and several others, in a letter to Governor Thomas, requesting friendly relations on the part of the Colony with the Miamis, with whom the Shawnees had entered into a treaty.

There are two other letters which Neucheconneh had a part in sending.   The one is a letter from the "Chiefs of the Shawnees at Allegheny" which James Logan laid before the Provincial

Council on August 10th, 1737, which was, in substance, that they were strongly solicited by the French, who were supplying them with some powder and lead to fight the Southern Indians; that they (the Allegheny Shawnees) were so far away that they could go no farther without falling into the hands of their enemies or going over to the French; and that, if they should return to the Susquehanna, as the Colony had often insisted, they must starve, as there was little game there.   The letter ended with a request that the Colony furnish them with arms and ammunition to defend themselves against their enemies   The other is a message from "Nuckegunnah, King of the Shawnees living at Allegheny", dated August 4th, 1738, and sent to the Governor of Virginia, advising that, the Catawbas had made an attack upon them, killing several and taking others prisoners; and that this attack had happened after the Shawnees had refrained from sending war parties against the Catawbas upon learning that the Governor of Virginia was endeavoring to make peace between the Catawbas and the Northern Indians.

Another reference to this famous chief, who ended his days in the valley of the Ohio, is when Captain William Trent and Andrew Montour found him near the mouth of the Miami, on August 4th, 1752.   Trent and Andrew Montour had attended the Virginia treaty at Logstown in June, and from there had gone down the Ohio past the Lower Shawnee Town with a present for the Miamis.   His last appearance in history is when he attended the Carlisle treaty of October, 1753.

In closing this chapter, we call attention to the fact that Chartier's Town, founded by Peter Chartier and Neucheconneh, and the scene of their principal activities until they led the Shawnees from that place down the Ohio to the French, in 1744, figured little in the Indian history of Pennsylvania after that event. When Celeron came down the Allegheny and Ohio in the summer of 1749, burying leaden plates at the mouths of the tributary streams, proclaiming that the region drained by the "Beautiful River" belonged to France, his detachment stopped at Chartier's Town, on August 6th, where he found six English traders, with fifty horses and one hundred and fifty bales of furs, who were returning from there to Philadelphia.   He ordered them to withdraw from this territory claimed then by France, and sent with them a letter to the Governor of Pennsylvania warning him to forbid the traders of the Colony to come into the valleys of the Ohio and Allegheny.

CHAPTER IX.

Shikellamy

SHIKELLAMY (Shikellimmy, Shikillimus, Swateny, etc.), who has been mentioned several times thus far, holds a high place in the Indian annals of Pennsylvania. His name literally means, "He causes it to be light, or daylight"; or "He enlightens us." Hence he has frequently been called "Our Enlightener." He was an Oneida chieftain, though he claimed he was born a Cayuga and was adopted by the Oneidas. It has also been said that he was a Frenchman, born in Montreal and taken captive, when a child two years old by the Oneidas, by whom he was reared.

Shikellamy was the great exponent of the policy of the Six Nations, and was sent by the Great Council at Onondaga to the Forks of the Susquehanna, then called Shamokin, (Sunbury, Pennsylvania), in 1727 or 1728, to conserve the interests of the Six Nations in the Susquehanna Valley, and to keep a watchful eye on the tributary Shawnees, Delawares, and other Indians in that region. The exact date of his coming to the Forks of the Susquehanna as the over-lord of the Shawnees, Delawares, and others is not known, but it is clear it was prior to June, 1728; for in that month, he, Sassoonan, and several other chiefs of the Delawares and Shawnees attended a conference with Governor Gordon and the Provincial Council at Philadelphia, with reference to the troubles between the Shawnees of Pechoquealin and the settlers, as related in Chapter VIII.

The first definite reference in the Colonial Records to Shikellamy's vice-gerency is in the minutes of a meeting of the Provincial Council held on September 1, 1728. This conference after discussing the endeavors of Manawkyhickon to set the Miamis and the Five Nations at variance with the English, as related in Chapter VII, was informed by Governor Gordon that two Indian traders from the region of Pechoquealin had advised him that the Shawnees of that place during the month of August had received a message from the Susquehanna, which caused them to remove to the Wyoming Valley, leaving their corn standing—the removal of Kakowatcheky's Clan as related in Chapter VIII. The Council then decided to send a message to Kakowatcheky asking why he had left Pechoquealin and "to acquaint Shikellima [Shikellamy] that, as he is appointed, as it is said, by the Five Nations to preside over the Shawnees, it is expected that he will give a good account of them."

The importance of Shikellamy's office as the over-lord or vice-gerent of the Six Nations over the Indians of the Susquehanna is seen from the fact that, after the Iroquois subjugated the Susquehannas, or Conestogas, in 1675 or 1676, they assigned the valley of this river as a hunting ground for the Shawnees, Delawares, Conoy, Nanticokes, Tutelo, and Conestogas. Moreover, Shikellamy's coming to the Forks of the Susquehanna, probably marks the date of the complete subjugation of the Delawares by the Iroquois.

Shikellamy was a man of dignity, sobriety, and prudence, and a great friend of the whites, especially the Moravian Missionaries, by whom he was converted to Christianity near the close of his life. He was not baptized by the Moravians, because he had been baptized many years before by a Jesuit priest in Canada. In the execution of his trust, he conducted many important conferences and treaties between the Government of Pennsylvania and the Council of the Six Nations. In 1745, he was promoted to the full vice-gerency of all the tributary tribes in the Susquehanna region.

Shamokin

Before proceeding further, attention is called to the fact that the term "Shamokin" was a regional name applied to the territory at and around the Forks of the Susquehanna with its center at the present town of Sunbury, Northumberland County, where the *town* of "Shamokin" was located on the level ground south of the mouth of the North Branch of the Susquehanna. The term "Shamokin" is Delaware and probably another form of the word "Shackamaxon". The Iroquois name "Chenasky", or "Chenastry" (now generally called Otzinachse, or Otzinachson) was given at least to the northern part of the Shamokin region.

The town of Shamokin (Sunbury) and the surrounding country were strategically located. It was in this region that the Catawba War Trail leading from the central seat of the Six Nations, through the valleys of Lycoming Creek and the West Branch, intersected with the trail leading from Wyoming to the Allegheny Valley; and it was no doubt the strategic location of the Shamokin region that caused Shikellamy to select it as his seat, when he was sent by the Great Council of the Six Nations as vice-gerent over he Indians of the Susquehanna Valley. In fact, from 1728 and possibly prior thereto, until 1737 or 1738, he resided at the intersection of the Catawba and Wyoming trails, in a village called Shikellamy's Town located on the West Branch of the Susquehanna, in Northumberland County, opposite the mouth of Sinking Run, or Shikellamy's Run, about half a mile below the present town of Milton. Here Conrad Weiser found him, as will presently be seen, when going to Onondaga in 1737. About 1738, Shikellamy removed to Shamokin proper, the Shamokin of Pennsylvania history (Sunbury), where he resided until his death. Here, also, it will be recalled, resided the great sachem of the Turkey Clan of Delawares, Sassoonan, from about the latter part of 1718 until his death in 1747.

Shikellamy Delivers Ultimatum on the Rum Traffic

While Shikellamy on October 10th, 1728, attended the conference with Governor Gordon and the Provincial Council, mentioned in Chapter VII, which resulted in a settlement of the troubles in that year with Kakowatcheky's Clan of Shawnees at Pechoquealin, his first great act after coming into the vice-gerency of the Iroquois over the Indians of the Susquehanna, was to deliver an ultimatum to the Colonial Authorities of Pennsylvania, in 1731, to the effect that, unless the liquor trade should be better regulated with regard to its sale to the Indians under his jurisdiction, friendly relations between the Colony of Pennsylvania and the powerful Six Nations would cease.

Shikellamy Sent to Onondaga to Arrange a Treaty

As has been seen in former chapters, the abuses of the liquor traffic among the Shawnees were among the causes which forced a large number of this tribe to migrate from the Susquehanna to the Ohio and Allegheny valleys several years prior to 1730, when French emissaries seized upon this opportunity to alienate the Shawneees from the English interest. Therefore, Governor Gordon at a council held at Philadelphia on August 16th, 1731, decided to adopt the suggestion of Secretary James Logan that a treaty be arranged with the Six Nations "to renew and maintain the same good-will and friendship for the Five Nations which the Honorable William Penn always expressed to them in his lifetime", and to prevail upon the Six Nations to assist in holding the Shawnees in their allegiance to the English. Accordingly, at this same conference, it was decided to send Shikellamy, "a trusty, good man and a great lover of the English" to Onondaga, the capital of the Six Nations, to invite them to send deputies to Philadelphia to arrange a treaty.

In keeping with Pennsylvania's efforts to retain the friendship of the Shawnees on the Allegheny, Governor Gordon sent them a message in December, 1731, reminding them of the benefits they had received from William Penn and his successors, while they lived in the eastern part of the Province, to which message Neucheconneh and other Shawnee chiefs on the Allegheny, replied in their letter to the Governor, of June, 1732, giving the reasons why they had removed from the Susquehanna, which letter was quoted in Chapter VIII.

Shikellamy returned to Philadelphia from his journey to Onondaga, on December 10th, 1731, accompanied by a Cayuga chief named Cehachquely, and Conrad Weiser and John Scull as interpreters. He reported that the Six Nations were very much pleased to hear from the Governor of Pennsylvania, but that, as winter was now coming on and their chiefs were too old to make such a fatiguing journey in the winter time, they would come to Philadelphia in the spring to meet the Governor.

Conrad Weiser

On his way to meet the Governor at this time, Shikellamy stopped at the home of Conrad Weiser, near Womelsdorf, in the present county of Berks, took him along to Philadelphia and introduced him to Governor Gordon as "an adopted son of the Mohawk Nation"; and as this conference (December 10, 1731,) is Weiser's first connection with the Indian affairs of Pennsylvania, it will be well to pause long enough, at this point, to give a short sketch of the history of this noted man of the frontier, who later had so much to do with bringing about the ascendency of the Anglo-Saxon in the Western World.

This sturdy German was born at Afsteadt, in Herrenberg, near Wurtemberg, Germany, in 1696. At the age of thirteen, he accompanied his father to America, and, for several years, assisted him in making tar and raising hemp on Livingston Manor, New York. The Weiser family spent the winter of 1713 and 1714 with several of the Iroquois at Schenectady, New York, where Conrad doubtless secured his first lessons in the Iroquois tongue. In the spring of 1714, he accompanied his father to the Schoharie Valley, where they endured much hardship in company with the other Palatines in that valley.   When he was seventeen years old, young Weiser went to live with Quagnant, a prominent Iroquois chief, who, taking a great fancy to Conrad, requested the father that the young man might dwell with him for a time.   He remained with the Iroquois chief for eight months, learning the Iroquois language and customs thoroughly, and was adopted by them.

In 1729, Conrad Weiser and his young wife followed the elder Weiser into the Tulpyhocken Valley, Pennsylvania, where, as has been related, a number of Palatines from the Schoharie Valley had settled, under the leadership of Conrad Weiser, Sr.   The young couple built their home about one mile east of Womelsdorf, Berks County, where Weiser continued to reside until a few years before his death, when he removed to Reading.   It is said that while on a hunting trip he met the great Iroquois chief, Shikellamy, the vice-gerent of the Six Nations, who was well pleased with Weiser on account of his being able to speak the Iroquois tongue, and they became fast friends.

While visiting his old home near Womelsdorf, he died July 13, 1760, much lamented by the Colony of Pennsylvania as well as by the Indians.   Said a great Iroquois chieftain, commenting on the death of Weiser: "We are at a loss, and sit in darkness."

If all white men had been as just to the Indians as was this sturdy German, the history of the advance of civilization in America undoubtedly would not contain so many bloody chapters. Conrad Weiser's home is still standing, and in the orchard above the house, rests all that is mortal of this distinguished frontiersman; while beside him are the graves of several Indian chiefs. Having loved him in life, they wished to repose beside him in death.   A beautiful monument has been erected to his memory in Womelsdorf, having thereon the words which George Washington uttered concerning him, while standing at his grave, in 1793: "Posterity Will Not Forget His Services."

Conrad Weiser was the progenitor of one of the most noted families of Pennsylvania.   His daughter, Anna, became the wife of Henry Melchoir Muhlenberg, founder of the Lutheran Church in America, was the mother of Frederick A. Muhlenberg and General John Peter Gabriel Muhlenberg.   Frederick A. Muhlenberg became a distinguished Lutheran clergyman and later was elected to the Legislature of Pennsylvania.   He was also chosen President of the Pennsylvania Convention, in 1787, which ratified the Constitution of the United States. From 1789 to 1797, he served in the Congress of the United States, and was speaker of the First and Third Congresses.

John Peter Gabriel Muhlenberg also became a distinguished Lutheran clergyman, and, at the outbreak of the Revolutionary War, was pastor of the German Lutheran congregation at Woodstock, Virginia. While serving this parish, he became well known to George Washington, and was selected to command the Eighth Virginia Regiment. His farewell sermon, preached to his congregation in January, 1776, is memorable in the annals of America. On the appointed day, an immense congregation greeted him. Clad in his clerical gown, he preached a burning sermon on the duty of the hour, at the close of which he made the statement: "There is a time to pray and a time to fight; now is the time to fight." The benediction pronounced amidst a deathlike silence, he threw aside his gown, revealing himself clad in the full uniform of a Continental officer, and ordered the drums to beat for recruits. With the noble men who there gathered around him by the hundreds, he started on his undying career as a soldier.

He endured the rigors of the terrible winter at Valley Forge, and fought valiantly at Germantown, Monmouth, and Stony Point. He was the leader of the American final assault at Yorktown, when the American arms finally triumphed.

He was promoted to Major General, and, after the close of the Revolution, removed from Virginia to Pennsylvania, where he was elected a member of the Supreme Executive Council of the state. He was a member of the First, Third, and Sixth Congresses, and was elected United States Senator in 1801, but resigned this post to receive the appointment by President Jefferson as Supervisor of Internal Revenue for Pennsylvania. At the time of his death in July, 1802, he was collector of the port of Philadelphia. His statue is placed in the rotunda of the Capitol at Washington, with that of Robert Fulton, the two representing the State of Pennsylvania. This statue shows him throwing aside his clerical robe and revealing the uniform of a Continental officer.

The Treaty of 1732

The Six Nations, no doubt mistrusting the motives of the English, failed to send deputies to Philadelphia in the spring of 1732, as they had promised Shikellamy. In the meantime, traders in the valleys of the Ohio and Allegheny reported that the French were rapidly gaining the friendship of the Shawnees in the Ohio Valley; that these Indians complained bitterly about the great quantities of rum brought to them by the English traders; and that they would have declared war against the English, on this account, save for the influence of Peter Chartier. The Shawnees said, furthermore, that it had been only five years since the Six Nations themselves had endeavored to persuade the Ohio Indians to declare war on the English. In view of these facts, there was much anxiety on the part of the Provincial Council of Pennsylvania, over the failure of the deputies of the Six Nations to make their appearance in Philadelphia in the spring of 1732.

Finally, on August 18th, 1732, the deputies of the Six Nations arrived, consisting of a number of Oneida, Cayuga, and Onondaga chiefs, among whom was the celebrated Shikellamy. A few days' time being given the chiefs in which to refresh themselves after their long and toilsome journey, the famous treaty of August 23rd to September 2nd, 1732, was entered into between the Six Nations and the Colony of Pennsylvania.

We have stated that Secretary James Logan suggested this treaty; but Logan's knowledge of the influence and importance of the Six Nations and their power over the Shawnees, Delawares and other tributary tribes, was gotten from Conrad Weiser. Not until the coming of Weiser did the Colony fully realize the importance of this powerful confederation.

The deputies of the Six Nations, who arrived in Philadelphia some days before the opening of the conference, as we have seen, were chiefs of only the Oneida, Cayuga, and Onondaga tribes; but they claimed that they were authorized to speak for the other members of the Iroquois Confederation. In the early stages of the conference, complaints were made, possibly by members of the Assembly, against the private nature of the council; and Conrad Weiser, the interpreter, was selected to interview the Iroquois deputies to learn their pleasure in the matter. The chiefs replied that they were content to continue in secret session, but were willing to deal in a more public manner, if such was desired. Thomas Penn, son of the founder of the Colony, having lately arrived in Philadelphia, spoke for the Province. He called the attention of the chiefs to the policy which his father had pursued in dealing with the Indians, and assured them that he came to the Province with a desire and design to follow in the footsteps of his parent. He then asked the Iroquois deputies how their Confederation stood toward the French, their former enemies. He inquired how the French behaved toward the Six Nations, and how all the other nations of Indians to the northward or the westward were affected toward the Iroquois.

The Iroquois deputies replied through their speaker, Hetaquantagechty, that they had no great faith in the governor of Canada, or the French, who had deceived them. "The Six Nations", said they, "are not afraid of the French. They are always willing to go and hear what they have to propose. Peace had been made with the French. A tree had been planted big enough to shelter them both. Under this tree, a hole had been dug, and the hatchets had been buried therein. Nevertheless, the chiefs of the Six Nations thought that the French charged too much for their goods, and, for this reason, they recommended their people to trade with the English, who would sell cheaper than the French." The deputies confided to the Governor that, when representatives of the Six Nations were at Montreal, in 1727, the governor of Canada told them that he intended to make war upon Corlear (the term applied to the governors of New York), and that he desired the Six Nations to remain neutral. On this occasion, one of the chiefs answered, saying: "Onontejo [the Indian name for the governor of Canada], you are very proud. You are not wise to make war with Corlear, and to propose neutrality to us. Corlear is our brother; he came to us when he was very little and a child. We suckled him at our breasts; we have nursed him and taken care of him till he is grown up to be a man. He is our brother and of the same blood. He and we have but one ear to hear with, one eye to see with, and one mouth to speak with. We will not forsake him nor see any man make war upon him without assisting. We shall join him, and, if we fight with you, we may have our own father, Onontejo, to bury in the ground. We would not have you force us to this, but be wise and live in peace."

The Iroquois deputies were told, through Conrad Weiser, that the Shawnees who were settled to the southward, being made uneasy by their neighbors, had come up to Conestoga about thirty-five years before, and desired leave of the Conestoga Indians located at that place, to settle in the neighborhood; that the Conestogas applied to the Government of Pennsylvania that the Shawnees might be permitted to settle there, and that they would become answerable for their good behavior; that William Penn, shortly after the arrival of the Shawnees, agreed to their settlement, and the Shawnees thereupon came under the protection of the Pennsylvania Colony; that, from that time, greater numbers of the Shawnee Indians followed, settling upon the Susquehanna and the Delaware. The deputies were further told that the Colony of Pennsylvania had held several treaties with the Shawnees, treating them from their first coming as "our own Indians", but that some of their young men, four or five years previously, being afraid of the Six Nations, had removed to the Allegheny Valley, and put themselves under the protection of the French, who had received them as children; that the Colony had sent a message asking them to return, and to encourage them, had laid out a large tract of land on the west side of the Susquehanna near Paxtang, and desired, by all means, that they would return to that place.

The Iroquois answered that they never had intended to harm the Shawnees, and that, as they were coming on their way to Philadelphia, they had spoken with Kakowatcheky, their (the Shawnees') old chief, then at Wyoming, and told him that he should not "look to Ohio, but turn his face to us." They had met Sassoonan, too, the old chief of the Delawares, then at Shamokin, and told him that the Delawares, too, should not settle in the Ohio and Allegheny valleys, upon which Sassoonan had sent messengers to the Delawares lately gone to the Ohio and Allegheny valleys, requiring them to return. It will be remembered that, in the times of which we are writing, and for a long period thereafter, the Allegheny River was considered simply as a continuation of the Ohio, and was generally called the Ohio.

The deputies were then told that, as they were the chiefs of all the northern Indians in the Province, and the Shawnees had been under their protection, they should oblige them to return nearer the Pennsylvania settlements; whereupon the chiefs asked if the Six Nations should do this themselves, or join with the Authorities of Pennsylvania. They were told that it was the desire of the Pennsylvania Colony that the Six Nations should join with the Colonial Authorities in efforts to have the Shawnees return.

The representatives of the Six Nations told the Governor that they believed that they could bring the Shawnees back, if Pennsylvania would prohibit her traders from going to the Allegheny Valley, explaining that, as long as the Shawnees were supplied at that place with such goods as they needed, they would be more unwilling to remove. It was finally agreed that Pennsylvania would remove such traders, and that the Six Nations would see that the French traders in the Ohio region were also removed.

The main purpose of this treaty was to secure the aid of the

Six Nations in efforts to bring the Shawnees from the Allegheny Valley; but it contained other provisions, notably the one obligating the Six Nations to "forbid all their warriors, who are often too unruly, to come amongst or near the English settlements, and especially that they never, on any account, rob, hurt, or molest any English subjects whatsoever, either to the Southward or elsewhere."

The Iroquois delegation having requested that, in their future dealings with Pennsylvania, Conrad Weiser should continue to be the interpreter, this request was granted, and the conference came to an end by the giving of many presents to the deputies, among which were six japanned and gilt guns, which were to be delivered one to each chief of the Six Nations. These guns were the gift of Thomas Penn, which he had brought with him from England for this purpose.

Shikellamy at Conference June, 1733

Shikellamy's next appearance before the Provincial Council was at a conference held at Philadelphia with Governor Gordon on June 18, 1733. Three matters were taken up at this conference. The first was a report which Shikellamy gave the Governor of the news of a plot on the part of the whites to take up arms against the Indians. Shikellamy said that he had received this news from "an Indian who lives in his neighborhood, named Katarioniecha (Peter Quebec), who is married to one Margaret, a daughter of Mrs. Montour." The second was a complaint on the part of Shikellamy that "since the Indian traders were prohibited to bring rum among the Indians, Cheaver, beyond all others, has brought in very large quantities, and gives out that he will not regard the orders of the Government on this head; that his behavior is such as gives just apprehension some mischiefs may happen if he is not called away from these parts; that formerly an order was given to the Indians to stave rum brought among them, but Cheaver threatens any Indians that shall offer to touch his; that it is to be feared he may either kill an Indian or some Indian him; that Cheaver intends this summer to go to Allegheny, contrary to what was agreed upon between this Government and the Six Nations last fall [at the treaty of 1732]." The third was a letter which Sassoonan had sent to John Harris asking him to desist from making a plantation at the mouth of the Juniata where Harris had built a house and cleared some fields.

Shikellamy Tells of Efforts of Six Nations to
Have Shawnees Return to the Susquehanna

The Six Nations were faithful to their promise, in the treaty of 1732, to induce the Shawnees in the Allegheny Valley to take up their adobe in the valley of the Susquehanna; and they used every means short of war in efforts to accomplish this result. On September 10th, 1735, Shikellamy and Hetaquantagechty, with three other Iroquois chiefs, reported at a meeting of the Provincial Council, that, in accordance with the treaty of 1732, the Six Nations had sent some of their chief men to the valley of the Allegheny, who met the Shawnees and urged them to return to the valley of the Susquehanna, assuring them that the Six Nations would protect them, but that the Shawnees had utterly refused to leave their western home, which, they said, was more commodious than was their home on the Susquehanna. This was the same conference referred to in Chapter VIII, in which Shikellamy and Hetaquantagechty advised the Governor of the murder of Sagohandechty by the Asswikales clan of Shawnees.

But before giving the Provincial Council this definite information as to the refusal of the Shawnees to return, Shikellamy had made two other visits to Philadelphia after the treaty of 1732, as follows:

On August 15th, 1733, Shikellamy and Hetaquantagechty, a Seneca chief, coming to Philadelphia, as messengers from the Six Nations, accompanied by Conrad Weiser from the latter's home in the Tulpehocken Valley, and advised the Provincial Council that, owing to a pestilence among the Six Nations, they could not send a delegation to consult with the Governor this year concerning the matters mentioned in the treaty of August, 1732. Hetaquantagechty stated that, before he left home, a great meeting of the Iroquois chiefs was appointed at Onondaga.

Also, on October 15th, 1734, Hetaquantagechty, accompanied by Shikellamy and Conrad Weiser, appeared before the Provincial Council at Philadelphia, and advised that the Six Nations, being delayed in waiting for a message from the Conoys at Conoy Town, near the mouth of the creek of the same name in Lancaster County, advising them that they had been wrongly accused of having killed two people in Virginia, could not send a deputation to Philadelphia this year to confer with the Governor and Council concerning the carrying out of the promises the Iroquois had made in the treaty of 1732. He stated, however, that the Six Nations had sent messengers to the Shawnees on the Allegheny, desiring them to return to the Susquehanna, who answered that they would remove farther north and nearer the French; whereupon some chiefs of the Six Nations went to confer with the Shawnees; and that he did not know what happened at their meetings with them.

What happened was the refusal of the western Shawnees to comply with the demand of the Iroquois that they return to the Susquehanna, and the murder of Sagahandechty by the Asswikales band of Shawnees, as was related in Chapter VIII. These facts were brought to the attention of the Provincial Council by Shikellamy and Hetaquandechty at the conference of September 10th, 1735. The Six Nations, said Shikellamy, greatly resented this barbarous and inhuman act, and thought it ought not to pass unrevenged, but they were willing to receive the advice of the Provincial Council on the matter. Shikellamy also suggested that, as that particular clan of Shawnees had fled southward, it would perhaps be well to write the Governor of Virginia, acquainting him with what they had already done and what mischief they might still do.

John and Thomas Penn replied, urging them to keep the peace at all hazards. They said they had learned that this particular band of Shawnees had entered the Allegheny Valley only a few years before they so cruelly murdered the Iroquois chieftain, coming from the South, and were practically strangers. The Penns, dissuading, further argued that since the murderers fled to the South, no one knowing exactly where, it would be better to let the matter drop. They said that the traders need not be withdrawn from the Allegheny. Then they presented the chief "six handkerchiefs to wipe and dry away [the] tears."

CHAPTER X.

Shikellamy

(Continued)

THE TREATY OF 1736

T the instigation of Shikellamy and Conrad Weiser, the Colonial Authorities of Pennsylvania were very anxious to have the treaty of August, 1732, confirmed by deputies representing all the members of the Iroquois Confederation, and Conrad Weiser was directed to employ his influence with Shikellamy to the end that these two mediators between the Colony of Pennsylvania and Great Council of the Six Nations might bring about a conference that would represent every member of that great Confederation. The summers came and went, and still the promised visit of the Iroquois was deferred. Finally, at a conference of Delaware and Conestoga chiefs, among whom were Sassoonan, representing the Delawares, and Civility, representing the Conestogas, held at Philadelphia on August 20, 1736, an appeal was made to them to explain why the Iroquois did not send deputies to Philadelphia, as they had promised. Sassoonan said that he knew nothing particularly of the Iroquois; that he had been in expectation to see them for three years past, but understood that they had been detained by nations that came to treat with them. He further stated that he expected that they would be on hand the next spring. The Provincial Council made a very liberal present to the Delawares and Conestogas on the occasion of this conference, accompanying it with the special request that they make an effort to ascertain from the Six Nations why they had not sent their deputies as they promised the preceding year, or at least to send a message stating the reasons for their delay.

This present to the Delawares had the desired effect, and in less than six weeks thereafter, Conrad Weiser sent word to the Provincial Council from his home near Womelsdorf, in the Tulpehocken Valley, that he had received intelligence that one hundred chiefs, representing all members of the Iroquois Confederation, had arrived at Shamokin (Sunbury) on their way to Philadelphia. On the 27th of September, Weiser arrived at Philadelphia, accompanied by this delegation of one hundred Iroquois. At this time, smallpox was raging in Philadelphia, on account of which Weiser took the Indians to James Logan's mansion at Stenton, a few miles from the city (now in the Twenty-second Ward, Philadelphia), and invited the provincial officers and proprietors out to meet them. The Indians were greatly pleased with Weiser's care for their health, and the esteem in which they held him increased by this act of solicitation on his part. The Iroquois had told the Colonial Authorities at the treaty of 1732 that Weiser and Shikellamy were the proper persons "to go between the Six Nations and this government." They said that their bodies were to be equally divided between "the Sons of Onas and the Red Men, half to the Indian and half to the white man." Weiser, said they, was faithful, honest, good, and true; that he had spoken their words for them, and not his own.

The Iroquois delegation, by far the largest that ever appeared at Philadelphia at a treaty, was entertained for three nights at Stenton. The sessions of the different conferences connected with the making of this treaty lasted until the 25th of October. They were held in the great meeting house at Fifth and Arch Streets. The Iroquois deputies reported that, following the suggestion of the Provincial Council at the treaty of 1732, they had strengthened their confederation by entering into firm leagues of friendship and alliance with other nations around them, to-wit: Onichkaryagoes, Sissaghees, Troumurtihagas, Attawantenies, Twechtwese, and Oachtaumghs. All these tribes, said the deputies, had promised to acknowledge the Iroquois as their elder brother and to act in concert with them.

The Iroquois deputies made the request that the Pennsylvania traders be removed from the Ohio and Allegheny country, but the Provincial Council politely refused this request, arguing that its Indians there could not live without being supplied with goods, and that, if the Pennsylvania traders did not supply them with goods, others from Maryland and Virginia would. The Iroquois also asked that no strong drink be sold at Allegheny by the traders. This petition was evaded. James Logan, President of the Council, upon which the administration of the government devolved since the death of Governor Gordon, on August 5th, 1736, rebuked the Indians for not controlling their appetite for rum. "All of us here," said he, "and all you see of any credit in this place, can every day have as much rum of their own to drink as they please, and yet scarce one of us will take a dram, at least not one man will, on any account, be drunk, no, not if he were hired to it with great sums of money."

But the most important part of this treaty was the execution and delivery of two deeds by the Iroquois to the Proprietaries of the Province of Pennsylvania—a momentous transaction brought about by that astute Iroquois statesman, Shikellamy, assisted by Conrad Weiser.

Deed of Susquehanna Lands

The first was a deed to all the lands on both sides of the Susquehanna, extending as far east as the heads of the streams running into the Susquehanna, as far west "as the setting of the sun" (afterwards interpreted by the Indians to mean as far as the crest of the Allegheny Mountains), as far south as the mouth of the Susquehanna, and as far north as the Blue, Kittatiny, or Endless Mountains.   As related in Chapter VI, William Penn, in order to get undisputed title to the lands he had purchased from the Susquehanna or Conestoga Indians, thought it advisable to get the consent of the (then) Five Nations; and, on January 13th, 1696, he purchased these same Susquehanna lands from Governor Thomas Dongan of New York, who had gotten his title from the Iroquois. Penn, thus recognized a feudal lordship of the Susquehanna lands in the Iroquois; and his deed to the same from Dongan was "confirmed" by the treaty with the Susquehannas, or Conestogas, at Philadelphia, on April 23, 1701.   The Six Nations, however, contended that they had deeded the Susquehanna lands to Dongan simply in trust and did not release any control over or rights in the same.   At the time of this treaty of 1736, the Colonial Authorities of Pennsylvania were impressed by Conrad Weiser with the power and influence of the Six Nations, and, accordingly, did not dispute with their deputies when they claimed indemnity for all the Susquehanna lands south and east of the Blue Mountains.

The consideration of the deed for these lands, dated October 11th, 1736, was 500 pounds of powder, 600 pounds of lead, 45 guns, 100 blankets, 200 yards of cloth, 100 shirts, 40 hats, 40 pairs of shoes and buckles, 40 pairs of stockings, 100 hatchets, 500 knives, 100 hoes, 100 tobacco tongs, 100 scissors, 500 awls, 120 combs, 2000 needles, 1000 flints, 20 looking glasses, 2 pounds of vermillion, 100 tin pots, 25 gallons of rum, 200 pounds of tobacco, 1000 pipes, and 24 dozens of garters.   That part of these goods which represented the consideration for the lands on the east side of the Susquehanna, was delivered, but that which represented the consideration for the lands on the west side of the river, was, at the Indians' desire, retained, and was finally delivered in 1742.

Deed of Delaware Lands

On October 25th, just two weeks after the signing of the deed of the Susquehanna lands, when most of the influential deputies of the Iroquois had left Philadelphia, and after those who remained had been drinking heavily, another deed was drawn up embracing all the Six Nations' claim to lands within Pennsylvania "beginning eastward on the River Delaware, as far northward as the ridge or chain of Endless Mountains as they cross ye country of Pennsylvania, from eastward to the West." This deed established a precedent for an Iroquois claim to all the lands owned by the Delaware Indians, and was the cause, as we shall see, of greatly embittering the Delawares.

Effects of Sale of Delaware Lands By Iroquois

It is clear that, while William Penn recognized the claim of the Six Nations to the lands of the Susquehannas or Conestogas, yet he never recognized any claim on the part of the Six Nations to the lands of the Delawares; and, prior to this treaty of 1736, it cannot be found that the Iroquois themselves ever made any claim to the lands of the Delawares, although of course, they had exercised an overlordship over them, "declaring them women and forbidding them to make war." It is very probable that, at the time of making the Iroquois deed for the Delaware lands, no one realized what the outcome of such a deed would be. It was an indirect way of denying to the Delaware Indians all title to their lands. The Iroquois had promised that in the future they would never sell any land within the limits of Pennsylvania to anyone except Penn's heirs, and, probably, the chief purpose in securing this deed was to place this promise of the Six Nations permanently in writing.

Shikellamy and Weiser Cause Change in the Indian Policy of Colonial Pennsylvania

This action in purchasing the Delaware lands from the Iroquois marked a great change in the Indian policy of Pennsylvania —a change brought about by Shikellamy and Conrad Weiser. Weiser interpreted the deed to the Iroquois, and they were evidently aware that they had gained a most important point; that, henceforth, the Colony of Pennsylvania would be a sponsor for their claims on the Delaware River; and that all the ancient disputes with the Delawares in this matter were settled. Furthermore, by this action, the Colony of Pennsylvania had taken sides in the age-long quarrel between the Iroquois on the one hand and the Delawares on the other. William Penn had refused to take sides in any Indian differences, but his sons were more bent on personal profit than on public justice and public security.

From the date of this purchase, it was no longer possible for the Colony of Pennsylvania to treat the Delawares as formerly. The Six Nations had been recognized as the favorite people and the Delawares, the affectionate friends of William Penn, as underlings. The Delawares had already been offended through the long delay in purchasing from them the Tulpehocken lands, which had been settled many years before the Colony got an Indian title for the same. Now, in purchasing their lands from the Iroquois, the Colony started that long series of events with the Delawares, which resulted in the bloodiest invasion in colonial history—an invasion which drenched Pennsylvania in blood from 1755 to 1764; but at the same time, while thus bringing upon herself a Delaware and Shawnee war, she escaped a Six Nation war, which no doubt would have been much more serious in its consequences.

Sale of Susquehanna Lands Involves Maryland and Virginia

"Since Pennsylvania had paid the Six Nations for their Susquehanna claims south of the Blue Mountains, the shrewd Iroquois became aware that neither Maryland nor Virginia had ever paid them for lands to the southward which lay within the western borders of those States. They stated that their claims to this region were based upon the conquests of their fathers. They now insisted that Pennsylvania should assist them in securing this land from Virginia and Maryland. The Governor, who was evidently following the advice of Conrad Weiser, put the Indians off until he could secure better information about these claims." (J. S. Walton's "Conrad Weiser and the Indian Policy of Colonial Pennsylvania").

This matter dragged along until the Lancaster treaty of 1744, when Maryland and Virginia formally purchased the Iroquois lands in their dominions.

Sale of Susquehanna Lands Offends Shawnees

"The growing discontent among the Shawnese seized upon the recent Iroquois land sale as another source of their dissatisfaction. When these Shawanese heard of the treaty of 1736, one hundred and thirty of their leaders sent a belt to the French, saying, 'Our land has been sold from under our feet; may we come and live with you?' The French not only readily consented, but offered to come and meet them with provisions. This information came from the Mohawks, who received no share from the recent Iroquois land sale. In the treaty of 1736, the Six Nations had promised to send all the Shawnees back from the Ohio, and compel them to live on the Susquehanna lands, where forty-five years before they had asked permission to live. The Iroquois found this a difficult thing to do, especially since the Mohawks received nothing from the late treaty. The Shawanese, moreover, were learning valuable lessons in diplomacy from the Iroquois and the French. In August, 1737, a message and a belt came to Philadelphia from the Shawanese on the Ohio, saying that the French had always been their friends, that each year they gave them powder, lead and tobacco, that these presents enabled them to hold their own against their Indian enemies in the South. Now if they should go back to their Susquehanna lands, as the leading men in Pennsylvania, and the Iroquois chiefs desired, they must starve, and lay themselves open to their enemies. With genuine shrewdness the Shawnees declared that they had no desire to join the French, and if the Pennsylvania authorities would send them a present as compensation for the land they had lost, they could keep back their enemies, and avoid falling into the hands of the French.

"The Pennsylvania Council, after 1736, always consulted Conrad Weiser on all Indian affairs. Weiser had little or no respect for a Shawnees Indian. The Council, while it realized that the Shawnees had no legal claims on the Susquehanna land, from a white man's standpoint in reference to land tenure, inclined to take Weiser's advice, and believed that it would be establishing a dangerous precedent to recognize Shawnees claims when they were but sojourners in the country. The Indians had a quite different conception of land tenure, and the Shawnees held that occupancy did, in time, become possession. Therefore, when they received a present of ten pounds from the Province, and an invitation to a treaty, they swallowed their chagrin, and found solace in the sympathy of the French. This paltry present was the beginning of a series of misunderstandings with these tribes which finally led to their total alienation from the English cause."—(J. S. Walton's "Conrad Weiser and the Indian Policy of Colonial Pennsylvania").

The two deeds gotten from the Iroquois at the treaty of 1732 embraced the counties of York, Adams, and Cumberland, that part of Franklin, Dauphin, and Lebanon southeast of the Blue or Kittatiny Mountains, and that part of Berks, Lehigh, and Northampton not already possessed.

Shikellamy and Weiser's Terrible Journey to Onondaga in Effort on Part of Virginia to Make Peace Between the Iroquois and the Catawbas

Shortly after the treaty of 1736, Virginia's difficulties with the Iroquois, on account of the damage done by their war parties against the Catawbas and other southern tribes, became so acute that Governor Gooch of Virginia decided that the only solution of the problem was to arrange a peace between the Six Nations and the Catawbas and their allied tribes. Gooch succeeded, in the autumn of 1736, in securing the consent of one of the southern tribes to make peace, and, finally, later in the winter, the entire Southern Confederacy of Indians agreed to send deputies the next spring to Williamsburg, the capital of Virginia, to meet similar deputies from the Iroquois. Governor Gooch then decided to secure an armistice between the two great confederations and to persuade the Iroquois to send deputies to Williamsburg. In his effort to accomplish these things, he appealed to the Colonial Authorities of Pennsylvania, as a result of which, Conrad Weiser was selected to proceed to the Great Council of the Six Nations at Ondaga, New York, to arrange an armistice and, if possible, to secure the promise of the Six Nations to send their deputies to Virginia.

It was now mid-winter (1737), and the snow lay several feet deep on the mountains of Pennsylvania and New York; yet it was very important that Weiser should arrive at the Great Council of the Six Nations before the opening of spring, as, at that time, war parties of Iroquois would already be on their way to Virginia. He started on his journey on the 27th of February, 1737, accompanied by a white man, named Stoffel Stump. They rode on horseback to Shikellamy's Town, where they found the Indians on the verge of starvation, and were unable to get the horses across the Susquehanna. Finally, after a day's delay an Indian succeeded in taking Weiser and Stump over the river in a canoe. At Shikellamy's Town, Weiser and Stump were joined by Shikellamy

and two other Indians, who acted as guides; and they set forth, on
foot, on their journey through the trackless and snow clad forest to
Onondaga. They followed the north bank of the West Branch of
the Susquehanna, called "Otzinachson" by the Indians, and proceeded to the mouth of Loyalsock Creek, in Lycoming County,
where they found Madam Montour at her village called Ostonwacken, near the mouth of the Loyalsock, and near the present
site of Montoursville. Weiser and his companions were almost
starved. At first Madam Montour told Weiser that she had no
food; but, when the Indians had withdrawn from her cabin, she
raised a board from the floor and fed him bountifully from a supply which she had concealed.

Bidding Madam Montour good-bye, the little party of four
left the West Branch of the Susquehanna, and followed what the
Indians called the "Lost, or Bewildered Stream." This was a dismal region. Said Weiser: "The woods was so thick that for a
mile at a time we could not find a place the size of a hand where
the sunshine would penetrate, even on the clearest day." In one
valley, probably Loyalsock Creek, they encountered such storms
that the Indians believed that an evil spirit, called Otkon, ruled
in that place. They were now traveling northward through
Lycoming and Sullivan counties.

On March 25th Shikellamy almost met his death on this terrible journey. Weiser describes the incident as follows:

"After we had gone óne hundred and fifty miles on our
journey, we came to a narrow valley, about half a mile broad, and
thirty miles long, both sides of which were encompassed by high
mountains, on which the snow lay about three feet deep; in it ran
a stream of water also three feet deep. The stream was so crooked
that it kept a continual winding from one side of the valley to the
other. In order to avoid wading so often through the water, we
endeavored to pass along the slope of the mountain—the snow
now being three feet deep, and so hard frozen on the top that we
walked upon it, but were obliged to make holes into the snow
with our hatchets, that we would not slide down the mountain,
and thus we crept on. It happened that the old Indian's
[Shikellamy's] foot slipped, and the root of the tree by which he
held breaking, he slid down the mountain, as from the roof of a
house; but happily he was stopped in his fall, by the string which
fastened his pack, hitching on the stump of a small tree. The two
Indians could not go to his aid, but our Dutch fellow traveler did;
yet not without visible danger of life. I also could not put a foot
forward, till I was helped; after this we took the first opportunity

to descend into the valley, which was not till after we had labored hard for half an hour with hands and feet. Having observed a tree lying directly off from where the Indian fell, when we were got into the valley again, went back about one hundred paces, where we saw that, if the Indian had slipped four or five paces farther, he would have fallen over a rock one hundred feet perpendicular, upon craggy pieces of rocks below. The Indian was astonished, and turned quite pale; then with outstretched arms, and great earnestness, he spoke these words: 'I thank the Great Lord and Governor of this World, in that He had mercy upon me, and has been willing that I should live longer.' "

On the 28th of March, their food supply became exhausted, but they hoped to reach the North Branch of the Susquehanna before night, expecting to find there an abundant supply of provisions. Near the middle of the forenoon, they came to Sugar Creek, Bradford County, and were detained a considerable time in an effort to cross the same. Finally, reaching the North Branch of the Susquehanna, several miles above the site of Towanda, Bradford County, instead of finding an abundant food supply as they had hoped, they found the Indians at that place on the verge of starvation. All the able bodied men were searching for game, and the old men, squaws, and children had been living for weeks upon maple juice and sugar. The only food offered Weiser's party at this place was a weak soup made of corn meal and ashes, but Weiser was unable to partake of any of it, giving his portion "to the bony little children who crowded around with tears on their stolid faces." However, later in the evening he succeeded in buying about a pound of corn bread.

Weiser had been at this place about twelve years before, and, at that time, found an abundance of game. He asked the old men why game had become so scarce; whereupon, they replied that the Great Spirit had resolved to destroy all the Indians. One old, gray-haired chief told Weiser that he recently had a vision of the Great Spirit of whom he inquired why game was so scarce, and received the following reply: "Your inquiry after the cause why game has become so scarce, I will tell you. You kill it for the sake of the skins, which you give for strong liquor and drown your senses, and kill one another, and carry on dreadful debauchery. Therefore, I have driven the wild animals out of the country, for they are mine. If you will do good, and cease from your sins, I will bring them back; if not, I will destroy you from off the earth."

Proceeding on their way, Weiser's party, on the 8th of April, reached the "Great Water Shed", dividing the basin of the Susquehanna from that of the Hudson on the east, the Mississippi on the west, and the St. Lawrence on the north. The forest seemed endless, and a fresh snow of about twenty inches had recently fallen. They were still three days' journey from Onondaga. At this time, the spirit of the resolute Weiser was almost broken. "I went to one side," said he, "and sat down under a tree, Intending to give up the ghost there, to attain which end, I hoped the cold of the night then approaching would assist me. My companions soon missed me, and the Indians came back and found me sitting there. I would not go any further, but said to them in one word: 'Here I will die;' they were silent a while; at last the old man [Shikellamy] began: 'My dear companion, take courage; thou hast until now encouraged us; wilt thou now give up entirely? Just think that the bad days are better than the good ones, and when we suffer much, we do not sin, and sin is driven out of us by suffering. But the good days cause men to sin, and God cannot be merciful; but on the other hand, when it goes badly with us, God takes pity on us.' I was, therefore, ashamed and stood up and journeyed on as well as I could."

They crossed the "Water Shed" the following day, and on the next, having traveled forty miles, they reached the Onondaga Council. Weiser gives no report of the conference and negotiations which he there had with the Six Nations. He gives only the results. The Six Nations consented to an armistice, but refused to send deputies to Williamsburg, claiming that it was too far to travel. They suggested that, if the Southern Indians wished to meet the Iroquois, they should come to Albany.

It is thus seen that Weiser failed to accomplish everything desired, but the armistice which he secured saved Virginia from an Iroquois invasion that spring. Upon making a report to the Provincial Council, the Governor immediately advised the Governor of Virginia of the results of Weiser's mission; whereupon, Governor Gooch at once sent deputies to the Cherokees and Catawbas. However, while these deputies were in session, a band of Iroquois warriors, possibly in ignorance of the decision of the Onondaga Council, attacked a hunting party of Cherokees, killing three of them; and this deed so angered the Southern Indians that they declared all further peace negotiations to be at an end. Once more Virginia appealed to the Colonial Authorities of Pennsylvania, and the matter was turned over to Weiser to secure a lasting peace, if possible, between the Six Nations and the Southern Indians. This question did not come up again for several years, and history

is silent as to whether Conrad Weiser, in the interim, did anything
or not.

The next mention of Shikellamy, in the Colonial Records, is
his presence at the conference with Thomas Penn, Governor
Thomas, and the Provincial Council, August 1st to 6th, 1740, being
accompanied by Sassoonan from Shamokin, Captain Hill from
Kittanning, and Shannopin from Shannopin's Town, which conference was described in Chapter VII, and needs no further reference at this point.

The Treaty of 1742

Shikellamy attended the conference or treaty held in Philadelphia in July, 1742, called for the purpose of paying the Six Nations
for that part of the land purchased from them in the treaty of
1736 which lay west of the Susquehanna River. It will be recalled
that, at the time of the Treaty of 1736, the Six Nations accepted
pay for that portion of their lands lying east of the Susquehanna,
and desired that the purchase price of that part lying west of the
Susquehanna should be paid at a future date. The deputies of the
Six Nations were expected to arrive in Philadelphia in May, 1742,
but it was not until June 30th that the deputies, representing all
tribes of the Confederation, except the Senecas and the Mohawks,
arrived at Philadelphia, empowered to receive the pay for the lands
west of the Susquehanna. The Senecas were not present at this
treaty, because of a great famine among them; nor were the
Mohawks, because they were not considered to have any claims
upon the Susquehanna lands. The sessions of the treaty began on
July 2nd. The three remaining nations of the Iroquois confederacy, early in the conference, received the goods in payment of that
part of the Susquehanna lands lying west of the Susquehanna
River, comprising the counties of York, Cumberland, Adams, and
most of Franklin.

Soon after the goods in payment of the Susquehanna lands
were divided, the Iroquois deputies expressed their dissatisfaction
with the amount, although admitting that it was as agreed upon.
They said they felt sure that, if the sons of William Penn, who
were then in England, were present, they would agree to giving a
large amount out of pity for the Indians on account of their poverty and wretchedness. Through their chief speaker, Canassatego,
an Onondago chieftain, they begged Governor Thomas, inasmuch
as he had the keys to the Proprietors' chest, to open the same and
take out a little more for them. Governor Thomas replied that
the Proprietors had gone to England and taken the keys with

them; whereupon, the Indians, as an additional reason for their request, called attention to the increasing value of the lands sold, and also to the fact that the whites were daily settling on Indian lands that had not been sold. They called attention to the fact that, at the last treaty with the Colony, the Iroquois had complained about the whites settling on unsold lands, and that the Governor, at that time, agreed to remedy this wrong.

Said Canassatego: "Land is everlasting, and the few things we receive for it are soon worn out and gone; for the future, we will sell no lands but when Brother Onas [meaning the sons of William Penn] is in the country, and we will know beforehand the quality of goods we are to receive. Besides, we are not well used with respect to the lands still unsold by us. Your people daily settle on these lands and spoil our hunting. We must insist on your removing them, as you know they have no right to the north-ward of the Kittochtinny Hills [Kittatinny, or Blue Mountains]. In particular, we renew our complaints against some people who are settled at Juniata, a branch of the Susquehanna, and all along the banks of that river as far as Mahaniay, and desire that they be forthwith made to go off the land, for they do great damage to our cousins, the Delawares."

Canassatego further called attention to the fact that Maryland and Virginia had not paid the Iroquois for lands within their bounds upon which the whites were settling, and that, at the treaty of 1736, the Governor of Pennsylvania had promised to use his influence with Maryland and Virginia in their behalf in regard to this matter. "This affair," said Canassatego, "was recommended to you by our chiefs at our last treaty and you then, at our earnest desire, promised to write a letter to that person who has authority over those people, and to procure us an answer. As we have never heard from you on this head, we want to know what you have done in it. If you have not done anything, we now renew our request, and desire you will inform the person whose people are seated on our lands that that country [western Maryland and Virginia] belongs to us by right of conquest, we having bought it with our blood, and taken it from our enemies in fair war." Canassatego threatened that, if Maryland and Virginia did not pay for these lands, the Iroquois would enforce payment in their own way.

Governor Thomas replied that he had ordered the magistrates of Lancaster County to drive off the squatters from the Juniata lands, and was not aware that any had stayed. The Indians interrupted, and said that the persons who had been sent to remove the squatters, did not do their duty; that, instead of removing them from the Juniata lands, they were in league with the squatters, and had made large surveys for themselves. The earnest arguments of Canassatego had the desired effect. The Provincial Council decided to add to the value of the goods a present of three hundred pounds.

The Governor advised Canassatego that, shortly after the treaty of 1736, James Logan, President of the Council, had written the Governor of Maryland about the lands, but received no reply. Now the Governor promised to intercede with Maryland and Virginia, and, if possible, to secure payment for the lands of the Iroquois upon which the whites of those colonies were settling. He also renewed his promise to remove the squatters from the Juniata Valley.

At this treaty of July, 1742, Canassatego, the principal speaker of the Iroquois deputation, ordered the Delawares of the Munsee Clan to remove from the territory of the "Walking Purchase" of 1737. This will be discussed in the chapter on the Munsee Delaware chief, Nutimus (Chapter XII).

More Troubles Between the Iroquois and Virginia

Hardly had the Iroquois deputies to the treaty of 1742 returned home when a war party of Iroquois started southward, afterwards claiming to have gone against their old enemies, the Catawbas. Coming down the Susquehanna River in canoes to John Harris' Ferry, the first important white settlement on their route, they secured from a magistrate of Lancaster County a pass for their safe passage through the inhabited parts of Pennsylvania. With this pass, they proceeded across the country in a southwestern direction toward the Shenandoah Valley, traveling without molesting anyone until they reached Virginia, where they had a severe engagement with a party of settlers, and several lives were lost on each side. They then retreated hastily to New York.

The first word that the Colonial Authorities of Pennsylvania had of this fresh trouble between the Iroquois and the Colony of Virginia was received on January 24th, 1743, from Thomas McKee, a trader then living on the Susquehanna at Big Island, (Lock Haven). McKee made a deposition on January 24th, stating as follows: "Being concerned in the Indian trade, he has a store settled at an Indian town on the South Branch Sasquehanna River, near an Island called the Big Island, inhabited by the Shawna [Shawnee] Indians; and that on the 12th or 13th of this instant,

January, about seven o'clock in the morning, the Indians of the Town came to this Deponent's store, and told him they had heard the Dead Halloa, and were much surprised at it. And soon after, the same halloa, as from the Big Island, was repeated in the hearing of this Deponent. Whereupon, he, with a servant of his, took a canoe and went over to the Island, and in his passage, heard the Indians belonging to the Town call over to those on the Island, and ask them what was the matter. To which they answered, that the white men had killed some of their men. And on this Deponent coming to them on the Island, he saluted them according to the usual way, saying, 'How do you do, my friends?' At which they shook their heads, and made no answer; but went over to the Shawnas' town. And this Deponent further saith, that there were ten in number of those Indians, and that they belonged to the Five Nations; and on their coming to town, immediately a council was called; and this Deponent attended at the Council House, and was admitted."

At this council, the leader of the band of the Iroquois who had made the expedition to Virginia informed the Shawnees of the misfortune that had befallen his band. The leader's speech was delivered in the Iroquois language, and interpreted to McKee in Shawnee. Whereupon, McKee addressed the council, and reminded them that none of the disorders of which the Indians complained had happened in Pennsylvania. One of the Shawnees made the remark that the white people were all of one color and, in case of war, would stand together. Another Shawnee asked the warriors if they had met any of McKee's men, who had been sent to the Juniata on a trading expedition. "They could not have met them," said a third warrior, "for if they had, they would have cut them off."

McKee adds in his affidavit: "On hearing these discourses, he [McKee] rose up, and called out an old Shawna, with whom he was best acquainted, and took him to his store; made him a present of two or three twists of tobacco, and desired him to press to the Indians in Council their treaty of peace with Pennsylvania, and the ill consequences of breaking it in cutting him off, as he apprehended he had great reason to fear they intended. That some short time after, the same Indian called this Deponent from his store, and told him that he had offered in Council what he had requested, and it was approved, though it seemed disagreeable to some of the Shawnees. And in a short time after, this Deponent [McKee] was informed by a white woman, who had been taken prisoner by the Indians in their Carolina wars, that it was left to the Shawnees to deal with him as they pleased; and that they were gone to hold a council concerning him at some distance from the town; and that if he did not make his escape, he would certainly be cut off.   Upon which last information, together with some observations he had made of their behavior, he thought it not safe to trust his life in their hands, and notwithstanding a considerable quantity of goods which he had carried up there to trade, he determined to withdraw, and leave his effects among them; and accordingly communicated his designs to his man; and they came off privately, traveling by night and day through the uninhabited parts of the country, till they apprehended themselves to be out of danger, being out three days and three nights."

Shikellamy and Weiser Go to Onondaga to Arrange for Treaty

The foregoing matters caused the Provincial Council to send Conrad Weiser to Shamokin, where on February 4th and April 9th, 1743, he held the conferences with Shikellamy, Sassoonan, and Great Hominy, chief of the Shawnees, mentioned in Chapter VII. At the first of these conferences, Weiser, learning that Shikellamy's cousin had been killed in the recent skirmish in Virginia, presented the old chief with "two Strowds" to wpie away his tears. He also sent a present to Kakowatcheky, then head of the Shawnees at Wyoming, with a message asking him, "as he lived about half way between Philadelphia and the Six Nations, to take care of the chain of friendship betwixt the Six Nations and Pennsylvania." A grand-son of Shikellamy, who was present at the skirmish, gave Weiser a full account of the expedition, and of the fight, in which it appeared that the whites were the aggressors.   At this conference, Shikellamy ordered the Shawnees to return the goods they had stolen from the trader, Thomas McKee.

Weiser returned to Philadelphia, and made a report of his conference with Shikellamy, but, before he returned, Governor Thomas had received a letter from Governor Gooch of Virginia, offering to accept the mediation of Governor Thomas in the matter. Weiser was then sent again to Shamokin, where he met Shikellamy in council on April 9th, and told him of the desire of the Governor of Virginia to come to an agreement with the Iroquois in this matter.

At this council, (April 9th), Weiser learned that the Indians who had been sent to Onondaga as deputies on behalf of the Virginia affair had returned, among whom were Shikellamy's son and Sachsidowa, a Tuscarora chief. They brought word that the Iroquois were willing to meet the Governor of Virginia at a council at the mouth of the Conodoguinet, opposite Harrisburg, the next spring, and, in the meantime, had ordered their warriors not to make expeditions into Virginia. Shikellamy told Weiser that the Six Nations could not meet Virginia in Council "with a hatchet stuck in their head; the Governor of Virginia must wash off the blood first, and take the hatchet out of their head, and dress the wound, (according to the custom that he who struck first must do it), and the Council of the Six Nations will speak to him and be reconciled to him, and bury that affair in the ground that it never may be seen nor heard of any more so long as the world stands." "But if the Virginians would not come to do that," said Shikellamy, "he [Shikellamy] believed there would be war." Shikellamy further told Weiser that, if war with Virginia should come, the Six Nations would not disturb the people of Pennsylvania, but their warriors would go directly to Virginia from Big Island (Lock Haven).

Shikellamy, Sachsidowa, several other chiefs, and Conrad Weiser brought this information to Philadelphia, laying it before the Provincial Council on April 22nd and 23rd. They also brought with them the message of Sassoonan commending Governor Thomas in his efforts as mediator, mentioned in Chapter VII. The Indian delegation was entertained free, and the Governor gave to Shikellamy a present of ten pounds; to Shikellamy's two sons, six pounds; and to Sachsidowa, five pounds.

When Virginia received the report, she lost no time in coming to terms, and a present of one hundred pounds' value was placed by her in the hands of Governor Thomas for the Iroquois. Governor Gooch of Virginia writing Governor Thomas, in May, said: "We request that you will be pleased to send your honest Interpreter [Weiser] once more to the Indian chiefs, and if possible, prevail with them to accept through your hands a present of one hundred pounds sterling value, in such goods as you may think proper, as a token of our sincere disposition to preserve peace and friendship with them, and as an earnest that we will not fail to send commissions next spring, at a time and place that shall be agreed upon, to treat with them." Thus did Virginia prepare to "take the hatchet out of the head" of the Iroquois, put there by her settlers in the unfortunate skirmish, and to "wash away the blood, and dress the wound."

The Provincial Council then sent Weiser and Shikellamy to

the Great Council of the Iroquois at Onondaga to arrange for the time and place of meeting, and to deliver Virginia's present. They arrived at Onondaga late in July where Taconte, the "Black Prince" of the Onondagas expressed great satisfaction at Weiser's arrival. Said he: "You never come without good news from our brethren in Philadelphia." "I smiled," says Weiser, "and told him it was enough to kill a man to come such a long and bad road over hills, rocks, old trees, and rivers, and to fight through a cloud of vermin, and all kinds of poisoned worms and creeping things, besides being loaded with a disagreeable message, at which they laughed." The Great Council of the Six Nations, after several days of oratory and imposing ceremonies, accepted the offer of Governor Thomas of Pennsylvania and Governor Gooch of Virginia for a confernce or treay at Harris Ferry (Harrisburg) the next spring. Later, on account of the inconvenience of meeting at Harrisburg, it was decided to hold the treaty at Lancaster, a small town then sixteen years old.

At Onondaga, the Iroquois chief, Zillawallie, gave the cause of the war between the Six Nations and the Catawbas. Addressing Weiser, he said; "We are engaged in a great war with the Catawbas, which will last to the end of the world; for they molest us, and speak contemptuously of us, which our warriors will not bear, and they will soon go to war against them again. It will be in vain for us to dissuade them from it."

On this mission to Onondaga, Conrad Weiser prevented a war between Virginia and the Six Nations—a war which would eventually have involved the other colonies.

Before describing the Lancaster Treaty, we call attention to the fact that, scarcely had the treaty of 1742 been concluded, when the Colonial Authorities of Pennsylvania were asked by the Governor of Maryland for advice and assistance in that Colony's trouble with the Six Nations. It appeared that, in the early part of the summer of 1742, some Nanticokes in Maryland were imprisoned, and that their friends, the Shawnees and Senecas, threatened to make trouble unless they were released. Governor Thomas of Pennsylvania engaged Conrad Weiser to accompany the Maryland messenger to the region of the Six Nations, as interpreter, for the purpose of inviting the Six Nations to a treaty to be held at Harris' Ferry (Harrisburg) in the spring of 1743. It does not appear that the Iroquois did any more than simply deliberate on this matter; but Maryland's advances at least had the virtue of opening negotiations at the Great Council of the Six Nations on the part of that Colony.

CHAPTER XI.

Shikellamy

(Continued)

THE LANCASTER TREATY OF 1744

ON FRIDAY, June 22nd, 1744, the long expected delegation of the Six Nations arrived at Lancaster for the purpose of entering into a treaty with Pennsylvania, Maryland, and Virginia. The delegation consisted of two hundred and forty-two, and was headed by Canassatego. There were many squaws and children mounted on horseback. Arriving in front of the Court House, the leaders of the delegation saluted the commissioners from Pennsylvania, Maryland, and Virginia, with a song. This was an invitation to the whites to renew former treaties and to make good the one now proposed.

Maryland Purchases Land from Iroquois

When the Maryland commissioners came to the Lancaster treaty, they had no intention whatever of recognizing any Iroquois claims to lands within the bounds of their province, basing their position upon the following facts: (1) Maryland had bought from the Minquas, or Susquehannas, in 1652, all their claims on both sides of the Chesapeake Bay as far north as the mouth of the Susquehanna River. (2) The Minquas, aided by troops from Maryland, had, in 1663, defeated eight hundred Senecas and Cayugas from the Iroquois Confederation.

But the Iroquois never abandoned their war on the Minquas until they overwhelmingly defeated this tribe in 1675, when they were reduced by famine and Maryland had withdrawn her alliance. Now, in view of their conquest of the Minquas, the Six Nations claimed a right to the Susquehanna lands to the head of Chesapeake Bay.

The Maryland commissioners receded from their position. The release for the Maryland lands was signed, on Monday, July 2nd, at George Sanderson's Inn, instead of at the Court House. Conrad Weiser signed in behalf of the absent member of the Iroquois Confederation, (Mohawk), both with his Indian name of Tarach-a-wa-gon, and that of Weiser. By his dexterous management, the lands released were so described as not to give Maryland a title to lands claimed by Pennsylvania, the boundary dispute between Maryland and Pennsylvania being at the time still pending. The release was for all "lands lying two miles above the uppermost forks of Patowmack or Cohongoruton River, near which Thomas Cresap has his hunting or trading cabin, [at Old Town fourteen miles east of Cumberland, Maryland,] by a line north to the bounds of Pennsylvania. But, in case such limits shall not include every settlement or inhabitant of Maryland, then such other lines and courses from the said two miles above the forks to the outermost inhabitants or settlements, as shall include every settlement and inhabitant in Maryland, and from thence by a north line to the bounds of Pennsylvania, shall be the limits. And, further, if any people already have or shall settle beyond the lands now described and bounded, they shall enjoy the same free from any disturbance of us in any manner whatsoever, and we do and shall accept these people for our Brethren, and as such will always treat them." Thus was the purchase happily effected.

However, Shikellamy refused to sign the deed of the Maryland lands, being determined not to recognize that Maryland had any land claims north of the disputed boundary line between herself and Pennsylvania.

Virginia Purchases Land from Iroquois

The Virginia commissioners had their negotiations with the Iroquois deputies in progress at the same time as Maryland. They found the Iroquois very determined not to yield any part of their claim to the Virginia lands. Said Tachanoontia, an Onondaga chieftain: "We have the right of conquest—a right too dearly purchased, and which cost us too much blood to give up without any reason at all." Finally, after much oratory, the Six Nations released all their land claims in Virginia for a consideration of two hundred pounds in goods and two hundred pounds in gold, with a written promise to be given additional remuneration as the settlements increased to the westward; and the Virginia commissioners guaranteed the Indians an open road to the Catawba country, promising that the people of Virginia would do their part if the Iroquois would perform theirs. The Iroquois understood this to mean that the Virginians would feed their war parties, if they (the Iroquois) would not shoot the farmers' cattle, chickens, etc., when passing to and from the Catawba country.

"When the treaty was over, the Indians believed that they had established land claims in Virginia, that the open road was guaranteed, that their warrors were to be fed while passing through the state, and that they had sold land only to the head-waters of the streams feeding the Ohio River.   The Virginians, on the other hand, believed that they had extinguished all Iroquois land claims forever within the charter limits of their colony."   The western bounds of the Virginia purchase were set forth as "the setting sun", leading Virginia to believe that the purchase included the Ohio Valley, but the Iroquois afterwards explained that by "the setting sun" was meant the crest of the Allegheny Mountains.   It was after the treaty that large tracts of land were granted the Ohio Company; and it was not until the year 1768 that the Six Nations, by the treaty of Fort Stanwix, New York, relinquished all their rights to the region on the east and south side of the Ohio, from the Cherokee River, in Tennessee, to Kittanning, Pennsylvania.

Pennsylvania, the Peacemaker

In the Lancaster Treaty, Pennsylvania was the mediator and peacemaker, inducing Maryland and Virginia to lay aside their opposition to Iroquois land claims, and settle in such a manner as to secure the friendship of the Six Nations.   Thus the French were thwarted, and the English frontier from New England to the Carolinas was protected.   Pennsylvania also confirmed her former treaties with the Iroquois.

But while Pennsylvania was acting as peacemaker, she had trouble of her own to adjust with the Iroquois deputies.   On April 9th, 1744, John (Jack) Armstrong, a trader on his way to the Allegheny, and his two servants, James Smith and Woodward Arnold, were murdered at Jacks Narrows (named for "Jack" Armstrong), on the Juniata, in Huntingdon County, by a Delaware Indian named Musemeelin.   It appeared that Musemeelin owed Armstrong some skins, and Armstrong seized a horse and rifle belonging to the Indian in lieu of the skins.   Later Musemeelin met Armstrong near the Juniata and paid him all his indebtedness except twenty shillings, and demanded his horse, but Armstrong refused to give the animal up until the entire debt was paid.   Shortly after this, Armstrong and his servants passed the cabin of Musemeelin on their way to the Allegheny, and Musemeelin's wife demanded the horse, but by this time Armstrong had sold it to James Berry. Musemeelin was away on a hunting trip at the time his wife made the demand on Armstrong, and, when he returned, she told him about it. This angered him and he determined on revenge. Taking two young Indians with him, Musemeelin went to the camp of Armstrong, shot Smith who was there alone and Arnold whom they found returning to camp, and, meeting Armstrong, who was sitting on an old log, he demanded his horse. Armstrong replied: "He will come by and by." "I want him now", said Musemeelin. "You shall have him. Come to the fire and let us smoke and talk together," said Armstrong. As they proceeded, Musemeelin shot and tomahawked him.

The matter was placed by Governor Thomas in the hands of Shikellamy at Shamokin, who caused the murderers to be apprehended, and, after a hearing, ordered two of them to be sent to the Lancaster jail to await trial. Conrad Weiser was the bearer of the Governor's message to Shikellamy and Sassoonan. While Shikellamy's sons were conveying the prisoners to Lancaster, the friends of Musemeelin, who was related to some important Delaware chiefs, induced Shikellamy's sons to allow Musemeelin to escape. The other Indian was locked in jail.

At the Lancaster treaty, Governor Thomas demanded of the Iroquois that they command their subjects, the Delawares, to surrender Musemeelin to the Provincial Authorities, and the Indians were invited to Lancaster to witness the trial. The Iroquois deputies replied that the Provincial Authorities should not be too much concerned; that three Indians had been killed at different times on the Ohio by the whites, and the Iroquois had never mentioned anything concerning them to the Colony. However, they stated that they had severely reproved the Delawares, and would see that the goods which the murderers had stolen from Armstrong be restored to his relatives, and Musemeelin be returned for trial, but not as a prisoner. Later, on August 21st, 1744, Shikellamy brought the two prisoners to the Provincial Authorities at Philadelphia. Musemeelin was not convicted. He returned to his wigwam.

Importance of the Lancaster Treaty

No Delawares, the friends of William Penn, were present at the Lancaster Treaty, the Iroquois having forbidden them to attend.

It is difficult to overstate the importance of the Lancaster Treaty—in many respects the most important Indian Council ever held in Pennsylvania up to this time. War between England and

France, King George's War, was then raging. At the opening of this conflict, the question uppermost in the minds, not only of the Governors of Pennsylvania, Maryland, and Virginia, but of all the colonies, was, "What will be the attitude of the powerful Six Nations?" The successful settling of the disputed land claims of the Iroquois in Maryland and Virginia, by this treaty, through the mediation of Pennsylvania, with Weiser as mentor, had much to do with making possible the success of Weiser's future negotiations with the Onondaga Council, negotiations that resulted in the neutrality of the Iroquois during King George's War. Had not the Iroquois deputies, at the Treaty of Lancaster, promised to inform the Governor of Pennsylvania as to the movements of the French? Had this great Confederation sided with the French, the English colonies would have been swept into the sea.

Disquieting Reports

The Six Nations faithfully kept their promise, made to Pennsylvania at the treaty of Lancaster, to advise the Colony of the movements of the French. In September following the treaty, Conrad Weiser had gone to Shamokin, with eight young Germans, and built Shikellamy a house "49½ feet long, 17½ feet wide, and covered with shingles." While engaged in this work, he received some disquieting news from the aged sachem. Weiser wrote Secretary James Logan, concerning it, on September 29th, 1744, as follows: "Shikellamy informed me that the Governor of Canada hath sent an embassy to Onondaga, to lament over the death of Tocanuwarogon, a chief of the Onondagas, who died last spring (in whose house I used to lodge), and to let the Council of the Six Nations know that the French had made war against the English, whom they would soon beat, and as they, the Six Nations, loved their brethren, the English, their father, Onontio, [the generic name for the Governors of Canada] desired them to take no offense nor be on either side concerned, but stand neutral, and they should be supplied by the French with powder, lead, and other commodities, at their several trading houses, as usual, as cheap as before, and as the English had run away from Oswego, cowards as they were, Onontio would take the house [fort] of Oswego to himself, as his people are the oldest settlers in the Northern countrys, and would supply his children, all the Indians, with all sorts of goods very cheap."

Shikellamy further told Weiser that the Council of the Six

Nations had resolved to notify the Governor of Canada that they
did not approve of his "intention to take the House at Oswego to
himself, which could not be done without bloodshed." They insinuated that the French were cowardly to attack the English "in
their backs." Said Shikellamy: "They [the Six Nations] would
therefore advise him [the Governor of Canada] to act more hon-
orably, as becometh a warrior, and go around by sea, and face the
English."

The Catawbas Willing to Make Peace

In the latter part of 1744, the news of Peter Chartier's desertion reached the Colonial Authorities of Pennsylvania and Virginia, and it was believed that the Catawbas were the instigators
of Chartier's action. Fearing that, not only the Catawbas, but the
whole Muskokee Confederation would join the French, Virginia
and Carolina renewed their efforts to bring about a peace between
the Catawbas and Iroquois; and Governor Gooch of Virginia wrote
Governor Thomas of Pennsylvania in November of that year advising that the Catawbas were willing to make peace, and requesting that Conrad Weiser get in touch with the Six Nations in the
matter.

Shikellamy and Weiser Once More Journey
to Onondaga

Governor Thomas made the recommendation to the Assembly
that Conrad Weiser should be sent to the Great Council of the Six
Nations at Onondaga to ascertain if it were possible to bring about
peace between the Catawbas and Iroquois. To make a journey at
this time when King George's War was raging and French intrigue
working among the Indians, was fraught with much danger; besides, it looked as if the attempt to work out a peace would not be
successful, inasmuch as the Six Nations declared at the Lancaster
treaty of 1744 that the war between them and the Catawbas must
go on "to the end of the world." Conrad Weiser was the one white
man in the colonies courageous enough to undertake the journey.

Weiser realized that Shikellamy was the key to the door of the
Six Nations. Late in 1744, Weiser had sent his son, Sammy, to
Virginia to collect a debt for him. While in Virginia, Sammy
Weiser met a band of Iroquois returning from an expedition
against the Catawbas, who told him that "Unhappy Jake", one of
Shikellamy's sons, had been killed in a fight with the Catawbas.
Weiser feared that this unhappy incident would so harden the

heart of Shikellamy that it would be useless to attempt to work out a peace between the Iroquois and the Catawbas. He then suggested to the Colonial Authorities, in a letter written on January 2nd, 1745, that it would be the part of policy to give old Shikellamy a present "to wipe away his tears", explaining that "it is customary with the Indians that, let what will happen, the chiefs or people in trust with them, don't stir to do any service or business to the public when they are in mourning, till they have in a manner a new commission as before said in being fetched out of mourning and invested with new courage and dispositions."

Weiser accordingly set out for Shamokin taking with him a present for Shikellamy purchased by the Colony, consisting of three match-coats and half a dozen silk handkerchiefs. Realizing the importance of Shikellamy's position Weiser had always made it a point to pay the old chief every attention. Three years before this time he had recommended the Moravian missionaries to build a free blacksmith shop at Shamokin, and we have already seen how he built a house for Shikellamy in the latter's declining years.

Finally, on the 19th of May, 1745, Weiser in company with Shikellamy, Shikellamy's son, Andrew Montour (son of Madam Montour), Bishop Spangenberg, of the Moravian Church, and two other Moravian missionaries, set out from Shamokin for Onondaga, at which place they arrived on the 6th day of June. At Tioga, a messenger had been sent ahead to apprise the Iroquois of their coming.

Representatives of all the members of the Iroquois Confederation, except the Mohawks, assembled in great numbers to hear what Weiser and Shikellamy had to say. There was a great stir among the Six Nations inasmuch as they were arranging to meet at Oswego and go to Canada to hold a treaty with the French Governor. Indeed, they would have started a day before Weiser's arrival, if his messenger had not appeared. Weiser asked the Great Council of the Iroquois whether they believed that their going to Canada to meet the French Governor would comport with the promises which they had made at the Lancaster treaty the year before. The sachems replied that they knew perfectly well what they were doing. Said they: "The French Governor of Canada will try to gain upon us. . . . . The French are known to be a crafty people. but it will be in vain for him, as we have already agreed what to say to him and will not go from it." Weiser and Shikellamy then delivered the message of the Catawbas suggesting Williamsburg, Virginia, as the place of meeting of the deputies from the opposing

tribes. Weiser made the best apology he could for the past conduct of the Catawbas, and urged the Iroquois to send deputies for
the sake of the Governors of Virginia and Pennsylvania, if for no
other reason. After a few minutes delay the Black Prince of the
Onondagas, the speaker of the Iroquois, replied that no council fire
had ever been kindled at Williamsburg, but that the Iroquois
would be willing to send deputies to Philadelphia. However, the
Black Prince further advised that the deputies could not be sent
that summer, but that they would be sent during the summer of
1746.

At this point we call attention to the fact that, at the Albany
Treaty, held in October, 1745, between the Six Nations and New
York, Connecticut, Massachusetts, and Pennsylvania, the matter
of the Catawba war again came up, but was not pressed. On that
occasion, Canassatego explained to Thomas Laurence, John Kinsey,
and Isaac Norris, the Commissioners from Pennsylvania, that the
chiefs of the Six Nations were not able to restrain their young
warriors from making raids into the Catawba country until peace
was declared. The Great Council of the Six Nations had all it
could do, at that time, to preserve neutrality in the struggle between the French and English, known as King George's War.

Shikellamy and Weiser found the Great Council at Onondaga
very much incensed at the conduct of Peter Chartier, in deserting
to the French and leading a band of Shawnees down the Ohio.
They asked why Pennsylvania did not declare war against him at
once.

When the Council was over, the Black Prince invited Shikellamy and Weiser's party and all the chiefs of the Onondagas to a
great dinner. All the company went directly to the house of the
Black Prince and partook of hominy, dried venison, and fish,
after which they were "served with a dram round." While they
were feasting, Weiser ascertained that many of the Iroquois were
in favor of a war with the Shawnees and peace with the Catawbas.
He also learned, in a confidential conversation with one of the old
sachems, that the Six Nations believed it to be to their best interests
to maintain strict neutrality in the war beween the English and the
French. This chief said that the Iroquois would not join with
either nation unless compelled to it for their own preservation;
that, hitherto, from their situation and alliance, they had been
courted by both the French and the English, but should either
party prevail so far as to drive the other out of the country, the
Iroquois would not be considered by the victorious   nation.

Presents would no longer be made to them, and, in the end, they would be obliged to submit to such laws as the conquerors should think fit to impose on them.

At this point, we call attention to the fact that, while there was a strong English party among the Mohawks, and a strong French party among the Senecas, the great Confederation of the Iroquois remained neutral throughout King George's War. Had the Confederation sided with the French in this conflict, there is little doubt that the career of the Anglo-Saxon on the North American Continent would have been put to an end. There is little doubt, also, that, if Shikellamy and Conrad Weiser had not brought the Iroquois Confederation into such friendly relations with the English in bringing about the treaties of 1732, 1736, 1742, and 1744, the Iroquois would have taken the part of the French in King George's War.

The reason why Bishop Spangenberg and the other Moravian missionaries accompanied Shikellamy and Weiser on this journey, was that the Moravians at that time had a project on foot to transfer their mission at Shekomeko, New York, to the Wyoming Valley, on the North Branch of the Susquehanna, in Pennsylvania; and this necessitated negotiations with the Great Council at Onondaga to whose dependencies Wyoming belonged. Count Zinzindorf had held a conference with the great Iroquois chieftain, Canassatego, at Weiser's home near Womelsdorf, in August, 1742, when the Iroquois deputies were returning from the treaty of 1742, at which conference the Moravians were given permission by the Iroquois to establish their missions in Pennsylvania. Now the Onondaga Council replied to the request of Bishop Spangenberg that they were glad to renew their contract with Count Zinzindorf and the Moravians, and they gave their consent to the proposed Moravian settlement at Wyoming.

The Moravians founded the town of Bethlehem in December, 1741, which has ever since been the central seat of the Moravian Church in America. Later, they established a mission at Friedensheutten, near Bethlehem, another called Friedensheutten, (Tents of peace), the Indian town of Wyalusing, Bradford County, another at Gnadenhuetten (Tents of grace), near Weissport, in Carbon County, another at Shamokin, the great Indian capital, and another at Wyoming, Luzerne County. They also established missions in the western part of the state. These were at and in the vicinity of the Munsee Delaware town of Goschgoschunk, near Tionesta, Forest County, and Friedenstadt (City of peace) on the Beaver, in Lawrence County. In 1772, the Moravian missionaries,

John Etwein and John Roth, conducted the congregation from Wyalusing to Friedenstadt on the Beaver. The efforts of the Moravian Church to convert the Delawares and other Indians of Pennsylvania to the Christian faith is one of the most delightful chapters in the history of the Commonwealth.

Incidents of Shikellamy's Journey Home

De Schweinitz, in his "Life of David Zeisberger", relates the following incidents of Shikellamy's journey home:

"After a stay of twelve days, the visitors began their homeward journey. At the first village they separated. Conrad Weiser and Andrew Montour took a circuitous trail; Spangenberg, Zeisberger, Shebosh, and Shikellamy and his son followed that which had brought them to Onondaga. The experiences of this latter party were even more trying than when they had come that way the first time. Not only had they to contend with the same horrors of the swamps, but a succession of rainstorms occurred that made traveling almost unendurable; and, the greatest calamity of all, their provisions failed. They braved these hardships for eight days until they reached Ostonwacken almost exhausted, hearts full of hope. A bitter disappointment awaited them. There was not a morsel of food to be had in the village, and not even a fire burning in a single lodge. Riding on in garments wringing-wet and barely alleviating the worst pangs of hunger with a few fishes which they had got in the Susquehanna, they lay down on the bank of the river at noon of the 7th of July utterly overcome. They could go no farther. It was an hour to try their souls. A handful of rice constituted the remnant of their provisions. Faint and silent, the Bishop and his young companions waited to see what God would do; while Shikellamy and his son, with the stoicism of their race, resigned themselves to their fate. Presently an aged Indian emerged from the forest, sat down among them, opened his package, and gave them a smoked turkey. While they proceeded, he joined their party, camped with them at night, and produced several pieces of delicious venison. They could not but recognize in this meeting a direct interposition of their Heavenly Father. The next day they reached Shamokin, where a trader supplied their wants.

"On their way to this town they came upon a rattlesnake nest, amid the hills of the Susquehanna. At first but a few of the reptiles were visible, basking in the sun. No sooner, however, did they kill these than the whole neighborhood seemed to be alive with them, and a rattling began which was frightful. Snakes crawled out of holes, from crevices in the rocks, and between loose stones, or darted from thickets, and lifted up their heads above patches of fern, until there was a multitude in motion. They completely surrounded the travelers, who hastened from the spot. It was a place where the reptiles had gathered in autumn and lain torpid, coiled together in heaps during the winter. From Shamokin, Spangenberg and his associates hastened to Bethlehem."

Shikellamy Opposes Weiser's Ohio Journey

While Shikellamy conferred with Weiser at Chamber's Mill, near Harrisburg, in the summer of 1747, concerning the dishonesty of a number of the traders, his next important action was to oppose Conrad Weiser's journey to the Ohio, in the summer of 1748, as the agent of the Colony of Pennsylvania in making a treaty at Logstown with the Ohio tribes. Shikellamy insisted that no present should be sent by the Colony to the Western Indians, inasmuch as they had not actually gone to war against the French, and could not do so without the permission of the Six Nations, their overlords. When Weiser asked the old chief to accompany him to the Ohio, Shikellamy stated that Weiser's attendance as interpreter would be necessary at the Great Council of the Six Nations in the spring of 1748, for the purpose of deciding upon a successor to Sassoonan. Shikellamy's opposition, while unsuccessful, postponed Weiser's journey for a time.

Last Days of Shikellamy

In the summer of 1747, Shikellamy's health began to fail. In July of that year, Weiser, in a report to the Provincial Council of a journey to Shamokin, says:

"I was surprised to see Shikellamy in such a miserable condition as ever my eyes beheld; he was hardly able to stretch forth his hand to bid me welcome; in the same condition was his wife, his three sons not quite so bad but very poorly, also one of his daughters and two or three of his grandchildren all had the fever; there was three buried out of the family a few days before . . . . . Next morning I administered the medicine to Shikellamy and one of his sons, under the direction of Dr. Grome, which had a very good effect on both. Next morning I gave the same medicine to two more (who would not venture at first); it had the same effect, and the four persons thought themselves as good as recovered, but above all Shikellamy was able to walk about with me with a stick in his hand before I left Shamokin. He, (Shikellamy), is extremely poor; in his sickness the horses have eaten all his corn; his clothes he gave to the Indian doctor to cure him and his family, but all in vain; he has nobody to hunt for him, and I cannot see how the poor old man can live. He has been a true servant to the Government and may perhaps still be, if he lives to be well again. As the winter is coming on again, I think it would not be amiss to send him a few blankets or match-coats and a little powder and lead. If the Government would be pleased to do it, and you could send it up soon, I would send my sons with it to Shamokin before the cold weather comes." The Council then resolved that a present of goods to the value of sixteen pounds be made to Shikellamy, and that it be sent to Weiser at his home near Womelsdorf with a request to dispatch it immediately by one of his sons to the aged sachem.

Death of Shikellamy

On the 6th day of December, of the eventful year of 1748, occurred the death of Shikellamy, the most picturesque and historic Indian character who ever lived in Pennsylvania. As we have seen, his residence was at Sunbury, and Conrad Weiser, in the later years of the old chief's life, had built him a substantial house which rested upon pillars for safety, and in which he always shut himself up when any drunken frolic was going on in the village. He had been taken ill in Philadelphia, but so far recovered that he had visited his old friend, Conrad Weiser, at his home near Womelsdorf, in April, 1748, and was able to complete his journey to Shamokin. Upon his return to Shamokin, he was again taken ill, and in June the Provincial Council was advised that he he was so ill that he might lose his eyesight; but he recovered sufficiently to make a trip to Bethlehem early in December. On his return from that place, he became so ill that he reached home only by the assistance of the Moravian missionary, Bishop Zeisberger. His daughter and the good bishop were with him during his last illness and last hours. Bishop Zeisberger and Henry Frye made the old chief a coffin, and the Indians painted the body in their gayest colors, bedecked it with his choicest ornaments, and placed with it the old chief's weapons according to the Indian custom. Then, after Christian burial services conducted by Bishop Zeisberger,

Shikellamy was buried in the Indian burying ground of his people in the present town of Sunbury.

The Moravian missionary, Watteville, visited Shamokin in October, 1748, where he was warmly welcomed by Shikellamy. We quote the following from De Schweinitz's "Life of David Zeisberger", giving an account of Watteville's visit and the last days of Shikellamy:

"Watteville's visit made a deep impression upon this sachem. Zeisberger had sent him a costly gift (a silver knife, fork and spoon, together with an ivory drinking cup, heavily mounted with silver), and an affectionate message entreating him to remember the Gospel, which he heard from his lips, and to turn to Christ. Watteville urged the subject with all the glowing warmth of his own love, Zeisberger interpreting his words into the Mohawk language. The heart of the old chief was touched; and several weeks after the departure of the party, he [Shikellamy] arrived at Bethlehem, in order to hear more of Christ. He was daily instructed in the plan of salvation, until he experienced the power of divine grace and could make a profession of personal faith. He had been baptized by a Jesuit father in Canada many years before this. Laying aside a manitou, last relic of his idolatry, he took his way rejoicing to his forest home. At Tulpehocken, however, he fell ill, and had barely strength to reach Shamokin. There he stretched himself on his mat, and never rose again. Zeisberger, who had returned to his post while Watteville and Cammerhoff had gone to Bethlehem, faithfully ministered to his body and soul. He died on the 6th of December, conscious to the last, but unable to speak, a bright smile illuminating his countenance."

Shikellamy left to mourn him his three sons and a daughter. We have already seen how another son, Unhappy Jake, was killed in the war with the Catawbas. The three sons who survived were: (1) Taghneghdoarus, also known as John Shikellamy, who succeeded his honored and distinguished father in authority, but never gained the confidence with which the father was held by both the Indians and the whites; (2) Taghahjute, or Sayughdowa, better known in history as Logan, Chief of the Mingoes, having been given the name of James Logan by Shikellamy, in honor of the distinguished secretary of the Provincial Council; (3) John Petty. His daughter was the widow of Cajadies, known as the "best hunter among all the Indians", who died in November, 1747. After the death of Shikellamy, Shamokin (Sunbury) rapidly declined as a center of Indian affairs, as his son who succeeded him was not able to restrain the Indians under his authority.

Among the tributes which have been paid to this great chieftain are the following: "He was a trustly, good man, and a great lover of the English", said Governor Hamilton, of the Colony of Pennsylvania. Said Count Zinzindorf, Moravian missionary, who, like all the prominent leaders of the Moravian Church, had been kindly received by Shikellamy: "He was truly an excellent and good man, possessed of many noble qualities of mind, that would do honor to many white men, laying claims to refinement and intelligence. He was possessed of great dignity, sobriety and prudence, and was particularly noted for his extreme kindness to the inhabitants with whom he came in contact." Also, the Moravian historian, Loskiel, says of him: "Being the first magistrate, and the head chief of all the Iroquois Indians living on the banks of the Susquehanna, as far as Onondaga, he thought it incumbent upon himself to be very circumspect in his dealings with the white people. He assisted the Missionaries in building, and defended them against the insults of the drunken Indians; being himself never addicted to drinking, because, as he expressed it, he never wished to become a fool."

The dust of this astute Iroquois statesman reposes at Sunbury on the banks of his long loved Susquehanna; and, as one stands near his grave and looks at the high and rocky river hill on the opposite side of the river, he beholds a strange arrangement of the rocks on the mountainside, resembling the countenance of an Indian warrior, and known locally as "Shikellamy's Profile." Thus, his face carved by nature's hand in the imperishable rock, gazes on the region where "Our Enlightener" had his home for so many years.

CHAPTER XII.

Nutimus and Manawkyhickon

NUTIMUS

NUTIMUS was a chief of the Munsee Clan of Delawares residing near the Forks of the Delaware. He has a firm place in the Indian history of Pennsylvania on account of his connection with the "Walking Purchase" of 1737, which we shall now describe.

The Walking Purchase

While the Six Nations at the treaty held at Philadelphia in October, 1736, described in Chapter X, went on record in declaring that the Delaware nation had no lands to sell, yet the Colonial Authorities of Pennsylvania depended for quiet enjoyment upon the old deeds from the Delawares to William Penn and his heirs, mentioned in an earlier chapter. In 1734, Thomas Penn, son of the founder of the Colony, claimed to have found a copy of a certain deed from the Delaware chiefs, Mayhkeerickkishsho, Taughhoughsey, and Sayhoppy, to his father, dated August 30, 1686, calling for a dimension "as far as a man can go in a day and a half", and thence to the Delaware River and down the courses of the same. The original of this deed, Thomas Penn claimed, had been lost for many years. The alleged description set forth in the original deed was as follows:

"All those lands lying and being in the province of Pennsylvania, beginning upon a line formerly laid out from a corner spruce tree, by the river Delaware, and from thence running along the ledge or the foot of the mountains west northwest (west southwest) to a corner white oak marked with the letter P. standing by the Indian path that leadeth to an Indian town called Playwiskey, and from thence extending westward to Neshaminy creek, from which said line, the said tract or tracts thereby granted doth extend itself back into the woods, as far as a man can go in one day and a half, and bounded on the westerly side with the creek called Neshaminy, or the most westerly branch thereof, and from thence by a line to the utmost extent of said creek one day and a half's journey to the aforesaid river Delaware, and thence down the several courses of the said river to the first mentioned spruce tree."

The dimension set forth in the foregoing alleged deed was never "walked" in the lifetime of William Penn. Thomas Penn and the other Colonial Authorities were anxious that the lands described in the alleged deed should be measured without further delay. Some of the Delawares did not wish the line measured, but, on August 25, 1737, the more influential chiefs of the Munsee Clan, among whom were "King Nutimus" and Manawkyhickon, entered into a treaty with Thomas Penn by the terms of which they agreed that the land should be measured by a walk according to the provisions of the deed. This agreement of August 25th was virtually a deed of release of the lands claimed to have been granted by the deed of August 30, 1686. We shall now see how well Thomas Penn and his associates were prepared for the "walk" and how it was accomplished:

The 19th day of September, 1737, was the day appointed for the "walk." It was agreed that the starting point should be a chestnut tree standing a little above the present site of Wrightstown, Bucks County. Timothy Smith, the sheriff of Bucks County, and Benjamin Eastburn, the surveyor-general, supervised the so-called walk. The persons employed by the Colonial Authorities to perform the walk, after the Proprietaries had advertised for the most expert walkers in the Province, were athletes famous for their abilities as fast walkers; and, as an inducement for their making this walk a supreme test of their abilities, a compensation of five pounds in money and 500 acres of land was offered the one who could go the longest distance in the allotted time. Their names were Edward Marshall, a native of Bucks County, a noted chain carrier, hunter and backwoodsman; James Yates, a native of the same county, a tall and agile man, with much speed of foot; and Solomon Jennings, also a man of remarkable physique. These men had been hunted out by the Proprietaries' agents as the fastest backwoodsmen in the Province, and as a preliminary measure, they had been taken over the ground before, spending some nine days, during which their route was marked off by blazing the trees and clearing away the brush.

At sunrise on the day appointed, these three athletes, accompanied by a number of Indians and some white persons, some of whom carried refreshments for them, started from the chestnut tree above Wrightstown; and, at first, they walked moderately, but before long they set such a pace that the Indians frequently called upon them to walk and not run. The remonstrance of the Indians producing no effect, most of them left in anger and disgust, asserting that they were basely cheated. By previous arrangement, a number of white people were collected about twenty miles from the starting point, to see the "walkers" pass. Yates was much in the lead, and was accompanied by several persons on horseback; next came Jennings, but out of sight; and lastly, Marshall, proceeding in an apparently careless manner, eating a biscuit and swinging a hatchet from hand to hand, evidently to balance the motion of his body. The above mentioned body of whites bet strongly in favor of Yates. Jennings and two of the Indians who accompanied him were exhausted before the end of the first day, and were unable to keep up with the other two. Jennings never thereafter recovered his health. However, Yates and Marshall kept on, and, at sunset, had arrived at the north side of the Blue Mountains.

At sunrise of the next day, Yates and Marshall started again, but, when crossing a stream at the foot of the mountain, Yates fell into the water, and Marshall turned back and supported him until some of the attendants came up, and then continued on his way alone. Yates was stricken with blindness and lived only three days. At noon Marshall threw himself full length upon the ground and grasped a sapling which stood on a spur of the Second or Broad Mountain, near Mauch Chunk, Carbon County, which was then declared to mark the distance that a man could travel on foot in a day and a half—estimated to be about sixty-five miles from the starting point. Thus, one man out of three covered this distance, and lived.

An Eye-Witness Describes the "Walk"

The following account of the walk is given by an eye-witness, Thomas Furniss:

"At the time of the walk I was a dweller at Newtown, and a near neighbor to James Yeates. My situation gave him an easy opportunity of acquainting me with the time of setting out, as it did me of hearing the different sentiments of the neighborhood concerning the walk; some alleging it was to be made by the river, others that it was to be gone upon a straight line from somewhere in Wrightstown, opposite to a spruce-tree on the river's bank, said to be a boundary to a former purchase.

"When the walkers started I was a little behind, but was informed they proceeded from a chestnut tree near the turning out of the road from Durham road to John Chapman's; and, being on horseback, overtook them before they reached Buckingham, and kept company for some distance beyond the Blue Mountains, though not quite to the end of the journey. Two Indians attended, whom I considered as deputies appointed by the Delaware Nation, to see the walk honestly performed. One of them repeatedly expressed his dissatisfaction therewith. The first day of the walk, before we reached Durham Cr., where we dined in the meadows of one Wilson, an Indian trader, the Indian said the walk was to have been made up the river, and complaining of the unfitness of his shoe-packs for traveling, said he expected Thomas Penn would have made him a present of some shoes. After this, some of us that had horses, walked, and let the Indians ride by turns; yet in the afternoon of the same day, and some hours before sunset, the Indians left us, having often called to Marshall that afternoon, and forbid him to run. At parting they appeared dissatisfied, and said they would go no further with us; for as they saw the walkers would pass all the good land, they did not care how far or where we went to. It was said we traveled twelve hours the first day, and it being in the latter end of Sept., or beginning of Oct., to complete the time were obliged to walk in the twilight. Timothy Smith, then sheriff of Bucks, held his watch for some minutes before we stopped, and the walkers having a piece of rising ground to ascend, he called out to them, telling the minutes behind, and bid them pull up, which they did so briskly, that immediately upon his saying the time was out, Marshall clasped his arms about a sapling to support himself. Thereupon, the sheriff asking him what was the matter, he said he was almost gone, and that, if he had proceeded a few poles further, he must have fallen. We lodged in the woods that night, and heard the shouting of the Indians at a cantico, which they were said to hold that evening, in a town hard by.

"Next morning the Indians were sent to, to know if they would accompany us any further; but they declined it, although I believe some of them came to us before we started, and drank a dram in the company, and then straggled off about their hunting, or some other amusement. In our return we came through this Indian town or plantation, Timothy Smith and myself riding forty yards, more or less, before the company; and as we approached within about 150 paces of the town, the woods being open, we saw an Indian take a gun in his hand, and advancing towards us some distance, placed himself behind a log that laid by our way.

Timothy observing his motions, and being somewhat surprised, as I apprehended, looked at me, and asked what I thought that Indian meant. I said I hoped no harm, and that I thought it best to keep on; which the Indian seeing, he arose and walked before us to the settlement. I think Smith was surprised, as I well remember I was, through a consciousness that the Indians were dissatisfied with the walk—a thing the whole company seemed to be sensible of, and upon the way, in our return home, frequently expressed themselves to that purpose. And indeed, the unfairness practiced in the walk, both in regard to the way where, and the manner how it was performed, and the dissatisfaction of the Indians concerning it, were the common subjects of conversation in our neighborhood, for some considerable time after it was done. When the walk was performed, I was a young man in the prime of life. The novelty of the thing inclined me to be a spectator, and as I had been brought up most of my time in Burlington, the whole transaction to me was a series of occurrences almost entirely new; and which, therefore, I apprehend, made the more strong and lasting impression on my memory."

Course of the Line From the End of the "Walk" to the Delaware

In the agreement with Thomas Penn to have the bounds of the alleged deed made by a walk, the Delawares believed that as far as a man could go in a day and a half would not extend beyond the Lehigh Hills, or about thirty miles from the place of beginning; but the crafty and unprincipled Colonial Authorities had laid their plans to extend the walk to such a point as to include the land in the Forks of the Delaware and also farther up that river, it being their desire to obtain, if possible, the possession of that desirable tract of land along the Delaware River above the Blue Mountains, called the "Minisink Lands." Having, as we have seen, reached a point more than thirty miles farther to the northwestward than the Delawares had anticipated, the Colonial Authorities now proceeded to draw a line from the end of the walk to the Delaware River. The alleged deed did not describe the course that the line should take from the end of the walk to the river; but any fair-minded person would assume that it should follow the shortest distance between these two places. However, the agent of the Proprietaries, instead of running the line by the nearest course to the Delaware, ran it northeastward across the country so as to strike the river near the mouth of the Lackawaxen, which flows into the Delaware River in the northern part of Pike County. The extent of this line was sixty-six miles. The territory as thus measured was in the shape of a great triangle whose base was the Delaware River and whose apex was the end of the walk, and included the northern part of Bucks, almost all of Northampton, and a portion of Pike, Carbon, and Monroe counties. This fraudulent measurement thus took in all the Minisink Lands and many thousand acres more than if the line had been run by the nearest course from the end of the walk to the Delaware.

King Nutimus and His Clan Refuse to Remove
From Lands of the Walking Purchase

When the settlers began to move upon the lands covered by the Walking Purchase of 1737, which they did soon after the "walk" was made, King Nutimus and several of the other Delaware chiefs who had signed the treaty or deed of release of 1737, were not willing to quit the lands or to permit the new settlers to remain in quiet possession. Indeed, they remonstrated freely and declared their intention to remain in possession, even if they should have to use force of arms.

In the spring of 1741, a message was sent by the Colonial Authorities to the Six Nations, requesting them to come down and force the Delawares of the Munsee Clan to quit these lands. The Six Nations complied and sent their deputies to Philadelphia, where this and other matters were taken up in the treaty of July, 1742, which treaty was discussed in Chapter X. At this treaty, Governor Thomas called the attention of Canassatego, the speaker of the Iroquois delegation, to the fact that a number of the Delaware Indians, residing on the Minisink lands above the mouth of the Lehigh River, had refused to surrender peaceful possession of the territory secured to the Colony by the Walking Purchase. However, the Governor did not tell Canassatego that, when John and Thomas Penn were persuading the Delawares to confirm the deeds covered by the Walking Purchase, they had promised these Indians that the said papers "would not cause the removal of any Indians then living on the Minisink Lands." These Delawares had requested that they be permitted to remain on their settlements, though within the bounds of the Walking Purchase, without being molested, and their request was granted. Later, on August 24, 1737, just the day before the Delaware chiefs signed the deed, or treaty, confirming the alleged deed of August 30, 1786, the assurances given the Delawares by John and Thomas Penn were repeated and confirmed at a meeting of the Provincial Council at Philadelphia.

Canassatego, unaware of the assurances given the Delawares, replied as follows:

"You informed us of the misbehavior of our cousins, the Delawares, with respect to their continuing to claim and refusing to remove from some land on the River Delaware, notwithstanding their ancestors had sold it by deed under their hands and seals to the Proprietors for a valuable consideration, upwards of fifty years ago, and notwithstanding that they themselves had about five years ago, after a long and full examination, ratified that deed of their ancestors, and given a fresh one under their hands and seals; and then you requested us to remove them, enforcing your request with a string of wampum. Afterwards you laid on the table, by Conrad Weiser, our own letters, some of our cousins' letters, and the several writings to prove the charge against our cousins, with a draught of the land in dispute. We now tell you that we have perused all these several papers. We see with our own eyes that they [the Delawares] have been a very unruly people, and are altogether in the wrong in their dealings with you. We have concluded to remove them, and oblige them to go over the River Delaware, and to quit all claim to any lands on this side for the future, since they have received pay for them, and it has gone through their guts long ago. To confirm to you that we will see your request executed, we lay down this string of wampum in return for yours."

Canassatego Commands Delawares to Remove From Bounds of Walking Purchase

Attending the treaty were some Delawares from the Sunbury region, headed by Sassoonan, and a delegation from the Forks of the Delaware, headed by Nutimus. As soon as Canassatego finished the foregoing speech, taking a belt of wampum in his hand, he turned to the Delawares, and delivered the following humiliating address:

"COUSINS:—Let this belt of wampum serve to chastise you; you ought to be taken by the hair of the head and shaked severely till you recover your senses and become sober; you don't know what ground you are standing on, or what you are doing. Our Brother

Onas' case is very just and plain, and his intentions to preserve friendship; on the other hand your cause is bad; your head far from being upright, you are maliciously bent to break the chain of friendship with our Brother Onas. We have seen with our eyes a deed signed by nine of your ancestors above fifty years ago for this very land, and a release signed not many years since by some of yourselves and chiefs now living to the number of fifteen or upwards.

"But how came you to take upon you to sell land at all? We conquered you; we made women of you; you know you are women, and can no more sell land than women. Nor is it fit that you should have the power of selling land, since you would abuse it. This land that you claim is gone through your guts. You have been furnished with clothes and meat and drink by the goods paid you for it, and now you want it again like children, as you are. But what makes you sell land in the dark? Did you ever tell us that you had sold this land? Did we ever receive any part, even the value of a pipe shank for it?

"You have told us a blind story that you sent a messenger to inform us of the sale, but he never came amongst us, nor we never heard anything about it. This is acting in the dark, and very different from the conduct which our Six Nations observe in their sales of land. On such occasions, they give public notice and invite all the Indians of their united nations, but we find that you are none of our blood. You act a dishonest part, not only in this, but in other matters. Your ears are ever open to slanderous reports about our brethren . . . . . And for all these reasons we charge you to remove instantly; we don't give you liberty to think about it. You are women; take the advice of a wise man, and remove immediately. You may return to the other side of the Delaware, where you came from, but we don't know whether, considering how you have demeaned yourselves, you will be permitted to live there, or whether you have not swallowed that land down your throats, as well as the land on this side. We, therefore, assign you two places to go,—either to Wyoming or Shamokin. You may go to either of these places, and then we shall have you more under our eye, and shall see how you behave. Don't deliberate, but remove away, and take this belt of wampum."

Canassatego spoke with the air of a conqueror and one having authority; and both the manner of the delivery of his speech and the manner in which it was received by the trembling Delawares, would indicate that the Six Nations must have been right in their contention that they gained the ascendency over the Delawares, not by artifice, as the Delawares told Heckewelder, but by force of arms, some authorities asserting that, when the Iroquois conquered the Susquehannas in 1675, this conquest carried with it the subjugation of the Delawares, inasmuch as the Susquehannas were overlords of the Delawares. "When this terrible sentence was ended", says Watson, "it is said that the unfeeling political philosopher [Canassatego] walked forward, and, taking strong hold of the long hair of King Nutimus, of the Delawares, led him to the door and forcibly sent him out of the room, and stood there while all the trembling inferiors followed him. He then walked back to his place like another Cato, and calmly proceeded to another subject as if nothing happened. The poor fellows [Nutimus and his company], in great and silent grief, went directly home, collected their families and goods, and, burning their cabins to signify they were never to return, marched reluctantly to their new homes."

The Delawares Remove From Bounds
of Walking Purchase

Shortly after the treaty of 1742, the Delawares of the Munsee Clan left the bounds of the "Walking Purchase" and the beautiful river bearing their name, and began their march toward the setting sun. The greater part of them, under Nutimus settled on the site of Wilkes-Barre, opposite Wyoming Town, and at "Niskebeckon", on the left bank of the North Branch of the Susquehanna, not far from the mouth of Nescopeck Creek, in Luzerne County. The town which they established near the mouth of Nescopeck Creek was called "Nutimy's Town." Others went to the region around Sunbury; and others took up their abode on the Juniata, near Lewistown, Mifflin County. Later all went to the valleys of the Ohio and Allegheny with their wrongs rankling in their bosoms.

The Walking Purchase was the subject of much discussion between the Quaker and Proprietary parties as being one of the chief causes of the alienation of the Delawares and of their taking up arms against the Colony during the French and Indian War, until the charge of "fraud" was withdrawn and the Delawares were reconciled through the influence of the Moravian Missionary, Christian Frederick Post, at the treaty at Easton, in the summer of 1758, described in Chapter XXII. Says Dr. George P. Donehoo, in his recent great work, "Pennsylvania—A History": "It matters little whether the Delaware were influenced by the Quakers to complain of the 'fraud', or whether they themselves felt that they had been cheated, the fact still remains that the 'Walking Purchase' directly and indirectly, led to the gravest of consequences, so far as the warlike Munsee Clan of the Delaware was concerned."

The Sad Case of Captain John and Titami

In connection with the removal of the Delawares from the territory within the bounds of the Walking Purchase, is the case of Captain John and Titami, two worthy old Delaware chiefs who had always been warm friends of the white man. In November, 1742, they petitioned Governor Thomas, setting forth that they had embraced Christianity, and desired to live where they were, near the English. The Governor sent for them, and they appeared before the Provincial Council. Captain John did not own any ground, but advised the Governor that, if permitted to live among the English, he would buy some. Titami owned three hundred acres of land, granted him by the Proprietors; and he said he simply wanted to spend his few remaining years on his own plantation in peace with everybody. The Governor ordered that Canassatego's speech be read to these old men, refused their petition, and told them they would have to secure the consent of the Six Nations. To compel these aged chiefs to ask permission of the Iroquois was too much for Delaware pride. They sadly left their homes, and went farther into the forests. Their white friends never knew why the old men left their former homes. They were never heard of again by the whites.

Indian Hannah

In this connection, we state that a small number of the Delawares remained within the borders of Bucks County until the outbreak of the Revolution. In 1775, Isaac Still, a prominent Delaware, collected forty of his tribe and led them to the Wabash, as he said, "far away from war and rum." Also, at the outbreak of the Revolution a family of four Delawares dwelt in wigwams in Marlborough Township, Chester County. Later, three of these died, and the remaining one, known as Indian Hannah, took up her abode near the Brandywine. In the summer time, she traveled through the countryside, selling willow baskets of her own make, and visiting persons who would receive her kindly. When old age came upon her, she removed from her wigwam and dwelt among friendly families. Though she had been associated with the whites for many years, yet she retained her Indian character to the last. She had a proud, haughty spirit, and did not condescend to associate with the lower order of whites. Her kindred dead, and all the companions of her race gone, she was desolate and often spoke of the wrongs and misfortunes of the Indian race. She died in 1803 at the great age of almost one hundred years.

Nutimus Joins in Sale of Lands Between Susquehanna and Delaware

On July 1, 1749, a number of Seneca, Onondaga, Tutelo, Nanticoke, and Conoy chiefs came to Philadelphia to interview Governor Hamilton, with reference to the settlements which the white people were making "on the other side of the Blue Mountains." This delegation had gone first to Wyoming, the place appointed for the gathering of the deputies of the various tribes, had waited there a month for the other deputies, and then decided to go on to Philadelphia. Governor Hamilton advised the chiefs that the Province had been doing everything in its power to prevent persons from settling on lands not purchased from the Indians. Immediately after the conference the Governor issued a proclamation, which was distributed throughout the Province, and posted upon trees in the Juniata and Path valleys, and other places where settlers had built their homes beyond the Blue Mountains, ordering all such settlers to remove from these lands by the 1st of November.

The delegation of chiefs had left Philadelphia but a short time when Governor Hamilton received word from Conrad Weiser that the other Indian deputies, who had failed to join the previous delegation at Wyoming, were at Shamokin (Sunbury) on their way to Philadelphia. The Governor then sent word to Weiser, urging him to divert this new delegation from coming to the city. Weiser did all in his power to carry out the Governor's orders, but the Indians soon let him see that they were determined to go on to Philadelphia, at which place they arrived on the 16th of August, numbering two hundred and eighty, and led by Canassatego, the speaker at the former treaties at Lancaster and Philadelphia.

Canassatego was the speaker of the Indian delegation at the conferences which were then held with the Governor and Provincial Council. When advised of the efforts that Pennsylvania had made to prevent her people from settling on unpurchased land, Canassatego excused the Government for this, saying: "White people are no more obedient to you than our young Indians are to us."

He thus also excused the war parties of young Iroquois who went against the Catawbas. Canassatego further offered to remedy the situation by saying that the Iroquois were "willing to give up the Land on the East side of Sasquehannah from the Blue Hills, or Chambers' Mill to where Thomas McGee [McKee], the Indian trader, lives, and leave it to you to assign the worth of them." This great Iroquois statesman complained especially of the settlements on the branches of the Juniata, saying that these were the hunting grounds of the Nanticokes and other Indians under the jurisdiction of the Iroquois. He told the Governor that, when the Nanticokes had trouble with Maryland, where they formerly lived, they had been removed by the Six Nations and placed at the mouth of the Juniata, and that there were three settlements of the tribe still remaining in Maryland. These latter, he explained, wished to join their relatives in Pennsylvania, but that Maryland would not permit them to do so, "where they make slaves of them and sell their Children for Money." He then asked the Governor to intercede with the Governor of Maryland to the end that the Nanticokes in Maryland might be permitted to join their brethren on the Juniata. Explaining why the proposed treaty with the Catawbas had not taken place, Canassatego said that King George's War breaking out had prevented them from getting together, "and now we say we neither offer nor reject Peace." He also let it be known that he did not believe that the Catawbas were sincere in their offers of peace.

Governor Hamilton then took up with Canassatego the proposed sale of lands, and, after much discussion, the Six Nations' deputies sold to the Colony of Pennsylvania a vast tract of land between the Susquehanna and the Delaware, including all or parts of the present counties of Dauphin, Northumberland, Lebanon, Schuylkill, Columbia, Carbon, Luzerne, Monroe, Pike, and Wayne. This is known in Pennsylvania history as the "Purchase of 1749", the deed having been signed on the 22nd of August of that year. Nutimus joined in the deed as chief of the Delawares at Nutimus' Town, at the mouth of Nescopeck Creek, Luzerne County. Also, Paxinosa, then residing at Wyoming, and the leading chief of the Shawnees of Eastern Pennsylvania, joined in this deed.

Last Days of Nutimus

Nutimus attended the great Easton conference of July, 1757, an account of which is given in Chapter XXII. Soon thereafter, he disappears from history.

MANAWKYHICKON

Manawkyhickon was a chief of the Munsee or Wolf Clan of Delawares. We have seen, in the present Chapter, that he joined with Nutimus in the agreement and deed of release of August 25, 1737. We met him also in Chapter VII, in connection with the threatened uprising of the Five Nations and the Miamis, in 1727 and 1728, where he, resenting the hanging of his near relative, Wequeala, was alleged to have "sent a black belt to the Five Nations", who, in turn, sent it to the Miamis, with the request that the latter join them in attacking the English, "to which they agreed." This relative, Wequeala, who was hanged at Perth Amboy, New Jersey, June 30th, 1727, for the murder of Captain John Leonard of that town, is believed by some authorities to have been Owechela, or Weheelan, Tamanend's brother, who, as stated in Chapter IV, joined with Tamanend and others in the deed of July 5th, 1697, and, as stated in Chapter VII, probably acted as vice-regent during the minority of Tamanend's son, Weheequeckhon, alias Andrew. This is speculation, however.

We also met Manawkyhickon, in Chapter VIII, in connection with the fight between the settlers and Kakowatcheky's band of Shawnees from Pechoquealin and the murder of the Indian man and two women at Cucussea, in Chester County. At a meeting of the Provincial Council, on June 3rd, 1728, in reference to the above mentioned troubles, Governor Gordon informed the Council that he had received a message from Manawkyhickon to the effect: "That he believed the Governor knew nothing of the fight between the Shawnees and white people, and desires that the back inhabitants may be cautioned not to be so ready to attack the Indians as they were at that time; that he very well remembers the League between William Penn and the Indians, and hopes that the Governor may be careful thereof."

At that time, Manawkyhickon was living at "Catawasse", a town of the Conoy and Delaware Indians at the mouth of Catawissa Creek, on the North Branch of the Susquehanna, on or near the site of the present town of Catawissa, Columbia County; and at Chenastry, at the mouth of Chillisquaque Creek, on the West Branch of the Susquehanna, in Northumberland County. But for some years prior to this time, the habitat of himself and his band of Munsees was Muncy Creek and the Muncy Hills in the southern part of Lycoming County.

At a conference held at Philadelphia on August 6th, 1740, between the Colonial Authorities, Sassoonan, Shikellamy and other chiefs, Manawkyhickon was referred to as "the King of the Minisincks." This conference took up the matter of the grievous wounding of a white man, Henry Webb, on the Minisink lands, by a Mohican tributary to the Six Nations, named Awamameak, whom the Mohicans refused to surrender when the Governor of Pennsylvania demanded the person of the offender. Manawkyhickon, as "King of the Minisincks" wrote the "King" of the Mohicans, who lived near Esopus, New York, to deliver the offender up. Webb recovered from his injury, and the matter of delivering the offending Mohican was dropped.

When Manawkyhickon died is not known, but in 1756 many of the Delawares of the Munsee Clan who had formerly been under him were living at Tioga (now Athens, Bradford County, Pennsylvania), and chose the great Teedyuscung as their "king". An account of Teedyuscung will be found in Chapters XXI and XXII.

CHAPTER XIII

Tanacharison, the Half King

TANACHARISON (Scruniyatha, Seruniyattha, Tanngrishon) was an Oneida chief, sent by the Great Council of the Six Nations, about 1747, as vice-gerent of the Iroquois over the Delawares, Mohicans, and others in the Ohio Valley. He was born about 1700. His residence was at or in the vicinity of Logstown, according to most authorities, though others say it was at Sauconk, at the mouth of the Beaver River, about fifteen miles below Logstown. The first mention of Tanacharison in recorded history is when he, Neucheconneh, Kakowatcheky, Scarouady, and others wrote a letter from "Aleggainey", on April 20th, 1747, to the Governor of Pennsylvania, on behalf of the Twightwees, or Miamis of the Ohio Valley. He was called the Half King, because, like Shikellamy, he was simply the representative of the Iroquois Confederation.

Tanacharison was living at Logstown when Conrad Weiser came to that place in September, 1748, and entered into a treaty with the various tribes in that region, on the part of the Colony of Pennsylvania, as mentioned in Chapter VIII. He promised Weiser that he would keep Pennsylvania posted as to the movements of the French in the valleys of the Ohio and Allegheny. "Let us", said he, "keep up true correspondence, and always hear of one another." His protestation of friendship for the English was sincere. He remained faithful to the English interest to the end of his life.

No doubt he met George Croghan when the latter was at Logstown in April, 1748, to tell the Indians of the Ohio that Conrad Weiser was coming with the Pennsylvania present. It is likely, too, that he was at Logstown when Celeron stopped there on his way down the Allegheny and Ohio in the summer of 1749. At least, he was there when George Croghan arrived at that place a few days after Celeron's departure and succeeded in counteracting the influence of this French emissary. At this time, he and Scarouady deeded Croghan a large tract of land at the Forks of the Ohio. No doubt he again met George Croghan when the latter was at Logstown, in November, 1750, with Andrew Montour, in an effort to counteract the intrigues of the French. Once more, in May, 1751, he met Croghan and Montour when they visited this important Indian town, bringing the present from the Colony of Pennsylvania, which they had promised on their visit in the preceding November. It may be that Tanacharison met Christopher Gist, the agent of the Ohio Company, when the latter was at Logstown on November 25th and 26th, 1750, though Gist says in his journal that the Indians were nearly all out hunting at that time.

Tanacharison at Virginia Treaty at Logstown

As we have seen, Pennsylvania was following up the advantages gained by Croghan's and Weiser's embassy to Logstown in 1748. In the meantime the Colony of Virginia had not relinquished its claim to the Ohio Valley. In June, 1752, the commissioners of Virginia, Joshua Fry, L. Lomax, and James Patton, held a treaty with the Delawares, Shawnees, and Mingoes of the Ohio Valley, at Logstown. Christopher Gist, the agent of the Ohio Company, George Groghan, and Andrew Montour were present, the latter acting as interpreter. The Great Council of the Six Nations declined to send deputies to attend the treaty. Said they: "It is not our custom to meet to treat of affairs in the woods and weeds. If the Governor of Virginia wants to speak with us, and deliver us a present from our father [the king], we will meet him at Albany, where we expect the Governor of New York will be present."

The object of the treaty was to obtain from the Indians a confirmation of the Lancaster Treaty of 1744, by the terms of which Virginia claimed that the Iroquois had ceded their right to all lands in the Colony of Virginia. The task of the Virginia commissioners was not an easy one for the reason that the Pennsylvania traders had prejudiced the Indians against Virginia. However, the commissioners secured permission to erect two forts and to make some settlements. Tanacharison, who was present and took a prominent part in the negotiations, advised that his brothers of Virginia should build "a strong house" at the mouth of the Monongahela to resist the designs of the French. As related in Chapter VIII, a similar request had been made to the Governor of Pennsylvania by the chiefs at Logstown when George Crogan was at that place in May, 1751.

The Virginians laid claim to all the lands of the Ohio Valley by virtue of the purchase made at the treaty of Lancaster, in 1744, in

which the western limit of the Iroquois sale was set forth as the
"setting sun". Conrad Weiser had advised the Governor of Pennsylvania that the Six Nations never contemplated such sale, explaining that by the "setting sun" was meant the crest of the Allegheny Mountains, the divide between streams flowing to the Atlantic
Ocean on the East and the Mississippi River on the West. At this
Logstown treaty one of the Iroquois chiefs told the Virginia commissioners that they were mistaken in their claims. The chiefs
agreed with the commissioners not to molest any settlements that
might be made on the southeast side of the Ohio. At the treaty,
two old chiefs, through an interpreter, said to Mr. Gist: "The
French claim all on one side of the river [the Ohio], and the English all on the other side. Where does the Indian land lie?" This
question Gist found hard to answer.

Tanacharison Appoints Shingas Chief of the Delawares

During the proceedings of the Virginia treaty Tanacharison, as
representative of the Six Nations, bestowed the sachemship of the
Delawares upon Shingas, an account of whom is given in Chapter
XIX. The Journal of the Commissioners' proceedings makes note
of this fact, under date of June 11th, as follows:

"Afterwards the Half King [Tanacharison] spoke to the
Delawares: 'Nephews, you received a speech last year from your
brother, the Governor of Pennsylvania and from us, desiring you
to choose one of your wisest Councillors, and present him to us for
a King. As you have not done it, we let you know it is our right
to give you a King, whom you must look upon as your chief, and
with whom all public business must be transacted between you and
your brethren, the English.' On which the Half King placed a
laced hat on the head of the Beaver, who stood proxy for his
brother, Shingas, and presented him with a rich jacket and a suit
of English clothes, which had been delivered to the Half King by
the Commissioners for that purpose."

Murder of Old Britain

At this time the great chief of the Miamis, or Twightwees, was
a sachem whom the French called La Demoiselle (the Young
Lady), for what reason it is difficult to conjecture, and whom the
English called Old Britain, on account of his steadfast friendship
for them. His village stood near the confluence of Loramie Creek

with the Miami. When Celeron made his expedition down the Ohio in 1749, he endeavored to draw Old Britain into a French alliance, but without success. Three years later, when Celeron was commander of the French fort of Detroit, the Governor of Canada resolved that the British power in the valley of the Miami should be overthrown. Accordingly, on June 21, 1752, over two hundred Ottawa and Chippewa Indians, under the leadership of a French officer, named Charles Langlade, who had married an Indian squaw, attacked Old Britain's town when nearly all the warriors were absent on a hunting expedition. Those who remained were taken by surprise. Before Old Britain and the five English traders who were with him in the village, could get safely within the fort, the enemy were in their midst. One of the traders was stabbed and his heart eaten by his savage captors, as they said, "to increase their courage." Thirteen of Old Britain's warriors were killed and scalped, and he was killed, boiled, and eaten.

The Miamis sent a message to the Governor of Pennsylvania discribing this tragic affair, which was laid before the Governor and Provincial Council later in the summer. Said the message: "We still hold our integrity with our brothers, the English, and are willing to die for them, and will never give up this treatment, although we saw our great Piankashaw King, which commonly was called Old Britain by us, taken, killed, and eaten within a hundred yards of the fort before our faces. We now look upon ourselves as lost people, fearing that our brothers will leave us; but before we will be subject to the French, or call them our fathers, we will perish here." Later, as we shall see, the Governor made a present of condolence to the Miamis on account of this unhappy event.

Tanacharison and Croghan Hold Conference

In May, 1753, Sir William Johnson of New York, sent Governor Hamilton of Pennsylvania the intelligence that a large French expedition was headed for the Ohio for the purpose of erecting forts and expelling the English. Hamilton at once sent messengers to the governors of Maryland and Virginia and the traders on the Ohio, advising them of the message he had received from Johnson. Before this message was received, George Croghan's cousin and partner, William Trent, had written Governor Hamilton that the French attacks on traders near Lake Erie and along the great Miami had caused Croghan to return to his trading house on the

Allegheny near the mouth of Pine Creek, about six miles above the mouth of the Monongahela, with some Indians and white refugees with him.

On May 7, 1753, while these refugees were gathered at Croghan's Pine Creek storehouse, a message was received from the Pennsylvania trader, John Frazer, sent down from Venango, (Franklin) stating that the French were coming with eight brass cannon, ammunition and stores. Croghan and his associates were thrown into consternation. On the following day, two Iroquois runners from the Great Council House at Onondaga brought similar news; and on May 12th, Governor Hamilton's warning to the Allegheny and Ohio traders arrived. The entire party looked to Croghan as leader. A conference was at once held at Pine Creek with Tanacharison and Scarouady. After much deliberation these sachems decided "that they would receive the French as friends, or as enemies, depending upon their attitude, but that the English would be safe as long as they themselves were safe. Croghan's partners, Teafee and Calendar, with the two messengers that had been sent out by Hamilton returned to Philadelphia on May 30th to report in person." Governor Hamilton at once laid these reports before the Assembly which, on May 31st, made an appropriation of two hundred pounds for condolence presents to the Twightwees, and six hundred pounds for the "Necessities of Life" (guns and ammunition), for the other tribes on the Ohio.

Tanacharison Appeals to Virginia

For more than three months, Governor Hamilton held this money, and then apologized to the Pennsylvania Assembly for not having sent a portion of it as a present to the Miamis, explaining that there was danger of the present being stolen by the French while being transported to the Ohio Valley. In the meantime, on June 23rd, Tanacharison and Scarouady wrote Governor Dinwiddie of Virginia, from Logstown stating:

"We send you this by our brother, Mr. Thomas Burney [a blacksmith living at Logstown] to acquaint you that we, your brethren, together with the head men of the Six Nations, the Twightwees [Miamis], Shawnees, and Delawares, were coming down to pay you a visit, but were prevented by the arrival here of four men, two Mingoes and two Delawares, who informed us that there were three hundred Frenchmen and ten Connewangeroonas within two days journey of this place, and we do not know how soon they may come upon us. Therefore, our request is, that you would send out a number of your people, our brethren, to meet us at the Forks of Mohongiale [the Monongahela], and see what is the reason of their coming."

It is thus seen that since no reply came from the Colonial Authorities at Philadelphia, the Ohio Indians turned to Virginia, which colony had promised them arms and ammunition. They then sent a delegation of about one hundred deputies to Winchester, Virginia, in September, 1753, to arrange for aid and supplies at a treaty then and there held between Virginia, in the interest of the Ohio Company, and the Six Nations and their tributary tribes in the Ohio Valley,—the Delawares, Shawnees, Twightwees, or Miámis, and Wyandots. Tanacharison and Scarouady headed this delegation. Early in 1753, Andrew Montour, at the instance of Governor Dinwiddie of Virginia, had visited the Great Council at Onondaga, to invite the Six Nations to hold this treaty, and he (Montour) was the interpreter at the treaty. George Croghan was present to aid William Fairfax, the commissioner of Virginia. At the Winchester treaty Tanacharison and Scarouady withdrew the consent that they had given at the Virginia treaty at Logstown in the summer of 1742, to any settlements west of the Allegheny Mountains, but they decided that a "strong house" might be built in the vicinity of Logstown in which to store goods. Virginia, on the other hand, promised to supply the Indians with ammunition to defend themselves against the French.

Indian Conference at Carlisle

While attending the Winchester treaty, the Indians heard of the appropriation which had been voted by the Pennsylvania Assembly; and thereupon, although no invitation had been received by them, they sent a portion of their deputies to Carlisle, Pennsylvania, to ascertain whether the report were true. This delegation consisted of a number of the important chiefs of the Six Nations, Delawares, Shawnees, Twightwees, or Miamis, and the Owendats, or Wyandots. Governor Hamilton sent Conrad Weiser, Richard Peters, Isaac Norris, and Benjamin Franklin to Carlisle to meet these deputies, October 1st to 4th, 1753. George Croghan was present to give advice. These commissioners had gone to Carlisle without presents, and they had Conrad Weiser interview one of the chiefs to ascertain if it were not possible to go through the forms of condolence on the promise to pay when

---

Author's note on second paragraph, page 184

Scaróuady led the Indian delegation to Winchester, Tanacharison being then on journey to forbid French advance. These chiefs had recently conferred with Capt. Trent. at Logstown, relative to French encroachments. Virginia's Logstown treaty was June, 1752. Date 1742 is typograpical error.

the goods should arrive later. The chief replied that his people could and would not do any public business while the blood of their tribe remained upon their garments, and that "nothing would wash it unless the presents intended to cover the graves of the departed were actually spread upon the ground before them."

Tanacharison Forbids French to Advance

While the commissioners and Indians were awaiting for the goods to arrive, Conrad Weiser learned from Scarouady that, when the Ohio Indians received the messages in May, 1753, advising them of the threatened French invasion, they at once sent a warning to the French, who were then at Niagara, forbidding them to proceed further toward the Ohio Valley. This notice not deterring the French, the Indians then held a conference at Logstown, and sent a second notice to the French when they were approaching the headwaters of French Creek, as follows:

"Your children on Ohio are alarmed to hear of your coming so far this way. We at first heard that you came to destroy us. Our women left off planting, and our warriors prepared for war. We have since heard that you came to visit us as friends without design to hurt us, but then we wondered you came with so strong a body. If you have had any cause of complaint, you might have spoken to Onas or Corlear [meaning the Governors of Pennsylvania and New York], and not come to disturb us here. We have a Fire at Logstown, where are the Delawares and Shawnees and Brother Onas; you might have sent deputies there and said openely what you came about, if you had thought amiss of the English being there, and we invite you to do it now before you proceed any further."

The French replied to this notice, stating that they would not come to the council fire at Logstown; that they meant no harm to the Indians; that they were sent by command of the king of France, and that they were under orders to build four forts,—one at Venango, one at the Forks of the Ohio, one at Logstown, and another on Beaver Creek. The Ohio Indians then held another conference, and sent a third notice to the French, as follows: "We forbid you to come any farther. Turn back to the place from whence you came."

Tanacharison was the bearer of this third notice to the French, and very likely, of the other two. Before the conference at Carlisle ended, it was learned that Tanacharison had just returned to

Logstown from delivering the third notice; that he had been received in a very contemptuous manner by the French; and that, upon his return, had shed tears, and actually warned the English traders not to pass the Ohio.

Tanacharison's notice given the French was equivalent to a declaration of war. Conrad Weiser was consulted as to what was best to be done, and he urged that the entire appropriation which the Pennsylvania Assembly had made on May 31st be expended at once. Said he: "Only by a generous donation could we expect to hold the friendship of those Indians."

The goods were then brought, the forms of condolence properly observed, and then the conference was resumed. After expressing their thanks for the goods and their deep affection for the English, the Indians called attention to the fact that Virginia desired leave to build a fort on the Ohio, which, coming to the ears of the Governor of Canada, was, as the Indians supposed, the cause why the French were determined to invade the Ohio country. The Indians then requested that no Pennsylvania and Virginia settlements be made at present west of the Allegheny Mountains, and that all trade in the Ohio Valley be confined to three posts,— Logstown, the mouth of the Monongahela, and the mouth of the Kanawha; that the prices be reasonable; and that future conferences be held at Croghan's house at Aughwick. In order to keep trade and friendship open with Pennsylvania, the Indians urged that George Croghan and someone else to be chosen by the Governor of Pennsylvania, be stationed at George Croghan's trading house at Aughwick, or Aughwick Old Town, now the site of Shirleysburg, Huntington County, to whom goods and supplies for the Western Indians could be sent, and who should guide and control Indian affairs. Croghan had recently settled at Aughwick when he was forced by impending bankruptcy to leave the Cumberland Valley.

At the close of the Carlisle treaty, Tanacharison returned to the Ohio, and, on October 27th, joined with Scarouady in writing the Governors of Pennsylvania and Virginia urging that they join with the Indians of the Ohio and Allegheny in an effort to prevent the occupation of the valleys of these streams by the French. This letter was written from Shanoppin's Town.

Tanacharison Accompanies Washington on Mission to the French

On October 31st, 1753, Major George Washington, then a youth of twenty-one years, was commissioned by Governor Robert Dinwiddie of Virginia, to deliver the Governor's message to St. Pierre, commandant of the French forts on the headwaters of the Allegheny River, in Northwestern Pennsylvania, protesting against the encroachments of the French on territory claimed by the English. On the same day that Washington received his commission he set forth from Williamsburg, the capital of Virginia, on his journey of more than five hundred miles through the wilderness. The next day, he arrived at Fredericksburg, where he engaged Jacob VanBraam, a Dutchman, who had been his old fencing master, to act as French interpreter. He and VanBraam then proceeded to Alexandria, where they procured supplies. From there they went to Winchester, where they got baggage, horses, etc.

Leaving Winchester, they traveled to Will's Creek (Cumberland, Maryland), where they arrived on November 14th. Here Washington hired Christopher Gist, as Washington expressed it "to pilot us out", and also procured the services of four others, namely: Barnaby Curran and John McGuire, Indian traders; and Henry Stewart and William Jenkins, servants.

Leaving Will's Creek on November 15th, the party proceeded over the Nemacolin Indian Trail to Turtle Creek, near Braddock, Pennsylvania, where they met John Frazer, the English trader, who, as has already been seen, was driven away from Venango by the French. At Frazer's, they sent their baggage down the Monongahela by canoes to the Forks of the Ohio, while Washington and Gist rode to Shannopin's Town on the east bank of the Allegheny a few miles above the mouth of the Monongahela. From there, they proceeded to the mouth of the Monongahela where they met their baggage. They then called on the Delaware chief, King Shingas, at his town on the north and south banks of the Ohio about two miles below the mouth of the Monongahela. The principal part of this village was on the south bank of the Ohio near the mouth of Chartier's Creek and the present town of McKees Rocks; and Washington mentions in his journal that the Ohio Company intended to build a fort at that place. Shingas accompanied Washington's party to Logstown, where they arrived on the evening of November 24th.

Upon his arrival at Logstown, Washington learned that

Tanacharison was absent at his hunting cabin on the Beaver, some fifteen miles distant.   He therefore called upon Monacatootha, or Scarouady, and informed him by John Davidson, his Indian interpreter, that he was sent as a messenger to the French general, and was ordered to call upon all the sachems of the Six Nations to acquaint them with it.   Monacatootha sent a messenger to Tanacharison early on the morning of the 25th.

Washington's Journal, under date of November 25th, describes his meeting with Tanacharison at Logstown:

"About three o'clock this evening the Half King [Tanacharison] came to town. I went up and invited him with Davidson, privately, to my tent; and desired him to relate some of the particulars of his journey to the French commandant, and of his reception there; also, to give me an account of the ways and distance. He told me that the nearest and levelest way was now impassable, by reason of many large miry savannas; that we must be obliged to go by Venango, and should not get to the near fort in less than five or six nights sleep, good traveling. When he went to the fort, he said, he was received in a very stern manner by the late commander, who asked him very abruptly, what he had come about, and to declare his business."   Tanacharison then said that he delivered to the French commander the third notice to advance no further, as related earlier in this chapter, and that the commander disregarded it.

Washington's Journal further says, under date of November 25th:

"The Half King told me he had inquired of the general after two Englishmen, who were made prisoners, and received this answer:

" 'Child, you think it a very great hardship that I made prisoners of those two people at Venango. Don't you concern yourself with it; we took and carried them to Canada, to get intelligence of what the English were doing in Virginia.'

"He informed me that they had built two forts, one on Lake Erie, and another on French Creek, near a small lake, about fifteen miles asunder, [apart] and a large wagon road between.   They are both built after the same model, but different in size; that on the lake the largest. He gave me a plan of them of his own drawing."

Under date of November 26th, Washington's Journal says:

"We met in councl at the long house about nine o'clock, where I spoke to them as follows:

" 'Brothers, I have called you together in council, by order of
your brother the governor of Virginia to acquaint you that I am
sent with all possible despatch, to visit and deliver a letter to the
French commandant of very great importance to your brothers,
the English; and I dare say to you, their friends and allies.

" 'I was desired, brothers, by your brother, the governor, to call
upon you, the sachems of the nations, to inform you of it, and to
ask your advice and assistance to proceed the nearest and best
road to the French. You see, brothers, I have gotten thus far on
my journey.

" 'His honour likewise desired me to apply to you for some of
your young men to conduct and provide provisions for us on our
way; and be a safeguard against those French Indians who have
taken up the hatchet against us. I have spoken thus particularly
to you, brothers, because his honour our governor treats you as
good friends and allies, and holds you in great esteem. To confirm what I have said, I give you this string of wampum.'

"After they had considered for some time on the above dis-
course, the Half King got up and spoke:

" 'Now, my brother, in regard to what my brother, the governor, had desired of me, I return you this answer:

" 'I rely upon you as a brother ought to do; as you say we
are brothers, and one people. We shall put heart in hand and
speak to our fathers, the French, concerning the speech they made
to me; and you may depend that we will endeavor to be your
guard.

" 'Brother, as you have asked my advice, I hope you will be
ruled by it, and stay until I can provide a company to go with you.
The French speech belt is not here; I have it to go for to my
hunting cabin. Likewise, the people whom I have ordered in are
not yet come, and can not until the third night from this; until
which time, brother, I must beg you to stay.

" 'I intend to send the guard of Mingos, Shannoahs, [Shaw-
nees], and Delawares, that our brothers may see the love and loyalty we bear them.'

"As I had orders to make all possible despatch, and waiting
here was very contrary to my inclination, I thanked him in the
most suitable manner I could; and told him [Tanacharison] that
my business required the greatest expedition, and would not admit
of that delay. He was not well pleased that I should offer to go
before the time he had appointed, and told me that he could not
consent to our going without a guard, for fear some accident should

befall us and draw a reflection upon him. 'Besides,' said he, 'this is
a matter of no small moment, and must not be entered into without due consideration; for I intend to deliver up the French speech
belt, and make the Shannoahs and Delawares do the same.' And
accordingly he gave orders to King Shingiss, who was present, to
attend on Wednesday night with the wampum; and two men of
their nation to be in readiness to set out with us next morning.
As I found it was impossible to get off without affronting them in
the most egregious manner, I consented to stay."

Washington's Journal continues:

"November 27th. Runners were despatched very early for
the Shannoah [Shawnee] chiefs. The Half King set out himself
to fetch the French speech belt from his hunting cabin.

"Nov. 28th. He returned this evening, and came with
Monakatoocha and two other sachems to my tent; and begged as
they had complied with his honour the governor's request, in providing men, &c to know on what business we were going to the
French. This was a question I had all along expected and had
provided as satisfactory answers to as I could; which allayed their
curiosity a little.

"Nov. 29th. The Half King and Monakatoocha came very
early and begged me to stay one day more; for notwithstanding
they had used all the diligence in their power, the Shannoah chiefs
had not brought the wampum they ordered, but would certainly
be in tonight; if not, they would delay me no longer, but would
send it after us as soon as they arrived. When I found them so
pressing in their request, and knew that returning of wampum was
the abolishing of agreements, and giving this up was shaking off all
dependence upon the French, I consented to stay, as I believed an
offence, offered at this crisis, might be attended with greater ill
consequence than another day's delay. They also informed me
that Shingas could not get in his men; and was prevented from
coming himself by his wife's sickness; (I believe, by fear of the
French) but that the wampum of that nation was lodged with
Kustalogo, one of their chiefs, at Venango.

"In the evening, late, they came again, and acquainted me that
the Shannoahs were not yet arrived, but that it should not retard
the prosecution of our journey. He delivered in my hearing the
speech that was to be made to the French by Jeskakake, one of
their old chiefs, which was giving up the belt the late commandant
had asked for and repeating nearly the same speech he himself had
done before.

"He also delivered a string of wampum to this chief, which was sent by King Shingiss, to be given to Kustalogo, with orders to repair to the French, and deliver up the wampum.

"He likewise gave a very large string of black and white wampum, which was to be sent up immediately to the Six Nations, if the French refused to quit the land at this warning; which was the third and last time, and was the right of this Jeskakake to deliver.

"Nov. 30th. Last night, the great men assembled at their council house, to consult further about this journey, and who were to go; the result of which was, that only three of their chiefs, with one of their best hunters, should be our convoy. The reason they gave for not sending more, after what had been proposed at council the 26th, was, that a greater number might give the French suspicions of some bad design, and cause them to be treated rudely; but I rather think they could not get their hunters in.

"We set out about nine o'clock with the Half King, Jeskakake, White Thunder, and the Hunter [Guyasuta]; and traveled on the road to Venango, where we arrived the fourth of December, without anything remarkable happening but a continued series of bad weather.

"This is an old Indian town, situated at the mouth of French Creek, on Ohio [Allegheny], and lies near north about sixty miles from the Loggstown, but more than seventy the way we were obliged to go."

At Venango, Washington learned that he would have to proceed to Le Boeuf (Waterford, Erie County) to deliver his message. His Journal continues:

"Dec. 5th. Rained excessively all day, which prevented our traveling. Captain Joncaire [the French commandant at Venango], sent for the Half King, as he had just heard that he came with me. He affected to be much concerned that I did not make free to bring them in before. I excused it in the best manner of which I was capable, and told him I did not think their company agreeable, as I had heard him say a good deal in dispraise of Indians in general; but another motive prevented me from bringing them into his company; I knew that he was an interpreter, and a person of very great influence among the Indians, and had lately used all possible means to draw them over to his interest; therefore, I was desirous of giving him no opportunity that could be avoided.

"When they came in, there was great pleasure expressed at seeing them. He wondered how they could be so near without coming to visit him, made several trifling presents, and applied liquor so fast that they were soon rendered incapable of the business they came about, notwithstanding the caution which was given.

"Dec. 6th.   The Half King came to my tent, quite sober, and insisted very much that I should stay and hear what he had to say to the French.   I fain would have prevented him from speaking anything until he came to the commandant, but could not prevail.   He told me that at this place a council fire was kindled, where all their business with these people was to be transacted, and that the management of the Indian affairs was left solely to Monsieur Joncaire.   As I was desirous of knowing the issue of this, I agreed to stay; but sent our horses a little way up French Creek, to raft over and encamp; which I knew would make it near night.

"About ten o'clock, they met in council.   The King [Tanacharison] spoke much the same as he had before done to the general, and offered the French speech belt which had before been demanded, with the marks of four towns on it, which Monsieur Joncaire refused to receive, but desired him to carry it to the fort [Fort Le Boeuf, now Waterford, Erie County,] to the commander.

"Dec. 7th.   Monsieur LaForce, Commissary of the French stores, and three other soldiers, came over to accompany us up. We found it extremely difficult to get the Indians off today, as every stratagem had been used to prevent their going up with me. I had last night left John Davidson (the Indian interpreter) whom I brought with me from town, and strictly charged him not to be out of their company, as I could not get them over to my tent; for they had some business with Kustologa, chiefly to know why he did not deliver up the French speech belt which he had in keeping; but I was obliged to send Mr. Gist over today to fetch them, which he did with great persuasion.

"At twelve o'clock, we set out for the fort [Le Boeuf], and were prevented from arriving there until the eleventh day by excessive rains, snows, and bad traveling through many mires and swamps; these we were obliged to pass to avoid crossing the creek, which was impossible, either by fording or rafting, the water was so high and rapid.

"We passed over much good land since we left Venango, and through several extensive and very rich meadows, one of which, I believe, was nearly four miles in length, and considerably wide in some places.

Dec. 12th.   I prepared early to wait upon the commander, and was received, and conducted to him by the second officer in command. I acquainted him with my business and offered my commission and letter; both of which he desired me to keep until the arrival of Monsieur Reparti, captain at the next fort, who was sent for and expected every hour.

"This commander is a knight of the military order of St. Louis, and named Legardeur de St. Pierre. He is an elderly gentleman, and has much the air of a soldier. He was sent over to take the command, immediately upon the death of the late general, and arrived here about seven days before me.

"At two o'clock, the gentleman who was sent for arrived, when I offered the letter, &c. again, which they received, and adjourned into a private apartment for the captain to translate, who understood a little English. After he had done it, the commander desired I would walk in and bring my interpreter to peruse and correct it; which I did.

"Dec. 14th. As the snow increased very fast, and our horses daily became weaker, I sent them off unloaded, under the care of Barnaby Currin and two others, to make all convenient despatch to Venango, and there to wait our arrival, if there was a prospect of the river's freezing; if not, then to continue down to Shanapin's town, at the Forks of Ohio, and there to wait until we came to cross the Allegheny; intending myself to go down by water, as I had the offer of a canoe or two. This evening, I received an answer to his honour the governor's letter, from the commandant.

"Dec. 15th. The commandant ordered a plentiful store of liquor, provisions, &c. to be put on board our canoes, and appeared to be extremely complaisant, though he was exerting every artifice which he could invent to set our Indians at variance with us, to prevent their going until after our departure; presents, rewards, and everything which could be suggested by him or his officers. I can not say that ever in my life I suffered so much anxiety as I did in this affair. I saw that every stratagem, which the most fruitful brain could invent, was practised to win the Half King to their interest; and that leaving him there was giving them the opportunity they aimed at. I went to the Half King and pressed him in the strongest terms to go; he told me that the commandant would not discharge him until the morning. I then went to the commandant, and desired him to do their business, and complained of ill treatment; for keeping them, as they were part of my company, was detaining me. This he promised not to do, but to forward my journey as much as he could. He protested he did not keep them, but was ignorant of the cause of their stay; though I soon found it out. He had promised them a present of guns, &c.

if they would wait until the morning. As I was very much pressed by the Indians to wait this day for them, I consented, on a promise that nothing should hinder them in the morning.

"16th. The French were not slack in their inventions to keep the Indians this day, also. But as they were obliged, according to promise, to give the present, they then endeavored to try the power of liquor, which I doubt not would have prevailed at any other time than this; but I urged and insisted with the King [Tanacharison] so closely upon his word, that he refrained, and set off with us as he had engaged.

"We had a tedious and very fatiguing passage down the creek. Several times we had like to have been staved against rocks; and many times were obliged all hands to get out and remain in the water half an hour or more, getting over the shoals. At one place, the ice had lodged, and made it impassable by water; we were, therefore, obliged to carry our canoe across the neck of land, a quarter of a mile over. We did not reach Venango until the 22d, where we met with our horses.

"Dec. 23d. When I got things ready to set off, I sent for the Half King, to know whether he intended to go with us, or by water. He told me that White Thunder had hurt himself much, and was sick, and unable to walk; therefore he was obliged to carry him down in a canoe. As I found he intended to stay here a day or two, and knew that Monsieur Joncaire would employ every scheme to set him against the English, as he had before done, I told him I hoped he would guard against his flattery, and let no fine speeches influence him in their favour. He desired I might not be concerned, for he knew the French too well for any thing to engage him in their favour; and that though he could not go down with us, he yet would endeavour to meet at the Forks with Joseph Campbell, to deliver a speech for me to carry to his honour, the governor. He told me he would order the Young Hunter to attend us, and get provisions, &c. if wanted.

"Our horses were now so weak and feeble, and the baggage so heavy, (as we were obliged to provide all the necessaries which the journey would require) that we doubted much their performing it. Therefore, myself and others, except the drivers, who were obliged to ride, gave up our horses for packs, to assist along with the baggage. I put myself in an Indian walking dress, and continued with them three days, until I found there was no probability of their getting home in any reasonable time. The horses became less able to travel every day; the cold increased very fast; and the roads were becoming much worse by a deep snow, continually freezing; therefore, as I was uneasy to get back, to make report of my proceedings to his honour, the governor, I determined to prosecute my journey, the nearest way through the woods, on foot.

"Accordingly, I left Mr. Vanbraam in charge of our baggage, with money and directions to provide necessaries from place to place for themselves and horses, and to make the most convenient despatch in traveling.

"I took my necessary papers, pulled off my clothes, and tied myself up in a match coat. Then with gun in hand, and pack on my back, in which were my papers and provisions, I set out with Mr. Gist, fitted in the same manner, on Wednesday, the 26th."

History does not say how Tanacharison and the other members of the party whom Washington and Gist left behind when they set out on foot, reached Logstown. Nor shall we follow Washington further on his return trip. Every school child is familiar with the fact that he was shot at by a hostile Indian near Murdering Town, not far from Evans City, Butler County, on the afternoon of December 27th, as he and Gist were on their way back to Virginia, and that he was almost drowned in the icy waters of the Allegheny within the present limits of Pittsburgh.

A Personal Statement

At this point, the author asks that the reader indulge him in making the statement that he traces his love for the history of Pennsylvania to the story of the attack on Washington by the hostile Indian on that December evening of 1753, told him under the following circumstances: On the farm on which he was reared in Armstrong County, the ancestral home of his paternal forebearers since 1795, is a high hill, commanding a majestic sweep of the horizon in all directions. To the eastward, the blue outline of the Chestnut Ridge can be seen, on a clear day, almost fifty miles away, while to the westward, are the undulating hills of Butler County. One of his earliest recollections is that of his accompanying his revered mother to this hilltop on summer evenings and, with her, watching the sun set in floods of gorgeous and golden beauty behind the western hills. On those occasions she told him that the western region, where the sun was setting, was Butler County, and that it was in this county where George Washington was shot at by a hostile Indian in the dead of winter and in the depth of the forest. The author shall always cherish the recollection of those summer evenings, when, as a child in company with his mother in the grace and beauty of her young womanhood, he watched those golden sunsets bathe the Butler County hills in glory, and in his fancy, pictured the region of the sunset as an enchanted land, inhabited by the ghosts and shadows of the past and hallowed by the footsteps of Washington.

Nemacolin

We have stated earlier in this chapter that Washington and Gist followed the Nemacolin Indian Trail from Cumberland, Maryland, to the Forks of the Ohio. This trail was named for the Delaware chief, Nemacolin, who in 1752, was employed, with others, by Colonel Thomas Cresap and Christopher Gist, acting for the Ohio Company, in blazing the most direct route between Cumberland and the mouth of Redstone Creek (Brownsville, Fayette County), on the Monongahela River. This trail followed the route of Christopher Gist's second journey from Cumberland to the Forks of the Ohio, in November, 1751. It was much shorter than the path which the Virginia traders had used from a date as early as 1740, in traveling from the Potomac to the Ohio. It was the same course followed by Washington's army on its unsuccessful march against Fort Duquesne in the summer of 1754, described in Chapter XIV, and also, in part, the same followed by Braddock's army in the summer of 1755.

Nemacolin's residence at the time of blazing this trail was at the mouth of Dunlap's Creek, also, in early times, called Nemacolin's Creek, in Fayette County. How long Nemacolin resided at this place is unknown. In 1785, General Richard Butler, in company with Colonel James Monroe, (afterwards President Monroe), made an expedition down the Ohio to treat with the Miamis. In General Butler's journal of this expedition, he speaks of an island called Nemacolin's, between the mouths of the Little Kanawha and Hocking, no doubt a subsequent dwelling place of Nemacolin.

Nemacolin was the son of the Delaware chief, Checochinican, or Specokkenecan, who dwelt on Brandywine Creek about 1716, and removed to the Susquehanna before June 16, 1718, as on that date he accompanied Captain Civility and other chiefs of the Conestogas, Shawnees, and Delawares of the Susquehanna, to Philadelphia, and complained to Governor Keith "that they have reason to think the authority of this Government is not duly observed, for that notwithstanding all our former agreements that rum should not be brought amongst them, it is still carried in great quantities." Checochinican added "that the young men about

Paxtan [Paxtang] had been lately so generally debauched with rum carried amongst them by strangers, that they now want all manner of clothing and necessaries to go a hunting; wherefore, they wish it would be so ordered that no rum should be brought amongst them by any except the traders who furnish them with all other necessaries."

In the Pennsylvania Archives, (Vol. I, page 239), is a letter from Checochinican to Governor Patrick Gordon, dated June 24, 1729, in which he says that, when the Indians sold their lands on the Brandywine to William Penn, they reserved a part on the head of the creek, by a written instrument which later was lost. Checochinican complains that settlers are crowding the Indians out, and hopes that the Governor "will be pleased to take care and protect us."This is his last appearance in history.

Another Delaware chief living in Southwestern Pennsylvania at the time of the blazing of Nemacolin's Trail, was Catfish. He had his cabin where Washington, the county seat of Washington County, now stands.

Tanacharison Asks Pennsylvania to Build
Fort on the Ohio

In January, 1754, Gorge Croghan and Andrew Montour were sent to Logstown by Governor Hamilton of Pennsylvania, to ascertain from Tanacharison and Scarouady a full account of the activities of the French in the valleys of the Allegheny and Ohio, the attitude of the Western Indians, and what assistance in the way of arms and ammunition Virginia had given these Indians. Croghan and Montour found some French soldiers at Logstown and most of the Indians drunk. John Patten, a trader, who accompanied Croghan and Montour, was captured by the French, but Tanacharson caused his release. The Pennsylvania emissaries remained at Logstown until February 2nd. They found the Indians determined to resist the French. A few days before they left, Tanacharison, Scarouady, and Shingas addressed a speech to Governor Hamilton in which they said: "We now request that our brother, the Governor of Virginia, may build a strong house at the Forks of the Mohongialo [Monongahela], and send some of our young brethren, the warriors, to live in it. And we expect our brother of Pennsylvania will build another house somewhere on the river, where he shall think proper, where whatever assistance he will think proper to send us may be kept for us, as our enemies are just at hand, and we do not know what day they may come upon us."

CHAPTER XIV.

Tanacharison, the Half King

(Continued)

Tanacharison Sees French Commit First Overt Act of War

ARLY in 1754, Virginia decided to fortify the Forks of the Ohio (Pittsburgh). She sent Captain William Trent to this place with a company of men to erect a fort. Trent arrived on February 17, 1754, and immediately began the erection of a fort, called Fort Trent.

After the work was well started, Captain Trent returned to Will's Creek (Cumberland, Maryland), to secure supplies, leaving a young commissioned officer, an ensign, named Edward Ward, who was a half-brother of George Croghan, in command. The Indian trader, John Frazer, was among Ward's forces, having the commission of lieutenant. The French were promptly warned of the arrival of Trent's forces, and with the opening of spring, marshalled their forces to the number of about one thousand, including French-Canadians and Indians of various tribes, with eighteen pieces of cannon, in all a flotilla of about sixty battaux and three hundred canoes, and descended the Allegheny from LeBoueff and Venango. The French forces arrived at the Forks of the Ohio on the evening of the 17th of April, under command of Captain Contrecoeur. Planting his artillery, Contrecoeur sent Chevalier Le Mercier, Captain of the Artillery of Canada, with a summons to Ensign Ward, demanding immediate surrender. This was the first overt act of war on the part of the French, in the conflict known as the French and Indian War.

Ward thus found himself surrounded by a force of one thousand French and Indians with the fort still uncompleted.

The Half King, Tanacharison, was present, and advised Ensign Ward to reply to the demand of Contrecoeur that he was not an officer of rank to answer the demand, and to request a delay until he could send for his superior in command. Contrecoeur, however, refused to parley; whereupon, Ward, having less than forty men, and, therefore, being utterly unable to resist the opposing force, prudently surrendered the half-finished stockade without further hesitation.

Contrecoeur, upon the surrender of Ward, treated him with the utmost politeness, invited him to sup with him, and wished him a pleasant journey back to Virginia. The French commander permitted him to withdraw his men, and take his tools with him; and on the next morning, he started on his return to Virginia going up the Monongahela to the mouth of Redstone Creek (Brownsville, Fayette County), where the Ohio Company had a stockade, erected by Trent on his way to the Ohio Valley. George Croghan, about the time Trent began erecting the fort at the Forks of the Ohio, had contracted with the Ohio Company to furnish provisions for Trent's forces, valued at five hundred pounds, from the back parts of Pennsylvania; and half of these were on their way to the Ohio when Contrecoeur captured the fort.

The French then took possession of the half-finished fort, completed it early in June, and named it Fort Duquesne, in honor of Marquis DuQuesne, then the Governor General of Canada.

Tanacharison with Washington in Virginia's Campaign of 1754

While Captain Trent was pushing on toward the Forks of the Ohio in the early part of 1754, Colonel Joshua Fry, with George Washington second in command, was raising additional troops in Virginia to garrison the fort Trent was to build. Soon Washington, under the rank of Lieutenant-Colonel, hastened to Will's Creek (Cumberland, Maryland), to push forward the preparations to reinforce the fort at the Forks of the Ohio, when the news of its capture was brought to him in the latter part of April, 1754. A council of war was then called in which it was agreed that it would be impossible to march to the French fort without reinforcements, but that an advance should be made to the mouth of Redstone Creek, where a fortification should be made and reinforcements awaited.

Washington was not yet joined by Colonel Fry, and had only one hundred fifty men under his command. On the 25th of April, he sent a detachment of sixty men to open the road, which detachment was joined by the main body on May 1st. By the 9th of May, he reached a place called the Little Meadows. Learning from Indian scouts, which had been sent him by his ally, Tanacharison, that the French were rapidly marching toward him, Washington hastened to take a position in a place called the Great Meadows along the national pike, in Fayette County. "I hurried to this place," says Washington, "as a convenient spot. We have, with nature's assistance, made a good entrenchment, and by clearing the bushes out of these meadows, prepared a charming field for an encounter."

Christopher Gist visited Washington's camp at the Great Meadows early in the morning of May 27th, coming from his plantation at Mount Braddock, thirteen miles distant, and reporting that on May 26th, M. La Force, with fifty soldiers had been at his plantation the day before, and that on his way to Washington's camp, he had seen the tracks of the same party only five miles from the encampment at the Great Meadows. Tanacharison, with a number of his warriors was but six miles from the Great Meadows, and a little after eight o'clock on the night of the same day, May 27th, he sent Washington intelligence that he had seen the tracks of Frenchmen, and had traced them to an obscure retreat. Washington feared that this might be a stratagem of the French for attacking his camp, and so, placing his ammunition in a place of safety and leaving a strong guard to protect it, he set out before ten o'clock with forty men, and reached Tanacharison's camp a little before sunrise, marching through a heavy rain, a night of intense darkness and the obstacles offered by an almost impenetrable forest. In a letter to Governor Dinwiddie, he says: "We were frequently tumbled over one another, and often so lost that fifteen or twenty minutes' search would not find the path again."

Tanacharison Helps Washington Fight First Battle of His Career

At early dawn (May 28th), Washington held a council with Tanacharison at the latter's camp, which was near a spring, now known as Washington's Spring, about two miles north of the Summit on the old national pike, near Uniontown; and it was agreed at this council to unite in an attack upon the French, Washington's forces to be on the right and Tanacharison's warriors on the left. The French were soon traced to an almost inaccessible rocky glen in the Allegheny Mountains, about three miles north of the Summit. The forces of Washington and Tanacharison advanced until they came so near as to be discovered by the French, who instantly ran to their arms. The firing continued on both sides for about fifteen minutes, when the French were defeated with the loss of their whole party, ten of whom, including their commander, M. de Jumonville, were killed, one wounded, and twenty-one taken prisoners.   Of the prisoners, the two most important were an officer named Drouillon, and the redoubtable LaForce.   The prisoners were marched to the Great Meadows, and from there sent over the mountains to Virginia.   Of Washington's party, only one was killed, and two or three were wounded.   Tanacharison's warriors sustained no loss, as the fire of the French was aimed exclusively at Washington and his soldiers.   It is said that Washington fired the first shot in this skirmish, the opening conflict of the French and Indian War.   Jumonville was buried where he fell, and a tablet marks the spot where his remains lie.   The scene of this encounter, the first battle of Washington's illustrious career, is almost as wild and primitive as it was on that fateful morning of the 28th day of May, 1754.

At a council held at Philadelphia on December 19th, 1754, between Governor Morris of Pennsylvania, and Scarouady, Jagrea, a Mohawk, and Aroas, a Seneca, the said Scarouady gave the following account of events leading up to the fight with Jumonville and the part that the Indian allies took in the same:

"This belt [holding up a belt of wampum] was sent by the Governor of Virginia and delivered by Captain Trent.   You see in it the representation of an hatchet.   It was an invitation to us to join with and assist our brethren to repel the French from the Ohio.   At the time it was given, there were but four or five of us, and we were all that knew any thing about the matter; when we got it, we put it into a private pocket on the inside of our garment. It lay next to our breasts.

"As we were on the road going to Council with our brethren, a company of French, in number thirty-one, overtook us and desired us to go and council with them; and when we refused, they pulled us by the arm and almost stripped the chain of covenant from off it, but still I would suffer none to go with them.   We thought to have got before them, but they passed us; and when we saw they endeavored to break the chain of friendship, I pulled this belt out of my pocket and looked at it and saw there this hatchet, and then went and told Colonel Washington of these thirty-one French Men, and we and a few of our brothers fought with them.   Ten were killed, and twenty-one were taken alive whom we delivered to Colonel Washington, telling him that we had blooded the edge of his hatchet a little."

John Davidson, the Indian trader, acted as interpreter, at the above council.   He was in the action, and gave Governor Morris the following account of it:

"There were but eight Indians, who did most of the execution that was done. Colonel Washington and the Half King [Tanacharison] differed much in judgment, and on the Colonel's refusing to take his advice, the English and Indians separated. After which the Indians discovered the French in an hollow and hid themselves, lying on their bellies behind a hill; afterwards they discovered Colonel Washington on the opposite side of the hollow in the gray of the morning, and when the English fired, which they did in great confusion, the Indians came out of their cover and closed with the French and killed them with their tomahawks, on which the French surrendered."

In writing to his brother, John Augustine, Washington, referring to the engagement with Jumonville, said:

"I have heard the bullets whistle, and believe me, there is something charming in the sound."

This remark was reported later to George the Second, King of England, who commented: "He would not say so if he had been used to hearing many."

Washington Gives Tanacharison an English Name

Two days after the death of Jumonville, Colonel Fry died at the camp at Will's Creek on his way to join the army, and the chief command now devolved upon Colonel Washington. Washington immediately commenced enlarging the intrenchment at the Great Meadows, and erecting palisades, anticipating an attack from the French. The palisaded fort at the Great Meadows having been completed, Washington's forces were augmented to three hundred by the arrival from Will's Creek of the forces which had been under Colonel Fry. With these was the surgeon of the regiment, Dr. James Craik, a Scotchman by birth, who was destined to be a faithful friend of Washington's throughout the remainder of his life, and was present at his bedside, when he closed his eyes in death within the hallowed walls of his beloved Mount Vernon.

On the 9th of June, Washington's early instructor, Adjutant Muse, accompanied by Andrew Montour, now Provincial Captain, arrived at the Great Meadows. Adjutant, now Major Muse, brought with him a belt of wampum, and a speech from Governor Dinwiddie to Tanacharison, with medals and presents for the Indians under his command. Says Washington Irving in his classic "Life of Washington": "They were distributed with that grand ceremonial so dear to the Red Man. The chiefs assembled, painted and decorated in all their savage finery. Washington wore a medal sent to him by the Governor for such occasions. The wampum and speech having been delivered, he advanced, and, with all due solemnity, decorated the chiefs and the warriors with the medals, which they were to wear in remembrance of their father, the King of England." Among the warriors thus decorated, was Canachquasy, the son of old Queen Alliquippa, who, with her son, had arrived at the Great Meadows on June 1st. Upon his decoration Canachquasy was given the English name of Lord Fairfax. Tanacharison was given the English name of Dinwiddie on this occasion, and returned the compliment by giving Washington the Indian name of Connotaucarius.

On the 10th day of June, Washington wrote Governor Dinwiddie from the camp at the Great Meadows, concerning the decoration of Canachquasy, as follows:

"Queen Alliquippa desired that her son, who was really a great warrior, might be taken into Council, as she was declining and unfit for business; and that he should have an English name given him. I therefore called the Indians together by the advice of the Half-King, presented one of the medals, and desired him to wear it in remembrance of his great father, the King of England; and called him by the name of Colonel Fairfax, which he was told signified 'the First in Council.' This gave him great pleasure."

At the end of the ceremonies of giving English names to Tanacharison and Canachquasy, Washington read the morning service. Dr. James Craik, who was present, said, in a letter home, that the Indians "believed he was making magic."

Washington Advances to Gist's Plantation

On the 10th of June, there was great agitation in the camp over the report that a party of ninety Frenchmen were approaching, which report was later found to be incorrect. On the same day, Captain Mackay of the Royal Army, in command of an independent company of one hundred riflemen from South Carolina, arrived at the Great Meadows, increasing Washington's forces to about four hundred men. Leaving one company under Captain Mackay to guard the fort, Washington pushed on over the Laurel Hill as far as Christopher Gist's plantation at Mount Braddock, near Connellsville, Fayette County. So difficult was the passage over Laurel Hill that it took approximately two weeks for Washington's forces to reach Gist's plantation from Great Meadows, a distance of thirteen miles. Washington's Indian allies refused to accompany him as far as Gist's plantation, and returned to the Great Meadows. The trouble was that Washington and Tanacharison could not agree as to the method of conducting the campaign. On the 27th of June, Washington had sent a party of seventy men under Captain Lewis to clear a road from Gist's plantation to the mouth of the Redstone (Brownsville), and another party under Captain Polson was, on the same day, sent ahead to reconnoiter.

While these movements of Washington's forces were taking place, a force of five hundred French and some Indians, afterwards augmented to about four hundred, left Fort Duquesne on the 28th of June to attack Washington, the French being commanded by M. DeVilliers, a half brother of Jumonville, who it is said, sought the command from Contrecoeur as a special favor that he might avenge his half-brother's "assassination". This force went up the Monongahela in large canoes, and on the 30th of June, reached the mouth of Redstone, and encamped on the rising ground about half a mile from the stockade, which, it will be recalled, Captain Trent had erected during the preceding winter as a storehouse for the Ohio Company. M. DeVilliers described it as "a sort of fort built of logs, one upon another, well notched in, about thirty feet long and twenty feet wide."

While at the mouth of the Redstone, M. DeVilliers learned that Washington's forces were entrenching themselves at Gist's plantation. He thereupon disencumbered himself of all his heavy stores, and leaving a sergeant and a few men to guard the boats, pushed on in the night, cheered by the hope that he was about to capture the forces of Washington. Arriving at Gist's plantation in the early morning of July 2nd, he saw the intrenchments which Washington had there begun to erect, at once invested them, and fired a general volley. No response came from the intrenchments; for the prey had escaped. M. DeVilliers was then about to retrace his steps, when a deserter, coming from the Great Meadows, disclosed to him the whereabouts and the half-famished condition of Washington's forces. Having made a prisoner of the deserter with a promise to reward or hang him after proving his story true or untrue, M. DeVilliers continued the pursuit. While he is pursuing Washington, we will relate how the latter's forces escaped capture.

At Gist's plantation, on June 28th, Washington held a council of war, upon receipt of intelligence that the French in large numbers, accompanied by many Indians, were marching against him. At this council, it was resolved to send a message to Captain Mackay, who was then at the Great Meadows, desiring him to join Washington at once, and also to call in Captain Lewis and Captain Polson, who, as we have seen, had been sent forward to cut the road from Gist's to Redstone, and to reconnoiter. Captain Mackay and his company arrived on the evening of the 28th, and the foraging parties on the morning of the 29th, when a second council of war was held, and it was decided to retreat as speedily as possible.

Washington Surrenders at Fort Necessity

The troops, with great difficulty, succeeded in reaching the Great Meadows. Here they halted on July 1st. The suffering among Washington's forces was great. For eight days they had no bread, and had taken little of any other food. It was not the intention of Washington at first to halt at this place, but his men had become so fatigued from great labor and hunger that they could draw the swivels no further. Here, then, it was resolved to make a stand. Trees were felled, and a log breastwork was raised at the fort, in order to strengthen it in the best manner that the circumstances would permit. Washington now named the stockade "Fort Necessity" from the circumstances attending its erection. At this critical juncture, many of Washington's Indian allies, under Tanacharison, deserted him, being disheartened at the scant preparations of defense against the superior force, and offended at being subject to military command.

Early on the morning of July 3rd an alarm was received from a sentinel, who had been wounded by the enemy, and, at nine o'clock, word was received that the whole body of the French and Indian allies amounting, as some authorities say, to nine hundred men, was only four miles off. Before noon, distant firing was heard, and the enemy reached a woods about a third of a mile from the fort. Washington had drawn his men up on the open and level ground outside the trenches, and waited for the attack, which he thought would be as soon as the enemy emerged from the woods; and he ordered his troops to reserve their fire until they should be near enough to do execution. The French did not incline to leave the woods and to attack the fort by assault. Washington then drew his men back within the trenches, and gave them orders to fire at their discretion, as suitable opportunities might present themselves. The enemy remained on the side of the rising ground next to the fort, and were sheltered by the trees. They kept up a brisk fire of musketry, but never appeared in open view. In the meantime, rain was falling in torrents, the trenches were filled with water, and many of the arms of Washington's men were out of order. Until eight o'clock at night—the rain falling without intermission—both parties kept up a desultory fire, the action having started at about eleven o'clock in the morning. By that time, the French had killed all the horses and cattle at the fort.

At eight o'clock at night, the French requested a parley, but Washington, suspecting this to be a feint to procure the admission of an officer into the fort to discover his condition, declined. They repeated their request with the additional request that an officer might be sent to them, they guaranteeing his safety. Washington then sent Captain Jacob Van Braam, the only person under his command who understood the French language, with the exception of Chevalier de Peyrouny, an Ensign in the Virginia regiment, who was dangerously wounded. Van Braam returned and brought with him from D. DeVilliers, the French commander, the proposed articles of capitulation. Villiers was a half-brother of the ill-fated Jumonville. Owing to the overpowering number of the enemy, Washington decided to come to terms. After a notification of the proposed articles, he consented to leave the fort the next morning, July 4, 1754, but was to leave it with the honors of war, and with the understanding that he should surrender nothing but the artillery.

French Accuse Washington of Having Assassinated Jumonville

Considerable dissatisfaction was expressed with regard to several of the article of capitulation when they were made public. One of these was an article, by consenting to which Washington virtually admitted that Jumonville had been "assassinated" in the action of May 28th. Another was an article, by consenting to which, Washington virtually admitted the validity of the French claim to the Ohio Valley. M. DeVilliers, the commandant of the French forces, in his account of the marcn from Fort Duquesne and the affair at the Great Meadows said, "We made the English consent to sign that they had assassinated my brother in his camp." A copy of the capitulation was subsequently laid before the House of Burgesses of Virginia, with explanations. The conduct of Washington and his officers was properly appreciated, and they received a vote of thanks for their gallant defense of their country. However, from this vote of thanks, two officers were excepted— Major Muse, who was charged with cowardice, and Captain Jacob VanBraam, who was accused of treachery in purposely misinterpreting the articles of capitulation. The truth is that Washington had been greatly deceived by VanBraam, either through ignorance or design. An officer of his regiment, who was present at the reading and signing of the articles of capitulation, wrote a letter to a friend, in which he discusses the true intent and meaning of the articles and of their bungling translation by VanBraam, as follows:

"When Mr. VanBraam returned with the French proposals, we were obliged to take the sense of them from his mouth; it rained so hard that he could not give us a written translation of them; we could scarcely keep the candle lighted to read them by; and every officer there is ready to declare that there was no such word as 'assassination' mentioned. The terms expressed were 'the death of Jumonville.' If it had been mentioned, we would by all means have had it altered, as the French, during the course of the interview, seemed very condescending and desirous to bring things to a conclusion; and, upon our insisting, altered the articles relating to the stores and ammunition, which they wanted to detain; and that of the cannon, which they agreed to have 'destroyed', instead of 'reserved for their use.'

"Another article, which appears to our disadvantage, is that whereby we oblige ourselves not to attempt an establishment beyond the mountains. This was translated to us, not 'to attempt' buildings or 'improvements on the lands of his most Christian Majesty.' This we never intended, as we denied he had any there, and therefore thought it needless to dispute this point.

"The last article, which relates to the hostages, is quite different from the translation of it given to us. · It is metioned 'for the security of the performance of this treaty', as well as for the return of the prisoners. There was never such an intention on our side, or mention of it made on theirs, by our interpreter. Thus, by the evil intention or negligence of VanBraam, our conduct is scrutinized by a busy world, fond of criticizing the proceedings of others, without considering circumstances, or giving just attention to reasons which might be offered to obviate their censures."

"VanBraam was a Dutchman, and had but an imperfect knowledge of either the French or English language. How far his ignorance should be taken as an apology for his blunders, is uncertain. Although he had proved himself a good officer, yet there were other circumstances, which brought his fidelity in question. Governor Dinwiddie, in giving an account of this affair to Lord Albermarle says: 'In the capitulation they made use of the word 'assassination', but Washington, not understanding French, was deceived by the interpreter, who was a paltroon, and though an officer with us, they say he has joined the French."

Also, Washington expressed himself on Van Braam's translation, as follows:

"That we were willfully or ignorantly deceived by our interpreter in regard to the word 'assassination', I do aver and will to my dying moment; so will every officer who was present. The interpreter was a Dutchman little acquainted with the English tongue, and therefore might not advert to the tone and meaning of the word in English; but whatever his motives were for so doing, certain it is he called it the 'death' or the 'loss' of the Sieur Jumonville. So we received and so we understood it until, to our great surprise and mortification, we found it otherwise in a literal translation."

Washington Marches Out With Honors of War

On the morning of July 4th, Washington and his forces marched out of Fort Necessity with the honors of war, taking with them their regimental colors, but leaving behind a large flag, too cumberous to be transported. His forces set out for Will's Creek, but had scarcely left the Great Meadows when they encountered one hundred Indian allies of the French, who, in defiance of the terms of capitulation, began plundering the baggage, and committing other irregularities. Seeing that the French did not or could not prevent their Indian allies, Washington's men destroyed their powder and other stores, including even their private baggage, to prevent its falling into the hands of the Indians. M. DeVilliers sent a detachment to take possession of the fort as soon as Washington's forces defiled therefrom. Washington's regiment left twelve dead on the ground, and the number left by Captain Mackay's company is not known. DeVillier said that the number of dead excited his pity.

Thus ended the affair at the Great Meadows, Washington's first and last surrender, the location of which is along the National Pike, in Fayette County, a few miles east of the Summit. On reaching Will's Creek, where his half-famished troops found ample provisions in the military magazine, he hastened with Captain

Mackay, to Governor Dinwiddie, at Williamsburg. whom they particularly informed of the events of their expedition. Washington soon thereafter resigned his commission, and retired to private life at Mount Vernon. His first act, after relinquishing his command, was to visit his mother, inquire into the state of her affairs, and look after the welfare of his younger brother and his sister, Betty. He continued his residence at Mount Vernon until the following year, when he again entered the service of Virginia in the army of General Braddock.

Tanacharison Complains of Washington

After the defeat of Washington at the Great Meadows, Tanacharison and Scarouady, with some of their followers, "came down to the back parts of Virginia", and then with Seneca George and about three hundred Mingos (Iroquois), retreated to George Croghan's trading post at Aughwick, now Shirleysburg, Huntingdon County. At about the same time, many Shawnees, Delawares, and an inconsiderable number of renegades of the Seneca tribe of the Six Nations, joined the French. Tanacharison and Scarouady after retreating to Aughwick, sent out messages to assemble the friendly Delawares and Shawnees at that place, and asked the Colony of Pennsylvania to support their women and children while the warriors fought on the side of the English, whom they expected speedily to take decisive steps against the French. In response to these messages, great swarms of excited Indians came to Aughwick, clamoring for food, and were fed at the expense of the Colony throughout the fall and winter.

Angered by the charge of the Virginians that the friendly Indians were treacherous and secretly aided the French in this campaign, Tanacharison expressed himself as dissatisfied with the conduct of Colonel Washington. In August, 1754, the old chief came to John Harris' Ferry (Harrisburg) to meet Conrad Weiser and accompany him to Aughwick. "On the way," says Weiser, "Tanacharison complained very much of the behavior of Colonel Washington, (though in a very moderate way, saying the Colonel was a good-natured man, but had no experience); that he took upon him to command the Indians as his slaves, and would have them every day upon the Out Scout, and attack the Enemy by themselves, and that he would by no means take advice from the Indians; that he lay at one place from one full moon to another, and made no fortifications at all but that little thing upon the meadow, where he

thought the French would come up to him in open field; that had
he taken the Half King's advice and made such fortifications as the
Half King advised him to make, he would certainly have beat the
French off; that the French had acted as great cowards and the
English as fools in that engagement; that he [the Half King] had
carried off his wife and children; so did other Indians before the
battle begun, because Colonel Washington would never listen to
them, but was always driving them on to fight by his directions."

Tanacharison and Scarouady Protest
Albany Purchase

In order to combine the efforts of the colonies in their resistance of the encroachments of the French, a conference was ordered
by the British Ministry, at Albany, New York, which was held in
June and July, 1754, to which the Six Nations were invited. They
came, and peace was established with them.   Governor Hamilton
of Pennsylvania, unable to be present, commissioned John Penn
and Richard Peters of the Provincial Council, and Isaac Norris and
Benjamin Franklin of the Assembly, to attend the Council in his
stead.   At this conference, a plan was proposed for a political
union, and adopted on the 4th of July.   It was subsequently submitted to the Home Government and the Provincial Assemblies.
The British Government condemned it, according to Franklin, on
account of its being too democratic; and the various Provincial
Assemblies objected to it as containing too much power of the king,
Pennsylvania negativing the same without discussion.

Although the Albany Conference, therefore, was not satisfactory in all its results, the Pennsylvania commissioners secured a
great addition to the Province of Pennsylvania, to which the Indian
title was not extinct.   The deed, which was signed by chiefs of the
Six Nations on July 6, 1754, conveyed to Pennsylvania all the land
extending on the west side of the Susquehanna River from the
Blue Mountains to a mile above the mouth of Kayarondinhagh
(Penn's) Creek; thence northwest by west to the western boundary of the Province; thence along the western boundary to the
southern boundary; thence along the southern boundary to the
Blue Mountains; and thence along the Blue Mountains to the place
of beginning.

George Croghan was in charge of distributing provisions and
supplies to the friendly Indians, who had assembled at Aughwick
after Washington's surrender at Fort Necessity.   The bills which

he was sending the Colonial Authorities for feeding these Indians having grown rather large, Croghan was suspicioned as not being reliable, and finally there were hints that he was in league with the French. The Pennsylvania Assembly then cut down his bills, and he decided to leave Aughwick. Conrad Weiser was then directed by the Colonial Authorities to go to Aughwick, and make a report on Croghan. He reached this place on August 31st, 1754, being accompanied by Tanacharison from Harris' Ferry, as we have already seen.

Weiser found that Croghan was entirely worthy of being trusted. He also found that the inhabitants of Cumberland County caused much trouble in selling so much strong liquor to the Indians assembled at Aughwick. In the conferences which he held with Tanacharison, Scarouady, King Beaver, and various other chiefs, he completely won old Tanacharison and his people back to the English cause after their anger at Washington and the Virginians. Moreover, at these conferences, Weiser learned that the Shawnees and Delawares had formed an alliance; that the French had offered them presents, either to join them or to remain neutral, and that to these proposals, the Delawares made no reply, but at once sent their deputies to Aughwick for the purpose, as Weiser thought, of learning the attitude of the English.

Near the close of the conference, Tanacharison and Scarouady pressed Weiser to tell them what transpired at the Albany Treaty; and he then told them all about the purchase of the vast tract west of the Susquehanna. "They seemed not to be very well pleased," says Weiser, "because the Six Nations had sold such a large tract." Weiser then explained that the purchase was made in order to frustrate land schemes of the Connecticut interests, and of the French on the Ohio. This appeared to satisfy them, though they resented not receiving a part of the consideration. For a time they were content, not knowing that the purchase included most of the lands on the West Branch of the Susquehanna. The Shawnee and Delaware deputies then went back to the Ohio into danger and temptations, and to learn from the French that their vast hunting grounds on the West Branch of the Susquehanna had been sold to the Province of Pennsylvania at the Albany Treaty.

No wonder that Tanacharison and Scarouady complained to Weiser. The Albany purchase was a very powerful factor in alienating, not only the Delawares, but the other Indians, from Pennsylvania. The Shawnees and Delawares of the Munsee Clan (Monseys) in the valleys of the Susquehanna, Juniata, Allegheny, and Ohio, thus found their lands "sold from under their feet" which the Six Nations had guaranteed to them, so they claimed, on their migration to these valleys. It was provided in the contract of sale of these lands that half of the purchase price should be paid upon delivery of the deed, and the remainder was not to be paid until the settlers had actually crossed the Allegheny Mountains, and taken up their abode in the purchased territory. The Indians declared in July, 1755, that they would not receive the second installment, but the Mohawk chief, Hendricks, persuaded them to stand by the deed. After Braddock was defeated on July 9, 1755, the entire body of dissatisfied Indians on the Albany Purchase took bitter vengeance on Pennsylvania. After three years of bloodshed, outrage and murder, Conrad Weiser persuaded the Proprietaries of Pennsylvania to deed back to the Indians that part of the Albany purchase which lay west of the Allegheny Mountains. This was done at the treaty at Easton, in October, 1758, which treaty will be discussed in Chapter XXII.

Death of Tanacharison

After the series of conferences with Conrad Weiser at Aughwick, in September, 1754, Tanacharison returned to the trading house of John Harris, at Harris' Ferry, where he became dangerously ill; and a conjuror, or "medicineman", was summoned to make inquiry into the cause and nature of his malady. The "medicineman" gave it as his opinion that the French had bewitched Tanacharison, in revenge for the great blow he had struck them in the affair of Jumonville; for the Indians gave him the whole credit of that success, Tanacharison having made it clear that it was he who killed Jumonville, in revenge of the French, who, as he declared, had killed, boiled, and eaten his father. Furthermore, Tanacharison had sent around the French scalps taken at that action, as trophies. All the friends of the old chieftain concurred in the opinion of the "medicineman", and when Tanacharison died at the house of John Harris, on October 4, 1754, · there was great lamentation among the Indians, mingled with threats of immediate vengeance. Thus was this noted sachem gathered to his fathers in the "Happy Hunting Ground", at a time when his services and influence among the Western Indians were greatly needed by the English.

CHAPTER XV

Scarouady

SCAROUADY (Monacatuatha, Monacatoocha, etc.) was an Oneida chieftain who was sent by the Great Council of the Six Nations to the Ohio Valley, about 1747, as vicegerent over the Shawnees of that region. He was an elderly man at that time, but lived long enough to take a prominent part, on the side of the English, in the stirring events of King George's War and the French and Indian War. Upon his coming to the Ohio Valley, he took up his residence at Logstown.

The first mention of Scarouady in the recorded history of Pennsylvania is when he, Kakowatcheky, Neucheconneh, Tanacharison and others wrote a letter from "Aleggainey", on April 20th, 1747, to the Governor of Pennsylvania on behalf of the Twightwees, or Miamis, of the Ohio Valley, a letter which has already been mentioned in Chapters VIII and XIII.

In November of this year, he accompanied Canachquasy and a delegation of ten Mingo warriors from the Kuskuskies region to Philadelphia, when Canachquasy informed the Provincial Council that, while it was true that the Onondaga Council had taken a stand for neutrality in King George's War, yet the young men of that part of the Iroquois in the Ohio Valley, under his command, had determined to take up arms against the French,—information that caused Pennsylvania to send George Croghan and Conrad Weiser on their embassies to Logstown, Croghan in April, 1748, and Weiser, in September of that year, as related in Chapters VIII and XIII. In the minutes of this Council (November 13th, 1747), Scarouady is described as old and infirm and as having commended himself to "James Logan's and the Council's Charity." He advised the Council that he had visited Philadelphia many years before.

Conrad Weiser accompanied Scarouady, Canachquasy, and their delegation on their homeward journey as far as John Harris' Ferry (Harrisburg), where the old chief complained bitterly to Weiser concerning the abuses of the rum traffic among the Western Indians. Then Weiser wrote the Provincial Council, on November 28th, characterizing the abuses of the rum traffic among the

Indians as "an abomination before God and man."   On the way, the party stopped at Weiser's home, near Womelsdorf, where "Scarouady told Shikellamy very privately that Peter Chartier and his company had accepted the French hatchet, but kept it in their bosom till they would see what interest they could make in favor of the French."

But it is in connection with the return to Logstown and other parts of the upper Ohio Valley of a portion of Peter Chartier's band of Shawnees that Scarouady's name comes into prominence in the annals of Pennsylvania.   Indeed, it was owing to the subtle influence of Scarouady that a large number of Chartier's disaffected Shawnees were induced to desert Chartier and come back under dominion of the Six Nations.   As stated in Chapter VIII, the Shawnee chiefs, Kakowatcheky and Neucheconneh applied very submissively to Scarouady, in 1748, to itercede with the Colonial Authorities for those members of Chartier's band who had returned; and Scarouady's apology for them was laid before the Pennsylvania Commissioners at Lancaster, on July 21st, of that year, as also related in Chapter VIII.

Treaty with the Miamis, or Twightwees

This conference at Lancaster deserves additional mention for the reason that the Colony of Pennsylvania then and there entered into a treaty with the Twightwees, or Miamis.   These Indians became deeply interested in the English when Croghan carried the information to Logstown in April, 1748, that Weiser was coming later in the year with a substantial present from the Province to the western tribes.

Their fur market with the French was very poor, and they had heard of the profitable conferences of the Six Nations with Pennsylvania.   Accordingly, they sent word to the Colonial Authorities that their deputies were coming eastward with the hope of holding a conference with the Colony of Pennsylvania, at Lancaster. Weiser urged that a delegation be sent to meet them and conduct them to Lancaster.

In June, 1748, Weiser presented Andrew Montour, the son of Madam Montour, to the Provincial Council as a person "who might be of service to the Colony as Indian interpreter and messenger."   Andrew Montour was a prominent man among the Delawares, and well fitted to serve as interpreter.   In introducing Montour, Weiser said that "he had found him faithful, knowing and prudent." During the previous winter Weiser had sent Montour to the Indians on the Ohio and Lake Erie "to observe what passed among the Indians."

Montour was directed to meet the deputies of the Twightwees and, if possible, persuade them to come to Philadelphia instead of Lancaster. When he met the Ohio Indians, however, he found it impossible to persuade them to come to Philadelphia, because they feared that the city was "sickly". The Council, therefore, decided to appoint four commissioners to meet these Indians at Lancaster at the treaty of July, 1748. At this conference, Montour was the interpreter of the Twightwees, Conrad Weiser of the Six Nations, and Scarouady was to have been the speaker of the Ohio Indians, but was unable to speak on this occasion on account of being disabled by a fall. Therefore, Andrew Montour became the speaker for all the Western Indians.

After making an appeal on the part of the Shawnees who had accompanied Chartier down the Ohio, the Twightwee chief took a piece of chalk and drew on the court house floor a map of the Ohio, Mississippi, and Wabash. He represented that on the Wabash and another stream called the Hatchet, the Twightwees had twenty towns in which they had more than one thousand fighting men. After the Pennsylvania commissioners and the Twightwees had smoked the pipe of peace together, a treaty of peace was formally drawn up with the Twightwees, on condition that they would have no communication with the French. An exchange of presents then took place. Pennsylvania gave these Indians goods to the value of one hundred eighty-nine pounds, and the Twightwees gave the Pennsylvania commissioners many beaver and deer skins.

Before the Twightwees departed, they were told by the Pennsylvania commissioners that there was a prospect of peace between England and France, to which important statement the Indians made no answer. The Pennsylvania authorities greatly appreciated the value of this newly formed relation with the Twightwees, inasmuch as such an alliance tended to enlarge the Indian trade, and would seriously interrupt communication of the French in Quebec with their settlements on the Mississippi River, for the reason that the towns of the Twightwees lay on the route followed by the French in traveling between their Quebec and Mississippi settlements.

Scarouady at Logstown Conferences

Scarouady took part in the following conferences at Logstown:

1st. The conference which George Croghan held with the Indians of that place in April, 1748, advising them that Conrad Weiser was coming later in the year with a generous present from the Province of Pennsylvania.

2nd. The conferences which Conrad Weiser held with the Indians at Logstown in September, 1748, when he delivered the present above referred to, and allied them with Pennsylvania.

3rd. The conference which Celeron held with the Indians of Logstown in August, 1749, while on his way down the Ohio, burying leaden plates at the mouths of tributary streams, proclaiming that the region drained by the "Beautiful River" belonged to France.

4th. The conference which George Croghan held with the Indians at Logstown a few days after Celeron's departure, when he succeeded in counteracting the influence of the Frenchman. At about this time, he and Tanacharison deeded Croghan a large tract of land near the Forks of the Ohio, as mentioned in Chapter XIII.

5th. The conference which George Croghan and Andrew Montour had with the Indians at Logstown on November 15, 1750, in an effort to counteract the intrigues of the French, and in which they promised that a present for the Indians would be brought to that place the next spring from the Colony of Pennsylvania.

6th. The conference which Christopher Gist, the agent of the Ohio Company, had with the Indians at Logstown on November 25 and 26, 1750, though, as stated in Chapter XIII, Gist said in his journal that nearly all of the Indians were out hunting at that time.

7th. The treaty which the Commissioners from Virginia held with the Indians at Logstown in June, 1752, which was described in Chapter XIII.

8th. Scarouady also attended the conference which Croghan and Montour had with the Indians at Logstown in May, 1751, when they delivered the present from the Colony of Pennsylvania, which they had promised on their visit to this place in the preceding November. This conference was mentioned in Chapter XIII.

It was pointed out, in Chapter XIII, that Scarouady was present at the council held at George Croghan's trading house at the mouth of Pine Creek on May 12, 1753, at which he and Tanacharison, on learning that the French were descending the Allegheny River, decided "that they would receive the French as friends, or as enemies, depending on their attitude, but that the English would be safe as long as they themselves were safe."

Scarouady's next important act was to join with Tanacharison in writing a letter, on June 23d, 1753, to Governor Dinwiddie of Virginia, appealing to this colony for help to resist the French. This letter was mentioned in Chapter XIII; and, as stated in that chapter, Scarouady was one of the deputies of the western tribes at the treaty at Winchester, in September, 1753.

Scarouady at Carlisle Treaty

The treaty at Carlisle, in October, 1753, was described in Chapter XIII. . At this point, we call attention to the fact that Scarouady took a prominent part in this treaty, and was one of the principal speakers. His most important speech was a bitter complaint against the abuses of the rum traffic among the Indians of the Ohio Valley by the unlicensed traders. Said he:

"The rum ruins us. We never understood the trade was to be for whiskey and flour. We desire it may be forbidden, no more sold in the Indian country, but that if the Indians will have any, they may go among the inhabitants and deal with them for it. When whiskey traders come, they bring thirty or forty kegs and put them down before us and make us drink, and get all the skins that should go to pay the debts we have contracted for goods bought of the fair traders, and by this means we not only ruin ourselves, but them too. These wicked whiskey sellers, when they have once got the Indians in liquor, make them sell the very clothes from their backs. In short, if this practice be continued, we must inevitably be ruined. We most earnestly, therefore, beseech you to remedy it."

The Pennsylvania commissioners expressed their sympathy for these complaints of the Indians, and promised to lay them before Governor Hamilton. Then the Indians went to their forest homes, pleased with their presents and the promises, but the Colonial Authorities did not recall the traders. Neither was the rum traffic stopped, in spite of the Indians' most solemn protestations. In the meantime, the great French and Indian War was coming apace.

After the Carlisle Treaty, Scarouady returned to the Ohio, where he joined with Tanacharison, an Shannopin's Town, on October 27th, in writing letters to the Governors of Virginia and

Pennsylvania, urging that they join with the Indians of the Ohio and Allegheny in resisting the occupation of the valleys of those streams by the French.

Scarouady Meets Washington

Scarouady's next appearance in the history of Pennsylvania was when George Washington met him at Logstown, in November, 1753, when Washington was on his way to the commandant of the French forts on the headwaters of the Allegheny, bearing the message of Governor Dinwiddie of Virginia. This meeting was described in Chapter XIII, and needs no further reference at this point. Also, in January, 1754, he held council with George Croghan and Andrew Montour, at Logstown, and joined with Tanacharison and Shingas in sending a request to Governor Hamilton to build a fort on the Ohio, as stated at the end of Chapter XIII.

Scarouady in Washington's Campaign of 1754

In Chapter XIV, we found Scarouady assisting Washington in his unsuccessful campaign of 1754. This campaign marked the end of Scarouady's residence at Logstown. On June 26th, while Washington's forces were in the neighborhood of Gist's plantation (Mount Braddock), Washington made the following note in his journal: "An Indian arrived bringing news that Monacatoocha [Scarouady] had burned his village, Logstown, and was gone by water to Redstone [Brownsville, Fayette County], and might be expected there in two days." This was the end of "Old Logstown". The French, however, rebuilt the village before March, 1755, for the Shawnees who remained in the vicinity.

Scarouady Succeeds Tanacharison as Half King

In Chapter XIV, we saw that Scarouady, after the defeat of Washington at the Great Meadows, retreated with Tanacharison and the Indians remaining loyal to the English, to Aughwick, where the Indians were provisioned throughout the fall and winter at the expense of Pennsylvania. He took a prominent part in the conferences with Conrad Weiser at this place in September, 1754, in which, it will be remembered, he protested against the Albany purchase. Upon the death of Tanacharison (October 4th, 1754), Scarouady succeeded him, not only in the direction of Indian affairs at Aughwick, but as Half King generally.

Scarouady Goes to Onondaga Council in English Interest

We saw, in Chapter XIV, how Scarouady, at a Council in Philadelphia, on December 19th, 1754, gave Governor Morris an account of the skirmish in which Jumonville was killed. He was then on his way to the Great Council of the Six Nations, at Onondaga, as the representative of Pennsylvania, Virginia, and the Western Indians, to ask the Onondaga Council to send deputies to Winchester, Virginia, the next spring, to confer on matters of common interest. The old chief's heart was set on war against the French. He remained in Philadelphia until Christmas day, and, before leaving, was given a message by Governor Morris to deliver to the Onondaga Council, protesting against the sale of the Wyoming lands to Connecticut. This sale had been very irregularly made by the Mohawks at the time of the great Albany Conference of June and July, 1754; although the Great Council of the Six Nations had declared, at this conference, that they would not sell the Wyoming lands to either Pennsylvania or Connecticut, but would reserve them as a hunting ground and for the residence of such Indians as cared to remove from the French and settle there, and had appointed Shikellamy's son, John, in charge of this territory.

Scarouady Returns from His Mission

Scarouady returned to Philadelphia in March, 1755, from his journey to the Six Nations. At a meeting of the Provincial Council held on March 31st, he gave a report of his mission. He had gone no farther than to the Oneidas, who told him that the Onondagas were not well disposed at that time toward the English. He had held council with the representatives of the Oneidas, Mohawks, Tuscaroras, and Nanticokes, who desired him, in the name of the Six Nations, to deliver to them what he had to say, assuring him that it would be as good and effectual as if delivered at the Great Council House at Onondaga. Scarouady said to the Provincial Council:

"I asked how the French came to set down on the Ohio. Is it by the advice of the counsellors or is it by the orders of the warriors of the Six Nations? I have it in charge from the Indians with whom I live at the Ohio, to make this my first question and not to proceed farther till I am informed of this fact. nor shall I say a word more till you give me your answer. On which the chiefs withdrew to council and then returned and spoke as follows:

" 'Brother: Our four nations are no ways concerned in the

settlement of the French on the Ohio, nor is it with our advice or well-liking. Our fathers, the Mohawks, when they first heard of the French going to the Ohio, sent a message with a large belt to the other nations, wherein they set forth that this proceeding of the French was extremely disagreeable to them and desired that it might be obstructed and that none of the Nations would suffer it, but do all in their power to prevent any settlement of the French in those parts. This message came first to our castles and was readily agreed to, and then we sent it forward to Onondaga where it has remained ever since; for the Onondagas said they approved of what the French were doing, that it was good and would do no hurt to the Indians, and by this means stopped the belt so that it went no further.'

"I then delivered Assaragoa's [Virginia's] belt, inviting the chiefs of the Six Nations to a Council at Winchester, and along with it and tyed to it, the large belt that was given me jointly by the Governments of Maryland and Pennsylvania, desiring them to agree to the Governor of Virginia's proposal, and assuring them, if they would come to Virginia, they would give them the meeting there. These invitations they received very gladly, and said they would lay them before the Great Council that was to meet in a little time at Onondaga, and did not doubt but that they should prevail with the Six Nations to comply with the invitation, and that great numbers would go; but then, as there were several old people, they could not take upon them to say that they could be got to come as far as Winchester, but would rather choose Conodogiunet [near Harrisburg], on Sasquehannah: but I said there were no conveniences there, and that this was but a little way from John Harris' Ferry where a large company might be accommodated, and I believe they will readily come there.

"The next thing I have to communicate to you is a message from these four nations to their brethren, the Shawnees, and their cousins, the Delawares. They desire them to consider themselves as under the protection of the Six Nations, and that they are well affected towards them. They bid them be quiet, easy, and still, nor be disturbed at what is going on, nor meddle at all on any side till they see or hear from them, and that it will not be long before they shall see one another and hold conversation together. In the meantime, as the English were their brethren and their cause was much favored by the Indians, they desired them to have their eyes and ears towards the Six Nations and their brethren, the English, as they had hitherto done, and not to look towards the French."

Closing his address to the Provincial Council, Scarouady gave the following good advice, not only to Pennsylvania but Virginia and Maryland as well:

"You think you prefectly well understand the management of Indian affairs, but I must tell you that it is not so, and that the French are more politick than you. They never employ an Indian on any business but they give him fine clothes, besides other presents, and this makes the Indians their hearty friends and do anything for them. If they invite the Indians to Quebec, they all return with laced clothes on, and boast of the generous treatment of the French Governor.

"Now, Brethren, some of the Six Nations are going to Canada, and some say a great number are coming to Virginia. Let me advise you, as you have time enough, to open those large pieces of goods that your city is full of, and cut them up into fine clothes, and have them ready against the treaty at Virginia, for you may depend upon it those who go to Canada will be finely clothed, and if your Indians, at their return, do not appear finer than they, they will be laughed at and made ashamed.

"Further, Brethren:

"I have brought with me three or four warriors, Mohawks and Oneidas; they are in King George's service; they are valiant men and faithful friends; I have a particular duty for them to do, of great consequence to the general cause. These you will be pleased to take notice of and give them clothes, that they may perform their business cheerfully, and leave your city well pleased."

A few days later Governor Shirley and Governor Delancey came to Philadelphia on their way to Annapolis, Maryland, to meet General Braddock, Governor Dinwiddie, and Governor Sharp. Scarouady was presented to the visiting governors, and made many complaints that the Indians whom he had brought with him from the country of Six Nations to serve in the operations against the French, were "naked", and that he would be ashamed to take them with him to Aughwick in so miserable condition. He pointed out that, if they should be permitted "to go so bare to Aughwick," it would prejudice the Indians there very much against the people of Pennsylvania.

The proposed treaty at Winchester, Virginia, in the spring of 1755 did not take place. General Braddock had his army on the march toward Fort Duquesne early in the spring. On April 23rd, Governor Morris of Pennsylvania, wrote George Croghan at Aughwick advising:

"Let the Indians know that there is no meeting of Governors at Winchester, but that as the General is on his march, all true friends of the English are desired not to proceed to Winchester, but to repair to the army, and distinguish themselves agreeable to their repeated professions."

Scarouady in Braddock's Campaign

Scarouady took an important part in the fateful campaign of General Edward Braddock against Fort Duquesne, in the summer of 1755. We shall not give the details of this campaign, more or less familiar to all students of Pennsylvania history. All of Braddock's forces were finally collected at Will's Creek, (Cumberland, Maryland), on the 19th day of May, at which place he remained until the 10th of June, before setting out for Pennsylvania.

In the latter part of May, George Croghan reached Braddock's camp at Will's Creek with about fifty warriors whom he had brought from Aughwick. Among the chiefs assembled to assist Braddock were: Scarouady, White Thunder, the keeper of the speech-belts, and Silver Heels, so called, probably, from being swift of foot. Braddock had expected not only a large delegation of the Indians from the Ohio Valley, but also a number of Cherokees and Catawbas, whom Governor Dinwiddie of Virginia, had given him reason to expect. He was therefore disappointed in the number of his Indian allies. Scarouady addressed the assembled chiefs and urged them to take up the English cause with vigor.

Washington Irving's "Life of Washington" contains the following interesting paragraphs concerning the assembling of Scarouady and his warriors at Will's Creek:

"Notwithstanding his secret contempt for the Indians, Braddock, agreeably to his instructions, treated them with great ceremony. A grand council was held in his tent, at Fort Cumberland, where all his officers attended. The chiefs, and all the warriors, came painted and decorated for war. They were received with military honors, the guards resting on their firearms. The general made them a speech through his interpreter, expressing the grief of their father, the great King of England, at the death of the Half King, Tanacharison, and made them presents to console them. They in return promised their aid as guides and scouts, and declared eternal enemity to the French, following the declaration with the war song, 'making a terrible noise.'

"The general, to regale and astonish them, ordered all the artillery to be fired, 'the drums and fifes playing and beating the point of war'; the fete ended by their feasting in their own camp on a bullock which the general had given them, following up their repast by dancing the war dance round a fire, to the sound of their uncouth drums and rattles, 'making night hideous', by howls and yellings.

"For a time all went well. The Indians had their separate camp, where they passed half the night singing, dancing, and howling. The British were amused by their strange ceremonies, their savage antics, and savage decorations. The Indians, on the other hand, loitered by day about the English camp, fiercely painted and arrayed, gazing with silent admiration at the parade of the troops, their marchings and evolutions; and delighted with the horse-races, with which the young officers recreated themselves.

"Unluckily the warriors had brought their families with them to Will's Creek, and the women were even fonder than the men of loitering about the British camp. They were not destitute of attractions; for the young squaws resemble the gypsies, having seductive forms, small hands and feet, and soft voices. Among those who visited the camp was one who no doubt passed for an Indian princess. She was the daughter of the sachem, White Thunder, and bore the dazzling name of Bright Lightning. The charms of these wild-wood beauties were soon acknowledged. 'The squaws,' writes Secretary Peters, 'bring in money plenty; the officers are scandalously fond of them.'

"The jealousy of the warriors was aroused; some of them became furious. To prevent discord, the squaws were forbidden to come into the British camp. This did not prevent their being sought elsewhere. It was ultimately found necessary, for the sake of quiet, to send Bright Lightning, with all the other women and children, back to Aughwick. White Thunder, and several of the warriors, accompanied them for their protection.

"As to the Delaware chiefs, they returned to the Ohio, promising the general they would collect their warriors together, and meet him on his march. They never kept their word. 'These people are villians, and always side with the strongest,' says a shrewd journalist of the expedition.

"Either from disgust thus caused, or from being actually dismissed, the warriors began to disappear from the camp. It is said that Colonel Innes, who was to remain in command at Fort Cumberland, advised the dismissal of all but a few to serve as

guides; certain it is, before Braddock recommended his march, none
remained to accompany him but Scarouady and eight of his warriors."

Scarouady Captured

On the 19th of June, when Braddock's first division, with
whom the Indian allies were marching as an advanced party, was
near or within the limits of Somerset County, Pennsylvania, and
not far from the Maryland line, Scarouady and his son being at a
small distance from the line of march, were surrounded and taken
by some French and Indians. The son escaped and brought the
intelligence to the warriors, who hastened to rescue or avenge the
aged chief, but found him tied to a tree. The French had been
disposed to kill him; but the Indians with them declared that they
would abandon the French should they do so, thus showing some
tie of friendship or kindred with Scarouady, who then rejoined
Braddock's forces unharmed.

Scarouady's Son Killed

On the 6th of July, three or four soldiers, loitering in the rear
of Braddock's forces, were killed and scalped by the Indian allies
of the French, and several of the grenadiers set off to take revenge.
These came upon a party of the Indians who held up boughs and
grounded their arms as the sign of amity. Either Braddock's
grenadiers did not perceive this sign, or else misunderstood it. At
any rate, they fired upon the Indians and one of them fell, who
proved to be the son of Scarouady. The grenadiers brought the
body of the young warrior to camp. Braddock then sent for Scarouady and the other Indians, and condoled with them on the la-
mentable occurrence, making them the customary presents to wipe
away their tears. He also caused the young man to be buried with
the honors of war, and at his request the officers attended the funeral and fired a volley over the grave. The camp that night, located
about two miles southeast of Irwin, Westmoreland County, was
given the name of Camp Monacatoocha, in honor of Scarouady.
Says Irving:

"These soldier-like tributes of respect to the deceased and
sympathy with the survivors, soothed the feelings and gratified the
pride of the father, and attached him more firmly to the service.
We are glad to record an anecdote so contrary to the general contempt for the Indians with which Braddock stands charged. It
speaks well for the real kindness of his heart."

What part Scarouady played in the remaining part of Braddock's march, or in the disastrous battle with the French and Indians at the site of the present town of Braddock, Allegheny County, on the afternoon of July 9th, is clouded in obscurity.

The story of Braddock's defeat has often been told and needs no further reference at this place, except to point out that Braddock was not ambushed, as many historians have stated. It is true that Beaujeu, the French commander, had planned an ambush, and picked a place for it on the evening of July 8th. In the meantime, Braddock had crossed the Monongahela, and started up the slopes of the field of encounter, before the French and Indians had reached the place which they had selected for ambushing him. The French account of the battle, after giving the plans of Beaujeu's detachment, says that he had orders to lie in ambush at a favorable spot which had been reconnoitered the previous evening; that the detachment, before it could reach the place selected for ambush, found itself in the presence of Braddock's army; that Beaujeu, finding his plan of ambush had failed, decided on an attack; and that he made this attack with so much vigor as to astonish Braddock's forces. Surely, if the French and Indians had been lying in ambush, Braddock's scouts would have found them.

Beaujeu fell early in the action, and the command of the French and Indians then devolved upon M. Dumas, who with great presence of mind rallied the Indians when they had begun to waver upon the death of Beaujeu. They were terrified at the sound of the English cannon. Dumas then ordered his officers to lead the Indians to the wings and attack Braddock's forces in the flank, while he, with the French troops, would maintain a position in front. This order was promptly obeyed, resulting in the overwhelming and inglorious defeat of Braddock's army.

Washington saved the army from total destruction. Two horses were shot under him, and four balls passed through his clothing. An Indian chief and his braves, after firing at him many times, concluded that he was protected by the Great Spirit. In 1770, when Washington, in company with Dr. Craik and William Crawford, made a journey down the Ohio River to examine lands given the Virginia soldiers, he met this chief, who, hearing that Washington was coming down the Ohio Valley, made a long journey to see the man at whom he and his warriors fired so often in the battle on the Monongahela fifteen years before.

At the time of the battle Colonel Dunbar, who followed in the rear of Braddock's army with his division, artillery, and heavy stores, had reached a point in the Allegheny Mountains not far from the place where Jumonville was killed in the first skirmish of the French and Indian War, and near the former Soldiers' Orphans' Home at Jumonville. Here he encamped. Here also the survivors of Braddock's defeat joined him on the 11th. Everything in the camp was in the greatest confusion. Some of his forces had deserted upon hearing the reports of the battle, and "the rest", says Orme, "seemed to have forgot all discipline." Destroying and burying most of his ammunition, Dunbar then began his disgraceful retreat. General Braddock, who had been carried with the retreating troops, died at the Orchard Camp near the Great Meadows on the 13th.

Colonel James Smith's Account of Happenings at Fort Duquesne on the Day of Braddock's Defeat

In May, 1755, the Colony of Pennsylvania began cutting a wagon road from Fort Loudon to join Braddock's road at Turkey Foot. James (later Colonel) Smith, then a young man eighteen years of age, was one of the force of three hundred men engaged in this work. At a point four or five miles above Bedford, he was captured by the Indians and carried to Fort Duquesne, where he was a prisoner at the time of Braddock's defeat. He gives the following description of the happenings at the fort on the day of the battle:

"Shortly after this, on the 9th day of July, 1755, in the morning, I heard a great stir in the fort. As I could then walk with a staff in my hand, I went out of the door, which was just by the wall of the fort, and stood upon the wall and viewed the Indians in a huddle before the gate, where were barrels of powder, bullets, flints, &c., and every one taking what suited; I saw the Indians also march off in rank entire—likewise the French Canadians, and some regulars. After viewing the Indians and French in different positions, I computed them to be about four hundred, and wondered that they attempted to go out against Braddock with so small a party. I was then in high hopes that I would soon see them fly before the British troops, and that General Braddock would take the fort and rescue me.

"I remained anxious to know the advent of this day; and, in the afternoon, I again observed a great noise and commotion in the fort, and though at that time I could not understand French, yet I found that it was the voice of joy and triumph, and feared that they had received what I called bad news.

"I had observed some of the old country soldiers speak Dutch [German]; as I spoke Dutch, I went to one of them, and asked him, what was the news? He told me that a runner had just arrived, who said that Braddock would certainly be defeated; that the Indians and French had surrounded him, and were concealed behind trees and in gullies, and kept a constant fire upon the English, and that they saw the English falling in heaps, and if they did not take the river, which was the only gap, and make their escape, there would not be one man left alive before sundown. Some time after this, I heard a number of scalp halloos, and saw a company of Indians and French coming in. I observed they had a great many bloody scalps, grenadiers' caps, British canteens, bayonets, &c., with them. They brought the news that Braddock was defeated. After that, another company came in, which appeared to be about one hundred, and chiefly Indians, and it seemed to me that almost every one of this company was carrying scalps; after this, came another company with a number of wagon horses, and also a great many scalps. Those that were coming in, and those that had arrived, kept a constant firing of small arms, and also the great guns in the fort, which were accompanied with the most hideous shouts and yells from all quarters; so that it appeared to me as if the infernal regions had broke loose.

"About sundown I beheld a small party coming in with about a dozen prisoners, stripped naked, with their hands tied behind their backs, and part of their bodies blackened,—these prisoners they burned to death on the bank of the Allegheny river opposite the fort. I stood on the fort wall until I beheld them begin to burn one of these men; they had him tied to a stake, and kept touching him with fire-brands, red-hot irons, &c., and he screaming in the most doleful manner,—the Indians in the meantime yelling like infernal spirits. As this scene appeared too shocking for me to behold, I retired to my lodgings both sore and sorry.

"When I came into my lodgings, I saw Russel's Seven Sermons, which they had brought from the field of battle, which a Frenchman made a present of to me. From the best information I could receive, there were only seven Indians and four French killed in this battle, and five hundred British lay dead on the field, besides what were killed in the river on their retreat. The morning after the battle, I saw Braddock's artillery brought into the fort; the same day I also saw several Indians in British officers' dress, with sash, half moons, laced hats, &c., which the British then wore."

Smith was a native of Franklin County, Pennsylvania. He remained in captivity among the Indians at Fort Duquesne, Mahoning, and Muskingum. He was adopted by his captors. During his captivity among the Indians, he was carried from place to place, spending most of his time at Mahoning and Muskingum. In about 1759, he accompanied his Indian relatives to Montreal, where he managed to secrete himself on board a French ship. He was again taken prisoner and confined for four months, but was finally exchanged and reached his home in 1760, to find the sweetheart of his boyhood married, and all his friends and relatives supposing him dead. He became a very prominent man on the Pennsylvania frontier, and during the Revolution, was a captain on the Pennsylvania line, being promoted, in 1778, to the rank of colonel. In 1788, he removed to Kentucky, where he at once took a prominent part in public affairs, serving in the early Kentucky conventions and in the legislature. He died in Washington County, Kentucky, in 1812, leaving behind him as a legacy to historians a very valuable account of his Indian captivity.

In the autumn following Braddock's inglorious defeat, the Delawares and Shawnees began their bloody invasion of Eastern Pennsylvania. However, there were few, if any, of these tribes fighting on the side of the French during the Braddock campaign. The Indians fighting on the side of the French in this campaign were mostly from the region of the Great Lakes. The Delawares and Shawnees were simply waiting to see which side would be victorious.

In closing this sketch of Scarouady's part in Braddock's campaign, it may be interesting to state the route followed by Braddock's army after entering Pennsylvania.

On June 19th the army reached Bear Camp, which was almost directly on the Pennsylvania and Maryland line, about three miles southeast of Addison, Somerset County. By the 23rd of June, it had reached Squaw Fort, situated a short distance southeast of Somerfield, Somerset County. On June 24th, the army passed over the Great Crossing of the Youghiogheny and encamped three or four miles east of the Great Meadows, the site of Fort Necessity, where Washington surrendered the year before. On June 25th, the army marched over the very spot where Braddock was buried a fortnight later, and encamped at the Orchard Camp, where he died on the night of July 13th. Both the Orchard Camp and the place of Braddock's burial are not far from the Summit on the National Pike, in Fayette County. On June 26th, the army encamped at Rock Fort Camp, not far from Washington's Spring, where, as stated in Chapter XIV, Tanacharison was encamped with his warriors when he and Washington set out to make the attack on Jumonville. On June 27th, the army reached Gist's Plantation, the present Mount Braddock, in Fayette County. On June 28th, the army reached Stewart's Crossing on the Youghiogheny, at Connellsville, Fayette County, where it encamped on the western side of this stream. The army remained in camp all day during the 29th, crossing the river on the 30th and encamping on the flats above the river at the mouth of Mount's Creek, Fayette County. On July 1st, the army encamped at what is known as the Camp at the Great Swamp, the location of which was near the old Iron Bridge, southeast of Mount Pleasant, Westmoreland County, and near the headwaters of Jacob's and Mount's creeks. On July 2nd, the army encamped at Jacob's Cabin, making a march of about six miles. This "cabin" belonged to the famous Delaware chief, Captain Jacobs, whose biography is given in Chapter XVIII. On July 3rd, the army passed near Mount Pleasant, and encamped at the headwaters of Sewickley Creek, about five miles southeast of Madison, Westmoreland County. The camp at this place was called Salt Lick Camp. On July 4th, the army encamped at Thicketty-Run (Sewickley Creek), about a mile west of Madison. From this camp two Indians were sent forward as scouts, as was also Christopher Gist. All three returned on the 6th, the Indians bringing the scalp of a French officer they had killed near Fort Duquesne. On July 6th, the army reached Camp Monacatoocha, located as we have seen in this chapter, not far from Irwin, Westmoreland County. Here Braddock abandoned his plan to approach Fort Duquesne by the ridge route or Nemacolin's Trail, in order to avoid the Narrows of Turtle Creek; and turning sharply westward, the army followed the valley of Long Run at or near Stewartsville, and encamped on the night of July 8th, about two miles from the Monongahela and an equal distance from the mouth of the Youghiogheny, near McKeesport, Allegheny County. This was the last camp of the army before the fatal encounter. Here George Washington, who had been left at the Little Crossing, near Grantsville, Maryland, on June 19th, on account of illness, rejoined the army on the morning of July 9th.

Scarouady's Opinion of Braddock

On August 15, 1755, Scarouady and six other chiefs who had fought with the English at Braddock's defeat, appeared before the Provincial Council at Philadelphia, received the thanks of the Council, and were given rewards for their fidelity. At a council held on August 22nd, Scarouady informed Governor Morris why most of the Indians with Braddock's army had left him before he reached the battlefield. Said he: "It is now well known to you how unhappily we have been defeated by the French near Monongahela. We must now let you know that it was the pride and ignorance of that great general [Braddock] that came from England. He is now dead; but he was a bad man when he was alive; he looked upon us as dogs; would never hear anything that was said to him. We often endeavored to advise him, and to tell him of the danger he was in with his soldiers; but he never appeared pleased with us, and that was the reason a great many of our warriors left him, and would not be under his command. We would advise you not to give up the point; though we have in a manner been chastised from above. But let us unite our strength. You are very numerous, and all the English Governors along your seashore can raise men enough. Don't let those that come from over the great sea be concerned any more. They are unfit to fight in the woods. Let us go ourselves, we that came out of this ground. We may be assured to conquer the French. The Delawares and Nanticokes have told me that the French never asked them to go on the late expedition against Braddock; one word of yours will bring the Delawares to join you. I am going to the Nanticokes, and shall pass by the Delawares, and any message you have to send or answer you have to give to them I will deliver to them."

Scarouady insisted that, if the Governor did not avail himself of this opportunity to engage these Indians as allies, they would go over to the French. He endeavored to impress upon the Governor and Provincial Council that it was impossible to remain neutral and live in the woods. Moreover, he claimed to have great influence among, not only the Indians on the Susquehanna, but also the Western Indians and the Wyandots in Ohio.

Governor Morris was at a loss to know how to reply to Scarouady's request that the Delawares be asked to take up arms against the French. The King of England had not yet declared war, and so the Governor did not feel at liberty to employ the Delawares in warlike measures. In his embarrassment he turned to Conrad Weiser, who advised him to give Scarouady a general answer thanking him for his advice and soliciting the lasting friendship of the old chief and his followers, begging them in the meantime to await until the decision of the Great Council of the Six Nations could be learned.

After holding conferences with the Governor on August 18th and 22nd, Scarouady went by way of Harris' Ferry (Harrisburg) to Shamokin (Sunbury) to hunt and await developments, from which place he sent a message to Governor Morris on September 11th, advising him that the Six Nations had sent a black belt of wampum to the Delawares and Shawnees, ordering them "to lay aside their petticoats, and clap nothing on but a breech-clout"; to come with speed to their assistance in the war against the French; and that he [Scarouady] was assembling a force of Indians to go against the French among whom were John, James-Logan, and John-Petty, the three sons of Shikellamy. The Seneca chief, the Belt, was Scarouady's authority as to the message of the Six Nations, but it is not known to what extent the Belt's information was true.

In the meantime, Conrad Weiser had gone to Harris' Ferry, where, early in September, he distributed a wagonload of flour and other supplies among the friendly Indians. Scarouady's wife was one of the recipients of this bounty. She informed Weiser that, shortly after Braddock's defeat, she had aroused her brothers, Moses and Esras, to go to the Ohio and bring her some French scalps in revenge for Braddock's death.

CHAPTER XVI.

Scarouady
(Continued)

Penn's Creek Massacre

T is the autumn of 1755. By this time nearly all the Delawares and Shawnees have gone over to the French. The bitter fruitage of the Walking Purchase of 1737 and the Albany Purchase of 1754 is about to be gathered. The Delawares and Shawnees are about to let loose the dogs of war on defenseless Pennsylvania.

On the 16th of October of this year, occurred the first Indian outrage in Pennsylvania after Braddock's defeat. This was an attack upon the German settlers near the mouth of Penn's Creek, which flows into the Susquehanna at Selinsgrove, in Snyder County. It is known in history as the "Penn's Creek Massacre." It was the first actual break of the treaty of peace which Penn had entered into with Tamanend shortly after his arrival in the Province; and it is significant that the massacre took place almost on the line of the Albany Purchase of 1754, which so angered the Delawares. The Indians killed, scalped and carried away all the men, women and children, amounting to about twenty-five in number, and wounded one man, who fortunately made his escape, and carried the word to George Gabriel's, at the mouth of Penn's Creek. The company who went out to bury the dead found the corpses of thirteen men and elderly women and one child two weeks old. One of the leaders of the Indians on this occasion was Keckenepaulin, a Delaware chief, who lived near Jenner's Cross Roads, in Somerset County. His name has been applied, as stated in Chapter VI, to the Shawnee town at the mouth of the Loyalhanna, possibly due to the fact that he resided there for a time. The prisoners were taken to Kittanning, among them being Barbara Leininger and Marie LeRoy (Mary King).

Only two days after the Penn's Creek Massacre, or on October 18th, another occurred only a short distance to the eastward, at the mouth of Mahanoy Creek, about five miles south of Sunbury, where twenty-five inhabitants were killed or carried into captivity and every building of the settlement was burned. This massacre

differed from that of October 16th in that none escaped the massacre of the 18th, whereas one escaped the massacre of the 16th.

Scarouady Warns Settlers

On the 23rd of October, John Harris, Thomas Forster, Captain
McKee, and Adam Terence went to Penn's Creek with a force of
forty men to bury the dead of the massacre of October 16th.
When they arrived, they found that this had already been done.
They then decided to return immediately to the settlements at
Paxtang (Harrisburg), but were urged by John Shikellamy, son
of the vice-gerent of the Six Nations, and the Belt, a Seneca chief,
to go to Shamokin (Sunbury), in order to ascertain the feelings of
the Indians at that place, which they did. They stayed at
Shamokin during the night of the 24th, and heard much in the talk
of the Delawares at that place to alarm them. Scarouady was
present, and advised the party to follow the eastern side of the river
on their return. They left on the morning of the 25th, but fearing
an ambush on the east side of the river they marched down the
western bank; and when they reached the mouth of Penn's Creek,
they were fired upon by a large number of Delawares hidden in
the bushes.

John Harris describes this attack as follows:

"We were attacked by about twenty or thirty Indians, received
their fire, and about fifteen of our men and myself took to the trees
and attacked the villians, killed four of them on the spot, and
lost but three men, retreating about half a mile through the woods
and crossing the Susquehanna, one of which was shot from off an
horse riding behind myself through the river. My horse before
was wounded, and falling in the river, I was obliged to quit and
swim part of the way. Four or five of our men were drowned
crossing the river." Harris further says that the Belt became enraged when he heard of this attack, and gathered up a party of
thirty friendly Indians, and pursued the enemy.

The same day that the attack was made on John Harris and
his force, or probably on the next day, the Indians crossed the
Susquehanna and killed many people from Thomas McKee's to
Hunter's Mill. Conrad Weiser gave an account of the massacre
in a letter written at eleven o'clock on the night of October 26th
from his home near Womelsdorf, to James Reed at Reading.

John Harris further advised in the above letter, which was
written from Paxtang on the 28th of October: "The Indians are

all assembling themselves at Shamokin to counsel; a large body of them were there four days ago. I cannot learn their intentions, but it seems Andrew Montour and Scaraouady are to bring down the news from them. There is not a sufficient number of them to oppose the enemy; and perhaps they will all join the enemy against us. There is no dependence on Indians, and we are in imminent danger.

"I got information from Andrew Montour and others that there is a body of French with fifteen hundred Indians coming upon us,—Picks, Ottawas, Orandox, Delawares. Shawnees, and a number of the Six Nations,—and are not many days march from this Province and Virginia, which are appointed to be attacked. At the same time, some of the Shawnee Indians seem friendly, and others appear like enemies. Montour knew many days ago of the Indians being on their march against us before he informed; for which I said as much to him as I thought prudent, considering the place I was in."

Massacres in Fulton and Perry Counties

On October 31st the Delaware chief, Shingas, began incursions into Fulton County which lasted for several days. Nearly all of the settlers of the Great Cove and Little Cove were murdered or taken captive, and their houses and barns were burned. The same was true of the settlements at McDowell's Mill and Conococheague. Most of the prisoners were taken to Kittanning where many of them were burned to death.

Shortly after the incursion into Fulton County, occurred the murder of the Woolcomber family, Quakers, in Perry County, thus described in "Loudon's Narratives":

"The next I remember of was in 1755, the Woolcombers family on Shearman's Creek; the whole of the inhabitants of the valley was gathered at Robinson's, but Woolcomber would not leave home, he said it was the Irish [Scotch-Irish] who were killing one another; these peaceable people, the Indians would not hurt any person. Being at home and at dinner, the Indians came in, and the Quaker asked them to come and eat dinner; an Indian announced that he did not come to eat, but for scalps; the son, a boy of fourteen or fifteen years of age when he heard the Indian say so, repaired to a back door, and as he went out he looked back, and saw the Indian strike the tomahawk into his father's head. The boy then ran over the creek, which was near the house, and heard

the screams of his mother, sisters and brother. The boy came to
our Fort [Robinson] and gave us the alarm; about forty went to
where the murder was done and buried the dead."

Cause of Indian Alienation Investigated

The news of these various massacres was laid before the Provincial Assembly by Governor Morris; whereupon the Assembly
answered with a request to the Governor to inform the House "if
he knew of any injury which the Delawares and Shawnees had received to alienate their affections, and whether he knew the part
taken by the Six Nations in relation to this incursion."

Robert Strettell, Joseph Turner, and Thomas Cadwalader,
were appointed a committee to inspect all "minutes of Council and
other books and papers" relating to Pennsylvania's transactions
with the Delawares and Shawnees from the beginning of the
Colony. The committee made an elaborate report, which was
approved and sent to the House on November 22nd, setting forth
the findings of the committee that "the conduct of the Proprietaries
and this Government has been always uniformly just, fair, and
generous towards these Indians."

Scarouady Threatens to Go to the French

While the terrible things related above were happening,
Scarouady was exerting his utmost influence on behalf of the English. On November 1st, he was at Harris' Ferry where he delivered a message to John Harris, who forwarded it to the Governor,
advising, among other things, that "about twelve days ago the
Delawares sent for Andrew Montour to go to Big Island [Lock
Haven], on which he [Scarouady] and Montour with three more
Indians went up immediately, and found there about six of the
Delawares and four Shawnees, who informed them that they had
received a hatchet from the French, on purpose to kill what game
they could meet with, and to be used against the English if they
proved saucy."

On November 8th, Scarouady and Montour appeared before
the Provincial Council, and gave additional details of their trip to
Big Island. Scarouady said that two Delawares from the Ohio
appeared at the meeting at Big Island and spoke as follows: "We,
the Delawares of Ohio, do proclaim war against the English. We
have been their friends many years, but now have taken up the

hatchet against them, and will never make it up with them whilst there is an English man alive.

"When Washington was defeated, we, the Delawares, were blamed as the cause of it. We will now kill. We will not be blamed without a cause. We make up three parties of Delawares. One party will go against Carlisle; one down the Susquehanna; and . . . . . another party will go against Tulpehocken to Conrad Weiser. And we shall be followed by a thousand French and Indians, Ottawas, Twightwees, Shawnees, and Delawares."

It will be noted that the Delawares gave their being blamed for Washington's defeat at the Great Meadows, in the summer of 1754, as the cause of their having taken up arms against Pennsylvania. Later they told the Shawnee chief, Paxinosa, of Wyoming, that the cause of their hostility was the Walking Purchase of 1737 and the Albany Purchase of 1754; and the great Delaware chief, Teedyuscung, stoutly insisted that it was these wrongs upon the Delawares that caused these friends of William Penn to take up arms against the Colony he founded.

On the afternoon of the same day, November 8th, Scarouady appeared before the Governor, his Council, and the Provincial Assembly, and told them of the journey which he had recently made in the interest of the English, up the North Branch of the Susquehanna "as far as the Nanticokes live." He stated that he had told the Nanticokes and other Indians on the Susquehanna that the defeat of General Braddock had brought about a great turn of affairs; that it was a great blow, but that the English had strength enough to recover from it. He further said that there were three hundred friendly Indians on the Susquehanna. (Delawares and Nanticokes) "who were all hearty in the English interest." For these he desired the Colony's assistance with arms and ammunition. He insisted that they should be given the hatchet, and that a fort should be built for the protection of their old men, women, and children. They had told him, he said, that whichever party, the French or English, would seek their assistance first, would be first assisted; and that he "should go to Philadelphia and apply immediately to the Government and obtain explicit answer from them whether they would fight or no." These Indians "waited with impatience to know the success of his application."

Then the old chief threw down his belts of wampum upon the table before the members of the Assembly and said: "I must deal plainly with you, and tell you if you will not fight with us, we will go somewhere else. We never can nor ever will put up the affront. If we cannot be safe where we are, we will go somewhere else for protection and take care of ourselves. We have no more to say, but will first receive your answer to this, and as the times are too dangerous to admit of our staying long here, we therefore entreat you will use all the dispatch possible that we may not be detained." It is possible that Scarouady meant that he and his followers would go to one of the other colonies, but he was understood as meaning that, unless the Pennsylvania Authorities acted promptly, he and his followers would go over to the French.

Governor Morris then said to the Provincial Assembly: "You have heard what the Indians have said. Without your aid, I can not make a proper answer to what they now propose and expect of us." The Assembly replied that, as Captain General, the Governor had full authority to raise men, and that "the Bill now in his hands granting Sixty Thousand Pounds will enable him to pay the expenses." This was a bill just passed by the Assembly, granting this sum for the defense of the Colony, to be raised by a tax on estates. The Governor opposed the bill on the ground that the Proprietary estates should not be taxed. He then explained to Scarouady how his controversy with the Assembly stood, and that he did not know what to do. Scarouady was amazed and said that Pennsylvania's failure to comply with his (Scarouady's) request in behalf of his three hundred friendly Indians would mean their going over to the French. However, he still offered his own services and counseled the Governor not to be cast down, but to keep cool.

After long consultations between Scarouady and Conrad Weiser, it was determined that Scarouady could render an important service to the Colony by visiting the Six Nations and Sir William Johnson, and, after gaining what intelligence he could on his way to New York, as to the actions of the Indians on the Susquehanna, by laying before the Great Confederation such intelligence as well as the recent conduct of the Delawares.

Scarouady Sent on Mission to Six Nations

Scarouady's decided stand had a good effect on the Governor and Council. On November 14th, the old chief and Andrew Montour were sent by the Governor on a mission to the Six Nations. They were instructed to convey the condolence of Pennsylvania to the Six Nations on the death of several of their warriors who had joined General Shirley and General Johnson and had

fallen in battle with the French, and to advise the Six Nations how
the Delawares had, in a most cruel manner, fallen upon and murdered so many of the inhabitants of Pennsylvania.   In a word,
Scarouady was to give the Six Nations a complete account of the
terrible invasion of the Delawares and Shawnees and to ascertain
whether or not this invasion was made with the knowledge, consent,
or order of the Six Nations, and whether the Six Nations would
chastise the Delawares.

Massacres in Berks County

Berks County, the home of Conrad Weiser, suffered terribly
during this dreadful autumn.   On November 14th, as six settlers
were on their way to Dietrick Six's plantation, near what is now
the village of Millersburg, they were fired upon by a party of
Indians.   Hurrying toward a watch-house, about half a mile distant, they were ambushed before reaching the same, and three of
them killed and scalped.   A settler named Ury, however, succeeded
in shootng one of the Indians throught the heart, and his body was
dragged off by the other savages.   The Indians then divided into
two parties.   The one party, lying in ambush near the watch-
house, waylaid some settlers who were fleeing toward that place,
and killed three of them.

The next night some savages crept up to the home of Thomas
Bower, on Swatara Creek, and pushing their guns through a window of the house, killed a cobbler who was repairing a shoe.   They
set fire to the house before being driven off.   The Bower family,
having sought refuge through the night at the home of a neighbor,
named Daniel Snyder, and returning to their home in the morning,
saw four savages running away and having with them the scalps of
three children, two of whom were still alive.   They also found the
dead body of a woman with a two week's old child under her body,
but unharmed.

Scarouady in Danger From Settlers

Conrad Weiser returned home from Philadelphia on November 17th, accompanied by Scarouady and Andrew Montour on
their way to the Six Nations.   He found the Berks County settlers
in a state of great excitement, on account of the Indian outrages.
The settlers of Berks County knew that he had frequently accompanied delegations of friendly Indians to Philadelphia.   To many
of the settlers whose homes and barns were destroyed and whose

dear ones were murdered or carried into captivity, all Indians looked alike. Consequently, many of the settlers were now suspicious of Weiser, and believed that he was protecting Indians who did not deserve it. Consequently, also, he had now great difficulty in conducting Scarouady and Montour towards the Susquehanna. Said he, in a letter to Governor Morris on November 19th: "I made all the haste with the Indians [Scarouady and Montour] I could, and gave them a letter to Thomas McKee, to furnish them with necessaries for their journey. Scarouady had no creature to ride on. I gave him one. Before I could get done with the Indians, three or four men came from Benjamin Spikers to warn the Indians not to go that way for the people were so enraged against all the Indians and would kill them without distinction. I went with them. So did the gentlemen before named. When we came near Benjamin Spikers, I saw about 400 or 500 men, and there was loud noise. I rode before, and in riding along the road and armed men on both sides of the road, I heard some say: 'Why must we be killed by the Indians, and not kill them? Why are our hands so tied?' I got the Indians into the house with much ado, where I treated them with a small dram, and so parted in love and friendship. Captain Diefenback undertook to conduct them, with five of our men, to the Susquehanna."

Weiser in Danger

Continuing the above letter, Weiser says:

"After this, a sort of a counsel of war was held by the officers present, the before named, and other Freeholders.

"It was agreed that 150 men should be raised immediately to serve as out scouts, and as Guards at Certain Places under the Kittitany Hills for 40 days. That those so raised to have 2 Shillings a Day & 2 Pounds of Bread, 2 Pounds of Beaff and a jill of rum, and Powder and lead. Arms they must find themselves.

"This Scheme was signed by a good many Freeholders, and read to the people. They cried out that so much for an Indian scalp would they have, be they friends or enemies, from the Governor. I told them I had no such power from the Governor nor Assembly. They began some to curse the Governor; some the Assembly; called me a traitor of the country, who held with the Indians, and must have known this murder beforehand. I sat in the house by a lowe window; some of my friends came to pull me away from it, telling me some of the people threatened to shoot me.

"I offered to go out to the people and either pasefy them or
make the King's Proclamation. But those in the house with me
would not let me go out. The cry was, The Land was betrayed
and sold. The common people from Lancaster [now Lebanon
County] were the worst. The wages they said was a Trifle and
some Body pocketed the Rest, and they would resent it. Some
Body had put it in their head that I had it in my power to give
them as much as I pleased. I was in danger of being shot to death.

"In the meantime, a great smoke arose under Tulpenhacon
Mountain, with the news following that the Indians had committed
a murder on Mill Creek (a false alarm) and set fire to a barn;
most of the people ran, and those that had horses rode off without
any order or regulation. I then took my horse and went home,
where I intend to stay and defend my own house as long as I can.
The people of Tulpenhacon all fled; till about 6 or 7 miles from
me some few remains. Another such attack will lay all the country waste on the west side of Schuylkill."

Moravians Massacred

Scarouady was hardly started on his journey to the Six
Nations when the tomahawk and scalping knife of the Delawares
became stained anew with the blood of the settlers of Eastern
Pennsylania. On November 24th, the Moravian missionaries at
Gnadenhuetten, Carbon County, were cruelly murdered by a band
of twelve warriors of the Munsee Clan of Delawares, led by
Jachebus, chief of the Assinnissink, a Munsee town in Steuben
County, New York. The bodies of the dead were placed in a
grave. A monument marks the spot where the dust of these victims of savage cruelty reposes, a short distance from Lehighton,
and bears the following inscription:

"To the memory of Gottlieb and Joanna Anders, with their
child, Christiana; Martin and Susanna Nitschnann; Anna Catherine Senseman; John Gattermeyer; George Fabricius, clerk;
George Schweigert; John Frederick Lesly; and Martin Presser;
who lived here at Gnadenhuetten unto the Lord, and lost their lives
in a surprise from Indian warriors, November 24, 1755. Precious
in the sight of the Lord is the death of his saints.—Psalm 96
CXVI 15".

Attack on Hoeth and Broadhead Families

On December 10th and 11th, occurred the attack on the
Hoeth and Broadhead families. The Hoeth family lived on Poco-
Poco Creek, afterwards known as Hoeth's Creek, and now generally

known as Big Creek, a tributary of the Lehigh above Weissport. This family was almost exterminated.

After committing the outrages on the Hoeths, the same band proceeded to the Broadheads, who lived near the mouth of Broadhead Creek, not far from the site of Stroudsburg, Monroe County. In the attack on the Broadhead family, they met with determined resistance, and were finally obliged to retire. All the members of the Broadhead family were noted for their bravery. Among the sons was the famous Colonel, later General Broadhead, of the Revolutionary War.

Also on New Year's Day, 1756, a guard of forty militia, who had been sent to erect a fort near the Moravian town of Gnaden-huetten, above mentioned, were attacked by hostile Delawares, and the greater number of them killed. The Indians on the same day laid waste the country between Gnadenhuetten and Nazareth, Northampton County, killing many settlers and burning farm houses and barns.

Assembly and Governor Dispute While Settlers Die

Indeed, from the Penn's Creek massacre until well into the year of 1756, terror reigned throughout the Pennsylvania settlements. It is a sad fact that while the Indians were thus burning and scalping on the frontier, the Assembly and Governor, instead of putting the Colony in a state of defense, spent their time in disputes as to whether or not the Proprietary estates should be taxed to raise money to defend the Province,—a disgusting chapter in the history of Pennsylvania. The smoke of burning farm houses darkened the heavens; the soil of the forest farms of the German and Scotch-Irish settlers was drenched with their blood; the tomahawk of the savage dashed out the brains of the aged and the infant; hundreds were carried into captivity, many of whom were tortured to death by fire at Kittanning and other Indian towns in the valleys of the Allegheny and the Ohio to which they were taken—all of these dreadful things were taking place as the disputes between the Governor and the Assembly continued.

Says Egle, in his "History of Pennsylvania": "The cold indifference of the Assembly at such a crisis awoke the deepest indignation throughout the Province. Public meetings were held in various parts of Lancaster and in the frontier counties, at which it was resolved that they would repair to Philadelphia and compel the Provincial authorities to pass proper laws to defend the country and oppose the enemy. In addition, the dead bodies of some of the murdered and mangled were sent to that city and hauled about the streets, with placards announcing that these were the victims of the Quaker policy of non-resistance. A large and threatening mob surrounded the house of Assembly, placed the dead bodies in the doorway, and demanded immediate relief for the people of the frontiers. Such indeed were the desperate measures resorted to for self defense."

Finally, on November 26th, the very day that the news reached Philadelphia of the slaughter of the Moravian missionaries at Gnadenhuetten, "An Act For Granting 60,000 pounds to the King's Use" was passed, after the Proprietaries had made a grant of 5,000 pounds in lieu of the tax on the Proprietary estates.

Benjamin Franklin Begins Erection of Chain of Forts

Pennsylvania then began erecting a chain of forts and block-houses to guard the frontier. These forts extended along the Kittatinny or Blue Mountains from the Delaware River to the Maryland line, and the cost of erection was eighty-five thousand pounds. They guarded the important mountain passes, were garrisoned by from twenty-five to seventy-five men in pay of the Province, and stood almost equi-distant, so as to be a haven of refuge for the settlers when they fled from their farms to escape the tomahawk and scalping knife. The Moravians at Bethlehem cheerfully fortified their town and took up arms in self-defense. Benjamin Franklin and James Hamilton were directed to go to the Forks of the Delaware and raise troops in order to carry the plan into execution. On December 29th, 1755, they arrived at Easton, and appointed William Parsons major of the troops to be raised in the county of Northampton. In the meantime, Captain Hays had been ordered to New Gnadenhuetten, the scene of the massacre of the Moravian missionaries on November 24th, with his militia from the Irish settlement in the county. The attack on these militia on New Year's Day, 1756, has been narrated. Finally, the Assembly requested Franklin's appearance, and, responding to this call, he turned his command over to Colonel William Clapham.

This chain of forts began with Fort Dupui, erected on the property of the Hugenot settler, Samuel Dupui, in the present town of Shawnee, on the Delaware River, in Monroe County. Next came Fort Hamilton, on the site of the present town of Stroudsburg, in Monroe County. Fort Penn was also erected in the eastern part of this town. These three forts were in the heart of the territory of the Munsee Clan of Delawares. Next was Fort

Norris, about a mile southeast of Kresgeville, Monroe County; and fifteen miles west was Fort Allen where Weissport, Carbon County now stands. Then came Fort Franklin in Albany Township, Berks County; and nineteen miles west was, Fort Lebanon, also known at Fort William, not far from the present town of Auburn, in Schuylkill County. Then came Fort Henry at Dietrick Six's, near Millersburg, Berks County. This post is sometimes called "Busse's Fort" from its commanding officer, also the "Fort at Dietrick Six's". Fort Lebanon and Fort Henry were twenty-two miles apart, and midway between them was the small post, Fort Northkill. Next came Fort Swatara, located in the vicinity of Swatara Gap, or Tolihaio Gap; then Fort Hunter, on the east bank of the Susquehanna River at the mouth of Fishing Creek, six miles north of Harrisburg; then Fort Halifax at the mouth of Armstrong Creek, half a mile above the present town of Halifax, on the east bank of the Susquehanna, in Dauphin County. While there were numerous block-houses, these posts were the principal forts east of the Susquehanna.

Crossing the Susquehanna, we find Fort Patterson in the Tuscarora Valley at Mexico, Juniata County; Fort Granville, near Lewistown, Mifflin County; Fort Shirley, at Shirleysburg, Huntingdon County; Fort Lyttleton at Sugar Cabins, in the northeastern part of Fulton County; Fort McDowell, where McDowell's Mill, Franklin County, now stands; Fort Loudoun, about a mile distant from the town of Loudoun, Franklin County; and Fort Lowther, at Carlisle, Cumberland County. Like the forts east of the Susquehanna, these forts were supplemented with block-houses in the vicinity. The erection of the entire chain of forts was completed in 1756.

Regina Hartman, the German Captive

As an example of the tragedies which the invasion of the Delawares brought upon the settlers of Eastern Pennsylvania, at the time of which we are writing, we deem it not inappropriate to insert, at this place, the account of the capture of Regina Hartman. The story of her capture, captivity among the Indians, and release has been told in many works dealing with the early history of Pennsylvania; and we quote as it is related in the "Frontier Forts of Pennsylvania":

"The Rev. Henry Melchior Muhlenberg [a son-in-law of Conrad Weiser] relates in the 'Hallische Nachrichten,' p. 1029, a touching incident, which has been frequently told, but is so 'apropos' to this record that it should not be omitted. It was of the widow of John Hartman who called at his house in February, 1765, who had been a member of one of Rev. Kurtz's [a Lutheran pastor in Berks County] congregations. She and her husband had emigrated to this country from Reutlingen, Wurtemberg, and settled on the frontiers of Lebanon County. The Indians fell upon them in October, 1755, killed her husband, one of the sons, and carried off two small daughters into captivity, whilst she and the other son were absent. On her return she found the home in ashes, and her family either dead or lost to her, whereupon she fled to the interior settlements at Tulpehocken and remained there.

"The sequel to this occurrence is exceedingly interesting. The two girls were taken away. It was never known what became of Barbara, the elder, but Regina, with another little girl two years old, were given to an old Indian woman, who treated them very harshly. In the absence of her son, who supplied them with food, she drove the children into the woods to gather herbs and roots to eat, and, when they failed to get enough, beat them cruelly. So they lived until Regina was about nineteen years old and the other girl eleven. Her mother was a good Christian woman, and had taught her daughters their prayers, together with many texts from the Scriptures, and their beautiful German hymns, much of which clung to her memory during all these years of captivity.

"At last, in the providence of God, Colonel Bouquet brought the Indians under subjection in 1764, [at the end of Pontiac's War] and obliged them to give up their captives   More than four hundred of these unfortunate beings were gathered together at Carlisle; amongst them the two girls, and notices were sent all over the country for those who had lost friends and relatives, of that fact. Parents and husbands came, in some instances, hundreds of miles, in the hope of recovering those they had lost, the widow being one of the number. There were many joyful scenes, but more sad ones. So many changes had taken place, that, in many instances, recognition seemed impossible. This was the case with the widow. She went up and down the long line, but, in the young women who stood before her, dressed in Indian costume, she failed to recognize the little girls she had lost. As she stood, gazing and weeping, Colonel Bouquet compassionately suggested that she do something which might recall the past to her children. She could think of nothing but a hymn which was formerly a favorite with the little ones:

'Allein, und doch nicht ganz allein,
Bin ich in meiner Einsamkeit.'

[The English translation of the first stanza of this hymn is as follows:

'Alone, yet not alone am I,
Though in this solitude so drear;
I feel my Saviour always nigh,
He comes the very hour to cheer;
I am with Him, and He with me,
E'en here alone I cannot be.']

"She commenced singing, in German, but had barely completed two lines, when poor Regina rushed from the crowd, began to sing also and threw her arms around her mother. They both wept for joy and the Colonel gave the daughter up to her mother. But the other girl had no parents, they having probably been murdered. She clung to Regina and begged to be taken home with her. Poor as was the widow she could not resist the appeal and the three departed together."

The Murder of Frederick Reichelsdorfer's Daughters

"The Frontier Forts of Pennsylvania" contains, also, the following account of one of the saddest tragedies of the autumn of 1755:

"The Rev. Henry Melchior Muhlenberg, D. D., in the Hallische Nachrichten, tells the soul-stirring story of Frederick Reichelsdorfer, whose two grown daughters had attended a course of instruction, under him, in the Catechism, and been solemnly admitted by confirmation to the communion of the Ev. Lutheran Church, in New Hanover, Montgomery County.

"This man afterwards went with his family some distance into the interior, to a tract of land which he had purchased in Albany township, Berks County (see under Fort Everett also). When the war with the Indians broke out, he removed his family to his former residence, and occasionally returned to his farm, to attend to his grain and cattle. On one occasion he went, accompanied by his two daughters, to spend a few days there, and bring away some wheat. On Friday evening, after the wagon had been loaded, and everything was ready for their return on the morrow, his daughters complained that they felt anxious and dejected, and were impressed with the idea that they were soon to die. They requested their father to unite with them in singing the familiar German funeral hymn,

'Wer weiss wie nahe meine Ende?'
[Who knows how near my end may be?]

after which they commended themselves to God in prayer, and retired to rest.

"The light of the succeeding morn beamed upon them, and all
was yet well. Whilst the daughters were attending to the dairy,
cheered with the joyful hope of soon greeting their friends, and being out of danger, the father went to the field for the horses, to prepare for their departure home. As he was passing through the
field, he suddenly saw two Indians, armed with rifles, tomahawks
and scalping knives, making towards him at full speed. The sight
so terrified him that he lost all self command, and stood motionless
and silent. When they were about twenty yards from him, he
suddenly, and with all his strength, exclaimed 'Lord Jesus, living
and dying, I am thine!' Scarcely had the Indians heard the words
'Lord Jesus' (which they probably knew as the white man's name
of the Great Spirit), when they stopped short, and uttered a
hideous yell.

"The man ran with almost supernatural strength into the
dense forest, and by taking a serpentine course, the Indians lost
sight of him, and relinquished the pursuit. He hastened to an adjoining farm, where two German families resided, for assistance,
but on approaching near it, he heard the dying groans of the
families, who were falling beneath the murderous tomahawks of
some other Indians.

"Having providentially not been observed by them, he hastened back to learn the fate of his daughters. But, alas! on arriving within sight, he found his home and barn enveloped with
flames. Finding that the Indians had possession here too, he hastened to another adjoining farm for help. Returning, armed with
several men, he found the house reduced to ashes and the Indians
gone. His eldest daughter had been almost entirely burnt up, a
few remains only of her body being found. And, awful to relate,
the younger daughter though the scalp had been cut from her head,
and her body horribly mangled from head to foot with the tomahawk, was yet living. 'The poor worm,' says Muhlenberg, 'was
able to state all the circumstances of the dreadful scene.' After
having done so she requested her father to stoop down to her that
she might give him a parting kiss, and then go to her dear Saviour;
and after she had impressed her dying lips upon his cheek, she
yielded her spirit into the hands of that Redeemer, who, though

His judgments are often unsearchable, and His ways past finding out, has nevertheless said, 'I am the resurrection and the life; if any man believe in me, though he die yet shall he live.' "

Murder of the Kobel Family

On November 24th, 1755, Conrad Weiser wrote Governor Morris concerning the murder of the Kobel family, as follows:

"I cannot forbear to acquaint your Honor of a certain Circumstance of the late unhappy Affair: One .... Kobel, with his wife and eight children, the eldest about fourteen Years and the youngest fourteen Days, was flying before the Enemy, he carrying one, and his wife and a Boy another of the Children, when they were fired upon by two Indians very nigh, but hit only the Man upon his Breast, though not Dangerously. They, the Indians, then came with their Tomahawks, knocked the woman down, but not dead. They intended to kill the Man, but his Gun (though out of order so that he could not fire) kept them off. The Woman recovered so farr, and seated herself upon a Stump, with her Babe in her Arms, and gave it Suck, and the Indians driving the children together, and spoke to them in High Dutch, 'Be still; we won't hurt you.' Then they struck a Hatchet into the woman's Head, and she fell upon her Face with her Babe under her, and the Indian trod on her neck and tore off the scalp. The children then run; four of them were scalped, among which was a Girl of Eleven Years of Age, who related the whole Story; of the Scalped, two are alive and like to do well. The Rest of the Children ran into the Bushes and the Indians after them, but our People coming near to them, and hallowed and made noise; the Indians Ran, and the Rest of the Children were saved. They ran within a Yard by a Woman that lay behind an Old Log, with two Children; there was about Seven or Eight of the Enemy."

Scarouady Returns From Mission to the Six Nations

As stated earlier in this chapter, Scarouady and Andrew Montour had been sent by the Governor of Pennsylvania as messengers to the Six Nations, late in 1755. They returned to Philadelphia from this mission on March 21, 1756, and on the 27th of that month, they appeared before the Provincial Council, and made a report of their journey. They had gone by way of Tulpehocken and Thomas McKee's trading post to Shamokin; and from there through Laugpaughpitton's Town and Nescopeck to Wyoming

(Plymouth, Luzerne County). At Wyoming they found a large number of Delawares, some Shawnees, Mohicans, and members of the Six Nations. They next came to Asserughney, a Delaware Town, twelve miles above Wyoming, on the north side of the Lackawanna River at its mouth. Their next stop was at Chinkannig (Tunkhannock), twenty miles farther up the Susquehanna, where they found the great Delaware chief, Teeduscung, with some Delawares and Nanticokes. Their next stop was at Diahogo (Tioga), a town composed of Mohicans and Delawares of the Munsee Clan, located where Athens, Bradford County, now stands, at which place they found ninety men. About twenty-five miles beyond, they came to the deserted town of Owegy. Leaving this place they arrived at Chugnut, about twenty miles distant. About five miles above Chugnut, was the town of Otseningo, where they found thirty cabins and about sixty warriors of the Nanticokes, Conoys, and Onondagas. Fourteen miles beyond this place they came to Oneoquagque, where they sent a message to the Governor of Pennsylvania, written by Rev. Gideon Hawley. From there they proceeded to Teyonnoderre and Teyoneandakt, and next to Caniyeke, the Lower Mohawk Town, located about two miles from Fort Johnson, and about forty miles from Albany, New York. At Fort Johnson, they held a conference in February, 1756, with Sir William Johnson and the chiefs of the Six Nations, who expressed great resentment over the action of the hostile Delawares.

This was a very dangerous journey for Scarouady and Montour. While they were at Wyoming, their lives were threatened by a party of eighty Delaware warriors, who came soon after their arrival. While Scarouady was consulting with the oldest chief in the evening, the rest cried out of doors: "Let us kill the rogue; we will hear of no mediator, much less of a master; hold your tongue, and be gone, or you shall live no longer. We will do what we please." Said Scarouady: "All the way from Wyoming to Diahogo, a day never passed without meeting some warriors, six, eight, or ten in a party; and twenty under command of Cut Finger Pete, going after the eighty warriors which we saw at Wyoming. . . . . . . All the way we met parties of Delawares going to join the eighty warriors there."

Scarouady reported that, at Wyoming he and Montour found John Shikellamy, son of the great vice-gerent of the Six Nations, with the hostile Delawares. They took him aside, and upbraided him severely for his ingratitude to Pennsylvania, "which had ever

been extremely kind to his father when alive." Then John
Shikellamy explained that he was with the enemies of the Colony,
because he could not help it, as they had threatend to kill him if
he did not join them.

Scarouady again appeared before the Provincial Council on
April 3rd and gave additional details of his journey. Said he:
"You desired us in your instructions to inquire the particular reasons assigned by the Delawares and Shawnees for their acting in
the manner they do against this Province. I have done it and all
I could get from the Indians is that they heard them say their
brethren, the English, had accused them very falsely of joining
with the French after Colonel Washington's defeat, and if they
would charge them when they were innocent, they could do no
more if they were guilty; this turned them against their brethren
and now indeed the English have good reason for any charge they
may make against them, for they are heartily their enemies."

As to the attitude of the Six Nations, Scarouady reported:
"The Six Nations in their reply expressed great resentment of the
Delawares; they threatened to shake them by the head, saying they
were drunk and out of their senses and would not consider the
consequences of their ill behavior and assured them that, if they
did not perform what they had promised they should be severely
chastized." At this meeting of the Provincial Council and at
others held early in April, Scarouady expressed himself as favoring
a declaration of war by Pennsylvania against the Delawares, and
ventured the opinion that the Six Nations would approve of such
action.

Pennsylvania Declares War Against the Delawares

As a result of the foregoing conferences with Scarouady, Governor Morris and the Provincial Council on April 14, 1756, made a
formal declaration of war against the Delawares, and offered rewards for Indians' scalps, as follows:

"For every male Indian enemy above twelve years old, who
shall be taken prisoner and delivered at any fort, garrisoned by the
troops in pay of this Province, or at any of the county towns to
the keepers of the common jail there, the sum of 150 Spanish dollars or pieces of eight; for the scalp of every male enemy above
the age of twelve years, produced to evidence of their being killed
the sum of 130 pieces of eight; for every female Indian taken
prisoner and brought in as aforesaid, and for every male Indian
prisoner under the age of twelve years, taken and brought in as

aforesaid, 130 pieces of eight; for the scalp of every Indian woman, produced as evidence of their being killed, the sum of fifty
pieces of eight, and for every English subject that has been killed
and carried from this Province into captivity that shall be recovered and brought in and delivered at the City of Philadelphia, to
the Governor of this Province, the sum of 130 pieces of eight, but
nothing for their scalps; and that there shall be paid to every
officer or soldier as are or shall be in the pay of the Province who
shall redeem and deliver any English subject carried into captivity
as aforesaid, or shall take, bring in and produce any enemy prisoner, or scalp as aforesaid, one-half of the said several and respective premiums and bounties."

The Scalp Act had the effect of causing hundreds of brave
warriors of the Delawares and Shawnees who were up to that time
undecided, to take up arms against the Colony. "A mighty shout
arose which shook the very mountains, and all the Delawares and
Shawnees, except a few old sachems, danced the war dance."

James Logan, a prominent Quaker member of the Provincial
Council, and former Secretary of the same, opposed the declaration
of war, though he was a strict advocate of defensive warfare.
Conrad Weiser was in favor of the declaration of war, but strongly
opposed to offering rewards for scalps. He said that the Colony
might offer rewards for Indian prisoners, but that a bounty for
scalps would certainly tend to aggravate existing affairs. He
argued that anyone could bring in these scalps, and there was no
means of distinguishing the scalps of friendly Indians. "Indeed,"
says Walton, "this was the core of the whole difficulty. Scalps of
friendly Indians were taken, and the peace negotiations with the
Eastern Indians frustrated."

Scarouady Favors Peace

The declaration of war against the Delawares was very distasteful to the Quaker members of the Provincial Assembly. They
believed that the entire Indian policy of the Colony had been reversed by such declaration and that the Delawares and Shawnees
would not have taken up arms against the Colony without a
grievance. Furthermore, they believed that adequate efforts had
not been made towards reconciliation before war was declared.
Therefore, when some friendly Indians were in Philadelphia a few
days after the declaration of war, Israel Pemberton waited upon
the Governor on behalf of numerous members of the Society of

Friends, and asked the Governor's permission to invite the Indians to dine with a committee of Quakers, to the end that the Indian grievances might be ascertained and additional efforts made to bring about peace. The Quakers offered to bear all expenses, to conduct the negotiations as a private matter, and do nothing without the approval of the Governor. The Governor granted permission on condition that Conrad Weiser should be informed of everything said to the Indians by the Quakers and everything said to the Quakers by the Indians. Pemberton then set forth at a dinner the well known peace principles of the Society of Friends. The Indians, especially Scarouady, their speaker, were greatly pleased. The old chief declared that the Six Nations would join eagerly in a project for establishing peace.

Following the dinner, Weiser and Pemberton had a long conference with Scarouady, in which it was decided to send messengers to the Six Nations "setting forth their conferences with the Quakers, their religious principles and their characters, and the influence they had as well with the Government as a people, their desiring to bring about a peace, and their offer to become mediators between them and the Government; that he [Scarouady] and the other Six Nations had heard what they said with pleasure and desired that they would hearken to it, cease their hostilities and accept this mediation, and lest they (the Delawares and Shawnees) might be afraid that they had done too much mischief and taken too many lives, even more than could be possibly forgiven, he assured them that these peaceable people would, notwithstanding this, obtain their pardon if they would immeditaely desist, send the English prisoners to some place, and deliver them up to the Governor, and request peace of him and forgiveness for what was passed."

Pemberton and Weiser laid the report of the conference before the Governor, who called the Provincial Council together and submitted four questions:

1st. Whether it were proper to permit the Society of Friends to act as mediators. 2nd. Whether or not a peace should be proposed on conditions of forgiveness and return of prisoners taken. 3rd. Whether or not such a message would obstruct the establishing of a fort which the Colony contemplated building at Shamokin. 4th. Whether or not it would be better to invite such friendly Indians as Paxinosa, chief of the Shawnees of Wyoming, to come near the settlements and be out of danger.

The Provincial Council being opposed to the Government's

assuming any responsibility, advised the Governor to leave the matter entirely with the Quakers. Scarouady, Captain New Castle, and several other friendly Indians agreed to carry the peace message among the hostile Delawares and the Six Nations. They were instructed to ask the Six Nations to solicit the influence of Sir William Johnson, of New York, in persuading the Colony of Pennsylvania to recall the declaration of war and the act providing a bounty for scalps.

Weiser advised the Governor that the declaration of war should stand, believing that it would influence the Delawares to ask for peace. He believed further that the Six Nations would agree to this, and called the attention of both the Governor and the Provincial Council to the fact that Scarouady as the representative of the Six Nations was not offended at the "Scalp Act."

The Delaware chiefs, Captain New Castle, Jonathan, and Andrew Montour were very eager for peace and offered to risk their lives in carrying the overtures of the Governor. However, while the Delawares had virtually thrown off the yoke of Iroquois bondage, yet the hatred of these three Delaware chiefs for their former masters was so strong that they positively declared that they would do nothing for Scarouady and the Six Nations. The Governor then decided to have no professional connection with the matter, but the day following his decision, he received a letter from Sir William Johnson, of New York, criticizing Pennsylvania's declaration of war and the Scalp Bounty Act. Governor Morris then changed his mind once more, and decided that he would send the peace message in his own name. The messengers then went forth among the Delawares and the Shawnees of the Susquehanna.

Scarouady also went to the territory of the Six Nations, carrying the Governor's peace message to Sir William Johnson, attending many conferences and making speeches in an effort to bring about peace. One of these was delivered at a meeting at Fort Johnson, New York, on May 10, 1756, between Sir William Johnson and a number of Oneida chiefs. Another was delivered on July 1, 1756, at the conference of the Six Nations with Sir William Johnson in behalf of the Shawnees and Delawares. Another was made at the German Flats, New York, on August 26, 1756, when Sir William Johnson spoke to the two parties of Indians, one under the command of Scarouady and Montour and another under command of Thomas, an Oghquaga chief. On this occasion Johnson asked the two bands of Indians to go to the Oneida Carrying Place to meet the army of General Webb. He said that he would send Croghan with them to this place.   Scarouady and Montour promised to accompany Croghan, but delayed their departure from day to day.   In the meantime General Webb having destroyd his forts and abandoned the Carrying Place, returned to the German Flats.   The proposed expedition under Croghan therefore did not start.

Final Conferences of Scarouady

While Scarouady was in New York exerting all the powers of his eloquence in behalf of peace, the French and Indian War went on in Pennsylvania.   A line of forts with intervening block houses was erected along the base of the Blue Mountains from Easton to the Maryland line; but the savages broke through this line of fortifications and continued their work of blood and death on the frontier.   On April 4, 1756, they burned McCord's Fort on the Conococheague, in Franklin County, and the entire garrison of twenty-seven was killed or captured.   On August 1, 1756, they burned Fort Granville, near Lewistown, Mifflin County, and captured the entire garrison after killing Lieutenant Edward Armstrong, the commander.   The Indian forces were Delawares under command of Captain Jacobs of Kittanning.   The prisoners were carried to that place where some of them were tortured to death, among these being John Turner, who had opened the gates at Fort Granville to the enemy.   Lieutenant Armstrong's brother, Colonel John Armstrong, then raised a force of three hundred soldiers from Cumberland County, marched over the Allegheny Mountains, and on September 8th, burned the great Delaware town of Kittanning, which had been the starting point for so many expeditions that spread terror and death on the frontier.   An account of the destruction of Kittanning will be given more fully in Chapter XVIII.

Scarouady returned to Pennsylvania and held a conference with George Croghan and one hundred and sixty Indians, chiefly chiefs from the Six Nations, at Harris' Ferry, on April 1st and 2nd, 1757.   He then accompanied them to Lancaster, where they remained until the end of the month and where additional conferences were held in the hope of establishing permanent peace. Many of the chiefs died of smallpox while at Lancaster.

On April 26, 1757, Scarouady, with a party of Mohawk warriors, set forth for Fort Augusta which had been erected at Shamokin, to reconnoiter the wilderness in that vicinity, and then to proceed toward the Ohio on a scouting expedition.   Scarouady proposed this expedition, stating that he was very apprehensive that the French would make an attempt against Fort Augusta; and so he believed it well to reconnoiter the country between that place and the Ohio, and if he found any French in the region, he would return and give notice to the commander of the fort.

The Colonial Records are not clear as to whether Scarouady actually went to the region of the Ohio and Allegheny, but on May 9th, Croghan reported that "three of the messengers I sent to the Ohio, returned." They had gone to Venango (Franklin) and other points in the western region. They reported that they were advised by the Indians of Venango, Kuskuskies, and those who had formerly lived at Kittanning, that the French were determined to make another trial against the English, but that they could not tell where they intended to strike next.

Death of Scarouady

The date of Scarouady's death is not known, but it was prior to August 26th, 1758, on which day several Mohawks came to Philadelphia from the territory of the Six Nations, bringing with them Scarouady's wife and all her children. She presented Governor Denny with "her husband's Calumet Pipe, and desired that he and the Indians might smoke it together; she intended to have gone into the Cherokee country, but had altered her mind, and would stay here with her children." Probably the old chief lost his life in one of Johnson's expeditions in New York.

It is with sincere regret that we take leave of Scarouady, an admirable character, a forceful orator, the leading speaker at many important conferences, the wise counselor, the strong enemy of the French, the firm friend of the English. Far past the prime of life when he first appears upon the scene, his aged shoulders bore a mighty burden to the end of his eventful career.

CHAPTER XVII.

Queen Allaquippa, Canachquasy and Paxinosa

NTERRUPTING, for a moment, the recital of the atrocities and battles of the French and Indian War, we devote this chapter to the biographies of three great Indian personages who were loyal to Pennsylvania before and during this bloody conflict.

QUEEN ALLAQUIPPA

Queen Allaquippa (Aliquippa), for whom the town of Aliquippa, in Beaver County, is named, and near which she is said to have at one time lived, is generally spoken of as a Seneca, though some authorities say that it is probable that she was a Mohawk. The weight of authority, however, is in favor of the contention that she was a Seneca. Conrad Weiser says that she belonged to this tribe. If she were a Mohawk, Weiser certainly would have known it, as he himself was an adopted son of the Mohawk nation.

By many authorities Queen Allaquippa is said to have been the mother of Canachquasy, the account of whom is given later in this chapter, and that she and her husband visited William Penn at New Castle, Delaware, shortly before he sailed for England the last time, in the autumn of 1701. There is no doubt that the parents of Canachquasy, whoever they were, went with their child to New Castle to bid farewell to the founder of the Colony; and if Queen Allaquippa were the mother of Canachquasy, the bidding of farewell to William Penn is her first appearance in history.

Distinguished Personages Visit Queen Allaquippa

When Conrad Weiser made his journey to the Ohio in the summer of 1748, in order to enter into a treaty on behalf of Pennsylvania with the western tribes, at Logstown, as mentioned in Chapter VIII, Queen Allaquippa was living at a village on the north bank of the Allegheny, a short distance above the mouth of the Monongahela. Weiser makes mention of his visit in a note in his journal, under date of August 27th, as follows: "Set off again in the morning early. Rainy weather. We dined at a Seneca town where an old Seneca woman [Queen Allaquippa] reigns with great authority. We dined at her house and they all used us very well."

Weiser reached Logstown on the evening of that same day (August 27th), at which place he made George Groghan's trading house his headquarters until he left for the settlements, on September 19th, in the meantime having visited Sauconk, at the mouth of the Beaver, and gotten in touch with the Indians of Kuskuskies, who were to receive part of the Pennsylvania present. Before leaving Logstown, he made another notation in his journal concerning Queen Allaquippa, as follows:

"The old Sinicker Queen from above, already mentioned, came to inform me some time ago that she had sent a string of wampum of three fathoms to Philadelphia by James Dunnings, to desire her brethren would send her up a cask of powder and some small shot to enable her to send out the Indian boys to kill turkeys and other fowls for her, whilst the men were gone to war against the French, that they may not be starved. I told her I had heard nothing of her message, but if she had told me of it before I had parted with all the powder and lead, I could have let her have some, and promised I would make inquiry; perhaps her messenger had lost it on the way to Philadelphia. I gave her a shirt, a Dutch wooden pipe and some tobacco. She seemed to have taken a little affront because I took not sufficient notice of her in coming down. I told her she acted very imprudently not to let me know by some of her friends who she was, as she knew very well I could not know by myself. She was satisfied, and went away with a deal of kind expressions."

When Celeron led his expedition down the Allegheny and Ohio in the summer of 1749, he found her living as nearly as can be determined at Shannopin's Town, on the east bank of the Allegheny, a few miles above the mouth of the Monongahela and within the present limits of Pittsburgh, though some assert that her residence was at McKees Rocks. He noted in his journal under date of August 7th as follows: "I re-embarked and visited the village which is called the Written Rock. The Iroquois inhabit this place, and it is an old woman of this nation who governs it. She regards herself as sovereign. She is entirely devoted to the English."

When Messrs. Patten, Fry and Lomax, the Commissioners of Virginia, who entered into a treaty with the Western Indians at

Logstown in 1752, as referred to in former chapters, were on their way to Logstown, they called on this old Indian Queen at Allaquippa's Town, located on the south bank of the Ohio below the mouth of Chartier's Creek, where she was living at that time. The journal of the Commissioners under date of May 30, 1752, describes their visit as follows:

"The goods being put on board four large canoes lashed together [at Shannopin's Town], the Commissioners and others went on board also, to go down the river with colors flying. When they came opposite the Delaware town, they were saluted by the discharge of firearms, both from the town and opposite shore where Queen Allaquippa lives; and the compliment was returned from the canoes. The company then went on shore to wait on the Queen, who welcomed them, and presented them with a string of wampum, to clear their way to Logstown. She presented them also with a fine dish of fish to carry with them, and had some victuals set, which they all ate of. The Commissioners then presented the Queen with a brass kettel, tobacco and some other trifles and took their leave."

When Washington made his journey to the French forts in the latter part of 1753, Queen Allaquippa was living at the present site of McKeesport, Allegheny County. When he and Christopher Gist reached Frazer's cabin at the mouth of Turtle Creek late in December, he learned from Frazer that Queen Allaquippa was offended by his failure to call on her on his way from Virginia to LeBouef. He then determined to visit her on his way back. He makes the following notation in his journal without giving a specific date, but from the context it is clear that it was some time between December 28th and the last day of the year: "As we intended to take horse here [at Frazer's], and it required some time to find them, I went up about three miles to the mouth of the Youghiogheny to visit Queen Alliquippa, who had expressed great concern that we passed her in going to the fort. I made her a present of a match-coat and a bottle of rum, which latter was thought much the better present of the two."

As has been seen in Chapter XIV, Queen Allaquippa was at the Great Meadows during Washington's campaign in the summer of 1754, and no doubt witnessed the conferring of the name of Colonel Fairfax upon Canachquasy by Washington at that place on the 10th day of June.

After Washington's surrender at Fort Necessity, July 4th, 1754, Queen Allaquippa went to Aughwick with the other Indians of the Ohio still friendly to Pennsylvania. Here she died some time prior to December 23rd, 1754, as, on that date, George Croghan, then in charge of Indian affairs at Aughwick, wrote the Colonial Authorities: "Alequeapy, ye old quine, is dead." .

CANACHQUASY (CAPTAIN NEW CASTLE)

As stated earlier in this chapter, it is probable that Canachquasy was the son of Queen Allaquippa. But whether he was her son or not, there is no doubt, as will be seen later, that, when a child, he accompanied his parents to New Castle, Delaware, in the autumn of 1701, when they went to that place to bid farewell to William Penn. His first appearance in Colonial history after attaining manhood was when he led a band of ten Mingo (Iroquois) warriors from Kuskuskies to Philadelphia in November, 1747, and brought the Provincial Council the first authentic news of the operations of the French in that quarter. In his speech delivered to the Provincial Council on November 13th, he advised the Governor that, although the Onondaga Council had taken a stand for neutrality during King George's War, which was then raging, yet the young warriors of the Iroquois in the Kuskuskies region had determined to take up arms against the French. The gist of his speech was given in the first part of Chapter XV. After apprising the Provincial Authorities of the attitude of the young Iroquois under his command, he asked for assistance by way of arms and ammunition from the Colony. "The French," said he, "have hard heads, and we have nothing strong enough to break them. We have only little sticks and hickories and such things that will do little or no service against the hard heads of the French."

Canachquasy was then told that a present had been prepared for them and the Cuyahogas. He then thanked the Council on behalf of his own delegation and the Cuyahogas, who, he said were of their own flesh and blood, and were pleased for the regard shown to them. The Council then purchased two hundred pounds worth of goods, a present for these Indans, and sent them as far as Harris' Ferry, where they were held until the following spring. Additions thereto were made so as to bring the total value up to about one thousand pounds. George Croghan was sent to Logstown the next spring, with a portion of these goods, to advise the Indians of that place and of Kuskuskies that Conrad Weiser would bring the balance later in the year. This Weiser did, as has already been seen, in the summer of 1748, when as agent of Pennsylvania, he entered into a treaty at Logstown with the Western Indians. Therefore, it is seen that Canachquasy's visit to the Provincial Council in November, 1747, was the means of the Colony's getting information which led to its sending Croghan and later Weiser the following year on the first embassy on the part of Pennsylvania to the Indians of the valleys of the Ohio and Allegheny.

Canachquasy spent the winter of 1747-48 with the Nanticokes at their village at the mouth of the Juniata. Just where he resided from this time until Washington's campaign in the summer of 1754 is uncertain; but it is probable that, during a large part of this period, his residence was at Kuskuskies or in that vicinity.

Canachquasy Given Name of New Castle

Canachquasy was the recipient of two English names. We have already seen, in Chapter XIV, that he was given the name of Lord Fairfax by Washington at the camp at the Great Meadows, on June 10, 1754. Later, he attended Weiser's conferences at Aughwick, in September, 1754. Likewise, we saw, in Chapter XV, that he was one of the chiefs who fought on the side of the English in Braddock's campaign in 1755, and that, at a meeting of the Provincial Council on August 15th of that year, he was thanked by the Council and rewarded for his fidelity. He was also present at a meeting of the Provincial Council on August 22, 1755, when Scarouady complained of the obstinacy of General Braddock. At this meeting, Canachquasy was given the name of New Castle. In the minutes of the Council, on this occasion, we read:

"The Governor [Governor Morris] addressing himself to Kanuksusy [Canachquasy], the son of old Allaguipas, whose mother was now alive and living near Ray's Town, desired him to hearken for he was going to give him an English name, then spoke as follows: 'In token of our affection for your parents and in expectation of you being a useful man in these perilous times, I do, in the most solemn manner, adopt you by the name of New Castle, and order you to be called hereafter by that name, which I have given to you, because, in 1701, I am informed that your parents presented you to the late Mr. William Penn at New Castle.' "

In this connection, we call attention to the fact that the minutes of the meeting of the Provincial Council above quoted (Colonial Records, Vol. VI, pages 588 and 589), refer to Canachquasy as "the son of old Allaguipas, whose mother was now alive and living near Ray's Town." That eminent authority on the Indian history of Pennsylvania, Dr. George P. Donehoo, points out that, inasmuch as George Croghan wrote from Aughwick, on December 23d, 1754, that "Alaqueapy, ye old quine, is dead," the "old Allaguipas," mentioned in the minutes of the Council of August 22nd, 1755, was not the mother of Canachquasy, but evidently an Indian chief, the father of Canachquasy, having a name similar, in sound, to that of Queen Allaquippa.

Canachquasy at Carlisle Council

An important Indian Council was held at Carlisle from January 13th to 16th, 1756, which was attended by Governor Morris, Richard Peters, William Logan, Joseph Fox, Conrad Weiser, George Croghan, and the following Indians: Canachquasy, The Belt, Aroas (Silver Heels), Jagrea, Seneca George, and others.

This Council had reference to Indian affairs on the Ohio and Allegheny at that time. Croghan reported that he had sent a friendly Indian, Delaware Jo, to the Ohio to get intelligence as to the situation there. Delaware Jo had gone to Kittanning, where the Delaware chief, Beaver, brother of Shingas, told him that the Six Nations had given the war hatchet to the Delawares and Shawnees. From Kittanning, Delaware Jo had gone to Logstown, where he was told the same thing by the Shawnees of that place. Furthermore, Delaware Jo had found some members of the Six Nations living in the Delaware towns on the Ohio and Allegheny, who always accompanied them in their war parties against the Pennsylvania settlements.

James Hamilton told the members of the conference how he had sent Aroas in the preceding November among the Indians of the Susquehanna to gain information, and that Aroas had learned from his uncle, who lived between Nescopeck and Wyoming, that the Delawares and Shawnees on the Ohio were persuaded by the French to strike the English, and had "put the hatchet into the hands of the Susquehanna Indians." After Croghan had listened to these accounts, he gave it as his opinion that the hostile Delawares and Shawnees were acting by the advice and approval of the Six Nations.

The Belt reviewed the events on the Ohio from the time of its first occupation by the French until the attacks upon Pennsylvania by the Delawares and Shawnees. He said that the French had entered into a secret treaty with the Delawares and Shawnees of the Ohio, who were in alliance with the Six Nations and were occupying the valleys of the Ohio and Allegheny by permission of the Six Nations, by the terms of which the Delawares and Shawnees permitted the French occupation and agreed to assist the French against the English.

Therefore, the thing uppermost in the mind of Canachquasy and his associates at the Carlisle Council was how to win back to the English interest the hostile Shawnees and Delawares, especially since it appeared, on the surface at least, that the Six Nations countenanced their hostility. But it must be remembered that those members of the Six Nations, living on the Ohio and Allegheny, at that time, and to whom Delaware Jo referred, were not true representatives of the Great Confederation of the Six Nations. They were a mongrel population, a mixture of all the Iroquoian stock on the outskirts of the territory of the Senecas. This mongrel population of the Ohio and Allegheny valleys was known as "Mingoes," and was really beyond the jurisdiction of the Six Nations.

Canachquasy Attends Other Conferences

Canachquasy attended a conference at Harris' Ferry on January 31, 1756, between Conrad Weiser, representing the Colony of Pennsylvania, and the friendly Indians of the Susquehanna. There was great danger, at this time, that the Pennsylvania settlers would not distinguish between good Indians and bad Indians; and Weiser's mission was for the purpose of retaining the friendship of the few that had not taken up arms against the Colony. In his report of this conference, written at his home at Womelsdorf on February 4th, and laid before the Governor on February 10th, he said:

"I had a good deal of trouble to quiet their minds (if I did at all). Satacarkoyies and New Castle went to Michael Taef's that night [January 31st], and New Castle got in the night lightheaded. He looked upon every person as an enemy, and did persuade Satacarkoyies to run away with him. He himself made off privately next morning, and had not been heard of when I left John Harris', which was on the second instant on the afternoon. . . . . . . I sent word about it to the people to take care of the said

New Castle if he should be seen anywhere; he had no arms with him. I think it highly necessary that the said Indians should be taken care of deeper within the Inhabitants; for should they suffer by our foolish people, we should lose all confidence and honor with the rest of the Indians."

On February 24th, Canachquasy attended a Council at Philadelphia. It seems that, shortly after his disappearance from the council held by Weiser at Harris' Ferry, on January 31st, he returned to that place. At any rate, he accompanied the delegation from Harris' Ferry which attended the conference at Philadelphia on the 24th of February.

Canachquasy also attended the councils at Philadelphia mentioned in Chapter XVI, held between the Colonial Authorities and the friendly Indians prior to and following the declaration of war against the Delawares, following which he offered, with Jonathan, and Andrew Montour, to carry the Governor's peace proposals among the Delawares.

Peace Missions of Canachquasy

Shortly after Pennsylvania's declaraton of war against the Delawares, Canachquasy carried the Governor's proposals of peace to these Indians. He spent four days at Wyoming, and then went on to Tioga, an important town of the Six Nations, Nanticokes, and Munsee Clan of Delawares, situated on the site of Athens, Bradford County. It was the southern gateway to the country of the Iroquois, and all the great war paths and hunting trails from the South and Southwest centered there. He held conferences with the Indians of this place and the surrounding towns, and made known to them the Governor's message. These Indians agreed to lay aside the hatchet and enter into negotiations for peace; but they cautioned Canachquasy not to charge them with anything that may have been done by the Delawares of the Ohio and Allegheny valleys under the influence of the French.

Canachquasy then returned to Philadelphia early in June, and laid his report before the Governor and Provincial Council. The Governor and Council, upon hearing the favorable report, drafted a proclamation for a suspension of hostilities with the enemy Indians of the Susquehanna Valley for a period of thirty days, and desired that a conference with them for the purpose of making peace, should be held at the earliest possible date.

Canachquasy then left once more for Tioga, bearing the Governor's message, advising the Susquehanna Indians that the

Colony would agree to a truce of thirty days and that, as one of the conditions of making peace, the prisoners taken on both sides should be delivered up. Shortly after he left, messengers were sent to him by the Governor carrying a few additional instructions, which were delivered to him at Bethlehem. In the meantime, Sir William Johnson, of New York, was holding a peace conference with the Six Nations at Otseningo, at which the assembled sachems of the Iroquois decided that the Delawares were acting like drunken men, and sent deputies to order them to become sober and cease their warfare against the English. This conference was composed of only a portion of the Iroquois, and the Delawares replied very haughtily saying that they were no longer women but men. "We are determined," said they, "to cut off all the English except those that make their escape from us in ships."

After a dangerous journey over the mountains and through the wilderness, Canachquasy reached Tioga, held conferences with the great Delaware chieftain, Teedyuscung, and persuaded him to bury the hatchet,—a most remarkable victory.

Canachquasy then returned to Philadelphia in the middle of July, 1756, and laid before the Governor and Provincial Council the results of his second mission to Tioga. Addressing the Governor and Council he said:

"As I have been entrusted by you with matters of highest concern, I now declare to you that I have used all the ability I am master of in the management of them, and that with the greatest cheerfulness. I tell you in general, matters look well. I shall not go into particulars. Teedyuscung will do this at a public meeting, which he expects will be soon. The times are dangerous. The swords are drawn and glittering all around you; numbers of enemies in your borders. I beseech you, therefore, not to give any delay to this important affair; we hear the council fire is to be kindled; come to a conclusion immediately; let us not wait a moment, lest what has been done should prove ineffectual. The times are very precarious; not a moment is to be lost without the utmost danger to the good cause we are engaged in. The Delaware King [Teedyuscung] wants to hear from your own mouth a confirmation of the assurances of peace and good will given him by me in your name; he comes well disposed to make you the same declarations. The Forks [Easton] is believed to be the place of meeting. What need of any altercation? Let it be. Tarry not, but hasten to meet him."

Arrangements were then completed for a conference with the hostile Delawares at Easton, and Conrad Weiser was ordered to concentrate his soldiers in the vicinity of that place and to furnish a guard for the Governor, who, with his Council, reached Easton on the 24th of July. Nothing of any moment could be done until the 27th of that month, inasmuch as Weiser had not arrived. Teedyuscung, on opening the conference, insisted on having his own interpreter. This request was granted, and the treaty was formally opened on July 28th. Teedyuscung claimed to have been appointed King over all the Clans of Delawares and to have been authorized by the Six Nations to negotiate for peace. The details of the treaty will be set forth more fully in the account of Teedyuscung, Chapter XXI. At this point, however, we call attention to the fact that Canachquasy's advice and activities during the treaty were very valuable; that the treaty resulted in a temporary peace, and that Canachquasy and Teedyuscung were to go back among the Delawares and give the "Big Peace Halloo." At the end of the conferences, Teedyuscung lingered at Fort Allen, which had been erected where the town of Weissport, Carbon County, now stands. At this place, Teedyuscung's inordinate appetite for rum, the curse of the Red Man, was taken advantage of, and he remained intoxicated for a considerable time. Canachquasy then went away in disgust.

The Pennsylvania Authorities were apprehensive that Teedyuscung was not sincere in the peace proposals that he had made at the treaty at Easton. Besides, a number of Indians on the border insinuated that the Easton treaty was but a ruse to gain time; and that Teedyuscung was a traitor working in the interest of the French. Finally, the Governor, becoming suspicious of Teedyuscung's long delay at Fort Allen, sent Canachquasy secretly to New York to learn from the Six Nations whether or not they had deputized Teedyuscung to represent them in public treaties. Canachquasy returned to Philadelphia in October with the report that the Six Nations denied Teedyuscung's authority. At a meeting of the Provincial Council on the 24th of that month, he said:

"I have but in part executed my commission, not having opportunity of having done it so fully as I wished. I met with Canyase, one of the principal counsellors of the Six Nations, a Mohawk chief, who has a regard for Pennsylvania. . . . . . I related to this chief very particularly the manner in which Teedyuscung spoke of himself and his commission and authority from the Six Nations at the treaty at Easton. I gave him a true notion of all he said on this head and how often he repeated it to the Governor, and then asked whether he knew anything of this matter.

Canyase said he did; Teedyuscung did not speak the truth when he told the Governor he had a regular authority from the Six Nations to treat with Onas.   Canyase then proceeded and said: 'Teedyuscung on behalf of the Delawares did apply to me as chief of the Six Nations.   He and I had long discourses together and in these conversations, I told him that the Delawares were women and always treated as such by the Six Nations.' "

Death of Canachquasy

While attending the Easton treaty, Canachquasy had a presentiment of impending death,—a presentiment soon to be fulfilled, the account of which is thus given in Volume II of the Pennsylvania Archives, Series 1, under date of July 27, 1756:

"Mr. Weiser coming to Town, the Governor proposed to open the conferences, but on his saying he was a stranger to Teedyuscung and it would take up some time, at least a day, to be rightly informed of his temper and expectations, it was deferred till tomorrow. Captain New Castle (Canachquasy) came to the Governor, much in liquor, tho' otherwise a very sober man, and requested a Council might be called, saying he had something of a particular nature to communicate . . . . . . with which being obliged, he acquainted the Governor that the Delawares had bewitched him and he should die soon; the Governor would have rallied it off, but he grew more serious and desired this information might be committed to writing and inserted in the minutes of Council, and sent to the Six Nations; that if any harm came to him, they might know to whom to impute it, and not charge others with it.   Teedyuscung, he declared, had warned him in a friendly manner, that he would not live long, having overheard two Delawares say they would put an end to his life by witchcraft.   And whilst he was speaking, Teedyuscung mistrusting what New Castle was upon, bolted into the room, fell into a violent passion with New Castle, who he supposed had been telling the Governor foolish words, and desired he might not be regarded in anything he should say on such a foolish subject, exclaiming, 'He bewitched!' The Governor was too wise to hearken to such silly stories, and then left the room in as abrupt a manner as he had entered it. After he was gone, the Governor endeavored to show New Castle that he was in no danger, but he made no impression.   New Castle still urging that information might be taken down, and, in case of his death, be communicated in a special message to the Six Nations, which was promised; and he then withdrew, to appearance, more composed."

Shortly after Canachquasy's appearance before the Provincial Council on October 24, 1756, he contracted small-pox, at Philadelphia, and before the middle of November, this great peace apostle among the Indians was no more. Canachquasy's devotion to the cause of the English commands our great admiration and respect. He said that he would die for the sons of Onas. In the following chapter (Chapter XVIII), we shall see some of the terrible atrocities, committed by the Delawares, while this firm friend of Pennsylvania was wroking for peace.

PAXINOSA (PAXNOUS, PAXIHOS)

Paxinosa was a noted chief of the Shawnees. His first appearance in history is among the Shawnees at Pechoquealin, near the Delaware Water Gap, and it is probable that he was one of the band of this tribe which Arnold Viele conducted to that region from the lower Ohio Valley, in 1794, as set forth in Chapter II. He removed from the Pechoquealin and Minisink region, and took up his abode just below Plymouth, Luzerne County, among the other Shawnees who had removed from Pechoquealin to that place. The date of his removal from Pechoquealin, however, is not known. As stated in Chapter VIII, Kakowatcheky, who had been chief of the Shawnees at Wyoming, removed to the Ohio Valley in 1743. A few years later, Paxinosa succeeded him as chief of the Shawnees at Wyoming.

Paxinosa Joins in Sale of Lands Between
Susquehanna and Delaware Rivers

As stated in Chapter XII, the Six Nations, on August 22nd, 1749, sold to the Colony of Pennsylvania, a vast tract of land between the Susquehanna and the Delaware, including all or parts of the present counties of Dauphin, Northumberland, Lebanon, Schuylkill, Columbia, Carbon, Luzerne, Monroe, Pike and Wayne. Paxinosa, as chief of the Shawnees at Wyoming, joined in the sale of these lands. The sale was made at Philadelphia.

Paxinosa Befriends Moravians

In the summer of 1754, when most of the Shawnees and Delawares of the valleys of the Ohio and Allegheny began to waver in their allegiance to the English, attempts were made to induce the Christian Delawares at Gnadenhuetten to remove from that place and come nearer the dissatisfied Indians. Paxinosa was one of the chiefs who endeavored to induce the Christian Delawares of Gnadenhuetten to move. At first, he was not friendly toward the Moravian missionaries, but later his wife, for whom he had great affection and to whom he had been married almost forty years, was converted to the Christian faith by the gentle Moravians and baptized by Bishop Spangenberg, with Paxinosa's concent. A deep impression of the truths of the Christian religion was thus made upon the heart of the old chief, causing him to change his attitude toward the Moravians and their converts.

At the time of the Penn's Creek Massacre and the attack upon John Harris and his band, the Moravian missionary, Keifer, was residing at Shamokin and exposed to imminent danger. Paxinosa, who was then at Shamokin, sent two of his sons who rescued the missionary and conducted him safely to Gnadenhuetten.

In the summer of 1757, he greatly befriended the Moravians. A report had been circulated among the hostile Delawares and Shawnees that the Moravian missionaries at Bethlehem were killing the Indian converts there, and sending their heads in bags to Philadelphia. This report greatly excited the Delawares and Shawnees, and they gathered a force of two hundred warriors for the purpose of destroying the Moravians. Paxinosa and Teedyuscung pacified the enraged Delawares and Shawnees, and persuaded them to desist from their design.

Paxinosa Loyally Supports the English

Paxinosa attended the conference which Scarouady held with the Indians at Wyoming on the latter's journey as the messenger of Pennsylvania to the Six Nations, described in Chapter XVI. On this occasion, he spoke boldly in favor of the English, but was silenced by the Delawares, who threatened to knock him on the head if he said anything more. He was also present at the conference which Canachquasy held with the Indians of Tioga, when the latter visited that place as the peace messenger of Pennsylvania shortly after the declaration of war against the Delawares in the spring of 1756. Shortly before this time, he and the Shawnees under his command at their town on the Shawnee Flats, now Plymouth, Luzerne County, had removed, through compulsion of the hostile Delawares, to Tioga. He sat for days meditating on

the waywardness of his people in taking up arms against the sons
of "Brother Onas."

Paxinosa Removes to the Ohio

In April, 1757, Paxinosa was living at Osteningo, now Binghampton, New York; and, in August of that year, he attended the
third conference with Teedyuscung at Easton, more particularly
described in Chapter XXII. In the early part of May, 1758, he
was met by Benjamin, a Mohican Indian, of Bethlehem, near
Tioga, with his entire family. He told Benjamin that he had
heard that the English had very bad designs against the Indians,
and that he therefore was going with his family to the Ohio "where
he was born." Benjamin tried to persuade him not to go, but
without avail. Paxinosa had heard that his hated enemies, the
Cherokees, had been sent for by the English to destroy all the
Indians on the Susquehanna. As a matter of fact, there were a
few Cherokees and Catawbas at that time joining the expedition
of General Forbes against Fort Duquesne. Not only the recently
pacified Eastern Delawares, but also the Iroquois, were becoming
aroused because of the presence of their hated enemies in Forbes'
expedition. Paxinosa told Benjamin that he had recently been
asked to attend a great council at Onondaga, at which it would be
determined whether the Iroquois would side with the English or the
French, but, as he had already resolved to move to the Ohio, he
would not attend the council at Onondaga. The old chief then
went back to the land of his birth.

Final Conferences of Paxinosa

On the 29th of June, 1760, General Monckton arrived at Fort
Pitt for the purpose of taking possession of the posts on the Allegheny, as well as those along the frontier to Detroit, at the close
of the French and Indian War. On August 12th of that year,
Monckton held a great conference at Fort Pitt, with the chiefs of
the Six Nations, Miamis, Delawares, Ottawas, Wyandots, and
Shawnees. General Monckton advised the assembled chiefs that
he had come to take possession of the western region; that he did
not intend to drive the Indians from their lands, nor to take their
lands from them, but he desired to establish once more peaceful
relations between the western tribes and the British Government.
Paxinosa attended this conference.

Not long thereafter, he ended his days on the Scioto Plains in
Ohio.

CHAPTER XVIII.

Captain Jacobs

APTAIN JACOBS was one of the Delaware chiefs who took up arms against Pennsylvania shortly after Braddock's defeat. He had at one time resided near Lewistown, where he sold lands to Colonel Buchanan, who gave him the name of Captain Jacobs, because of his close resemblance to a burly German in Cumberland County. Later he resided at "Jacob's Cabin," not far from Mount Pleasant, Westmoreland County. His principal residence was at the famous Indian town of Kittanning, Armstrong County, which, as we have seen in an earlier chapter, was the first town established by the Delawares on their migration into the Allegheny Valley with the consent of the Iroquois Confederation. From this town, he and that other noted chief, Shingas, led many an expedition against the frontier settlements. For a time, in the autumn of 1755, they made their headquarters at Nescopeck, in Luzerne County, and at that place, also, planned many a bloody expedition.

Captain Jacobs Captures Fort Granville

Reference was made, in Chapter XVI, to the capture of Fort Granville, near Lewistown, Mifflin County, by Captain Jacobs, on August 1, 1756. We quote the following account of this event from the "Frontier Forts of Pennsylvania":

"The attack upon Fort Granville was made in harvest time of the year 1756. The Fort at this time was commanded by Lieut. Armstrong, a brother of Colonel Armstrong, who destroyed Kittanning. The Indians, who had been lurking about this fort for some time, and knowing that Armstrong's men were few in number, sixty of them appeared, July 22nd, before the fort, and challenged the garrison to a fight; but this was declined by the commander in consequence of the weakness of his force. The Indians fired at and wounded one man, who had been a short way from it, yet he got in safe; after which they divided themselves into small parties, one of which attacked the plantation of one Baskins, near the Juniata, whom they murdered, burnt his house and carried off his wife and children. Another made Hugh Carroll and his family prisoners.

"On the 30th of July, 1756, Capt. Edward Ward, the commandant of Granville, marched from the fort with a detachment of men from the garrison, destined for Tuscarora Valley, where they were needed as guard to the settlers while they were engaged in harvesting their grain. The party under Capt. Ward embraced the greater part of the defenders of the fort, under command of Lieut. Edward Armstrong. Soon after the departure of Capt. Ward's detachment, the fort was surrounded by the hostile force of French and Indians, who immediately made an attack, which they continued in their skulking, Indian manner through the afternoon and following night, but without being able to inflict much damage on the whites. Finally, after many hours had been spent in their unsuccessful attacks, the Indians availed themselves of the protection afforded by a deep ravine, up which they passed from the river bank to within twelve or fifteen yards of the fort, and from that secure position, succeeded in setting fire to the logs and burning out a large hole, through which they fired on the defenders, killing the commanding officer, Lieut. Armstrong, and one private soldier and wounding three others.

"They then demanded the surrender of the fort and garrison, promising to spare their lives if the demand was acceded to. Upon this, a man named John Turner, previously a resident in the Buffalo valley, opened the gates and the besiegers at once entered and took possession, capturing as prisoners twenty-two men, three women and a number of children. The fort was burned by the chief, Jacobs, by order of the French officer in command, and the savages then departed, driving before them their prisoners, heavily burdened with the plunder taken from the fort and the settlers' houses, which they had robbed and burned. On their arrival at the Indian rendezvous at Kittanning, all the prisoners were cruelly treated, and Turner, the man who had opened the gate at the fort to the savages, suffered the cruel death by burning at the stake, enduring the most horrible torment that could be inflicted upon him for a period of three hours, during which time red hot gun barrels were forced through parts of his body, his scalp torn from his head and burning splinters were stuck in his flesh, until at last an Indian boy was held up for the purpose who sunk a hatchet in the brain of the victim and so released him from this cruel torture."

Captain Jacobs Killed at the Destruction of Kittanning

Kittanning, in addition to being the center from which Captain Jacobs and Shingas sent their expeditions against the frontier settlements, was the place for the detention of English prisoners. George Croghan reported at the Carlisle Council of January 13, 1756, that he had sent the friendly Indian, Delaware Jo, in December, 1755, to the Ohio for intelligence; and that this friendly Indian had visited Kittanning, where he found more than one hundred English prisoners taken from various parts of Pennsylvania and Virginia. In order, therefore, to break up this harboring place of the Delawares, an expedition was authorized by the representatives of Governor Morris and the Provincial Council, to be conducted by Lieutenant-Colonel John Armstrong, of the Second Battalion of the Pennsylvania Regiment. Colonel Armstrong was a brother of the ill-fated Lieutenant Edward Armstrong, who was killed by Jacobs in the attacks on Fort Granville.

The capture of Fort Granville greatly elated Captain Jacobs. He said: "I can take any fort that will catch fire, and I will make peace with the English when they teach me to make gun powder."

The following description of Colonel Armstrong's march over the mountains to Kittanning and the destruction of that place is quoted from Egle's "History of Pennsylvania":

"On the 20th of August, 1756, William Denny arrived in the Province, superseding Governor Morris. He was hailed with joy by the Assembly, who flattered themselves that, with a change of government, there would be a change of measures. Upon making known the Proprietary instructions, to which he stated he was compelled to adhere, all friendly feeling was at an end, and there was a renewal of the old discord.

"Before Governor Morris was superseded, he concerted with Colonel John Armstrong an expedition against the Indian town of Kittanning, on the Allegheny, the stronghold of Captain Jacobs and Shingas, the most active Indian chiefs, and from whence they distributed their war parties along the frontier. On the arrival of Governor Denny, Morris communicated the plan of his enterprise to him and his Council.

"Colonel Armstrong marched from Fort Shirley [Shirleysburg, Huntingdon County], on the 30th of August, with three hundred men, having with him, besides other officers, Captains Hamilton, Mercer, Ward, and Potter. On the 2nd of September, he joined an advance party at the Beaver dams, near Frankstown. On the 7th, in the evening, within six miles of Kittanning, the scouts discovered a fire in the road, and around it, as they reported, three, or at most, four Indians. It was deemed prudent not to attack this party; but lest some of them should escape and alarm the town, Lieutenant Hogg and twelve men were left to watch them, with orders to fall upon them at day-break. The main body, making a circuit, proceeded to the village. Guided by the whooping of the Indians at a dance, the army approached the place by the river, about one hundred perches below the town, at three o'clock in the morning, near a cornfield, in which a number of the enemy were lodged, out of their cabins, on account of the heat of the weather. As soon as the dawn of day made the town visible, the troops attacked it through the cornfield, killing several of the enemy. Captain Jacobs, their principal chief, sounded the war-whoop, and defended his house bravely through loop-holes in the logs; and the Indians generally refused quarter, which was offered them, declaring that they were men, and would not be prisoners.

"Colonel Armstrong, who had received a musket ball in his shoulder, ordered their houses to be set on fire over their heads. Again the Indians were required to surrender, and again refused, one of them declaring that he did not care for death, as he could kill four or five before he died, and as the heat approached, some of them began to sing. Others burst from their houses, and attempted to reach the river, but were instantly shot down. Captain Jacobs, in getting out of a window, was shot, as also a squaw, and a lad called the king's son. The Indians had a number of small arms in their houses, loaded, which went off in quick succession as the fire came to them; and quantities of gunpowder, which were stored in every house, blew up from time to time, throwing some of the bodies of the enemy a great height in the air. A party of Indians on the opposite side of the river fired on the troops, and were seen to cross the river at a distance, as if to surround them; but they contented themselves with collecting some horses which were near the town to carry off their wounded, and then retreated without attempting to take from the cornfield those who were killed there in the beginning of the action. Several of the enemy were killed in the river as they attempted to escape by fording it, and between thirty and forty, in the whole, were destroyed.

"Eleven English prisoners were released, who informed that, besides the powder, of which the Indians boasted they had enough for ten years' war with the English, there was a great quantity of

goods burned, which the French had presented to them but ten
days before; that two batteaux of French Indians were to join
Captain Jacobs to make an attack upon Fort Shirley, and that
twenty-four warriors had set out before them on the preceding
evening.   These proved to be the party discovered around the fire,
as the troops approached Kittanning.   Pursuant to his orders,
and relying upon the report made by the scouts, Lieutenant Hogg
had attacked them, and killed three at the first fire.   He, however,
found them too strong for his force, and having lost some of his best
men, the others fled, leaving him wounded, overlooked by the
enemy in their pursuit of the fugitives.   He was saved by the
army on their return.   [He afterwards died of his wounds].
Captain, afterwards General, Mercer was wounded in the action
at Kittanning, but was carried off safely by his men.

"The corporation of Philadelphia, on occasion of this victory,
on the 5th of January following, addressed a complimentary letter
to Colonel Armstrong, thanking him and his officers for their
gallant conduct, and presented him with a piece of plate.   A medal
was also struck, having for device an officer followed by two soldiers, the officer pointing to a soldier shooting from behind a tree,
and an Indian postrate before him; in the background Indian
houses in flames.   Legend: Kittanning, destroyed by Colonel
Armstrong, September the 8th, 1756.   Reverse device: The arms of
the corporation.   Legend: The gift of the corporation of Philadelphia.

"The destruction of the town of Kittanning, and the Indian
families there, was a severe stroke on the savages.   Hitherto the
English had not assailed them in their towns, and they fancied
that they would not venture to approach them.   But now, though
urged by an unquenchable thirst of vengeance to retaliate the
blow they had received, they dreaded that, in their absence on war
parties, their wigwams might be reduced to ashes.   Such of them
as belonged to Kittanning, and had escaped the carnage, refused
to settle again on the east of Fort Duquesne, and resolved to place
that fortress and the French garrison between them and the English."

Many blankets were afterwards found on the ground where
Lieutenant Hogg and his party were defeated.   Hence the battle-
field has ever since borne the name of "Blanket Hill."   It is in
Kittanning Township, Armstrong County.

The English prisoners recovered from the Indians at the destruction of Kittanning were:

Ann McCord, wife of John McCord, and Martha Thorn, a child seven years of age, both captured at Fort McCord, on April 1st, 1756; Barbara Hicks, captured at Conolloways; Catherine Smith, a German child captured near Shamokin; Margaret Hood, captured near the mouth of the Conococheague, Maryland; Thomas Girty, captured at Fort Granville; Sarah Kelly, captured near Winchester, Virginia; a woman, a boy, and two little girls, who were with Captain Mercer and Ensign Scott, and had not reached Fort Littleton when Colonel Armstrong made his report.

It will be recalled that among the prisoners captured by the Delawares at the Penn's Creek Massacre of October 16th, 1755, were Barbara Leininger and Marie LeRoy (Mary King). They were carried to Kittanning and were there when Colonel Armstrong made the attack; but in order to prevent their being rescued by Armstrong's forces, they were taken ten miles westward into the wilderness, and thence to Fort Duquesne, where they stayed for two months. They were then taken to Sauconk, at the mouth of the Beaver; and in the spring of 1757, they were carried to Kuskuskies, where they remained until the Indians of that place learned during the next summer that General Forbes was marching on Fort Duquesne. They were then taken to the Muskingum, where they made their escape on March 16, 1759, and reached Fort Pitt on the 31st of that month.

SOME OTHER EVENTS OF THE TERRIBLE YEAR 1756

Massacre at Fort Allen

Reference was made, in Chapter XVI, to the massacre of a number of militia at Fort Allen (Weissport, Carbon County) on New Year's Day, 1756. The Governor had ordered the soldiers to this place to protect the property of those Delawares who had been converted to the Christan religion by the Moravians and to defend the country in general. A temporary stockade had been built, and, on this day, while the soldiers were amusing themselves skating on the Lehigh River, they saw two Indians farther up the stream. They gave chase, but the Indians proved to be decoys, and skillfully maneuvered to draw the soldiers into an ambush. After proceeding some distance, a band of Indians rushed out behind the soldiers, cutting off their retreat, and massacreing almost all. The Indians then fired the stockade and surrounding houses and mills of the Moravians.

On the same day, the Delaware chief, Teedyuscung led a band of about thirty Indians into lower Smithfield Township, Monroe County, destroying the plantation of Henry Hess, killing Nicholas Colman and a laborer named Gotlieb, and capturing Peter Hess and young Henry Hess, son of Peter Hess and nephew of Henry Hess, the owner of the plantation. This attack took place about nine o'clock in the morning. Teedyuscung's band then went over the Blue Mountains and overtook five Indians with two prisoners, Leonard and William Weeser, and a little later killed Peter Hess in the presence of his son.

In a few days the Indians over-ran the country from Fort Allen as far as Nazareth, burning plantations, and killing and scalping settlers. During this same month, the Delawares entered Moore Township, Northampton County, burning the buildings of Christian Miller, Henry Shopp, Henry Diehl, Peter Doll, Nicholas Scholl, and Nicholas Heil, and killing one of Heil's children and John Bauman. The body of Bauman was found two weeks later, and buried in the Moravian cemetery at Nazareth.

Massacre Near Schupp's Mill

On January 15th, some refugees at Bethlehem went out into the country to look after their farms and cattle, among them being Christian Boemper. The party and some friendly Indians who escorted them, were ambushed by hostile Delawares near Schupp's Mill, and all were killed except one named Adam Hold, who was so severely wounded that it was necessary later to amputate his arm. Those killed were Christian Boemper, Felty Hold, Michael Hold, Laurence Knuckel, and four privates of Captain Trump's Company then stationed at Fort Hamilton (Stroudsburg).

At about the same time, a German, named Muhlhisen while breaking flax on the farm of Philip Bossert, in Lower Smithfield Township, Monroe County, was fatally wounded by an unseen Indian. One of Bosserts's sons, hearing the report of the Indian's rifle, ran out of the house and was killed. Then old Philip Bossert, the owner of the farm, appeared on the scene, wounded one of the Indians, and was himself wounded badly. Neighbors then arrived upon the scene, and the Indians retreated.

Massacre of Settlers in the Juniata Valley

On January 27th, a party of Indians from Shamokin made an incursion into the Juniata Valley, attacked the house of Hugh

Mitcheltree, near Thompsontown, Juniata County, killing Mrs.
Mitcheltree and a young man named Edward Nicholas, Mr. Mitcheltree being then absent at Carlisle.   This same party of savages
then went up the Juniata River to the house of Edward Nicholas,
Sr., where they killed Nicholas and his wife, and captured Joseph
Thomas, Catherine Nicholas, John Wilcox, and the wife and two
children of James Armstrong.   While these atrocities were being
committed, an Indian named John Cotties, who had failed in his
effort to be chosen captain of the party, took with him a young
warrior and went to Sherman's Creek, where the two killed William
Sheridan and his entire family, thirteen in all.   Proceeding down
the creek to the home of two old men and an elderly woman
named French, they took the lives of these aged people.   Cotties
made the boast afterwards that he and his young companion had
taken more scalps than all the others of the party.   It will be
noted that these massacres took place within the bounds of the
purchase of 1754, which so angered the Delawares and Shawnees.

Capture of John and Richard Coxe and John Craig

In February, 1756, occurred the capture of John Coxe, his
brother Richard, and John Craig, thus described in the "Frontier
Forts of Pennsylvania":

"At a council, held at Philadelphia, Tuesday, September 6th,
1756, the statement of John Coxe, a son of the widow Coxe, was
made, the substance of which is: He, his brother Richard, and
John Craig were taken in the beginning of February of that year
by nine Delaware Indians from a plantation two miles from Mc-
Dowell's mill, [Franklin County], which was between the east and
west branches of the Cononocheague Creek, about 20 miles west of
the present site of Shippensburg, in what is now Franklin County,
and brought to Kittanning on the Ohio.   On his way hither he
met Shingas with a party of 30 men, and afterward Capt. Jacobs
and 15 men, whose design was to destroy the settlements on
Cononcocheague.   When he arrived at Kittanning, he saw here
about 100 fighting men of the Delaware tribe, with their families,
and about 50 English prisoners, consisting of men, women and children.   During his stay here, Shingas' and Jacobs' parties returned,
the one with nine scalps and ten prisoners, the other with several
scalps and five prisoners.   Another company of 18 came from
Diahogo with 17 scalps on a pole, which they took to Fort Duquesne to obtain their reward.   The warriors held a council,

which, with their war dances, continued a week, when Capt. Jacobs left with 48 men, intending as Coxe was told, to fall upon the inhabitants at Paxtang. He heard the Indians frequently say that they intended to kill all the white folks, except a few, with whom they would afterwards make peace. They made an example of Paul Broadley, who, with their usual cruelty, they beat for half an hour with clubs and tomahawks, and then, having fastened him to a post, cropped his ears close to his head, and chopped off his fingers, calling all the prisoners to witness the horrible scene."

Additional details of the incursion during which the Coxe boys and John Craig were captured are given in Egle's "History of Pennsylvania", as follows:

"In February, 1756, a party of Indians made marauding incursions into Peters Township. They were discovered on Sunday evening, by one Alexander, near the house of Thomas Barr. He was pursued by the savages, but escaped and alarmed the fort at McDowell's mill. Early on Monday morning a party of fourteen men of Captain Croghan's company, who were at the mill, and about twelve other young men, set off to watch the motion of the Indians. Near Barr's house they fell in with fifty, and sent back for a reinforcement from the fort. The young lads proceeded by a circuit to take the enemy in the rear, whilst the soldiers did attack them in front. But the impetuosity of the soldiers defeated their plan. Scarce had they got within gunshot, they fired upon the Indians, who were standing around the fire, and killed several of them at the first discharge. The Indians returned fire, killed one of the soldiers, and compelled the rest to retreat. The party of young men, hearing the report of firearms, hastened up; finding the Indians on the ground which the soldiers had occupied, fired upon the Indians with effect; but concluding the soldiers had fled, or were slain, they also retreated. One of their number, Barr's son, was wounded, would have fallen by the tomahawk of an Indian, had not the savage been killed by a shot from Armstrong, who saw him running upon the lad. Soon after soldiers and young men being joined by a reinforcement from the mill, again sought the enemy, who, eluding the pursuit, crossed the creek near William Clark's, and attempted to surprise the fort; but their design was discovered by two Dutch lads, coming from foddering their master's cattle. One of the lads was killed, but the other reached the fort, which was immediately surrounded by the Indians, who, from a thicket, fired many shots at the men in the garrison, who appeared above the wall, and returned the fire as often as they obtained sight of the enemy. At this time, two men crossing to the mill, fell into the middle of the assailants, but made their escape to the fort, though fired at three times. The party at Barr's house now came up, and drove the Indians through the thicket. In their retreat they met five men from Mr. Hoop's, riding to the mill; they killed one of these and wounded another severely. The sergeant at the fort having lost two of his men, declined to follow the enemy until his commander, Mr. Crawford, who was at Hoop's, should return, and the snow falling thick, the Indians had time to burn Mr. Barr's house, and in it consumed their dead. On the morning of the 2nd of March, Mr. Crawford, with fifty men, went in quest of the enemy, but was unsuccessful in his search."

Attack on Andrew Lycans and John Rewalt

On March 7th, Andrew Lycans and John Rewalt, settlers in the Wiconisco, or Lykens Valley in Dauphin County, went out early in the morning to feed their cattle when they were fired upon by savages. Hastening into the house, they prepared to defend themselves. The Indians concealed themselves behind a pig-pen some distance from the dwelling. Lycans' son, John, John Rewalt, and Ludwig Shutt, a neighbor, upon creeping out of the house, in an effort to discover the whereabouts of the Indians, were fired upon and each one wounded, Shutt very dangerously. At this point Andrew Lycans discovered an Indian named Joshua James and two white men running away from their hiding place near the pig-pen. The elder Lycans then fired, killing the Indian; and he and his party then sought safety in flight, but were closely pursued by at least twenty of the Indians. John Lycans and John Rewalt, although badly wounded, made their escape with the aid of a negro servant, leaving Andrew Lycans, Ludwig Shutt, and a boy to engage the Indians. The Indians then rushed upon these and, as one of their number, named Bill Davis, was in the act of striking the boy with his tomahawk, he was shot dead by Shutt, while Andrew Lycans killed another and wounded a third. Andrew Lycans also recognized two others of the band, namely, Tom Hickman and Tom Hays, members of the Delaware tribe. The Indians then momentarily ceased their pursuit, and Lycans, Shutt, and the boy, weak from the loss of blood, sat down on a log to rest, believing that they were no longer in imminent danger. Later, Lycans managed to lead his party to a place of concealment and then over the mountain into Hanover Township, where they were given assistance by settlers. Andrew Lycans, however, died from his wounds and terrible exposure. His name has been given to the charming valley of the Wiconisco.

Attack on Zeislof and Kluck Families

On March 24th, some settlers with ten wagons went to Albany, Berks County, for the purpose of bringing a family with their effects to a point near Reading. As they were returning, they were fired upon by a number of Indians on both sides of the road. The wagoners, leaving the wagons, ran into the woods, and the horses, frightened at the terrible yelling of the Indians, ran off. The Indians on this occasion, killed George Zeislof and his wife, a boy aged twenty, another aged twelve, and a girl aged fourteen. Another girl of the party was shot through the neck and mouth, and scalped, but made her escape.

On the same day the Indians burned the home of Peter Kluck, about fourteen miles from Reading, and killed the entire family. While the Kluck home was burning, the Indians assaulted the house of a settler named Lindenman nearby, in which there were two men and a woman, all of whom ran upstairs, where the woman was killed by a bullet which penetrated the roof. The men then ran out of the house. Lindenman was shot through the neck. In spite of his wound, Lindenman succeeded in shooting one of the Indians.

At about the same time a boy named John Schoep, who lived in this neighborhood, was captured and taken seven miles beyond the Blue Mountains where, according to the statement of Schoep, the Indians kindled a fire, tied him to a tree, took off his shoes, and put moccasins on his feet. They then prepared themselves some mush, but gave him none. After supper they took young Schoep and another boy between them, and proceeded over the second mountain. During the second night of his captivity, when the Indians were asleep, young Schoep made his escape, and returned home.

During the raid in which the above outrages occurred, the Indians killed the wife of Baltser Neytong, and captured his son aged eight. And in November, the Indians entered this region, and carried off the wife and three children of Adam Burns, the youngest child being only four weeks old. They also killed a man named Stonebrook, and captured a girl in this raid.

Shingas Captures Fort McCord

On April 1st, 1756, Shingas attacked and burned Fort Mc-Cord, a private fort located several miles northwest of Fort Loudon, Franklin County, and all the inmates, twenty-seven in number, were either killed or carried into captivity. At the time of the capture of the fort, Dr. Jamison was killed near that place; and at about the same time, a number of persons, employed by William Mitchell to harvest his crops, were likewise killed or captured in the field while at work. After the destruction of the fort, Shingas' band was pursued by three parties of settlers. The third party overtook them at Sidling Hill, where a brisk engagement took place for two hours, but Shingas being reinforced, the settlers retreated. Hance Hamilton, in a letter written to Captain Potter, dated Fort Lyttleton, April 4th, 1756, at eight o'clock in the evening, describes this engagement:

"These come to inform you of the melancholy news of what occurred between the Indians, that have taken many captives from McCord's Fort and a party of men under the command of Captain Alexander Culbertson and nineteen of our men, the whole amounting to about fifty, with the captives, and had a sore engagement, many of both parties killed and many wounded, the number unknown. Those wounded want a surgeon, and those killed require your assistance as soon as possible, to bury them. We have sent an express to Fort Shirley for Doctor Mercer, supposing Doctor Jamison is killed or mortally wounded in the expedition. He being not returned, therefore, desire you will send an express, immediately, for Doctor Prentic to Carlisle; we imagining Doctor Mercer cannot leave the fort under the circumstances the fort is under."

Likewise, Robert Robinson thus describes the attack on McCord's Fort and the pursuit of the savages:

"In the year 1756 a party of Indians came out of the Conococheague to a garrison named McCord's Fort, where they killed some and took a number prisoners. They then took their course near to Fort Lyttleton. Captain Hamilton being stationed there with a company, hearing of their route at McCord's Fort, marched with his company of men, having an Indian with him who was under pay. The Indians had McCord's wife with them; they cut off Mr. James Blair's head and threw it into Mrs. McCord's lap, saying that it was her husband's head; but she knew it to be Blair's."

As related earlier in this chapter, Mrs. McCord was taken to

Kittanning, where she was recaptured by Colonel Armstrong when he destroyed that Indian town on September 8, 1756.

An appropriate monument now marks the site of Fort Mc-Cord.

Attack on Wuench and Dieppel Families

On June 8th, a band of Indians crept up on Felix Wuench as he was ploughing on his farm near Swatara Gap, and shot him through the breast. The poor man cried lamentably and started to run, defending himself with a whip; but the Indians overtook him, tomahawked and scalped him. His wife, hearing his cries and the report of the guns, ran out of the house, but was captured with one of her own and two of her sister's children. A servant boy who saw this atrocity ran to a neighbor named George Miess, who, though he had a crippled leg, ran directly after the Indians and made such a noise as to scare them off.

On June 24th, Indians attacked the home of Lawrence Dieppel, in Bethel Township, Berks County, carrying off two of the children, one of whom they later killed and scalped.

Attack on Bingham's Fort

On June 12th occurred the attack on Bingham's Fort, located in the Tuscarawa Valley, in Tuscarawa Township, Juniata County. The Delaware chief, King Beaver, was the leader of the Indians on this occasion. On that day, as John Gray and Francis Innis were returning from Carlisle, where they had gone for salt, Gray's horse scared at a bear, threw him off, and ran away. While he was catching his horse and gathering up his pack of salt, Innis pressed on rapidly toward the fort, where his wife and three children, George Woods, Mrs. John Gray and her little daughter, Jane, and others, were carried off by King Beaver of the Turkey Tribe of Delawares. The Pennsylvania Gazette gave the following account of the capture of this fort: "George Woods, Nathaniel Bingham, Robert Taylor, his wife and children, and John McDonell, were missing. Some of these it was supposed were burnt as a number of bones were found. Susan Jiles was found dead and scalped; Alexander McAlister and wife, James Adams, Jane Cochran and two children were missed. McAlister's house had been burned, and a number of cattle and horses had been driven off."

All the prisoners taken at Bingham's Fort were marched to Kittanning and from there to Fort Duquesne, where they were parceled out and adopted by the Indians. George Woods, one of the prisoners, was a very remarkable man. The French commander gave him to an old Indian named John Hutson, who removed him to his own wigwam. Woods later purchased his own ransom, and returned to the settlements. He was a surveyor, and followed this business in the counties of Juniata, Bedford, and Allegheny. When Pittsburgh was laid out, in 1765, he assisted in this work, and one of its principal streets, Wood Street, is named after him.

Capture of John McCullough

On July 26th the Indians entered the valley of the Conococheague, in Franklin County, killing Joseph Martin, and taking captive two brothers, John and James McCullough. James McCullough, the father of these boys, had only a few years before removed from Delaware into what is now Montgomery Township, Franklin County. At the time of this Indian incursion, the McCullough family were residing temporarily in a cabin three miles from their home, and the parents and their daughter, Mary, on the day of the capture, went home to pull flax. A neighbor, named John Allen, who had business at Fort Loudon, accompanied them to their home, and promised to return that way in the evening, and accompany them back to their cabin. However, he did not keep his promise, and returned by a circuitous route. When he reached the McCullough cabin on his return, he told John and James to hide, that Indians were near and that he supposed they had killed Mr. and Mrs. McCullough. John was but eight years old, and James but five at the time. They alarmed their neighbors, but none would volunteer to go to the McCullough home to warn Mr. and Mrs. McCollough, being too much interested in making preparations to hurry to the fort a mile distant for safety.

Then the boys determined to warn their parents themselves. Leaving their little sister, Elizabeth, aged two, asleep in bed, they proceeded to a point where they could see the McCullough home, and began to shout. When they had reached a point about sixty yards from the house, five Indians and a Frenchman, who had been secreted in the thicket, rushed upon them and took them captive. The parents were not captured, inasmuch as the father, hearing the boys shout, had left his work and thus the Indians missed him, and they failed to notice the mother and Mary at work in the field.

John and James were taken to Fort Duquesne. From this place James was carried to Canada, and all trace of him became lost. John was taken to Kittanning, Kuskuskies, and the Musk-ingum, was adopted by the Delawares, and remained among them for nine years until liberated by Colonel Bouquet in the autumn of 1764. At one time his father came to Venango (Franklin) to liberate him, but the boy had been so long among the Indians that he preferred the Indian life to returning with his father, and succeeded in eluding him. After his liberation by Colonel Bouquet, he returned to the community from which he had been taken nine years before, and lived there nearly sixty years. He wrote a most interesting account of his captivity, which sheds much light on the manners and customs of the Delawares at that time.

During the same month (July), Hugh Robinson was captured and his mother killed at Robinson's Fort, in Perry County. Hugh, after being carried to the western part of the state, made his escape. Also, during this same month a number of Indians appeared near Fort Robinson, killed the daughter of Robert Miller, the wife of James Wilson, and a Mrs. Gibson, and captured Hugh Gibson and Betty Henry.

Also, during July, Samuel Miles and Lieutenant Atlee were ambushed by three Indians near a spring about half a mile from Fort Augusta, at Sunbury. A soldier named Bullock, who had come to the spring for a drink, was killed. Miles and Atlee made their escape. A rescuing party came out from the fort, and found the soldier scalped, with his blood trickling into the spring, giving its waters a crimson hue. The spring was ever afterwards called the Bloody Spring.

Massacre Near Brown's Fort

On August 6th, a soldier named Jacob Ellis, of Brown's Fort, about two miles north of Grantville, Dauphin County, desired to cut some wheat on his farm a few miles from the fort, and, accordingly, took with him a squad of about ten soldiers as a guard. At about ten o'clock a band of Indians crept up on the reapers, shot the corporal dead, and wounded another of the soldiers. A little after this attack, a soldier named Brown was found missing, and the next morning his body was found near the harvest field. On October 12th, the Indians made an incursion into this same neighborhood, killing Noah Frederick who was ploughing his field, and capturing three children that were with him. A little later, Peter Stample and Frederick Henley were killed in the same neighborhood.

Conococheague Valley Again Invaded

On August 27th, another incursion was made into the beautiful valley of the Conococheague, resulting in the slaying of thirty-nine settlers near the mouth of this stream. Also, early in November, some soldiers of the garrison at Fort McDowell, in the western part of Franklin County, where McDowell's Mill now stands, were ambushed, Privates James McDonald, William McDonald, Bartholomew McCafferty, and Andrew McQuoid being killed and scalped, and Captain James Corkin and Private William Cornwall carried into captivity. At the same time, the following settlers in the neighborhood were killed: John Culbertson, Samuel Perry, Hugh Kerrel, John Woods and his mother-in-law, and Elizabeth Archer; also four children of John Archer, and two boys named Sam Neily and James Boyd, were carried into captivity.

Attack on the Boyer Family

Sometime during the summer of 1756, though authorities differ as to the exact date, occurred the attack on the Boyer family, who lived in the vicinity of Fort Lehigh, at Lehigh Gap. The "Frontier Forts of Pennsylvania" thus describes this event:

"His [Boyer's] place was about 1½ miles east of the Fort, on land now owned by Josiah Arner, James Ziegenfuss and George Kunkle. With the other farmers he had gathered his family into the blockhouse for protection. One day, however, with his son Frederick, then thirteen years old, and the other children, he went home to attend to the crops. Mr. Boyer was ploughing and Fred was hoeing, whilst the rest of the children were in the house or playing near by. Without any warning they were surprised by the appearance of Indians. Mr. Boyer, seeing them, called to Fred to run, and himself endeavored to reach the house. Finding he could not do so, he ran towards the creek, and was shot through the head as he reached the farther side. Fred, who had escaped to the wheat field, was captured and brought back. The Indians, having scalped the father in his presence, took the horses from the plough, his sisters and himself, and started for Stone Hill, in the rear of the house. There they were joined by another party of Indians and marched northward to Canada. On the march the sisters were separated from their brother and never afterwards heard from. Frederick was a prisoner with the French and Indians in Canada for five years, and was then sent to Philadelphia. Of Mrs. Boyer, who remained in the blockhouse, nothing further is known. After reaching Philadelphia, Frederick made his way to Lehigh Gap, and took possession of the farm. Shortly after he married a daughter of Conrad Mehrkem, with whom he had four sons and four daughters. He died October 31, 1832, aged 89 years."

Expedition Against Great Island and Other Indian Strongholds

During the summer of 1756, Fort Augusta was built and garrisoned at Sunbury. The Delawares and Shawnees in the valley of the West Branch of the Susquehanna were committing so many atrocities that Colonel William Clapham, commander of the fort, sent an expedition against the Indian towns on the Juniata, Chincklamoose (Clearfield, Clearfield County), Great Island (Lock Haven, Clinton County), and other places on both branches of the Susquehanna. During October, Colonel Clapham received the intelligence that the Indians at Great Island were making incursions against the settlements. He then directed Captain John Hambright, of Lancaster, to lead a company of thirty-eight men, and destroy that Indian stronghold. There is no doubt that Captain Hambright carried out his instructions, but, unhappily, no records giving the details of his expedition are to be found. In this connection, we state that Colonel Clapham was one of the most conspicuous figures on the frontier. In the early spring of 1763, he removed with his family to Sewickley Creek, where the town of West Newton, Westmoreland County, now stands. Here he and his entire family were cruelly murdered on the afternoon of May 8, 1763, by The Wolf, Kekuscung, and two other Indians, one of whom was called Butler.

Attack on a Friendly Delaware

This chapter has been devoted largely to a recital of atrocities committed by the Indians during the French and Indian War, —atrocities that make our flesh creep and cause chills to run down our pulses. Yet this history would be incomplete and unfair if we neglected to say that the white men were not always fair and honorable, on their part. The following instance of an attack on a friendly Delaware who had been converted to Christianity by the Moravian missionaries was reported to Governor Denny by Timothy Horsefield, in a letter dated November 29th, 1756:

"I beg leave to mention to your Honour, that a few Days Since as one of our Indians was in the Woods a Small distance from Bethlehem, with his Gun, hoping to meet with a Deer, on his return home he met with two men, who (as he Informs) he Saluted by taking off his Hat; he had not gone far before he heard a gun fired, and the Bullet whistled near him, which terefied him very much, and running thro' the thick Bushes, his gun lock Catched fast, and went off; he dropt it, his Hat, Blanket, &c., and came home much frightened. The Indians came to me complaining of this Treatment, Saying they fled from amongst the Murthering Indians, and come here to Bethlehem, and Adresst his Honour the Late Governor, and put themselves under His protection, which the Governor Answered to their Satisfaction, Desireing them to Sit Still amongst the Brethren, which they said they had done, and given offence to none. I told them I would do all in my Power to prevent such Treatment for the future, and that I would write to the Governor and inform him of it, and that they might be Assured the Governor would use proper measures to prevent any mischief happening. I thought at first to write a few Advertisements to warn wicked People for the future how they Behave to the Indians, for if one or more of them should be kill'd in such a manner, I fear it would be of very bad consequence; but I have since considered it is by no means proper for me to advertise, for as the Late Governor's proclamation is Expired, the first Proclamation of War against the Indians I conceive is still in force. I thought it my Duty to Inform your Honor of this Affair, and Doubt not you will take the matter into your wise Consideration."

CHAPTER XIX.

Shingas, King Beaver and Pisquetomen

SHINGAS

SHINGAS (Chingas, Shingiss, etc.) was a noted chief of the Turkey Clan of Delawares, a brother of King Beaver and Pisquetomen. By many authorities he is believed to have been a nephew of the great Sassoonan. He was a very cruel warrior. Heckewelder says of him: "Were his war exploits all on record, they would form an interesting document, though a shocking one. Conococheague, Big Cove, Sherman's Valley, and other settlements along the frontier, felt his strong arm sufficiently that he was a bloody warrior, cruel his treatment, relentless his fury. His person was small, but in point of courage and activity, savage prowess, he was said to have never been exceeded by anyone."

Shingas Made King of the Delawares

Shingas did not come into the kingship of the Delawares until 1752, on which date, at the Virginia treaty at Logstown, he was made head chief of the Delawares by Tanacharison as representative of the Six Nations. The Journal of the Virginia Commissioners to this treaty, under date of June 11th, describes his coronation as follows: "Afterwards the Half King [Tanacharison] spoke to the Delawares: 'Nephews, you received a speech last year from your brother, the Governor of Pennsylvania and from us, desiring you to choose one of the wisest councellors, and present him to us for a King. As you have not done it, we let you know it is our right to give you a King, and we think proper to give you Shingas for your King, whom you must look upon as your head chief, and with whom all public business must be transacted between you and your brethren, the English. On which the Half King put a laced hat on the head of The Beaver, who stood proxy for his brother, Shingas, and presented him with a rich jacket and a suit of English clothes, which had been delivered to the Half King by the Commissioners for that purpose.'"

Attention is called to the fact that, while Shingas is called "King" of the Delawares, it is hardly likely that either he or his brother, Beaver, who upon his death or abdication, became "King" could have been the leading chief of this tribe as they belonged to the Turkey Clan.   According to immemorial custom the "King" of the three Delaware Clans had to be a member of the Turtle Clan, as were Tamanend and Sassoonan.

As has been seen in earlier chapters, a treaty between Pennsylvania and the Delawares, Shawnees and other Indians of the valleys of the Ohio and Allegheny, was held at Carlisle in October, 1753.   Shingas was present at this treaty, as was also his brother, Pisquomen, representing the Delawares.

Washington Meets Shingas

When George Washington made his journey to the French forts in November, 1753, he found Shingas living where the town of McKees Rocks, Allegheny County, now stands.   We read the following in Washington's Journal: "About two miles from this [the Forks of the Ohio], on the Southeast side of the River at a place where the Ohio Company intended to erect a fort, lives Shingas, King of the Delawares.   We called upon him to invite him to council at the Logs Town.   Shingas attended us to the Logs Town, where we arrived between sun setting and dark on the 25th day after I left Williamsburg."

Shingas took part in the conferences which Washington held with the Indians of Logstown before setting forth from that place to Venango and Le Boueff.

Croghan and Montour Meet Shingas at Logstown

When George Croghan and Andrew Montour were at Logstown in January and February, 1754, Shingas was one of the chiefs with whom they had conferences.   On this occasion, Shingas joined with Scarouady, Delaware George, and several other chiefs on the Ohio, in requesting that the Governor of Virginia might build a "strong house" at the Forks of the Ohio and that the Governor of Pennsylvania might build "another house" somewhere on the Ohio.   Just before these Pennsylvania messengers left Logstown (February 2nd), Shingas delivered to them the following speech:

"Brother Onas: I am glad to hear all our people here are of one mind.   It is true I live on the river side, which is the French road, and I assure you by these strings of wampum [gave them strings of wampum] that I will neither go down or up, but will remove nearer to my brethren, the English, where I can keep our women and children safe from the enemy."

This promise Shingas did not keep, but deserted to the French. We have seen, in Chapter XVIII, that, at Kittanning, on the Allegheny, and at Nescopeck, on the North Branch of the Susquehanna, he and Captain Jacobs planned many bloody expeditions which they made against the frontier settlements after Braddock's defeat. He spent much of his time, during the French and Indian War, inciting the Indians of Kittanning, Kuskuskies, Logstown, and Sauconk against the English. The latter town, at the mouth of the Beaver, is sometimes called Shingas' Old Town.

Shingas Ravages the Frontier

As stated in Chapter XVI, on October 31st, 1755, Shingas began incursions into Fulton County, which lasted for several days, and were the beginning of those incursions which made his name "a terror to the frontier settlements of Pennsylvania." The following letters describe these initial incursions:

Adam Hoops wrote Governor Morris from Conococheague November 3rd:

"I am sorry I have to trouble you with this melancholy and disagreeable news, for on Saturday I received an express from Peters Township that the inhabitants of the Great Cove were all murdered or taken captive, and their houses and barns all in flames. Some few fled, upon notice brought them by a certain Patrick Burns, a captive, that made his escape that very morning before this sad tragedy was done.

"Upon this information, John Potter, Esq., and self, sent express through our neighborhood, which induced many of them to meet with us at John McDowell's Mill, where I with many others had the unhappy prospect to see the smoke of two houses that were set on fire by the Indians, viz, Matthew Patton's and Mescheck James', where their cattle were shot down, the horses standing bleeding with Indian arrows in them, but the Indians fled.

"The Rev. Mr. Steel, John Potter, Esq., and several others with us, to the number of about an hundred, went in quest of the Indians, with all the expedition imaginable, but to no success. These Indians have likewise taken two women capitves, belonging to said township. I very much fear the Path Valley has undergone the same fate.

"We, to be sure, are in as bad circumstances as ever any poor Christians were in, for the cries of the widowers, widows, fatherless and motherless children, with many others, for their relations, are enough to pierce the hardest of hearts; likewise it's a very sorrowful spectacle to see those that escaped with their lives with not a mouthful to eat, or bed to lie on, or clothes to cover their nakedness, or keep them warm, but all they had consumed into ashes.

"These deplorable circumstances cry aloud for your Honour's most wise consideration, that you would take cognizance of and grant what shall seem most meet, for it is really very shocking, it must be, for the husband to see the wife of his bosom, her head cut off, and the children's blood drank like water by these bloody and cruel savages as we are informed has been the fate of many."

On the same day, John Potter, Sheriff of Cumberland County, wrote Richard Peters:

"Sir: This comes ye melancholy account of the ruin of the Great Cove, which is reduced to ashes, and numbers of the inhabitants murdered and taken captives on Saturday last about three of the clock in the afternoon. I received intelligence in conjunction with Mr. Adam Hoopes, and sent immediately and appointed our neighbors to meet at McDowell's. On Sunday morning, I was not there six minutes till we observed, about a mile and half distant, one, Matthew Patton's house and barn in flames, on which we sat off with about forty men, tho' there was at least one hundred and sixty there. Our old officers hid themselves for (ought as I know) to save their scalps until afternoon when danger was over; we went to Patton's with a seeming resolution and courage but found no Indians there, on which we advanced to a rising ground, where we immediately discovered another house and barn on fire belonging to Mesach James, about one mile up the creek from Thomas Bar's; we set off directly for that place, but they had gone up the creek to another plantation left by one widow Jordan the day before, but had unhappily gone back that morning with a young woman, daughter to one William Clark, for some milk for childer, were both taken captives but neither house nor barn hurt. I have heard of no more burnt in that valley yet, which makes me believe they have gone off for some time, but I much fear they will return before we are prepared for them, for it was three of the clock in the afternoon before a recruit came of about sixty men. Then we held council whether to pursue up the valley all night or return to McDowell's, the former of which I and Mr. Hoop and some others plead for, but could not obtain without putting it to votes, which done, we were out voted by a considerable number, upon which I and my company was left by them that night and came home, for I will not guard a man that will not fight when called in so eminent manner, for there was not six of these men that would consent to go in pursuit of the Indians.

"I am much afraid that Juniata, Tuscaroro, and Sherman's Valley hath suffered. There is two-thirds of the inhabitants of this valley who hath already fled, leaving their plantations, and, without speedy succor be granted, I am of opinion this county will be lead dissolute without inhabitant. Last night I had a family of upwards of an hundred of women and children who fled for succor. You cannot form no just idea of the distressed and distracted condition of our inhabitants unless your eyes seen and your ears heard their crys. I am of opinion it is not in the power of our representatives to meet in assembly at this time. If our Assembly will give us any additional supply of arms and ammunition, the latter of which is most wanted, I could wish it were put into the hands of such persons as would go out upon scouts after the Indians rather than for the supply of forts."

Benjamin Chambers, on November 2nd, wrote the following "to the inhabitants of the lower part of the County of Cumberland":

"If you intend to go to the assistance of your neighbours, you need wait any longer for the certainty of the news. The Great Cove is destroyed; James Campbell left this company last night and went to the fort at Mr. Steel's meeting house, and there saw some of the inhabitants of the Great Cove, who gave this account that, as they came over the hill, they saw their houses in flames. The messenger says that there is but 100, and that they divided into two parts. The one part to go against the Cove and the other against the Conolloways, and that there are no French among them. They are Delawares and Shawnees. The part that came against the Cove are under the command of Shingas, the Delaware King; the people of the Cove that came off saw several men lying dead; they heard the murder shout and the firing of guns, and saw the Indians going into the houses that they had come out of before they left sight of the Cove. I have sent express to Marsh Creek at the same time that I send this, so I expect there will be a good company from there this day, and as there is but 100 of the enemy, I think it is in our power (if God permit) to put them to flight, if you turn out well from your parts. I understand that the west settlement is designed to go if they can get any assistance to repel them."

Likewise, John Armstrong wrote Governor Morris from Carlisle, on November 2nd:

"At four o'clock this afternoon by expresses from Conegochego, we are informed that yesterday about 100 Indians were seen in the Great Cove. Among whom was Shingas, the Delaware King; that immediately after the discovery, as many as had notice fled, and looking back from an high hill, they beheld their houses on fire, heard several guns fired and the last shrieks of their dying neighbours; 'tis said the enemy divided and one part moved towards Canallowais. Mr. Hamilton was here with 60 men from York County when the express came, and is to march early tomorrow to the upper part of the county. We have sent out expresses everywhere, and intend to collect the forces of this lower part, expecting the enemy every moment at Sherman's Valley, if not nearer hand. I'm of opinion that no other means than a chain of block houses along or near the south side of the Kittatinny Mountain, from Susquehannah to the temporary line, can secure the lives and properties even of the old inhabitants of this county, the new settlement being all fled except Sherman's Valley, whom (if God do not preserve) we fear will suffer very soon."

Sherman's Valley and numerous other frontier settlements were desolated by this scourge of the frontier. Finally, Governor Denny, in 1756, set a price of two hundred pounds upon Shingas' head, but unhappily he was not killed or captured.

Capture of the Martin and Knox Families

Among the outrages committed by Shingas during the above incursion into Fulton County, was the capture of the family of John Martin, a settler in the Big Cove. On Saturday morning, November 1, 1755, Mrs. Martin learned that Indians were in the neighborhood, and, thereupon, sent her son, Hugh, aged seventeen, to their neighbor, Captain Stewart, requesting him to come and take her family with his to the block-house, as her husband, John Martin, had gone to Philadelphia for supplies for the family, and had not returned. When Hugh came in sight of his home on his way back from Captain Stewart's, whose house was burned, he saw the Indians capture his mother; his sister, Mary, aged nineteen; his sister, Martha, aged twelve; his sister, Janet, aged two; his brother, James, aged ten; and his brother, William, aged eight.

Hugh hid where a fallen tree lay on the bank of Cove Creek not far from the Martin house, which the Indians now burned to the ground.

After the Indians left, Hugh started toward Philadelphia to meet his father. All that day he found nothing but desolation, and in the evening, he came to a stable with some hay in it. Here he lay until morning. During the night something jumped on him, which proved to be a dog. In the morning he found some fresh eggs in the stable, which he ate. When he was ready to leave, a large colt came to the stable. Making a halter of rope, he mounted the colt and rode on his way. In the afternoon, he met some men who had gathered to pursue the Indians, among them being the owner of the colt, who was much surprised to find it so easily managed, as it was considered unruly. It is not known when Hugh met his father, but, at any rate, they returned and rebuilt the house.

Mrs. Martin and her children were taken to the Indian town of Kittanning. A warrior wished to marry Mary, which made the squaws jealous and they beat her dreadfully, so much so that her health rapidly declined, and one morning she was found on her knees dead in the wigwam. An Indian squaw claimed little Janet, and tied her to a rope fastened to a post. While she was thus confined, a French trader named Baubee came to the child, and she reached out her arms and called him father. He then took her in his arms, and the Indian woman who claimed her sold her to the trader for a blanket, who carried her to Quebec intending to adopt her. Later, Mrs. Martin was bought by the French, and also taken to Quebec, not knowing her child was there. Still later, Mrs. Martin bought her own freedom, and one day she found little Janet on the streets of Quebec. Janet was well dressed and had all appearances of being well cared for, but did not recognize the mother. Mrs. Martin followed Janet to the home of the French family who had her, identified her by some mark, and the family reluctantly gave up the child to the mother, who paid them what they had paid the Indians for her.

Mrs. Martin then sailed with Janet to Liverpool, England, from which place she took ship to Philadelphia, and joined her husband.

The boys, James and William, and the daughter, Martha, were taken to the Tuscarawas and Musknigum, in the state of Ohio. After Mrs. Martin and Janet returned to their home in the Big Cove, Mr. Martin, upon the close of the French and Indian War, endeavored to recover his child from the Indians. Traveling on horseback to the Ligonier Valley, he found an encampment of Indians, and tried to make arrangements with them for the return of his children, when they claimed to have raised his family and wanted pay. Being unable to pay them, he said something about not having employed them to raise his family; thereupon, they became angry, and he made his escape as fast as he could, being chased by two Indians on horseback to a point on the Allegheny Mountain, where the sound of the bells of the Indian horses ceased.

Mr. Martin eventually recovered his children when ten Shawnee chiefs, with about fifty of their warriors, together with a large body of Delawares, delivered to George Croghan, then deputy agent of Sir William Johnson, at Fort Pitt, on May 9th, 1765, the remainder of their prisoners that had not been delivered to Colonel Henry Bouquet when the latter made his expedition to the Muskingum, in the autumn of 1764, for the purpose of recovering the prisoners taken by the Indians during the French and Indian and the Pontiac-Guyasuta Wars,—just nine years and six months after their capture. Martha could read when captured, but during her captivity, she had forgotten this art. William and James, during their captivity, assisted the squaws in raising vegetables, caring for the children and old people, and grew up as Indians, in contrast to their brother, Hugh, who had escaped capture and became a man of considerable influence on the Pennsylvania frontier. Before being taken to the Muskingum, Martha, James, and William spent some time with their Indian captors on Big Sewickley Creek, in Westmoreland County. The boys became attached to the locality, and after their return, they patented two tracts of land in that vicinity, and lived there most of their lives.

Janet Martin, in 1774, married John Jamison. She has many descendants in Western Pennsylvania, especially in Westmoreland County, among them being the well-known Robert S. Jamison family, of Greensburg.

During the same incursion, occurred the capture of the Knox family, who lived some distance from the Big Cove. On Sunday morning, November 2nd, 1755, while the family were engaged in morning worship, they were alarmed by the barking of their dogs. Then, two men of their acquaintance, who had come to the Knox home on Saturday evening for the purpose of attending religious services the next day, went to the door. They were immediately shot down by the Indians, and the rest of the family taken prison-

ers. After the Indians returned to the town from which they had
come, no doubt Kittanning, each warrior who had lost a brother
in the incursion was given a prisoner to kill. As there were not
enough men to go around, little Jane Knox was given to one of the
warriors as his victim. Placing her at the root of a tree, this savage commenced throwing his tomahawk close to her head, exclaiming that his brother, who was killed, was a warrior, and that
the other Indians had given him only a squaw to kill. Jane expected that every moment would be her last. Presently, an Indian
squaw came running and claimed Jane as her child, thus saving
her life. She later returned to the settlements, and became the
wife of Hugh Martin, mentioned above. Later Hugh Martin was
one of the commissioners who located the first court house in
Greensburg.

Shingas Burns Fort McCord

In the spring of 1756, Shingas again scourged the Pennsylvania frontier. His principal act in the incursions of this spring
was the capture and burning of Fort McCord, in Franklin County,
on April 1st. This atrocity was described in Chapter XVIII, and
needs no further reference here.

Post Meets Shingas on Peace Mission
To Western Indians

When the Moravian missionary, Christian Frederick Post, as
the agent of Pennsylvania, made his two journeys to the Ohio and
Allegheny in the summer of 1758, he met and conferred with
Shingas. During this summer Shingas was located most of the
time at Kuskuskies, Logstown, and Sauconk, but shortly prior
thereto had been residing, for a time, on the Muskingum in Ohio.
The object of Post's mission was to make peace with the Western
Indians. The neutrality of the Delawares on the Susquehanna had
already been secured by treaties with Teedyuscung, an account of
which will be given in the chapters on Teedyuscung (Chapters
XXI and XXII), and now the problem was to secure the neutrality
of the Delawares and Shawnees of the valleys of the Ohio and
Allegheny.

It is doubtful whether any more suitable person could have
been found in all the colonies for carrying the peace proposal to
the Western Delawares than Christian Frederick Post. Born in
Germany, he came to America and labored as a Moravian missionary among the Delawares. For a time he was located at Wyoming.

The Delawares loved and trusted him. For years he had lived among them in all the intimacy of friends and companions. His first wife was Rachael, an Indian convert, whom he married in 1743, and who died at the Moravian mission at Bethlehem in 1747 In 1749, he chose as his second wife, Agnes, a dusky daughter of the Delawares, who was baptized by Bishop Cammerhof March 5, 1749, and who died at Bethlehem in 1751. So that the Delawares, in dealing with Post, looked upon him as of their own flesh and blood.

At Kuskuskies, on the 18th day of August, Shingas, Delaware George, and King Beaver advised Post that before they could enter into a treaty of peace with Pennsylvania, it would be necessary for them to get in touch with the tribes living as far as beyond the Lakes, but that they would work steadfastly to this end.

Some of Post's conferences on this first mission to the Ohio were held under the very guns of Fort Duquesne. On the 24th of August his party arrived on the bank of the Allegheny River directly opposite the fort, where King Beaver introduced the missionary to a number of Indians, all of whom were glad to hear his message of peace, except an old, deaf Onondaga, who objected strongly to both Post's message and his presence. At the same place, on August 25th, Post was told "not to stir from the fire, that the French had offered a great reward for my [Post's] scalp, and that several parties were out for that purpose." "Accordingly," says Post, "I stuck constantly as close to the fire as if I had been charmed there." At a council held here on the 26th, the intrepid missionary gave his message of peace. There were present altogether three hundred French and Indians. That aftrnoon, the French in council at the fort, demanded that Post be delivered to them, but their Indian allies objected. In fact the French were anxious to kill him, and had bribed one of his Indian companions named Daniel "to leave me there."

Says Dr. Donehoo: "It is a marvel that Post ever returned from this mission at the site of Fort Duquesne, from which place no Englishman had returned alive since Braddock's defeat, except a few prisoners who had escaped. Post was in a hostile country, with a large reward offered for his scalp, and there were many Indians about him who were not entirely friendly, and one of his own companions had been bribed to kill him—yet he came through it all. On the night of 26th of August the Indians who had taken Post to Fort Duquesne realized it was no longer safe for him to remain there, so before daybreak on the 27th, Post left with a party of six Indians taking a different trail than the ones over which they had come. The main body of Indians remained behind to know whether the French would make any attempt to take him by force. . . . . . . They [Post and his party] reached Sauconk that night, where they were gladly received."

A Significant Question

Post notes in the journal of his first mission to the Ohio, under date of August 28th, the following in regard to Shingas and Daniel:

"We set out from Sauconk in company with twenty for Kus- kuskies. On the road Shingas addressed himself to me and asked if I did not think that, if he came to the English, they would hang him, as they had offered a great reward for his head. He spoke in a very soft and easy manner. I told him that was a great while ago; it was all forgotten and wiped away; that the English would receive him very kindly. Then Daniel interrupted me and said to Shingas: "Don't believe him; he tells nothing but idle lying stories. Wherefore did the English hire one thousand two hundred Indians to kill us?' I protested it was false; he said: 'G—d d—n you for a fool; did you not see the woman lying in the road that was killed by the Indians that the English hired?' I said: 'Brother, do consider how many thousand Indians the French have hired to kill the English and how many they have killed along the frontier.' Then Daniel said: *'D—n you. Why do not you and the French fight on the sea? You come here only to cheat the poor Indians and take their land from them.'* Then Shingas told him to be still, for he did not know what he said. We arrived at Kus- kuskies before night, and I informed Pisquetomen of Daniel's be- havior, at which he appeared sorry."

Shingas Kind to Prisoners

Also, under date of August 29th, Post notes again in his jour- nal:

"I dined with Shingas. He told me, though the English had set a great price on his head, he never thought to revenge himself, but was always very kind to any prisoners that were brought him; and that he assured the Governor he would do all in his power to bring about an established peace, and wished he could be certain of the English being in earnest."

We state in this connection that Heckewelder testifies that

Shingas, though a terrible warrior in battle, was never known to treat prisoners cruelly. "One day," says Heckewelder, "in the summer of 1762, while passing with him near by where two prisoners of his, boys about twelve years of age, were amusing themselves with his own boys, as the chief observed that my attention was arrested by them, he asked me at what I was looking. Telling him in reply that I was looking at his prisoners, he said: 'When I first took them, they were such; but now they and my children eat their food from the same bowl, or dish.' Which was equivalent to saying that they were, in all respects, on an equal footing with his own children, or alike dear to him." Shingas was, at that time, living on the Muskingum.

The Indians' Point of View

On September 1st, at Kuskuskies, Shingas, King Beaver, Delaware George, and Pisquetomen unburdened their hearts, and frankly told Post the cause of their hostility to the English during the French and Indian War. Their statements, also, revealed the real reason why, after the close of this conflict, they again took up arms against the English in Pontiac's War, which, in 1763, drenched the frontier with the blood of the pioneers. Post reports the truly patriotic speeches of these great chiefs, as follows:

"Brother, we have thought a great deal since God has brought you to us; and this is a matter of great consequence, which we cannot readily answer; we think on it, and will answer you as soon as we can. Our feast hinders us; all our young men, women and children are glad to see you; before you came, they all agreed together to go and join the French; but since they have seen you, they all draw back; *though we have great reason to believe you intend to drive us away, and settle the country; or else, why do you come to fight in the land that God has given us?*"

"I said, we did not intend to take the land from them; but only to drive the French away. *They said, they knew better;* for that they were informed so by our greatest traders; and some Justices of the Peace had told them the same, and the French, said they, tell us much the same thing,—'that the English intend to destroy us, and take our lands; but the land is ours, and not theirs; therefore, we say, if you will be at peace with us, we will send the French home. It is you that have begun the war, and it is necessary that you hold fast, and be not discouraged, in the work of peace. We love you more than you love us; for when we take any prisoners from you, we treat them as our own children. We are poor, and yet we clothe them as well as we can, though you see our children are as naked as at the first. By this you may see that our hearts are better than yours. It is plain that you white people are the cause of this war; *why do not you and the French fight in the old country, and on the sea? Why do you come to fight on our land? This makes every body believe you want to take the land from us by force, and settle it.'*

"I told them, 'Brothers, as for my part, I have not one foot of land, nor do I desire to have any; and if I had any land, I had rather give it to you, than take any from you. Yes, brothers, if I die, you will get a little more land from me; for I shall then no longer walk on that ground, which God has made. We told you that you should keep nothing in your heart, but bring it before the council fire, and before the Governor, and his council; they will readily hear you; and I promise you, what they answer they will stand to. I further read to you what agreements they made about Wyoming, and they stand to them.'

"They said, 'Brother, your heart is good; you speak always sincerely; but we know there are always a great number of people that want to get rich; they never have enough; look, we do not want to be rich, and take away that which others have. God has given you the tame creatures; we do not want to take them from you. God has given to us the deer, and other wild creatures, which we must feed on; and we rejoice in that which springs out of the ground, and thank God for it. Look now, my brother, the white people think we have no brains in our heads; but that they are great and big, and that makes them make war with us; we are but a little handful to what you are; but remember, when you look for a wild turkey you cannot always find it, it is so little it hides itself under the bushes; and when you hunt for a rattlesnake, you cannot find it; and perhaps it will bite you before you see it. However, since you are so great and big, and we so little, do you use your greatness and strength in completing this work of peace. This is the first time that we saw or heard of you, since the war begun, and we have great reason to think about it, since such a great body of you comes into our lands. It is told us, that you and the French contrived the war to waste the Indians between you; and that you and the French intended to divide the land between you; this was told us by the chief of the Indian traders; and they said further, brothers, this is the last time we shall come among you; for the French and the English intend to kill all the Indians, and then divide the land among themselves.'

"Then they addressed themselves to me, and said: 'Brother, I suppose you know something about it; or has the Governor stopped your mouth, that you cannot tell us?'

"Then I said: 'Brothers, I am very sorry to see you so jealous. I am your own flesh and blood, and sooner than I would tell you any story that would be of hurt to you, or your children, I would suffer death; and if I did not know that it was the desire of the Governor, that we should renew our old brotherly love and friendship, that subsisted between our grandfathers, I would not have undertaken this journey. I do assure you of mine and the people's honesty. If the French had not been here, the English would not have come; and consider, brothers, whether, in such a case, we can always sit still.'

"Then they said: 'It is a thousand pities we did not know this sooner; if we had, it would have been peace long before now.'

"Sept. 2nd.—I bade Shingas to make haste and dispatch me, and once more desired to know of them, if it was possible for them to guide me to the General. [General Forbes, who was then marching against Fort Duquesne]. Of all which they told me they would consider; and Shingas gave me his hand, and said, 'Brother, the next time you come, I will return with you to Philadelphia, and will do all in my power to prevent any body's coming to hurt the English more.'

"6th.—Pisquetumen, Tom Hickman and Shingas told me, 'Brother, it is good that you have stayed so long with us; we love to see you, and wish to see you here longer; but since you are so desirous to go, you may set off tomorrow; Pisquetumen has brought you here, and he may carry you home again; you have seen us, and we have talked a great deal together, which we have not done for a long time before. Now, Brother, we love you, but cannot help wondering why the English and French do not make up with one another, and tell one another not to fight on our land.'

"King Beaver and Shingas spoke to Pisquetumen. 'Brother, you told us that the Governor of Philadelphia and Teedyuscung took this man [Post] out of their bosoms, and put him into your bosom, that you should bring him here; and you have brought him here to us; and we have seen and heard him; and now we give him into your bosom, to bring him to the same place again, before the Governor; but do not let him quite loose; we shall rejoice when we shall see him here again.' They desired me to speak to the Governor, in their behalf, as follows:

" 'Brother, we beg you to remember our oldest brother, Pis-quetumen, and furnish him with good clothes, and reward him well for his trouble; for we shall look upon him when he comes back.'"

While at Kuskuskies, on this first peace mission to the Western Indians, Post received from Shingas, King Beaver, Delaware George, Pisquetomen, John Hickman, Killbuck, Keckenapaulin, and eight other chiefs, a "speech belt" of eight rows, by which the western tribes agreed to the peace with the English. The accept-ance of this belt by the Governor of Pennsylvania would make peace effective with these Indians. Pisquetomen and John Hick-man delivered the belt at the Grand Council at Easton, in October, 1758.

On Post's second journey to the Ohio (Autumn of 1758), he again met Shingas and held council with him at Kuskuskies, Sau-conk, and Logstown, finding him anxious to make peace with the English on behalf of the Western Indians. Before Post left for Eastern Pennsylvania, the French had abandoned and set fire to Fort Duquesne, November 24th. The next day the advance troops of the army of General John Forbes took possession of its smould-ering ruins, and this "Gateway of the West", which had cost Pennsylvania and the English great sacrifies of blood and treasure to possess, was named Pittsburgh, in honor of William Pitt. Had not Shingas and his associate chiefs, welcomed the peace message of the gentle Moravian missionary, who can tell how different would have been the result? Would the Anglo-Saxon today have the ascendancy in the Western World? Would America be speak-ing French today? Logstown and Sauconk were filled with war-riors, and in the villages in the valleys of the Tuscarawas and Muskingum were hundreds of others. One word from Shingas or King Beaver, and they would have arisen in savage wrath. But that word was not spoken, because Post, whom they loved and in whom they had confidence, held them silent and kept them from assisting the French, as the army of General Forbes marched over the mountains and through the wilderness to dislodge the French from the beautiful and fertile valleys of the Ohio and Allegheny, and to end the French and Indian War in Pennsylvania.

Shingas at Fort Pitt

On July 5th, 1759, a council was held, at the newly erected Fort Pitt, between George Croghan, Captain William Trent, and Captain Thomas McKee, on the one hand, and the representatives

of the Six Nations, Delawares, Shawnees, and Wyandots. This
was the first large gathering of Indians at Fort Pitt. Andrew
Montour was the interpreter, while Colonel Hugh Mercer and the
garrison were also present. The Delawares were represented by
Shingas, King Beaver, Delaware George, Killbuck, and The Pipe;
and the Six Nations by Guyasuta. Croghan informed the assembled chiefs of the terms of the Treaty of Easton. These were confirmed, and the Indians promised to return the captives held in
their villages.

On August 12th, 1760, General Monckton held a conference
at Fort Pitt with the Western Indians, for the purpose of assuring
them that the English had no design of taking the Indians' lands.
In the first part of September, Shingas and Andrew Montour went
to Presque Isle (Erie) to join Croghan and Major Robert Rogers
in leading an expedition to take possession of Detroit and other
western posts surrendered by the French.

Shingas Attends Lancaster Treaty of 1762

After the erection of Fort Pitt in 1759 Shingas retired to Kuskuskies, and later to the Muskingum and the Tuscarawas.

Early in February, 1762, Governor James Hamilton received
a letter from Shingas and King Beaver, through their faithful
friend, Christian Frederick Post, advising the Governor that they
desired to hold a treaty with him in the following spring.

The Colonial Authorities had made many efforts after Post's
mission to the Western Indians in 1758, to induce Shingas and
King Beaver to come to Philadelphia for a conference. Shingas
had declined to come, fearing that the English would retaliate
upon him for the terrible atrocities that he had committed upon
the frontier settlements during the French and Indian War. Now,
however, that peace was secure and the Indian raids upon the border had stopped, Shingas wanted to meet the Governor in conference.

In March, the Governor sent a reply to Shingas and Beaver
through Post, inviting these two chiefs to come to Lancaster to
hold a conference at that place, inasmuch as smallpox was
raging in Philadelphia. Post was appointed as the guide
and escort, not only for the two chiefs and their delegation of
Indians, but also for the captives which were to be returned by the
Indians from the villages on the Muskingum and Tuscarawas, as
well as the villages on the Beaver and Ohio. Post immediately

went to the villages of Shingas and Beaver on the Tuscarawas, and
began preparations for their return on the 25th of June.   He was
beset with many troubles.   He had difficulty in getting Shingas
and Beaver to return with him and also in keeping the captives
from running away and returning to the Indian villages.   Dr.
George P. Donehoo, in "Pennsylvania A History" thus comments
upon the reluctance of the white captives to return to the settlements:

"One of the most remarkable facts in the relation of the English with the Indians during this entire period is that these captives, whose parents or husbands or wives had been most cruelly
killed and scalped by Indians, had to be guarded and oftentimes
fettered in order to keep them from running back to the captivity
from which they had been released.   One explanation of this most
peculiar condition has been attempted by some writers, who have
dealt with the topic, saying that the captives were men and women
of the lower sort, and had not been accustomed to anything different from that which had been their condition in the villages of
their Indian masters.   But this is an absolutely false statement.
Some of them had been taken from the best class of frontier families.   The great majority of them, as shown by their names, belonged to the hardy, religious Scotch-Irish families along the
frontiers of Pennsylvania and Virginia, which furnished the leading men and women of the Colonial period.   The only explanation
is to be found in the statements made by the captives and by the
Indians, that these adopted relations were treated with the utmost
kindness and respect by their captors."

When Post, Shingas, Beaver, the other Indians, and the white
captives reached Fort Pitt, Post held a conference with King
Beaver in which this chief advised him that the Indians had
already delivered seventy-four prisoners at that fort.   After many
difficulties, Post, Shingas, Beaver, the other Indians, and the remaining captives reached Lancaster, on August 8th, where the
great conference began on the 12th of that month.   Further details
of this conference are given in Chapter XXII, but in this connection, we state that the principal matters discussed were the return
of the prisoners and the claim on the part of the Delawares that
they had been defrauded out of their lands by the Pennsylvania
authorities.   The conference was closed by giving the Indian
delegation many presents.

Shingas in Pontiac's War

After a few year's of peace between Pennsylvania and the Indians, Pontiac's War, which opened in May, 1763, desolated the frontier. On the opening of this war, Shingas was living on the Tuscarawas, and Fort Pitt was commanded by Captain Simon Ecuyer. On May 31st, Captain Ecuyer received the following account from Shingas and King Beaver, which they had delivered to Thomas Calhoun, a trader at Tuscarawas, at eleven o'clock, on the night of May 27, 1763:

"Brother, King Beaver, with Shingas, Windohala, Wingenum, Daniel, and William Anderson, out of regard to you and the friendship that formerly subsisted between our grandfathers and the English, which has been lately renewed by us, we come to inform you of the news we had heard, which you may depend upon as true. All the English that were at Detroit were killed ten days ago; not one left alive. At Sandusky, all the white people there were killed five days ago, nineteen in number, except the officer, who is a prisoner, and one boy who made his escape, whom we have not heard of. At the mouth of the Mamee River, Hugh Crawford with one boy was taken prisoner and six men killed. At the Salt Licks [on the Mahoning in Ohio], five days ago, five white men were killed. We received the account this day. We have seen a number of tracks on the road between this and Sandusky, not far off, which we are sure is a party come to cut you and your people off; but as we have sent a man to watch their motions, request you may think of nothing you have here, but make the best of your way to some place of safety; as we would not desire to see you killed in our town. Be careful to avoid the road, and every part where Indians resort. Brother, what goods and other effects you have here, you need not be uneasy about them. We assure you that they will take care to keep them safe for six months. Perhaps by that time we may see you, or send you word what you may expect of us."

As set forth in Chapter XXIII, Shingas took part in the siege of Fort Pitt, in July, 1763. On July 26th, he and Turtle Heart, held a parley with Captain Ecuyer, the commandant, under a flag of truce, and requested him to withdraw the troops from that place. Soon after this Shingas disappears from history. What became of him or when he died is not known, though some authorities have endeavored to identify him with Buckongehelas, a Delaware chief, who was living in Ohio as late as 1800.   Some have suggested, too, that Shingas commanded the Indians at the battle of Bushy Run, Westmoreland County, on August 6th, 1763, but this is very improbable, as both he and King Beaver were not in entire sympathy with Pontiac's uprising.   It is much more likely that Guyasuta, an account of whom is given in Chapter XXIII, commanded the Indians at this battle.

KING BEAVER

King Beaver, or Tamaque, a chief of the Turkey Clan of Delawares, was, as has been seen in this chapter, a brother of Shingas and Pisquetomen, and possibly a nephew of the great Sassoonan. Upon the death or abdication of Shingas, he succeeded to the kingship of the Delaware tribe.

King Beaver's first important appearance in history is when George Croghan and Andrew Montour were at Logstown, in May, 1751, delivering the present of Pennsylvania to the tribes of the Ohio and Allegheny.   On this occasion, King Beaver requested that Pennsylvania would build a "strong house on the River Ohio, so that in case of war with the French, the Indians of the Ohio Valley might have a place of security."

On this occasion, too, he replied to a suggestion that the Delawares should comply with the promise that they had made the Governor of Pennsylvania, three years before to choose a new chief to succeed Sassoonan, who, as we have seen, died in the autumn of 1747.   King Beaver said that, inasmuch as all the wise men of the Delawares were not gathered together, it would take considerable time to select a man competent to rule over them, but that as soon as possible they would make a selection, which he trusted would be satisfactory, not only to the English, but also to the Six Nations.

He was also present at the treaty which the Virginia commissioners held with the Western Indians at Logstown, in June, 1752.   On this occasion he stood proxy for his brother, Shingas, when Tanacharison as the representative of the Six Nations crowned Shingas King of the Delawares, as was seen earlier in this chapter.

King Beaver at Aughwick Conferences

As was related in the latter part of Chapter XIV, King Beaver attended the conferences with Conrad Weiser, George Croghan, Tanacharison, and Scarouady, held at Aughwick in September,

1754. It will be recalled that upon Washington's defeat at the Great Meadows in the early part of July of that year, the friendly Indians assembled at Aughwick, where supplies were distributed to them by George Croghan, and that Weiser was sent to Aughwick to investigate the manner in which Croghan was distributing the supplies, and make a report thereon to the Pennsylvania Authorities.

Tanacharison and Scarouady were the principal Indian speakers at these conferences; but King Beaver, as the representative of the Delawares, also took part. A speech which he made at Aughwick on this occasion sheds some light on the time of the subjugation of the Delawares by the Iroquois.

Said he: "I must now go into the depth and put you in mind of old histories and our first acquaintance with you when William Penn first appeared in his ship on our lands. We looked in his face and judged him to be our brother and gave him a fast hold to tie his ship to; and we told him that a powerful people called the Five Nations had placed us here and established a fair and lasting friendship with us, and that he, the said William Penn, and his people shall be welcome to be one of us, and in the same union, to which he and his people agreed; and we then erected an everlasting friendship with William Penn and his people, and we on our side, so well as you, and observed as much as possible to this day. We desire you will look upon us in the same light, and let that treaty of friendship, made by our forefathers on both sides, subsist and be in force from generation to generation."

King Beaver in the French and Indian War

There are very few records of the activities of King Beaver during the French and Indian War; but there is no doubt that he assisted in many an incursion against the Pennsylvania frontier. Egle in his "History of Pennsylvania" states that it was King Beaver who led the band of Delawares who captured Bingham's Fort in the Tuscarora Valley in Juniata County, on June 12, 1756, an account of which was given in Chapter XVIII. We have already seen, in this chapter, the important part that he played in the peace missions of Christian Frederick Post to the Western Indians in the summer and autumn of 1758.

King Beaver was the principal speaker at the great council held at Fort Pitt on July 5, 1759, referred to earlier in this chapter, which gathered the fruits of Post's mission of the preceding year.

He was also present at the great Indian conference with General Monckton at Fort Pitt on August 12, 1760, held for the purpose of assuring the Western Indians that the English had no design of taking their lands upon the close of the French and Indian War. In the spring of 1761 he sent White Eyes, (also known as Grey-Eyes) and Wingemund to meet Governor Hamilton in council at Philadelphia and to advise him that a number of chiefs of the Western Indians proposed coming to Philadelphia to cement the bond of peace established between them and the Colony at the close of the French and Indian War.

As we have seen in the present chapter, in 1762 King Beaver, Shingas, and a number of other chiefs from the Mukingum, Tuscarawas, and Ohio, accompanied Christian Frederick Post to the great conference which was held at Lancaster in August of that year, where they delivered up the white captives which had been taken during the French and Indian War, and held in various villages on the Muskingum and Tuscarawas. His speech at this conference, that he knew nothing of the basis of the charge which Teedyuscung made as to the fraudulent character of the Walking Purchase, had no doubt much to do with Teedyuscung's finally agreeing to withdraw the charge of fraud.

On the outbreak of Pontiac's War, in May, 1763, King Beaver was one of the chiefs who, as related earlier in this chapter, warned Thomas Calhoun, a trader at Tuscarawas, to flee toward the eastern settlements. What part, if any, he took in Pontiac's uprising is not definitely known, though both he and Shingas had warned the English that a war would result if they remained on the Ohio. From all the data that can be found, we are justified in assuming that King Beaver was not in hearty sympathy with Pontiac's aims and purposes, at least at the beginning of the uprising. When Colonel Bouquet led his expedition to the Muskingum and Tuscarawas in the summer and autumn of 1764, King Beaver was one of the principal Delaware chiefs in that region, and Colonel Bouquet compelled him and the other chiefs of the western tribes to surrender the prisoners which had been taken in Pontiac's War.

King Beaver's next appearance in the history of Pennsylvania is when he, with New Comer, Wingenund, Custaloga, Guyasuta, White-Eyes, Captain Pipe, and other chiefs of the western tribes, attended the great conference which opened at Fort Pitt, on May 10th, 1765, held for the purpose of resuming trade relations between Pennsylvania and these Indians after the close of Pontiac's

War.   Andrew Montour, it will be remembered, was the interpreter on this occasion.

King Beaver also attended the great council at Fort Pitt April 26th to May 9th, 1768, held between Pennsylvania, the western tribes, and Six Nations, for the purpose of adjusting the difficulties growing out of the fact that settlements were being established in the valleys of the Youghiogheny and Monongahela, on territory not purchased from the Indians.   Over one thousand Indians attended this council, which led to the great purchase at Fort Stanwix (Rome, New York), on November 5th of this year, more particularly described in Chapter XX.

King Beaver had various residences during that part of his life spent in Western Pennsylvania—Logstown, Sauconk, and Kuskuskies.   The Beaver River bears his name.   As early as 1756, he established the town of Tuscarawas on the river of the same name in Ohio, a town which was later known as King Beaver's Town. Here he died in 1771, admonishing his people to accept Christianity.   In the latter years of his life, he had come under the influence of the Moravians, and invited them to establish missions among the Delawares of Ohio.   Upon his death, Captain Johnny, or Straight Arm, succeeded to the kingship of the Turtle Clan of Delawares, but White Eyes, an account of whom is given in Chapter XXV, was the actual ruler.

PISQUETOMEN

As we have seen also, in this chapter, Pisquetomen, a chief of the Turkey Clan of Delawares, was a brother of Shingas and King Beaver, and possibly a nephew of Sassoonan.   His first important appearance in Pennsylvania history is when he, Sassoonan, and other Delaware chiefs conveyed to the Penns, in September, 1732, "all the land along the Schuylkill between the Lechay Hills and Kittochtinny Hills, from the Branches of the Delaware to the Branches of the Susquehanna."   He was also one of the chiefs who attended the great conference at Carlisle in October, 1753, mentioned in former chapters.

We have seen in this chapter the important part that Pisquetomen played in Post's mission to the Western Indians in the summer and autumn of 1758.   It is on account of these services that this chief especially claims our remembrance.

We close this sketch of these three distinguished brothers by calling attention to the statement which King Beaver and Shingas made to Pisquetomen at Kuskuskies just before Post left for the East upon the completion of his first mission to the Western Indians:

"Brother, you told us that the Governor of Pennsylvania and Teedyuscung took this man [Post] out of their bosoms and put him into your bosoms, that you should bring him here; and you have brought him to us; and we have seen and heard him; and now we give him into your bosom, to bring him to the same place again before the Governor."

CHAPTER XX.

Madam Montour and Her Son, Andrew Montour

MADAM MONTOUR

MADAM MONTOUR was the first of a family whose name is closely connected with the Indian annals of Pennsylvania. There is much doubt as to her birth. She claimed to be the daughter of an Indian woman, probably a Huron, and one of the governors of Canada. Whether this is true or not, about 1664, a Frenchman, Montour by name, settled in Canada, where he married an Indian woman by whom he became the father of a son and two daughters. The son grew up among the Indians, who were, at that time, allies of the French. In 1685, while in the service of the French, he was wounded in a fight with two Mohawks on Lake Champlain. Later, he deserted the French, and, in 1709, he was killed while inducing twelve of the western tribes to support the English.

So much for the son of the nobleman, Montour. One of the daughters married a Miami Indian, and became lost to history. The other daughter, the noted Madam Montour, was born prior to 1684. When a child of ten years, she was captured by the Iroquois, and adopted, probably by the Seneca tribe, for, upon reaching womanhood, she married a Seneca, named Roland Montour, according to the "Hand Book of American Indians," by whom she had the following children: Andrew, Robert, Louis, and Margaret. Upon the death of her Seneca husband, she married the noted Oneida chief, Carondowanen, or "Big Tree", who later took the name of Robert Hunter, in honor of the Governor of New York. He was killed, about the year 1729, in North Carolina, in the war between the Iroquois and the Catawbas.

Madam Montour's first appearance as an official interpreter was at the Albany Treaty, in August, 1711. Her first appearance as an official interpreter in Pennsylvania was at a conference held in Philadelphia, July 3rd to 5th, 1727, between the Provincial Council and chiefs of the Six Nations, mostly Cayugas, in which the chiefs requested that no English settlements be made up the Susquehanna farther than Paxtang (Harrisburg), explaining that this territory was on the road by which the Six Nations went to war against the Catawbas, and that they feared that misfortunes would befall their warlike activities, if their warriors were furnished with rum by the settlers along the route.   She became a noted interpreter, and was uniformly friendly to the Colony of Pennsylvania.   Her sons, too, were loyal to the Colony, and Andrew, received large grants of donation lands lying along Chillisquaque Creek, in Northumberland County, and on the Loyalsock, where Montoursville, Lycoming County, is situated.   A creek, a river, a town, a county, and a mountain range—all in Pennsylvania—are named for her, or members of her family.   She lived for many years at the village of Ostonwackin, sometimes called Frenchtown, at the mouth of Loyalsock Creek, in Lycoming County.

She was living at Ostonwackin when she and her son, Andrew, welcomed Count Zinzindorf, the Moravian missionary, upon his visit to that place, in 1742.   Upon hearing the Count preach the Gospel and relate the history of the Saviour's life upon earth, she burst into a flood of tears, as the almost forgotten truths flashed upon her mind.   It was learned that she believed that Bethlehem, the birthplace of Christ, was situated in France, and that it was the English who crucified Him,—a perversion of the truth that it is believed, she had heard in her youth from French teachers among the Indians.   It is thought that she died in 1752 at the home of her son, Andrew.

Madam Montour and two of her daughters attended the Lancaster Treaty of June and July, 1744.   One daughter, known as French Margaret, was the wife of Keteriondia, alias Peter Quebec, and lived near Sunbury prior and subsequent to 1733.   Another daughter was one of the converts at the Moravian Mission, at New Salem, Ohio, April 14th, 1791.   This daughter spoke English, French, and six Indian languages.   A granddaughter was Catherine, of Catherine's Town, near the head of Seneca Lake, New York, destroyed by General Sullivan, on September 3rd, 1779. Catherine was a daughter of French Margaret.   Esther Montour, known as Queen Esther, "the fiend of Wyoming," was a granddaughter of Madam Montour and a daughter of French Margaret.

It is claimed that Madam Montour was a lady of education, of genteel manners, and handsome of face and form.   It is said, too, that, on her various trips to Philadelphia as interpreter at Indian conferences, she was entertained by ladies of the best society.   But, inasmuch as she was twice married to an Indian warrior, it is probable that her education and refinement have been overstated. Some have made the claim that she had no Indian blood, and that, for some unknown reason, she preferred the life and dress of the Indian. Near the end of her life, she became blind, but had sufficient bodily vigor to go on horseback from Logstown to Venango in two days, a distance of about seventy miles, her son, Andrew, leading the horse. She and this son are among the most picturesque characters in the Indian history of Pennsylvania.

ANDREW MONTOUR

Andrew Montour, whose Indian name was Sattelihu, was the oldest and most noted of the children of Madam Montour. We have met Andrew many times thus far in these sketches, but we devote the remainder of this chapter to additional information concerning this interesting character.

The first glimpse that we get of the "Half Indian", as Montour is frequently called, is when Count Zinzindorf, the Moravian missionary, visited Ostonwackin in September of 1742. Zinzindorf writes of his meeting with Montour as follows:

"On September 30, 1742, as we were not far from Ostonwackin, Conrad Weiser rode to the village. He soon returned in company with Andrew, Madam Montour's oldest son. Andrew's cast of countenance is decidedly European, and had his face not been encircled with a broad band of paint applied with bear's fat, we would certainly have taken him for one. He wore a brown broadcloth coat, a scarlet damasken lapel waistcoat, breeches, over which his shirt hung, a black cordovan neckerchief decked with silver bangles, shoes and stockings, and a hat. His ears were hung with pendants of brass and other wires plaited together, like the handle of a basket. He was very cordial; but on addressing him in French, he, to my surprise, replied in English."

Montour's Activities Prior to Braddock's Campaign

Andrew Montour's first important appearance in Colonial history was in February, 1743, at a conference held at Shikellamy's house, in Shamokin, between Conrad Weiser and the Indians of that place. At this conference Montour acted as interpreter for the Delawares. In 1744, he was captain of a party of warriors of the Six Nations, who marched against the Catawbas of Carolina. On this expedition, he fell sick on his way to the James River in Virginia, and was obliged to return to Shamokin.

In May, 1745, as has already been seen, he accompanied

Shikellamy, Conrad Weiser, and Bishop Spangenberg on their mission to the Onondago Council, in an effort to induce the Six Nations to make peace with the Catawbas. In June, 1748, Conrad Weiser introduced him to the President and Provincial Council of Pennsylvania, and informed them that he had employed Montour in various matters of importance and found him faithful and prudent; "that he [Weiser] had, for his own private information, as Andrew lives among the Six Nations between the branches of Ohio and Lake Erie, sent a message to him in the winter, desiring him to observe what passed among those Indians on the return of Scarouady, and come down to his home in the spring, which he did." The Council then voted Montour a reward for his trouble, and employed him to meet a deputation of Shawnee chiefs from the Allegheny then on their way to Philadelphia. He then assisted as interpreter at the conference held with these chiefs and others of the Six Nations and Miamis (Twightwees) at Lancaster in July, 1748, as was related in Chapter XIII. In August, 1748, he accompanied Weiser on his mission to Logstown. In May, 1750, he came from the Allegheny Valley, possibly Kuskuskies, and took part in the conference held at George Croghan's house at Pennsboro, Cumberland County, with some chiefs of the Six Nations and Conestogas.

Montour's next appearance in the history of Pennsylvania is when he accompanied George Croghan to Logstown in November, 1750, as was also related in Chapter XV, where they succeeded in counteracting, in a measure, the intrigues of the French, and promised the Indians of that place that a present from the Colony of Pennsylvania would be brought for them the following spring. After leaving Logstown, Montour and Croghan proceeded by way of the Lower Shawnee Town, at the mouth of the Sioto, to the Miami village of Pickawillany in the lower Ohio Valley, on a mission to strengthen the alliance between the English and Ohio Indians. They returned in the spring of 1751, and were sent in May of that year to carry the present to the Indians at Logstown, which had been promised on their visit to that place in the preceding November. As stated in Chapter VII, Montour and Croghan, by means of the Pennsylvania present, were able to make quite a favorable impression upon the Indians of Logstown in favor of the English on this occasion, and some French, who were present, were virtually ordered away by a speech which a certain speaker of the Six Nations delivered to the French Indian agent, Joncaire.

Montour and Croghan returned to Pennsboro early in June.

In a letter which George Croghan wrote the Governor on June 10th, enclosing a journal of his and Montour's transactions at Logstown, he said: "Mr. Montour has exerted himself very much on this occasion, and as he is not only very capable of doing the business, but looked on amongst all the Indians as one of their chiefs, I hope your Honor will think him worth notice, as he has employed all his time in the business of this Government."

Montour then returned to the Ohio some time in the summer or autumn of 1751, where he remained until near the beginning of the year 1752. His next act of importance was to act as interpreter at the Virginia treaty at Logstown, in June, 1752. In April of that year, he had received a grant of one hundred forty-three acres of land lying on what is still called Montour's Run, near its junction with Sherman's Creek, in Perry County; and on the same day that he received the grant, he requested of Governor Hamilton permission to interpret for the Governor of Virginia at the Logstown Treaty. The Virginians were so well pleased with his services that they allowed him thirty pistoles, and offered to give him a tract of one thousand acres if he would remove to Virginia and settle within the grant of the Ohio Company. At this treaty Montour was addressed by the Six Nations as one of their counsellors.

Early in 1753 we find Montour visiting the Great Council of the Six Nations at Onondaga, at the instance of Governor Dinwiddie, to invite the Iroquois to hold a treaty with Virginia at Winchester. In August of that year, he stopped at John Frazer's trading post near Braddock, Allegheny County, on his way back to Virginia with a number of chiefs of the Six Nations, Picks, Shawnees, Wyandots, and Delawares. Captain William Trent accompanied the party and spent some time in viewing the ground near the Forks of the Ohio, on which the Ohio Company contemplated erecting a fort. As we have already seen, Virginia made a treaty with the Iroquois chiefs at Winchester in September of that year. Andrew Montour was the interpreter on the occasion, as has been seen in former chapters.

The Indians who had attended the Winchester Treaty in September held a treaty with the Pennsylvania Commissioners at Carlisle in October. Andrew Montour also attended this treaty. Toward the close of the conference, Scarouady presented a large belt of wampum to Montour, addressing the Pennsylvania commissioners as follows: "Since we are now here together, with a great deal of pleasure, I must acquaint you that we have set a horn on Andrew Montour's head; and that you may believe what he says to be true between the Six Nations and you, they have made him one of their counsellors and a great man among them, and they love him dearly."

At the close of the Carlisle conference, Montour went to his home on Sherman's Creek, where he remained until early in November. He was then joined, at that place, by his brother, Louis, bringing two messages from the Indians of the Ohio, one for the Governor of Pennsylvania, and the other for Governor Dinwiddie of Virginia. These messages were sent by Tanacharison and Scarouady from Old Town, which Louis Monour explained was Shannopin's Town, on October 27th. Andrew then sent messengers to carry the Virginia message to its destination, and Louis brought the other to Governor Hamilton. These messages, which have been referred to in Chapters XIII and XV, contained the urgent request that Pennsylvania and Virginia join with the Indians on the Ohio in prohibiting the French from occupying the valleys of those streams.

Governor Hamilton replied to Tanacharison and Scarouady's letter on November 20th, advising that he would communicate with the Governor of Virginia in an effort to carry out their wishes. The Governor's letter was sent to Andrew Montour and George Croghan to be taken by them to the Ohio. On January 13, 1754, Croghan reached Shannopin's Town, at which place he was overtaken by Montour, and they proceeded to Logstown the next day, where, as stated at the end of Chapter XIII, they held council with Tanacharison and Scarouady, who requested both Pennsylvania and Virginia to build forts on the Ohio. Montour then left for Philadelphia, leaving Croghan at Logstown to interpret for Captain William Trent, who had "just come out with the Virginia goods and has brought a quantity of tools and workmen to begin a fort."

On February 20th, 1754, Montour was closely examined by the Governor and Assembly as to the location of Shannopin's Town, Logstown, and Venango. Montour proved that these towns were all within the limits of the Province of Pennsylvania; but the Assembly decided that the encroachments of the French on the Ohio and Allegheny did not concern Pennsylvania any more than Virginia. Montour then returned to his home on Sherman's Creek, at which place he wrote to Secretary Richard Peters, on May 16th, advising that the Indians of the Ohio did not look upon their friendship with Virginia as sufficient to engage them in war with the French, and urged Pennsylvania to send assistance to these Indians at once, as if they were to be retained in the interest of

Pennsylvania. "I have delayed my journey to the Ohio," said he, "and waited with great impatience for advices from Philadelphia, but have not yet received any. I am now obliged to go to Colonel Washingon, who has sent for me many days, to go with him to meet the Half-King [Tanacharison], Monacatooth [Scarouady], and others, that are coming to meet the Virginia Commissioners, and, as they think, some from Pennsylvania."

Before the above letter was written, Governor Dinwiddie had given Montour a captain's commission "to head a select company of friendly Indians, as scouts, for our small army." Montour, however, did not organize a company of Indians, as he had been instructed, but raised a company of traders and woodsmen, who had been driven from the valley of the Ohio on the approach of the French. His company consisted of eighteen men, and with these, he and Croghan joined Washington at the Great Meadows on the 9th of June. Montour and his forces assisted Washington in the battle of Fort Necessity, on July 3rd and 4th, where two of his men, Daniel Lafferty and Henry O'Brien, were taken prisoners.

On August 31st, Montour met Weiser at Harris' Ferry and accompanied him and Tanacharison to Aughwick, where, as has been seen in Chapter XIV, Weiser held conferences with Croghan, Tanacharison, and Scarouady, in September. On the way to Aughwick, Montour became intoxicated several times, and abused Governor Hamilton for not paying him for is trouble and expenses. Weiser reprimanded him when sober, and he begged Weiser's pardon and desired him not to mention the matter to the Governor. "I left him drunk at Aughwick," said Weiser; "on one leg he had a stocking and no shoe; on the other, a shoe and no stocking. From six of the clock till past nine, I begged him to go with me, but to no purpose. He swore terrible when he saw me mount my horse." On Weiser's way home Montour met him at Carlisle, having arrived there the day before. He again begged Weiser's pardon, and left for Virginia.

Montour either remained in Maryland or Virginia until the middle of December, or else returned there before that time, inasmuch as Governor Sharp mentions his being at Wills Creek (Cumberland, Md.,) on December 10th. He then came back to his home in Sherman's Valley.

We next hear of him in the spring of 1755, when he and George Croghan joined Braddock's army at Fort Cumberland with about fifty warriors. After Braddock's army began to advance on Fort Duquesne, many of the Indian allies under Montour and Croghan deserted, or were dismissed by Braddock; and when the army reached the Little Meadows, near Grantsville, Maryland, there were but seven in the company. Both Montour and Croghan continued with Braddock and took part in the terrible defeat at the mouth of Turtle Creek, on the Monongahela, on July 9th. We have already seen how the seven faithful Indians were thanked by the Provincial Council, in August, 1755, for the assistance which they rendered in Braddock's campaign.

Montour's Activities in the French and Indian War

Montour and Scarouady, after leaving Philadelphia, in August, 1755, went to Shamokin, from which place Scarouady sent a message to the Governor, on September 11th, advising that the Six Nations had ordered the Delawares at Shamokin to take up arms against the French.

The next glimpse we get of Montour is when he met John Harris at Shamokin, on the night of October 24th, in full war paint, and he and Scarouady advised Harris' party to keep on the east side of the Susquehanna on their return to Paxtang. It will be recalled that, as stated in Chapter XVI, John Harris had led a party to bury the dead of the Penn's Creek Massacre of October 16th, but finding that they were already buried, had come to Shamokin to ascertain the sentiments of the Indians at that place. During the month of October, Montour and Scarouady, as was also seen in Chapter XVI, attended the Indian council at Big Island (Lock Haven), where they found six Delawares and four Shawnees, who informed them that they had received a hatchet from the French to be used against the English "if they proved saucy."

Montour and Scarouady then went to Philadelphia, where, on November 8th, they gave the Governor the details of their trip to Big Island. In the middle of November, Montour and Scarouady left Philadelphia on a trip up the North Branch of the Susquehanna to Onondaga, on a mission from Pennsylvania to the chiefs of the Six Nations. The details of this trip have already been given in Chapter XVI, and need not be stated at this point. We have also seen, in Chapter XVI, that Montour and Scarouady returned to Philadelphia in March, 1756, from their mission to the Six Nations, and held conferences with the Governor and Provincial Council, which resulted in Pennsylvania's declaring war against the Delawares, April 14, 1756.

We saw in Chapter XVI that shortly after Pennsylvania's declaration of war against the Delawares, Scarouady went to the territory of the Six Nations, carrying Pennsylvania's peace message. He was accompanied on this mission by Montour, who, before leaving Philadelphia, put his children under the Governor's care, "as well the three that are here, to be independent of the mother, as a boy twelve years old, that he had by a former wife, a Delaware granddaughter of Allompis [Sassoonan]".

Montour acted as interpreter at the conference at Fort Johnson, on May 10, 1756, between Sir William Johnson, Scarouady, and a number of other Oneida chiefs. In June, he acted as interpreter at the camp on Lake Onondaga; and on July 25th, at Fort Johnson, he was appointed Captain of the Indian allies of Sir William Johnson. On September 10th, he appears once more as interpreter at Fort Johnson, and on the 20th of that month, he marched with Sir William Johnson to the relief of the army besieged at Fort Edward. He was ordered back, however, by General Webb, and reached Fort Johnson on the 2nd of November, where on the 17th to the 23rd of that month, he acted as interpreter at a conference with a number of chiefs and warriors of the Six Nations.

We find Montour at Fort Johnson once more, on June 13, 1757, attending a conference in which it was brought out that he had been sent during the preceding winter by Sir William Johnson to Onondaga Castle, to let the Six Nations know that he "expected that they should use the hatchet against the French." Another conference was held at Fort Johnson, on September 12, 1757, at which Montour offered five chiefs of the Mohawks and Senecas and four deputies of the Cherokees, the calumet of peace.

On November 12th, 1757, the French burned the settlement at the German Flats, in the Mohawk Valley; whereupon General Johnson sent Montour and Croghan to the Oneida Castle to learn why the Oneidas had not given the English notice of the approach of the French. They met the leading Oneida chiefs at Fort Herkimer, on November 30th, who advised them and also some German officers present, that the Oneidas had sent a warning to the settlers at the German Flats more than two weeks before, and that the settlers had paid no attention to it.

It is not clear as just how long Montour remained in the service of Sir William Johnson; but it is likely that he took part in the attack on Fort Ticonderoga and witnessed the terrible slaughter of the English troops under General Abercombie. Montour then returned to Pennsylvania, and with George Croghan, took part in the Great Council at Easton in October, 1758, between the Governors of Pennsylvania and New Jersey, on the one hand, and the chiefs of the Six Nations, Delawares, Nanticokes, Tutelos, and other tribes on the other hand. He acted as the interpreter of the

Delawares and Six Nations at this Council, but in the minutes of the same, his name is erroneously set forth as Henry Montour.

At the close of the treaty, Montour and Croghan at once went to the Ohio. As has been seen in Chapter XIX, the French burned Fort Duquesne on November 24th, and General Forbes' army occupied its site the next day. Two days later (November 27th), Montour and Croghan crossed the Allegheny, and reached Logstown on November 28th. On the 29th they reached Sauconk, at the mouth of the Beaver, where they were joined by some Delawares from Kuskuskies, accompanied by Christian Frederick Post. Here they conferred with Post, Shingas, and King Beaver, respecting the message that General Forbes had sent to these Indians. On December 2nd they returned to Logstown, and on the 3rd, reached Killbuck, or Smoky Island, opposite Pittsburgh. On the 4th, they crossed the river to Fort Pitt and held a conference with Colonel John Armstrong and Colonel Henry Bouquet.

Montour and Croghan then returned to Philadelphia, where the former was interpreter at a conference on February 8th and 9th, 1759, between General Forbes and some Indians from Buccaloons, an Indian town in Warren County. On February 20th, Montour reported to the Governor that these Indians were dissatisfied with the answer that they had received from General Forbes, and desired that he should return with them to the Allegheny, but that he had told them that he was an officer subject to General Forbes and could not go without his written consent. These Indians wished to learn fully the intentions of the English after driving the French from the Ohio and Allegheny.

Montour's Activities From the Close of the French and Indian War to the Outbreak of the Pontiac-Guyasuta War

In May, 1759, Montour was sent by Croghan to collect all the Indians he could for the purpose of meeting the latter in council at Fort Pitt; and on July 5th to 11th the conference took place there between Croghan as Sir William Johnson's deputy, Col. Hugh Mercer, and Captain William Trent, and the chiefs of the Six Nations, Delawares, Shawnees and Wyandots, at which conference Montour acted as interpreter. The chiefs were advised of the terms of the Treaty of Easton, and promised to return the prisoners taken during the French and Indian War. On October 24, 1759, he acted as interpreter at a conference at Fort Pitt between General Stanwix and the Western Indians. Still another conference with these Indians was held at the same place, by General Monckton, on August 12, 1760, at which Montour acted as interpreter.

Montour then accompanied Shingas to Presque Isle (Erie) to join the expedition which Major Robert Rodgers and George Croghan were leading to Detroit to take possession of the western posts, which had been surrendered by the French. On November 4th, 1760, Rodger's expedition left Presque Isle, consisting of a flotilla of nineteen whale boats and batteaux and a shore party of forty-two rangers, as well as twenty Indians of the Six Nations, Shawnees, and Delawares, under the command of Montour. Detroit surrendered on November 29th, and on December 8th, Major Rodgers and Montour set off with a party of Indians to take possession of Mackinaw. After proceeding about ninety miles, the Indians declared that it was impossible to proceed further without snow-shoes, and returned to Detroit.

Montour's next important work was to act as interpreter at a conference held at Philadelphia, on May 22, 1761, between the Governor and a number of Indians from the Allegheny. In the summer and autumn of this year, he accompanied Sir William Johnson to Detroit, narrowly escaping death by drowning, when his boat overturned on Lake Erie. On December 22nd of this year, he received a grant of two hundred acres of land in Sakson's Cove, between Kishacoquillas Creek and the Juniata River. He also acted as interpreter at the great conference at Lancaster on August 23, 1762, between the Provincial Authorities and King Beaver, Shingas, and other chiefs of the western tribes, who accompanied Christian Frederick Post to that place, as related in Chapter XIX.

Montour's Activities in Pontiac's War

Pontiac's War began in May, 1763. On the 5th of this month, Sir William Johnson directed Montour to proceed to Chillisquaque, on the West Branch of the Susquehanna, to endeavor to allay the fears of the Indians of that vicinity concerning their lands and to co-operate with Thomas McKee, the assistant deputy Indian Agent. In July, John Harris wrote Colonel Bouquet, at Carlisle, that Montour had arrived at Paxtang from a tour of the villages of the upper Susquehanna, where he found the Indians "inveterate and inclined for war", and that he, (Harris), would have Montour go to Carlisle and give this information to Colonel Bouquet personally. Soon thereafter Colonel Bouquet wrote Governor Hamilton from Carlisle that Montour reported that at the time of his leaving, neither he nor Johnson knew anything of Pontiac's uprising. Montour, on July 23rd, was at Fort

Augusta (Sunbury) on his way up the Kest Branch of the Susquehanna, returning on August 7th with the news of the attack on
Fort Pitt and Fort Ligonier.

Montour's next important act was to deliver, on December 19,
1763, to the newly arrived Governor, John Penn, an address of
welcome from the Conestoga Indians, of Conestoga, Lancaster
County. The unfortunate Conestogas had sent this address just a
few days before this massacre, on December 14th, by the Paxtang
boys.

Early in 1764, Sir William Johnson sent Montour with a
force of nearly two hundred Tuscaroras, Oneidas, and a few
rangers, against the Delawares on the upper Susquehanna, to punish them for their hostility against the settlers. On their way to
Kanestio, (a Delaware village in Steuben County, New York,) they
encountered a force of Delawares going against the English settlements, and captured twenty-nine of them. These prisoners,
among whom was Captain Bull, son of the famous Teedyuscung,
were sent by way of Fort Stanwix (Rome, New York), to Johnson
Hall; and later Captain Bull and thirteen of his associates were
sent to New York, and confined in jail. On April 7th, Montour
wrote from Tioga concerning the success of his expedition, stating
that the Delawares had fled before his arrival at Kanestio, but
that, with one hundred and forty warriors, he had destroyed three
large Delaware towns, all the outlying villages, and one hundred
and thirty scattered Delaware houses, together with horses and
cattle. The houses were well built of square logs, with good
chimneys, and many had four fire places.

Later Activities of Montour

We hear little of Montour for the next three years. Part of this
time, he assisted Sir William Johnson in New York, and part was
spent in Pennsylvania. By many it is thought that he accompanied George Croghan and his party from Fort Pitt to New
Orleans in the summer and autumn of 1766. On May 19, 1767,
he received a large grant of land on the head of Penn's Creek, above
the Great Spring. Montour's next appearance in history is when
he attended the council at Fort Pitt, April 26th and May 9th, 1768,
between George Croghan, Deputy Agent of Indian affairs, John
Allen, and Joseph Shippen, Commissioners of Pennsylvania, and
eleven hundred and three chiefs and warriors of the Six Nations,
Delawares, Munsees, Shawnees, Mohicans, and Wyandots. He
acted as interpreter on this occasion. The matters taken up at
this conference or treaty were the difficulties growing out of the

fact that the whites were settling on lands west of the Allegheny Mountains that had not been purchased from the Indians. It led to the purchase at Fort Stanwix, in October, 1768, to be mentioned presently.

Atrocious Murder of Indians By Frederick Stump

Shortly before the treaty at Fort Pitt, above mentioned, great consternation was caused throughout Pennsylvania and great fear of Indian outrages following the atrocious murders committed by Frederick Stump. On Sunday morning, January 10, 1768, six Indians, namely, White Mingo, Cornelius, John Campbell, Jones, and two squaws, came to Stump's cabin on Stump's Run, near Middleburg, Snyder County, in a drunken condition. Stump and his servant, John Ironcutter, after endeavoring without success to persuade them to leave, killed them all, dragging their bodies to the creek, where they cut a hole in the ice, and pushed them into the stream. Then fearing that the news of these murders might be carried to other Indians in the vicinity, Stump went the next day to their cabin fourteen miles up the creek, where he found a squaw, two girls, and a child, killed them all and threw their bodies into the cabin and burned it. One of the bodies which he had pushed through the hole in the ice on the preceding day, floated down Middle Creek to the Susquehanna, and then down this stream, finally lodging against the shore opposite Harrisburg, just below the location of the present bridge on Market Street of that city.

Several Indians who had escaped the murderous wrath of Stump, chased him toward Fort Augusta, at Sunbury. Stump did not enter this fort, but ran to a house occupied by two women, whose protection he implored, alleging that he was pursued by Indians. The women did not believe his story, but he begged very piteously. They then hid him between two beds. His pursuers were only a moment behind him. To their questioning, the women replied that they knew nothing of Stump. Before the Indians left the house of the two women, they seized a cat, pulled out its hair, and tore it to pieces, thus illustrating what they would have done with Stump, had they found him.

Shortly after the atrocious murder committed by Stump, the Delaware chief, Newahleeka, residing at the Great Island (Lock Haven), sent a message to Governor John Penn, advising that the Delawares and other Indians at the Great Island were much displeased on account of the fact that five white men had lately been seen marking trees and surveying land in that region not yet purchased from the Indians.   This message was delivered by a Delaware named Billy Champion.   Governor Penn then took occasion to send a message to Newahleeka, advising him that the Province had offered two hundred pounds as a reward for the capture of Stump.   Said Penn: "Brother, I consider this matter in no other light than as the act of a wicked, rash man, and I hope you will also consider it in the same way. . . . . . There are among you and us some wild, rash, hot-headed people who commit actions of this sort."   Then Shawnee Ben, a chief of the Shawnees at Great Island, sent word to Captain William Patterson: "As it was the Evil Spirit who caused Stump to commit this bad action, I blame none of my brothers, the English, but him."

Stump and Ironcutter were apprehended and lodged in jail at Carlisle on Saturday evening, March 23rd.   On the following Friday, a company of settlers from Sherman's Valley, where he had lived, marched to Carlisle, surrounded the jail, entered it with drawn pistols, and released the murderers.   After their rescue, they both returned to the neighborhood of their shocking crime, where they found their presence very disagreeable to the inhabitants.   They then left the neighborhood.   They were never again arrested for their crime.   Both went to Virginia, where Stump died at an advanced age.

Penns Make Last Purchase at Fort Stanwix

Montour was also one of the interpreters at the Great Congress with the Indians at Fort Stanwix (Rome, New York), in October, 1768, in which the Six Nations conveyed to the Proprietaries of Pennsylvania all the land, within the boundaries of the Province, extending from the New York line on the Susquehanna River, past Towanda and Tyadahgon Creeks, up the West Branch of the Susquehanna, over to Kittanning, and thence down the south side of the Allegheny and the Ohio to the mouth of the Tennessee River.

By this purchase, for a consideration of ten thousand pounds, the Proprietaries acquired the present counties of Green, Washington, Fayette, Somerset, Westmoreland, Cambria, Susquehanna, Sullivan, and Wyoming, and parts of Beaver, Allegheny, Armstrong, Indiana, Clearfield, Center, Clinton, Lycoming, Bradford, Lackawanna, Wayne, Luzerne, Columbia, Montour, Union, Pike, and Snyder.   The date of executing and delivering the deed was November 5, 1768.   This was the last purchase made by the Penns.

During the year 1769, Montour was granted a tract of three hundred acres situated on the south side of the Ohio River opposite Montour's Island, about nine miles below the mouth of the Monongahela. This is the last definite reference that we have to this distinguished and picturesque character, except that, on September 7, 1771, Richard Brown made an affidavit in which he mentioned that a certain Andrew McConnell had recently seen and talked with Montour at Fort Pitt concerning the murder of two Indians by a white man. His death occurred some time prior to 1775. Some claim that he ended his days at the home of his niece, who was the wife of White Mingo, a Six Nation's chief, who lived near the mouth of Pine Creek on the Allegheny, five or six miles above the mouth of the Monongahela, from 1759 to 1777. Others believe that he died on Montour's Island in the Ohio River

GEORGE CROGAN

We have met George Crogan, the "King of Traders," frequently in these sketches. At this point, it will be well to devote a few paragraphs to this influential man of the frontier. His name was one of the most conspicuous in the western annals in connection with Indian affairs at the time of which we are writing, and for many years thereafter. Bore in Ireland and educated at Dublin, he came to America somewhere between the years 1740 and 1744. He engaged in the Indian trade and appears to have been first licensed as an Indian trader in Pennsylvania, in 1744. In 1746, he was located in Silver Spring Township, in the present county of Cumberland, a few miles west of Harris' Ferry, now Harrisburg. During the same year, he was made a counsellor of the Six Nations at Onondaga, according to his sworn statement; and in March, 1749, he was appointed by the Governor and Council of Pennsylvania one of the justices of the peace in Common Pleas for Lancaster County.

As early as the years 1746 and 1747, he had gone as far as the southwestern border of Lake Erie in his trading expeditions. In 1748, he had a trading house at Logstown, which was made the headquarters of Weiser upon his visit to the Indians of that place, in the month of September, 1748. He had also branch trading establishments at the principal Indian towns in the valleys of the Ohio and Allegheny, one being on the northwestern side of the Allegheny River, at the mouth of Pine Creek, five or six miles above the forks of the Ohio. From this base of operations and from Logstown, trading routes "spread out like the sticks of a fan." One of these routes went up the Allegheny past Venango, (Franklin), where Crogan had a trading house and competed with John

Frazer, another Pennsylvania trader, who for some years, had traded at this place, maintaining both a trading house and a gunsmith shop.

Croghan's abilities and influence among the Indians soon attracted the attention of Conrad Weiser, who, in 1747, recommended him to the Council of Pennsylvania, and, in this way, he entered the public service of the Colony. We have already seen the part he played in Washington's campaign of 1754. The outbreak of the French and Indian War ruined his prosperous trading business, and brought him to the verge of bankruptcy. To add to his financial troubles, the Irish traders, because most of them were Roman Catholics, fell under suspicion of acting as spies for the French, and Croghan was unjustly suspicioned by many in authority. He was granted a captain's commission to command the Indian allies during Braddock's campaign. He resigned his office early in the year 1756, and retired from the Pennsylvania service, going to New York where his distant relative, Sir William Johnson, chose him deputy Indian agent, and appointed him to manage the Susquehanna and Allegheny tribes. From this time forward, he was engaged in important dealings with the Western Indians, and had much to do in swaying them to the British interest and making possible the success of Forbes in 1758. In 1763, he went to England on private business, and was shipwrecked upon the coast of France. Upon his return to America in 1765, he was dispatched to Illinois, going by way of the Ohio River, and was taken prisoner near the mouth of the Wabash, and carried to the Indian towns upon that river. Here he not only secured his own release, but conducted negotiations putting an end to Pontiac's War. He also took part in the Great Treaty of Fort Stanwix (Rome, New York), in 1768, and, as a reward, was given a grant of land in Cherry Valley, New York. Shortly prior to this, however, he had purchased a tract on the Allegheny, about four miles above the mouth of the Monongahela, where he entertained George Washington in 1770. When the Revolutionary War came on, it seems he embarked in the patriotic cause, and later was an object of suspicion; and, in 1778, Pennsylvania proclaimed him a public enemy, and his place as Indian agent was conferred upon Colonel George Morgan. He continued, however, to reside in Pennsylvania—the scene of his early activities and the Colony which he rendered such signal service—and died at Passayunk on August 31, 1782. His funeral was conducted at the Episcopal Church of St. Peter's in Philadelphia, but the place of his burial remains unknown.

CHAPTER XXI.

Teedyuscung

EEDYUSCUNG was one of the famous, able chiefs of the Delawares. He was the son of the Delaware chief, Captain John Harris, of the Turtle Clan, and was born at Trenton, New Jersey, about 1705. The early part of his life is clouded in obscurity; but, when he was about fifty years of age, he was chosen chief of the Delawares on the Susquehanna, and from that time until his tragic death on April 16th, 1763, he was one of the chief figures in the Indian history of Pennsylvania.

He was one of the founders, if not the actual founder, of the Delaware town of Wyoming, in 1742 or 1743. He came under the influence of the Moravian missionaries, and was baptized by them as Brother Gideon. Honest John was also a name applied to him by the Moravians and others. Later he became an apostate, and endeavored to induce the Christian Delawares of Gnadenhuetten to remove to Wyoming, actually succeeding in gaining a party of seventy of the converts, who left Gnadenhuetten, April 24th, 1754, and took up their abode at Wyoming.

In April, 1755, he attended a conference with the Provincial Authorities at Philadelphia, assuring them of his friendship for the English. At that time, he was still living at Wyoming. His friendship for the English and Pennsylvania did not continue long after the conference of April, 1755. When the Delawares and Shawnees took up arms against Pennsylvania following Braddock's defeat, Teedyuscung, at Nescopeck with Shingas and other leaders of the hostile Indians, planned many a bloody expedition against the frontiers of Eastern Pennsylvania. In Chapter XVIII, we saw that, on New Year's Day, 1756, he led a band of twenty-five hostile Delawares into Lower Smithfield Township, Monroe County, attacking the plantation of Henry Hess, killing several persons and capturing several others.

In March, 1756, he and the Delawares under. him left the town of Wyoming and removed to Tioga (now Athens, Bradford County), followed at about the same time by the Shawnees from their town where Plymouth, Luzerne County, now stands, under the leadership of Paxinosa. After the death of Shikellamy, in

1749, some of the Shamokin Delawares had settled at Tioga, and upon Teedyuscung's removal to that place, they and the Delawares of the Munsee Clan chose him "King of the Delawares". He was at that time busily engaged in forming an alliance between the three clans of Delawares and the Shawnees, Nanticokes, and Mohicans of Northwestern Pennsylvania.

Teedyuscung Agrees to Enter Into Peace Negotiations

As was stated in Chapter XVI, Scarouady and Andrew Montour were sent by the Governor of Pennsylvania, in November, 1755, on a mission to the Six Nations, going as far as Fort Johnson, New York, where, in February, 1756, they held council with the Iroquois chiefs. On their way up the Susquehanna Valley, they found Teedyuscung with a number of Delawares and Nanticokes at the Indian town of Chinkanning, now Tunkhannock, Wyoming County, shortly before taking up his residence at Tioga. We have also seen, in Chapter XVII, that Canachquasy, shortly after Pennsylvana's declaration of war against the Delawares, in April, 1756, carried the Governor's peace message to the Indians at Tioga, at which place he held conference with Teedyuscung. We saw also, in the same chapter, that Canachquasy returned from this mission early in June, and laid before the Governor and Provincial Council the favorable report that the Delawares, Nanticokes, and Shawnees under Teedyuscung, were willing to enter into negotiations for peace. Likewise it was seen, in the same chapter, that the Governor then drafted a proclamation for a suspension of hostilities against the Indians in the Susquehanna Valley, for a period of thirty days, and sent Canachquasy once more to Tioga with this information, where he held a number of conferences with Teedyuscung, persuaded this renowned warrior to lay aside the hatchet, and returned to Philadelphia in July, where he laid before the Provincial Council the result of his second mission to Tioga.

Teedyuscung at Easton Treaty of July, 1756, Declares Delawares are No Longer Slaves of the Six Nations

Immediately upon Canachquasy's return to Philadelphia from his second mission to Tioga, arrangements were made for a conference with Teedyuscung at Easton, which place Governor Morris with the Provincial Council, reached on July 24, 1756. The conference formally opened on July 28th, Conrad Weiser in the meantime having posted his troops in the vicinity of Easton. Teedyuscung's insistent request that he have his own interpreter was granted. He and the fourteen other chiefs accompanying him were formally welcomed by Governor Morris. Teedyuscung made the following reply:

"Last spring you sent me a string [of wampum], and as soon as I heard the good words you sent, I was glad, and as you told us, we believed it came from your hearts. So we felt it in our hearts and received what you said with joy. The first messages you sent me came in the spring; they touched my heart; they gave me abundance of joy. You have kindled a council fire at Easton. I have been here several days smoking my pipe in patience, waiting to hear your good words. Abundant confusion has of late years been rife among the Indians, because of their loose ways of doing business. False leaders have deceived the people. It has bred quarrels and heart-burnings among my people.

"The Delaware is no longer the slave of the Six Nations. I, Teedyuscung, have been appointed King over the Five United Nations and representative of the Five Iroquois Nations. What I do here will be approved by all. This is a good day; whoever will make peace, let him lay hold of this belt, and the nations around shall see and know it. I desire to conduct myself according to your words, which I will perform to the utmost of my power. I wish the same good that possessed the good old man, William Penn, who was the friend to the Indian, may inspire the people of this Province at this time."

In the conferences that followed, the Governor insisted that, as a condition for peace, Teedyuscung and the Indians under his command should return all the prisoners that they had captured since taking up arms against the Colony. But, inasmuch as only a small delegation of chiefs had accompanied Teedyuscung to Easton, it was desired that he and Canachquasy should go back among the Indians, give the "Big Peace Halloo", and gather their followers together for a larger peace conference that would be more representative of the Indians, and to be held in the near future.

The Governor then gave Teedyuscung a present, informing him that a part of it "was given by the people called Quakers, who are descendants of those who first came over to this country with your old friend, William Penn, as a particular testimony of their regard and affection for the Indians, and their earnest desire to promote the good work of peace, in which we are now engaged."

What Caused Teedyuscung to Declare That the Delawares Were No Longer Women?

We saw in, Chapter XVII, that, at the council held at Otseningo (Binghampton, New York), in the spring of 1756, the Delawares broke away from the Iroquois and declared: "We are men and are determined not to be ruled any longer by you as women; and we are determined to cut off all the English except those that make their escape from us in ships." Teedyuscung, therefore, at the Easton conference, simply was the spokesman expressing the determination of the Delawares to remain free from the domination of the Iroquois; and he also made the statement that the Iroquois had authorized him as their spokesman at this conference.

What were the causes of Teedyuscung's assertion that the Delawares were no longer women but men? Many answers have been given to this question. The Quakers endeavored to make the Delawares ascribe their bold stand against their conquerors, the Iroquois, and the taking up of arms against the Colony, to the Walking Purchase of 1737, in which they had undoubtedly been overreached; and as we shall see, Teedyuscung bitterly complained of this notorious purchase.

Others, including George Croghan, were of the opinion that it was because the Quaker Assembly, of 1751, had refused to build a "strong-house" at the Forks of the Ohio, when the Delawares and Shawnees of the Ohio Valley were still united in the English interest, and, as we have seen in former chapters, had repeatedly asked that a fort be built in that region.

The Governor of Pennsylvania said that it was because, when Scarouady appeared before the Governor and Assembly on November 8, 1755, and implored that Pennsylvania give the hatchet to the Shawnees and Delawares on the Susquehanna, then faithful in the English interest and anxious to take up arms against the French, the Assembly did not permit Governor Morris to give these Indians the hatchet and join them against the French, the consequence being that the Delawares and Shawnees of the Susquehanna became greatly dissatisfied and went over to the French.

The great English statesman, Edmund Burke, said that it was because it was "an error to have placed so great a part of the Government in hands of men who hold principles directly opposite to its end and design; as a peaceable industrious people the Quakers cannot be too much cherished; but surely they cannot themselves complain that, when by their opinions they make themselves sheep, they should not be entrusted with office, since they have not the nature of dogs."

Benjamin Franklin said it was because "these public quarrels were at the bottom owing to the Proprietaries, our hereditary Governors, who, when any expense was to be incurred for the defense of their Province, with increditable meanness, instructed their deputies to pass no act for levying the necessary taxes, unless their vast estates were in the same act expressly excused."

No doubt all of the reasons, enumerated above, contributed to the remarkable change in the character of the Delawares, as did also the Albany purchase of 1754, which, as we have seen in Chapter XIV, caused the Delawares and Shawnees of the West Branch of the Susquehanna and of the valleys of the Ohio and Allegheny to complain bitterly that their lands had been sold from under their feet.

Then, the Delawares received a message purporting to come from the Six Nations that their petticoats should be shortened to reach only to their knees, and that they should again receive the hatchet to defend themselves; but this was no doubt a message from the Senecas and not from the whole Iroquois Confederation.

Teedyuscung Boastful

Teedyuscung was very boastful at this Easton conference of July, 1756, conceiving himself to be a great man, and pompously asserting that he appeared in the name of ten nations, meaning the six clans of the Iroquois and the four tribes on the Susquehanna. The Moravian missionary, Zeisberger, attended the conference, and, during the six days of negotiations, moved among the Indian delegation pleading that they accept Christianity; but Teedyuscung had no ear for this message.

After Teedyuscung was given a present by the Governor, at the Easton conference, he and his followers were given a grand entertainment with which he was greatly pleased, and declared frequently that he would go forth, and do all in his power for peace. After the entertainment, when some of the Quakers, who attended the conference, came to bid him farewell, "he parted with them in a very affectionate manner." He plead strongly for peace, insisting that he and his people on the Susquehanna were not responsible for the actions of the Indians on the Ohio.

The peace belt, which he had brought to the conference and to which he urged that the white people hold fast, was then produced.

It contained "a square in the middle, meaning the lands of the Indians, and at one end the figure of a man, indicating the English, and at the other end another, meaning the French." Teedyuscung said that the Iroquois told the Delawares that both the English and the French coveted their lands, and urged the Delawares to join the Iroquois in defending against both the English and the French. Governor Morris was suspicious of this statement, called together his Council, and secretly consulted with Conrad Weiser as to whether it would be proper to keep the belt. Weiser said that he doubted the statement of Teedyuscung and sought advice from New Castle (Canachquasy), who told him that the Six Nations had sent the belt to the Delawares, who, in turn, sent it to the Governor of Pennsylvania. Canachquasy advised that Teedyuscung be liberally supplied with wampum, if peace was expected to be brought about. Weiser seconded this advice, and called attention to the fact that the French gave great quantities of wampum to their Indians, and that the English would have to outbid the French in the length of wampum belts. A messenger was then sent to the Moravian mission at Bethlehem to bring material for making a belt to be given Teedyuscung, and the Indian women converts were called in and set to work making the belts. The belt that was to be given to Teedyuscung was to be a fathom long and sixteen beads wide, in the center of which was to be the figure of a man, typifying the Governor of Pennsylvania, and on each side five other figures typifying the ten nations, which Teedyuscung claimed to represent.

While the Indian women were making the belts, Teedyuscung became very angry. He supposed that the Governor had invited Indian women into his councils. Said he: "Why do you council in the dark? Why do you consult with women? Why do you not talk in the light?" The Governor replied: "My councils are set on a hill; I have no secrets. The Governor never sits in swamps, but speaks his mind openly. The squaws are here making belts, not holding council." This answer appeased the anger of the great chief.

Before the end of the conference, the Governor, holding the two belts in his hands and addressing Teedyuscung and Canachquasy, declared them to be messengers of peace for the Province of Pennsylvania, to go among the hostile tribes on the Susquehanna in an effort to persuade them to desert the French and unite with the English. Giving each of these peace messengers an armload of wampum, the Governor bade them Godspeed on the important mission undertaken by these two chiefs,—a mission fraught with much difficulty and danger, as the secret emissaries of the French were using every device to thwart their designs.

As was related in Chapter XVII, Teedyuscung and Canachquasy, after the conference, started to give the "Big Peace Halloo" among the hostile tribes, but Teedyuscung remained for a time at Fort Allen, where he secured liquor and remained intoxicated for a considerable time. Lieutenant Miller was in charge of the fort at this time, and Teedyuscung brought sixteen deer skins which he said he was going to present to the Governor "to make him a pair of gloves." Lieutenant Miller insisted that one skin was enough to make the Governor a pair of gloves, and after supplying Teedyuscung liberally with rum, he secured from him the entire sixteen deer skins for only three pounds. The sale was made while the chief was intoxicated, and afterwards he remained at the fort demanding more rum, which Miller supplied, Canachquasy in the meantime having gone away in disgust.

On August 21st, Teedyuscung and his retinue went to Bethlehem, where his wife, Elizabeth, and her three children desired to remain while the "King" went on an expedition to the Minisinks, for the purpose of putting a stop to some depredations which they were committing in New Jersey. Returning from this expedition, he went to Wyoming, where he sent word to Major Parsons at Easton requesting that his wife and children be sent to join him. Upon Parson's making known the King's desire, the wife determined to stay at Bethlehem. He then made frequent visits to this place, much to the annoyance of the Moravian missionaries.

When the Provincial Authorities learned of the cause of Teedyuscung's detention at Fort Allen, Lieutenant Miller was discharged, and Teedyuscung went to Wyoming, thence up the North Branch of the Susquehanna, persuading the Indians to lay down their arms, and to send deputies to a second conference to be held at Easton, in October. However, in the meantime, the Governor, becoming suspicious of the chief's long delay at Fort Allen and being influenced, no doubt by the statements of many Indians on the border that Teedyuscung was not sincere in his peace professions, that he was a traitor, and that the Easton conference was but a ruse to gain time, sent Canachquasy secretly to New York to ascertain from the Six Nations whether or not they had deputized Teedyuscung to represent them in important treaties. Canachquasy returned with the report that the Six Nations denied Teedyuscung's authority, as was related more fully in Chapter XVII.

Obstacles in the Way of Peace

J. S. Walton, in his "Conrad Weiser and the Indian Policy of Colonial Pennsylvania", thus sets forth the obstacles which confronted Pennsylvania in her efforts to make peace with the hostile Delawares:

"The prospects of peace were growing more and more embarrassing. England, now that war was declared with France (April, 1756) sent Lord Loudon to America to take charge. Indian affairs were placed under the control of two men, Sir William Johnson for the northern, and Mr. Atkins for the southern colonies. Loudon's policy was to secure as many Indians as possible for allies, and with them strike the French. To this end Mr. Atkins secured the alliance of the Cherokee and other southern tribes. These were immediately added to the armies of Virginia and Western Pennsylvania. This act stirred the Northern Indians. The Iroquois and the Delawares declared that they could never fight on the same side with the despised Cherokees. This southern alliance meant northern revolt, and threatened to crush the peace negotiations at Easton. At this critical juncture, Lord Loudon, whose ignorance of the problem before him was equalled only by his contempt for provincialism, ordered the Governor of Pennsylvania to have nothing whatever to do with Indian affairs. Sir William Johnson, only, should control these things. Moreover, all efforts towards peace were advantages given to the enemy. Johnhon, however was inclined towards peace, but he seriously complicated affairs in Pennsylvania by appointing George Croghan his sole deputy in the Province. Croghan and Weiser had quite different views upon Indian affairs. The Indians were quick to notice these changes. Jonathan, an old Mohawk chief, in conversation with Conrad Weiser said: 'Is it true that you are become a fallen tree, that you must no more engage in Indian affairs, neither as counsellor nor interpreter? What is the reason? Weiser replied, 'It is all too true. The King of Great Britain has appointed Warruychyockon [Col. William Johnson] to be manager of all Indian affairs that concern treaties of friendship, war, etc. And that accordingly the Great General (Lord Loudon) that came over the Great Waters, had in the name of the King ordered the Government of Pennsylvania to desist from holding treaties with the Indians, and the Government of Pennsylvania will obey the King's command, and consequently I, as the Government's servant, have nothing more to do with Indian affairs.' Jonathan and his com-

panion replied in concert, 'Ha! Ha!' meaning 'Oh ,sad.'   The two
Indians then whispered together a few minutes, during which
Weiser politely withdrew into another room.   When he returned
Jonathan said, 'Comrade, I hear you have engaged on another
bottom.   You are made a captain of warriors and laid aside coun-
cil affairs and turned soldier.'

"To this Weiser replied with some spirit, setting forth his
reasons for self-defense, the bloody outrages of the Indians, the
reception of the first peace messengers.   'You know,' said Weiser,
'that their lives were threatened.   You know the insolent answer
which came back that caused us to declare war.   I was at Easton
working for peace and if I had my wish there would be no war at
all. . . . . . So, comrade, do not charge me with such a thing as
that.'   The Indians thanked Weiser for the explanation and went
away satisfied.   But at the same time Weiser was shorn of his
power among the Indians.   Making him commander of the Provincial forces robbed Pennsylvania of her most powerful advocate
at the council fires of the Indians."

Teedyuscung at the Second Easton Conference

In August, 1756, Governor Morris was superseded by Governor William Denny.   Governor Denny endeavored to have
Teedyuscung attend a conference in Philadelphia, in an effort to
continue the peace work begun at the Easton Conference of July
of that year.   Teedyuscung sent the following reply by Conrad
Weiser to Governor Denny's invitation: "Brother, you remember
very well that in time of darkness and danger, I came in here at
your invitation.   At Easton, we kindled a small council fire. . . .
If you should put out this little fire, our enemies will call it only a
jack lantern, kindled on purpose to deceive those who approach it.
Brother, I think it by no means advisable to put out this little
fire, but rather to put more sticks upon it, and I desire that you
will come to it [at Easton] as soon as possible, bringing your old
and wise men along with you, and we shall be very glad to see
you here."

Upon Teedyuscung's refusal to go to Philadelphia, Governor
Denny decided to meet the chief at Easton, where the second great
conference with him and the Indians under his command opened
on November 8, 1756.   "The Governor marched from his lodgings
to the place of conference, guarded by a party of Royal Americans
on the front and on the flanks, and a detachment of Colonel

Weiser's provincial's in subdivisions in the rear, with colors flying, drums beating, and music playing, which order was always observed in going to the place of conference." Says Dr. George P. Donehoo, in his "Pennsylvania—A History":

"Teedyuscung opened the council with a speech and with all of the usual formalities of an Indian council. This Indian chief, called a 'King', was a most gifted orator and talented diplomat. His one most bitter enemy was his own vice of drunkenness which led to all of his troubles and to his death. The one marvel about him was that when he had been on a drunken spree all night and kept so by his enemies, he would appear the next day with a clear head, fully fit to deal with all of the complex problems which arose. His foes among the Indians and among the English kept him filled with rum in the hope that he could be rendered so drunk that he could not attend to his business. He would sleep out all night, under a shed, anywhere, in a drunken stupor, and appear the next day with a clear head and an eloquent tongue to 'fight for peace, at any price.' In his opening address, in referring to the tales which had been told about him he says: 'Many idle reports are spread by foolish and busy people; I agree with you that on both sides they ought to be no more regarded than the chirping of birds in the woods.' What great orator today could express himself more perfectly and beautifully?"

In his opening address, Teedyuscung gave the following additional assurances of his desire to make peace with Pennsylvania:

"I remember well the leagues and covenants of our forefathers. We are but children in comparison with them. What William Penn said to the Indians is fresh in our minds and memory, and I believe it is in yours. The Indians and Governor Penn agreed well together; this we all remember, and it is not a small matter that would then have separated us, and now you fill the same station he did in this Province; it is in your power to act the same part. I am sorry for what our foolish people have done. I have gone among my people pleading for peace. If it cost me my life, I would do it."

Teedyuscung Charges That Delawares Were Defrauded Out of Their Lands

Governor Denny in his reply to Teedyuscung's speech, asked him why the Delawares had gone to war against the English. Teedyuscung in his reply stated that great injustice had been done the Delawares in various land purchases. The Governor then asked him to be specific in his statements and point out what land sales, in his opinion, had been unjust. Then Teedyuscung stamped his foot upon the ground and made the following heated reply:

"I have not far to go for an instance; this very ground that is under me [striking it with his foot] was my land and inheritance, and is taken from me by fraud. When I say this ground, I mean all the land lying between Tohiccon Creek and Wyoming, on the River Susquehannah. I have not only been served so in this Government, but the same thing has been done to me as to several tracts in New Jersey over the River. When I have sold lands fairly, I look upon them to be really sold. A bargain is a bargain. Tho' I have sometimes had nothing for the lands I have sold but broken pipes or such triffles, yet when I have sold them, tho' for such triffles, I look upon the bargain to be good. Yet I think that I should not be ill used on this account by those very people who have had such an advantage in their purchases, nor be called a fool for it. Indians are not such fools as to bear this in their minds."

Governor Denny then asked him if he (Teedyuscung) had ever been dealt with in such a manner, and the chief replied:

"Yes, I have been served so in this Province; all the land extending from Tohiccon, over the great mountain, to Wyoming, has been taken from me by fraud; for when I agreed to sell the land to the old Proprietary, by the course of the River, the young Proprietaries came and got it run by a straight course by the compass, and by that means took in double the quantity intended to be sold. . . . . I did not intend to speak thus, but I have done it at this time, at your request; not that I desire now you should purchase these lands, but that you should look into your own hearts, and consider what is right, and that do."

It is thus seen that Teedyuscung referred directly to the notorious Walking Purchase of 1737. Governor Denny then consulted Richard Peters and Conrad Weiser about the transactions complained of. Peters said that Teedyuscung's charges should be considered, inasmuch as they had been made before; but Weiser advised that none of the Indians attending Teedyuscung at this second Easton conference had ever owned any of the lands in question; that if any were living who had at one time owned the lands, they had long since removed to the valleys of the Ohio and Allegheny. Weiser further told the Governor that the land in question had been bought by the Proprietaries when John and Thomas

Penn were in the Colony; that a line was soon after run by Indians and surveyors; and that, when a number of the chiefs of the Delawares complained about the Walking Purchase afterwards, the deeds were produced and the names of the grantors attached to them examined at the council held in Philadelphia, in 1742, at which council, after a long hearing, Canassatego as the speaker of the Six Nations declared that the deeds were correct, and ordered the Delawares to remove from the bounds of the purchase.

The Governor then advised Teedyuscung that the deeds to which he referred were in Philadelphia; that he would examine them upon his return to the city, and if any injustice had been done the Delawares, he would see that they should receive full satisfaction. Some days later, however, Governor Denny denied that any injustice had been done the Delawares by the Walking Purchase, but offered a very handsome present to make satisfaction for the injuries which they complained of. This present Teedyuscung refused to receive; and the matter was then placed in charge of an investigating committee.

It was then decided that a general peace should be proclaimed, provided that the white prisoners were delivered up, and that the declaration of war and Scalp Act should not apply to any Indians who would promise to lay down their arms.

Teedyuscung then made the following promise in regard to the delivery of the captives:

"I will use my utmost endeavors to bring you down your prisoners. I have to request you that you would give liberty to all persons and friends to search into these matters; as we are all children of the Most High, we should endeavor to assist and make use of one another, and not only so, but from what I have heard, I believe there is a future state besides this flesh. Now I endeavour to act upon both these principles, and will, according to what I have promised, if the Great Spirit spare my life, come next spring with as great a force of Indians as I can get to your satisfaction."

At the close of the conference, Teedyuscung's delegation was given a present to the value of four hundred pounds, the Governor advising that the larger part of it was from the Quakers. Teedyuscung in his reply urged that the work of peace be continued. Said he:

"Hear me with patience; I am going to use a comparison in order to represent to you better what we ought to do.

"When you choose a spot of ground for planting, you first prepare the ground, then you put the seed into the earth; but if you don't take pains afterwards, you will not obtain fruit. To instance, in the Indian corn, which is mine, I, as is customary, put seven grains in one hill, yet without further care it will come to nothing, tho' the ground be good; tho' at the beginning I take prudent steps, yet if I neglect it afterwards, tho' it may grow up to stalks and leaves, and there may be the appearance of ears, there will be only leaves and cobs. In like manner in the present business, tho' we have begun well, yet if we hereafter use not prudent means, we shall not have success answerable to our expectations. God that is above hath furnished us both with powers and abilities. As for my own part, I must confess to my shame I have not made such improvements of the power given me as I ought; but as I look on you to be more highly favored from above than I am, I would desire you that we would join our endeavours to promote the good work, and that the cause of our uneasiness, begun in the times of our forefathers, may be removed; and if you look into your hearts, and act according to the abilities given you, you will know the grounds of our uneasiness in some measure from what I said before in the comparison of the fire; tho' I was but a boy, yet I would according to my abilities bring a few chips; so with regard to the corn; I can do but little; you may a great deal; therefore, let all of us, men, women, and children, assist in pulling up the weeds, that nothing may hinder the corn from growing to perfection. When this is done, tho' we may not live to enjoy the fruit ourselves, yet we should remember our children may live and enjoy the good fruit, and it is our duty to act for their good."

The second conference at Easton closed on November 17th. In the minutes of this great council, we read: "Teedyuscung showed great pleasure in his countenance, and took a kind leave of the Governor and all present."

Teedyuscung's Activities After the Second Easton Conference

Conrad Weiser accompanied Teedyuscung and the Indian delegation to Fort Allen at the close of the conference, reaching that place after dark. The old chief's wife was at that time among the Moravians at Bethlehem, and the next morning she declared that she would not live with Teedyuscung any longer on account of his drunkenness. Teedyuscung then took all the children away from her but one. Whereupon Weiser, induced by the Moravians, urged his influence in persuading the wife to live once more with her husband. In this task Weiser succeeded, and he and the Indian delegation left Bethlehem for Fort Allen. At Hessey's Inn at Bethlehem, the Indian delegation had dined on cider and beef, and a ten gallon keg of rum had been sent along for them to drink after they had gotten beyond Fort Allen. However, when the party came near the fort, some Indians came to meet Teedyuscung, to receive their share of the presents which had been given at the Easton conference, constantly importuning that the chief treat them with rum. In spite of all that Weiser could do, five gallons of rum were consumed by them before they reached the fort; and then Teedyuscung demanded that the remaining five gallons be given him to have a frolic with the Indians. After much importuning, Weiser surrendered the keg, on condition that the Indians stay away from the fort while engaged in their frolic, to which terms Teedyuscung agreed.

"I ordered a soldier to carry it [the rum] down to the fire," said Weiser. "About the middle of the night he [Teedyuscung] came back and desired to be let in and it was found that he was alone; orders were given to let him in, because his wife and children were in the fort; he behaved well. After awhile we were alarmed by one of the drunken Indians that offered to climb over the stocaddoes. I got on the platform and looked out the porthole and saw the Indian and told him to be gone, else the sentry should fire upon him. He ran off as fast as he could and cried, 'damn you all, I value you not;' but as he got out of sight immediately we heard no more of it."

After the rum was consumed, Teedyuscung parted with tears in his eyes, desiring Weiser "to stand a friend to the Indians and give good advice, till everything that was desired was brought about." "Though he is a drunkard and a very irregular man," wrote Weiser, "yet he is a man that can think well and I believe him to be sincere in what he says."

Teedyuscung then went out among the Delawares and other Indians of the Susquehanna Valley, to hunt up the white captives and to work for peace. By this time, as we say in Chapter XVII, his great collaborator in the work of peace, Canachquasy, was no more. Teedyuscung continued pleading for peace. The charge that he had made concerning the Walking Purchase caused considerable civil strife in the Colony. The Governor had promised that the chief's charges would be investigated, and the Quakers were determined that the committee in charge of the investigation should not shirk their duty.

The Lancaster Treaty of May, 1757

At about this time, Sir William Johnson, who, as we have seen, had been put in charge of Indian affairs in the colonies, appointed George Croghan as his deputy in charge of Indian affairs in Pennsylvania. Following Croghan's desire, a treaty with a large number of the Susquehanna Indians was held at Lancaster during May, 1757. Teedyuscung, however, did not attend, being still among the Indians, working for peace. It was the desire of Johnson and Croghan that all friendly Indians should take up the hatchet in the English cause; but Teedyuscung opposed this, and contended that the friendly Indians should be asked no more than to remain neutral. While the delegation of chiefs were waiting near Lancaster for Teedyuscung, Governor Denny received orders from Lord Loudon not to take part in Indian treaties, and to forbid the Quakers from attending such treaties or contributing thereto in any manner. The Governor then declined to take part in the Lancaster treaty.

Says Walton: "Letters and petitions now poured in upon the Governor. William Masters and Joseph Galaway, of Lancaster, voiced the sentiment of that vicinity in a letter urging the Governor to come to Lancaster immediately, and use every possible means to ascertain the truth or falsity of Teedyuscung's charges. 'The Indians now present have plainly intimated that they are acquainted with the true cause of our Indian war.' The Friendly Society for the Promotion of Peace Among the Indians asked permission of the Governor to examine the minutes of the Provincial Council and the Proprietaries' deeds, in order to 'assist the Proprietaries in proving their innocence of Teedyuscung's charges.' The Governor positively refused to show them any papers. The Commissioners in charge of Indian affairs were also refused the same request. The Governor then lost his temper and charged the Quakers of Pennsylvania with meddling in affairs which did not concern them. The Assembly then sent a message to the Governor, denying that the people of the Province ever interfered with his majesty's prerogative of making peace and war. . . . . Their known duty and loyalty to his majestiy, notwithstanding the pains taken to misrepresent their actions, forbids such an attempt. It is now clear by the inquiries made by your Honor, that the cause of the present Indian incursions in this Province, and the dreadful calamities many of the inhabitants have suffered, have arisen in a great measure from the exorbitant and unreasonable purchases made or supposed to have been made of the Indians, that the natives complain that there is not a country left to hunt or subsist in.' "

Governor Denny was compelled by pressure of the people to go to the Lancaster conference. At this time, the Cherokees, who were serving in the army at Fort Loudon and Fort Cumberland, were particularly opposed to any peace with the Delawares, and as a consequence, while the conferences were in progress at Lancaster, some Indian outrages occurred within a few miles of that place, so exasperating the people that they brought the mutilated body of a woman, whom the Indians had scalped, and left it on the court house steps as the silent witness, as they said, of the fruits of an Indian peace. All these matters, together with the absence of the great Teedyuscung, made it impossible to accomplish anything definite at Lancaster. George Croghan was anxious that the Western Indians be taken into a treaty of peace at Lancaster, and this question was therefore postponed on account of the absence of Teedyuscung.

While Teedyuscung did not attend the Lancaster treaty, he sent a message complaining bitterly of the Moravians at Bethlehem, as follows:

"Brothers, there is one thing that gives us a great deal of concern, which is our flesh and blood that live among you at Bethlehem and in the Jersies, being kept as if they were prisoners. We formally applied to the minister at Bethlehem [probably meaning Bishop Spangenberg] to let our people come back at times and hunt, which is the chief industry we follow to maintain our families; but that minister has not listened to what we said to him, and it is very hard that our people have not the liberty of coming back to the woods where game is plenty, and to see their friends. They have complained to us that they cannot hunt where they are. If they go to the woods and cut down a tree, they are abused for it, notwithstanding that very land we look upon to be our own; and we hope, brothers, that you will consider this matter and let our people come back into the woods, and visit their friends, and pass and repass, as brothers ought to do."

The Moravian missionaries resented this message of Teedyuscung, claiming that he well knew the sentiments of the Indian converts at Bethlehem, and that they were there of their own free

will. The Colonial Government paid no attention, however, to
this message. In June, 1757, the Governor received a message
from Teedyuscung, asking that four or five horseloads of provisions be sent to Wyoming, not by white people, but by Indians.
Said he:

"I desire you to be careful. I have heard and have reason to
think it will grieve both you and me to the heart. Though many
nations belonging to the French can go round me, and as I have
heard and have reason to believe that they know and have understood that I have taken hold of your hand, their aim is to break
us apart and to separate us. When I visited the Indians over the
Great Swamp and told them my message of peace, they said it was
a bait, and that the English would kill us all; but, however, when
they saw me come back safe the first time, they dropped their
tomahawks and said, 'If the English are true to you they will be
true to us.'"

The matter of the fradulent land sales came up at this conference at Lancaster. One of the chiefs of the Six Nations, Little
Abraham, spoke as follows concerning the frauds upon the Delawares:

"They lived among you, brothers, but upon some difference
between you and them, we [the Six Nations] thought proper to
remove them, giving them lands to plant and hunt on at
Wyoming and Juniata on Susquehanna. But you, covetous of
land, made plantations there and spoiled their hunting grounds.
They then complained to us, and we looked over those lands and
found the complaints to be true.. . . . . . The French became
acquainted with all the causes of complaint that the Delawares
had against you; and as your people were daily increasing their
settlements, by this means you drove them [the Delawares] back
into the arms of the French, and they took the advantage of
spiriting them up against you by telling them: 'Children, you
see, and we have often told you, how the English, your brethren,
did serve; they plant all the country, and drive you back; so that
in a little time you will have no land. It is not so with us.
Though we built trading houses on your land, we do not plant it.
We have our provisions from over the great waters.'"

The Six Nations' chiefs at this conference then advised that
part of the lands of the Delawares be given back to them and
promised to make both the Delawares and Shawnees return the
captives. They further urged that another invitation be sent to
Teedyuscung to come and bring some Senecas with him, in order

that the land question might be fully settled. Governor Denny followed the suggestion of the chiefs of the Six Nations made at the Lancaster conference, and accordingly arranged for the third council or treaty at Easton, where the complaints of the Delawares might be more fully heard. This treaty we shall discuss in the next chapter.

We close this chapter by calling attention to the following events which took place in the spring of 1757, while Teedyuscung was working for peace:

Atrocities in Monroe County

On March 25th, the Delawares made an incursion into Monroe County, in which Sargeant Leonard Den was killed. This was followed by another on April 20th when Andreas Gundryman, a boy aged seventeen, who had gone to bring some fire wood from the neighborhood of Fort Hamilton to his father's house near the fort, was killed. In the same incursions, Peter Soan and Christian Kline were killed and several others carried into captivity.

Murder of John Spitler and Barnabas Tolon

On May 16th, John Spitler while fixing up a pair of bars on his farm a few miles from Stumpton, was shot and his body cruelly mangled. His body was buried in the graveyard at Hebron, near Lebanon. The following account of his murder and burial is contained in the records of the Hebron church:

"1757, May den 16, wurde Johannes Spitler, Jr., ohnweit von seinem Hause, an der Schwatara von moerderischen Indianern ueberfallen und ermordert. Er war im acht unddreisigsten Jahr seines Alters, und verwichenes Jahr im April, an der Schwatara aufgenommen. Seine uebelzugerichtette Leiche wurde den 17ten May hieher gebracht, und bei einer grossen Menge Leute begleitet auf unsern hiesigen Gottesacker beerdigt."

The following is the translation of the record:

"On the 16th of May, 1757, John Spitler, Jr., was fallen upon and murdered by savage Indians not far from his house on the Swatara. He was in the thirty-eighth year of his age, and had taken up his residence on the Swatara in the preceding April. His badly mangled body was brought here on the 17th of May, accompanied by a large concourse of people, and buried in the graveyard of this place."

On May 22nd, Barnabus Tolon was killed and scalped in

Hanover Township, Lebanon County. "We are," says the editor of the Pennsylvania Gazette, "well informed that 123 persons have been murdered and carried off from that part of Lancaster [Lebanon] County by Indians since the war commenced, and that lately three have been scalped and are yet living."

Massacre on Quitapahilla Creek

"Londonderry Township (Lebanon County) being more towards the interior, was not so much exposed to the depredations of the savages as those on the northern frontiers. Nevertheless, in the more sparsely settled parts they committed various murders. June 19, 1757, nineteen persons were killed in a mill on the Quitapahilla Creek, and on the 9th of September, 1757, one boy and a girl were taken from Donegal Township, a few miles south of Derry. About the same time, one Danner and his son Christian, a lad of twelve years, had gone into the Conewago hills to cut down trees; after felling one, and while the father was cutting a log, he was shot and scalped by an Indian, and Christian, the son, taken captive into Canada, where he remained until the close of the war when he made his escape. Another young lad, named Steger, was surprised by three Indians and taken captive whilst cutting hoop-poles, but, fortunately, after remaining with the Indians some months made his escape."—(Frontier Forts of Pennsylvania).

Murder of Adam Trump

On June 22nd occurred the murder of Adam Trump, in Albany Township, Lancaster Cunty, thus referred to in a letter of James Read, from Reading, on June 25th:

"Last night Jacob Levan, Esq., of Maxatawney, came to see me and showed me a letter of the 22d inst. from Lieutenant Engel, dated in Allemangel, by which he advised Mr. Levan of the murder of one Adam Trump in Allemangel, by Indians, that evening, and that they had taken Trump's wife and his son, a lad nineteen years old, prisoners; but the woman escaped, though upon her flying, she was so closely pursued by one of the Indians, (of which there were seven) that he threw his tomahawk at her, and cut her badly in the neck, but 'tis hoped not dangerously. This murder happened in as great a thunderstorm as has happened for twenty years past; which extended itself over a great part of this and Northampton counties. * * * *

"I had almost forgot to mention (but I am so hurried just

now, 'tis no wonder), that the Indians after scalping Adam Trump left a knife, and a halbert, or a spear, fixed to a pole of four feet, in his body."

News From Fort Duquesne

In the spring of 1757 Lieutenant Baker with five soldiers and fifteen Cherokee Indians made a scouting expedition into the vicinity of Fort Duquesne. His force encountered a party of three French officers and seven men on the headwaters of Turtle Creek, about ten miles from the fort. They killed five of the Frenchmen and took one officer prisoner, who gave the information that Captain Lignery was then commandant of the fort, and that there were six hundred French troops and two hundred Indians at that place. This is the latest definite information received as to the conditions of Fort Duquesne until it was captured in November of the next year by General Forbes.

CHAPTER XXII.

Teedyuscung
(Continued)

Teedyuscung at the Third Easton Council

THE third council with Teedyuscung at Easton opened on July 21, 1757, and continued until August 7th. There were almost endless discussions about Teedyuscung's having a secretary of his own, deeds, frauds, and other matters which had come before Indian councils for many years prior to this council. Finally, John Pumpshire was selected by Teedyuscung as his interpreter, and Charles Thomson, master of the Quaker school in Philadelphia, as his clerk. Thomson, in writing of this affair to Samuel Rhodes, says:

"I need not mention the importance of the business we are come about. The welfare of the Province and the lives of thousands depend upon it. That an affair of such weight should be transacted with soberness, all will allow; how, then, must it shock you to hear that pains seem to have been taken to make the King [Teedyuscung] drunk every night since the business began. The first two or three days were spent in deliberating whether the King should be allowed the privilege of a clerk. When he was resolute in asserting his right and would enter into no business without having a secretary of his own, they at last gave it up, and seem to have fallen on another scheme which is to unfit him to say anything worthy of being inscribed (?) by his secretary. On Saturday, under pretense of rejoicing for the victory gained by the King of Prussia and the arrival of the fleet, a bonfire was ordered to be made and liquor given to the Indians to induce them to dance. For fear they should get sober on Sunday and be fit next day to enter on business, under pretense that the Mohawks had requested it, another bonfire was ordered to be made, and more liquor given them. On Monday night the King was made drunk by Conrad Weiser, on Tuesday by G. Croghan; last night he was very drunk at Vernon's, and Vernon lays the blame on Comin and G. Croghan. He did not go to sleep last night. This morning he lay down under a shed about the break of day and slept a few hours. He is to speak this afternoon. He is to be sure in a fine capacity to do business. But thus we go on. I leave you to make reflections. I for my part wish myself at home."

Teedyuscung Renews Charge of Fraud

Teedyuscung entered this third Easton council with his mind made up not to reiterate the charge of fraud concerning the Walking Purchase, doubtless fearing the Six Nations. His advisors told him that he could afford to wait until peace was fully established, before asserting the Delaware rights to lands drained by the Delaware River. However, Governor Denny was determined to make the great chief deny that any fraud had been practiced upon the Delawares in land purchases. When pressed for the cause of the alienation of the Delawares, Teedyuscung unequivocally asserted that it was the land purchases. Said he:

"The complaint I made last fall I yet continue. I think some lands have been bought by the Proprietors or his agents from Indians who had not a right to sell. . . . . . I think, also, when some lands have been sold to the Proprietors by Indians who had a right to sell to a certain place, whether that purchase was to be measured by miles or hours walk, that the Proprietors have contrary to agreement or bargain, taken in more lands than they ought to have done, and lands that belonged to others. I therefore now desire that you will produce the writings and deeds by which you hold the land, and let them be read in public, and examined, that it may be fully known from what Indians you have bought the lands you hold; and how far your purchases extend; that copies of the whole may be laid before King George, and published to all the Provinces under his Government. What is fairly bought and paid for I make no further demand about. But if any lands have been bought of Indians to whom these lands did not belong, and who had no right to sell them, I expect a satisfaction for those lands; and if the Proprietors have taken in more lands than they bought of true owners, I expect likewise to be paid for that."

Teedyuscung Requests Benefits of Civilization

Said Teedyuscung: "We [the Delawares] intend to settle at Wyoming, and we want to have certain boundaries fixed between you and us, and a certain tract of land fixed which it shall not be lawful for us or our children ever to sell, nor for you or any of your children ever to buy. . . . . . To build different houses from what we have done before, such as may last not only for a little time, but for our children after us; we desire you will assist us in making our settlements, and send us persons to instruct us in building houses and making such necessaries as shall be needed, and that persons be sent to instruct us in the Christian religion, and to instruct our children in reading and writing, and that a fair trade be established between us, and such persons appointed to conduct and manage these affairs as shall be agreeable to us."

Walton's Account of the Council

The remaining matters taken up at this great conference are thus succinctly set forth by J. S. Walton, in his "Conrad Weiser and the Indian Policy of Pennsylvania":

"Teedyuscung then asked that the territory of Wyoming be reserved to the Indians forever. That it might be surveyed and a deed given to the Indians, that they might have something to show when it became necessary to drive the white men away. After these charges were again made the Governor called Croghan and Weiser together to know what was the best thing to do. Each of these men with his large share of experience in Indian affairs agreed in the opinion that some outside influence had induced Teedyuscung to revive these charges. They also united in the opinion that the Indians merely wanted a glimpse of the old deeds, and would be satisfied with a cursory examination of the signatures.

"Upon these assertions the Governor and Council were induced to grant Teedyuscung's request and to show him the deeds of 1636 and 1637 from the Delawares, and of 1749 from the Iroquois. When the Governor applied to Mr. Peters for the papers and deeds they were again refused. Peters declared that he held them as a sacred trust from the Proprietors and would neither surrender them nor permit himself to be placed under oath and give testimony. These two things could only be done, he insisted, in the presence of Sir William Johnson, before whom as a final arbitrator, the Proprietors desired that these charges should be laid. James Logan immediately opposed Richard Peters. He insisted that all deeds relating to lands which the Indians claimed were fraudulently purchased, sould be shown. To refuse this would be unjust to the Indians and dangerous to the cause of peace. Logan explained that the Proprietary instructions should not be too literally construed and obeyed. The Indians were opposed to having their case settled before Sir William Johnson. After an animated discussion in council it was reluctantly agreed that the deeds should be shown. The Council only consented to this after Conrad Weiser had assured them that Teedyuscung did not insist upon seeing all the deeds, but only those pertaining to the back lands. R. Peters again protested, but was overruled. The deeds were laid on the table August 3, 1757.

"Charles Thomson, at Teedyuscung's request, copied these deeds. The chief said he would have preferred to have seen the deeds of confirmation given to Governor Keith in 1718, but the great work of peace was superior to the land dispute, and if the Proprietors would make satisfaction for the lands which had been fraudulently secured, he would return the English prisoners held captive among the Indians. The peace belt was then grasped by the Governor and Teedyuscung, and the two years' struggle for peace was crowned with victory. After much feasting and dancing, drinking and burning of bonfires the treaty closed.

"Teedyuscung promised to fight for the English on condition that his men should not be commanded by white captains. The Governor and his party returned to Philadelphia, deeply worried over the publicity of the Indian charges of fraud which had occurred at the Easton conference. Peace to the Proprietors was dearly purchased, if the people of the Province were confirmed in their belief that the Indian outrages had been caused by fraud in land purchases."

The council ended on Sunday, August 7th. Governor Denny then returned to Philadelphia realizing that two things were imperative. One was to disprove Teedyuscung's charge of fraud, in order to remove from the Proprietaries of the Colony the responsibility for the hostility of the Delawares and Shawnees; the other was to make peace with the Indians of the valleys of the Ohio and Allegheny, in order that the expedition of General Forbes then planned might be a success. The Governor was very apprehensive that, on account of the allegiance of the Western Indians with the French, the proposed expedition of General Forbes would meet with the same fate as the expedition of the ill-fated Braddock in the summer of 1755. Besides, unless the hostile Indians of the Ohio and Allegheny could be persuaded to sever their allegiance with the French, there was little chance of ending the barbarous raids which they were making on the frontier settlements. How these Western Indians were induced by the Moravian missionary, Christian Frederick Post, to sever their allegiance with the French, as General Forbes was marching on Fort Duquesne in the autumn of 1758, has already been told in Chapter XIX.

Atrocities of the Summer of 1757

Indian atrocities still continued as Teedyuscung worked for peace. In August, 1757, incursions were made into Lebanon County. John Andrews' wife and child were captured while going to a neighbor's house. John Winklebach's two sons and Joseph Fischbach were fired upon by fifteen Indians, while bringing in the cows at sunrise. The boys were killed, and Fischbach was badly wounded. At about the same time, Leonard Long's son was killed and scalped while plowing in his father's field, and Isaac Williams' wife was killed. In September, Christian Danner was killed and his son, aged twelve, captured and carried to Canada, where he made his escape after three years, as related in Chapter XXI.

During this summer, incursions were also made into Dauphin County. At the time of one of these incursions, a Mr. Barnett and a Mr. Mackey were at work on the former's farm near Manada Creek, when news reached them that their families were murdered in the block house nearby. They at once started for the scene of horror, but had not gone far until they were ambushed by a party of Indians who killed Mackey and severely wounded Barnett who, nevertheless, was able to escape, owing to the swiftness of his horse. He concealed himself until the Indians left the neighborhood the next day, when he learned that his family was safe with the exception of his son, William, aged nine, whom the Indians had captured, together with Mackey's son about the same age. The Indians proceeded westward with the two little boys. Upon learning that one of the boys was the son of Mackey, whom they had just killed, they forced him to stretch his father's scalp. For a time, the little Mackey boy carried his father's scalp, which he would often stroke with his little hand, and say, "My father's pretty hair."

Mr. Barnett at length recovered from his wound. In the hope of recovering his son, he accompanied George Croghan to Fort Pitt, and attended the council which Crogan, Colonel Hugh Mercer, Captain William Trent, and Captain Thomas McKee held with the Shawnees, Delawares, and other Indians at that place on July 5th, 1759. One day during his stay at the fort, he wished to get a drink of water from Grant's Spring, above the fort, so named from the defeat of Major James Grant at that place in the preceding September. He had proceeded only a short distance, when something told him to turn back. At the same instant, he heard the report of a rifle, and looking towards the spring, saw the smoke of the same and an Indian scalping a soldier, who had gone to the spring for a drink.

Mr. Barnett returned home without recovering his son, but Crogan promised to use every endeavor to obtain the child. At length the boy was brought to Fort Pitt, but so great was his inclination to return to the Indians that it was necessary to guard him closely until there would be an opportunity to send him to his father. On one occasion, he jumped into a canoe, and was half way across the Allegheny River before he was observed. Quick pursuit followed; but he reached the other side and hid in the bushes, where it took a search of several hours to find him. Soon thereafter, he was sent to Carlisle, where the father received him with tears of joy, and took him home to the arms of the mother. During his captivity, the Indians frequently broke the ice on rivers and creeks, and dipped him in "to make him hardy". This treatment impaired his constitution. He sank into the grave in early manhood, leaving a wife and daughter. Shortly thereafter, the mother died. Then Mr. Barnett, the elder, removed to Allegheny County, where he died at the great age of eighty-two years. His dust reposes in the church yard of Lebanon, Mifflin Township, Allegheny County.

But, to return to the Mackey boy. The Indians gave this child to the French, and at the close of the French and Indian War, he passed into the hands of the English, was taken to England, and later, became a soldier in the British army, and was sent to America during the Revolutionary War. He procured a furlough, and sought out his widowed mother, who had mourned him as dead. As he stood before her in the strength of robust manhood, she was unable to see in him any trace of her long lost boy. "If you are my son," said she, "you have a mark upon your knee that I will know." He then exposed his knee to her view; whereupon she threw her arms around his neck in unrestrained joy. He never returned to the British army, but remained with his mother to the end of her days, often meeting William Barnett, and recounting with him their experiences while captives among the Indians.

Teedyuscung's Activities After the Third Easton Council

Two days after the third Easton conference closed, Teedyuscung and his family went to Bethlehem, where he tarried for several days. Reichel, in his "Memorials of the Moravian Church," says of this visit:

"Some of these unwelcome visitors halted for a few days, and some proceeded as far as Fort Allen and then returned, undecided as to where to go and what to do. During the month full 200 were counted—men, women and children—among them lawless crowds who annoyed the brethren by depredations, molested the Indians at the Manakasy, and wrangled with each other over their cups at 'The Crown'."

After the third Easton treaty was over, and as Teedyuscung was returning to Tioga, he met three messengers from the Ohio Indians, who stated to him that they were sorry that they had taken up arms against the English, and would do whatever he told them; whereupon, he informed them of the peace that had been established by the treaty at Easton, and that he would give them the tomahawk against the French, and bring them down to Philadelphia for a treaty. He then proceeded to Philadelphia, where he laid this information before the Governor and Provincial Council on August 30th, and advised them that he had sent his son, Amos, and another Delaware back to the Ohio with the three messengers.

Teedyuscung again appeared before the Governor and Provincial Council on September 5th, and asked for a copy of the Delaware deed of release, which Sassoonan and six other chiefs of the Delawares had executed on September 17, 1718, by the terms of which they acknowledged that their ancestors had conveyed to Pennsylvania, in fee, and had then paid for all the land between "the Delaware and the Susquehanna, from Duck Creek to the mountains on this side of Lechay [Lehigh River]". He also asked why the Easton treaty had not been published. Governor Denny explained that it was Sir William Johnson's business to order any publication of the treaty, and that George Croghan had reminded the Governor of this fact. Teedyuscung then declared that Croghan was a rogue, and that he (Teedyuscung) would have nothing to do with either Croghan or Johnson. The Governor then handed over the copy of the deed of 1718, and assured Teedyuscung that the treaty would be published.

Teedyuscung appeared before the Governor and Provincial Council on December 1st to urge that, as winter was coming on, houses should speedily be built for the Indians at Wyoming. He also visited the Governor and Provincial Council on January 17, 1758, in which he advised them that they might be assured that: "I shall use my utmost endeavors to establish the peace so happily concluded at Easton between the people of this Province and their brethren, the Indians."

Teedyuscung Again Asks for Benefits
of Civilization

Teedyuscung again came to Philadelphia on March 13, 1758. On this visit he was very spirited and asked for a clerk. The Council having debated for more than an hour whether this request should be granted, Teedyuscung sent a message that he was tired of waiting, was at dinner, and would bring his clerk, or would not speak at all. A public conference was then held in the council chamber of the State House, which many persons of the city attended. He advised the Council that, in compliance with his promise at the third Easton conference, he had given the "Big Peace Halloo", and had secured the alliance of eight nations of the Western Indians, who had taken hold of the peace belt, in addition to the ten for which he had spoken at the Easton treaty. The calumet which these recent allies had sent Teedyuscung in reply to the publication of peace was smoked by himself, the Governor, and members of the Provincial Council and the Assembly.

A week later, when Governor Denny made his reply accepting the alliance of the eight nations and thanking Teedyuscung for his great work in behalf of peace, the great chief repeated the request for the benefits of civilization, which he had made at the third Easton treaty. Said he:

"Brother, you must consider I have a soul as well as another, and I think it proper you should let me have two masters to teach me, that my soul may be instructed and saved at last. Brother, I desire moreover two school masters, for there are a great many Indian children who want school masters. One therefore is not sufficient to teach them all, so that they may be sufficiently instructed in the Christian way. Brother, I have a body as well as a soul. I want two men to instruct me and show me the ways of living, and how to conduct temporal affairs, who may teach me in everything to do as you do yourselves, that I may live as you do, and likewise who may watch over me and take care of my things, that nobody may cheat me. You tell us the Christian religion is good, and we believe it to be so, partly upon the credit of your words, and partly because we see that some of our brother Indians who were wicked before they became Christians live better lives now than they formerly did."

He added that he asked the liberty of choosing the masters and that he wanted two instructors in temporal affairs, so that if one should prove dishonest, the other might prevent him from doing injury to or impose upon the Indians.

Teedyuscung's Appeal Led to Post's Being Sent
on Mission to the Western Indians

During the conferences that attended the above visit of Teedyuscung to the Governor and Provincial Council, the old chief
urged that the Provincial Authorities should not neglect the opportunity to do everything possible to strengthen the alliance with the
eight western nations who had agreed to his peace proposal. He
said: "I have received every encouragement from the Indian
nations. Now, brother, press on with all your might in promoting
the good work we are engaged in. Let us beg the God that made
us to bless our endeavours, and I am sure if you assert yourselves,
God will grant a blessing, and we shall live."

Teedyuscung then urged that a messenger should be sent to his
friends on the Ohio and Allegheny, warning them to sever their
allegiance with the French. Teedyuscung's appeal was the first
move towards the daring mission of Christian Frederick Post to
the Indians of the Ohio in the summer and autumn of 1758, in
which he succeeded in persuading the western tribes not to give
further assistance to the French.

At this same conference, he also requested that a messenger be
sent to stop the Cherokees from coming any further. These Indians
were coming to assist in the expedition of General Forbes against
Fort Duquesne, much to the displeasure of the Delawares and
Shawnees. We have already seen, in Chapter XVII, that it was
the coming of the Cherokees to assist the English that caused
Paxinosa to leave for the Ohio. At the time of which we are writing, there was great danger that the presence of the Cherokees at
Fort Cumberland, Fort Littleton, Carlisle, and other places, with
the English forces, would seriously complicate any proceedings for
peace. Therefore, the Governor and General Forbes later sent
Christian Frederick Post on a mission to Wyoming, for the purpose
of explaining the situation concerning the Cherokees, and to request
the Indians on the Susquehanna to call the friendly Indians east
of the mountains while the General advanced against Fort Duquesne.

Post, accompanied by Charles Thomson and three friendly
Indians, left Philadelphia on June 7th and, reaching Bethlehem
the next day, they employed three others to accompany them.
From that place they went to the Nescopeck Mountain, about
fifteen miles from Wyoming, where they met a party of nine
Indians on their way to Bethlehem, who warned them not to go to

Wyoming, as the woods were full of strange Indians. It was then decided to go back to the east side of the mountain, and to send two messengers forward to invite Teedyuscung to meet them. The next day Teedyuscung came from his new residence at Wyoming. Post complained to him that the path to Wyoming was closed, and it was his (Teedyuscung's) business to keep it open. The Delaware "King" replied that the road had been closed by the Six Nations. He told Post that he expected a great many Mohicans and Wanamis to come during the summer to live with him at Wyoming; and he begged for corn and flour for them, and that arms and ammunition might be sent to Shamokin, whence they might be transported by way of the river to Wyoming. He assured Post that a belt repeating an invitation to the Senecas to join in the English interest would reach their head chief in eight days, and that there must be a great treaty during the summer.

Post got much valuable information from Teedyuscung as to the situation among the Indians of the Allegheny and Ohio. He then returned to Philadelphia on June 16th, and delivered his report to the Governor. On June 20th, a peace message from the Cherokees was delivered to the Governor, who desired to send it at once to Teedyuscung at Wyoming. Post was the messenger selected for this purpose, who set out for Wyoming over the same course that he had recently traveled, at which place he arrived on June 27th, and delivered the message to Tedyuscung. At Wyoming Post met a number of chiefs from the Allegheny, to whom he explained all about the peace measures that were under way. An old sachem, named Katuaikund, upon hearing the good news, "lifting up his hands to heaven wished that God would have mercy upon them, and would help them to bring them and the English together again, and to establish an everlasting ground foundation for peace among them. He wished further that God would move the Governor and the people's hearts toward them in love, peace, and union. . . . He said further that it would be well if the Governor sent somebody with them at their return home, for it would be of great consequence to them who lived above Allegheny to hear from the Governor's mind from their own mouths." At Wyoming, Post learned that the garrison at Fort Duquesne consisted of about eleven hundred French, almost starved, who would have abandoned the fort, had not the Mohawks sent them assistance, and that the commander had recently said that, "if the English come too strong upon me, I will leave." Two of the messengers who had come from the Allegheny with news concern-

ing the situation of the French were Pisquetomen and Keekyuscung.

Post then returned to Fort Allen (Weissport) on June 30th;
and after the Governor heard his report and had talked with
Pisquetomen and Keekyuscung, it was decided to send these two
Indians to the Ohio, in order to gain information as to the situation
among the Indians there, and to advise them of the peace measures.
Post was requested to accompany these messengers, and he agreed
to do so, if Charles Thomson were permitted to go with him.   The
Governor replied that "he might take any other person."   Post
then left Philadelphia on June 15th, reaching Bethlehem on the
17th, at which place he made preparations for his journey to the
Ohio.   On the 19th he reached Fort Allen (Weissport), where
Teedyuscung tried to dissuade him from going on his dangerous
mission. Post says: "He [Teedyuscung] was afraid I should
never return, that the Indians would kill me."   Post replied to
Teedyuscung that he was obliged to go, even if he should lose his
life.   On the 22nd, when Post again prepared to set out, Teedyuscung again protested saying that he was afraid that the Indians
would kill Post, or that the French would capture him.   Post then
made the final reply to Teedyuscung that he would go on this peace
mission to the Ohio, even if he died in the undertaking, and that,
if, unhappily, he should die before completing the mission, he
hoped that his death would be the means of saving many hundreds
of lives.   Without further delay, he therefore set forth on his first
mission to the Ohio, accompanied by Pisquetomen and Keekyuscung, as related in Chapter XIX.

Teedyuscung Continues Working for Peace

During all the time between the close of the third council at
Easton, in the summer of 1757, to the opening of the fourth council
at Easton, on October 7, 1758, Teedyuscung worked steadfastly for
peace, and insisted from time to time that a strong fort be
built at Wyoming.   However, he was unable to remain neutral,
and he petitioned the Governor for reward on scalps, believing that
if the white man could enjoy the profits of such a bounty, there was
no reason why the Indians friendly to the Province should not
come in for their share.   He even sent friendly Indians to protect
the frontiers.   When Will Sock, a Conestoga, had been over the
country carrying a French flag, and had murdered Chagrea and a
German in Lancaster County, Teedyuscung took away the flag,

sent it to Philadelphia, and gave him an English flag. In the
meantime, also, he kept urging the Provincial Authorities to build
houses for the friendly Indians at Wyoming, in accordance with
Pennsylvania's promise at the Easton conference of 1757 to enact
a law which would settle the Wyoming lands upon him and his
people forever.

Mary Jemison, White Woman of Genesee

While Teedyuscung was thus working for peace, two atrocities
were committed in Adams County during the month of April, 1758.
The first of these was the attack on the home of Thomas Jemison
near the confluence of Sharp's Run and Conewago Creek, Adams
County, on April 5th, by Indians from the Ohio and Allegheny
valleys. On the morning of that day, Jemison's daughter, Mary,
aged about fifteen, had returned from an errand to a neighbor's,
and a man took her horse to go to his house after a bag of grain.
Her father was busy with chores about the house, her mother was
getting breakfast, her two older brothers were at the barn, while
she, with the smaller children of the family and a neighbor woman,
were in the house. Suddenly they were alarmed by the discharge
of a number of guns. Opening the door they found the man and
the horse lying dead. The Indians then captured Mr. Jemison, his
wife, his children, Robert, Matthew, Betsy, and Mary, together
with the neighbor woman and her three children, the two brothers
in the barn making their escape. The attacking party consisted
of six Indians and four Frenchmen. They set out with their
prisoners in single file, using a whip when anyone lagged behind.
At the end of the second day's march, Mary was separated from
her parents. During the night her parents and all the other prisoners, except Mary and a neighbor boy, were cruelly put to death,
and their bodies left in the swamps to be devoured by wild beasts.
During the next day's march, the unhappy girl had to watch the
Indians scrape and dry the scalps of her parents, brothers, sisters,
and neighbors. Her mother had an abundance of beautiful, red
hair, and she could easily distinguish her scalp from the others,—
a sight which remained with her to the end of her days. The
neighbor boy was given to the French, and Mary was given to two
Shawnee squaws, and carried to the Shawnee towns on the Scioto.
Here these squaws adopted her, replacing a brother who had been
killed during the French and Indian War.

In the autumn of 1759, she was taken to Fort Pitt, when the

Shawnees and other western tribes went to that place to make peace with the English. She accompanied them with a light heart, as she believed she would soon be restored to her brothers who had made their escape when she was captured. The English at Fort Pitt asked her a number of questions concerning herself, which so alarmed her adopted Indian sisters that they hastily took her down the Ohio in a canoe. Afterwards she learned that some settlers had come to the fort to take her away, but could not find her.

She married two Indian chiefs of renown. The first was a Delaware named Sheninjee, of whom she spoke as "noble, large in stature, elegant in appearance, generous in conduct, courageous in war, a friend of peace, and a great lover of justice." To this husband she bore two children. The first died soon after birth, but the second, who was born in the fourth year of her captivity, she named in memory of her father, Thomas Jemison. Her first husband died while they were enroute with her child to her new home in the Genesee Valley in New York. Several years after the death of her first husband, she married Hiokatoo, also known as Gardow, by whom she had four daughters and two sons. This second husband was a cruel and vindictive warrior.

Two great sorrows came into her life. The first was when her son, John, killed his brother, Thomas, her comforter and namesake of her father. The second was when this same John a few years later killed his other brother, Jesse. Her grief became somewhat assuaged when John was murdered later in a drunken quarrel with two Indians.

Mary Jemison continued to live in the German Flats, New York, and upon the death of her second husband, she became possessed of a large tract of valuable land. She was naturalized April 19, 1817, and received a clear title to her land. In 1823, she sold a major portion of her holdings, reserving a tract two miles long and one mile wide.

This remarkable lady who preserved the sensibilities of a white woman amidst the surroundings of barbaric life, died September 19, 1833, at the age of ninety-one years, and was buried, with Christian rites, in the cemetery of the Seneca Mission on the Buffalo Creek Reservation, in New York. On March 17, 1874, her body was removed to the Indian Council House Grounds at Letchworth Park, where a beautiful bronze statue marks the grave of "The White Woman, The Genesee."

Capture of the Family of Richard Bard

The second atrocity committed by the Indians while Teedyuscung was working for peace, was the attack on the home of Richard
Bard, on April 13, 1758. The Bard family resided near a place
later known as Marshall's Mills, in Adams County. A little girl,
named Hannah McBride, was at the door when the Indians
approached. She ran screaming into the house where there were
Bard and his wife and six months' old child, an apprentice boy,
and a relative of the Bards, Lieutenant Thomas Potter by name, a
brother of General James Potter. One of the Indians attacked
Lieutenant Potter with a cutlass, but he succeeded in wresting it
from the savage. Mr. Bard seized a pistol and snapped it at the
breast of one of the Indians, but it failed to fire. As there was no
ammunition in the home, the occupants of the house, fearing a
slaughter or being burned alive, surrendered, as the Indians
promised no harm would be done to them. The savages then went
into the field nearby, where they captured Samuel Hunter, Daniel
McManiny, and a boy named William White, who was coming to
a mill near the Bard home.

The Indians then secured the prisoners, plundered the house,
and burned the mill. At a point about seventy rods from the
home, contrary to their promises, they killed Lieutenant Potter,
and having proceeded over the mountain for several miles, one of
them sunk the spear of his tomahawk into the breast of the child,
and scalped it. When they had proceeded with their prisoners
past the fort into Path Valley, they encamped for the night. The
next day they discovered a party of settlers in pursuit. They then
hastened the pace of their prisoners under threat of tomahawking
them. Reaching the top of Tuscarora Mountain, the party sat
down to rest, and one of the Indians, without giving any warning
whatever, buried his tomahawk in the head of Samuel Hunter, and
scalped him. They then passed over Sidling Hill and the Allegheny Mountains by Blair's Gap, and encamped beyond Stony
Creek. Here they painted Bard's head red on one side, indicating
that a council had been held; that an equal number were for killing
him and for saving his life, and that his fate would be determined
in the next council.

Bard then determined to attempt his escape and, while assisting his wife in plucking a turkey, he told her of his intentions.
Some of the Indians were asleep, and one was amusing the others
by parading around in Mrs. Bard's gown. As this Indian was

thus furnishing amusement for the others, Bard was sent to the spring for water, and made his escape. After having made an unsuccessful search for Bard, the party proceeded to Fort Duquesne and then to Kuskuskies, where Mrs. Bard, the two boys and the girl were compelled to run the gauntlet, and were beaten in a most inhuman manner. Here also Daniel McManiny was put to death by being tied to a post, scalped alive, and pierced through the body with a red-hot gun barrel.

Mrs. Bard was separated from the other prisoners, led from one Indian town to another, and finally adopted by two warriors, to take the place of a deceased sister. Finally she was taken to the headwaters of the Susquehanna, and during the journey, suffered greatly from fatigue and illness. She lay for two months, a blanket her only covering and boiled corn her only food. She remained in captivity two years and five months.

Mr. Bard, after having made his escape and after a terrible journey of nine days, during which his only food was a few buds and four snakes, finally reached Fort Littleton, Fulton County. After this, he wandered from place to place throughout the frontier, seeking information concerning his wife. After having made several perilous journeys to Fort Duquesne for the same purpose, and in which he narrowly escaped capture on several occasions, he finally learned that she was at Fort Augusta (Sunbury), where he redeemed her.

During Mrs. Bard's captivity, she was kindly treated by the warriors who had adopted her. Before the Bards left Fort Augusta, Mr. Bard requested one of his wife's adopted brothers to visit them at their home. This he did some time afterwards, when the Bards were living about ten miles from Chambersburg, remaining at the Bard home for some time; but finally he went one day to McDowell's Tavern, where he became intoxicated and got into a quarrel with a rough frontier character by the name of Newgen, who stabbed him dangerously in the neck. Newgen fled from the vicinity in order to escape the wrath of Bard's neighbors. The wounded Indian, however, recovered after being tenderly nursed by his adopted sister, Mrs. Bard. He then returned to his people, who put him to death on the pretext of having, as they claimed, joined the white people.

Other atrocities than the attacks on the Jemison and Bard families, were committed in Eastern Pennsylvania in the month of April, 1758. A man, named Lebenguth, and his wife were killed in the Tulpehocken Valley. Also, at Northkill, Nicholas Geiger's wife and two children and Michael Ditzelar's wife were killed.

Teedyuscung at the Grand Council at Easton

While Christian Frederick Post was on his first mission to the Ohio Indians, Teedyuscung was persuading the Six Nations to send deputies to a fourth grand peace conference at Easton. His purpose was to draw all the Indians into an alliance with the English, and to secure a general and lasting peace. As a preliminary, he had induced the Minisink Indians and a number of Senecas to go to Philadelphia in August and hold a conference with the Governor.

The Grand Council at Easton, known as the Fourth Easton Council, opened on Sunday, October 8, 1758, with more than five hundred Indians in attendance, representing all the tribes of the Six Nations, the Delawares, Conoys, Tuteloes, and Nanticokes. Governor Denny, members of the Provincial Council and Assembly, Governor Bernard, of New Jersey, Commissioners for Indian affairs in New Jersey, Conrad Weiser, George Crogan, and a number of Quakers from Philadelphia, made up the attendance of the whites.

Pennsylvania Deeds Back Albany Purchase of 1754

Three great land disputes came before this council. The first was the Albany purchase of 1754, which, as we have already seen, caused the Delawares of the West Branch of the Susquehanna and the valleys of the Ohio and Allegheny to go over to the French. To the credit of Conrad Weiser, it must be said that he had all along insisted that this was not a just purchase; that the Indians were deceived, and that the running of the lines had been greatly misrepresented. Furthermore, the Six Nations had declared to Sir William Johnson in 1755, that they would never consent to this sale, pointing out that the West Branch of the Susquehanna was held by them simply in trust as a hunting ground for their cousins, the Delawares. The matter was adjusted at this treaty by Governor Denny, on behalf of the Proprietaries, telling the Six Nations that Conrad Weiser and Richard Peters would deed back to them all of the Albany Purchase west of the summits of the Allegheny Mountains, if the Six Nations would confirm the residue of the purchase. This they agreed to, and the mutual releases were executed October 24th.

But before the releases were executed, Christian Frederick Post had succeeded in drawing the Shawnees and Delawares of the Ohio away from the French,—a fact that shows the greatness of his achievement. On his way back from his first mission to the Ohio

Indians, he sent Pisquetomen and John Hickman to Philadelphia to deliver the speech belt which Shingas, Beaver, and other chiefs had given him, while he went on from Harris' Ferry to see General Forbes. Pisquetomen and Hickman then went to the Great Council at Easton, where Pisquetomen delivered the belt.

On the afternoon of October 22nd, just as Pisquetomen and Hickman were leaving Easton, Post arrived at the Council with the news from General Forbes that the General's advance guard, on October 12th, was attacked at Loyal Hanning, later known as Fort Ligonier, at the present town of Ligonier, Westmoreland County, by twelve hundred French and two hundred Indians. Post then left Easton on October 25th on his second mission to the Ohio Indians, to make known to them the results of the Easton Council.

The success of Post's second mission to the Ohio has already been told, as has the fact that, in July, 1759, a great conference was held at Fort Pitt with all the Ohio tribes by George Croghan, Colonel Hugh Mercer, then commander at Fort Pitt, Captain William Trent, and Captain Thomas McKee, which gathered the fruit and glory of the peace missions of this Moravian missionary. King Beaver was the principal speaker of the Indians on this occasion. Guyasuta was also present, and Andrew Montour was the interpreter.

The second land dispute taken up at the Grand Council was the complaint of the Munsee Clan of Delawares (Munseys) that their lands in New Jersey had never been purchased. Governor Bernard, of New Jersey, when asked by the Munseys what he should pay for the New Jersey land, offered them eight hundred dollars, saying that it was a very extraordinary offer. The Munseys then asked the Iroquois deputies for their opinion as to the price. The Iroquois replied that the offer was fair and honorable; that if it were their own case, they would cheerfully accept it; but, as there were a great many of the Munseys to share in the purchase money, they would recommend that the Governor add two hundred dollars more. To this Governor Bernard agreed, and so this second great land dispute was settled.

The third land dispute to come before the Grand Council was the old complaints made by Teedyuscung concerning the Walking Purchase. The Six Nations had not met with the Delawares at any public treaty with Pennsylvania since the treaty of 1742, in which Canassatego, as the spokesman of the Six Nations, ordered the Delawares to remove from the bounds of the Walking Purchase. Three questions called for an answer at the Grand Council:

(1) Was the Walking Purchase just? (2) Had the Six Nations any right to sell lands on the Delaware? (3) Were the Delawares subject to the Iroquois, or were they independent?

Teedyuscung Humbled By Iroquois Chiefs

Before taking up the matter of the Walking Purchase, the Iroquois deputies concluded that the first thing to do was to humble Teedyuscung, and break down his influence and standing. The great Delaware had entered this council more humbly than he did the councils of 1756 and 1757, realizing that his bitter enemy, Nickas, a Mohawk chief, was in attendance.

Nickas began the attack on Teedyuscung, designed to break down his influence. Pointing to Teedyuscung, he spoke with great vigor and bitterness. Conrad Weiser was ordered to interpret Nickas' speech, but declined, and desired that Andrew Montour should do it. Weiser clearly saw that the interpretation of his speech would cause great discord, and he planned to have the interpreation postponed until the anger of the Iroquois had time to cool. He therefore advised that the speech be interpreted at a private conference, which was arranged to take place the next morning, October 14th. The next morning came; but there was no conference. Weiser had succeeded in causing more delay to avert the threatening storm. However, on the morning of the 15th, Nickas, at a private conference, said: "Who made Teedyuscung chief of the nations? If he be such a great man, we desire to know who made him so? Perhaps you have, and if this be the case, tell us so. It may be the French have made him so. We want to inquire and know where his greatness arose."

Nickas was followed by Tagashata, chief of the Senecas, who said: "We do not know who made Teedyuscung this great man over ten nations, and I want to know who made him so." Then Assarandonquas, chief of the Onondagas, said: "I never heard before now that Teedyuscung was such a great man, and much less can I tell who made him so. No such thing was ever said in our towns." Then Thomas King, in behalf of the Oneidas, Cayugas, Tuscaroras, Nanticokes, and Conoys, said: "I now tell you we, none of us, know who has made Teedyuscung such a great man. Perhaps the French have, or perhaps you have, or some among you, as you have different governments and are different people. We for our parts entirely disown that he has any authority over us, and we desire to know from whence he derives his authority."

Under this concerted attack upon his kingly pretensions, Teedyuscung sat like a stoic, never saying a word in reply, and his features betraying no signs of emotion.

The following day, October 16th, after Conrad Weiser had time to advise Governor Denny and Governor Bernard as to the proper reply to make to these speeches of the Iroquois deputies, Governor Denny advised them that he had never made Teedyuscung a great chief. He further told the deputies that, at the former Easton conferences, Teedyuscung had spoken of the Iroquois as his uncles and superiors; and Governor Bernard also denied making Teedyuscung a great chief, or king. Thus, the skillful guidance of Conrad Weiser, in delaying the outburst of Iroquois anger and in framing the proper speeches for the Governors, smoothed matters over, and prevented the cause of peace from suffering a serious setback.

After the apologies of Governor Denny and Governor Bernard, Teedyuscung arose to speak on his land claims. Said he:

"I did let you know formerly what my grievance was. I told you that from Tohiccon, as far as the Delawares owned, the Proprietaries had wronged me. Then you and I agreed that it should be laid before the King of England, and likewise you told me you would let me know as soon as ever he saw it. You would lay the matter before the King, for you said he was our Father, that he might see what was our differences; for as you and I could not decide it, let him do it. Now let us not alter what you and I have agreed. Now, let me know if King George has decided the matter between you and me. I don't pretend to mention any of my uncles' [Iroquois'] lands. I only mention what we, the Delawares, own, as far as the heads of Delaware. All the lands lying on the waters that fall into the Susquehanna belong to our uncles."

He then took another belt and turned to address the Iroquois, but these proud sachems had, during his speech to Governors Denny and Bernard, noiselessly left the room. Teedyuscung then declined to speak further. The next day, October 17th, the Indians spent in private conferences. On October 18th, after Governor Denny had had a private interview with the Six Nations, Teedyuscung came to his headquarters, stating that the Delawares did not claim the land high up on the Delaware, as those belonged to their uncles, the Iroquois, but that the land which he did specifically complain about, was included in the Walking Purchase. Governor Denny avoided giving Teedyuscung a direct reply until he would lay the land dispute before the Six Nations' deputies.

He then explained to the deputies that Pennsylvania had bought land from them which the Delawares claimed, advising that this was a matter which should be settled among themselves. The Six Nations replied that they did not understand the Governor. They said that he had left matters in the dark; that they did not know what lands he meant; that if he meant the lands on the other side of the Blue Mountains, he knew that the Proprietaries had a deed for them (the Purchase of 1749), which ought to be produced and shown to them; that their deeds had their marks, and when they should see them, they would know their marks again. Conrad Weiser then brought the deed. The Iroquois examined it and said: "The land was ours and we can justify it."

Teedyuscung said no more at the Easton conference concerning the Walking Purchase, but he charged the Six Nations with selling his land at Wyoming to the Connecticut interests at the Albany treaty of 1754. In fact, one of the conditions upon which he was willing to make peace was that he and his Delawares be settled at Wyoming, and that a deed be given to them for these lands. Addressing the Iroquois deputies, he said:

"Uncles, you may remember that you placed us at Wyoming and Shamokin, places where Indians have lived before. Now, I hear since that you have sold that land to our brethren, the English, [meaning the Connecticut commissioners]. Let the matter now be cleared up in the presence of our brothers, the English. I sit here as a bird on a bough. I look about and do not know where to go. Let me therefore come down upon the ground and make that my own by a good deed, and I shall then have a home forever; for if you, my uncles, or I, die, our brethren, the English, will say they bought it from you, and so wrong my posterity out of it."

The Grand Council ended on October 26th. Peace was secured, and through the efforts of Post, the Ohio Indians had been drawn away from the French. Thus the good work inaugurated by Canachquasy and furthered by Teedyuscung reached a happy consummation.

The Murder of Dr. John and Family

In February, 1760, a friendly Delaware, named Doctor John, his wife, and two children were massacred near Carlisle. Captain Callender, a member of the inquest, was summoned by the Assembly, and after interrogating him, the Governor offered a reward of

one hundred pounds for the apprehension of each person connected
with the murder.   Great excitement prevailed throughout the
Province, on account of the assassination of these friendly Indians;
for it was feared that the recently pacified Shawnees and Delawares
would retaliate by attacking the settlements on the frontiers.   A
letter was sent to Christian Frederick Post, the Moravian missionary, desiring him "forthwith to make Teedyuscung and the Indians
at Wyoming acquainted with these murders and the issuing of the
proclamation, and to assure him that no pains would be spared to
discover and punish the authors."   Similar messages were sent to
the Delawares and Shawnees in the valleys of the Ohio and Allegheny.

Teedyuscung Makes Journey to Western Indians

Christian Frederick Post and John Hays, under instructions
from Governor Hamilton, left Easton in May, 1760, for the purpose of making a journey with Teedyuscung up the North Branch
of the Susquehanna, thence across to the headwaters of the Allegheny, and thence down this stream to "some principal Indian
town over the Ohio", where a great Indian council was to be held.
Teedyuscung joined Post and Hays at Wyoming, and the party
then went up the Susquehanna as far as Pasigachkunk, on
Cowanesque Creek, in Tioga County, where they were stopped by
Senecas, and the white men were forced to turn back; "for," said
Hays, "there was an old agreement that no white man should pass
through their country for fear of spies to see their land."   However, Teedyuscung and a few Indian companions, among whom
was his son, Amos, kept on, and attended the great council of the
western tribes in Ohio.

On September 15th, Teedyuscung appeared before Governor
Hamilton and the Provincial Council, and related to them the results of his western mission as follows:

"You may remember that I often promised you to give the
halloo through all the Indian nations.   I have been a long way
back, a great way indeed, beyond the Allegheny, among my friends
there.   When I got as far as the Salt Lick Town towards the head
of Beaver Creek [River], I stopped there and sent messengers to
the chiefs of all the Indians in those parts, desiring them to come
and hold council.   It took three weeks to collect them together; and
then, having a large number gathered together, I communicated to
them all that had passed between me and this government for four

years past, at which they were glad and declared that this was the first time they had a right understanding of these transactions. They said they had heard now and then that we were sitting together about peace, but they were not acquainted till now with the particulars of our several conferences. I concealed nothing from them, and when they had heard all, they were right glad. It gave joy to their very hearts. This is all I have to say at this time. Tomaquior [Tamaque], the Beaver King (who is the head man of the Delawares at the Ohio), did not give me anything in charge to say to the Governor. We were all present at the great council held at Pittsburgh, and heard him [King Beaver] tell the General that he would go to Philadelphia in the summer, and hold a council with this government, in compliance with the several invitations that he had received from it. I told Tamaque that Pittsburgh was no place to hold council as the old fire was there; that Pittsburgh was only a place for warriors to speak in, and that he should do no council business at Pittsburgh. And accordingly Tamaque told the General that he would not say anything to him, but say it at the place where their grandfathers were always used to hold council with the English."

The council referred to by Teedyuscung as being held at Pittsburgh, was the great conference held at Fort Pitt, by General Monckton, with the western tribes on August 12, 1760. The purpose of this conference was to assure the Western Delawares, Shawnees, and other tribes that the English had no design of taking their lands. Reference was made to this conference in Chapter XIX.

In 1761, Teedyuscung wished to leave Wyoming, inasmuch he despaired of securing a title to that region, for his people. Fortunately the Governor was able to persuade him not to do such a rash act, and he continued then to reside at Wyoming until the end of his days.

Teedyuscung is Paid for Withdrawing Charge of Fraud

On April 26, 1762, Teedyuscung attended a conference with Governor Hamilton at Philadelphia, in which he was told that, if he would withdraw his charges against the Proprietors of fraud in the Walking Purchase, he would be given four hundred pounds. Teedyuscung replied that he "never did charge the Proprietors with fraud, but had only said that the French had informed them that the English had cheated them out of their land, that his young men desired him to mention it at the treaty of Easton, and that he did it to please them, and was sorry it had reached their hearts." Governor Hamilton then told him that, if he would acknowledge this in public, he would make him a present, not on account of the lands, which had been bought and paid for, but on account of the chief's needy circumstances. Then, when Teedyuscung made his public acknowledgment, the Governor made him the present of four hundred pounds.

Reference was made, in Chapter XIX, to the fact that a great conference was held at Lancaster beginning August 12, 1762, between the Provincial Authorities and Shingas, King Beaver, and other western chiefs whom Christian Frederick Post had brought from the Muskingum, Tuscarawas, and the Ohio. King Beaver, who was at the head of the Western Indians at this conference, was advised "that about six years ago your brother, Teedyuscung, made a complaint to the Proprietaries wherein he charged them of defrauding the Delawares of a tract of land lying on the River Delaware, between Tohiccon Creek and the Kittatiny Hills. He alleged that this complaint was not made by him on his own account, but on behalf of the owners of the lands, many of whom he said lived on Allegheny. This dispute, brethren, was by mutual consent, referred to our great King George, who ordered Sir William Johnson to inquire fully into the matter, and make his report to him, that justice might be done you, if you had been wronged. Accordingly, Sir William Johnson, about two months ago (June, 1762), came to Easton, whereupon the Proprietaries' commissioners producing and reading sundry writings and papers, Teedyuscung was convinced of his error, and acknowledged that he had been mistaken with regard to the charge of forgery made against the Proprietaries, having been misinformed by his ancestors, and desired that all future disputes about land should be buried under ground, and never heard of more, offering that such of the Indians as were then present should sign a release for the land in question, and that he would endeavour to persuade the rest of his brethren who were concerned to do the same at this treaty at Lancaster. Now, brethren of Allegheny, as we are face to face, be plain and tell whether you are satisfied with and approve of what was done at the last treaty of Easton, and whether you lay any claims to those lands, that there may be no room left for any future dispute about it among our children."

To this King Beaver replied: "As to my own part, I know nothing about the lands upon the River Delaware, but since you request it I will first speak to my own people about it." Then King Beaver, having consulted with his counsellors, further replied: "I must acknowledge I know nothing about lands upon the Delaware, and I have no concern with lands upon that river. We know nothing of the Delawares' claim to them. I have no claim myself nor any of my people. I suppose there may be some spots or pieces of land in some part of the Province that the Delawares claim, but neither I nor any of my people know anything of them. As to what you and our brother, Teedyuscung, have done, if you are both pleased, I am pleased with it. As to my part, I want to say nothing about land affairs. What I have at heart and what I came down about, is to confirm our friendship and make a lasting peace, so that our children and grandchildren may live together in everlasting peace after we are dead."

Teedyuscung and the Eastern Delawares then conferred together, but what was said by them was not made known. The old chief then addressed Governor Hamilton as follows: "Before all these Allegheny Indians here present, I do now assure you that I am ready and willing to sign a release to all the lands we have been disputing about, as I told you I would at Easton and desire no more may be ever said or heard of them hereafter."

Then Teedyuscung was given another present, being two hundred Spanish dollars, and the value of two hundred pounds in goods,—the last chapter in the history of the charge of fraud, made by this able Delaware chief to the embarrassment of the Colonial Authorities.

Teedyuscung was now approaching the end of his earthly career. He was really a great man. It was but natural that he should, for a time, have taken up arms against the Province which, by unfair means, it must be admitted, had gotten possession of the hunting grounds of his ancestors. In appraising his conduct, all honor must be given him for his untiring labors in behalf of peace. Indeed, the prominence that was his, in these labors, caused him to be the object of the hatred of the Mohawks, who could not brook the fact that one so much beneath them, a Delaware, should occupy such an exalted position. This hatred led to Teedyuscung's death.

But this grave and dignified chieftain had a sense of humor. There is a tradition that, on one occasion, he met, at Stroudsburg, a blacksmith, named McNabb, a worthless fellow, who thus addressed the great Delaware: "Well, cousin, how do you do?" "Cousin, cousin", said Teedyuscung, "how do you make that out?"

"Oh, we are all cousins from Adam," said McNabb. "Ah," said Teedyuscung, "then I am glad it is no nearer."

Death of Teedyuscung

This great leader of the Eastern Delawares, the last of their great chiefs, was burned to death on the night of April 16, 1763, as he lay in a drunken debauch on a couch in his house at Wyoming, which was set on fire by some of his Indian enemies, either Senecas or Mohawks. A monument has been erected to this noted chief, in Fairmont Park, Philadelphia, which represents him, bow and spear in hand, a plume of eagle feathers on his brow, as stepping forth on his journey towards the setting sun.

CHAPTER XXIII.

Guyasuta

GUYASUTA (Kiasutha) has generally been called a Seneca chief, but he was probably of the mongrel Iroquois known as the Mingoes, who inhabited the Allegheny Valley and region to the westward. We have already met him as one of the chiefs who accompanied George Washington from Logstown to Fort LeBouef, when the latter went to that place in November, 1753, carrying the protest of Governor Dinwiddie of Virginia to St. Pierre, the commandant of the French forts. He is referred to in Washington's journal of this trip as the Hunter.

Long years afterward, Washington met Guyasuta near the mouth of the Muskingum, when, in October, 1770, accompanied by his friend, neighbor, and former companion in arms, Dr. Craik, and William Crawford, he journeyed down the Ohio Valley to examine the lands apportioned among the Virginia soldiers. Guyasuta was at his hunting camp when Washington met him. Seventeen years had matured the young ambassador to thoughtful manhood; yet Guyasuta held a perfect recollection of him. With a hunter's hospitality, he gave Washington, Dr. Craik, and Crawford a quarter of a buffalo, just killed. He insisted that they should encamp together for the night, and not wishing to detain Washington, he moved his hunting party to another camp some miles down the Ohio. Here the great Virginian and Guyasuta held long talks around the council-fire that night. During the intervening years, Guyasuta had fought against the English, in the French and Indian War, had helped Pontiac form his great conspiracy, in 1763, and was one of the most vindictive in carrying it into terrible and bloody execution upon the English forts and settlements; while Washington, in both these conflicts, was one of the powerful leaders on the side of the English. We cannot but wonder what were the subjects of conversation of Washington and Guyasuta around that council-fire.

Guyasuta Goes Over to the French

Guyasuta was one of the western chiefs, who went over to the French shortly after Braddock's defeat. At the head of a party of twenty Senecas, he visited Marquis de Vaudreuil, Governor of Canada, at Montreal, Joncaire accompanying him as interpreter, where they were received with much ceremony, so pleasing to the Indians. Guyasuta, as the chief and orator of the Seneca delegation, addressed the Governor on this occasion. He and his warriors remained near Montreal during the winter, it being too late in the year to make the journey back to the Ohio.

Grant's Defeat

The most important service Guyasuta rendered the French during the French and Indian War was leading the Indians in the attack on Major James Grant, where the Allegheny County Court House, in the city of Pittsburgh, now stands, on September 14, 1758. When Forbes' army was advancing on Fort Duquesne in the autumn of this year, and the advance, under Colonel Bouquet, had reached the Loyalhanna and Ligonier, Westmoreland County, Major Grant, with a force of thirty-seven officers and eight hundred and five privates, was sent by Bouquet to reconnoiter the fort and adjacent country. Grant's instructions were not to approach too near the fort and not to attack it. The wilderness between Ligonier and Fort Duquesne was filled with Indians constantly watching the movements of Grant's little army; yet he succeeded in coming within sight of the fort without being discovered. Late at night he drew up his troops on the brow of the fatal hill in the city of Pittsburgh, which still bears his name, about a quarter of a mile from the fort.

Not having met with either French or Indians on the march, and believing from the stillness of the enemy's quarters that the forces in the fort were small, Grant at once determind to make an attack. Accordingly, two officers and fifty men were directed to approach the fort and fall upon the French and Indians that might be outside. They saw none and were not challenged by the sentinels; and as they returned, they set fire to a large storehouse, but the fire was extinguished. At the break of day, September 14th, Grant sent Major Lewis with two hundred regulars and Virginia volunteers to take a position about a half mile back, and lie in ambush where they had left their baggage. Four hundred men were posted along the hill facing the fort, while Captain McDonald's company, with drums beating and bagpipes playing. marched toward the fort in order to draw out the garrison. The music of the drums and bagpipes aroused the garrison from their slumber, and both the French and Indians sallied out in great numbers, the latter led by Guyasuta.

The French and Indians separated into three divisions. The first two were sent under the cover of the banks of the Monongahela and Allegheny to surround the main body of Grant's troops, while the third was delayed awhile to give the others time, and then lined up before the fort as if exhibiting the whole strength of the garrison. This plan worked admirably. Captain McDonald was obliged to fall back on the main body, and at the same time, Grant found himself flanked by the detachments on both sides. A desperate struggle ensued. The highlanders, exposed to the enemy's fire without cover, fell in great numbers. The provincials, concealing themselves among the trees, made a good defense for a while, but not being supported and being overpowered by numbers, were compelled to fall back. The result was that Grant's forces were overwhelmingly and ingloriously defeated. Many of his brave troops were driven into the Allegheny River and drowned. The total loss was two hundred and seventy killed, forty-two wounded, and several taken prisoners. Among the latter was Major Grant himself.

Grant's expedition was a monstrous blunder. General Forbes, with the main body of the army was as far in the rear as Bedford, and neither he nor Colonel Bouquet had any definite knowledge of the strength of the French and Indians at Fort Duquesne. In view of these facts, it seems strange, indeed, that Colonel Bouquet permitted Grant to advance into a death trap. Grant himself showed utter lack of judgment in playing the bagpipes and beating the drums at daylight, which had only the effect of telling the enemy of his advance. Neither the French nor the Indians knew of Grant's presence until the music broke the stillness of the autumn morning. How Grant's conduct impressed the Indians was expressed by one of their chiefs in a conversation with James Smith, at that time a captive among them. This chief told Smith that the Indians believed that Grant "had made too free with spiritous liquors during the night, and had become intoxicated about daylight."

French and Indians Attack the Camp on the Loyalhanna

Emboldened by the defeat of Major Grant, Captain DeLignery, then commander of Fort Duquesne, sent about one thousand French and two hundred Indians, the latter most likely led by Guyasuta, against the English camp on the Loyalhanna, at

Ligonier, hoping to compel them to retreat as did Dunbar after the defeat of Braddock. They attacked the camp on October 12th, but were repulsed by Colonel James Burd, who was then in command of the camp, the English loss being twelve killed, eighteen wounded, and thirty-one missing. Colonel Bouquet was not at the camp at the time of the engagement, being at Stony Creek with seven hundred men and a detachment of artillery.

Before Forbes' army left Ligonier, a thrilling event in the life of George Washington took place. He was a colonel in the army, and, on November 12th, was out with a scouting party which attacked a number of the enemy about three miles from the camp, killing one and taking three pisoners, an Indian man and woman, and an Englishman, named Johnson, who had been captured by the Indians several years before, in Lancaster County. Captain Mercer, hearing the firing, was sent with a party of Virginians to the assistance of Washington. The two parties approaching each other in the dusk of the evening, each mistook the other for the enemy, and fired upon each other, killing several Virginians and wounding about a dozen others. Washington, upon recognizing the terrible mistake, rushed between the two parties, and knocked up the presented muskets with his sword.

Washington's skirmish, on November 12th, was the last clash of arms between the French and Indians on the one side and the English on the other, in the Ohio Valley during the French and Indian War. It will be remembered that Washington was a leading figure in the opening conflict in this war, the attack on Jumonville, May 28th, 1754.

The Englishman, Johnson, gave Forbes the information relative to the conditions at Fort Duquesne that caused the General to decide to press forward against the fort at once, instead of going into winter quarters on the Loyalhanna. His army accordingly left the Loyalhanna on November 17th, finding the way to the fort strewed with the bodies of Major Grant's soldiers who had died on the retreat. On the 24th, the French set fire to Fort Duquesne and fled, and on the 25th, Forbes, army took possession of its smouldering ruins. Says Bancroft: "As the banners of England floated over the waters, the place, at the suggestion of Forbes, was with one voice called Pittsburg(h). It is the most enduring monument to William Pitt. America raised to his name statues that have been wrongfully broken, and granite piles of which not one stone remains upon another; but, long as the Monongahela and the Allegheny shall flow to form the Ohio, long as the English tongue shall be the language of freedom in the boundless valley which their waters traverse, his name shall stand inscribed on the gateway of the West."

Forbes' troops found many of the dead of Grant's defeat within a quarter of a mile of the fort. They also found a number of stakes driven into the ground on which were stuck the heads and kilts of the Highlanders, captured on that fateful September morning. Detachments then buried Grant's dead and the bones of those who were slain at Braddock's defeat over three years before.

Guyasuta at Council of July, 1759

Guyasuta's next act of importance was to attend the council held at Fort Pitt, July 5, 1759, mentioned in Chapters XIX, XX, and XXII, between George Croghan, Colonel Hugh Mercer, Captain William Trent, and Captain Thomas McKee, on the one hand, and the representatives of the Six Nations, Delawares, Shawnees, and Wyandots, on the other, at which the terms of the Easton treaty of October, 1758, were confirmed, and the Western Indians promised to surrender the prisoners taken in the French and Indian War.

Guyasuta in Pontiac's War

The fall of Quebec, in the autumn of 1759, practically ended the French and Indian War. Then the English came to take possession of the surrendered French forts. The Indians soon found that their new masters had a very different attitude towards them than had the French. While the French had lavished presents upon them, the English now doled out blankets, ammunition, and guns with a sparing hand. The proud-spirited western tribes were exasperated at the patronizing air of the English, and their indignation was encouraged by the Frenchmen among them.

A few years of discontent, and then Pontiac, the great chief of the Ottawas, formed a conspiracy, bold in its design and masterful in its execution, to drive the English into the sea. In this plan and in its execution, he was ably assisted by Guyasuta. The Delawares, Shawnees, and, in fact almost all the tribes of the great Algonquin family, and one tribe of the Six Nations, the Senecas, joined in this uprising, known as Pontiac's Conspiracy, also as the Pontiac and Guyasuta War.

In carrying the Pontiac and Guyasuta Conspiracy into execution, these chiefs were ably assisted by Custaloga or Kustaloga, a chief of the Munsee or Wolf Clan of Delawares. Custaloga was living at Venango when John Frazer, the English trader, was driven from that place by the French late in the summer of 1753, and when Washington stopped there in November of that year on his way to St. Pierre, at Fort LeBoueff. However, Custaloga's principal seat was Custaloga's Town, located about twelve miles above the mouth of French Creek and near the mouth of Deer Creek, in French Creek Township, Mercer County. He also ruled over the Delawares at the town of Cussewago, or Cassewago, on the site of the present town of Meadville, the county seat of Crawford County. He was one of the chiefs with whom Colonel Bouquet dealt when he made his expedition to the Muskingum in the autumn of 1764. His successor was Captain Pipe of the Wolf Clan of Delawares.

In May, 1763, the dogs of war were once more let loose on the English forts and settlements. Almost every fort along the Great Lakes and the Ohio was instantly attacked. Those that did not fall under the first onslaught were resolutely besieged. On June 15th, Fort Presqu' Isle (Erie), commanded by Ensign Price, was attacked, and all of the garrison who were not killed, were taken to Detroit, except Benjamin Gray, who escaped to Fort Pitt and gave the news. On June 18th, Fort LeBouef (Waterford, Erie County) was captured; and at about the same time, Fort Venango Franklin, commanded by Lieutenant Gordon, was burned and the entire garrison put to death. Lieutenant Gordon was tortured over a slow fire for several successive nights.

Fort Pitt was attacked on June 22nd, and later the siege of the place was commenced. On the 26th of July a party of Indians approached the gate, displaying a flag of truce, among whom were Shingas and Turtle Heart. They were admitted, and Captain Simeon Ecuyer, the commandant, held a parley with them. The Indian delegation complained that the English were the cause of the war, saying that they had marched their armies into the country and built forts against the repeated protests of the Indians. Said the Indian speaker: "My brothers, this land is ours, and not yours." Captain Ecuyer refused to leave the place, and told the Indians if they would not abandon the siege, he would "throw bomb shells, which will burst and blow you to atoms, and fire cannon among you loaded with a whole bag full of bullets."

Says Parkman: "Disappointed of gaining a bloodless possession of the fort, the Indians now, for the first time, began a general attack. On the night succeeding the conference, they

---

Author's note on second paragraph, page 376
Inadvertantly it was stated in above paragraph that Ensign Price was in command of Fort Prequ' Isle. He was in command of Fort LeBeouf, and Ensign Christie was in command at Fort Presqu' Isle.

approached in great multitudes, under cover of the darkness and completely surrounded it; many of them crawling beneath the banks of the two rivers, which ran close to the rampart, and, with incredible perseverance, digging, with their knives, holes in which they were completely sheltered from the fire of the fort. On one side, the whole bank was lined with these burrows, from each of which a bullet or an arrow was shot out whenever a soldier chanced to expose his head. At daybreak, a general fire was opened from every side, and continued without intermission until night, and through several succeeding days. Meanwhile, the women and children were pent up in the crowded barracks, terror-stricken at the horrible din of the assailants, and watching the fire-arrows as they came sailing over the parapet, and lodging against the roofs and sides of the buildings. In every instance, the fire they kindled was extinguished. One of the garrison was killed, and seven wounded. Among the latter was Captain Ecuyer, who, freely exposing himself, received an arrow in the leg. At length, an event hereafter to be described put an end to the attack, and drew off the assailants from the neighborhood of the fort, to the unspeakable relief of the harassed soldiers, exhausted as they were by several days of unintermitted vigilance."

Fort Bedford, commanded by Captain Wendell Ourry (Uhrig) was also attacked as was Fort Ligonier, commanded by Lieutenant Archibald Blane. Indeed, terror reigned on the whole Pennsylvania frontier. From many fertile valleys rose the smoke of burning settlements. The mutilated bodies of slain settlers were torn and devoured by hogs and wild beasts. Hundreds of families fled over the mountains to the extreme eastern settlements.

Battle of Bushy Run

Then Colonel Bouquet was sent with an army to the relief of Fort Pitt, composed of five hundred regulars, lately returned from the West Indies, and two hundred rangers from Lancaster and Cumberland Counties. On his way to Fort Pitt, Bouquet fought the terrible battle of Bushy Run, about a mile east of Harrison City, Westmoreland County, August 5th and 6th, 1763. Inasmuch as it is almost a certainty that Guyasuta commanded the Indians at this bitterly contested engagement, we give the following description of Bouquet's advance and of the battle, from the classic pen of Francis Parkman, the great authority on Pontiac's Conspiracy:

"Orders were therefore sent to Colonel Bouquet, who commanded at Philadelphia, to assemble as large a force as possible, and cross the Alleghenies with a convoy of provision and ammunition. With every effort, no more than five hundred men could be collected for this service. They consisted chiefly of Highlanders of the 42nd Regiment, which had suffered less than most of the other corps, from West Indian exposure. Having sent agents to the frontier to collect horses, wagons, and supplies, Bouquet soon after followed with the troops, and reached Carlisle about the first of July. He found the whole country in a panic. Every building in the fort, every house, barn, and hovel in the little town, was crowded with the families of settlers, driven from their homes by the terror of the Indian tomahawk. None of the enemy, however, had yet appeared in the neighborhood, and the people flattered themselves that their ravages would be confined to the other side of the mountains. Whoever ventured to predict the contrary drew upon himself the indignation of the whole community.

"On Sunday, the third of July, an incident occurred which redoubled the alarm. A soldier, riding express from Fort Pitt, galloped into the town, and alighted to water his horse at the well in the centre of the place. A crowd of countrymen were instantly about him, eager to hear the news. 'Presqu'Isle, Le Boeuf, and Venango are taken, and the Indians will be here soon.' Such was the substance of the man's reply, as, remounting in haste, he rode on to make his report at the camp of Bouquet. All was now consternation and excitement. Messengers hastened out to spread the tidings, and every road and pathway leading into Carlisle was beset with the flying settlers, flocking thither for refuge. Soon rumors were heard that the Indians were come. Some of the fugitives had seen the smoke of burning houses rising from the valleys, and these reports were fearfully confirmed by the appearance of miserable wretches, who half frantic with grief and dismay, had fled from the sight of blazing dwellings and slaughtered families. A party of the inhabitants armed themselves and went out, to warn the living and bury the dead. Reaching Shearman's Valley, they found fields laid waste, stacked wheat on fire, and the houses yet in flames, and they grew sick with horror, at seeing a group of hogs tearing and devouring the bodies of the dead. As they advanced up the valley, everything betokened the recent presence of the enemy, while columns of smoke, rising among the surrounding mountains, showed how general was the work of destruction.

"On the previous day, six men, assembled for reaping the harvest, had been seated at dinner at the house of Campbell, a settler on the Juniata. Four or five Indians suddenly burst the door, fired among them, and then beat down the survivors with the butts of their rifles. One young man leaped from his seat, snatched a gun which stood in a corner, discharged it into the breast of the warrior who was rushing upon him, and, leaping through an open window, made his escape. He fled through the forest to a settlement at some distance, where he related his story. Upon this, twelve young men volunteered to cross the mountain, and warn the inhabitants of the neighboring Tuscarora Valley. On entering it, they found that the enemy had been there before them. Some of the houses were on fire, while others were still standing, with no tenants but the dead. Under the shed of a farmer, the Indians had been feasting on the flesh of the cattle they had killed, and the meat had not yet grown cold. Pursuing their course, the white men found the spot where several detached parties of the enemy had united almost immediately before, and they boldly resolved to follow, in order to ascertain what direction the marauders had taken. The trail led them up a deep and woody pass of the Tuscarora. Here the yell of the war-whoop and the din of firearms suddenly greeted them, and five of their number were shot down. Thirty warriors rose from their ambuscade, and rushed upon them. They gave one discharge, scattered, and ran for their lives. One of them, a boy named Charles Eliot, as he fled, plunging through the thickets, heard an Indian tearing the boughs behind him, in furious pursuit. He seized his powder-horn, poured the contents at random down the muzzle of his gun, threw in a bullet after them, without using the ramrod, and, wheeling about, discharged the piece into the breast of his pursuer. He saw the Indian shrink back and roll over into the bushes. He continued his flight; but a moment after, a voice earnestly called his name. Turning to the spot, he saw one of his comrades stretched helpless upon the ground. This man had been mortally wounded at the first fire, but had fled a few rods from the scene of blood, before his strength gave out. Eliot approached him. 'Take my gun,' said the dying frontiersman. 'Whenever you see an Indian, kill him with it, and then I shall be satisfied.' Eliot, with several others of the party, escaped, and finally reached Carlisle, where his story excited a spirit of uncontrollable wrath and vengeance among the fierce backwoodsmen. Several parties went out, and one of them, commanded by the sheriff of the place, encountered a band of Indians, routed them after a sharp fight, and brought in several scalps.

"The surrounding country was by this time completely
abandoned by the settlers, many of whom, not content with seeking refuge at Carlisle, continued their flight to the eastward, and
headed by the clergyman of that place, pushed on to Lancaster,
and even to Philadelphia. Carlisle presented a most deplorable
spectacle. A multitude of the refugees, unable to find shelter in
the town, had encamped in the woods or on the adjacent fields,
erecting huts of branches and bark, and living on such charity as
the slender means of the townspeople could supply. Passing
among them, one would have witnessed every form of human
misery. In these wretched encampments were men, women, and
children, bereft at one stroke of friends, of home, and the means
of supporting life. Some stood aghast and bewildered at the sudden and fatal blow; others were sunk in the apathy of despair;
others were weeping and moaning with irrepressible anguish.
With not a few, the craven passion of fear drowned all other
emotion, and day and night they were haunted with visions of the
bloody knife and the reeking scalp; while in others, every faculty
was absorbed by the burning thirst for vengeance, and mortal
hatred against the whole Indian race.

"The route of the army lay along the beautiful Cumberland
Valley. Passing here and there a few scattered cabins, deserted
or burnt to the ground, they reached the hamlet of Shippensburg,
somewhat more than twenty miles from their point of departure.
Here, as at Carlisle, was congregated a starving multitude, who
had fled from the knife and the tomahawk.

"By the last advices from the westward, it appeared that Fort
Ligonier, situated beyond the Alleghenies, was in imminent
danger of falling into the enemy's hands before the army could
come up; for its defences were slight, its garrison was feeble, and
the Indians had assailed it with repeated attacks. The magazine
which the place contained made it of such importance that
Bouquet resolved at all hazards to send a party to its relief.
Thirty of the best men were accordingly chosen, and ordered to
push forward with the utmost speed, by unfrequented routes
through the forests and over the mountains, carefully avoiding the
road, which would doubtless be infested by the enemy. The party
set out on their critical errand, guided by frontier hunters, and
observing a strict silence. Using every precaution, and advancing
by forced marches, day after day, they came in sight of the fort
without being discovered. It was beset by Indians, and, as the
party made for the gate, they were seen and fired upon; but they

threw themselves into the place without the loss of a man, and Ligonier was for the time secure.

"In the meantime, the army, advancing with slower progress, entered a country where as yet scarcely an English settler had built his cabin. Reaching Fort Loudon, on the declivities of Cove Mountain, they ascended the wood-encumbered defiles beyond. Far on their right stretched the green ridges of the Tuscarora, while, in front, mountain beyond mountain rose high against the horizon. Climbing heights and descending into valleys, passing the two solitary posts of Littleton and the Juniata, both abandoned by their garrisons, they came in sight of Fort Bedford, hemmed in by encircling mountains. Their arrival gave infinite relief to the garrison, who had long been beleaguered and endangered by a swarm of Indians, while many of the settlers in the neighborhood had been killed, and the rest driven for refuge into the fort. Captain Ourry, the commanding officer, reported that, for several weeks, nothing had been heard from the westward, every messenger having been killed, and the communication completely cut off. By the last intelligence, Fort Pitt had been surrounded by Indians, and daily threatened with a general attack.

"Having remained encamped, for three days, on the fields near the fort, Bouquet resumed his march on the twenty-eighth of July, and soon passed beyond the farthest verge of civilized habitation. The whole country lay buried in foliage. Except the rocks which crowned the mountains, and the streams which rippled along the valleys, the unbroken forest, like a vast garment, invested the whole. The road was channelled through its depths, while, on each side, the brown trunks and tangled undergrowth formed a wall so dense as almost to bar the sight. Through a country thus formed by nature for ambuscades, not a step was free from danger, and no precaution was neglected to guard against surprise. In advance of the marching column moved the provincial rangers, closely followed by the pioneers. The wagons and cattle were in the centre, guarded in front, flank, and rear by the regulars, while a rear-guard of rangers closed the line of march. Keen-eyed riflemen of the frontier, acting as scouts, scoured the woods far in front and on either flank, so that surprise was impossible. In this order the little army toiled heavily on, over a road beset with all the obstructions of the forest, until the main ridge of the Alleganies, like a mighty wall of green, rose up before them, and they began their zigzag progress up the woody heights, amid the sweltering heat of July. The tongues of the panting oxen hung lolling from their jaws, while the pine trees, scorching in the hot sun, diffused their resinous odors through the sultry air. At length, from the windy summit the Highland soldiers could gaze around upon a boundless panorama of forest-covered mountains, wild as their own native hills. Descending from the Alleganies, they entered upon a country less rugged and formidable in itself, but beset with constantly increasing dangers. On the second of August, they reached Fort Ligonier, about fifty miles from Bedford, and a hundred and fifty from Carlisle. The Indians who were about the place vanished at their approach; but the garrison could furnish no intelligence of the motions and designs of the enemy, having been completely blockaded for weeks. In this uncertainty, Bouquet resolved to leave behind the oxen and wagons, which formed the most cumbrous part of the convoy, since this would enable him to advance with greater celerity, and oppose a better resistance in case of attack. Thus relieved, the army resumed its march on the fourth, taking with them three hundred and fifty pack horses and a few cattle, and at nightfall encamped at no great distance from Ligonier. Within less than a day's march in advance, lay the dangerous defiles of Turtle Creek, a stream flowing at the bottom of a deep hollow, flanked by steep declivities, along the foot of which the road at that time ran for some distance. Fearing that the enemy would lie in ambuscade at this place, Bouquet resolved to march on the following day as far as a small stream called Bushy Run, to rest here until night, and then, by a forced march, to cross Turtle Creek under cover of the darkness.

"On the morning of the fifth, the tents were struck at an early hour, and the troops began their march through a country broken with hills and deep hollows, everywhere covered with the tall, dense forest, which spread for countless leagues around. By one o'clock, they had avanced seventeen miles, and the guides assured them that they were within half a mile of Bushy Run, their proposed resting place. The tired soldiers were pressing forward with renewed alacrity, when suddenly the report of rifles from the front sent a thrill along the ranks; and, as they listened, the firing thickened into a fierce, sharp rattle, while shouts and whoops, deadened by the intervening forest, showed that the advanced guard was hotly engaged. The two foremost companies were at once ordered forward to support it; but far from abating, the fire grew so rapid and furious as to argue the presence of an enemy at once numerous and resolute. At this, the convoy was halted, the troops formed into line, and a general charge was ordered. Bearing down through the forest with fixed bayonets, they drove the yelping assailants before them, and swept the ground clear. But at the very moment of success, a fresh burst of whoops and firing was heard from either flank, while a confused noise from the rear showed that the convoy was attacked. It was necessary instantly to fall back for its support. Driving off the assailants, the troops formed in a circle around the crowded and terrified horses. Though they were new to the work, and though the numbers and movements of the enemy, whose yelling resounded on every side, were concealed by the thick forest, yet no man lost his composure; and all displayed a steadiness which nothing but implicit confidence in their commander could have inspired. And now ensued a combat of a nature most harassing and discouraging. Again and again, now on this side and now on that, a crowd of Indians rushed up, pouring in a heavy fire, and striving, with furious outcries, to break into the circle. A well-dircted volley met them, followed by a steady charge of the bayonet. They never waited an instant to receive the attack, but, leaping backwards from tree to tree, soon vanished from sight, only to renew their attack with unabated ferocity in another quarter. Such was their activity that very few of them were hurt, while the English, less expert in bush fighting, suffered severely. Thus the fight went on, without intermission, for seven hours, until the forest grew dark with approaching night. Upon this, the Indians gradually slackened their fire, and the exhausted soldiers found time to rest.

"It was impossible to change their ground in the enemy's presence, and the troops were obliged to encamp upon the hill where the combat had taken place, though not a drop of water was to be found there. Fearing a night attack, Bouquet stationed numerous sentinels and outposts to guard against it, while the men lay down upon their arms, preserving the order they had maintained during the fight. Having completed the necessary arrangements, Bouquet, doubtful of surviving the battle of the morrow, wrote to Sir Jeffrey Amherst, in a few clear, concise words, an account of the day's events. His letter concludes as follows: 'Whatever our fate may be, I thought it necessary to give your excellency this early information, that you may, at all events, take such measures as you will think proper with the provinces, for their own safety, and the effectual relief of Fort Pitt; as, in case of another engagement, I fear insurmountable difficulties in protecting and transporting our provisions, being already so much weakened by the losses of this day, in men and horses, besides the additional necessity of carrying the wounded, whose situation is truly deplorable.'

"The condition of these unhappy men might well awaken sympathy. About sixty soldiers, besides several officers, had been killed or disabled. A space in the centre of the camp was prepared for the reception of the wounded, and surrounded by a wall of flour-bags from the convoy, affording some protection against the bullets which flew from all sides during the fight. Here they lay upon the ground, enduring agonies of thirst, and waiting, passive and helpless, the issue of the battle. Deprived of the animating thought that their lives and safety depended on their own exertions; surrounded by a wilderness, and by scenes to the horror of which no degree of familiarity could render the imagination callous, they must have endured mental sufferings, compared to which the pain of their wounds was slight. In the probable event of defeat, a fate inexpressibly horrible awaited them; while even victory would by no means insure their safety, since any great increase in their numbers would render it impossible for their comrades to transport them. Nor was the condition of those who had hitherto escaped an enviable one. Though they were about equal in numbers to their assailants, yet the dexterity and alertness of the Indians, joined to the nature of the country, gave all the advantages of a greatly superior force. The enemy were, moreover, exulting in the fullest confidence of success; for it was in these very forests that, eight years before, they had well-nigh destroyed twice their number of the best British troops. Throughout the earlier part of the night, they kept up a dropping fire upon the camp, while, at short intervals, a wild whoop from the thick surrounding gloom told with what fierce eagerness they waited to glut their vengeance on the morrow. The camp remained in darkness, for it would have been highly dangerous to build fires within its precincts, which would have served to direct the aim of the lurking marksmen. Surrounded by such terrors, the men snatched a disturbed and broken sleep, recruiting their exhausted strength for the renewed struggle of the morning.

"With the earliest dawn of day, and while the damp, cool forest was still involved in twilight, there rose around the camp a general burst of those horrible cries which form the ordinary prelude of an Indian battle. Instantly from every side at once, the enemy opened their fire, approaching under cover of the trees and bushes, and levelling with a close and deadly aim. Often, as on the previous day, they would rush up with furious impetuosity, striving to break into the ring of troops. They were repulsed at every point; but the English, though constantly victorious, were beset with undiminished perils, while the violence of the enemy seemed every moment on the increase. True to their favorite tactics, they would never stand their ground when attacked, but vanish at the first gleam of the levelled bayonet, only to appear again the moment the danger was past. The troops, fatigued by the long march and equally long battle of the previous day, were maddened by the torments of thirst, more intolerable, says their commander, than the fire of the enemy. They were fully conscious of the peril in which they stood, of wasting away by slow degrees beneath the shot of assailants at once so daring, so cautious, and so active, and upon whom it was impossible to inflict any decisive injury. The Indians saw their distress, and pressed them closer and closer, redoubling their yells and howlings, while some of them sheltered behind trees, assailed the troops, in bad English, with abuse and derision.

"Meanwhile the interior of the camp was a scene of confusion. The horses, secured in a crowd near the intrenchment which covered the wounded, were often struck by the bullets, and wrought to the height of terror by the mingled din of whoops, shrieks, and firing. They would break away by half scores at a time, burst through the ring of troops and the outer circle of assailants, and scour madly up and down the hillsides; while many of the drivers, overcome by the terrors of a scene in which they could bear no active part, hid themselves among the bushes and could neither hear nor obey orders.

"It was now about ten o'clock. Oppressed with heat, fatigue, and thirst, the distressed troops still maintained a weary and wavering defence, encircling the convoy in a yet unbroken ring. They were fast falling in their ranks, and the strength and spirits of the survivors had begun to flag. If the fortunes of the day were to be retrieved, the effort must be made at once; and happily the mind of the commander was equal to the emergency. In the midst of the confusion he conceived a stratagem alike novel and masterly. Could the Indians be brought together in a body, and made to stand their ground when attacked, there could be little doubt of the result; and to effect this object, Bouquet determined to increase their confidence, which had already mounted to an audacious pitch. Two companies of infantry, forming a part of the ring which had been exposed to the hottest fire, were ordered to fall back into the interior of the camp, while the troops on either hand joined their files across the vacant space, as if to cover the retreat of their comrades. These orders given at a favorable moment, were executed with great promptness. The thin line of troops who took possession of the deserted part of the circle, were, from their small numbers, brought closer in towards the centre. The Indians mistook these movements for a retreat. Confident that their time was come, they leaped up on all sides, from behind the trees and bushes, and, with infernal screeches, rushed headlong toward the spot, pouring in a most heavy and galling fire. The shock was too violent to be long endured. The men struggled to maintain their posts, but the Indians seemed on the point of breaking into the heart of the camp, when the aspect of affairs was suddenly reversed. The two companies, who had apparently abandoned their position, were in fact destined to begin the attack; and they now sallied out from the circle at a point where a depression in the ground, joined to the thick growth of trees, concealed them from the eyes of the Indians. Making a short detour through the woods, they came round upon the flank of the furious assailants, and discharged a deadly volley into their very midst. Numbers were seen to fall; yet though completely surprised, and utterly at a loss to understand the nature of the attack, the Indians faced about with the greatest intrepidity, and boldy returned the fire. But the Highlanders, with yells as wild as their own, fell on them with the bayonet. The shock was irresistible, and they fled before the charging ranks in a tumultuous throng. Orders had been given to two other companies, occupying a contiguous part of the circle, to support the attack whenever a favorable moment should occur; and they had therefore advanced a little from their position, and lay close crouched in ambush. The fugitive multitude, pressed by the Highland bayonets, passed directly across their front, upon which they rose and poured among them a second volley, no less destructive than the former. This completed the rout. The four companies, uniting, drove the flying savages through the woods, giving them no time to rally or reload their empty rifles, killing many, and scattering the rest in hopeless confusion.

"While this took place at one part of the circle, the troops and the savages had still maintained their respective positions at the other; but when the latter perceived the total rout of their comrades, and saw the troops advancing to assail them, they also lost heart, and fled. The discordant outcries which had so long deafened the ears of the English soon ceased altogether, and not a living Indian remained near the spot. About sixty corpses lay scattered over the ground. Among them were found those of several prominent chiefs, while the blood which stained the leaves of the bushes showed that numbers had fled severely wounded from the field. The soldiers took but one prisoner, whom they shot to death like a captive wolf. The loss of the English in the two battles surpassed that of the enemy, amounting to eight officers and one hundred and fifteen men.

"Having been for some time detained by the necessity of making litters for the wounded, and destroying the stores which the flight of most of the horses made it impossible to transport, the army moved on, in the afternoon, to Bushy Run. Here they had scarcely formed their camp, when they were again fired upon by a body of Indians, who, however, were soon repulsed. On the next day, they resumed their progress towards Fort Pitt, distant about twenty-five miles, and though frequently annoyed on the march by petty attacks, they reached their destination, on the tenth, without serious loss. It was a joyful moment, both to the troops and to the garrison. The latter, it will be remembered, were left surrounded and hotly pressed by the Indians, who had beleaguered the place from the twenty-eighth of July to the first of August, when, hearing of Bouquet's approach, they had abandoned the siege, and marched to attack him. From this time, the garrison had seen nothing of them until the morning of the tenth, when, shortly before the army appeared, they had passed the fort in a body, raising the scalp-yell, and displaying their disgusting trophies to the view of the English.

"The battle of Bushy Run was one of the best contested actions ever fought between white men and Indians. If there were any disparity of numbers, the advantage was on the side of the troops, and the Indians had displayed throughout a fierceness and intrepidity matched only by the steady valor with which they were met. In the provinces, the victory excited equal joy and admiration, more especially among those who knew the incalculable difficulties of an Indian campaign. The assembly of Pennsylvania passed a vote expressing their high sense of the merits of Bouquet, and of the important service which he had rendered to the province. He soon after received the additional honor of the formal thanks of the king.

"In many an Indian village, the women cut away their hair, gashed their limbs with knives, and uttered their dismal howlings of lamentation for the fallen. Yet though surprised and dispirited, the rage of the Indians was too deep to be quenched, even by so signal a reverse, and their outrages upon the frontier were resumed

with unabated ferocity. Fort Pitt, however, was effectually relieved, while the moral effect of the victory enabled the frontier
settlers to encounter the enemy with a spirit which would have been
wanting, had Bouquet sustained a defeat."

Andrew Byerly

In this connection, we call attention to the fact that Andrew
Byerly, at the head of a detachment of eighteen of the Royal
Americans, was in the advance of Bouquet's army when the battle
of Bushy Run commenced. Also, during the terrible night of
August 5th, he, at great risk, brought several hatfuls of water from
a neighboring spring to allay the thirst of Bouquet's wounded.
This noted man of the Westmoreland frontier had settled in the
Brush Creek Valley along the Forbes road, in 1759. In the latter
part of May, 1763, the Indians had warned Byerly to leave this
settlement. Captain Ecuyer, in a letter written to Colonel
Bouquet, on May 29th, refers to this fact as follows:

"Just as I had finished my letter three men came in from
Clapham's [Colonel William Clapham, who lived near West
Newton, Westmoreland County] with the melancholy news that
yesterday, at three o'clock in the afternoon, the Indians murdered
Clapham and everybody in his house. These three men were out at
work, and had escaped through the woods. I immediately armed
them and sent them to assist our people at Bushy Run. The
Indians have told Byerly to leave his place in four days, or he and
his family would all be murdered."

Later, Mr. Byerly and his family escaped to Fort Ligonier,
as thus related in Cort's "Colonel Henry Bouquet":

"As Ecuyer states, Byerly had received warning; but his
family was in no condition to be moved. Mrs. Byerly had just
been confined and the departure was delayed as long as possible,
indeed until certain death was imminent, if the flight should be
any longer postponed. Byerly had gone with a small party [per-
haps Clapham's men referred to above] to bury some persons who
had been killed at some distance from his station. A friendly
Indian who had often received a bowl of milk and bread from Mrs.
Byerly came to the house after dark, and informed the family that
they would all be killed, if they did not make their escape before
daylight. Mrs. Byerly got up from her sick couch and wrote the
tidings on the door of the house for the information of her husband when he should return. A horse was saddled on which the

mother with her tender babe three days old in her arms, was placed, and a child not two years old was fastened behind her.

"Michael Byerly was a good sized lad, but Jacob was only three years old and had a painful stone bruise on one of his feet. With the aid of his older brother who held him by the hand and sometimes carried him on his back, the little fellow, however, managed to make good time through the wilderness to Fort Ligonier, about thirty miles distant. But although he reached his ninety-ninth year, he never forgot that race for life in his childhood, nor did he feel like giving quarter to hostile Indians, one of whom he killed on an island in the Allegheny in a fight under Lieutenant Hardin in 1779, although the savage begged for quarter.

"Milk cows were highly prized by frontier families in those days, and the Byerly family made a desperate effort to coax and drive their small herd along to Fort Ligonier. But the howling savages got so close that they were obliged to leave the cattle in the woods to be destroyed by the Indians. Byerly in some way eluded the Indians and joined his family in the retreat. They barely escaped with their lives. The first night they spent in the stockade, and in the morning the bullets of the pursurers struck the gates as the family pressed into the fort."

Attempt to Inoculate Indians with Small-pox

When Colonel Bouquet was preparing to lead his army over the mountains to the relief of forts Bedford, Ligonier, and Pitt, General Sir Jefferey Amherst, then in command of all the English troops in the colonies, wrote him as follows: "I wish to hear of no prisoners, should any of the villians be met with in arms. . . . Could it not be contrived to send the small-pox among those disaffected tribes of Indians?" To this Bouquet replied: "I will try to inoculate them with some blankets, and take care not to get the disease myself. As it is a pity to expose good men against them, I wish we could use the Spanish method, to hunt them with English dogs who would, I think, effectually extirpate or remove that vermin." Then Amherst replied: "You will do well to try to inoculate the Indians by means of blankets, as well as to try every other method that can serve to extirpate this exorable race."

Parkman calls attention to the fact that, while there is no direct evidence that Bouquet carried into effect the shameful plan of infecting the Indians with small-pox, yet a few months after Amherst's suggestion, this disease made havoc among the tribes of the Ohio. Also, on June 24th, Captain Ecuyer, the commandant at Fort Pitt, after narrating the fact that he and Alexander McKee held a short parley that day with Turtle Heart and another Delaware chief who had come to the fort for the purpose of terrifying the garrison by reports of great numbers of Indians marching against the place, noted the following in his journal: "Out of our regard to them [Turtle Heart and his companion], we gave them two blankets and a handkerchief out of the Small-pox Hospital. I hope it will have the desired effect."

Murder of Colonel William Clapham

In closing the account of Bouquet's expedition to the relief of forts Ligonier, Bedford, and Pitt, we call attention to the fact that Colonel William Clapham, mentioned above, had taken his family to the frontier near the present town of West Newton, in the early spring of 1763. On May 28th, the Indians rushed into his house, killed and scalped his wife and three children, and another woman. The two women were treated with shocking indecency. At the time of the murders, three men who were working at some distance from the Clapham house, hastened to Fort Pitt, and carried the news to the garrison. Two soldiers who were in Clapham's detail of scouts, who were stationed at a saw-mill near the fort, were also killed and scalped by the same party. It would appear that others were slain in this same massacre, for Colonel Burd entered in his journal on June 5th that, "John Harris gave me an account of Colonel Clapham and twelve men being killed near Pittsburgh and two Royal Americans being killed at the saw-mill." Thus it is seen that the Indians visited terrible retribution upon Colonel Clapham for the expedition which he sent against them in the summer of 1756, as related in Chapter XVIII.

Guyasuta Confers with Bradstreet and Bouquet

Guyasuta, in August, 1764, attended a conference with Colonel Bradstreet, near Erie, in which Bradstreet concluded a peace with the Delawares and Shawnees. However, Colonel Bouquet, upon learning of this fact, while at Fort Loudon, Franklin County, and perceiving that the Delawares and Shawnees were not sincere in their intentions, as they continued their depredations, refused to ratify the treaty, and pushed on with his army to the Muskingum, as referred to in Chapter XIX, where he compelled Guyasuta and the other chiefs of the western tribes to surrender the prisoners captured during Pontiac's War, as well as many captured during the French and Indian War. Bouquet dealt sternly with the chiefs, and they were glad to make peace.

More than two hundred prisoners were yielded up to Bouquet by Guyasuta and his associate chiefs. Some of the captives had been among the Indians since the early days of the French and Indian War, and in many cases, it was with extreme reluctance that they consented to accompany Bouquet's army back to the Pennsylvania settlements. Indeed, in some cases it was found necessary to deliver the captives bound to Bouquet. The Indians had become greatly attached to these captives, and had adopted them into their families. They shed torrents of tears when they were compelled to deliver them up.

However, Colonel Bouquet, on account of the lateness of the season, was obliged to return to Pennsylvania without having secured all the prisoners held by the Shawnees. On November 12th, he held a conference with a number of their chiefs, among whom were Nimwha and Red Hawk. At this conference, he took hostages from the Shawnees, and laid them under the strongest obligation for the delivery of the rest of the prisoners at Fort Pitt in the ensuing spring. These hostages escaped soon afterwards, thus giving reason to doubt the sincerity of the intentions of the Shawnees with respect to performance of their promises. But to the credit of the Shawnees it must be said that they punctually fulfilled all their promises. Ten of their chiefs, with about fifty of their warriors, met George Croghan, then deputy agent to Sir William Johnson, at Fort Pitt, on May 9, 1765, and delivered the remainder of their prisoners, "brightened the chain of friendship, and gave every assurance of their firm intentions to preserve the peace inviolable forever."

CHAPTER XXIV.

Guyasuta

(Continued)

OTHER EVENTS OF THE PONTIAC-GUYASUTA WAR IN PENNSYLVANIA

Maiden Foot and Miss Means

DURING the spring of 1763 Lieutenant Blane, in command of Fort Ligonier, was visited by several parties of friendly Indians, among whom was a young brave named Maiden Foot. When Maiden Foot was at the fort on one of these occasions, a settler named Means with his wife and little daughter, Mary, aged eleven, were there also. Maiden Foot seemed much pleased with the girl. The Means' home was about a mile south of the fort. On leaving the fort, Maiden Foot gave Mary Means a string of beads. He seemed sad and heartbroken at the time.

In the latter part of May or early in June, after the Pontiac and Guyasuta War had started, Mrs. Means and Mary started for the fort on hearing a rumor that the Indians had become hostile. On their way to the fort, they were captured by two Indians, who took them into the woods and tied them to saplings. Soon they heard the report of rifles, which was the first Indian assault on the fort. Later in the afternoon, Maiden Foot appeared before Mrs. Means and her daughter, no doubt being the Indian selected to scalp them. He recognized them, cut the bands which bound them to the tree, and conducted them by a roundabout way to their home, where Mr. Means met them. Maiden Foot then told the family to flee to the mountains, and pointed to a ravine in which they could hide until after the Indian band left the neighborhood. On leaving them Maiden Foot took the little girl's handkerchief, on which was worked in black silken thread her name "Mary Means".

Some years afterwards the Means family moved to a point near Cincinnati, Ohio, where the parents died; and the girl having grown to womanhood, married an officer named Kearney, who commanded a company under Wayne at the battle of the Fallen

Timbers, August 20, 1794. After this battle, Kearney and some companions found an elderly Indian sitting on a log on the battle-field and waving a white handkerchief. On their approaching him, the Indian said that he had been a warrior all his life; that he had fought at Ligonier, at Bushy Run, the Wabash against St. Clair, and at the recent battle against Wayne. He then explained that he had enough of war, and desired henceforth to live in peace with all mankind. Searching in his pouch he brought forth the handkerchief of Mary Means. Officer Kearney had often heard his wife tell the story of Maiden Foot. He took the old Indian home with him. Mrs. Kearney and the Indian immediately recognized each other, although thirty-one years had elapsed since they parted near Fort Ligonier. Maiden Foot now explained that shortly before he met Mary Means, he had lost a sister about her age and size, and that the giving of the string of beads to her was in effect the adopting of her as his sister. He was taken into the Kearney family, according to Boucher's "History of Westmoreland County", and upon his death four years later, was buried in a graveyard at Cincinnati, where a tablet was erected at his grave bearing the following inscription:

> "In memory of Maiden Foot, an Indian Chief of the
> Eighteenth Century, who died a Civilian and a Christian."

Expedition Against Great Island

At the time of Colonel Bouquet's expedition for the relief of Fort Pitt, the Delawares, Shawnees, and other tribes composing Pontiac and Guyasuta's confederation, planned to attack the interior settlements of Pennsylvania as far as Tulpehocken, their main object being to capture Fort Augusta, at Sunbury. Reports reaching Carlisle, Paxtang, and other places that Fort Augusta would be attacked by a great force of Indians, Colonel John Armstrong, with about three hundred volunteers from Cumberland and Bedford counties marched from Carlisle to destroy the Indian town at Great Island, [Lock Haven.] At Jersey Shore, Lycoming County, Armstrong's force advanced so suddenly upon the Indian village located there, that the Indians were scarcely able to escape, leaving their food, hot upon their bark tables, which they had pre-pared for dinner. Arriving at Great Island, Armstrong found the place had been deserted a few days before. His army then de-stroyed the village at Great Island together with a large quantity of grain and provisions.

As part of Armstrong's army was returning down the West

Branch of the Susquehanna, on August 26th, 1763, they encountered a force of Indians at Muncy Creek Hill, Lycoming County. A
hot skirmish followed in which four of Armstrong's men were
killed and four wounded; while the Indians suffered as severely,
and carried away their dead and wounded.

Captains Patterson, Sharp, Bedford, Laughlin, and Crawford,
with seventy-six of their comrades arrived at Fort Augusta the
next day, and other stragglers came in that night and the following
day. These soldiers reported the details of the battle at Muncey
Creek Hill and also that, after the battle, a party of twelve Indians
returning to Great Island from a mission to Bethlehem, were
attacked by them on a hill north of the present town of Northumberland, and, they believed, all were killed.

Attacks on Friendly Indians

In September and October, 1763, Indian outrages were committed as far into the heart of the settled parts of the Province as
the neighborhood of Reading and Bethlehem; and many of the
settlers believed that the Moravian Indians were secretly giving
assistance to their brethren at war against the Province. A party
of rangers murdered a number of the Moravian Indians as they
were found asleep in a barn. Among these were an Indian woman
named Zippora, who was thrown down upon the threshing floor
and killed, and an Indian man named Zachari, his wife and little
child, who were put to the sword, although the mother begged
upon her knees that the life of her child might be spared.

About the middle of October a party of rangers marched
against the Moravian Indians at Wichetunk, in what is now Polk
Township, Monroe County, intending to surprise them by night,
but their plans were frustrated by a violent storm in the evening.
The Moravian missionary, Bernard Adam Grube, then led these
Indians to Nazareth, but Governor Penn suggested that, in order
to watch their behavior, it would be better to disarm them and
bring them into the interior parts of the Province. They were
accordingly taken to Province Island on the Delaware by the
Moravian missionary, John Roth.

Among the troops under the command of Captain Jacob
Wetterhold, stationed at Fort Allen during the summer and
autumn of 1763, was Lieutenant Jonathan Dodge, "a most precious
scoundrel", who committed many atrocious acts against his fellow
soldiers, and particularly against friendly Indians. One of the
wrongs he committed against the Indians, is thus described in a

letter which he wrote to Timothy Horsfield, on August 4th, 1763:
"Yesterday there were four Indians came to Ensign Kern's. . . . .
I took four rifles and fourteen deer skins from them, weighed them,
and there were thirty-one pounds." After these Indians had left,
Dodge continues: "I took twenty men and pursued them; then I
ordered my men to fire, upon which I fired a volley on them; could
find none dead or alive." These were friendly Indians, who were
on their way from Shamokin (Sunbury) to the Moravian mission
at Bethlehem.

In the "Frontier Forts of Pennsylvania", we read of another
attack made by Dodge upon friendly Indians:

"Jacob Warner, a soldier in Nicholas Wetterholt's company
made the following statement September 9th: 'That he and
Dodge were searching for a lost gun, when, about two miles above
Fort Allen, they saw three Indians painted black. Dodge fired
upon them and killed one; Warner also fired upon them, and
thinks he wounded another; but two escaped; the Indians had not
fired at them. The Indian was scalped, and, on the 24th, Dodge
sent Warner with the scalp to a person in Philadelphia, who gave
him eight dollars for it. These were also friendly Indians."

The Killing of Captain Jacob Wetterholt

Determined to avenge themselves on account of the atrocious
acts of Dodge, the Delawares attacked Captain Jacob Wetterholt
on October 8th, as thus described in Egle's "History of Pennsylvania":

"Before daybreak in the morning of the 8th of October, some
Delawares attacked the house of John Stenton, in Allen Township,
(Northampton County), on the main road from Bethlehem to Fort
Allen, eight miles northwest from the former place, where Captain
Jacob Wetterhold, of the Province service, with a squad of men,
was lodging for the night. Meeting with Jean, the wife of James
Horner, who was on her way to a neighbors for coals to light her
morning fire, the Indians, fearing lest she should betray them or
raise an alarm, dispatched her with their tomahawks. Thereupon
they surrounded Stenton's house. No sooner had Captain Wetterhold's servant stepped out of the house (he had been sent to saddle
the captain's horse) than he was shot down. The report of the
Indian's piece brought his master to the door, who, on opening it,
received a mortal wound. Sergeant Lawrence McGuire, in his
attempt to draw him in, was also dangerously wounded and fell,
whereupon the lieutenant advanced. He was confronted by an

Indian, who, leaping upon the bodies of the fallen men, presented a pistol, which the lieutenant thrust aside as it was being discharged, thus escaping with his life, and succeeding also in repelling the savage. The Indians now took a position at a window, and there shot Stenton as he was in the act of rising from bed. Rushing from the house, the wounded man ran for a mile, and dropped down a corpse. His wife and two children had meanwhile secreted themselves in the cellar, where they were fired upon three times, but without being struck. Captain Wetterhold, despite his sufferings, dragged himself to a window, through which he shot one of the savages while in the act of applying a torch to the house. Hereupon, taking up the dead body of their comrade, the besiegers withdrew. Having on their retreat plundered the house of James Allen, they attacked Andrew Hazlitt's, where they shot and scalped a man, shot Hazlitt after a brave defence, and then tomahawked his fugitive wife and two children in a barbarous manner. Finally they set fire to his house, and then to that of Philip Kratzer, and crossing the Lehigh above Siegfried's bridge, passed into Whitehall Township.

"In this maraud twenty-three persons were killed, and many dangerously wounded. The settlers were thrown into the utmost distress, fleeing from their plantations with hardly a sufficiency of clothes to cover themselves, and coming into the town of Northampton (now Allentown), where, we read, there were but four guns at the time, 'and three of them unfit for use, with the enemy four miles from the place.' At the same time, Yost's mill, about eleven miles from Bethlehem, was destroyed, and all the people at the place, excepting a young man, cut off.

"This was the last invasion of the present Northampton County by a savage foe. Old Northampton, and especially that part of it which was erected into Monroe, by act of Legislature, in April, 1836, suffered subsequently, at intervals, from the Indians as late as 1765."

The Murder of the Conestogas

One of the events of the Pontiac and Guyasuta War, which, as Dr. Geo. P. Donehoo remarks, "attracted wide attention and has been a source of discussion ever since," was the murder of six members of the Conestoga tribe at the town of Conestoga, Lancaster County, on December 14, 1763, by a band of Scotch-Irish settlers, "The Paxton Boys", from the neighborhood of Paxtang church not far from Harrisburg. Edward Shippen, in a letter to Governor Penn, dated at Lancaster December 14th, gives the fol-

lowing account of this event: "One, Robert Edgar, a hired man
to Captain Thomas McKee, living near the Borough acquainted
me today that a Company of People from the Frontier had killed
and scalped most of the Indians at the Conestoga Town early this
morning; he said he had his information from an Indian boy who
made his escape; Mr. Slough has been to the place and held a
Coroner's inquest on the corpses, being Six in number; Bill Sawk
and some other Indians were gone towards Smith's Iron Works to
sell brooms; but where they are now we can't understand. . . . . .
Warrants are issued for the apprehending of the murderers, said to
be upwards of fifty men, well armed and mounted."

Great excitement was caused in Philadelphia by the murder of
these Indians. Just a short time before, on November 30th, they
sent a letter to John Penn, in which they congratulated him on his
arrival in the Province and asked his favor and protection. The
Quakers especially were loud in their denunciation of this atrocity,
seemingly unmindful of the fact that John Harris and Colonel
John Elder, pastor of the Presbyterian Church at Paxtang, had
frequently appealed to the Colonial Authorities to remove the
Conestogas to a place of safety, owing to the excitement prevailing
in the Paxtang region on account of the many raids of the hostile
Indians.

Furthermore, during October, Captain Bull, the son of the
great Teedyuscung, had led a band of one hundred thirty-five
Delawares from the Ohio and Allegheny, with whom he had lived
for ten years, into the Wyoming Valley. They committed many
atrocities. Many of the Paxton Boys had just returned from an
expedition against Captain Bull's band and, as Rev. Elder said, in
a letter written on October 25th, had seen "the mangled carcasses
of these unhappy people", which "presented to our troops a melancholy scene, which had been acted not above two days before their
arrival." The Paxton Boys were therefore in a state of excitement and rage against all Indians, especially when they discovered
that some of the Indians who were committing outrages along the
Susquehanna had been traced to Conestoga. Likewise, it must be
said to the credit of Rev. Elder that, when he learned that a large
number of the Paxtang settlers were assembling to march against
the Conestogas, he sent a messenger to them urging them to desist.

Governor Penn issued a proclamation on December 22nd,
calling upon judges, justices, sheriffs, and other civil and military
officers, to make diligent search for the perpetrators of this crime,
and to place them in the public jails of the Province, the remaining Conestogas, fourteen in number, in the meantime having been

placed in the Lancaster workhouse for protection. How the Paxton Boys replied to this proclamation of the governor is thus set
forth in a letter of Edward Shippen to Governor John Penn written
from Lancaster on December 27th: "I am to acquaint your
Honor that between two and three of the clock this afternoon, upwards of a hundred armed men from the westward rode very fast
into town, turned their horses into Mr. Slough's (an In-keeper)
yard, and proceeded with the greatest precipitation to the work
house, stove open the door and killed all the Indians, and took
to their horses and rode off. All their business was done, and they
were returning to their horses before I could get half way down to
the Work House."

The details of the massacre of these unarmed and defenseless
Conestogas are most shocking and revolting. Protesting their
innocence and their love for the English, they prostrated themselves with their children before their infuriated murderers, and
plead for their lives. Their appeal was answered by the rifle,
hatchet, and scalping knife. Some had their brains blown out,
others their legs chopped off, and others their hands cut off. Bill
Sawk (Sock) and his wife, Mollie, with their two children, had
their heads split open, and were scalped. The mangled bodies of
these Indians, who had never been at war with the whites and had
always been claimed as friendly Indians, were buried at Lancaster.

Thus perished the last remnant of the once mighty tribe of
Susquehannas. The excitement on the frontier at the time, and
the laxity on the part of the Colonial Assembly in providing for
the defense, may, in a measure, explain why the harassed frontiersmen committed such a horrid and notorious act; but the historian
searches the records of the time in vain for any justification for
this atrocity, which is a black spot on the pages of the history of
Pennsylvania.

Not content with the butchery of the Conestogas, the Paxton
Boys threatened to go to Philadelphia and kill the Moravian Indians on Province Island. These Indians were then lodged in the
barracks in Philadelphia. A report reached the city that the
Paxton Boys were on the march. Cannon were then planted
around the barracks, volunteers were called into service, and alarm
bells were rung. About two hundred of the Paxton Boys actually
crossed the Schuylkill at Swedsford, and advanced to Germantown, when hearing of the preparations which had been made, they
wisely proceeded no further.

Pennsylvania Offers Bounty For Scalps

On July 7th, 1764, Pennsylvania offered a bounty for Indian scalps, even the scalps of children, "for the better carrying on of offensive operations against our Indian enemies", as follows:

"For every male Indian enemy above ten years old, who shall be taken prisoner and delivered at any forts garrisoned by the troops in the pay of this Province, or at any of the county towns, to the keeper of the common gaols there, the sum of one hundred & fifty Spanish dollars, or pieces of eight; for every female Indian enemy taken prisoner and brought in as aforesaid, and for every male Indian enemy ten years old, or under, taken prisoner, and delivered as aforesaid, the sum of one hundred and thirty pieces of eight; for the scalp of every male Indian enemy above the age of ten years, produced as evidence of their being killed, the sum of one hundred and thirty-four pieces of eight; and for the scalp of every female Indian enemy above the age of ten years, produced as evidence of their being killed, the sum of fifty pieces of eight; and that there shall be paid to every officer, or officers, soldier, or soldiers, as are or shall be in the pay of this Province, who shall take, bring in, and produce any Indian enemy prisoner, or scalp, as aforesaid, one half of the said several and respective premiums & bounties."

As a result of the scalp bounties, "secret expeditions", say the Pennsylvania Archives, "were set on foot by the inhabitants which were more effectual than any sort of defensive operations."

Murder of Schoolmaster Brown and His Pupils

One of the most terrible atrocities committed within the bounds of Pennsylvania by the Delawares during the Pontiac-Guyasuta War is thus described in "Colonel Henry Bouquet and His Campaigns", by Cort:

"In 1764, July 26, three miles northwest of Greencastle, Franklin County, was perpetrated what Parkman, the great historian of Colonial times, pronounces 'an outrage unmatched in fiend-like atrocity through all the annals of the war.' This was the massacre of Enoch Brown, a kindhearted exemplary Christian schoolmaster, and ten scholars, eight boys and two girls. Ruth Hart and Ruth Hale were the names of the girls. Among the boys were Eben Taylor, George Dustan and Archie McCullough. All were knocked down like so many beeves, and scalped by the merciless savages. Mourning and desolation came to many homes in the valley, for each of the slaughtered innocents belonged to a different family. The last named boy, indeed, survived the effects of the scalping knife, but in somewhat demented condition. The teacher offered his life and scalp in a spirit of self-sacrificing devotion, if the savages would only spare the lives of the little ones under his charge and care. But no! the tender mercies of the heathen are cruel, and so a perfect holocaust was made to the Moloch of war by the relentless fiends in human form. . . . . . It is some relief to know that this diabolical deed, whose recital makes us shudder even at this late date, was disapproved by the old warriors, when the marauding party of young Indians came back with their horrid trophies. Neephaughwhese, or Night Walker, an old chief or half-king, denounced them as a pack of cowards for killing and scalping so many children. . . . . Who can describe the horror of the scene in that lonely log school house, when one of the settlers chanced to look in at the door to ascertain the cause of the unusual quietness? In the center lay the faithful Brown, scalped and lifeless, with a Bible clasped in his hand. Around the room were strewn the dead and mangled bodies of seven boys and two girls, while little Archie, stunned, scalped and bleeding, was creeping around among his dead companions, rubbing his hands over their faces and trying to gain some token of recognition. A few days later the innocent victims of savage atrocity received a common sepulchre. All were buried in one large rough box at the border of the ravine, a few rods from the school house where they had been so ruthlessly slaughtered. Side by side, with head and feet alternately, the little ones were laid with their master, just as they were clad at the time of the massacre."

John McCollough, a cousin of Archie, had been captured in the same neighborhood just nine year previously, and was living among the Delawares at Muskingum when the young warriors returned with the scalps of the schoolmaster and his pupils. He was among the prisoners surrendered to Bouquet, and is the authority for the statement concerning the indignation expressed by old Night Walker.

During the same incursion in which Schoolmaster Brown and his pupils were killed, Susan King Cunningham, who lived in the same neighborhood, was brutally murdered while on her way through the woods to call on a neighbor. As she did not return when expected, a search was made, and her body was found near her home. Not content with murdering and scalping the poor woman, the fiends performed a Caesarian operation, and placed her child on the ground beside her.

Guyasuta at the Council at Fort Pitt

But to return to Guyasuta. His next act of importance was to attend the great council at Fort Pitt which opened on May 10th, 1765, relative to resuming trade relations between Pennsylvania and the Western Indians after Pontiac's War. He was one of the principal speakers on this occasion, and represented the Senecas. The Delawares were represented by New Comer, King Beaver, Wingenund, Turtle Heart, White Wolf, Sun Fish, Thomas Hickman, and many others. George Croghan, as deputy agent of Indian affairs, had arrived at the fort on February 28th, accompanied by Lieutenant Alexander Frazer. At the council Guyasuta made the following speech:

"When you first came to drive the French from this place, the Governor of Pennsylvania sent us a Message that we should withdraw from the French, & that when the English was settled here, we should want for nothing. It's true, you did supply us very well, but it was only while the War was doubtful, & as soon as you conquer'd the French you did not care how you treated us, as you did not then think us worth your Notice; we request you may not treat us again in this manner, but now open the Trade and do not put us off with telling us you must first hear from your great man before it can be done. If you have but little goods, let us have them for our skins, and let us have a part of your rum, or we cannot put dependence on what you tell us for the future."

To the above speech of Guyasuta and the speeches of the other chiefs, Croghan faithfully promised that trade relations would be opened without delay.

When Croghan set out from Philadelphia for Fort Pitt, he gave a pass for a large number of wagons and pack horses belonging to Boynton and Wharton of Philadelphia, loaded with guns, knives, blankets, and other goods intended as presents for the Indians at Fort Pitt. However, the people of Cumberland County and the valley of the Conococheague, upon whom such terrible atrocities had been so recently committed by the Indians, determined to prevent these war-like supplies being carried to the Indians. Accordingly, on March 6th, when the pack train had reached Sidling Hill, about seventeen miles beyond Fort Loudon, sixty-three horse loads were either burned or pillaged by the force of infuriated settlers, since known as the "Sidling Hill Volunteers", led by Colonel James Smith, who, it will be remembered, was a captive at Fort Duquesne at the time of Braddock's defeat. This action of Smith and his followers obstructed communication with Fort Pitt for some time.

Guyasuta Attends Council at Fort Pitt,
April and May, 1768

Guyasuta also attended the great conference held at Fort Pitt from April 26th to May 9th, 1768, for the purpose of adjusting the difficulties due to the fact that many settlements had been made in the valleys of the Youghiogheny and the Monongahela on land not purchased from the Indians. This conference led to the purchase at Fort Stanwix (Rome, New York), November 5th, 1768, more particularly described in Chapter XX, and needing no additional reference at this point, except to point out that, shortly after the treaty and purchase of Fort Stanwix, marauds were made into Western Pennsylvania. On February 26, 1769, eighteen persons were either killed or taken prisoner in the Brush Creek settlement, in Westmoreland County. Whether Guyasuta had anything to do with these outrages is not known.

Guyasuta Arouses Anger of White Eyes

In May, 1774, Guyasuta attended a conference with George Croghan at Ligonier. On October 27th, 1775, he was the principal speaker at the treaty held at Fort Pitt between the Commissioners of the Continental Congress and a few of the chiefs of the Senecas, Delawares, Shawnees, and Wyandots, in an effort to secure their neutrality during the Revolutionary War. He represented the Iroquois, or Mingoes, in the Allegheny Valley and Ohio. As an Iroquois, he assumed to speak for all the western tribes, and thereby aroused the anger of White Eyes, the great Delaware chief, who thereupon declared the absolute indpendence of the Delawares. This council was far from harmonious, but the chiefs declared their intention to remain neutral; and Guyasuta promised to use his influence at the Great Council of the Iroquois in New York, to obtain a decision in favor of peace.

Guyasuta in the Revolutionary War

In May, 1776, Sir Guy Johnson and Colonel John Butler held a great council with the Iroquois chiefs at Fort Niagara, New York, when the overwhelming majority of the sachems voted to accept the war hatchet against the Americans. Guyasuta then came from his home near Sharpsburg, Allegheny County, to a council at Fort Pitt on July 6th of that year, and declared that neither the English nor the Americans should be permitted to pass through the territory of the Six Nations. This was a conference between Majors Trent and Ward, and Captain Neville, on the one hand, and Guyasuta, Captain Pipe, a Delaware chief, Shade, a

Shawnee chief, and other Western Indians. The object of the conference seems to have been to enable Guyasuta, as the outstanding representative of the Six Nations in the Ohio and Allegheny valleys, to define his position in the struggle between England and her American Colonies.

"I am appointed," said Guyasuta, "by the Six Nations to take care of this country, that is of the nations on the other side of the Ohio [meaning the present Allegheny River], and I desire you will not think of an expedition against Detroit, for, I repeat, we will not suffer an army to pass through our country." Captain Neville replied that the Americans would not invade Guyasuta's domain, unless the British should try to come through the same towards Fort Pitt. Detroit was then in the possession of the British, and, no doubt, as an actual ally of the British, it was the task assigned Guyasuta to prevent an advance against this post by the Americans.

At any rate soon thereafter this great chief of the Senecas took up arms against the Americans, and led many a bloody expedition against the settlements of Western Pennsylvania. During the summers of 1778 and 1779, he was especially active against the settlements of New York and Pennsylvania, and decorated the Seneca towns of the upper Allegheny with the scalps of hundreds of settlers.

Broadhead's Expedition Against Guyasuta's Warriors

In order to put a stop to the raids of Guyasuta's warriors Colonel Broadhead, who was in command of Fort Pitt during the summer of 1779, begged General Washington for permission to lead an expedition into the Seneca country. Early in the same summer, Washington directed General John Sullivan to invade the territory of the Iroquois from the East; and about the middle of July, Broadhead received permission from Washington to undertake a co-operating movement up the Allegheny. With sixty boats, two hundred pack horses and six hundred and five soldiers, he left Fort Pitt on August 11th. Small garrisons were placed at Fort McIntosh (Beaver), Fort Crawford (New Kensington, Westmoreland County), and Fort Armstrong (Kittanning, Armstrong County). A band of friendly Delawares, under Captain Samuel Brady and Lieut. John Hardin, accompanied the expedition as scouts. Broadhead's small army ascended the beautiful Allegheny, whose banks were now clothed in the verdure of midsummer.

Majestic stood the river hills,
Clothed in living green,
While Allegheny gently rolled
Its winding way between.

Reaching the mouth of the Mahoning, Broadhead left the river and followed the Indian trail running almost due north through the wilderness of what is now Clarion County, and reached the Allegheny near the mouth of Tionesta Creek, Forest County. A few miles below the mouth of Brokenstraw Creek, Warren County, Broadhead's force encountered a party of thirty Seneca's, under Guyasuta, descending the Allegheny on their way to raid the frontier settlements. Both sides discovered each other at about the same time, took position behind trees and rocks, and a sharp fight commenced, which lasted but a few minutes, when a party of Broadhead's scouts, moving over the river hill, attacked the Senecas on the flank. The Indians then took to flight, leaving five of their number dead on the field. It has been said that Corn-planter was the commander of the Indians at this engagement, but it is clear that he was at this time in the Genesee country endeavoring to oppose the advance of Sullivan's army. Broadhead then marched up the river, destroyed the Seneca towns, and burned one hundred thirty of their houses, some of them large enough for three or four families. They also destroyed five hundred acres of corn, of which Broadhead said: "I never saw finer corn, although it was planted much thicker than is common with our farmers."

Guyasuta Burns Hannastown

The hardest blow dealt by the Indians during the Revolutionary War, within the limits of Western Pennsylvania, was the burning of Hannastown, the county seat of Westmoreland, by Guyasuta, on Saturday, July 13th, 1782. This historic frontier village was located about three miles north of Greensburg. The town grew up around the tavern of Robert Hanna, on the old Forbes Road, before the Revolutionary War.

At the time of its destruction, Hannastown contained thirty log houses, and, at the northern end, was a stockade fort of logs set upright, and erected in 1773. In the centre was a spring whose waters still gush forth to quench the thirst of the lover of Pennsylvania history, who makes a pilgrimage to the spot where the frontier village stood.

Guyasuta, with a band of one hundred Seneca warriors and sixty Canadian rangers, left Lake Chautauqua, New York, descended the Allegheny River to a point a short distance above

Kittanning, and leaving the canoes on the bank of the river, marched overland into the settlements of Westmoreland. While the expedition was making its visitation of death and destruction, many of these canoes broke loose from their moorings, and floated down the river to Fort Pitt, where some of them were picked up by the garrison.

On this midsummer day when Guyasuta's warriors destroyed the historic town, one of the harvesters, who were cutting wheat on the farm of Michael Huffnagle, the county clerk, about a mile north of the village, discovered a band of Indians, in war paint, creeping through the woods. He informed his companions, and all fled unseen to the stockade. The alarm was spread throughout the Hannastown settlement by Sheriff Matthew Jack. About sixty persons were in the village, and they took refuge within the fort. Huffnagle carried most of the county records safely into the fort.

Four young men were sent out to scout. Coming upon the Indians creeping through the thick woods in the valley of Crabtree Creek, they narrowly escaped death, and fled back to the fort, followed closely by the Indians. It seems that Guyasuta intended to take the fort by storm; for his warriors did not shoot or yell until they rushed into the village. One man was wounded before he reached the fort.

The Indians then drove into the woods all the horses found in the pasture lots and stables, killed one hundred cattle, and plundered the deserted houses. From the shleter of the houses, they opened a hot rifle fire upon the stockade, defended by twenty men with seventeen rifles, only nine of which were fit for use. With these, the frontiersmen took turns at the loopholes, and succeeded in preventing the Indians from assaulting and battering down the gates. At least two of the savages were killed, and others wounded; while only one person inside the stockade was wounded, a maiden of sixteen summers named Margaret Shaw, who received a bullet in her breast while exposed before a hole in one of the gates, as she was rescuing a child, who had toddled into danger. The young lady died from the effects of her wound about two weeks later. Her dust reposes in the soil of "Old Westmoreland", a short distance north of Mt. Pleasant.

The attack on the fort continued until night, when the Indians set fire to the village, and danced in the glare of the flames. The county jail and all the other buildings, except the court house and one dwelling, were reduced to ashes. These two had been set on fire, but the fire went out; and, as they stood near the fort, the unerring rifles of the frontiersmen frustrated an attempt to set fire to them again. Happily, the wind blew strongly from the north, carrying the flames and burning embers away from the fort. After the buildings were burned, the Indians and their white allies retired to the valley of Crabtree Creek, and reveled and feasted until late at night.

The attack was not renewed in the morning, and Guyasuta and his forces made good their escape. It was not until Monday morning that a force of sixty frontiersmen took up the pursuit, following them to the crossing of the Kiskiminetas.

Other places in the neighborhood of Hannastown were also attacked with deadly effect. A wedding had taken place, on July 12th, at the home of Andrew Cruikshank at Miller's Station, two miles south of Hannastown; and on July 13th, many friends of the happy couple were gathered at the Cruikshank home for the wedding party, when Guyasuta's warriors fell upon them, killing several and making prisoners of fifteen. Among the latter were Lieutenant Joseph Brownlee, his wife and several children, Mrs. Robert Hanna and her daughter, Jennie, and a Mrs. White and two of her children. As these prisoners were being taken through the woods, Mrs. Hanna addressed Lieutenant Brownlee as "Captain"; whereupon the Indians killed him, his little son whom he was carrying, and nine other captives. The others were taken to Canada.

Also, on Sunday morning, some of Guyasuta's force attacked the Freeman settlement on Loyalhanna Creek, a few miles northeast of Hannastown, killing one of Freeman's sons and capturing two of his daughters. On the same day, an attack was made on the Brush Creek settlement west of Hannastown, where many farm animals were killed, and several farm buildings burned. This attack was promptly reported to General William Irvine, then the commander at Fort Pitt, by Michael Huffnagle, the defender of the Hannastown fort.

Hannastown never arose from its ashes. Court was held there for a few sessions after the burning of the village. Then a new road was laid out from Bedford to Pittsburgh, following the course of the present Lincoln Highway; and, in January, 1787, the Westmoreland Court began its sessions in the town of Greensburg, on the new road, the present county seat of the historic county of Westmoreland.

It appears that there was a previous attack on Hannastown.

Boucher, in his "History of Westmoreland County," refers to this former attack, as follows:

"Eve Oury was granted a special pension of forty dollars per year by Act of April 1, 1846. The act itself recites that it was granted for heroic bravery and risking her life in defense of the garrison of Hannastown Fort in 1778, when it was attacked by a large number of Indians, and that by her fortitude, she performed efficient service in driving away the Indians, and thus saved the inmates from a horrid butchery by the merciless and savage foe."

Eve Oury (Uhrig) was the daughter of Francis Oury. She died at Shieldsburg, Westmoreland County, in 1848, and is buried at Congruity, in the same county.

Reference has been made to the fact that the Six Nations, owing principally to the influence of Sir Guy Johnson, Colonel John Butler, and other British sympathizers and agents, were overwhelmingly on the side of the British during the Revolutionary War. The British offered the Iroquois great plunder and bounties for American scalps, as an inducement for them to attack the Americans. To be specific, the League of the Iroquois voted to take no part in the great conflict, but allow each tribe to decide for itself. A large part of the Tuscaroras and nearly all the Oneidas, owing to the influence of Rev. Samuel Kirkland, remained neutral; but the other four tribes of the historic confederation went over to the British, and brought desolation and death upon the frontiers of New York and Pennsylvania. Witness Cherry Valley, in New York, and Wyoming and Hannastown, in Pennsylvania.

Guyasuta's tribe, the Senecas, were the most numerous and warlike of the Six Nations. A recital of the bloody outrages committed by them upon the Americans struggling for liberty during the American Revolution would fill many pages. While it is not to be wondered at that Guyasuta sided along with his nation in the American Revolution, it is sincerely to be regretted that one of the most noted chiefs that ever trod the soil of Pennsylvania took the side of the British in this conflict Terrible was the retribution visited upon the Senecas and their allies by General Sullivan—a retribution that led to the final extinction of the Iroquois Confederation. No wonder that the old chief's declining years were embittered.

Last Days of Guyasuta

After the Revolutionary War, Guyasuta lived in the vicinity of Fort Pitt. As old age crept upon him, he became virtually destitute. In 1790, he sent a pathetic message to the Quakers of Philadelphia, addressing them as the sons of his beloved "Brother Onas" and imploring their assistance. Said he: "When I was young and strong, our country was full of game which the good Spirit sent for us to live upon. The lands which belonged to us were extended far beyond where we hunted. Hunting was then not tiresome; it was diversion; it was pleasure. When your fathers asked land from my nation, we gave it to them, for we had more than enough. Guyasuta was among the first people to say, 'give land to our brother Onas for he wants it; and he has always been a friend to Onas and his children. But you are too far off to see him. Now he is grown old. He is very old and he wonders at his own shadow; it has become so little. He has no children to take care of him and the game is driven away by the white people. . . . I have no other friends but you, the children of our beloved Brother Onas."

From December, 1792, to the middle of April, 1793, General Anthony Wayne trained the Legion of the United States at that place on the Ohio River, twenty miles below Pittsburgh, since known as Legionville. Before leading the Legion from that place against the Western Indians, he was visited by Guyasuta.

In May, 1793, Captain Samuel Brady was tried at Pittsburgh for the murder of certain Indians near the mouth of the Beaver, in the spring of 1791. Due at least in part to the testimony given in his behalf by Guyasuta, he was acquitted. Guyasuta's testimony was so strongly in favor of the defendant that even Brady's counsel, James Ross, Esq., was abashed. At the close of the trial, Mr. Ross spoke to Guyasuta, expressing his surprise at the decided tone of his testimony. The aged chief then clapped his hand upon his breast, and said: "Am I not the friend of Brady?"

General James O'Hara bought Guyasuta's interest in the large tract of land on the west side of the Allegheny near Sharpsburg, Allegheny County, and gave the old chief a home on the plantation during his declining years. Here he died some time in the closing years of the eighteenth century, and his body was placed in the old Indian mound on the estate by General O'Hara. Guyasuta station on the Pennsylvania Railroad nearby bears the name of this noted chieftain.

The claim has been made, however, that Guyasuta died at Custaloga's Town on French Creek about twelve miles above its mouth and near the mouth of Deer Creek in French Creek Township, Mercer County, and was buried at that place. (See Frontier Forts of Pennsylvania, Volume Two, pages 322, 323).

CHAPTER XXV.

New Comer, White Eyes and Killbuck

NEW COMER

NEW COMER, or Nettawatwees, was a chief of the Turtle Clan of Delawares, his authority being limited, it seems, to that Clan alone, though he was the nominal head of the Delaware nation. His first appearance in history is when he was a witness to the deed which Sassoonan and six other chiefs gave to William Penn, on September 17th, 1718, by the terms of which they released all the land "between the Delaware and the Susquehanna from Duck Creek to the Mountains [the South Mountain] on this side of Lechay [the Lehigh River]", mentioned more particularly in Chapter VII.

New Comer was one of the chiefs who met George Croghan at Logstown in January, 1754, and joined with Scarouady, Tanacharison, Shingas, and Delaware George, in requesting both Pennsylvania and Virginia to build forts near the Forks of the Ohio as a place of security for the Indians of that region in case of war with the French. He went to the Muskingum and Tuscarawas near the close of the French and Indian War, from which place he joined with King Beaver and Shingas in sending White Eyes and Wingenund to Philadelphia in May, 1761, to advise the Governor that a large delegation of chiefs from Ohio proposed coming to meet him in order to cement the bond of peace.

When Colonel Bouquet led his expedition to the Muskingum and Tuscarawas in the summer and autumn of 1764, to quell Pontiac's uprising and to force the Western Indians to deliver up the prisoners which they had captured, New Comer, as chief of the Turtle Clan was nominally the head of the Delaware nation at that time. Bouquet deposed him on this occasion for refusing to attend the conference between this resolute soldier and the chiefs of the hostile tribes. The deposition, however, was never accepted by the Delawares.

New Comer attended the conference at Fort Pitt, beginning May 10th, 1765, relative to resuming trade relations with the western tribes after the close of Pontiac's War; also the great council at the same place, April 26th to May 9th, 1768, relative to the settlements made at Redstone and other places in the valleys of the Monongahela and Youghiogheny, on land not purchased from the Indians—the council which led to the Great Congress at Fort Stanwix, (Rome, New York,) in October of that year, at which Pennsylvania purchased from the Six Nations that part of the state known as the "Purchase of 1768", the counties included in which were set forth in Chapter XX.

In his latter years, New Comer came under the influence of the Moravian missionaries, and granted them lands on the Tuscarawas, in 1772. He was especially friendly to Bishop Zeisberger of the Moravian Church. He was much perplexed, however, on account of the lack of unity among Christians. He could not understand why there were so many different denominations; and, in the latter part of 1772, he advised the Governor of Pennsylvania that he intended to go to England to consult the King on this matter which was disturbing his heart, a journey which he did not take, however.

Last Days of New Comer

When William Wilson, as the ambassador of George Morgan, then in charge of Indian affairs at Fort Pitt, was sent in the summer of 1776 on a mission to invite the Delawares, Shawnees, and Wyandots of Ohio to a conference to be held at Fort Pitt in October of that year, he was greatly befriended by New Comer at the Delaware town of Coshocton, located on the site of the present town of that name, in Coshocton County, Ohio. Wilson, in spite of the interference of Hamilton, commander of the British fort at Detroit, succeeded in persuading a number of the chiefs of the western tribes to attend the conference at Fort Pitt in October Among these chiefs was the venerable New Comer. Unusual solemnity was given to the conference by the fact that he breathed his last at Fort Pitt before the treaty was concluded.

WHITE EYES

White Eyes, also sometimes Grey Eyes, became the ruler of the Turkey Clan of Delawares upon the death of King Beaver. During the winter of 1776-1777, he was elected chief sachem of the Delaware nation, following the death of the aged New Comer in Pittsburgh in the autumn of 1776. His Delaware name was Coquetakeghton.

While White Eyes met Post on the latter's first mission to the

Ohio in the summer of 1758, his first appearance of importance in Pennsylvania history is when he and the Delaware chief, Wingenund, as the ambassadors of King Beaver and New Comer, met Governor Hamilton in council at Philadelphia, on May 22nd, 1761, and delivered the promise of these "chief men at Allegheny" to meet the Provincial Authorities in the near future further to confirm the peace "that was begun at Easton" [Treaty of Easton, October, 1758], "a peace", said White Eyes, "that has a good face, and seems to be as well established as that made by William Penn. . . . . at the first settlement of the Province." Andrew Montour was the interpreter. The Governor received White Eyes and Wingenund very cordially, and requested them to advise their superior chiefs to make arrangements for the delivery of the white prisoners taken in the French and Indian War, a request, which, as was seen in Chapter XIX, was carried out by King Beaver and Shingas, at the Lancaster conference of August, 1762.

Nothing definite is known as to the part taken by White Eyes in Pontiac's War. But in Lord Dunmore's War, in the autumn of 1774, we find him an earnest advocate of peace. Many of his people reviled him and accused him of ingratiating himself with the Virginians in his efforts to persuade the Shawnees to make peace with Dunmore; but the great chieftain's purpose was to save the Shawnees from destruction. Taunts and abuse did not swerve him. He was Lord Dunmore's advisor; and, when peace was concluded between the Virginians and the Shawnees, at Camp Charlotte, near Circleville, Ohio, in October, Lord Dunmore took occasion to extol White Eyes and his people, saying that they had been the unflinching advocates of peace, and telling the Shawnees that only out of regard for them, the Delawares, as "grandfathers" of the Shawnees, had he made the terms of peace so lenient. Both the Shawnees and the Virginians had suffered severe losses at the battle of Point Pleasant, West Virginia, described in the sketch of Cornstalk, Chapter XXVII.

Reference was made, in Chapter XXIV, to the fact that White Eyes attended the treaty held at Fort Pitt on October 27th, 1775, in an effort to secure the friendship of the western tribes in the Revolutionary War, at which he resented Guyasuta's claim to represent the Delawares. White Eyes' sympathy for the Americans gave offense to Guyasuta, who reminded him that the Delawares were "women".

"Women!" was the scornful reply of White Eyes. "Yes, you say that you conquered me, that you cut off my legs, put a petti-

coat on me, and gave me a hoe and cornpounder in my hands.
. . . . . Look at my legs. If, as you assert, you cut them off,
they have grown again to their proper size. The petticoat I have
thrown away; the corn-hoe and pounder I have exchanged for
these firearms; and I declare that I am a man. Yes, all the
country on the other side of that river"—waving his hand in the
direction of the Allegheny—"is mine."

White Eyes Accompanies William Wilson to Detroit

In the sketch of New Comer, reference was made to the fact
that, in the summer of 1776, William Wilson, as agent of George
Morgan, made a journey among the Indians of Ohio, to invite
them to a treaty at Fort Pitt in October, and that he was befriended
by New Comer at Coshocton. On this occasion, New Comer, believing it unsafe for Wilson to proceed to the Wyandots at Sandusky, sent Killbuck to carry his message to them. Killbuck returned in eleven days with word from the Wyandot chiefs that
they wanted to see Wilson and hear his message from his own
mouth. Wilson then decided to go to see them, and New Comer
directed Killbuck to accompany him. Scarcely had the journey
begun when Killbuck became ill, and his place was taken by White
Eyes. Proceeding, Wilson and White Eyes learned that the
Wyandot chiefs had gone to Detroit. Wilson then boldly pressed
on to the neighborhood of the British post, where he and White
Eyes met the Wyandots. Both he and White Eyes addressed them
urging them to attend the treaty. The Wyandot chiefs betrayed
Wilson's presence to the British commander, Colonel Henry Hamilton, Lieutenant Governor, to whom Wilson frankly told the object of his mission. Though greatly angered, Hamilton respected
Wilson's character as an ambassador, and gave him a safe conduct through the Indian country to Fort Pitt; but scathingly denounced White Eyes, and ordered him to leave Detroit within
twenty-four hours, if he valued his life.

White Eyes Makes Alliance With the Americans

The Delawares on the Tuscarawas and Muskingum, owing
principally to the influence of White Eyes, having maintained
neutrality between the Americans and the British, during the early
years of the Revolutionary War, and this remarkable chieftain
having shown an intelligent sympathy with the American cause and
expressed the hope that the Delaware Nation might form the four-

teenth state in the American union, Congress, in June, 1778, ordered a treaty to be held at Fort Pitt, on July 23rd, for the purpose of forming an alliance with these Indians, and requested Virginia to choose two commissioners and Pennsylvania, one, for this purpose. Pennsylvania neglected to choose a commissioner; but Virginia appointed General Andrew Lewis, the conqueror of Cornstalk, at Point Pleasant, and his brother, Thomas Lewis, a civilian. The time of the treaty was postponed to September, owing to the inability of the American troops to reach Fort Pitt in July.

Messengers had been sent to the Shawnees, inviting them to come with the Delawares to the treaty, but they declined, except a small band under Nimwha, who lived with the Delawares at Coshocton.

The conference began on September 12th, and the treaty was signed on the 17th. Besides White Eyes, the Delawares were represented by Killbuck, successor to New Comer of the Turtle Clan, Captain Pipe, successor to Custaloga, of the Wolf Clan, and Wingenund, the Delaware "wise man." These three chiefs appeared at the councils, in all their gaudy attire, painted, feathered, and beaded; while General McIntosh and his staff officers attended in new uniforms. The interpreter was Job Chilloway, a Delaware from the Susquehanna, who had learned the English language from having lived for a number of years among the white people.

General Lewis advised the Delaware chiefs of his intention to send an army against the British at Detroit, and asked the permission of the Delawares for the army to pass through the territory over which they claimed control, bounded on the east by the Ohio and Allegheny, and on the west by the Hocking and Sandusky.

By the terms of the treaty as finally concluded, all offenses were mutually forgiven; a perpetual friendship was pledged; each party agreed to assist the other in any just war; the Delawares gave permission for an American army to pass through their territory, and agreed to furnish meat, corn, warriors and guides for the army. The United States agreed to erect and garrison a fort, within the Delaware country, for the protection of the old men, women, and children; and each party agreed to punish offenses committed by citizens of the other, according to a system to be arranged later. The United States promised the establishment of fair and honest trade relations; and lastly, the United States guaranteed the integrity of the Delaware nation, and promised to admit it as a state of the American Union, "provided nothing contained in this article be considered as conclusive until it meets the approbation of congress." With reference to the promise to admit the Delaware nation as a state of the Union, the commissioners must have known that this was an impossibility.

But the guileless White Eyes never suspected that he and his people were being imposed upon. Said he: "Brothers, we are become one people. We [the Delawares], are at a loss to express our thoughts, but we hope soon to convince you by our actions of the sincerity of our hearts. We now inform you that as many of our warriors as can possibly be spared will join you and go with you."

The great courage of White Eyes in forming this alliance of the Delawares with the Americans is seen when it is recalled that all the other western tribes were on the side of the English, and, for some time, had been endeavoring, by solicitation and threats, to draw the Delawares into a British alliance. Governor Hamilton, at Detroit, who had charge of the operations of the British against the frontiers, had been ordered, on October 6th, 1776, to enlist the various western tribes and have them ready for a campaign against the frontier the next spring. Hamilton gave the savages fifty dollars for each American scalp taken by them. The Americans held him in abhorrence, and called him the "hair-buyer" general. For more than two years before White Eyes allied his people with the Americans, the other western tribes, instigated by the British and induced by the scalp bounty, were desolating the Pennsylvania frontier. The terrible situation of the settlers in this region is shown by the following letter written to President Wharton, in November, 1777, by Archibald Lochry, County Lieutenant of Westmoreland:

"The distressed situation of our country is such, that we have no prospect but desolation and destruction. The whole country on the north side of the road [Forbes Road] from the Allegheny Mountains to the river is all kept close in forts; and can get no subsistance from their plantations; they have made application to us requesting to be put under pay, and receive rations. . . . . . As we could see no other way to keep these people from flying and letting the country be evacuated, we were obliged to adopt these measures."

Then, on March 28th, 1778, the Pittsburgh Tories, Captain Alexander McKee, Matthew Elliott, Robert Surphlit, and Simon Girty, deserted the American force at Fort Pitt, and went over to the British. McKee was a man of education, and had long been in secret correspondence with British officers in Canada. General

Hand, the commandant at Fort Pitt, had received a hint of Mc-Kee's intention, early in the evening, and he ordered a squad of soldiers to go to the deserter's house the next morning, and remove him to the fort.   When the troops arrived the next morning, they found that the renegades had escaped from McKee's house during the night.   For a number of years, Captain McKee had lived on a plantation of fourteen hundred acres, at the mouth of Chartiers Creek, granted to him by Colonel Bouquet, in 1764, the site of the town of McKees Rocks, on the left bank of the Ohio, in Allegheny County.   It was from the house on this plantation that he made his escape.

He and his companions made their way to the chief town of the Delawares, Coshocton, Ohio, where they endeavored to arouse this tribe against the Americans.   A great debate took place in the Delaware council between Captain Pipe, who advocated that the Delawares give McKee's request favorable consideration, and White Eyes, who, by his oratory thwarted the plans of the renegades.

The renegades then went to the Shawnees on the Scioto, where they were welcomed.   James Girty, a brother of Simon, was there with the Shawnees, having been sent by the commandant of Fort Pitt on a peace embassy.   This natural savage at once joined his brother and the other tories.   Then Governor Hamilton, learning that McKee and his companions were among the Shawnees, sent Edward Hazle to the Scioto, who conducted them safely to Detroit, where Hamilton gave them commissions in the British service, and they became the merciless scourgers of the frontiers.

Thus, it is seen that White Eyes, in daring to form an alliance with the Americans, exposed the Delawares to destruction by the British and their savage allies.   But he had the courage to do what he believed to be right.

White Eyes' Grand Plan

At this treaty, White Eyes avowed that his people had embraced Christianity.   During the few years prior to this treaty, the Moravian missionaries made good progress in Christianizing the Delawares, under White Eyes, in their villages on the Tuscarawas.   White Eyes told the Moravians, in 1774, that he sincerely believed the Gospel.   He then unfolded to Bishop Zeisberger this grand plan: Christianity should be the national religion.   He would go to England and lay before the king the differences between the Delawares and the white people, tell the king of the rapid westward march of the whites, and induce him to guarantee to the Delawares the country they then possessed, which should be their home to all generations. There the Delawares would live as a civilized and Christian people. To bring about this happy result should be the work of the Moravian missions. Then White Eyes journied to Philadelphia and requested the Continental Congress to send the Delawares teachers and clergymen of the Episcopal Church. Lord Dunmore had promised this remarkable chief his assistance; but later, on account of the disturbed condition of the colonies, persuaded him to give up his projected visit to England.

The noble aspirations of the great chieftain command our admiration. Behold the contrast between the plans of Pontiac and those of White Eyes. Pontiac desired the Indian to remain for all time a warrior and hunter; and, in an attempt to carry his plans into execution, and drive the English into the sea, he drenched the frontiers with the blood of the settlers. White Eyes, on the other hand, deeming the plow a blessing and all the implements of industry good, hoped, by statesman-like negotiations, to secure for his people a home, where they might enjoy the benefits of civilization.

Plot Against Friendly Delawares

Due to the alliance between the Delawares and the United States, Colonel Broadhead, then commandant at Fort Pitt, in the autumn of 1780 received the aid of more than forty friendly Delawares, who had come to assist him in his operations against the hostile tribes. In a letter to President Reed, dated November 2nd, 1780, he says: "I believe I could have called out near an hundred. But as upwards of forty men from the neighborhood of Hannastown have attempted to destroy them whilst they consider themselves under our protection, it may not be an easy matter to call them out again, notwithstanding they [the Hannastown settlers] were prevented from executing their unmanly intention, by a guard of regular soldiers posted for the Indians' protection. I was not a little surprised to find that the late Captains Irwin and Jack, Lieutenant Brownlee, and Ensign Guthrie concerned in this base attempt. I suppose the women and children were to suffer an equal carnage with the men."

It was very fortunate for Colonel Broadhead that he was able to save the lives of these friendly Delawares. Provisions at Fort Pitt had become very scarce, and Colonel Broadhead had sent

Captain Samuel Brady through the Chartier's Creek settlement for the purpose of procuring cattle and sheep for the hungry garrison. The Scotch-Irish settlers of this region greatly resented Brady's activities, and his mission was a failure.   Then Colonel Broadhead sent many of the friendly Delawares, whose lives he had saved, to the Great Kanawha to spend the winter there hunting buffaloes, and to bring the meat to Fort Pitt.

White Eyes and Heckewelder

White Eyes was a very warm friend of the Moravian missionary, Heckewelder.   They first met when Heckewelder visited him at his home near the mouth of the Beaver, when the missionary was on his way to the Tuscarawas in the spring of 1762.   Heckewelder relates the following incidents in the life of this noted chieftain:

"In the year 1777, while the Revolutionary War was raging, and several Indian tribes had enlisted on the British side, and were spreading murder and devastation along our unprotected frontier, I rather rashly determined to take a journey into the country on a visit to my friends.   Captain White Eyes, the Indian hero, whose character I have already described, resided at that time at the distance of seventeen miles from the place where I lived.   Hearing of my determination, he immdiately hurried up to me, with his friend Captain Wingenund, whom I shall presently have occasion further to mention, and some of his young men, for the purpose of escorting me to Pittsburgh, saying, 'that he would not suffer me to go, while the Sandusky warriors were out on war excursions, without a proper escort and himself at my side.'   He insisted on accompanying me, and we set out together.   One day, as we were proceeding along, our spies discovered a suspicious track.   White Eyes, who was riding before me, inquired whether I felt afraid.   I answered that while he was with me, I entertained no fear.   On this he immediately replied: 'You are right; for until I am laid prostrate at your feet, no one shall hurt you.' 'And even not then,' added Wingenund, who was riding behind me; 'before this happens, I must be also overcome, and lay by the side of our friend Koguethagechton [the Indian name of White Eyes].' I believed them, and I believe at this day that these great men were sincere, and that, if they had been put to the test, they would have shown it, as did another Indian friend by whom my life was saved in the spring of the year 1781.   From behind a log in the bushes where he was concealed, he espied a hostile Indian at the very moment he was leveling his piece at me.   Quick as lightning he jumped between us, and exposed his person to the musket shot just about to be fired, when fortunately the aggressor desisted, from fear of hitting the Indian whose body thus effectually protected me, at the imminent risk of his own life. Captain White Eyes, in the year 1774, saved in the same manner the life of David Duncan, the peace messenger, whom he was escorting. He rushed, regardless of his own life, up to an inimical Shawanese, who was aiming at our ambassador from behind a bush, and forced him to desist."

Death of White Eyes

Immediately after the forming of the alliance with the Delawares, General McIntosh, then in command at Fort Pitt, prepared to lead an expedition against the British at Detroit. With an army of thirteen hundred troops, he moved down the Ohio to the mouth of the Beaver early in October, 1778. Here he built Fort McIntosh on the high bluff overlooking the Ohio, on the western side of the Beaver. Four weeks were consumed in erecting the fort, and the sixty Delaware warriors who accompanied the army, could not understand why so much time was spent in erecting a fortification that would not be needed when Detroit was taken. However, on November 5th, the army began its march through the wilderness towards Detroit. In accordance with the provisions of the treaty with the Delawares, General McIntosh intended to erect a fort for the protection of their women and children at the Delaware capital of Coshocton at the junction of the Tuscarawas and the Walhonding. On the march to the Tuscarawas, White Eyes was treacherously put to death, it is believed by a Virginia militiaman, causing dismay among the warriors, most of whom returned to Coshocton. Such is the account of his death, given by most authorities. However, DeSchweinitz, in his "Life of David Zeisberger", says that this greatest and best of the later Delaware chiefs died of small-pox on November 10th, in the camp on the Tuscarawas. But whatever the manner of his death, whether by the hand of an assassin or by small-pox, the sudden ending of his earthly career had the effect of causing General McIntosh to abandon the attempt to take Detroit that winter.

Says DeSchweinitz: "Where his [White Eyes'] remains are resting, no man knows; the plowshare has often furrowed his grave. But his name lives; and the Christian may hope that in the resurrection of the just, he, too will be found among the great multitude redeemed out of every kindred, and tongue, and people, and nation."

KILLBUCK

Upon the death of White Eyes, Killbuck, the firm friend of the Americans, was elected as his successor. However, he soon found himself in the minority, and Captain Pipe, the head of the war faction among the Delawares, influenced the great Delaware council at Coshocton, as will be seen in Chapter XXVI, in February, 1781, to join the hostile tribes in alliance with the British. Killbuck was absent at Fort Pitt when this action was taken, and on account of threats against his life, was afraid to return to Coshocton. He went to Salem, located on the Tuscarawas about fourteen miles below New Philadelphia. Here, on February 26th, he wrote a long letter by the hand of Missionary Heckewelder, to Colonel Broadhead, advising him of the action taken by the Delaware council. Then, as will be seen in Chapter XXVI, Broadhead determined to punish the Delawares for their perfidy, and in April, 1781, led an expedition against the Delaware capital of Coshocton. As Broadhead's troops were on their way back from the attack at Coshocton and while resting at New Comer's Town, Killbuck appeared in the camp and threw at Broadhead's feet the scalp of "one of the greatest villians" among the hostile Delawares.

After Broadhead's expedition against Coshocton, the hostile Delawares, under their leader, Captain Pipe, went to the headwaters of the Sandusky, while those friendly to the United States moved, with Killbuck, to Smoky Island (also known as Killbuck's Island) within sight of Fort Pitt. Here Killbuck remained until after the Revolutionary War.

Killbuck's Indian name was Gelelemend (i. e. a leader). He was a grandson of the great New Comer. In consequence of his friendship for the United States during the Revolutionary War, he incurred the hatred of the war faction among the Delawares, which continued even after the general peace concluded between the Delawares and the United States by the treaty of Greenville, August 3rd, 1795. Most authorities say he was born near the Lehigh Water Gap, Carbon County, Pennsylvania, in 1737. In the summer of 1788, he united with the Moravian Indians at Salem, on the Petquotting, in Tuscarawas County, Ohio, being given, in baptism, the name ,William Henry, after Judge William Henry of Lancaster, Pennsylvania. Here he died in the early winter of 1811. Says DeSchweinitz: "The vices of the generation, which he had lived to see, caused him deep sorrow, and he protested, even with his dying breath, against their degeneracy."

CHAPTER XXVI.

Captain Pipe and Glikkikan

CAPTAIN PIPE

APTAIN PIPE was a chief of the Wolf Clan of Delawares, and succeeded Custaloga. He was "a very artful and designing man, and a chief of considerable ability and influence." He was very active in Pontiac's War; and when Colonel Bouquet left Fort Pitt, in the summer of 1764, on his way to bring the western tribes into subjection, and compel them to surrender the prisoners taken in that memorable uprising, he had this chief detained at the fort as a hostage.

Shortly after the treaty held at Fort Pitt on October 27, 1775, at which White Eyes, replying to the taunts of Guyasuta, boldly asserted the independence of the Delawares, Captain Pipe seceded from the tribe with a number of his followers. His ostensible reason for this action was that he feared that the speech of White Eyes would arouse the anger and vengeance of the Iroquois; but his real reason seems to have been that he was not in sympathy with the friendly attitude of the Delawares towards the American cause; for later on he boldly declared against the Americans.

When the renegades, McKee, Elliott, and Girty, came to the Delaware capital of Coshocton in the spring of 1778, they reported that the American armies on the Atlantic Seaboard had been overwhelmed by the English. This false report encouraged Captain Pipe to renew vigorously his attempts to have the Delawares take up arms against the Americans. It has already been related how he was opposed in the Delaware council by White Eyes, whose oratory prevailed. The Moravian missionary, Rev. John Hecke-welder, left Bethlehem, Pa., on March 23, 1778, to visit the Moravian missions in Ohio. Arriving at Fort Pitt, he found the garrison much disturbed over the flight of the tories, McKee, Elliott, and Girty, and hastened to the Ohio Delawares as fast as his horse could carry him. Upon his arrival, he gave the Delaware council the true state of affairs as to military operations in the East, advising them of the recent capture of General Burgoyne and his army. Captain Pipe then left the council in chagrin and went back to his village.

On the death of White Eyes, Captain Pipe continued as head of the war faction among the Delawares; and so great was his influence that he succeeded in persuading the majority of the tribe, in violation of the alliance which they had made with the Americans, to go over to the British. The Delaware council at Coshocton took this action in February, 1781, during the absence of Killbuck at Fort Pitt. Colonel Broadhead, then in command at Fort Pitt, determined to attack the Delaware town of Coshocton, and punish them for their perfidy. He proceeded to Wheeling with his little army of three hundred troops, from which place he took up the march toward the Delaware capital, on April 10th. On April 20th, Broadhead's advance having come upon three Delawares about a mile from Coshocton, captured one, but the other two escaped and gave the alarm. Broadhead's force then dashed into the Delaware capital, where they found but fifteen warriors, every one of whom was put to death in the resistless rush of the American troops; but no harm was done to the old men, women and children. Broadhead's troops then set fire to the town after having "taken great quantities of peltry and other stores", and destroyed about forty head of cattle. The reason that Broadhead found so few warriors in Coshocton was that a band of forty who had just returned from a raid on the settlements, laden with scalps and prisoners, had crossed to the farther side of the river, a few miles above the town, to enjoy a drunken revel. On account of the swollen condition of the stream and the fact that the war parties had taken their canoes with them, the troops were unable to cross to the farther side. Broadhead wished to send a detail to the Moravian towns farther up the river, for the purpose of procuring boats; but the volunteer soldiers protested, saying that they had done enough, suffered severely from the weather, had almost worn out their horses, and proposed to return to fort Pitt. The Colonel, finding that he could not help himself, inasmuch as the troops were not subject to strict military discipline, consented to their proposal.

On the return march, Broadhead followed the Tuscarawas to New Comer's Town, at which place he found about thirty friendly Delawares who had withdrawn from Coshocton when the Delaware council voted to espouse the British cause. "The troops," said Broadhead in his report of the expedition, "experienced great kindness from the Moravian Indians and those at New Comer's Town, and obtained a sufficient supply of meat and corn to subsist the men and horses to the Ohio River."

Captain Pipe Befriends the Moravian Missionaries

When the Delaware council at Coshocton voted to take up arms against the United States, the Moravian converts renounced all fellowship with them. The British, believing that the converts were being instigated by the Moravian missionaries to take an active part on the American side, set on foot measures to punish them. A treaty with the Iroquois took place at Niagara, at which the renegade, McKee, as agent of Indian affairs, proposed, by authority of the commandant of Detroit, an expedition against the Moravian towns. The Six Nations were not willing themselves to take part in the expedition, but sent a message to the Chippewas and Ottawas, saying: "We give you the believing Indians and their teachers to make broth of." These tribes declined, and then the same message was sent to the Wyandots, whose chief accepted it, but, as he protested, merely in order to save the lives of the Christian Indians. The expedition was then planned at a great feast among the Shawnees on the Scioto "in the presence and by the help of British officers and under the folds of the British flag. Wyandots, Mingoes, and Delawares, together with a few Shawnees, formed the troop. To the captains only was the real object of the expedition made known. They received secret instructions to drive the Christian Indians from their seats, to seize their teachers, and either convey them as prisoners to Detroit, or put them to death and bring their scalps."

The result of the expedition was that the Moravian missions were broken up, the Christian Delawares taken to the north bank of the Sandusky, in Wyandot County, Ohio, and the Moravian missionaries taken to Detroit for trial, on the charge that they had rendered assistance to the Americans. The exodus from the missions began in September, 1781; and the trial took place in November, before Major De Pyster, who had succeeded to the command of Detroit after the capture of Hamilton, the "hair buyer", by George Rogers Clark, in February, 1779. De Pyster opened the council by rehearsing the charges against the missionaries, and then addressing Captain Pipe, asked him whether the accusations were correct and founded in fact, and especially whether the missionaries had corresponded with the Americans.

"There may be some truth in the accusations," said Captain Pipe. "I am not prepared to say that all that you have heard is false. But now nothing more of that sort will occur. The teachers are here." De Pyster replied: "I infer, therefore, that these

men have corresponded with the rebels, and sent letters to Fort
Pitt. From your answer this seems to be evident. Tell me, is it
so?"

Captain Pipe then sprang to his feet and exclaimed: "Father,
I have said that there may be some truth in the reports that have
reached you; but now I will tell you exactly what has occurred.
These teachers are innocent. On their own account they never
wrote letters; they had to do it. I [striking upon his breast]
and the chiefs at Goshachgunk are responsible. We induced these
teachers to write letters to Pittsburgh, even at such times when
they at first declined. But this will no more occur, as I have said,
because they are now here."

Major De Pyster then acquitted the missionaries, explaining
that he was not opposed to the preaching of the Gospel among the
Indians and cautioned the missionaries not to meddle with the war.
He gave them permission to return to their converts as soon as they
pleased.

Andrew Poe's Fight with Big Foot

"A striking incident in the history of Washington County
was connected with the removal of the Moravians [to Sandusky,
just related]. While the exiles were being conducted up the
Walhonding, seven Wyandot warriors left the company and went
on a raid across the Ohio River. Among the seven were three sons
of Duquat, the half-king, and the eldest son, Scotosh, was the
leader of the party. They crossed the Ohio on a raft, which they
hid in the mouth of Tomlinson's run. They visited the farm of
Philip Jackson, on Harman's creek, and captured Jackson in his
flax field. The prisoner was a carpenter, about 60 years old, and
his trade made him valuable to the Indians, as he could build
houses for them. The savages did not return directly to their
raft, but traveled by devious ways to the river, to baffle pursuit.
The taking of the carpenter was seen by his son, who ran nine miles
to Ft. Cherry, on Little Raccoon Creek, and gave the alarm. Pursuit the same evening was prevented by a heavy rain, but the next
morning seventeen stout young men, all mounted, gathered at
Jackson's farm. Most of the borderers decided to follow the
crooked and half obliterated trail, but John Jack, a professional
scout, declared that he believed he knew where the Indians had
hidden their raft, and called for followers. Six men joined him,
John Cherry, Andrew Poe, Adam Poe, William Castleman,

William Rankin, and James Whitacre, and they rode on a gallop directly for the mouth of Tomlinson's run.

"Jack's surmise was a shrewd one, based on a thorough knowledge of the Ohio River and the habits of the Indians. At the top of the river hill, the borderers tied their horses in a grove and descended cautiously to the river bank. At the mouth of the run were five Indians, with their prisoner, preparing to shove off their raft. John Cherry fired the first shot, killed an Indian, and was himself killed by the return fire. Four of the five Indians were slain, Philip Jackson was rescued without injury, and Scotosh escaped up the river with a wound in his right hand.

"Andrew Poe, in approaching the river, had gone aside to follow a trail that deviated to the left. Peering over a little bluff, he saw two of the sons of the half-king sitting by the stream. The sound of the firing at the mouth of the run alarmed them, and they arose. Poe's gun missed fire, and he jumped directly upon the two savages, throwing them to the ground. A fierce wrestling contest took place. Andrew Poe was six feet tall, of unusual strength, and almost a match for the two brothers. One of them wounded him in the wrist with a tomahawk, but he got possession of the only rifle that was in working order and loaded, and fatally shot the one who had cut him. Poe and the other savage [His English name was Big Foot. He was a large and powerful Indian] contested for the mastery, awhile on the shore, and then in the water, where Andrew attempted to drown his antagonist. The Indian escaped, reached land and began to load his gun, when Andrew struck out for the opposite shore, shouting for his brother Adam. At the opportune moment, Adam appeared and shot the Indian through the body, but before he expired the savage rolled into the water and his corpse was carried away down the stream. One of the borderers, mistaking Andrew in the stream for an Indian, fired at him and wounded him in the shoulder. The triumphant return of the party to Ft. Cherry was saddened by the death of John Cherry, who was a man of great popularity and a natural leader on the frontier.

"Scotosh, the only survivor of the raiding band, succeeded in swimming the Ohio and hid over night in the woods. In the morning he made a small raft, recrossed the stream, recovered the body of his brother lying on the beach, conveyed it to the Indian side of the river and buried it in the woods. He then made his way to Upper Sandusky, with a sad message for his father and the tribe."
—(Hassler's "Old Westmoreland").

Moravian Delawares Murdered—Crawford Burned

The most dastardly act of Captain Pipe's career was the burning of Colonel William Crawford, the friend of Washington, at the stake, near Sandusky, Ohio, in June, 1782. But, before giving the details of this atrocious act, attention is called to the following facts which led to the same:

In the spring of 1781 Killbuck, after the destruction of Coshocton by Colonel Broadhead, removed with Nanowland and a few other friendly Delawares with their relatives to the vicinity of Fort Pitt, taking up their residence on a small island at the mouth of the Allegheny, known as Killbuck Island, later Smoky Island, and gave active assistance to the American cause. Killbuck became a colonel in the army, and some of his men received commissions as captains.

In the autumn of 1781, the Scotch-Irish settlers of Western Pennsylvania, believed that the Moravian converts on the Tuscarawas, even if they did not join the war parties, were giving food and shelter to the hostile Indians. David Williamson of Washington County, gathered up a force of about one hundred men, and marched to the Tuscarawas, in November, to compel the Moravians either to remove to Fort Pitt, or to migrate farther into the hostile country. Williamson was unaware that the missions had already been broken up, the converts taken to Sandusky, and the missionaries to Detroit. He found only a few Christian Indians who had wandered back to gather corn. These he conducted to Fort Pitt.

The spring of 1782 opened early, mild weather beginning about the first of February. This caused Indian raids in Southwestern Pennsylvania to begin as early as February 8th, greatly alarming and perplexing the settlers, as they could not believe that the Indians had come from a point farther away than the Moravian missions on the Tuscarawas. Among the outrages committed at this time were the murder of John Fink, on February 8th, near Buchanan's Fort on the upper Monongahela; the murder of Mrs. Robert Wallace, and the capture of her three children on February 10th, on Raccoon Creek, near Vance's Fort, Washington County; and the capture of John Carpenter, on February 15th, on the Dutch Fork of Buffalo Creek, in Washington County. Four of the Indians who captured Carpenter were Wyandots, but two others, who spoke German, informed Carpenter that they were Moravians. After his captors had taken him across the Ohio, Carpenter made his escape. Coming to Fort Pitt, he told Colonel Gibson the story of his capture, and then returned to his home on Buffalo Creek, where he told his story to the settlers.

Accordingly, the settlers of Washington County turned out to the number of one hundred sixty, under the command of Colonel Williamson, and crossing the Ohio at Mingo Bottom, a few miles below Steubenville, marched against the Moravian villages. On the evening of March 6th, they were within striking distance of the Moravian town of Gnadenhuetten, when their scouts brought the intelligence to the camp at night that the town was full of Indians. Williamson and his force believed that the occupants of the town were the savages who had been making the raids, but as a matter of fact they were Moravian converts who, after being compelled to go to Sandusky in the preceding autumn, had come back to their old homes to gather their corn.

Williamson attacked the town the next morning. The presence of women and children was plain notice to the frontiersmen that the town was not occupied by a war party. Furthermore, no resistance was made and there was no show of hostile action. Holding a council with a few of the converts who could speak English, Williamson advised them that they must go to Fort Pitt instead of returning to Sandusky. To this they agreed, and at his suggestion, sent messengers down the river to Salem to tell the converts of that place to come to Gnadenhuetten. While the Indians were being assembled and conducted to the church at Gnadenhuetten, an Indian woman was found to be wearing the dress of the wife of Robert Wallace, who, as we have seen, had been killed on February 10th on Raccoon Creek, Washington County, and three of her children captured by some hostile Indians. The Indian men were then examined, one at a time, but none of them acknowledged guilt. It developed, however, that some Wyandot warriors who had journeyed with the converts from Sandusky halted a short period at Gnadenhuetten, and then proceeded on their way to pillage the frontier settlements.

The frontiersmen then began to clamor for the execution of the whole band of Delawares, and Williamson put the question to vote whether they should be taken to Fort Pitt or put to death on the spot. All but eighteen voted to slay all the Indians in the morning.

Bishop Loskiel, in his "History of the Missions of the United Brethren", says that the converts were informed that evening of the fate which awaited them, and that they spent the night in praying, singing hymns, and exhorting one another to die with the fortitude of Christians.

Accordingly, on the morning of Friday, March 8th, 1782, the terrible decree was carried into execution. The Indian men were led two by two to the cooper shop, where they were beaten to death with mallets and hatchets. Many of them died with prayers on their lips, while others met their death chanting songs. Altogether eighty men, twenty women, and thirty-four children were inhumanly butchered. Only two escaped. One was a boy who hid himself in the cellar under the house in which the women and children were butchered, and crept forth during the night. The other was a boy who was scalped among the men, but later revived and crawled into the woods in the night time.

Before Williamson's troops left for home, they burned every building in Gnadenhuetten, "including the two slaughter houses with their heaped-up corpses." The neighboring Moravian villages of Schoenbrun and Salem were also reduced to ashes.

About two weeks after Williamson's forces reached home, the militiamen living in the valley of Chartier's Creek assembled again, and marched against the friendly Delawares on Killbuck Island. The attack was made on Sunday morning, March 24th The United States soldiers on the island were made prisoners, and several of the friendly Indians were shot down, among them being Nanowland, the friend of Captain Samuel Brady. Chief Killbuck, however, and most of his band, succeeded in making their escape to Fort Pitt, where Colonel Gibson, then in temporary command, protected them. Two warriors fled through the woods to Sandusky, one being Chief Big Cat, who ever afterward was the bitter foe of the Americans. Before the militiamen returned to their homes, they sent word to Colonel Gibson that they would kill and scalp him at the first opportunity, for no other reason than that he had protected the friendly Indians and saved them from a fate like that which befell the Christian Delawares at Gnadenhuetten.

Although many of the Western Pennsylvania frontiersmen approved Colonel Williamson's butchery of the Indian women and children at Gnadenhuetten, they felt that, after all it was not a glorious exploit. It was not long until there was a general desire throughout Washington County especially, for a campaign against the Western Indians, especially the Wyandot and Delaware towns on the Sandusky River. A general call then went out for volunteers to strike the stronghold of these Indians. The general muster was fixed for Monday, May 20th, at Mingo Bottom; and a few days later, four hundred and eighty horsemen assembled at that place, and elected Colonel William Crawford as leader of the expedition, he, through the influence of General Irvine, then in command at Fort Pitt, receiving five votes over Colonel David Williamson. General Irvine had been requested to lead the expedition, but declined. When he was pressed to give the expedition assistance, he agreed to furnish some gun flints and powder, on condition that the expedition would conform to military laws and regulations. He also detailed Surgeon John Knight and Lieutenant Rose to serve in the expedition.

While preparations were being made for this expedition, the Ohio Indians, aroused to greater hostility by the butchery at Gnadenhuetten, made many incursions into Washington and Westmoreland counties. "Thomas Edgerton was captured on Harman's Creek and John Stevenson near West Liberty. Five soldiers were ambushed in the woods near Fort McIntosh; two were killed and the three others were taken to Lower Sandusky, where they successfully ran the gauntlet. Two men were killed on the border of Washington County; at Walthour's Block House, near Brush Creek in Westmoreland, a man of name of Willard was killed and his daughter carried away and murdered in the woods. On Sunday, May 12th, Rev. John Corbly and his family, while walking to their meeting house on Muddy Creek, in what is now Green County, were attacked by the savages. The preacher alone escaped without injury. The wife and three children were killed and scalped. Two daughters were scalped, but survived to endure their suffering."—(Hassler's "Old Westmoreland").

On May 25th, the expedition left Mingo Bottom, and marched towards Sandusky. On the 28th, the troops turned aside to visit the ruins of the Moravian town at Shoenbrun, where they fed their horses on the standing corn. On the evening of June 13th, the troops reached the upper Indian town on the Sandusky finding the place deserted, the Indians having had warning of Colonel Crawford's approach. Crawford then advised a retirement, but was overruled in council. The next morning the command began the march toward the principal Wyandot town, proceeding through the beautiful plain on the west side of the Sandusky River.

In the afternoon, as the troops neared a large grove, they were fired upon by British and Indians in the grove. The Americans, however, charged, and driving out the enemy, occupied the grove themselves. Dismounting and forming a line along the northern side of the grove, they for several hours exchanged a brisk rifle fire with the British and Indians lying in the bushes. In this combat, five of Crawford's men were killed and nineteen wounded, while the enemy lost six killed, and eleven wounded, among the wounded being the British commander, Captain Caldwell.

During the night, Crawford's men were unable to get much rest owing to the hideous yells of the savages, and when the day dawned, the battle was resumed in long-range fighting. In the afternoon, a band of one hundred and forty Shawnees joined the other Indians. The Americans observed their arrival, and believing that they were greatly outnumbered by the savages, held a council of war in which it was decided to retreat during the night. As a matter of fact, however, the Indian forces, even when augmented by the arrival of the Shawnees, did not exceed the number of Crawford's forces.

No sooner had Crawford's men begun to retreat during the night, than a strange panic seized them. Many fired their guns into the darkness, and others leaving the ranks fled like maniacs across the prairie. Meanwhile, the savages were slaying and scalping the straggling fugitives. A few of the troops, exhausted by the long fighting, had fallen asleep in the grove and awoke to find themselves deserted. These were almost all overtaken and scalped

In the expedition were Crawford's only son, John, his nephew, William Crawford, and his son-in-law, William Harrison. In the wild retreat, the Colonel was unable to find them. Standing by the trail as the fugitives rushed by, he called for his son, and receiving no answer, fell to the rear and became lost. He then met with Dr. Knight, the surgeon, and nine other men; and together they wandered about for two days, when they were captured by a band of Delawares. Captain Pipe ordered them to be burned at the stake. In the meantime, Colonel Williamson had made good his escape, and with 300 soldiers, arrived at Mingo Bottom, on June 12th.

In the hope of escaping such a dreadful fate, Colonel Crawford asked that his old friend, the Delaware chief, Wingenund, might be sent for. Wingenund appeared before the Colonel, who entreated him to save his life, calling his attention to the fact that they had always been friends. Wingenund reluctantly advised the Colonel that it was beyond his power to save him. He told him that the Delawares and other tribes making up the Indian forces, were determined to avenge Colonel Williamson's butchery of the helpless women and children at Gnadenhuetten during the preceding March. He told Crawford that if Colonel Williamson had not been with Crawford's forces, it might be possible to save Crawford's life; that the Indians had their spies watching Crawford's march from the very beginning; and that these spies saw him turn aside from the line of march and visit the ruins at Shoenbrun. These things, said Wingenund, convinced the Indians that Crawford's expedition was simply seeking an opportunity to commit an outrage similar to the atrocity committed by Williamson's troops, especially since Williamson hastened to retreat. Failing to capture the hated Williamson, they determined that Crawford must pay the penalty. Then Wingenund burst into tears, and turned aside that he might not witness the torture of his friend.

The place of Crawford's torture was in the valley of Tymoochee Creek, about five miles west of upper Sandusky. He was tied by a long rope to a pole; his body was shot full of gun powder; his ears were cut off; burning fagots were pressed against his skin, and he was horribly gashed with knives. The unfortunate man endured this terrible agony for four hours in the presence of Dr. Knight and the renegades, Simon Girty and Matthew Elliott. He appealed to Girty to shoot him and end his misery, but in vain. Falling unconscious, his scalp was torn off, and burning embers were poured upon his bleeding head. The excruciating pain revived him; he rose to his feet and started once more to walk around the pole, then groaned and fell dead. The Indians then burned his body to ashes.

Thus perished this prominent man of the Western Pennsylvania frontier, the friend and land agent of George Washington. His residence was, for some years prior to his tragic death, at Connellsville, Fayette County. Crawford County bears his name.

The other prisoners were divided among the several Indian villages, and tortured to death. So far as is known, only two escaped, Dr. Knight, the surgeon, and John Slover, one of the guides.

Captain Pipe Rebukes the Shawnees

During the summer of 1793, commissioners representing the United States endeavored to establish peace between the Western Indians and the United States Government after the defeats of General Harmar and General St. Clair. In the latter part of July, these commissioners were met at the mouth of the Detroit River by about thirty chiefs of the Western Indians, who came to inquire whether the United States would consent to the Ohio River as the boundary line of the Indian territory. The commissioners replied that this was impossible, and offered large presents if the Indians would confirm the limits as agreed upon by the treaties of Fort McIntosh and Fort Harmar. This reply was reported to a grand council of the western tribes on the Maumee. Then a violent debate took place; some of the Indians were in favor of peace on these terms, and others advocated that the war go on. Among the latter were the Shawnees who were under the influence of Simon Girty and other British emissaries. Among those who were in favor of peace was Captain Pipe. Addressing Captain Henry, chief of the Mohawks, Pipe delivered the following sarcastic speech referring to the circumstances under which the Shawnees came to Pennsylvania in the early days of the history of the Province: "See the Shawnees. You brought him to me when he was a little boy; you gave him to me, saying, 'Have mercy on this child; receive him that he may live; you are old, and he may help you, fetch you a drink of water occasionally, and shoot you a squirrel!' Moved with pity, I consented; received the Shawnees; adopted him as my grandson, because, without a single friend in the world, he went about forsaken and forlorn. I kept him with me; I instructed him in that which is good; I educated him; he was always about me. But no sooner had he reached manhood than he became disobedient. I admonished him; I punished him; but he grew more wicked continually. And now he listens neither to me nor to any one else, but does evil only. Therefore I am of the opinion that the Great Spirit did not create the Shawnees, but that the devil created him."

Last Days of Captain Pipe

Little is recorded concerning Captain Pipe's activities from the time of the torture of Colonel Crawford. He remained friendly to the Moravian missionaries, and expressed regret that he had been a party to causing the removal of the Christian Delawares from the Tuscarawas to Sandusky, in the autumn of 1781. When Washington became first president of the United States, in 1789, the old chief urged the western tribes to maintain peaceful relations with the young republic. He ended his days shortly before the overwhelming defeat of these Indians by General Wayne, at the Battle of the Fallen Timbers, on the 20th day of August, 1794.

GLIKKIKAN

Among the Christian Delawares who were killed at the Gnadenhuetten massacre was Glikkikan. He had formerly lived in the

Kuskuskies region, in Lawrence County, and was the principal counsellor of the Delaware chief, Packanke, whose capital was New Kaskaskunk, which some authorities say stood on or near the site of New Castle, and others on or near the site of Edenburg, Lawrence County. In the summer of 1769, Glikkikan made a journey to the Moravian mission at Lawunakhannek, located on the east bank of the Allegheny, a short distance above Tionesta, Forest County, for the purpose of refuting the doctrines of Christianity. On his way to that place, he held a successful disputation with the French Jesuits at Venango, and was very confident that he could put the Moravian missionaries to confusion. Zeisberger, the head of the mission, was absent when Glikkikan arrived, but Anthony, a native convert and assistant, made such an impressive speech to Glikkikan, setting forth the doctrines of Christianity, as to astonish the chieftain. Zeisberger arrived shortly afterwards and confirmed Anthony's speech with the result that Glikkikan, instead of delivering the elaborate speech which he had prepared against Christianity, replied: "I have nothing to say. I believe your word." When he returned to his home, instead of boasting of a victory over the Moravians, he advised his associate warriors to go and hear the Gospel preached by the Moravians.

Soon afterwards he made another visit to the mission, informed the Moravians that he desired to embrace Christianity, and invited them in the name of his chief, Packanke, to come and settle on a tract of land on the Beaver near Kaskaskung, which he offered for the use of the mission. The Moravians accepted his invitation, and moved to the valley of the Beaver, in April, 1770, settling where the town of Moravia, Lawrence County, now stands. Soon thereafter Glikkikan became a devout Christian, and so continued until his death.

The conversion of this bravest warrior and most eloquent counsellor of Packanke exasperated this chief, and he reproached Glikkikan, and denounced the Moravians. He taunted Glikkikan with deserting him with his council, and with having a desire to turn white. To these reproaches Glikkikan replied: "I have joined the Brethren. Where they go I will go; where they lodge, I will lodge; their people shall be my people and their God my God." A few days later Packanke was so affected by the preaching of the Moravians that he sobbed aloud. Said Zeisberger: "A haughty warrior captain weeps publicly in the presence of his former associates. It is marvelous!" In the spring of 1773, the mission at Moravia removed to the Muskingum.

CHAPTER XXVII

Cornstalk

CORNSTALK was one of the greatest chiefs of the Shawnees, and was born at least as early as 1720. Some authorities have identified him with the Shawnee chief Tamenebuck, or Taming Buck.. Assuming the identity of these two chiefs, the first important appearance of Cornstalk in the history of Pennsylvania is when he attended a conference or treaty at Philadelphia, July 27th to August 1st, 1739, along with Neucheconneh, then living at Chartier's Old Town, Kakowatcheky, then living at Wyoming, and Kishacoquillas, then living at the mouth of the creek of the same name, on the Juniata, in Mifflin County. Cornstalk was no doubt living at Chartier's Old Town, on the Allegheny, at this time. Also, assuming the identity of these two chiefs, Cornstalk was one of the Shawnee chiefs who accompanied Peter Chartier when the latter deserted to the French in 1744, and as was seen, in Chapter VIII, he was one of the Shawnee chiefs who met the Pennsylvania commissioners in council at Lancaster, July 21st, 1748, when these chiefs asked the forgiveness of the Pennsylvania authorities for having been in Chartier's band. On this occasion, he made a speech imploring forgiveness, as was also seen in Chapter VIII.

Cornstalk Commands Shawnees at Battle of Point Pleasant

In the latter years of his life, Cornstalk was the head chief of the Shawnees who had settled in the valley of the Scioto. In July, 1773, the Iroquois sold to Virginia a large tract of land south of the Kanawha. The sale greatly incensed the Shawnees, as they claimed that the land did not belong to the Iroquois Confederation. Presently settlers came in great numbers, in many cases erecting their cabins close to the wigwams of the Indians. Consequently, the indignation of the Shawnees was increased. Murders on both sides followed, bringing on that great conflict between Virginia, on the one hand, and the Shawnees and their allies, on the other, known as Lord Dunmore's War,—a war whose coming was hastened by the wanton murder of the family of Logan, chief of the Mingoes, on April 30th, 1774.

Governor Dunmore raised an army of about three thousand troops to check the Indian uprising. General Andrew Lewis commanded one division and Dunmore the other. Lewis' division of eleven hundred troops marched down the Kanawha River to Point Pleasant, West Virginia, where they were attacked on the morning of October 10th, 1774, by one thousand Indians under the command of Cornstalk. Cornstalk had opposed the entrance of his tribe into war with Virginia, but the rest of the chiefs overruled him. It is claimed that on the evening before the battle he made another attempt to bring about peace, and was again overruled.

The battle raged throughout the entire day, and above its noise and din could be heard the voice of Cornstalk as he encouraged his warriors, and shouted, "Be Strong! Be Strong!" He displayed masterly generalship, so maneuvering the Indians that the Virginians were forced into a triangle whose sides were the Ohio and Great Kanawha rivers, and whose base was the Indian forces. His tactics won the admiration of General Lewis and his officers.

At nightfall Cornstalk's forces withdrew, crossed the Ohio, and headed for the Shawnee villages. What his losses were was never ascertained, but during the battle, the Shawnees were observed to throw many of their slain into the Ohio. As for the Virginians, seventy-five of their force lay dead on the field, and one hundred and forty were wounded. A council of the chiefs was held, and although Cornstalk was bitterly opposed by many of the chiefs, he was able to persuade them to seek a peace with the Virginians.

Accordingly, in November, Cornstalk entered into a treaty of peace with Lord Dunmore, at Chillicothe, Ohio. On this occasion, he made a very impressive speech, boldly charging the whites as being the cause of the war, and dwelling at length upon the atrocious murder of the family of Logan, chief of the Mingoes. It is said that his powerful, clarion voice could be heard distinctly over the whole camp of twelve acres. Among those present was Colonel Benjamin Wilson, who speaks thus of Cornstalk's address:

"When he arose he was in nowise confused or daunted, but spoke in a distinct and audible voice without stammering or repetition and with peculiar emphasis. His looks while addressing Dunmore were truly grand and majestic; yet graceful and attractive. I have heard the first orators in Virginia, Patrick Henry and Richard Henry Lee, but never have I heard one whose powers of delivery surpassed those of Cornstalk on that occasion."

Death of Cornstalk

After making the treaty of peace with Lord Dunmore, Cornstalk remained at peace with the whites. During the spring of 1777, when most of the Ohio tribes were going over to the English, the old chief came to the Moravian missionaries, and warned them that the Shawnees, except those in his own tribe, were going over to the British; that he was powerless to prevent them, and that ammunition was being sent them from Detroit, to be used against the Americans. On a previous visit to the Moravians with more than one hundred of his warriors, he adopted missionary Schmick and his wife, making Schmick his brother and Mrs. Schmick his sister.

Seeing that there was danger of a general Indian uprising, Cornstalk late in the summer of 1777, taking with him a young chief named Red Hawk, went to Point Pleasant to warn Captain Matthew Arbuckle of the threatened uprising. He and Red Hawk were then arrested and detained as hostages. While thus held, one afternoon his son, Ellinipisco, came to visit his father. Unhappily, on that same day two soldiers who were out hunting on the opposite side of the river, were attacked by two Indians, who killed and scalped one of them. A company of men brought the body of the dead soldier to the fort, and then the cry went up: "Let us go and kill the Indians." The company, under the command of Captain Hall, went to the house where Cornstalk was detained. Captain Arbuckle endeavored to restrain them, but was threatened with death, if he interfered. Cornstalk's son was blamed with having brought the hostile Indians with him, but this he strenuously denied. Turning to his son, Cornstalk said: "My son, the Great Spirit has seen fit that we should die together, and has sent you here to that end. It is His will and let us submit; it is all for the best." The old chief then arose and with great dignity advanced to meet the soldiers, receiving seven bullets in his body, and sinking in death without a groan. Ellinipisco was then instantly killed, and Red Hawk, who had hidden himself in the chimney, was dragged out and hacked to pieces.

Thus, one of the bravest and noblest of the Indian race, while a hostage and on a mission of mercy, was barbarously murdered by those whom he sought to befriend. His exalted virtues and his most unhappy fate "plead like angels, trumpet-tongued, against the deep damnation of his taking off", arousing the vindictive spirit of the Shawnees, never broken, until General Wayne defeated the western tribes at the battle of the Fallen Timbers, on the 20th day of August, 1794, and compelled them to sign the treaty of Greenville, by the terms of which they gave up possession to 25,000 square miles of territory north of the Ohio.

It seems that Cornstalk had a presentiment of approaching death. On the day before he was murdered, he was admitted to a council held at the fort, where he said: "When I was young and went to war, I often thought each might be my last adventure, and I should return no more. I still live. Now I am in the midst of you, and if you choose, may kill me. I can die but once. It is alike to me whether now or hereafter."

In 1896, a monument was erected in the Court House yard at Point Pleasant to the memory of this brave and energetic warrior, skillful general, and able orator. Here he fought courageously; here he died heroically. May his well deserved fame be as enduring as the granite of his monument—as enduring as the hills and mountains of the land he loved.

CHAPTER XXVIII.

Logan, Chief of the Mingoes

OGAN was the second son of Shikellamy, the vice-gerent of the Six Nations. His Indian name was Tah-gah-jute, which means, "His eyelashes stick out and above as if looking through or over something—hence spying." He was born at the Indian village of Osco, or Wasko, now Auburn, New York, in about 1725, where a large monument has been erected to his memory. When he was about three years old, his parents took up their residence at Shikellamy's Town, a short distance below Milton, Pennsylvania, upon Shikellamy's appointment by the Onondaga Council as the vice-gerent of the Six Nations over the Shawnees and other tribes of the Susquehanna Valley. Later, Shikellamy removed to Shamokin (Sunbury), where the son grew to manhood. The father re-named him James Logan after James Logan, Secretary of the Provincial Council of Pennsylvania, for whom he had a high regard.

Logan's mother was a Cayuga and he, too, married a Cayuga, who, after bearing him several children of whose after life nothing definite is known, died of fever at Shamokin, in October, 1747. Later, Logan married a second wife, a Shawnee, who survived him, but bore him no children.

During the French and Indian War, as well as during the uprising of Pontiac, Logan remained at peace with Pennsylvania, and rendered considerable service to the Colony. He was a close friend of Conrad Weiser, Scarouady, and Andrew Montour.

Logan Removes to the Juniata Valley

Early in the summer of 1765 Logan removed to the beautiful valley of the Juniata, building his cabin near Reedsville, Mifflin County. Nearby the cabin was a limestone spring, which is known to this day as "Logan's Spring". Here in the heart of the mountains he lived for the next five years, making an honest living by hunting and selling dressed deer skins to the traders, and much esteemed by his white neighbors. On one occasion during his sojourn at this place, he was cheated by a tailor, who traded him some spoiled wheat for good deer skins. Logan at once made complaint, and when Judge Brown decided in his favor, he said, "Law good, makes rogues pay."

The following letter written by Hon, R. P. Maclay of the state senate of Pennsylvania to George Darsie of the same body, revealing Logan's high sense of honor, was printed in the "Pittsburgh Daily American" of March 21, 1842:

"Allow me to correct a few inaccuracies as to place and names in the anecdote of Logan, the celebrated Mingo chief, as published in the 'Pittsburgh Daily American' of March seventeenth, to which you call my attention. The person surprised at the spring, now called Big Spring, and about four miles west of Logan's Spring, was William Brown—the first actual settler in Kishacoquillas Valley and one of the associate judges of Mifflin County from its organization till his death at the age of ninety-one or two, and not Samuel Maclay as stated by Dr. Hildreth. I will give you the anecdote as I heard it related by Judge Brown himself while on a visit to my brother, who then owned and occupied the Big Spring farm, four miles west of Reedsville:—

" 'The first time I ever saw the spring,' said the old gentleman 'my brother, James Reed, and myself had wandered out of the valley in search of land and finding it very good, we were looking for a spring. About a mile from this we started a bear and separated to get a shot at him. I was traveling along looking about on the rising ground for the bear, when I came suddenly on the spring; and being dry and more rejoiced to find so fine a spring than to have killed a dozen bears, I set my rifle against a bush and rushed down the bank and lay down to drink. Upon putting my head down, I saw reflected in the water on the opposite side the shadow of a tall Indian. I sprang to my rifle, when the Indian gave a yell whether for peace or war I was not just sufficiently master of my faculties to determine; but upon my seizing my rifle and facing him, he knocked up the pan of his gun, threw out the priming and extended his open palm toward me in token of friendship. After putting down our guns we again met at the spring and shook hands. This was Logan, the best specimen of humanity I ever met with, either white or red. He could speak a little English and told me there was another white hunter a little way down the stream and offered to guide me to his camp. There I first met your father.

"We visited Logan at his camp at Logan's Spring, and your father and he shot at a mark for a dollar a shot. Logan lost four or five rounds and acknowledged himself beaten. When we were about to leave him, he went into his hut and brought out as many deer skins as he had lost dollars and handed them to Mr. Maclay, who refused to take them, alleging that we had been his guests and did not come to rob him—that the shooting had been only a trial of skill and the bet merely nominal. Logan drew himself up with great dignity and said: 'Me bet to make you shoot your best; me gentleman and me take your dollar if me beat.' So he was obliged to take the skins or affront a friend whose sense of honor would not permit him to receive even a horn of powder in return.

" 'The next year,' said the old gentleman, 'I brought my wife up and camped under a big walnut tree on the bank of Tea Creek until I had built a cabin near where the mill now stands and have lived in the valley ever since. Poor Logan (and the big tears coursed each other down his cheeks) soon went to the Allegheny and I never saw him again."

Logan is said to have carved on a giant oak tree at Standing Stone, now Huntingdon, Pennsylvania, a full-length figure of an Indian brandishing a tomahawk. This was probably done while he made a visit to that place from his home near Reedsville.

Logan Moves to the Ohio

In 1770 Logan moved to the Ohio, taking up his residence at the mouth of the Beaver. Here he was visited by the Moravian missionary, John Heckewelder, in 1772. Logan had been accepted by that part of the Iroquois living in the Ohio Valley, and known as the Mingoes, as their chief; and he explained to Heckewelder on this visit that he had difficulty in holding his young men in check from making bloody reprisals upon the whites under the influence of liquor. He confessed to the missionary his own fondness for rum—a weakness which his father, the great Shikellamy, never indulged, because, as he said, he did not wish to be a fool. While living at the mouth of the Beaver, he was also visited, in 1773, by the missionary, McClure, who found him under the influence of rum and painted as a warrior. While living at this place Logan made many trips to Fort Pitt to trade, and no doubt visited Guyasuta at his village near Sharpsburg. He also frequently visited the traders at Venango, and was a visitor at Custaloga's Town on French Creek, in Mercer County.

After residing at the mouth of the Beaver for three years, Logan moved his family down the Ohio, and took up his residence on the north bank of this stream at the mouth of Yellow Creek, a few miles below where Wellsville, Ohio, now stands. The town of Mingo Junction, twenty miles farther down the river, perpetuates the name of his tribe and his memory on the strength of Logan's having resided at that place for a short time, at least.

The Murder of Logan's Family

On April 29, 1774, while Logan was away from his home at the mouth of Yellow Creek on a hunting trip, some of his men were trying to capture horses tethered on their ground in the neighborhood, and two were shot down by a man named Meyers, a Virginia land-grabber. It is said that Logan's camp planned revenge, and that a squaw, either Logan's sister or sister-in-law, informed Meyers' band of outlaws of the intention of Logan's followers. Meyers' band were lodged on the south side of the Ohio, under the command of Daniel Greathouse.

Greathouse then invited Logan's men across the river to be his guests at Baker's tavern for the next day. The invitation was accepted, and the band crossed the river and went to the tavern, leaving their guns in their tents, as it was to be a friendly visit. Upon their arrival, they were treated freely to rum and three of them became greatly intoxicated, the others refusing to drink, as it was a general custom among the Indians for at least one of the party to remain sober in order to take care of their intoxicated companions. The sober Indians, among whom was Logan's brother, John Petty, were challenged to shoot at a mark. The Indians shot first, and as soon as they had emptied their guns, Greathouse's band shot down the three sober Indians in cold blood. One of the party, a sister-in-law of Logan, endeavored to escape by flight, but was also shot down. She lived long enough to implore the murderers to spare the life of her little babe two months old, explaining to them that it was one of their kin; and its life was spared on that account. The whites then set upon the drunken Indians with tomahawks and butchered them all. Altogether ten Indians were killed by these white fiends, among whom were the mother, sister, and brother of Logan. As stated in Chapter XXVI, this cold-blooded murder of Logan's family was one of the prime causes of Lord Dunmore's War, which took place during the summer and autumn of 1774.

There has been lack of agreement among historians as to the exact date of this atrocity, but most authorities say that it was on the 30th of April; and this date must be correct, as on May 3rd,

Valentine Crawford, a brother of Colonel William Crawford, on writing from his home on Jacob's Creek, near Connellsville, says: "On Saturday last, about twelve o'clock, one Greathouse and about twenty men fell on a party of Indians at the mouth of Yellow Creek, and killed ten of them. They brought away one child a prisoner, which is not at my brother, William Crawford's." Also Colonel William Crawford, in a letter written to George Washington on May 8th, says: "Daniel Greathouse and some others fell on some Indians at the mouth of Yellow Creek and killed and scalped ten, and took one child about two months old, which is at my house. I have taken the child from a woman that it had been given to."

What eventually became of this Indian babe, nephew of Logan, and the grandson of the famous Shikellamy, is not known. Historians agree that it was the son of Colonel John Gibson who, as we shall presently see, translated Logan's great speech.

When Logan returned from his hunting trip and learned of the murder of his family and friends, he determined to avenge their death. Said he later, "Logan thought only of revenge; Logan will not weep." Like his famous father, he had always been a friend of the whites; and only a few days before the murder of his family a council of Mingo chiefs assembled, many of whom were in favor of war, but his counsel prevailed, and the chiefs decided not to take up the hatchet on this occasion. Logan said, "I admit that you have just cause of complaint. But you must remember that you, too, have sometimes done wrong. By war you can only harass and distress the frontier settlements for a time; and then the Virginians will come like the trees in the woods in number and drive you from the good lands you possess, from the hunting grounds so dear to you." Also when Heckewelder visited him in 1772 he said that while Logan complained "against the English for imposing liquor upon the Indians; yet he otherwise admired their ingenuity; spoke of gentlemen, but observed that the Indians unfortunately had but few of them as their neighbors."

Logan Takes Revenge

Therefore, from the friend of the whites and an advocate of peace, Logan changed into a fearless and terrible foe of the race that was gradually driving the Indian from his hunting grounds. He at once led a band of warriors against the traders at Canoe Bottom, on the Hockhocking River, but the Delaware chief, White

Eyes, foiled this attempt.   On the 19th of May, he set out once more with a band of eight chosen warriors, who were later joined by four more, and went to the neighborhood of Ten Mile, Dunkard and Muddy creeks, in Southwestern Pennsylvania, where, after waiting and watching for two weeks, he and his band killed a settler named Spicer, together with his wife and six children, taking prisoner two of the children, William, aged nine, and Betsy, aged eleven.   Betsy was afterwards released, but William grew to manhood among the Indians.   Two days later Logan's band killed two men on the site of the fort on Dunbar Creek.   On the 22nd of June, he returned to the Indian town of Wakatomica, now Dresden, Ohio, with sixteen scalps and two prisoners.

Several days later Logan started on the war-path the third time, leading a party of seven warriors to the Monongahela region where he thought the murderers of his family lurked.   On the 12th of July his band came upon William Robinson, Thomas Hellen, and Colman Brown, pulling flax in the field opposite to Simpson Creek.   Brown was killed on the spot and Robinson and Hellen started to run, but Logan succeeded in capturing both. Logan made himself known to Robinson, and told him that he would have to run the gauntlet, but gave him "such complete instruction and directions as they traveled together that Robinson ran the gauntlet safely and reached the stake without harm." The warriors then determined to burn Robinson at the stake; but Logan made three attempts, the last one successful, to prevent this atrocity.   He loosed the cords which bound the unfortunate man, placed a belt of wampum around his neck as a mark of adoption, introduced him to a young warrior, and said: "This is your cousin; you are to go home with him and he will take care of you." Robinson afterwards said that so fervent was Logan's impassioned eloquence on his behalf, that the saliva foamed at his mouth when he addressed the assembled warriors.   Hellen, after being un· mercifully beaten while running the gauntlet, was adopted into an Indian family.

Logan believed that Captain Michael Cresap was the leader of the outlaws who murdered his family; and three days after Robinson had been adopted, he dictated to him (Robinson) the following note to Cresap, dated July 21, 1774, which was written with suggestive ink made of gun-powder mixed with water:

"To Captain Cresap:

What did you kill my people on Yellow Creek for?
The White People killed my kin at Conestoga a great
while ago and I thought nothing of that; but you killed
my kin again on Yellow Creek and took my cousin prisoner. Then I thought I must kill too; and I have been
three times to war since; but the Indians are not angry,
only myself."

The "cousin" that Logan refers to in the above note was the
child of his sister. It is usual for the Indians to refer to relatives
generally as cousins.

Once more Logan went on the war-path, this time setting out
with a few chosen braves to the Holston and Clinch rivers in
Southwestern Virginia, where he had been informed Captain Cresap
made his home. He and his warriors reached the neighborhood in
the middle of September, where on Reedy Creek, a branch of the
Holston, they killed the whole family of John Robertson except
one young boy, whom they carried off captive. At least all the
circumstances point to this murder as having been committed by
Logan, inasmuch as the note which Logan addressed to Captain
Cresap was found tied to a club in the house of the unfortunate
settler, where, on the floor, were found the dead bodies of the
family.

About the middle of October, Logan's party came to Old
Chillicothe, Ohio, where a number of Delawares, who had taken
part in Lord Dunmore's War, were now located among the Shawnees, after having been driven from the Muskingum by the Virginia troops. The party brought with them five scalps and
Robertson's little boy, as well two other prisoners. It is said that
during these incursions, Logan had taken thirty scalps and prisoners. His thirst for revenge was now satisfied. He "sat still",
and refused to lead or accompany any more war parties.

Logan's Famous Speech

Logan arrived from the Holston raid at the time when Cornstalk's defeated warriors had returned from the terrible battle of
Point Pleasant (October 10th), and the chiefs were assembled in
council. Both Logan and Cornstalk argued for peace, and the
council decided not to continue the war. A deputation of chiefs
was then sent to Lord Dunmore to sue for peace. Dunmore
agreed to a conference, whereupon runners were sent out to invite

all the chiefs to assemble at Camp Charlotte, the place of the conference.

Logan refused to attend the conference. Then Lord Dunmore sent Colonel John Gibson, the alleged father of the infant of Logan's sister, whose life was spared when the rest of Logan's family was murdered, as a special messenger to invite and bring the great chieftain to the conference. Logan refused again to attend the conference, and proposed that he and Colonel Gibson take a walk into the woods to talk matters over. At length they sat down on a log under a large elm, still standing on the Pickaway plains, about six miles south of Circleville, Pickaway County, Ohio, and known to this day as Logan's Elm.

Here, with Colonel Gibson as his only auditor, and with tears rolling down his face, Logan delivered his famous speech, one of the finest specimens of eloquence in the English language, as follows:

"I appeal to any white man to say if ever he entered Logan's cabin hungry, and I gave him not meat; if ever he came cold or naked, and I gave him not clothing.

"During the course of the last long and bloody war, Logan remained in his tent, an advocate for peace. Nay, such was my love for the whites, that those of my own country pointed at me as they passed, and said, 'Logan is the friend of white men.' I had even thought to live with you, but for the injuries of one man. Colonel Cresap the last spring, in cold blood, and unprovoked, cut off all the relatives of Logan; not sparing even my women and children. There runs not a drop of my blood in the veins of any human creature. This called on me for revenge. I have sought it. I have killed many. I have fully glutted my vengeance. For my country, I rejoice at the beams of peace. Yet, do not harbor the thought that mine is the joy of fear. Logan never felt fear. He will not turn on his heel to save his life. Who is there to mourn for Logan? Not one."

Gibson wrote down the speech, and read it the next day at the conference at Camp Charlotte. Thomas Jefferson, in his "Notes on Virginia", published in 1781 and 1782, gave "Logan's Lament", as he called it, world-wide publicity. Colonel John Gibson, on April 4, 1800, made an affidavit before J. Barker, of Pittsburgh, as to the authorship of the great speech, and the accuracy of his translation of the same. Logan spoke in Delaware. Says Heckewelder, "For my part I am convinced that it was delivered precisely as it was related to us, with only this difference, that it possessed a force and expression in the Indian language which it is impossible to transmit to our own."

Thomas Jefferson challenges Cicero, Demosthenes, and both European and American statesmen to surpass this speech—the cry of the wrongs of the Indian race that came up from the breaking heart of Logan, and made his name immortal. It is at once bold, lofty, and sublime; and yet it is permeated with a note of sadness. It has been recited in the schools throughout the United States for more than a hundred years. It was copied in England, and has been translated in French, German, and other modern languages as a specimen of classic oratory. The Ohio Archaeological and Historical Society has erected a monument near Logan's Elm bearing the following inscription:

> "Under the spreading branches of a magnificent elm
> tree nearby is where Logan, a Mingo chief, made his
> celebrated speech."

Death of Logan

After the treaty with Lord Dunmore, Logan returned to his cabin at Old Chillicothe, now Westfall, on the banks of the Scioto. Before long he left there and took up his residence at Pluggy's Town, eighteen miles north of Columbus, Ohio. Here, on July 25, 1775, he was instrumental in saving the life of Captain Wood while on his way to invite the western tribes to the conference held in Pittsburgh in October of that year.

During the latter years of his life, he wandered from tribe to tribe, a broken man. He drank freely and suffered much from despondency. Often he was heard to say that it would have been better if he had never been born. There is a tradition that he wandered back to the Wyoming Valley on the Susquehanna. Here, according to the tradition, he arrived on July 2nd, 1778, just the day before the Wyoming massacre, and in time to give the alarm to a number of his friends among the whites. Campbell refers to this tradition in his poem, "Gertrude of Wyoming", in which the character Outalissi represents the great chief of the Mingoes.

In the autumn of 1778 he saved the life of Simon Kenton, the scout, and companion of Daniel Boone, who had been caught stealing horses of the Indians and was condemned to die at the stake. Kenton was lodged with Logan for safe keeping until the torture should commence. Logan addressed him and said: "Be strong,

I am a great chief. They talk of taking you to Sandusky and burning you there. I will send messengers to speak good for you." He then sent two runners to Sandusky, in the meantime holding the angry Indians in check, and with great difficulty got Kenton released.

Heckewelder says that during the year 1779, Logan adopted a white woman into his family as his sister to take the place of the sister who was killed at Yellow Creek five years before. During the remaining year he lived among the Mingoes on the Sandusky River, spending much of his time, however, roving from place to place. In 1780, he went over to the British side and joined the force of volunteers, regulars, and Indians, which Captain Henry Bird led to Kentucky and destroyed the settlements at Ruddell's and Martin's stations. As Captain Bird was conveying the prisoners to Detroit, Logan became very friendly with some of them, especially John Duncan to whom he said: "I know that I have two souls—the one good, the other bad. When the good has the ascendency I am kind and humane. When the bad soul rules, I am perfectly savage and delight in nothing but blood and carnage."

After he returned from this raid, he went to a council of chiefs at Detroit in the autumn. While the conference was in session Logan, crazed by drink, struck his wife such a terrible blow that it was thought he had killed her. He then fled towards his home on the Sandusky, but was pursued by a band of Indians, among whom were his wife's relatives and his own nephew, Tod-kah-dohs, Logan was overtaken at a camping place near Brownsville, Ohio. Suspecting that they had pursued him for the purpose of punishing him for striking his wife, he threatened to scalp the whole party. His nephew knowing his alertness and that the only way of escape was to strike first, shot the famous chief as he was leaping from his horse. The next morning his body was buried by a band of Wyandots.

The above is the account usually given of Logan's death. Another account is that he was killed on the way, while making this same journey from Detroit to Sandusky; that he had a quarrel with his nephew, Tod-kah-dohs, and that, while he was sitting by the camp fire with his face between his hands, in deep meditation, Tod-kah-dohs stole up behind him, and buried his tomahawk in his brain.

We close this sketch of the immortal Logan with the following lines composed for the occasion of the dedicating of the monument to his memory, erected near Logan's Elm:

"Logan, to thy memory here
White men do this tablet rear;
On its front we grave thy name,
In our hearts shall live thy fame.
While Niagara's thunders roar,
Or Erie's surges lash the shore;
While onward broad Ohio glides
And seaward roll her Indian tides,
So long their memory, who did give
These floods their sounding names shall live.
While time in kindness burries
The gory axe and warrior's bow.
O justice, faithful to thy trust,
Record the virtues of the just."

Murder of Joseph Wipey

As we have seen, it was in the spring of 1774 that the family of Logan was killed. During this same spring, occurred the murder of another friendly Indian, Joseph Wipey. The exact location of the murder is hard to determine; but it seems to have been near the mouth of Hinckston's Run, which flows southward through Cambria County, and empties into the Conemaugh at Johnstown, although some authorities say that the murder occurred in the southeastern part of Indiana County.

When, after the purchase at Fort Stanwix, in October, 1768, the Delawares left their towns on the Kittanning Trail, and the region of the purchase began to be rapidly settled by the white people, this elderly Delaware remained on the hunting grounds of his forefathers, and built his cabin by a stream north of the Conemaugh. He was an inoffensive, harmless old hunter and fisher, and had given many evidences of his friendship for the whites. At peace with all mankind, he was gently gliding down the stream of life, awaiting his summons to the Happy Hunting Grounds. John Hinckston and James Cooper wantonly murdered him, some time in May of this year, while he was fishing from his canoe. Arthur St. Clair, writing from Ligonier to Governor John Penn, on May 29th, concerning this murder, says: "It is the most astonishing thing in the world—the disposition of the common people of this country. Actuated by the most savage cruelty, they wantonly perpetrate crimes that are a disgrace to humanity, and seem, at the same time, to be under a kind of religious enthusiasm, whilst they want the daring spirit that usually inspires."

The murder of Logan's family had much to do with bringing on Lord Dunmore's War. And now, St. Clair feared that the wanton murder of Wipey would bring on a Delaware war that would devastate the western settlements. He advised Governor Penn that this atrocity gave him "much trouble and vexation." Happily, though, the Delawares did not again take up arms against the Province until the latter years of the Revolutionary War.

CHAPTER XXIX.

Bald Eagle

BALD EAGLE was a chief of the Wolf Clan of Delawares. Bald Eagle Township, in Clinton County, Bald Eagle Mountain, and Bald Eagle Valley, in Clinton and Center counties, are named for him. Early in the Revolutionary War, this chief espoused the British cause, and his war parties brought death and desolation to the settlements on the West Branch of the Susquehanna.

Bald Eagle Kills James Brady

One of the bloody deed of Bald Eagle was the fatal wounding of James Brady, son of Captain John Brady, and youngest brother of the famous Captain Samuel Brady, near Williamsport, Lycoming County, on August 8, 1778, an account of which is given in Menginess' "History of the West Branch Valley", as follows:

"A Corporal and four men, belonging to Colonel Hartley's regiment, and three militiamen, were ordered about two miles above Loyalsock, on the 8th of August, 1778, to protect fourteen reapers and cradlers, who went to assist Peter Smith, the unfortunate man that had his wife and four children murdered about a month previous, to cut his crop. Smith's farm was on Turkey Run, not far from Williamsport, on the opposite side of the river.

"James Brady, son of Captain John, the younger brother of Captain Sam Brady of the Rangers, was with the party. According to custom in those days, when no commissioned officer was present, the company generally selected a leader, whom they styled 'Captain', and obeyed him as such. Young James Brady was selected Captain of this little band of about twenty men.

"On arriving at the field, they placed two sentinels at the opposite ends, the sides having clear land around. The day being Friday, they cut the greater part of the grain, and intended to complete it the next morning. Four of the reapers improperly left that night, and returned to the fort. A strict watch was kept all night, but nothing unusual occurred. In the morning they all went to work; the cradlers, four in number, by themselves, near the house; the reapers in another part of the field. The reapers, except young Brady, placed their guns round a tree. He thought this was wrong, and placed his some distance from the rest. The morning proved to be very foggy, and about an hour after sunrise, the sentinels and reapers were surprised by a number of Indians, under cover of the fog, quietly approaching them. The sentinels fired and ran towards the reapers, when they all ran, with the exception of young Brady. He made towards his rifle, pursued by three Indians, and when within a few yards of it, was fired upon by a white man with a pistol, probably a tory, but falling over a sheaf of grain, the shot missed him. He rose again, and when almost within reach of the rifle, was wounded by a shot from an Indian. Here another sentinel fired his gun, but was immediately, with a militiaman, shot down. Brady succeeded in getting his rifle, however, and shot the first Indian dead. He caught up another gun, and brought down a second savage, when they closed around him in numbers, but being a stout active man, he struggled with them for some time. At length one of them struck a tomahawk into his head, when he fell, and was wounded with a spear in the hands of another. He was so stunned with the blow of the tomahawk, that he remained powerless, but strange as it may seem, retained his senses. They ruthlessly tore the scalp from his head as he lay in apparent death; and it was a glorious trophy for them, for he had long and remarkably red hair.

"The cradlers, who it appears were in a low spot, in a distant part of the field, on hearing the alarm, ascended an eminence and partly beheld this unhappy affair. The Indians, as soon as they accomplished their bloody work, left instantly, probably fearing an attack from the whites.

"The Corporal and three men, with the cradlers, proposed to make a stand; but the others thought it imprudent, and they all immediately left. The cradlers being acquainted with the country, took the nearest way to Wallis'; the Corporal and his three men pushed right down the road. At Loyalsock they were fired upon by a party of Indians, probably the same that killed Brady. They returned the fire, when the Indians fled; and they retook three horses from them, and brought them to the fort in safety.

"After Brady was scalped, he related that a little Indian was called and made to strike the tomahawk into his head, in four separate places. He was probably taking lessons in the art of butchery.

"After coming to himself, he attempted, between walking and creeping, to reach the cabin, where an old man named Jerome

Vaness, had been employed to cook for them. On hearing the report of the guns, he had hid himself; but when he saw Brady return, he came to him. James begged the old man to fly to the fort, saying, 'The Indians will soon be back and will kill you.' The worthy man positively refused to leave him alone, but stayed and endeavored to dress his frightful wounds. Brady requested to be assisted down the river, where he drank large quantities of water, when he still insisted on the old man leaving him and trying to save himself; but he would not do it. He then directed his faithful old friend to load the gun that was in the cabin, which was done, and put into his hands, when he lay down and appeared to sleep.

"As soon as the sad intelligence reached the fort, [Fort Muncy], Captain Walker mustered a party of men and proceeded to the spot. When they came to the river bank, Brady heard the noise, and supposing it was Indians, jumped to his feet and cocked his gun. But it was friends. They made a bier and placed him on it, and brought him away. He requested to be taken to Sunbury to his mother. His request was granted, and a party started with him, amongst whom was Robert Covenhoven. He became very feverish by the way, and drank large quantities of water, and became partly delirious. It was late at night when they arrived at Sunbury, and did not intend to arouse his mother; but it seemed she had a presentiment of something that was to happen, and being awake to alarms, met them at the river and assisted to convey her wounded son to the house. He presented a frightful spectacle, and the meeting of mother and son is described to have been heart-rending. Her heart was wrung with the keenest anguish, and her lamentations were terrible to be heard.

"The young Captain lived five days. The first four he was delirious, on the fifth his reason returned, and he described the whole scene he had passed through very vividly, and with great minuteness. He said the Indians were of the Seneca tribe, and amongst them were two chiefs; one of whom was a very large man, and from the description was supposed to be Cornplanter; the other he personally knew to be the celebrated chief Bald Eagle, who had his nest near where Milesburg, Center County, now stands.

"On the evening of the fifth day, the young Captain died, deeply regretted by all who knew him; for he was a noble and promising young man. Vengeance, 'not loud, but deep,' was breathed against the Bald Eagle, but he laughed it to scorn, till the fatal day at Brady's Bend on the Allegheny."

Samuel Brady's Vow

Lieutenant (later Captain) Samuel Brady, was at Carlisle accompanying his regiment, the Eighth Pennsylvania, to Fort Pitt, when he received word of the scalping of his brother. He had parted from him about a week before. Samuel now hastened to Sunbury, but arrived too late to find James alive.

Samuel Brady's rage over the murder of his beloved brother stirred the depths of his soul. He made a solemn vow that he would never make peace with the Indians of any tribe.

Captain John Brady Killed

Lieutenant Samuel Brady arrived at Fort Pitt on September 10th, 1778, accompanying his regiment. Here he was destined to achieve fame as an Indian fighter, but not before he received another crushing blow. On April 11, 1779, his father, Captain John Brady, was conveying supplies from Fort Wallis to Fort Muncy, when three Iroquois Indians, secreted in a thicket, shot him dead from his horse.

The body of Captain John Brady was buried in an old grave-yard near Halls, Lycoming County, where a heavy granite marker was erected at his grave, bearing the following inscription:

Captain John Brady
Fell in Defense of Our Forefathers
At Wolf Run, April 11, 1779
Aged Forty-six Years

One hundred years after his death, funds were raised for the erection of a large monument to his memory in the cemetery at Muncy, the shaft being unveiled on October 15, 1879.

Bald Eagle Killed By Samuel Brady

Samuel Brady received the news of the murder of his father at about the time he was chosen by Colonel Broadhead as a forest ranger, at Fort Pitt. In his frenzy of grief, it is said that he renewed the vow taken after the murder of his brother, raising his hand on high and saying:

"Aided by Him Who formed yonder sun and heavens, I will avenge the murder of my father; nor while I live, will I ever be at peace with the Indians of any tribe."

Samuel Brady did not have long to wait for an opportunity to avenge the death of his brother. In June, 1779, a band of the

Wolf Clan of Delawares and probably some Senecas, came down the Allegheny River and made a raid into Westmoreland County, killing a soldier between Fort Hand (near Apollo) and Fort Crawford (Parnassus), attacking the settlement at James Perry's Mill on Big Sewickley Creek, killing a woman and four children and carrying off two children, the latter possibly being the children of Frederick Heinrich (Henry), near Greensburg.

The attack on the home of Frederick Henry is thus described in Rev. W. A. Zundel's "History of Old Zion Church":

"Frederick Henry (Heinrich), of Northampton, Burlington County, New Jersey, settled, shortly after 1770, in the Herold settlement [in Hempfield Township, Westmoreland County]. In time, the new settlers cleared some land and erected a house and stables. Four children cheered this lonely settlement. During the spring of 1779, when the husband, Frederick Henry, was compelled to leave home to take some grist to a distant mill, a band of Indians, perhaps Senecas, descended upon the helpless home.

"As was their custom, the Indians sneaked up to the house to ascertain if the men were home and on guard. Now, the Henry's had a large cock that frequently came to the door of the home to be fed. Mrs. Henry, seeing some feathers moving near the door, sent one of the children to shoo away the big rooster; whereupon the Indians, decked out in the feathers of their war headgear, burst in upon the helpless family. Mrs. Henry bravely attempted to defend her little ones; whereupon she was tomahawked and scalped in the presence of her small children.

"One child, seeing the Indians coming at the door, fled into the corn field and hid among the corn, and thus escaped, the Indians being in a hurry, fearing the wrath of the settlers. The Indians now took the three children captive, and after firing the buildings, started on their journey toward the Indian country. It soon developed that the youngest child, a mere infant, would be too much bother to the Indians, so when it began to cry, a big Indian took it by its feet, and dashed its brains out against a maple tree on the Solomon Bender farm, now owned by William Henry. This tree was held sacred by the pioneers and it stood until recent times (about 1900). The other children were carried away.

"Immediately upon the return of Henry, a posse of settlers started out in pursuit of the Indians. One account relates that the Indians were in their camp above Pittsburgh on the Allegheny, and after a lively skirmish, the children were recaptured, and the murderer of the wife and child identified, tied to a tree, and dispatched by the daughter, Anna Margaret, then about nine years old. Another account agrees with the report of Colonel Broadhead, that Captain Brady, with twenty white men and a Delaware chief, effected the capture."

The news of this raid reaching Fort Pitt, two parties were sent out against these Indians, one marching into the Sewickley settlement and attempting to follow the Indian trail, and the other consisting of twenty men under Captain Samuel Brady, ascending the Allegheny River.

Brady's forces were painted and dressed like Indians. He had with him his "pet Indian", the unfortunate Nanowland, who, as we have seen, was killed at Killbuck Island, near Fort Pitt, in the spring of 1782, by the Scotch-Irish settlers living on Chartier's Creek. Brady's reason for going up the Allegheny was that he was satisfied that the Indians came from the north and would return that direction to get possession of their canoes, which they had no doubt hidden along the river bank when they had left the stream. Brady came upon the canoes of these Indians drawn up within the mouth of one of the creeks entering the Allegheny from the east. There is lack of agreement among historians as to the identity of this creek. Some say that it was the Big Mahoning; but Colonel Broadhead, in his report to General Washington, written on June 24th, says that the scene was "about fifteen miles above Kittanning", which agrees with the location of Red Bank Creek, not far from the beautiful bend on the Allegheny, which bears the name of Brady.

The Indians were in camp in the woods north of the creek and were preparing supper when Brady discovered them. They had hobbled the horses which they had stolen, and turned them loose to graze on the meadow near the creek. On account of the swollen condition of the creek, Brady's men were compelled to ascend it two miles before they were able to cross. Waiting until after nightfall, Brady and his men descended the northern side of the creek to a point near the camp, and then lay in the tall grass.

Laying aside their arms, Brady and Nanowland crept on their stomachs to within a few yards of the Indian camp, in order to count the number of the Indians and learn the position of the captives taken. As Brady and his faithful Delaware were lying in the grass, one of the warriors arose from his position near the fire, stepped forth to a few feet from where Brady lay, stood there for a while and then returned to his companions, and lay down to sleep. Then Brady and Nanowland crept back to their companions and prepared to attack the Indians at daybreak. As the first streaks of dawn floated over the verdant hills of the Allegheny, one of the Indians awoke and aroused his companions. The whole band then stood about the fire, when suddenly a sheet of flame blazed from the rifles of Brady and his men, and the chief of the seven Indians fell dead, while the others fled into the surrounding forest, two of them severely wounded. It was Brady's own rifle that brought down the chief, who was none other than Bald Eagle. With a shout of triumph, Brady leaped upon the fallen chieftain and scalped him. Thus, on the banks of the Allegheny, far from the harvest field near the banks of the Susquehanna, where Bald Eagle killed young James Brady, during the preceding summer, Captain Samuel Brady avenged the death of his youngest and favorite brother.

The children captured by Bald Eagle's band were recovered unharmed and returned to Fort Pitt. The death of Bald Eagle had a good effect in that the Indians made no more raids into Westmoreland during that summer. Three weeks later, Captain Brady returned to the neighborhood of the attack on Bald Eagle's band. Observing a flock of crows hovering above the thicket, he made a search and found the partially devoured body of one of the Indians that died of his wounds.

There seems, however, to have been another chief by the name of Bald Eagle. Withers, in his Chronicles of Border Warfare, says that this latter was an Indian of notoriety, not only among his own nation, but also the inhabitants of the northwestern frontier of West Virginia, with whom he was in the habit of associating and hunting. Says Withers: "In one of his visits among them he was discovered alone by Jacob Scott, William Hacker and Eliza Runner who, reckless of the consequences, murdered him solely to gratify a most wanton thirst for Indian blood. After the commission of this most outrageous enormity, they seated him in the stern of a canoe and with a piece of journey-cake thrust into his mouth, set him afloat on the Monongahela. In this situation he was seen descending the river by several who supposed him to be, as usual, returning from a friendly hunt with the whites in the friendly settlements, and who expressed some astonishment that he did not stop to see them. The canoe floated near to the shore below the mouth of George's Creek [in southwestern Fayette County, Pennsylvania], and was observed by Mrs. Province, who had it brought to the bank, and the friendly but unfortunate old Indian decently buried." The murder of this friendly Indian took place near New Geneva, Fayette County, in 1773.

Captain Samuel Brady

We close this chapter with a few additional references to Captain Samuel Brady. He was the most noted scout connected with Fort Pitt during the Revolutionary War; and his exploits would fill many pages. On one occasion he started from Pittsburgh with a few picked men on a scout toward the Sandusky villages. While they were on their return trip they were pursued by Indians and all killed except Brady, who succeeded in getting as far towards Fort Pitt as the hill named for him near Beaver. He was not wounded, but almost dead from fatigue. He well realized that he was being tracked by the Indians, and that if he did not resort to some trick to elude them, he would be lost. Having selected a large tree, lately been blown down having a leafy top, he walked back carefully in his tracks a few hundred yards, and then turned about and walked in his old steps as far as the tree. This was done in the hope and belief that the Indians would be sure to follow him thither. He then walked along the trunk of the tree, and hid himself in its leafy top. He believed that the Indians would track him to the tree, and finding no further trace of him, would sit on the trunk or log of the same for consultation. He had not long to wait. Presently three Indians with their eyes bent to the earth followed his tracks, came to the tree, which they closely examined for the trail beyond, but not finding any, sat down on the trunk to consult together just as Brady had anticipated. Quickly and silently Brady raised his rifle and shot the foremost Indian dead. The bullet passed through his body and wounded the other two. Springing upon these with clubbed rifle, Brady soon dispatched them both.

On another occasion, as this noted scout was returning to Fort Pitt, he realized that he was being tracked by an Indian with a dog. Occasionally he had seen the Indian in the distance passing from tree to tree and advancing on his trail. For his ambush he selected a large chestnut tree which had been blown out of root. He walked from the top of the tree along its trunk, and sat down in the hole made by the uprooting of the tree. In a short time he saw a small dog mount the log at the other end and with nose to the trunk approach him, closely followed by a plumed warrior. Brady had to make a choice between the dog and the Indian. He preferred shooting the former, which he did. As the dog rolled off the log dead, the Indian with a loud whoop ran into the forest and disappeared.

One of the well known stories concerning Brady is that of his famous leap. Historians are not in accord as to the exact location of this exploit. Some have placed it on Slippery Rock Creek, in Butler County, but there seems to be very little doubt that it took place in Portage County, Ohio. On this occasion he was hotly pursued by Indians, and coming to a stream with a high bank, summoning all his powers, leaped across the same, although the distance was more than twenty-five feet. His Indian pursuers stopped on the bank.

Brady's scouting covered a vast extent of territory, to the headwaters of the Allegheny, to Sandusky on the west, and to the West Branch of the Susquehanna, on the east. In "Meginness' History of the West Branch Valley", is an account of an "Indian hunt" which Brady and Peter Grove made, most likely in 1780, through the counties of Huntingdon, Clearfield, Center, Lycoming, Clinton, and Union. They would creep up on Indian camps, fire into the same, each killing an Indian, and then bound off through the woods like antelopes. They were matchless sprinters, and the Indians were never able to overtake them. In this "hunt", they killed many Indians, among them being Blacksnake, the Panther, the Greatshot, and Wamp. It is a terrible story of butchery. Grove says that his heart was wrung to tears with the cries of Wamp's squaw. Some time after they had shot the Panther and the Blacksnake, they returned to the camp where the massacre occurred. Says Grove: "We found the Panther dead, but the Blacksnake was yet alive, and vomiting blood. We made all dead shots that day."

After the Revolutionary War, Brady left Fort Pitt and the Chartier's settlement nearby, where he had spent much of his time, and went to West Liberty, West Virginia, where he died.

Cornplanter

CORNPLANTER, whose Indian name was Garganwahgah, or Gyantwachias, meaning "The Planter", was a noted chief of the Senecas, also known as John O'Bail, supposed to have been born at Ganawagus on the Genesee River, in New York, some time between 1732 and 1740. His father was a white trader named John O'Bail, or O'Beel, said by some historians to have been an Englishman, while others say that he was a Dutchman. Cornplanter's mother was a full-blood Seneca.

In a letter written by Cornplanter to the Governor of Pennsylvania, he gives the following facts of his early youth: "When I was a child, I played with the butterfly, the grasshopper, and the frogs; and as I grew up, I began to pay some attention and play with the Indian boys in the neighborhood, and they took notice of my skin being of a different color from theirs, and spoke about it. I inquired from my mother the cause, and she told me my father was a resident of Albany. I still ate my victuals out of a bark dish. I grew up to be a young man and married a wife, and I had no kettle or gun. I then knew where my father lived, and went to see him, and found he was a white man and spoke the English language. He gave me victuals while I was at his house, but when I started to return home, he gave me no provisions to eat on the way. He gave me neither kettle nor gun."

By some authorities he is said to have been among the Indians at Braddock's defeat, but this statement has been doubted. During the Revolutionary War, he went over with his tribe to the English side. Being a chief of high rank and in the full vigor of manhood, he no doubt participated in the principal engagements of the Senecas against the United States in that conflict. Some authorities have said that he was present at the massacres at Cherry Valley and Wyoming, in which the Seneca tribe took a prominent part. We saw in Chapter XXIX, that he was probably with Bald Eagle when young James Brady was killed, in August, 1778. Some authorities have said, too, that he was with Guyasuta when Colonel Broadhead defeated the forces of the latter at the mouth of the Broken Straw, in the summer of 1779. This can very well be doubted, inasmuch as it is clear that, at this time, Cornplanter was actively engaged in the Genesee country in New York in opposing the campaign of General Sullivan.

In 1780, under Brandt and Johnson, Cornplanter led the Senecas in their raids against the settlers in the valleys of the Schoharie and Mohawk. On one of these raids, his father fell into his hands as a prisoner. The father did not recognize the son, and after marching for some miles, Cornplanter stepped before him and addressed him as follows:

"My name is John O'Bail, commonly called Cornplanter. I am your son. You are my father. You are now my prisoner, and subject to the custom of Indian warfare; but you shall not be harmed. You need not fear. I am a warrior. Many are the scalps which I have taken. Many prisoners have I tortured to death. I am your son. I was anxious to see you and greet you in friendship. I went to your cabin and took you by force; but your life shall be spared. Indians love their friends and their kindred, and treat them with kindness. If you now choose to follow the fortunes of your yellow son and to live with our people, I will cherish your old age with plenty of venison, and you shall live easy. But if it is your choice to return to your fields and live with your white children, I will send a party of trusty young men to conduct you back in safety. I respect you, my father. You have been friendly to Indians, and they are your friends." The father preferred his white children, and chose to return to them.

Cornplanter at the Treaty of Fort Stanwix (Rome, N. Y.), in October, 1784

Notwithstanding the fact that Cornplanter was a bitter enemy of the United States during the Revolutionary War, he became a firm friend of the young Republic upon the conclusion of peace. He comprehended the growing power of America, and was incensed with the ingratitude which Great Britain showed to the Senecas for their fidelity during the American Revolution. He attended the treaty at Fort Stanwix (Rome, N. Y.), in October, 1784, between the Six Nations and the "Thirteen Fires", as the Indians called the United States, where he used all the energies of his brilliant intellect in favor of peace. At this treaty the Six Nations, on October 23rd, ceded to Pennsylvania that part of the state northwest of the boundary of the purchase of 1768, the description in the deed being set forth as follows:

"Beginning on the south side of the river Ohio, where the western boundary of the State of Pennsylvania crosses the said river, near Shingo's old town, at the mouth of Beaver Creek, and thence by a due north line to the end of the forty-second and the beginning of the forty-third degrees of north latitude; thence by a due east line separating the forty-second and the forty-third degree of north latitude, to the east side of the east branch of the Susquehanna River; thence by the bounds of the late purchase made at Fort Stanwix, the fifth day of November, Anno Domini one thousand seven hundred and sixty-eight, as follows: Down the said east branch of Susquehanna, on the east side thereof, till it comes opposite to the mouth of a creek called by the Indians Awandac, and across the river, and up the said creek on the south side thereof, all along the range of hills called Burnet's Hills by the English, and by the Indians ...., on the north side of them, to the head of a creek which runs into the west branch of Susquehanna, which creek is by the Indians called Tyadaghton, but by the Pennsylvanians Pine Creek, and down the said creek on the south side thereof to the said west branch of Susquehanna; thence crossing the said river, and running up the south side thereof, the several courses thereof to the forks of the same river, which lies nearest to a place on the river Ohio called Kittanning, and from the fork by a straight line to Kittanning aforesaid; and thence down the said river Ohio by the several courses thereof to where said State of Pennsylvania crosses the same river, at the place of beginning."

It will be noticed in the above deed of the Purchase of 1784, that the line was to run along the south bank of the West Branch of the Susquehanna; thence "crossing the said river, and running up the south side thereof, the several courses and distances thereof to the forks of the same river, which lies nearest to a place on the river Ohio called Kittanning, and from the fork by a straight line to Kittanning aforesaid." The name "Canoe Place" is given in the old maps of the state to designate the point on the West Branch of the Susquehanna from which the purchase line ran to Kittanning. The point also designated the head of navigation on the West Branch. A survey of that line was made by Robert Galbraith, in 1786, and a cherry tree, standing on the west branch of the river was marked by him as the beginning of his survey. The same cherry tree was also marked by William P. Brady as the southeast corner of a tract surveyed by him "at Canoe Place", in 1794, on a grant in the name of John Nicholson, Esq.   The town of Cherry Tree, Indiana County, now covers a part of this ground. The historic cherry tree disappeared many years ago. The Legislature of Pennsylvania, in 1893, granted an appropriation of fifteen hundred dollars for marking the historic site, and a substantial granite monument now stands where the tree stood.

Purchase at Fort McIntosh

The deed given at Fort Stanwix extinguished the Iroquois title to this region, but it became necessary to appease the Wyandots, Delawares and other western tribes, who likewise claimed title to the same lands. Therefore, the same commissioners who were at the treaty at Fort Stanwix, were sent to Fort McIntosh, the site of the present town of Beaver, Beaver County, where, on January 21, 1785, Pennsylvania received a deed from these Indians for the same land. The Fort Stanwix deed and the Fort McIntosh deed are identical as to boundaries, but the consideration in the former was five thousand dollars, and in the latter two thousand dollars. "Thus," says Meginness, "in a period of about one hundred and two years was the whole right of the Indians to the soil of Pennsylvania extinguished."

These deeds included all of the counties of Lawrence, Mercer, Crawford, Butler, Venango, Forest, Warren, Clarion, Jefferson, Elk, Kane, Cameron, Potter, and a part of Beaver, Allegheny, Armstrong, Erie, Indiana, Clearfield, Clinton, Tioga, and Bradford. That part of Erie County, called "the triangle," was ceded to Pennsylvania by the United States, in 1792.

Cornplanter Attends Other Treaties, and Appeals to Washington

Cornplanter also attended the treaty at Fort Harmar in 1789, in which extensive territory was conveyed to the United States in the present state of Ohio. However, his name does not appear among the signers of the treaty. He also attended the treaties of September 15, 1797, and of July 30, 1802. These acts rendered him unpopular with the Senecas, and for a time his life was in danger. The chief, Red Jacket, seized upon these matters as a means of promoting his own popularity at the expense of Cornplanter.

In 1790, Cornplanter, accompanied by his half-brother, the Seneca chief, Half-Town, visited Philadelphia to lay before President Washington certain complaints of the Senecas against Colonel John Gibson.

In a speech to Cornplanter on this occasion, Washington said:

"When you return to your country, tell your people that it is my desire to promote their prosperity by teaching them the use of domestic animals, and the manner in which the white people plow and raise so much corn; and, if upon consideration, it would be agreeable to the nation at large to learn those arts, I will find some means of teaching them at such places within their country as shall be agreed upon."

In 1792, Pennsylvania granted Cornplanter a tract of 500 acres of land on the Allegheny, at the mouth of Oil Creek, where Oil City, Venango County, now stands. This he sold in 1818.

"For his many valuables services to the whites", Pennsylvania again granted him a large tract of land on the Allegheny, in Warren County, on March 16, 1796. On the 8th of this same month, he appeared before the representatives of the United States Government appointed to meet him, at Franklin, where he spoke as follows:

"I thank the Almighty for giving us luck to meet together at this time, and in this place as brethren, and hope my brothers will assist me in writing to Congress what I have now to say.

"I thank the Almighty that I am speaking this good day. I have been through all Nations of America, and am sorry to see the folly of many of the people. What makes me sorry is they all tell lies, and I never found truth amongst them. All the western Nations of Indians, as well as white people, have told me lies. Even in Council I have been deceived, and been told things which I have told to my chiefs and young men, which I have found not to be so, which makes me tell lies by not being able to make good my word; but I hope they will all see their folly and repent. The Almighty has not made us to lie, but to tell the truth one to another; for when two people meet together, if they lie one to the other, the people cannot be at peace, and so it is with nations, and that is the cause of so much war.

"General Washington, the father of us all, hear what I have now to say, and take pity on us poor people. The Almighty has blest you, and not us. He has given you education, which enables you to do many things that we cannot do. You can travel by sea as well as by land, and know what is doing in any other country, which we poor people know nothing about. Therefore you ought to pity us. When the Almighty first put us on this land, He gave it to us to live on. And when the white people first came to it, they were very poor, and we helped them all in our power; did not kill them, but received them as brothers. And now it appears to me as though they were going to leave us in distress."

Sometime prior to 1795, Cornplanter and a few of his tribe resided for a while at the mouth of Cornplanter's Run which flows into Buffalo Creek, in South Buffalo Township, Armstrong County, near the present village of Boggsville. His village seems to have been on both sides of the creek. On the top of a wooded hill, about a mile to the west, the traces of the burial ground of the village can still be seen. Smith, in his excellent "History of Armstrong County", says that when Charles Sipe, Sr., great-great grandfather of the present author, and his sons hunted along Buffalo Creek and Cornplanter's Run, in 1794 and 1795, the corn fields of the village were still distinguishable. These were on the flats on both sides of the creek.

Day's "Historical Collections" Quoted

The following facts concerning this noted chieftain are quoted from Day's "Historical Collections":

"Having buried the hatchet, Cornplanter sought to make his talents useful to his people by conciliating the good-will of the whites, and securing from further encroachment the little remnant of his national domain. On more than one occasion, when some reckless and blood-thirsty whites on the frontier had massacred unoffending Indians in cold blood, did Cornplanter interfere to restrain the vengeance of his people. During all the Indian wars from 1791 to 1794, which terminated with Wayne's treaty, Cornplanter pledged himself that the Senecas should remain friendly to the United States. He often gave notice to the garrison at Fort Franklin of intended attacks from hostile parties, and even hazarded his life on a mediatorial mission to the western tribes. He ever entertained a high respect and personal friendship for General Washington, 'the great councillor of the Thirteen Fires,' and often visited him, during his presidency, on the business of his tribe. His speeches on these occasions exhibit both his talent in composition and his adroitness in diplomacy. Washington fully reciprocated his respect and friendship. . . . . . . When Washington was about retiring from the presidency, Cornplanter made a special visit to Philadelphia to take an affectionate leave of the great benefactor of the white man and the red.

"After peace was permanently established between the Indians and the United States, Cornplanter retired from public life, and devoted his labors to his own people. He deplored the evils of intemperance, and exerted himself to suppress it. The benevolent efforts of missionaries among his tribe always received his encouragement, and at one time, his own heart seemed to be softened by the words of truth; yet he preserved, in his later years, many of the peculiar notions of the Indian faith."

Colonel Thomas Proctor Meets Cornplanter

In the spring of 1791, Colonel Thomas Proctor was sent on a mission to the Indians of the Northwest. During his journey, when he had reached the "Great Bend" on the upper Allegheny on April 6th, he met four Indian runners going with belts from Cornplanter to the Indians at the headwaters of the Allegheny, to inform them that several Delawares had recently been killed near Fort Pitt by some white people, said to be a party of Virginians. The Indians who had escaped being killed turned against the whites and killed and scalped seventeen of them some miles above Pittsburgh. The Indians who thus fell upon the settlers were pursued by a band of militia which overtook them, and compelled the Seneca chief, Newarle, to accompany them to Fort Pitt. Newarle and the commander at Fort Venango (Franklin) were taking a boatload of supplies for Cornplanter's Indians at the time when he was overtaken by the militia, and these supplies were likewise taken by the militia to Fort Pitt, although they had been purchased by Cornplanter.

Colonel Proctor, after holding a conference with the four Indian runners, descended the Allegheny to Fort Venango, where he met Cornplanter and accompanied him up the Allegheny to his town in Warren County. Here Proctor was entertained by the great Seneca, with a feast in true Indian hospitality.

Cornplanter and General Irvine

Cornplanter entertained a high regard for General William Irvine who, for several years subsequent to 1792, was engaged in superintending the surveys of land northwest of the Allegheny. Indeed, an affectionate intimacy subsisted between the two, and reciprocal visits were often made by them. Cornplanter said that General Irvine was one of the few white men who spoke the truth. On one occasion, when some Delawares of the Wolf Clan had threatened the life of the General, Cornplanter sent some of his own Indians to watch their movements. General Irvine at this time took up large tracts of land on Brokenstraw Creek in Warren County, some miles below Cornplanter's Reservation.

Cornplanter Visits General Wayne

When General Anthony Wayne was drilling the Legion of the United States at that place, since known at Legionville, on the north bank of the Ohio, about twenty miles below Pittsburgh, preparatory to leading it against the Western Indians, in 1794, he was visited by both Cornplanter and Guyasuta. Afterwards Cornplanter went on a peace mission among the hostile western tribes, but in vain. He found them too much elated by the overwhelming and inglorious defeats which they had administered to the armies of Generals Harmar and St. Clair, and too much under the influence of British traders. While Cornplanter was on his peace mission, three of his people were basely attacked near the Genesee by some whites, who killed one and severely wounded another. On hearing this news, Cornplanter said: "It is hard when I and my people are trying to make peace with the whites that we should receive such a reward."

Cornplanter's Letter to Major Isaac Craig

In the early winter of 1795, Major Thomas Butler, then in command at Fort Franklin, informed Major Isaac Craig of Pittsburgh, that Cornplanter had at his saw mill a large quantity of boards. Craig immediately dispatched Marcus Hulings, an experienced waterman, with three bags of money and some other articles up the Allegheny to Cornplanter's town to purchase this lumber. Hearing the next day that some private persons had gone on the same errand, Major Craig dispatched James Beard on horseback with a letter, informing the great Seneca of Hulings' object. Mr. Beard arrived in time and secured the lumber. The following is the letter of Cornplanter to Major Craig in reply to the latter's letter:

"Genesadego, 3d December, 1795.

"I thank the States for making me such kind ofers. We have made peace with the United States as long as watter runs, which was the reason that I built a mill in order to suport my family by it. More so, because I am geting old and not able to hunt. I also thank the States for the pleashure I now feel in meeting them again in friendship, you have sent a man to make a bargain with me for

a sertain time which I do not like to do.   But as long as my mill
makes boards, the United States shall always have them in preference to any other, at the market price, and when you want no
more boards I can't make blankets of them.   As for the money you
have sent, if I have not boards to the amount, leave it and I will
pay it in boards in the Spring.

"I thank you kindly for the things you have sent me. I would
thank Major Craig or Col. Butler to let Col. Pickering and Gen.
Washington know that there is a grate deal of damage done in this
country by Liquor; Capt. Brant has kiled his son and other chiefs
has done the same, and when the drink was gone and they began
to think of the horid crime they had comited, they resigned their
command in the Nation; two Chiefs has been kiled, the one at
Fort Franklin the other at Genesee.   I have sent a speech to the
States conserning the Chief killed at Franklin, and has been waiting all summer to receive pay for him, but can see no sign of its
coming.   I am by myself to bear all the burden of the people.
Now father take pitty on me and send me 40 dollars worth of black
Wampum and 10 of white; and I expect to see it in two months
and an half, as I must make new Chiefs with it again that time, to
help me.   I wish to hear from my son and what progress he is
making in his learning, and as soon as he is learned enough I want
him at home to manage my business for me.   I will leave it all to
my father, Gen. Washington, to judge when he is learned enough.
My compliments to my father and the United States, and I wish
it was possible for me to live forever in the United States.

his
CAPT. X. O. BEAL.
mark"

It will be noted that, in the above letter, Cornplanter asks
what progress his son "is making in his learning".   This was his
favorite son, Henry O'Bail, who was carefully educated, but later
became a drunkard, and caused much sorrow to his aged father.

Cornplanter Offers to Assist Americans in War of 1812

Reference has been made to the fact that Cornplanter was a
firm friend of the United States.   He gave additional proof of this
friendship when, in 1812, he came from the retirement of his
sylvan retreat on the banks of the Allegheny, and offered himself
and two hundred warriors to Colonel Dale, at Franklin, for a
regiment which the Colonel was forming in Crawford and
Venango counties to go to the defense of Erie.   He was much dis-

appointed when he learned that his services could not be accepted. However, a number of the Senecas did take an active part in the War of 1812. Among them were Cornplanter's son, Major Henry O'Bail, and his half-brother, Half-Town. Both of these were conspicuous in several engagements on the Niagara frontier.

Reverend Timothy Alden Visits Cornplanter

Reverend Timothy Alden, then president of Allegheny College, visited Cornplanter at his village on the Allegheny, in Warren County, in 1816, and thus describes the chief and his village:

"Jennesedaga, Cornplanter's village, is on a handsome piece of bottom land, and comprises about a dozen buildings. It was grateful to notice the agricultural habits of the place, and the numerous enclosures of buckwheat, corn, and oats. We also saw a number of oxen, cows, and horses, and many logs designed for the saw mill and the Pittsburgh market. Last year, 1815, the Western Missionary Society established a school in the village, under Mr. Samuel Oldham. Cornplanter, as soon as apprised of our arrival, came over to see us, and took charge of our horses. Though having many around him to obey his commands, yet, in the ancient patriarchal style, he chose to serve us himself, and actually went into the fields, cut the oats, and fed our beasts. He appears to be about 68 years of age, and 5 feet 10 inches in height. His countenance is strongly marked with intelligence and reflection. Contrary to the aboriginal custom, his chin is covered with a beard three or four inches in length. His house is of princely dimensions compared with most Indian huts, and has a piazza in front. He is owner of 1,300 acres of excellent land, 600 of which encircle the ground-plot of his little town. He receives an annual stipend from the United States of $250.00. Cornplanter's brother, lately deceased, called the prophet, was known by the high-sounding name Guskukewanna Konnediu, or Large Beautiful Lake. Kinjuquade, the name of another chief, signified the place of many fishes;—hence probably the name of Kinjua."

Day's "Historical Recollections" Again Quoted

Once more we quote from Day's "Historical Collections":

"In 1821-22 the commissioners of Warren County assumed the right to tax the private property of Cornplanter, and proceeded to enforce its collection. The old chief resisted it, conceiving it not only unlawful, but a personal indignity. The sheriff again appeared with a small posse of armed men. Corn-planter took the deputation to a room around which were ranged about a hundred rifles, and with the sententious brevity of an Indian, intimated that for each rifle a warrior would appear at his call. The sheriff and his men speedily withdrew, determined, however, to call out the militia. Several prudent citizens, fearing a sanguinary collision, sent for the old chief in a friendly way to come to Warren and compromise the matter. He came, and after some persuasion, gave his note for the tax, amounting to $43.79. He addressed, however, a remonstrance to the Governor of Pennsylvania, soliciting a return of the note, and an exemption from such demands against land which the state itself had presented to him. [Cornplanter's note was never paid. The state exempted his lands from taxes]. He met them at the court house in Warren, on which occasion he delivered the following speech, eminently characteristic of himself and his race:

" 'Brothers: Yesterday was appointed for us all to meet here. The talk which the governor sent us pleased us very much. I think that the Great Spirit is very much pleased that the white people have been induced so to assist the Indians as they have done, and that He is pleased also to see the great men of this state and of the United States so friendly to us. We are much pleased with what has been done.'

" 'The Great Spirit first made the world, and next the flying animals, and found all things good and prosperous. He is immortal and everlasting. After finishing the flying animals, He came down on earth and there stood. Then He made different kinds of trees, and weeds of all sorts, and people of every kind. He made the spring and other seasons, and the weather suitable for planting. These He did make. But stills to make whiskey to be given to Indians He did not make. The Great Spirit bids me tell the white people not to give Indians this kind of liquor. When the Great Spirit had made the earth and its animals, He went into the great lakes, where He breathed as easily as anywhere else, and then made all the different kinds of fish. The Great Spirit looked back on all that He had made. The different kinds He made to be separate, and not to mix with and disturb each other. But the white people have broken His command by mixing their color with the Indians. The Indians have done better by not doing so. The Great Spirit wishes that all wars and fighting should cease.

" 'He next told us that there were three things for our people to attend to. First, we ought to take care of our wives and children. Secondly, the white people ought to attend to their farms and cattle. Thirdly, the Great Spirit has given the bears and deer to the Indians. He is the cause of all things that exist, and it is very wicked to go against His will. The Great Spirit wishes me to inform the people that they should quit drinking intoxicating drink, as being the cause of disease and death. He told us not to sell any more of our lands, for He never sold lands to any one. Some of us now keep the seventh day; but I wish to quit it, for the Great Spirit made it for others, but not for the Indians, who ought every day to attend to their business. He has ordered me to quit drinking any intoxicating drink, and not to lust after any woman but my own, and informs me that by doing so I should live the longer. He made known to me that it is very wicked to tell lies. Let no one suppose this I have said now is not true.

"I have now to thank the Governor for what he has done. I have informed him what the Great Spirit has ordered me to cease from, and I wish the Governor to inform others of what I have communicated. This is all I have at present to say.'

"The old chief appears, after this, again to have fallen into seclusion, taking no part even in the politics of his people.

"Notwithstanding his profession of Christianity, Cornplanter was very superstitious. 'Not long since,' says Mr. Foote, of Chautauqua County, 'he said the Good Spirit had told him not to have any thing to do with the white people, or even to preserve any mementoes or relics that had been given to him, from time to time, by the pale-faces, whereupon, among other things, he burnt up his belt, and broke his elegant sword.' "

Cornplanter Visits the Steamboat, Allegheny

In the "Pittsburgh Gazette" of May 28, 1830, we read an account of a trip of the steamboat, the "Allegheny", as follows:

"She left Pittsburgh on her third trip on the 14th of May, 1830, with sixty-four passengers and twenty-five or thirty tons of freight, and arrived at Warren at nine o'clock on the 19th,—three and one-half days' running time,—and on the same evening she departed from Warren for Olean. At nine o'clock the next day she arrived opposite the Indian village of Cornplanter. Here a deputation of gentlemen waited on this ancient and well-known Seneca chief, and invited him on board this new and, to him, wonderful visitor, a steamboat. He was in all his native simplicity of dress and manner of living, lying on his couch, made of rough pine boards, and covered with deer skins and blankets. His habitation, a two-story log house, was in a state of decay, without furniture, except a few benches, and wooden bowls and spoons to eat out of. He was a smart, active man, seemingly possessed of all his strength of mind and perfect health. He, with his son, Charles, sixty years of age, and his son-in-law, came on board and remained until she passed six miles up, and then returned in their own canoe, after expressing great pleasure.

Last Days of Cornplanter

Concerning the last days of this great leader of the Senecas, a gentleman wrote the following in "The Democratic Arch", a newspaper of Venango County:

"I once saw the aged and venerable chief, and had an interesting interview with him, about a year and a half before his death. I thought of many things when seated near him, beneath the widspreading shade of an old sycamore, on the banks of the Allegheny —many things to ask him—the scenes of the Revolution, the generals that fought its battles and conquered, the Indians, his tribe, the Six Nations, and himself. He was constitutionally sedate,—was never observed to smile, much less to indulge in the 'luxury of a laugh.' When I saw him, he estimated his age to be over 100 years. I think 103 was about his reckoning of it. This would make him near 105 years old at the time of his decease. His person was much stooped, and his stature was far short of what it once had been—not being over 5 feet 6 inches at the time I speak of. Mr. John Struthers, of Ohio, told me, some years since, that he had seen him near 50 years ago, and at that period, he was about his height—viz., 6 feet 1 inch. Time and hardship had made dreadful impressions upon that ancient form. The chest was sunken, and his shoulders were drawn forward, making the upper part of his body resemble a trough. His limbs had lost their size and become crooked. His feet, too, (for he had taken off his moccasins,) were deformed and haggard by injury. I would say that most of the fingers on one hand were useless; the sinews had been severed by a blow of the tomahawk or scalping knife. How I longed to ask him what scene of blood and strife had thus stamped the enduring evidence of its existence upon his person! But to have done so would, in all probability, have put an end to all further conversation on any subject,—the information desired would certainly not have been received,—and I had to forgo my curiosity.

"He had but one eye, and even the socket of the lost organ was hid by the overhanging brow resting upon the high cheek bone. His remaining eye was one of the brightest and blackest hue. Never have I seen one, in young or old, that equalled it in brilliancy. Perhaps it had borrowed lustre from the eternal darkness that rested on its neighboring orbit. His ears had been dressed in the Indian mode; all but the outside ring had been cut away. On the one ear this ring had been torn asunder near the top, and hung down his neck like a useless rag. He had a full head of hair, white as the 'diven snow', which covered a head of ample dimensions and admirable shape. His face was not swarthy; but this may be accounted for from the fact, also, that he was but half Indian.

"He told me that he had been at Franklin more than 80 years before the period of our conversation, on his passage down the Ohio and Mississippi, with the warriors of his tribe, on some expedition against the Creeks or Osages. He had long been a man of peace, and I believe his great characteristics were humanity and truth. It is said that Brant and the Cornplanter were never friends after the massacre of Cherry Valley. Some have alleged, because the Wyoming massacre was perpetrated by the Senecas, that the Cornplanter was there. Of the justice of this suspicion there are many reasons for doubt. It is certain that he was not the chief of the Senecas at that time; the name of the chief in that expedition was Ge-en-quah-toh, or He-goes-in-the-smoke.

"As he stood before me—the ancient chief in ruins—how forcibly was I struck with the truth of the beautiful figure of the old aboriginal chieftain, who, in describing himself, said he was 'like an aged hemlock, dead at the top, and whose branches alone were green.' After more than one hundred years of most varied life —of strife, of danger, of peace—he at last slumbers in deep repose, on the banks of his own beloved Allegheny."

Death of Cornplanter

This great leader of the Senecas died at Cornplanter Town, Warren County, on the banks of his long-loved Allegheny, on February 18th, 1836,—the passing of the last great Indian chief of Pennsylvania. "Whether at the time of his death he expected to go to the fair Hunting Grounds of his own people or to the Heaven of the Christians, is not known." It was his wish that his grave should remain unmarked. However, the State of Pennsylvania erected a monument at his grave, in 1866, the first monument erected by any state of the Union to an Indian chief, bearing the following inscription:

> "Gy-ant-wa-chia, The Cornplanter,
> JOHN O'BAIL, ALIAS CORNPLANTER,
> DIED
> At Cornplanter Town, Feb. 18, A. D. 1836,
> Aged About 100 Years.

"Chief of the Seneca tribe, and a principal chief of the Six Nations from the period of the Revolutionary War to the time of his death. Distinguished for talent, courage, eloquence, sobriety, and love for tribe and race, to whose welfare he devoted his time, his energy, and his means during a long and eventful life."

Three of Cornplanter's children were present at the dedication of his monument, the last of whom died in 1874, aged about one hundred years. Other descendants still reside on the Cornplanter Reservation, in Warren County, cherishing the memory of "one of the bravest, noblest and truest specimens of the aboriginal race."

CHAPTER XXXI.

Other Indian Events in Pennsylvania During the Revolutionary War

THOUGH not directly connected with any of the outstanding Indian chiefs of Pennsylvania whose biographies we have just concluded, we devote this chapter and the next to a narration of additional Indian events in Pennsylvania during the Revolutionary War—a story of outrages and terrible atrocities.

In weighing the conduct of an individual, of a group of individuals, or of a nation, we should take into consideration their mental endowment, moral standard, social aptitude, and the kind of temptations they meet or that may have been thrust upon them. And so, in reading the account of the Indian atrocities during the Revolutionary War, we should not lose sight of the fact that, as was pointed out in former chapters, the British, early in this struggle, stirred up the Indians against the Americans, offering them rewards for American scalps, well knowing that Indian warfare meant suffering and death to the innocent and the helpless. The aged father, whose form was bent by a life of toil and hardship on the frontier; the aged mother, whose hair was silvered by child-birth pain and a life full of care and rich in service; the widow, lingering by the grave of her buried love; the matron, devoted and ministering to her children; the young man of talent, promise, and joyous parental hope; the boy just opening into adolescence; the maiden in the loveliness of grace, beauty, and virtue; the child, angel-eyed and silken haired, prattling at its parent's knee; the tender and helpless babe on its mother's breast— the merciless Indian dashed out the brains of all these, tore off their reeking scalps, carried them to British agents, and received the British scalp bounty for their dreadful work.

As pointed out in former chapters, the British general, Henry Hamilton, who was in command at Detroit, was directed, on October 6th, 1776, to enlist the Indians in the British service, and have them ready for operations against the western frontier the next spring. Hamilton incited many Indian incursions against the frontier, and gave the Indians $50.00 for each scalp. About

June 1st, 1777, he began to enlist and send out war parties against the frontiers of Kentucky, Virginia, and Pennsylvania. About the end of July of that year, he reported to his superior commander at Quebec, that he had sent out fifteen war parties, consisting of 30 white men and 289 Indians, an average of 21 in each band. These Indians were chiefly Wyandots and Miamis, of Northwestern Ohio, and Shawnees of Southern Ohio. The Americans held Hamilton in abhorrence, and nick-named him the "hair-buyer" general. He continued his dreadful work until his capture by Colonel George Rodgers Clark, at Vincennes, Indiana, February 25th, 1779, who sent him to Richmond as a prisoner where he was confined in irons.

The British agents in New York were no better than Hamilton They sent the Senecas and various other tribes of the Six Nations in alliance with them, against the frontiers of New York and both Eastern and Western Pennsylvania. As will presently be seen, they gave their Indian allies ten dollars each for the two hundred and twenty-seven scalps of principally old men, women and children, killed at the Wyoming cassacre of July 3rd, 1778.

Franklin, in his list of twenty-six British atrocities, gives the 10th and 14th as follows:

"10th. The King of England, giving audience to his Secretary of War, who presents him a schedule entitled 'Account of Scalps'; which he receives very graciously.

"14th. The commanding officer at Niagara, sitting in state, a table before him, his soldiers and savages bring him scalps of the Wyoming families and presenting them. Money on the table with which he pays for them."

Who stands with the greater condemnation before the judgment seat of Almighty God? Is it the untutored Red Man with passions wild as the storms of his native mountains? Or, is it the anointed children of education and civilization, who were the instigators of his deeds of blood and death?

Attack on the Campbell Family

Robert Campbell lived with his parents near Pleasant Grove Church in Cook Township, Westmoreland County. In July, 1775, he and his brothers, William and Thomas, were working in the harvest field when they were captured by a band of Senecas. After capturing the boys, the Indians went to the Campbell home, where they killed and scalped the mother and her infant. Their bodies were found the next day. They also captured the girls, Polly, Isabella, and Sarah. The youngest girl, who had difficulty in riding a horse upon which the Indians placed her, was killed about a mile from the home, and her body was found a few days later. The three boys and two girls were then taken across the Kiskiminetas below the mouth of the Loyalhanna, and carried to New York. After four years, the two girls were released, and returned to their father. Robert escaped in 1782, and succeeded in returning to his home. At the close of the Revolutionary War, William was exchanged, and also returned home. Thomas never returned. What became of him is unknown.

The Easton Conference of January 27, 1777

Prior to entering into the treaty with the Delawares, an account of which was given in Chapter XXV, the Continental Congress as early as January, 1777, received information "that certain tribes of Indians living in the back parts of the country near the waters of the Susquehanna within the Confederacy and under the protection of the Six Nations, the friends and allies of the United States", intended coming to Easton to hold a conference with the Continental and Colonial Authorities. Thereupon, the Continental Congress appointed a commission, consisting of George Taylor, George Walton, and others, to purchase suitable presents and to conduct a treaty with these Indians; while the Assembly of Pennsylvania named Colonels Lowry and Cunningham as their commissioners, and the Council of Safety sent Colonels Dean and Bull. Thomas Paine was appointed to act as secretary of the commission.

Some of the Indians reached Wilkes-Barre on January 7th, and announced the coming of the larger delegation, which reached the same place on January 15th. They then proceeded to Easton, where the conference was opened on January 27th, in the German Reformed Church. It is claimed that, before proceeding to business, the members of the commission and the Indians shook hands with one another, and drank to the health of the Continental Congress and the Six Nations, as the notes of the organ filled the auditorium. There were seventy men and one hundred women and children in the Indian delegation; and among the chiefs were the following: Taasquah, or "King Charles", of the Cayuga; Tawanah, or "The Big Tree", of the Seneca; Mytakawha, or "Walking on Foot", and Kaknah, or "Standing by a Tree", of the Munsee; Amatincka, or "Raising Anything Up" of the Nanti-coke; Wilakinko, or "King Last Night" of the Conoy, and Thomas Green, whose wife was a Mohawk, as interpreter.

The conference did not proceed far until it became evident that the British, through the influence of Colonel John Butler, then at Niagara, were having great success in turning the Six Nations against the Americans. The results of this conference are thus set forth in the report of the treaty, made to the Supreme Executive Council of Pennsylvania: "The Indians seem to be inclined to act the wise part with respect to the present dispute. If they are to be relied upon, they mean to be neuter. We have already learned their good intentions." But, as has been seen, the overwhelming majority of the warriors of the Six Nations took the British side in the Revolutionary War.

Capture of Andrew McFarlane

In the autumn of 1774, Andrew McFarlane, with his brother, James, had started a trading post at Kittanning. The Revolutionary War having come on, the Continental Congress, in July, 1776, ordered the raising of a regiment of seven companies from Westmoreland, and one from Bedford, to erect and garrison forts at Kittanning, LeBoueff, and Erie, to protect the Allegheny Valley from the incursions of Tories and Iroquois. This regiment, under the command of Colonel Aeneas Mackey, with George Wilson as Lieutenant-Colonel, and Richard Butler, for whom Butler County is named, as Major, rendezvoused at Kittanning late in the fall, built Fort Armstrong at that place, and prepared to advance up the Allegheny to erect the other forts, when a call was received for the regiment to march eastward across the state, and join the army of General Washington near the Delaware. In spite of a storm of protest on the western frontier this regiment, afterwards known as the Eighth Pennsylvania, began its long and terrible march in January, 1777, to join Washington's army. After the regiment left Kittanning, McFarlane was deserted by all his neighbors except two clerks. In the meantime he had, without success, requested the Westmoreland commissioners to send some militia to guard the stores that Colonel Mackey left at Kittanning; and he and Samuel Moorehead, who lived at Black Lick Creek, Indiana County, undertook to raise a force of volunteer rangers, McFarlane being his lieutenant.

On February 25th, two British subalterns, two Chippewa, and

two Iroquois Indians, sent by the British commandant at Fort Niagara to descend the Allegheny, arrived on the west side of the Allegheny opposite McFarlane's trading post at Kittanning, and shouted toward the other shore, calling for a canoe. McFarlane, thinking that the Indians had come to trade or possibly to bring some important news, crossed in a boat to the western shore. Upon stepping from his boat, he was seized by the Indians and told that he was a prisoner, his capture being witnessed by his wife "and some men at the settlement". His captors carried him to Quebec where, through the efforts of his brother, James, then a lieutenant in the First Pennsylvania Regiment, he was exchanged, in the autumn of 1780, and rejoined his wife, Margaret Lynn Lewis, at Staunton, Virginia. Soon thereafter he opened another trading house on Chartier's Creek, Allegheny County, where he lived for many years.

Upon the capture of her husband, Mrs. McFarlane with her infant in her arms fled through the wilderness to Carnahan's block house, more than twenty miles distant, and located in Bell Township, Westmoreland County, about two miles from the Kiskiminetas River.

Andrew McFarlane's brother, James, as the leader of a band of insurrectionists during the Whiskey Rebellion, lost his life in July, 1794, in an attack upon the house of General Neville, Revenue Collector, near Bower Hill, Allegheny County. His dust reposes in the Old Mingo Creek Cemetery near Monongahela City, Washington County.

Indian Massacre Near Standing Stone

On June 19th, 1777, occurred the massacre at what was known as the Big Spring several miles west of the fort at Standing Stone, now Huntingdon, Pennsylvania. The Indians destroyed the plantations in the neighborhood, and the inhabitants fled to the fort. Felix Donnelly, his son, Francis, Bartholomew Maguire, and his daughter, Jane, residing near the mouth of Shaver's Creek, placed their effects upon horses, and with a cow started for the fort, when the Indians entered the neighborhood. Jane Maguire proceeded on ahead driving the cow, while her father and the Donnellys followed in the rear on horseback. When they had reached a point about opposite the Big Spring, an Indian fired from ambush and killed the younger Donnelly. His father who was close beside him, caught him as he was falling from his horse;

whereupon, Maguire rode to his side, and the two held the dead body of the boy upon the horse. The Indians then rushed from their hiding places and fired upon the party, one bullet striking Donnelly and another grazing Maguire's ear. Donnelly fell to the ground as did the body of his dead son. The Indians scalped the boy and pursued Jane Maguire, who succeeded in escaping after she had lost her dress in freeing herself from an Indian who attempted to capture her. Some men on the opposite side of Shaver's Creek hearing the firing, rushed to the scene, and the Indians then retreated into the woods, not knowing the strength of the party. Maguire and his daughter reached the fort and alarmed the garrison, which started in pursuit of the Indians, but failed to overtake them. The dead body of young Francis Donnelly was then buried at a spot now within the limits of the town of Huntingdon.

Outrages in Westmoreland County in 1777

During October and November, 1777, when General Edward Hand, who was then in command of Fort Pitt, was endeavoring to recruit his army for an invasion of the Indian country, many raids were made into Westmoreland County, principally by the Senecas. These raids were no doubt instigated by Guyasuta, and possibly some of them were led by him. An incursion was made into the Ligonier Valley about the middle of October, and eleven men were killed and scalped near Palmer's Fort, located in Fairfield Township, midway between the Chestnut Ridge and Laurel Hill Mountain. A few days later four children were killed within site of this fort; and three men were killed and a number captured within a few miles of Ligonier.

On November 1st, Lieutenant Samuel Craig, who lived near Shield's Fort, located near the town of New Alexandria, Westmoreland County, was riding toward Ligonier for salt, when he was waylaid and either killed or captured at the western base of Chestnut Ridge. Rangers found his mare lying dead near the trail with eight bullets in her body, but no trace of Craig was ever discovered.

At about the same time a band of Senecas led by a Canadian, attacked Fort Wallace, about a mile south of Blairsville, but their leader was killed and they were repulsed. At about the same time, also, Major James Wilson, hearing the firing of guns at the cabin of his neighbor while at work on his farm, got his rifle and went to investigate. He found the neighbor killed, the head being severed from his body. Wilson then hurriedly took his wife and children to Fort Barr, located on a tributary of the Loyalhanna, about five and one-half miles southeast of Fort Wallace.

On November 2nd, 1777, William Richardson was killed and scalped about three miles from Fort Ligonier. At the same time, two men were killed and a woman captured not far from the place where Richardson met his death.

Among the prisoners taken by the Indians during these incursions, were Major Charles Campbell and Randall Laughlin, who were carried to Quebec, where they were exchanged in the fall of 1778. The band of Indians perpetrating these outrages, was pursued by a party of rangers led by the celebrated Colonel James Smith, Captain John Hinkston, and Robert Barr. Smith and his rangers overtook the Indians on the east bank of the Allegheny River, near Kittanning, killed five of them, and returned in triumph to the settlements with the scalps of these Indians and with the horses which they had stolen.

The Squaw Campaign

General Hand, aroused by the above depredations, and learning that the British had built a magazine where Cleveland, Ohio, now stands, and had stored it with arms, ammunition, and clothing for use of the Indian incursions proposed to be made the next spring, determined to lead an expedition for the destruction of these supplies. His expedition left Fort Pitt in February, 1778, descending the Ohio to the mouth of the Beaver and then ascending the Beaver to the mouth of the Mahoning. By the time the Mahoning was reached that stream was almost impassable, and Hand was so disheartened that he was about to give up the expedition and return, when the footprints of some Indians were discovered on the high ground. These tracks led to a small Indian village, where Edinburg, Lawrence County, now stands. Hand's forces attacked the village, but found that it contained only one old man, and some squaws and children, the warriors being away on a hunt. The Indians escaped except the old man and one squaw, who were both shot, and another squaw, who was taken prisoner. This woman captive informed Hand that ten Delawares of the Wolf Clan were making salt ten miles farther up the Mahoning. Hand then dispatched a detachment after these Indians, who proved to be four squaws and a boy. The soldiers killed three of the squaws and the boy, and the other squaw was taken prisoner.

The condition of the weather making further progress impossible, General Hand led his army back to Fort Pitt with the two squaw captives. His formidable force of five hundred horsemen had slain one old man, four women, one boy, and captured two women. On Hand's arrival at Fort Pitt, the frontiersmen derided his recent exploits and dubbed the expedition the "Squaw Campaign." Discouraged and humiliated, he asked General Washington to relieve him, and on May 2nd, Congress voted his recall, and commissioned General Lachlan McIntosh to succeed him.

The Tories of Sinking Spring Valley

While the Tory plotting leading to the flight of the Tories, Captain Alexander McKee, Matthew Elliott, Robert Surphlit, and Simon Girty from Fort Pitt, during the winter of 1777 and 1778, as related in Chapter XXV, was going on, British agents from Niagara and Detroit visited several isolated settlements in the mountains of Pennsylvania, in an effort to persuade the mountaineers to espouse the British cause. One of these agents succeeded in deluding a number of frontiersmen in what is now Blair County, promising that any man who deserted the American cause should have two hundred acres of land on the conclusion of peace. He told these settlers that, if they would join a force of British and Indians coming down the Allegheny in the spring of 1778, they would be permitted to join in a general incursion against the frontier settlements, and receive their share of the pillage.

The frontiersmen who yielded to the persuasions of the British agent, held meetings in the isolated Sinking Spring Valley, in Blair County, in February and March, 1778, their leader being John Weston. In the meantime, after fully enlisting Weston, the British agent returned up the Allegheny, promising to come to Kittanning about the middle of April with a force of three hundred Indians and Tories to meet Weston's followers, and then attack Fort Pitt and the frontier settlements. By about the first of April, Weston had increased his band to thirty, and was joined about that time by a man named McKee, who came from Carlisle. At Carlisle, McKee had been in communication with a British officer who had been held at that place as a prisoner of war, who gave McKee a letter addressed to all British officers, vouching for the loyalty of McKee and his associates. This letter was to be used in securing the protection of the plotters of the Sinking Spring Valley, when they would meet the force of British and Indians at Kittanning.

Presently word reached the plotters that a force of Indians had gathered at Kittanning, and occupied the fort at that place, which had been deserted by the Americans the year before. Then Weston and his associates set out in their march over the mountains to Kittanning, crossing the main range of the Alleghenies at Kittanning Point, and following the Kittanning Indian Trail. On the afternoon of the second day, they encountered a band of one hundred Iroquois who were on a plundering raid of their own, and believed Weston and his men to be enemies. Weston ran forward waving his hand and shouting: "Friends! Friends!" The Iroquois being ignorant of the conspiracy, killed and scalped Weston, and then darted into the thickets. McKee waving in one hand the letter he had received from the British prisoner at Carlisle and in the other a white handkerchief, called out to the Indians: "Brothers! Brothers!" The Indians did not respond, but vanished into the forest.

Weston was buried where he fell, and his companions decided to proceed no further. Many perished from hunger in the wilderness. Some, after great suffering, reached British posts in the southern colonies. Five returned to their homes, and were later lodged in jail at Bedford. The leader of these, Richard Weston, brother of the dead plotter, was caught in the Sinking Spring Valley by a party of Americans, and lodged in jail at Carlisle to await trial, but later made his escape. Those who had fled were charged with treason, and their estates were forfeited. After the Revolutionary War was over, a few returned to Pennsylvania, succeeded in procuring the removal of the attainder, and got back their land.

Outrages in Westmoreland County in 1778

In April, 1778, the Senecas crossed the Kiskiminetas and Conemaugh, and once more entered Westmoreland County. On the 28th of that month about twenty rangers, commanded by Captain Hopkins who had gone out from Fort Wallace, were surprised by a larger force of Indians, and defeated. Nine of the rangers lay dead in the forest and their bodies were left behind, while Captain Hopkins was slightly wounded. Four of the Indians were killed in the engagement.

Hassler, in his "Old Westmoreland" suggests that this was probably the combat referred to by Dr. Joseph Smith in his "Old Redstone", in which Ebenezer Finley, son of the pioneer preacher, James Finley, took part. According to Smith, a horseman dashed into the fort with the word that he had seen two men and a woman fleeing through the woods from Indians. About twenty of the militia at Fort Wallace then sallied forth, and at about a mile and a half from the fort were ambushed. Presently, the militia retreated toward the fort, in the meantime many being shot down or tomahawked. Ebenezer Finley having fallen behind his companions while trying to prime his gun, exerted himself tremendously to prevent his being overtaken. In this effort he succeeded in passing a comrade by striking him on the shoulder with his elbow. At almost the same instant his comrade was brained with a tomahawk. Says Hassler: "Thus young Finley saved himself by sacrificing the life of another, and the pious author [Dr. Joseph Smith] would have it that Finley escaped by the interposition of Providence."

Hassler, in his "Old Westmoreland" describes another event which tradition says took place near Fort Wallace possibly in the summer of 1778, as follows:

"The story goes that signs of Indians were seen near Fort Barr, and the settlers throughout the southern part of Derry took refuge there. They were preparing to withstand an attack, when brisk firing was heard in the direction of Fort Wallace. Major James Wilson, at the head of about forty men, promptly set out from Barr's to the relief of the other post. They arrived within sight of Fort Wallace, which they found heavily besieged; but as soon as Wilson's company appeared, the savages turned upon it and assailed it in overwhelming force. The principal conflict took place on a bridge over a deep gully, about 500 yards from the fort. Several Indians were there slain and others were thrown over the bridge; but Wilson's party was forced to retreat and fought desperately all the way back to Fort Barr. During this retreat two of Robert Barr's sons, Alexander and Robert, were killed, but their bodies were saved from the scalping knife. All others gained the stockade in safety, and the Indians soon afterward disappeared from the settlement."

In 1778, a settler named Reed lived not far from Fort Ligonier. When Indian troubles threatened the settlement, Reed and his family moved to the fort, where his oldest daughter, Rebecca, distinguished herself in running foot races with various athletes of the garrison. Some time during the summer, Rebecca and her brother, George, a young man named Means, and his sister Sarah, left the fort to gather berries in a clearing about two miles away. On their way, the young men, who were walking ahead, met Major McDowell coming toward the fort. At that instant the party were fired upon by Indians. McDowell's rifle was splintered by a bullet, and young Reed was mortally wounded. Young Means ran back to protect the girls, and was captured. The girls started to run toward the fort, but the Indians soon caught Miss Means. Miss Reed, however, outdistanced her pursuers as she fled toward the fort.

The garrison hearing the firing, a relief party headed by a young man named Shannon, proceeded in the direction of the firing. These met Miss Reed a short distance from the fort, and Shannon conducted her to safety, while the others proceeded to the scene of the firing, where they found the lifeless bodies of young Reed and Miss Means. Three years later young Means returned from his captivity and reported that the warrior who had chased Miss Reed was renowned as an athlete among the Indians, but had lost his prestige on account of his failure to catch the "white squaw." Later young Shannon married Rebecca Reed, and they spent a long and happy life in the Ligonier Valley.

The Ulery family lived about two miles south of Ligonier. In the month of July, most likely in the year 1778, the three girls, Julian, aged twenty, Elizabeth, aged eighteen, and Abigail, aged sixteen, were raking hay a short distance from their home, when they were attacked by Indians. The girls ran toward the house with their pursuers close on their heels. Abigail was unable to keep up with her sisters, and when the latter got into the house, they immediately closed and barred the door, thinking that Abigail had been captured. The father then shot through the door, wounding one of the Indians. In the meantime, Abigail ran into the woods above the house, and hid herself among leaves and weeds in a depression made by the uprooting of a tree. The Indians came near where she lay concealed; but the wounded member of the band was moaning so piteously that his companions, without making further search for Abigail, carried him away, and soon disappeared over the brow of the hill above the Ulery home. No doubt this Indian died, for shortly afterwards a newly made grave was found at that place, and many years later the grave was opened and human bones exhumed by Isaac Slater.

The following day, Julian and Elizabeth went to work in the

same field, when Indians, evidently the same band that made the attack the day before, got between the girls and the house, and succeeded in capturing them.   Julian and Elizabeth struggled desperately with their captors.   Then, in the hope of making the girls reconciled to going along with them, the Indians gave them new moccasins.   The captives still struggled, and were dragged along to the rivulet near Brant's school house, when the Indians became desperate and told them to make a choice between captivity and death.   The girls struggled all the harder, and were then tomahawked and scalped on the spot.   The Indians then hurried on, but presently returned to remove the moccasins from the girls, when they found Elizabeth partly recovered, and sitting up against a tree.   An Indian then sunk his tomahawk into her brain.   Julian was conscious but lay still, and the Indians thought her dead.   She recovered but was never strong, and her scalp never healed.   She spent her days on the homestead with her sister Abigail.

The Harman family lived in 1777 near Williams' block house about midway between Stahlstown and Donegal, Westmoreland County.   Some time during the summer of this year, Mr. Harman and three of his neighbors were returning from some gathering in the neighborhood, when they were fired upon by Indians from ambush, and all killed except one, who, throwing his arms about his horse's neck, rode beyond the reach of the Indians.   His body was found the next day with his horse standing by its side.

Mrs. Harman and her sons, Andrew, John, and Philip, spent the next winter at the block house, and then returned to the farm on Four Mile Run.   One morning in the spring of 1778, Mrs. Harman sent John and Andrew to chase some horses of a neighbor out of a field of growing grain.   A band of Senecas who were watching, captured the boys, and carried them to the headwaters of the Allegheny.   A member of this Indian band had the tobacco pouch of Mr. Harman, which the boys recognized, and he was no doubt a member of the band who killed the father during the preceding summer.   Both John and Andrew were adopted by the Senecas.   John died among them about a year after his capture, but Andrew after two years was sold to a British officer for a bottle of rum, who took him to London where he was kept for another two years as a servant.   At the end of the Revolutionary War, he was exchanged and sent to New York, from which place he immediately went to his old home in the Ligonier Valley, where he found his mother overjoyed to meet him.   Andrew had many thrilling experiences during his captivity.   He was among the Senecas when Colonel Broadhead marched against them in the summer of 1779.

Massacre on Lycoming Creek

On June 10th, 1778, occurred the terrible massacre at Lycoming Creek, within the limits of the present town of Williamsport, Lycoming County.   On this day, Peter Smith, his wife and six children, William King's wife and his two daughters, Ruth and Sarah, Michael Smith, Michael Campbell, and David Chambers, and two men named Snodgrass and Hammond, were going to Lycoming in wagons; and when they arrived at Loyalsock Creek, John Harris met them, told them that he heard firing up the creek, and advised them to return to Fort Muncy.   Smith said that the firing would not stop him; and he and his party continued up the West Branch of the Susquehanna, while Harris proceeded to Fort Muncy and told the garrison of the firing which he had heard. A detail of fifteen soldiers then started from the fort in the direction of the firing.

When Smith and his party were within half a mile of Lycoming Creek, they were ambushed by Indians, and Snodgrass fell dead with a bullet through his forehead at the first fire.   The Indians then rushed toward the wagons, and the white men hurried toward the shelter of some trees, while two of the children, a boy and girl, escaped to the woods.   The Indians then endeavored to surround the party, and their movements being discovered, the other men fled leaving Campbell, who was fighting at too close quarters to join in the flight.   Campbell was killed and scalped on the spot.   Before the men were out of sight of the wagons, they saw the Indians attacking the women and children with their tomahawks.   This attack occurred just before sundown.   The boy who had escaped, fled to the stockade on Lycoming Creek, and informed the garrison what had happened.   In the meantime the detail of fifteen soldiers from Fort Muncy, under Captain William Hepburn, arrived at the scene of this massacree and found the bodies of Snodgrass and Campbell.   It was then too dark to pursue the Indians, but they pressed on toward Lycoming and met the party going out from that place.

On the following morning they returned to the scene of the massacre, and found the body of Peter Smith's wife.   She had been shot, stabbed, and scalped.   A little girl and a boy had also been killed and scalped.   The body of Snodgrass was also found,

shot through the head and scalped.   The boy who had made his escape insisted that Mrs. King must be somewhere in the thicket, as
he heard her scream and say that she would not go along with the
Indians when they were dragging her away.   The party then
made another search and found the body of Mrs. King near the
stream, to which she had dragged herself.   She had been tomahawked and scalped, but was not dead.   When her husband
approached her she arose to a sitting position, greeted him, and
then expired, not living long enough to relate the details of the
massacre.

Broken-hearted, William King returned to Northumberland,
and many years later, learning that his daughters were still alive,
he started on foot for Niagara, accompanied by a faithful old
Indian.   He soon found his daughter Sarah and later, after much
suffering and hardship, succeeded in finding the other daughter,
Ruth.   The three then returned to their home near Milton, Northumberland County.

Among those taken captive were Peter Wyckoff, his son,
Cornelius, Thomas Covenhoven, and a negro, the latter of whom
was burned at the stake in the presence of the other prisoners.
Wyckoff and his son remained among the Indians for two years,
when they were given their freedom.

A boulder bearing a bronze tablet has been erected in the
town of Williamsport telling of this melancholy event.

Outrages on the North Branch of the Susquehanna

We have just seen how outrages were committed on the West
Branch of the Susquehanna during the month of June.   During
this same month the North Branch of the Susquehanna was also
devastated.   On the 12th of the month, William Crooks and Asa
Budd went up the river to a point several miles above Tunkhannock.   Crooks was fired upon by some hostile Indians and
killed.   On the 17th, a party of six went up the river in canoes to
observe the movements of the Indians.   About six miles below
Tunkhannock, those in the forward canoe landed and ascended
the bank, when they saw an armed force of Indians and Tories
advancing against them.   Giving the alarm, they returned to their
boats, and endeavored to get behind an island to escape the fire of
the Indians.   In this canoe were Mina Robbins, Joel Phelps, and
Stephen Jenkins.   Robbins was killed and Phelps wounded, while
Jenkins escaped unharmed.   Captain Jewett went up the river with

a scouting party on the 26th, returning on the 30th with the news that the Indians and Tories were assembling in great force up the river. On the same day, June 30th, Benjamin Harding, Stuckely Harding, James Hadsall, and his sons, James and John, Daniel Weller, John Gardner, and Daniel Carr, went up the river into Exeter to their labor in the fields. Late in the afternoon they were attacked by Indians. Weller, Gardner and Carr were taken prisoners. Benjamin Harding, Stuckely Harding, James Hadsall, and his son James were killed. On July 1st, Colonel Nathan Denison and Lieutenant-Colonel George Dorrance with a small force marched from Forty Fort to Exeter, eleven miles distant, where the murders of the preceding day had been committed, and buried the dead.

The Wyoming Massacre

On July 3rd, 1778, occurred the terrible massacre of Wyoming. Late in June Colonel John Butler with his Tory rangers, a detachment of Sir John Johnson's Royal Greens, and a large body of Indians, chiefly Senecas, altogether a force numbering about four hundred British and Tories and seven hundred Indians, descended the North Branch of the Susquehanna, and entered the charming valley of the Wyoming, in Luzerne County. On July 2nd, Fort Jenkins, located within the present limits of the town of West Pittson, was attacked by these invaders, and capitulated after four of its defenders were killed and three taken prisoners. On the same day Wintermoot's fort, about a mile below Fort Jenkins, threw open its gates and here the British and Tories assembled.

There were several small stockades at Wyoming, but no cannon; and none of the forts was able to hold out against such a large force. Moreover most of the able-bodied men of Wyoming were in the American army. Colonel Zebulon Butler of the Continental army, happened to be at home at Wyoming at the time, and assumed command of the settlers, most of them being old men and boys who organized and formed themselves into companies to garrison the forts.

On July 3rd, Colonel Zebulon Butler's forces marched out to meet the invaders, Butler assisted by Major Garret, commanding the right wing, and Colonel Denison assisted by Lieutenant-Colonel George Dorrance, commanding the left. The engagement began between four and five o'clock in the afternoon. The enemy outnumbering the gallant defenders nearly three to one, were able to outflank them, especially on the left, where a swamp well suited

Indian warfare. The men of Wyoming fell in great numbers, and it soon becoming impossible to maintain their position, Colonel Dorrance gave an order to fall back, so as to present a better front to the enemy. His command, however, was mistaken as a signal for retreat. The defenders becoming demoralized, were slaughtered without mercy. Even those who surrendered as prisoners of war, were subjected to the most cruel torture. Sixteen Americans were arranged around a large stone, since known as the Bloody Rock, or Queen Esther's Rock, where Queen Esther Montour, a granddaughter of Madam Montour, dashed out their brains with a tomahawk as she passed around the circle. By a desperate effort three men, named Hammond, Evans, and Joseph Elliott, escaped her fury. In another similar ring nine persons were butchered in the same manner. Many were shot swimming the Susquehanna, and others were hunted out and killed in their hiding places. Only sixty of those who had marched out to give battle survived. The stockades were filled with widows and orphans. It has been said that one hundred and fifty widows and six orphans were the result of this battle, and that about two-thirds of the defenders were slaughtered. The Indians secured 227 scalps, for which the British afterwards paid ten dollars each. A monument has been erected marking the site of this, the most dreadful massacre in the annals of Pennsylvania.

At Forty Fort, located within the limits of the town of that name, the firing at Wyoming was distinctly heard, and the spirits of the defenders of that place were high until they learned the dreadful news of Wyoming, when the first fugitives reached there in the evening. Many other fugitives came to Forty Fort during the night, among them being Colonel Dennison, who rallied the little band for defense, and succeeded the next day in entering into terms of capitulation with the Tory leader, Colonel John Butler. The enemy marched into Forty Fort six abreast, the British and Tories at the northern gate, and the Indians at the southern. In violation of the terms of capitulation the Indians began immediately to rob, plunder, and destroy. Tory Butler did nothing to stop it. When night came on the blaze of burning dwellings lighted up the valley, and the terrified survivors of the massacre fled to the Pocono Mountains beyond Stroudsburg. Many of them however, perished in the dreadful wilderness on the way, and these places are still called "Shades of Death". In a few days Colonel John Butler led the first part of his force away, but the Indians continued their work of burning and plundering until almost every building in the beautiful valley was consumed.

Queen Esther, the fury in form of woman, was the most infamous of all the Montours. She became the wife of Eghohowen, a chief of the Wolf Clan of Delawares, at Asinsam, above Tioga, in 1760. After the death of her husband, she ruled as chieftainess of his tribe. At the time of the Wyoming massacre, she had her residence at Queen Esther's Town, opposite the western shore of Tioga Point, Bradford County. In the fall of that same year, Colonel Thomas Hartley led a force that destroyed her village, and she afterwards settled near the head of Cayuga Lake, New York, where she died.

The Great Runaway

The massacre of Wyoming was followed by the "Great Runaway" of the settlers on the West Branch of the Susquehanna, when they learned the fate of the settlers at Wyoming. Within two days following the massacre news had penetrated the entire North Branch Valley, and as far up the West Branch as Fort Antes, now Jersey Shore, Lycoming County. On July 12th, Colonel Matthew Smith wrote from Paxtang that he had just arrived at Harris' Ferry and beheld the greatest scenes of distress that he had ever seen, the place being crowded with settlers who had come down the river, leaving everything. Also William McClay, later the first United States senator from Pennsylvania, wrote from Paxtang on the same day as follows: "I left Sunbury and almost my whole property on Wednesday last. I will not trouble you with a recital of the inconveniences I suffered while I brought my family by water to this place. I never in my life saw such scenes of distress. The river and roads leading down it were covered with men, women and children, flying for their lives. In short. Northumberland County is broken up." At the same time, Robert Covenhoven wrote concerning the flight of the settlers: "I took my own family safely to Sunbury and came back in the keel boat to secure my furniture. Just as I rounded a point above Derrstown [now Lewisburg, Union County], I met the whole convoy from all the forts above. Such a sight I never saw in all my life. Boats, canoes, hog-troughs, rafts, hastily made of dry sticks, every sort of floating article had been put into requisition and was crowded with women, children, and plunder. Whenever an obstruction occurred at any shoal or ripple, the women would leap out into the water and put their shoulders to the boat or raft and launch it again into deep water. The men of the settlement came down in single file on each side of the river to guard the women and children. The whole convoy arrived safely at Sunbury, leaving the entire range of farms along the West Branch to the ravages of the Indians."

It is a remarkable fact that but few persons were killed by the Indians during this wild and precipitate flight of the settlers.

In answer to Colonel Hunter's appeal, Colonel Daniel Broadhead with the Eighth Pennsylvania Regiment, then on its march to Fort Pitt, was ordered to the West Branch, arriving at Fort Muncy on July 24th. Also Colonel Thomas Hartley with a small regiment arrived at Fort Augusta on August 1st and marched to the relief of Colonel Broadhead at Fort Muncy. After Colonel Hartley's expedition, which we shall now describe, some of the more venturesome settlers returned to their habitations.

Colonel Hartley's Expedition

Reference has already been made to Colonel Thomas Hartley's expedition in the autumn of 1778. Leaving Samuel Wallis' at Muncy on September 21, he led a force of two hundred men through swamps, over mountains, twenty times crossing the Lycoming River; and on the 26th, his advance party of nineteen fired upon an equal number of Indians, killed their leader, and put the rest to flight. This engagement caused the alarm to be given to the main body of the Indians against whom his expedition was aimed; and a few miles further he found where seventy warriors had slept the preceding night, from which place they had turned back. Furthermore, one of his men who had deserted him, had warned the Indians, as was learned when the expedition reached Sheshecununk, Bradford County, where fifteen Indians were taken prisoner.

From Sheshecununk, Hartley advanced to Tioga, destroyed the town, and captured a prisoner. Butler, the Tory leader, had been there with a force of three hundred Tories and Indians only a few hours before Hartley reached that place. Ascertaining at Tioga that a force of five hundred was fortifying itself at Chemung, only twelve miles distant, Hartley retreated to Sheshecununk, at which place he crossed the North Branch of the Susquehanna, and proceeded to the Indian town of Wyalusing, Bradford County. There with the supply of provisions exhausted, his force spent the night of September 28th, and devoted the next morning to killing and cooking beef. Seventy of his force left for home in canoes, and the remainder were attacked three times below Wyalusing, with the loss of four killed and wounded.   At Wyoming three men going out looking for potatoes, were scalped, and Hartley left half of his detachment as a garrison at that place.   He then returned to Sunbury and, the term of his militiamen having expired, he appealed to Congress and the Provincial Council for more troops. His expedition had marched three hundred miles in two weeks, devastating the country of Queen Esther, and destroying her town, as well as Tioga, Sheshecununk, and Wyalusing.   In the forests and groves he found where the Indians had dressed and dried the scalps of the frontier victims.

About the 1st of November, the Indians came down the North Branch of the Susquehanna, destroying the settlements as far as the mouth of the Nescopeck, and investing Wyoming.   Colonel Hartley then advanced from Fort Jenkins, (which was situated on the north shore of the North Branch of the Susquehanna about midway between Berwick and Bloomsburg, in Columbia County), with its garrison to the relief of Wyoming, clearing the country of the enemy.

Frances Slocum, the Lost Sister of Wyoming

On November 2nd, 1778, Jonathan Slocum and his sons, William and Benjamin, were at work harvesting their corn near Wyoming.   At the Slocum home were the other members of the family and a Mrs. Nathan Kingsley and her two sons.   About noon, the Kingsley boys, who were sharpening a knife on the grindstone in the front yard, were attacked by Indians.   Mrs. Slocum hastened to the door and was horrified to see the lifeless body of the elder Kingsley boy lying on the ground, and the Indian who had killed him, preparing to scalp him with the knife that the boys were sharpening.   Snatching her infant from the cradle and calling to the others to run for their lives, she fled out of the rear door of the house over a log fence into a swamp beyond, where she hid herself and her baby.   In the meantime, the younger Kingsley boy and Frances Slocum, a girl five and a half years old, hid themselves under a staircase, and Judith Slocum with her three year old brother, Isaac, also fled toward the swamp, while little Mary Slocum, a girl nine years of age, started to flee in the direction of the fort at Wyoming, carrying her baby brother, one and one-half years old, in her arms.   Ebenezer Slocum, a boy thirteen years old, was a cripple, and was unable to flee.

While the Slocums were fleeing from their home, the Indians

made their way into the house, dragging forth young Kingsley, Frances Slocum, and Ebenezer Slocum. Mrs. Slocum then, leaving her baby behind, rushed among the Indians and implored them to release the child. She pointed to the crippled feet of Ebenezer, and exclaimed: "The child is lame, he can do thee no good." The Indians then released Ebenezer, but in spite of the piteous pleadings of the mother, they refused to release little Frances. The leader of the Indians, throwing Frances athwart his shoulder, and another of the band doing likewise with young Kingsley, they dashed into the woods. Little Frances looked toward her mother and stretched out her little arms in a pitiful appeal. This was the last sight that the mother ever had of her little daughter,—a picture that was in her memory every waking moment until death.

Long years afterwards it was learned from Frances Slocum that she and the Kingsley boy were carried to a cave, where the Indians kept them that night. Setting out at sunrise the next morning, they traveled for many days before arriving at the Indian village to which the captors belonged. When they arrived at this village, the Kingsley boy was taken away, which was the last she ever saw or heard of him.

The chief who took Frances gave her to an aged Delaware couple, who adopted her, giving her the name of Weletawash, which was the name of the couple's youngest child, who had lately died. This Indian couple was living in Ontario, Canada, when the Revolution ended. They then moved to the site of the present city of Fort Wayne, Indiana, where Frances grew to womanhood, and in 1790 married the Delaware, Little Turtle. In 1794 her husband deserted her and went west. Later she married a chief of the Miamis called Shepoconnah, and in 1801 they, with their two sons and daughter removed to the Osage village about one mile from the confluence of the Mississineva and Wabash rivers in the state of Indiana. Here Shepoconnah was made a war chief of the Miamis and Frances was admitted into the Miami tribe, and given the name of Maconaquah, signifying "A Young Bear." Shepoconnah died in 1832.

After the capture of Frances her father was killed. Many efforts were made to obtain clues as to her whereabouts, but to no avail. Also, after peace was declared ending the Revolutionary War, her brothers made a journey to Fort Niagara, where they offered one hundred guineas for her recovery. The brothers never gave up the search for their sister. They visited many Indian villages and traveled thousands of miles, even enlisting the United

States Government in the search. They also attended every gathering of Indians where white children captives were given up.

Finally, in 1835, Colonel George W. Ewing, an Indian trader, was quartered in the home of Maconoquah, as Frances Slocum was now called, where she related the story of her life to him. Marveling at its mystery, Colonel Ewing wrote the postmaster at Lancaster, Pennsylvania, a letter containing the narrative of Maconoquah. No one however, was interested; but two years later John W. Forney, publisher of the Lancaster Intelligencer, ran across this letter and published it in July, 1837. Immediately the narrative was read by those who knew the story of the lost sister of Wyoming. A short time afterward Joseph Slocum journeyed to the home of Maconoquah, where he positively identified her as his long lost sister. She acknowledged him as her brother, but declined to leave her wigwam to enjoy the comforts of her brother's home in Wilkes-Barre. Said she: "No, I cannot. I have always lived with the Indians; they have always used me kindly; I am used to them. The Great Spirit has always allowed me to live with them, and I wish to live and die with them." The brother then returned to his home, and correspondence was kept up between the lost sister of Wyoming and her relatives until her death, which occurred March 9, 1847.

The Fatal Voyage of David Rodgers

In the spring of 1778, Governor Henry of Virginia, directed Captain David Rodgers, also a Virginian, then living at Redstone (Brownsville, Fayette County), to organize an expedition to bring powder from New Orleans by way of the Ohio River. Rodgers at once gathered up a force of forty settlers in the vicinity of Redstone, proceeded to Fort Pitt, and constructed two large flat boats. Among his force, was Basil Brown, one of the founders of Brownsville. Leaving Fort Pitt in June, Rodgers' force floated down to the mouth of the Arkansas River. At a Spanish fort near this place, he learned that the powder had been sent up the Mississippi to St. Louis. Leaving his boats and most of his men at the post, he, with six companions, floated in a canoe down to the Spanish capital of Louisiana, obtained there the proper papers, and then returned to St. Louis and secured the powder.

The voyage up the Ohio was uneventful until the mouth of the Licking was reached. Here, on an October afternoon, several Indians were seen crossing the Ohio to the Kentucky shore, about a mile up stream. Rodgers believed that the Indians did not see his boats, and decided to halt and attack them. Pulling his boats on the beach in the mouth of the Licking, he penetrated the forest, where a strong force of Indians, led by Simon Girty and Matthew Elliott, outnumbering Rodgers' party two to one, surrounded the voyagers and killed the entire party except thirteen. The Indians who had been seen crossing the Ohio were only decoys. Captain Rodgers was fatally wounded but, by the help of John Knotts, was able to hide in a dark ravine, where Knotts left the dying man in the morning, and returned through the wilderness to Redstone. Afterwards an unsuccessful search was made for the body of Rodgers, which had probably been devoured by wolves.

Robert Benham, commissary of the expedition, was wounded in both legs, but crawled into a tree-top. Here, on the afternoon of the second day, suffering greatly from hunger, he shot a raccoon which came within range of his rifle. At the sound of his gun, he heard a voice which he believed to be the shout of an Indian, and at once re-loaded his rifle. Footsteps were heard approaching, and a white man covered with blood came out of the thicket. This was Basil Brown. He was wounded in the right arm and left shoulder, both arms being helpless. Benham pointed out the dead raccoon, and Brown kicked it to where Benham reclined, who built a fire, dressed and cooked the animal, and fed both Brown and himself. Benham then placed his folded hat between Brown's teeth, and the latter, wading into the Licking, dipped the hat into the water, and carried it full to his thirsty companion. During the days which followed, Brown would drive rabbits, wild turkey, and other game, within the range of Benham's rifle, and when the latter had shot them, Brown kicked them to the fire, and Benham dressed and cooked the game. Thus, these two men lived in the wilderness for nineteen days, when a flat boat descending the Ohio, rescued them, and took them to what is now Louisville, Kentucky. Brown returned to the Redstone settlement; but Benham, when the war was over, settled at the place which was the scene of Rodgers' disaster, the site of Newport, Kentucky.

CHAPTER XXXII.

Other Indian Events in Pennsylvania During the Revolutionary War
(Continued)

The Prowess of Mrs. Experience Bozarth

ABOUT the middle of March, 1779, several families who were afraid to stay at home, gathered at the house of Mrs. Experience Bozarth on Dunkard Creek, Greene County. About April 1st, a band of Indians made an attack upon the house, when all the men except two were absent. Some of the children, who were playing near the house, came running in great haste, saying that "there were ugly red men". One of the men in the house stepped to the door, receiving a bullet in his side, causing him to fall back into the house. The Indian who shot him came in over his prostrate body, and engaged the other man in the house. This man tossed the Indian on a bed, and called for a knife to kill him. Mrs. Bozarth not finding a knife, took up an axe that lay nearby, and with it knocked out the brains of this Indian. At the same instant, a second Indian entered the door, and shot the man dead who was struggling with the Indian on the bed. Mrs. Bozart immediately attacked this second Indian with her axe, giving him several large gashes which let his entrails appear. He bawled with pain. Then one of several other Indians who had been engaged in killing the children out of doors, rushed to the relief of the wounded Indian, and Mrs. Bozarth split his head open with her axe as he came through the door. Another Indian dragged the wounded and bellowing savage out of doors; whereupon Mrs. Bozarth with the assistance of the man who had been shot, but by this time was a little recovered, shut the door and fastened it. The inmates of the house kept garrison for several days until a relief party arrived. In the meantime, the dead white man and the dead Indian were both in the house with them.

Capture of Assemblyman James McKnight

On April 26th, 1779, James McKnight was captured by the Indians at Fort Freeland, located about four miles east of Watson-

town, Northumberland County.   He was a member of the general
Assembly of Pennsylvania, having been elected to that office in
1778.   The following letter written by Colonel Samuel Hunter
from Fort Augusta (Sunbury), on April 27th, 1779, gives an
account of this event and other outrages on the frontier:

"I am really sorry to inform you of our present disturbances;
not a day, but there is some of the enemy makes their appearances
on our frontiers.   On Sunday last, there was a party of savages
attacked the inhabitants that lived near Fort Jenkins, and had
taken two or three familys prisoners, but the garrison being
appris'd of it, about thirty men turned out of the fort and rescued
the prisoners; the Indians collecting themselves in a body drove
our men under cover of the fort, with the loss of three men kill'd
and four badly wounded; they burned several houses near the fort,
kill'd cattle, and drove off a number of horses.

"Yesterday there was another party of Indians, about thirty
or forty, kill'd and took seven of our militia, that was stationed at
a little Fort near Muncy Hill, call'd Fort Freeland; there was two
or three of the inhabitants taken prisoners; among the latter is
James McKnight, Esqr., one of our Assemblymen; the same day
a party of thirteen of the inhabitants that went to hunt their
horses, about four or five miles from Fort Muncy was fired upon
by a large party of Indians, and all taken or kill'd except one man.
Captain Walker, of the Continental Troops, who commands at
that post, turned out with thirty-four men to the place he heard
the firing, and found four men kill'd and scalped and supposes
they captured ye remaind'r.

"This is the way our frontiers is harrassed by a cruel savage
enemy, so that they cannot get any spring crops in to induce them
to stay in the county.   I am afraid in a very short time we shall
have no inhabitants above this place unless when General Hand
arrives here, he may order some of the troops at Wyoming down
on our frontiers; all Col. Hartley's Regiment, our two months'
men, and what militia we can turn out, is very inadequate to guard
our country.

"I am certain everything is doing for our relief, but afraid it
will be too late for this county, as it's impossible to prevail on the
inhabitants to make a stand, upon account of their women and
childer.

"Our case is really deplorable and alarming, and our county
on ye eve of breaking up, as I am informed at the time I am writing this by two or three expresses that there is nothing to be seen

but desolation, fire and smoke; as the inhabitants is collected at particular places, the enemy burns all their houses that they have evacuated."

The family of James McKnight had other terrible experiences with the Indians. In the autumn of 1778 Mrs. James McKnight and Mrs. Margaret Wilson Durham, each with an infant in her arms, started on horseback from Fort Freeland to go to Northumberland when, near the mouth of Warrior Run, about two miles from the fort, they were fired upon by a band of Indians and ambushed. Mrs. Durham's child was killed in her arms, and an Indian rushed out of the bushes and scalped her. Alexander Guffy, Peter Williams, and Ellis Williams hastened to the scene of the shooting, and were greatly surprised to find Mrs. Durham alive and piteously calling for water. These men bound up her head as best they could and conveyed her in a canoe down the river to Sunbury, where Colonel William Plunkett, who was also a physician, dressed her wounded head. She recovered and lived to the mature age of seventy-four years, dying in 1829.

Mrs. McKnight was not injured. Her horse became frightened at the shooting, and ran back to the fort. As the horse wheeled, Mrs. McKnight's child fell from her arms; but she caught it by the foot, and thus held it until the fort was reached. Two of Mrs. McKnight's sons, who were accompanying her and Mrs. Durham on foot, were captured, as was Mr. Durham. The father and the two boys were taken to Canada, and returned home after the close of the Revolutionary War.

Outrages in Westmoreland County in 1779

Early in the spring of 1779, the inhabitants of Westmoreland County suffered terribly from Indian raids. In the latter part of April, a band of Senecas entered the Ligonier Valley, killed one man, and carried two families into captivity. On April 26th, Fort Hand, garrisoned by seventeen men under Captain Samuel Moorhead and Lieutenant William Jack, was attacked, possibly by the same band, estimated to be one hundred strong. At one o'clock in the afternoon, the Indians fired upon two ploughmen, who escaped to the fort. Then the fort was attacked, several women within making bullets while the riflemen fired at the Indians. The firing was kept up until nightfall. In the meantime, three of the garrison were wounded, one of them fatally. This was Sergeant Philip McGray, who occupied a sentry box. He died in a few days.

After McGraw had been shot and removed, a man named Mc-Cauley, who took his place, was also wounded.

During the night, the Indians shot at the fort, and mimicked the sentinel's cry, "All's well." At midnight, they set fire to John McKibbon's barn near the fort, and the tories among them cried: "Is all well now?" During the night, a messenger was sent to Fort Pitt for aid. The Indians gave up the siege the next forenoon, and forty soldiers who were hurried from Fort Pitt, arrived too late to intercept them.

The dreadful situation of the Westmoreland settlers during that spring is seen in the following statement in a letter sent to President Reed by Archibald Lochry, from Hannastown, on May 1st: "The savages are continually making depredations among us. Not less than forty people have been killed, wounded, or captured this spring, and the enemy have killed our creatures within three hundred yards of this town."

Charles Clifford lived on Mill Creek, about two and one-half miles northward from Ligonier. On April 22nd, 1779, he and his two sons went to work in the field. Leaving his sons to continue the work, he went in search of his horses. After searching for some time without success, he reached the Forbes Road leading to the stockade near Laughlintown, when five Indians who lay concealed behind a log, shot at him. One bullet splintered his gun and cut his face, which bled freely, but otherwise he was unharmed. The Indians believed that Clifford was protected by the Great Spirit. They approached him, wiped the blood from his face, and told him that they were glad that they had not killed him. They then took him along with them, and when they had reached a point near Fairfield, Westmoreland County, they met fifty-two others proceeding northward, having with them a prisoner named Peter Maharg. The chief of this band wore many silver trinkets on his head and arms. After a while the two bands separated, Clifford going with one, and Maharg with the other. Clifford was carried to the Seneca region on the headwaters of the Allegheny, and after six weeks, was delivered to the British at Montreal. He was well liked by the British officers, and from one he secured a compass, which he gave to James Flock, who with it made his way back to his home in Westmoreland, where he had been captured sometime before. After two and one-half years, Clifford was exchanged and returned to his home in the Ligonier Valley.

This was not the only experience that the Clifford family had with the Indians. On the 18th of October, 1777, Clifford's son,

James, shot an Indian while hunting with a dog near Bunger's spring about a quarter of a mile from the fort at Ligonier. The Indian was not killed outright, and a party of militia immediately turned out from the fort to search for him. They traced him by blood on the path for about forty rods, at which point the Indian seems to have stopped the wound with leaves. They were unable to find him.

Atrocities in Union County

After the Great Runaway of July, 1778, a few of the most venturesome of the inhabitants returned to the valley of the West Branch of the Susquehanna. The following year, in May, the Indians entered Union County, and killed John Sample and his wife on White Deer Creek. There were about twenty Indians in this band. Christian VanGundy and Henry Vandyke, with a small force of settlers, hastened to the scene to bring away those who had survived the massacre. While quartered in the Sample home, Indians made an attack during the night, endeavoring to break down the door with a log, and setting fire to the roof. Those inside fired upon them wounding two, whom the other Indians carried off. VanGunday was wounded in the leg while extinguishing the fire, and one of his companions was shot in the face. At daybreak, they decided to leave the house and seek safety in flight. On opening the door, they found the leader of the Indian band lying dead in front of it. VanGundy took his rifle and Vandyke his powder horn. The other Indians then came from ambush. VanGundy, with his two rifles, hastened to a ravine, and endeavored to get the others to follow him. They refused to follow, and then the Indians killed and scalped the old people of the place. Colonel John Kelly led a party which came upon five of these Indians sitting upon a log. Four were killed at one volley, and the fifth escaped. On July 8th, Indians again entered this neighborhood, destroying the mill of the widow of Peter Smith, near the mouth of White Deer Creek, and killing one man in the attack. This was a famous grist, saw and boring mill. Here many gun barrels were bored for the Continental army.

The Battle of Minisink

One of the most hotly contested engagements of the Revolutionary War was the battle of Minisink, which was fought July 22nd, 1779. The place of the battle was what is now Port Jervis,

New York, just across the Delaware River from the town of Lackawaxon, Pike County, Pennsylvania. Early in July the Mohawk chief, Joseph Brant, with four hundred of his warriors, left the Susquehanna and approached the settlements on the Delaware. On the 19th of July the Tories who were with Brant's forces, disguised as Indians, came to the village of Minisink, now Port Jervis, and set fire to the town. The fort, the mill, and twelve houses and barns were burned, and several persons were killed. Most of the inhabitants fled to the mountains for safety. The Tories then took their prisoners and booty to Grassy Brook, where Brant had left the main body of his Indians.

In the meantime, a force of one hundred and fifty volunteers had assembled to pursue the invaders. Colonel Tuesten, fearing the craftiness and treachery of Brant, opposed pursuit, but was overruled. Then Major Meeker mounted his horse and shouted: "Let the brave follow me; cowards may stay behind."

On July 22nd, the pursuers came upon the Indian encampment of the previous night at Halfway Brook. The smouldering fires gave plain evidence that the savages were in great force, and the two colonels very prudently advised against further pursuit, but were overruled. A captain was then sent forward with a scouting party, but being discovered, was slain. The volunteers eagerly pressed forward, and at nine o'clock, saw the enemy marching in the direction of the fording place on the Delaware. In the meantime, Brant had deposited much of his plunder in Pike County. The commander of the volunteer troops then decided to intercept Brant's forces at the fording place, but the wily chieftain, comprehending the designs of the Americans, wheeled his columns and, by skillful movement, brought his whole force in the rear of the volunteers. Indeed, he had formed an ambuscade and deliberately selected a battle ground suitable for his purpose.

The Americans surprised and disappointed at not finding Brant's forces where they expected them, were marching back, when they encountered the Indians. Brant's forces greatly outnumbered the Americans and, to make matters worse, the ammunition of the latter was limited, making it necessary for them to fire, not at random, but to make every shot count. The engagement began at eleven o'clock, and when night fell it was still undecided. By that time, the ammunition of the Americans was almost expended, and their line was broken. The Americans then began a retreat. Dr. Tuesten, who was dressing the wounds of seventeen who were injured, was fallen upon, and he and the entire seventeen were killed.   Many were shot while swimming the river. Some escaped under the cover of darkness.   A few succeeded in reaching the wilds of Pike County.   Only thirty of the force of one hundred and fifty that went out to battle, returned to tell the story of the engagement.   "The massacre of the wounded Americans", says Frederic A. Godcharles, "is one of the darkest stains upon the memory of Brant whose honor and humanity were often more conspicious than that of his Tory allies."

Capture of Fort Freeland

As related presently, General John Sullivan was sent by General Washington, in the summer of 1779, with an army to invade the territory of the Six Nations, in New York.   No sooner had General Sullivan started on his march from Easton than the Indians learned of his plan and, assisted by the Tories, took measures to defeat the expedition.   Captain John MacDonald, a Tory in command of a force of British and three hundred Senecas, marched from the vicinity of Wyalusing, Bradford County, and attacked the garrison at Fort Freeland on July 28th, where many settlers had gathered for protection.   The firing on the fort could be distinctly heard at Fort Boone, located about a mile above the town of Milton, Northumberland County; whereupon, Captain Hawkins Boone, a cousin of the famous Daniel Boone, hastened from the fort with a detail of thirty-two soldiers to the relief of the defenders at Fort Freeland.   However, in a few hours Fort Freeland was a mass of ruins, and its gallant defenders were either tomahawked or taken prisoners.   It is said that the resistance was so stubborn that the articles of capitulation were not accepted until Captain MacDonald had made the third proposal, and not even then, until all the ammunition in the fort was exhausted, the women even melting the pewter into bullets while the men fired them at the British and Indians.

Upon the surrender of the fort, the British and Indians gathered together the provisions and proceeded to the creek, where they made preparations for a feast.   While they were feasting Captain Boone's party arrived on the opposite bank of the creek and fired a volley into the midst of the revelers, killing about thirty of them. However, the British and Indians soon rallied and surrounded Boone's forces, killing thirteen of them, among whom was Captain Boone himself.   As a result of the capture of Fort Freeland, one hundred and eight settlers were killed or taken prisoner.   The enemy then ravaged the country in the vicinity, advancing as far as Milton, and burning everything before them.

Fifty-two women and children, and four old men were permitted by the British commander to go to Fort Augusta. The captives were taken to Niagara. The few who survived the hardships of the terrible march through the wilderness and the sufferings of long imprisonment, returned to the surviving members of their families after the close of the Revolutionary War.

The capture of Fort Freeland and the ravaging of the country in the vicinity was not strictly an Indian incursion. The Senecas under Hickatoo, the husband of Mary Jemison, White Woman of Genesee, were simply allies of the British detachment commanded by Captain John MacDonald.

General Sullivan's Expedition Against the Six Nations

General Washington, exasperated at the continued outrages of the Six Nations, determined that the power of that great Confederacy should be broken. Accordingly, in the summer of 1779, he sent General John Sullivan into the Iroquois country in Northeastern Pennsylvania and Southern New York with an army of five thousand men. Sullivan rendezvoused at Easton May 26th. His line of march passed through Wyoming, Tunkhannock, Wyalusing, Sheshecunk, Tioga, and Chemung. At Newtown on the present site of Elmira, New York, the Indians, fifteen hundred strong, under Joe Brant and Captain John McDonald, and the British and Tories, under Colonel John Butler and the two Johnsons, made a determined stand, on August 29th, but were overwhelmingly defeated. Sullivan then marched through the heart of the territory of the Six Nations, burning their houses, destroying their corn, killing their cattle, and felling their orchards which had been growing for generations. Terrible was the retribution which he visited upon them for siding with the British and devastating the American frontier.

We quote the following account of Sullivan's Expedition from Headley's "Washington and His Generals":

"Our Revolution called forth every variety of talent, and tried it in every mode of warfare. Perhaps there never was a war into which such various elements entered. We had not only to organize a government and army, with which to meet a powerful antagonist, and also quench the flames of civil war in our own land, but were compelled to meet a cloud of savages on their own field of battle—the impenetrable forest—and in their own way. The English enlisted them against us by promises of plunder, and appealing to their revenge; while their own bitter hatred prompted them to take advantage of the defenseless state of our frontiers, to fall on our settlements and massacre our people.

"The tragedies which were enacted at Cherry Valley and Wyoming, with all the heart-sickening details and bloody passages, finally aroused our government to a vigorous effort. Washington, being directed to adopt measures to punish these atrocities and secure our frontiers, ordered Sullivan to take an army and invade the Indian territories. The Six Nations, lying along the Susquehanna and around our inland lakes, extending to the Genesee flats, were to be the objects of this attack. His orders were to burn their villages, destroy their grain, and lay waste their land.

"A partisan warfare had been long carried on between the border inhabitants and the Indians, in which there had been an exhibition of bravery, hardihood, and spirit of adventure never surpassed. The pages of romance furnish no such thrilling narrative, examples of female heroism, and patient suffering, and such touching incidents as the history of our border war. For personal prowess, manly courage, and adventure, nothing can exceed it. Yet it had hitherto been a sort of hand-to-hand fighting, a measuring of the Indian's agility and cunning against the white man's strength and boldness; but now a large army, with a skillful commander at its head, was to sweep down everything in its passage.

"The plan adopted was for the main army to rendezvous at Wyoming, and from thence ascend into the enemy's country, while General James Clinton, advancing with one brigade along the Mohawk west, was to form a junction with it, wherever Sullivan should direct. The first of May, 1779, the troops commenced their march, but did not arrive at Wyoming till the middle of June. It was a slow and toilsome business for an army to cut roads, bridge marshes, and transport artillery and baggage through the wide expanse of forest between the Delaware and Susquehanna. At length, however, the whole force assembled at Wyoming; and on the thirty-first of July took their final departure.

"So imposing a spectacle those solitudes never before witnessed. An army of three thousand men slowly wound along the picturesque banks of the Susquehanna—now their variegated uniforms sprinkling the open fields with gay colors, and anon their glittering bayonets fringing the dark forest with light; while by their side floated a hundred and fifty boats, laden with cannon and stores—slowly stemming the sluggish stream. Officers dashing along in their uniforms, and small bodies of horse between the columns, completed the scene—while exciting strains of marital music rose and fell in prolonged cadences on the summer air, and swept, dying away, into the deep solitudes. The gay song of the oarsman, as he bent to his toil, mingled in the hoarse words of command; and like some wizard creation of the American wilderness, the mighty pageant passed slowly along. The hawk flew screaming from his eyrie at the sight; and the Indian gazed with wonder and affright, as he watched it from the mountain-top, winding miles and miles through the sweet valley, or caught from afar the deafening roll of the drums and shrill blast of the bugle. At night the boats were moored to the shore, and the army encamped beside them—the innumerable watchfires stretching for miles along the river. As the morning sun rose over the green forest, the drums beat the reveille throughout the camp, and again the pageant of the day before commenced. Everything was in the freshness of summer vegetation, and the great forest rolled its sea of foliage over their heads, affording a welcome shelter from the heat of an August sun.

"Thus, day after day, this host toiled forward, and on the twelfth from the date of their march, reached Tioga. Here they entered on the Indian settlements and the work of devastation commenced. Here also Clinton, coming down the Susquehanna, joined them with his brigade—and when the head of his column came in sight of the main army, and the boats floated into view, there went up such a shout as never before shook that wilderness.

"Sullivan, in the meantime, had destroyed the village of Chemung; and Clinton, on his passage, had laid waste the settlement of the Onondagas. The whole army, now amounting to nearly five thousand men, marched on the 26th of August up the Tioga River, destroying as it went. At Newtown the Indians made a stand. From the river to a ridge of hills, they had thrown up a breastwork a mile in extent, and thus defended, boldly withstood for two hours a heavy fire of artillery; but being at length attacked in flank by General Poor, they broke and fled. The village was immediately set on fire, and the rich fields of corn cut down and trodden under foot.

"On the first of September the army left the river, and struck across the wilderness, to Catherine's Town. Night overtook them in the middle of a swamp, nine miles wide; and the rear guard, without packs or baggage, were compelled to pass the whole night on the marshy ground. This town also was burned, and the fields ravaged. Having reached Seneca Lake, they followed its shores northward, to Kendaia, a beautiful Indian village, with painted houses, and monuments for the dead, and richly cultivated fields. It smiled like an oasis there in the wilderness; but the smoke of the conflagration soon wrapped it, and when the sun again shone upon it, a smoldering heap alone remained—the waving corn had disappeared with the dwellings, and the cattle lay slaughtered around.

"Our troops moved like an awful, resistless scourge through this rich country—open and fruitful fields and smiling villages were before them—behind them a ruinous waste. Now and then, detachments sent off from the main body were attacked, and on one occasion seven slain; and once or twice the Indians threatened to make a stand for their homes, but soon fled in despair, and the army had it all their own way. The capital of the Senecas, a town consisting of sixty houses, surrounded with beautiful cornfields and orchards, was burned to the ground, and the harvest destroyed. Canandaigua fell next, and then the army stretched away for the Genesee flats. The fourth day it reached this beautiful region, then almost wholly unknown to the white man. The valley, twenty miles long and four broad, had scarce a forest tree in it, and presented one of the most beautiful contrasts to the surrounding wilderness that could well be conceived.

"As the weary columns slowly emerged from the dark forest, and filed off into this open space, their admiration and astonishment knew no bounds. They seemed suddenly to have been transported into an Eden. The tall, ripe grass bent before the wind—cornfield on cornfield, as far as the eye could reach, waved in the sunlight—orchards that had been growing for generations, were weighed down under the profusion of fruit—cattle grazed on the banks of the river, and all was luxuriance and beauty. In the midst of this garden of nature, where the gifts of Heaven had been lavished with such prodigality, were scattered a hundred and twenty-eight houses—not miserable huts, huddled together, but large, airy buildings, situated in the most pleasant spots, surrounded with fruit trees, and exhibiting a civilization on the part of the Indians never before witnessed.

"Into this scene of surpassing loveliness the sword of war had now entered, and the approach of Sullivan's vast army, accompanied with the loud beat of the drum and shrill fife, sent consternation through the hearts of the inhabitants. At first they seemed resolved to defend their homes; but soon, as all the rest had done, turned and fled in affright. Not a soul remained behind; and Sullivan marched into a deserted, silent village. His heart relented at the sight of so much beauty; but his commands were peremptory. The soldiers thought, too, of Wyoming and Cherry Valley, and the thousand massacres that had made our borders flow in blood, and their hearts were steeled against pity. An enemy who felt no obligations, and kept no faith, must be placed beyond the reach of inflicting injury.

"At evening, that army of five thousand men encamped in the village; and just as the sun went down behind the limitless forest, a group of officers might be seen, flooded by its farewell beams, gazing on the scene. While they thus stood conversing, suddenly there rolled by a dull and heavy sound, which startled them into an attitude of the deepest attention. There was no mistaking that report—it was the thunder of cannon—and for a moment they looked on each other with anxious countenances. That solitary roar, slowly traversing the mighty solitudes that hemmed them in, might well awaken the deepest solicitude. But it was not repeated; and night fell on the valley of Genesee, and the tired army slept. The next morning, as the sun rose over the wilderness, that heavy echo again shook the ground. It was then discovered to be the morning and evening gun of the British at Niagara; and its lonely thunder there made the solitude more fearful.

"Soon after sunrise, immense columns of smoke began to rise the length and breadth of the valley, and in a short time the whole settlement was wrapt in flame from limit to limit; and before night those hundred and twenty-eight houses were a heap of ashes. The grain had been gathered into them, and thus both were destroyed together. The orchards were cut down, the cornfields uprooted, and the cattle butchered and left to rot on the plain. A scene of desolation took the place of that scene of beauty, and the army encamped at night in a desert.

"The next day, having accomplished the object of his mission, Sullivan commenced his homeward march. Ah! who can tell the famine, and disease, and suffering of those homeless Indians during the next winter? A few built huts amid the ashes of their former dwellings, but the greater part passed the winter around Fort Niagara.

"On the fifteenth of October, after having been absent since the first of May, or five months and a half, the army again reached Easton. Two hundred and eighty miles had been traversed over mountains, through forests, across swamps and rivers, and amid hostile Indians. The thanks of Congress were presented to Sullivan and his army for the manner they had fulfilled their arduous task."

The great Confederacy of the Six Nations never recovered from the terrible blow dealt them by General Sullivan. The following winter is known as "the winter of the deep snow", and was perhaps the severest winter in the history of the United States. In January, New York harbor was frozen over so solidly that the British drove laden wagons on the ice from the city to Staten Island. One heavy snowstorm followed another, and by February first, the snow lay four feet deep in the woods and mountains of Pennsylvania and New York. Their food supplies destroyed by Sullivan's army, great numbers of the Iroquois starved and froze to death during this terrible winter.

Lieutenant Samuel Brady Rescues Mrs. Jennie Stoops

The spring of 1780 had scarcely opened when the Indians began their incursions into the Western Pennsylvania settlements. On Sunday morning, March 12th, a party of Wyandots, falling upon five men and six children at a sugar camp on Raccoon Creek, in southern Beaver County, killed the men, and captured the children, three boys and three girls. Near the end of this month, a band of the Munsee Clan of Delawares, led by Washnash, captured a flatboat going down the Ohio River to Kentucky, killing three men and making prisoners of twenty-one men, women, and children.

Early in May, Colonel Broadhead, then in command at Fort Pitt, sent Godfrey Lanctot, a Frenchman, who spoke several Indian languages, to visit the Shawnees, Wyandots, and Delawares of the Munsee Clan in Ohio, in an effort to make peace; but his efforts were fruitless. During the same month the Senecas coming down the Allegheny invaded Westmoreland County, where they killed and captured five prisoners near Ligonier, burned Laughlin's Mill, killed two men on Bushy Run, and two on Braddock's Road near Turtle Creek.

Colonel Broadhead then received a report that an army of British and Indians was assembling on the Sandusky River in Ohio, intending to attack Fort Pitt. Accordingly, he directed Lieutenant (later Captain) Samuel Brady to go to Sandusky with a few scouts, in order to learn the plans of the proposed expedition

against Fort Pitt. Late in May, Brady set out for Sandusky with
five white companions and two Delawares, the whole company being dressed and painted like Indians. When Brady's company
approached the Wyandot country, they traveled only by night,
hiding in the forests by day. One of the Delawares became faint-
hearted and returned to Fort Pitt.

When Brady and his remaining companions drew near the
Wyandot capital near upper Sandusky, he and one Delaware
companion waded to a wooded island opposite the Indian town,
where they lay all the next day watching the Indians enjoy a horse
race near the bank of the river. They found the town full of
warriors. The indications were that the savages were preparing
for the warpath. During the night Brady and his companion rejoined the others, and started toward Fort Pitt. When they had
reached a point about two miles from Sandusky, they captured
two Indian maidens at a camp, and took them along, believing
that they might divulge valuable information. At the end of six
days, one of these squaws escaped. The food supply of Brady
and his men was now exhausted, and for an entire week they had
nothing to eat but berries. Brady succeeded in shooting an
otter; but even these hungry frontiersmen could not eat the rank
flesh.

When Brady and his companions reached a point near the old
Indian town of Kuskuskies, at the junction of the Mahoning and
Shenango rivers, in Lawrence County, Brady saw a deer and
attempted to shoot it; but his gun flashed in the pan. He was
preparing again to fire, when he heard the voices of Indians. Concealing himself, he saw an Indian captain riding a grey horse
followed by six warriors on foot, coming along the Indian trail.
On the same horse with the Indian captain, were a captive white
woman and her child, the woman riding behind the Indian, who
held her child in his arms. Brady at once recognized the woman
as Mrs. Jennie Stoops, who had been captured some time before on
Chartier's Creek, at a point near the present town of Crafton,
Allegheny County. Taking careful aim Brady shot the Indian
captain through the head. The savage fell from his horse, dragging the woman and child with him. Brady then dashed forward
shouting for his men to come on. The hostile Indians being surprised at the sudden death of their leader, fired a few shots, and
then fled. Being dressed like an Indian, Mrs. Stoops did not
recognize Lieutenant Brady, but thought him an Indian. "Why
did you shoot your brother?" she asked. Brady took the child in

his arms, saying, "Jennie Stoops, I am Captain Brady; follow me, and I will secure you and your child." Taking Mrs. Stoops by the hand and the child in his arms, Brady hastened into the thicket, where he found his companions cowering in fear, who had let the other Indian squaw escape.

After going a few miles further along the trail toward Fort McIntosh (now Beaver), Brady and his scouts met a band of settlers from the Chartier's Valley, pursuing the captors of Mrs. Stoops and her child. Mrs. Stoops and her infant were then restored unharmed to the husband and father; and Brady returned to the scene of the adventure, where he found and scalped the Wyandot captain.

Outrages in the Wyoming Valley in 1780

Terrible as was the retribution which General Sullivan visited upon the Six Nations in the summer of 1779, it did not prevent their entering the Wyoming Valley the next spring, and bringing terrible suffering to the settlers of Luzerne County. This incursion is thus described in Miner's "History of Wyoming":

"In the latter part of March an alarm was given that Indians were in the valley. On the 27th, Thomas Bennett and his son, a lad, in a field not far from their house, in Kingston, were seized and made prisoners by six Indians. Lebbeus Hammond, who had been captured a few hours before, they found tied as they entered a gorge of the mountain. Hammond had been in the battle, [the Wyoming Massacre of July 3rd, 1778] and was then taken prisoner, but had escaped from the fatal ring at bloody rock, where Queen Esther was pursuing her murderous rounds as previously related. He was a prize of more than ordinary value. No doubt could exist but that he was destined a victim to the cruelest barbarity. The night of the 27th they took up their quarters about twelve miles north from the valley. The next day, having crossed the river near the three islands, they pushed on toward Meshoppen with all the speed in their power. While on their march they met two parties of Indians and Tories, descending for murder and pillage upon the settlement. A man by the name of Moses Mount, whom they knew, was particular in his inquiries into the state of the garrison and the situation of the inhabitants. On the evening of the 28th they built a fire, with the aid of Mr. Bennett, who being an old man, was least feared, and permitted to go unbound. To a request from Mr. Bennett, of the Chief, to lend him an awl to put on a button, the savage, with a significant look replied, 'No want button for one night,' and refused his request. The purpose of the Indians could not be mistaken. Whispering to Hammond, while the Indians went to a spring near by, to drink, it was resolved to make an effort to escape. To stay was certain death; they could but die. Tired with their heavy march, after a supper of venison, the Indians lay around the fire, Hammond and the boy tied between them, except an old Indian who was set to keep the first watch. His spear lay by his side, while he picked the meat from the head of a deer, as half sleeping and nodding, he sat over the fire. Bennett was allowed to sit near him, and seemingly in a careless manner, took the spear, and rolled it playfully on his thigh. Watching his opportunity when least on his guard, he thrust the spear through the Indian's side, who fell with a startling groan upon the burning logs. There was not a moment to be lost. Age forgot its decrepitude. In an instant Hammond and young Bennet were cut loose, the arms seized, three of the remaining savages tomahawked, and slain as they slept, and another wounded. One only escaped unhurt. On the evening of the 30th the captive victors came in with five rifles, a silver mounted hanger, and several spears and blankets, as trophies of their brilliant exploit.

"Another band of ten Indians, on the same day that Bennett and Hammond were taken, shot Asa Upson in Hanover, (near where the bridge crosses the canal below Carey-Town). On the 28th, two men were making sugar about eight miles below Wilkesbarre, one was killed, the other taken prisoner. On the 29th, Jonah Rogers, a lad of fourteen or fifteen, was taken prisoner from the lower part of the valley. The Indians then pushed down the river to Fishing Creek, where, on the 30th they surprised the family of the Van Campens. Moses Van Campen was taken prisoner after they had murdered and scalped his father, his brother, and his uncle, and captured a boy named Pence. Directing their course northeast, the savages passed through Huntington, where they were met by a scout of four men under the orders of Capt. Franklin. Shots were exchanged, and two of his men wounded. Too few to cope with the Indian party, Capt. Franklin took up a position in an old log house; but the enemy preferred to pursue their course, and the same evening came to a camp where Abraham Pike, with his wife, were making sugar. Pike, who was a British deserter, was a most desirable acquisition. The wife and her child they painted, and sent into the settlements. The party now bent their way to the lake country, crossed the Susquehanna at the little Tunkhannock, and pursued their course up the east branch of the river.

"Lieut. Van Campen, a man of true courage, brave and enterprising, formed a plan, with Pike, Rogers, and Pence, to rise on the ten Indians, and effect their liberation, or die in the attempt. It was a bold and hazardous enterprise. The party had ascended to within fifteen miles of Tioga Point, where they encamped on the night of the 3rd of April. The Indians, beyond the probability of pursuit, all lay down to sleep, five on each side of the prisoners, who were carefully bound. Van Campen had observed that a knife, used by one of the Indians, fell near him, and placing his foot on it, secured the inestimable prize. About midnight, finding the enemy buried in profound sleep, Van Campen cut himself loose, and with noiseless celerity liberated the hands of his companions. Springing to their feet, placing the guns in a secure place, tomahawks were used with the utmost vigour. The Indians made a desperate, but unavailing effort for the mastery, but were overpowered, and several of the ten killed, two others wounded, and two or three escaped unhurt. After scalping the dead, recovering the scalps of those of our people whom the Indians had slain, making a hasty raft, the party, taking the guns, tomahawks, spears, and blankets of the foe, descended the Susquehanna, and on the evening of the 5th of April arrived with their spoils in triumph at Wyoming.

"No nobler deed was performed during the Revolutionary war. In a narrative of his life and services, written in 1837, and presented as a memorial to Congress, asking for a pension, Lieut. Van Campen represents his companions in this affair, except Pence, as terrified and inactive, thus impairing his own credit, and marring the beauty of a most chivalrous achievement. There was honour enough for all; there could be no motive but excessive self-glorification, for representing Pike and Rogers as cowards. But when that narrative was written Van Campen was an old man, Pike and Rogers were both dead, and he may have supposed no one remained to rescue their names from the odium. The writer of this knew Abraham Pike and Jonah Rogers well. Mr. Rogers was a highly respectable citizen, and was well understood, though quite a youth, to have performed his duty like a man. That he was collected and cool is evident from his observing that Pike struck his first blow with the head of his axe, then turned it and gave the edge. The former he has often heard recount the daring exploit, and until this recent statement of Van Campen, never heard a doubt of Pike's courage expressed. Familiarly he was called 'Serjeant Pike, the Indian killer,' and as such was every where welcome. An Irishman! A regularly disciplined soldier! The presumption would be strong against the charge of cowardice. But death was certain if taken to Niagara; even cowardice itself would have stimulated a man, so situated, to fight. That Van Campen's memory had become impaired, is apparent from the fact that he claimed to have killed nine of the ten Indians. Col. Jenkins, in a memorandum made at the time says: 'Pike and two men from Fishing Creek, and two boys that were taken by the Indians, made their escape by rising on the guard, killed three, and the rest took to the woods, and left the prisoners with twelve guns,' &c. No! without detracting from the bravery and good conduct of Van Campen, we cannot but conclude, that he had told the story of his own prowess, heightening the colouring in his own favour, as he found it gave him consideration with his wondering listeners, until, perhaps, he believed himself the sole hero of the victory.

"On the 30th of March, three persons, named Avery, Lyons, and Jones, were taken prisoners by the Indians, from Capouse.

"The unfortunate, or fortunate Hammond, who, twice in such fearful jeopardy, had twice escaped, had now the pleasure of appearing at Head-Quarters, having been sent on the 3rd of April, by Col. Butler, express, with despatches for his Excellency.

"In the course of these predatory excursions, the savages set fire to the simple log buildings which the settlers had erected for their temporary residence."

Capture of the Gilbert Family

On April 25th, 1780, occurred the capture of the family of Benjamin Gilbert, in what is now Carbon County. The following account of this event is quoted from Egle's, "History of Pennsylvania":

"As late as 1780 the Gilbert family, living on Mahoning Creek, five or six miles from Fort Allen, were carried into a bitterly painful captivity by a party of Indians, who took them to Canada, and there separated them. At the time of its occurrence, this event caused intense excitement throughout the State, and from an interesting narrative published shortly after their release from captivity, we append the following synopsis:

"Benjamin Gilbert, a Quaker from Byberry, near Philadelphia, in 1775, removed with his family to a farm on Mahoning creek, five or six miles from Fort Allen. His second wife was a widow Peart. They were comfortably situated, with a good log dwelling-house, barn, and saw and grist mill. For five years this peaceable family went on industriously and prosperously; but on the 25th of April, 1780, the very year after Sullivan's expedition, they were surprised about sunrise by a party of eleven Indians, who took them all prisoners. At the Gilbert farm they made captives of Benjamin Gilbert, Sr., aged 69 years; Elizabeth, his wife, 55; Joseph Gilbert, his son, 41; Jesse Gilbert; another son, 19; Sarah Gilbert, wife to Jesse, 19; Rebecca Gilbert, a daughter, 16; Abner Gilbert, a son, 14; Elizabeth Gilbert, a daughter, 12; Thomas Peart, son to Benjamin Gilbert's wife, 23; Benjamin Gilbert, a son of John Gilbert of Philadelphia, 11; Andrew Harrigar, of German descent, 26; a hireling of Benjamin Gilbert's; and Abigail Dodson, 14, a daughter of Samuel Dodson, who lived on a farm about one mile from Gilbert's mill. The whole number taken at Gilbert's was twelve. The Indians then proceeded about half a mile to Benjamin Peart's dwelling, and there captured himself, aged 27; Elizabeth, his wife, 20, and their child, nine months old.

"The last look the poor captives had of their once comfortable home was to see the flames and falling in of the roofs, from Summer Hill. The Indians led their captives on a toilsome road over Mauch Chunk and Broad mountains into the Nescopec path, and then across Quakake creek and the Moravian pine swamp to Mahoning Mountain where they lodged the first night. On their way they had prepared moccasins for some of the children. Indians generally secure their prisoners by cutting down a sapling as large as a man's thigh, and therein cut notches in which they fix their legs, and over this they place a pole, crossing it with stakes drove in the ground, and on the crotches of the stakes they place other poles or riders, effectually confining the prisoners on their backs; and besides all this they put a strap round their necks, which they fasten to a tree. In this manner the night passed with the Gilbert family. Their beds were hemlock branches strewed on the ground, and blankets for a covering. Andrew Montour was the leader of the Indian party. [Not the son of Madam Montour].

"The forlorn band were dragged on over the wild and rugged region between the Lehigh and the Chemung branch of the Susquehanna. They were often ready to faint by the way, but the cruel threat of immediate death urged them again to the march. The old man, Benjamin Gilbert, indeed, had begun to fail, and had been painted black—a fatal omen among the Indians; but when his cruel captors had put a rope around his neck, and appeared about to kill him, the intercessions of his wife softened their hearts, and he was saved. Subsequently, in Canada, the old man, conversing with the chief, observed that he might say what none of the other Indians could, 'that he had brought in the oldest man and the youngest child.' The chief's reply was impressive: 'It was not I, but the great God, who brought you through; for we were determined to kill you, but were prevented.'

"On the fifty-fourth day of their captivity, the Gilbert family had to encounter the fearful ordeal of the gauntlet. 'The prisoners,' says the author of the narrative, 'were released from the heavy loads they had heretofore been compelled to carry, and were it not for the treatment they expected on their approaching the Indian towns, and the hardship of separation, their situation would have been tolerable; but the horror of their minds, arising from the dreadful yells of the Indians as they approached the hamlets, is easier conceived than described—for they were no strangers to the customary cruelty exercised upon the captives on entering their towns. The Indians—men, women, and children—collected together, bringing clubs and stones in order to beat them, which they usually do with great severity, by way of revenge for their relations who have been slain. This is performed immediately upon their entering the village where the warriors reside, and cannot be avoided; the blows, however cruel, must be borne without complaint. The prisoners are sorely beaten until their enemies are weary with the cruel sport. Their sufferings were in this case very great; they received several wounds, and two of the women who were on horseback were much bruised by falling from their horses, which were frightened by the Indians. Elizabeth, the mother, took shelter by the side of one of them (a warrior), but upon his observing that she met with some favor upon his account, he sent her away; she then received several violent blows, so that she was almost disabled. The blood trickled from their heads in a stream, their hair being cropped close, and the clothes they had on in rags, made their situation truly piteous. Whilst the Indians were inflicting this revenge upon the captives, the chief came and put a stop to any further cruelty by telling them 'it was sufficient,' which they immediately attended to.

"Soon after this a severer trial awaited them. They were separated from each other. Some were given over to Indians to be adopted, others were hired out by their Indian owners to service in white families, and others were sent down the lake to Montreal. Among the latter was the old patriarch, Benjamin Gilbert. But the old man, accustomed to the comforts of civilized life, broken in body and mind from such unexpected calamities, sunk under the complication of woe and hardship. His remains were interred at the foot of an oak near the old fort of Coeur du Lac, on the St. Lawrence, below Ogdensburg. Some of the family met with kind treatment from the hands of British officers at Montreal, who were interested in their story, and exerted themselves to release them from captivity.

"Sarah Gilbert, the wife of Jesse, becoming a mother, Elizabeth left the service she was engaged in—Jesse having taken a house— that she might give her daughter ever necessary attendance. In order to make their situation as comfortable as possible, they took a child to nurse, which added a little to their income. After this, Elizabeth Gilbert hired herself to iron a day for Adam Scott. While she was at her work, a little girl belonging to the house acquainted her that there were some who wanted to see her, and upon entering the room, she found six of her children. The joy and surprise she felt on this occasion were beyond what we shall attempt to describe. A messenger was sent to inform Jesse and his wife that Joseph Gilbert, Benjamin Peart, Elizabeth his wife, and their young child, and Abner and Elizabeth Gilbert the younger, were with their mother.

"Among the customs, or indeed common laws, of the Indian tribes, one of the most remarkable and interesting was adoption of prisoners. This right belonged more particularly to the females than to the warriors, and well was it for the prisoners that the election depended rather upon the voice of the mother than on that of the father, as innumerable lives were thus spared whom the warriors would have immolated. When once adopted, if the captives assume a cheerful aspect, entered into their modes of life, learned their language, and, in brief, acted as if they actually felt themselves adopted, all hardship was removed not incident to Indian modes of life. But, if this change of relation operated as amelioration of condition in the life of the prisoner, it rendered ransom extremely difficult in all cases, and in some instances precluded it altogether. These difficulties were exemplified in a striking manner in the person of Elizabeth Gilbert the younger. This girl, only twelve years of age when captured, was adopted by an Indian family, but afterwards permitted to reside in a white family of the name of Secord, by whom she was treated as a child indeed, and to whom she became so much attached as to call Mrs. Secord by the endearing title of mamma. Her residence, however, in a white family, was a favor granted to the Secords by the Indian parents of Elizabeth, who regarded and claimed her as their child. Mr. Secord having business at Niagara, took Betsy, as she was called, with him; and there after long separation, she had the happiness to meet with six of her relations, most of whom had been already released and were preparing to set out for Montreal, lingering and yearning for those they seemed destined to leave behind, perhaps for ever. The sight of their beloved little sister roused every energy to effect her release, which desire was generously seconded by John Secord and Colonel Butler, who, soon after her visit to Niagara, sent for the Indian who claimed Elizabeth, and made overtures for her ransom. At first he declared that he 'would not sell his own flesh and blood;' but, attacked through his interest, or in other words, his necessities, the negotiations succeeded, and, as we have already seen, her youngest child was among the treasures first restored to the mother at Montreal.

Eventually they were all redeemed and collected at Montreal on the 22nd of August, 1782, when they took leave of their kind friends there, and returned to Byberry, after a captivity of two years and five months."

Pennsylvania Again Offers Bounties for Scalps

In Chapter XVI, we saw that Pennsylvania offered bounties for Indian scalps during the French and Indian War, the proclamation being made on April 14th, 1756. Also, in Chapter XXV, we saw that the Province offered similar bounties during the Pontiac and Guyasuta War, this proclamation being made on July 7th, 1764. Likewise, we saw in Chapters XXV and XXXI, that the British General, Henry Hamilton, "the hair buyer", who was in charge of operations against the American frontier during the Revolutionary War, gave his Indian allies fifty dollars for each American scalp they were able to get. Now, when the Indians in alliance with the British, urged on by the substantial bounties which the British and Tory commanders at Detroit and in New York were giving for American scalps, even the scalps of babes, were making the soil of the land of Penn red with the blood of its inhabitants, combatants and non-combatants alike, and torturing many of them to death in the Indian villages, Pennsylvania again offered bounties for Indian scalps. Colonel Samuel Hunter and Colonel Jacob Stroud were authorized to offer these rewards.

On April 7th, 1780, President Reed wrote Colonel Hunter as follows: "The council would and do for this purpose authorize you to offer the following premiums for every male prisoner whether white or Indian, if the former is acting with the latter, Fifteen Hundred Dollars, and One Thousand Dollars for every Indian scalp". And on April 11, 1780, he wrote to Colonel Jacob Stroud, "We have therefore authorized Lieutenant of the county (Northampton) to offer Fifteen Hundred Dollars for every Indian or Tory prisoner taken in arms against us, and One Thousand Dollars for every Indian scalp."

On June 27th, 1780, Colonel Hunter wrote to President Reed from Sunbury, stating that several small parties have "made attempts to get scalps or prisoners agreeable to the proclamation, but have returned without success in that way." President Reed then replied with a letter of "condolence", in which he said: "We are sorry to hear the attempts which have been made to get scalps and prisoners have been so unsuccessful and hope perseverance will in time produce better effects". "Better effects" were presently "produced". Many scalping parties were organized, which were quite successful. On one occasion thirteen scalps were sent to Fort Pitt in one package. Moreover, the scalp bounty law was brought into disrepute by the killing of friendly Indians to sell their scalps.

Captain Samuel Brady was a recipient of scalp bounties. In the minutes of a meeting of the Provincial Council on February 19th, 1781, we find an order to Colonel Lochry, Lieutenant of Westmoreland County, "for the sum of twelve pounds, ten shillings, state money, to be paid to Captain Samuel Brady as a reward for an Indian's scalp, agreeable to a late proclamation of this board."

Finally, when General Sir Guy Carleton, in the autumn of 1782, shocked by the cruel burning of Colonel William Crawford and other American prisoners, put an end to the British alliance with the Indians, Pennsylvania no longer gave money for the scalps of the Indians.

Outrages in Allegheny and Washington Counties

On September 4th, 1780, two settlers were killed near Robinson's Run, in Allegheny County, and on the same day, two men descending the Ohio in a canoe, were fired upon, and one of them was wounded. About the middle of September, the Wyandots killed and captured ten settlers on Ten Mile Creek, Washington County.

Attack on Stock Family

One of the principal Indian outrages of the Revolutionary War was the attack on the Stock, or Stuck, family near Selinsgrove, Snyder County, in 1781. Three of the sons of Mr. Stock were at work in a field when a band of thirty Indians appeared. The Indians did not attack these three, but found another son ploughing in the field, whom they killed. They then entered the Stock home, occupied at the time by Mrs. Stock and her daughter-in-law. Mrs. Stock defended herself with a canoe pole, in the meantime retreating toward the field where Mr. Stock was working. The Indians overtook her, however, and sank a tomahawk into her brain. Then, after plundering the house, they carried the daughter-in-law into the woods, and killed and scalped her.

When Mr. Stock returned and found the mutilated bodies of his wife, son, and daughter-in-law, he gave the alarm. Then Michael Grove, John Stroh, and Peter Pence pursued the enemy, coming upon them encamped on the North Branch of the Susquehanna on the side of the hill covered with fern. Grove crept close enough to the Indian band to discover that their rifles were stacked around a tree, and that all but three of the Indians were asleep. One was telling his companions in great glee how poor Mrs. Stock defended herself with the canoe pole. Lying quiet until all the Indians were asleep, Grove then returned to Stroh and Pence. The three frontiersmen then decided to attack, and creeping close to the camp, they dashed among the sleeping Indians, Grove applying his deadly tomahawk, while Stroh and Pence seized the rifles and fired among the sleeping warriors. After several Indians were killed the others, believing that they were attacked by a large force, fled into the forest. A captive white boy was liberated on this occasion, and the frontiersmen returned with the scalps of the slain Indians and their best rifles.

Colonel Lochry's Unfortunate Expedition

In the summer of 1781, the militia officers of Westmoreland County directed Colonel Archibald Lochry to raise three hundred men to assist in the western campaign of George Rogers Clark; but owing to the fact that the many Indian raids into Westmoreland had caused scores of families to seek safety east of the mountains, Colonel Lochry was able to muster less than one hundred men. These began to assemble at Carnahan's block house on August 1st, where the muster was held the next day. On August

---

Massacre of Settlers at Philip Klingensmith's

Just before Lochry's expedition, twenty men, women, and children were massacred at Philip Klingensmith's, in the Brush Creek Settlement, Westmoreland County, July 2nd, 1781, by a band of seventeen Indians, probably Senecas, or Munsee Clan of Delawares, or both. Only three settlers escaped. About the same time, the Indians killed two women in the Ligonier Valley.—Penna. Archives, Vol. IX, page 240.

3rd, the little band of eighty-three militiamen began its march to join Clark at Wheeling. Crossing the Youghiogheny at West Newton and the Monongahela at Monongahela City, Lochry's force went overland by the settlements on the headwaters of Chartiers and Raccoon creeks, Washington County, and reached the Ohio River at Wheeling, West Virginia, on August 8th, just a few hours after Clark's force left that place. Descending the Ohio in boats, the little flotilla on the forenoon of August 24th, approached a level spot at the mouth of the creek since known as Lochry's Run, and being the dividing line between Ohio and Dearborn counties, Indiana, Colonel Lochry at once ordered a landing; the boats were beached, and the men and horses were soon on the shore.

No sooner had they landed than half a hundred rifles blazed from the woods that flanked the level ground near the shore. Many of Lochry's men were killed and others wounded. Others hastened to the boats and pushed for the Kentucky shore. Says Hassler, in his "Old Westmoreland: "Painted savages then appeared, shrieking and firing, and a fleet of canoes filled with other savages shot out from the Kentucky shore, completely cutting off the escape of Lochry's men. The volunteers returned the fire for a few moments, but were entrapped, and Colonel Lochry offered to surrender. The fight ceased, the boats poled back to shore and the force landed the second time. Human blood was now mingled with that of the buffalo in the languidly flowing river. [The troops had shot a buffalo at the water's edge just before the attack.] . . . . . . The Westmoreland men found themselves the prisoners of Joseph Brant, the famous war chief of the Mohawks, with a large band of Iroquois, Shawnees, and Wyandots. George Girty, a brother of Simon, was in command of some of the Indians. The fierce Shawnees could not be controlled and began at once to kill their share of the prisoners. While Lochry sat on a log, a Shawnee warrior stepped behind him and sunk a tomahawk into the Colonel's skull, tearing off the scalp before life was gone. It was with great difficulty that Brant prevented the massacre of the men assigned to the Mohawks and Wyandots."

In this ill-fated expedition, forty of Lochry's force were slain. most of them after the surrender. The prisoners who were not butchered by the savages, were taken to Detroit and from there to Montreal, at which place a few escaped, and the remainder were released after the treaty of peace ending the Revolutionary War. Among the few who returned to Westmoreland County, were

Captain Robert Orr and Lieut. Samuel Craig, Jr., the latter a son
of Lieut. Samuel Craig who, as we have seen, was either killed or
captured at the base of the Chestnut Ridge on November 1st, 1777.

Murder of the Frantz Family

The murder of the Frantz family, who lived on the farm
which is now the home of the Greensburg Country Club, occurred,
most authorities assert, some time before the attack on Hannastown. This event is thus described in Boucher's "History of Westmoreland County":

"The murder of the Francis [Frantz] family was one of the
most inhuman and barbarous incidents in border warfare. The
family resided two miles or more east of Brush Creek. There had
been no special alarm on account of the Indians for some months,
and their usual vigilance was somewhat relaxed. On the day of
the murder, they did not have their cabin door barricaded, and a
party of Indians, therefore, very easily gained access. Two of
the family were killed at once and the remaining members were
taken prisoners. One was a young girl who lived to return to the
settlement, where she married and has left descendants in Hempfield Township. Her brothers and sisters were divided among
several tribes represented among the captors. Those who were
killed were scalped, and their bodies were found near the ruins of
the cabin the day following. They were buried in the garden, a
custom then prevalent among the pioneers and which lasted till
regular cemeteries or graveyards, as they were called, were established."

A tradition in the Frantz family is as follows:

"That Mr. Frantz was at work in a field when his horses gave
warning of the approaching of the Indians, becoming excited,
tearing themselves from the harness, and starting to run. Mr.
Frantz then ran to the house, quickly entered it, and seizing a musket, killed his closest pursuer. His wife and little daughter,
Emma, then seven years of age, were captured, after several other
occupants of the home had been killed. The Indians then started
carrying Mr. and Mrs. Frantz and Emma with them; but when
they had gotten as far as the boundary line of the farm, Mr. and
Mrs. Frantz refused to go further, whereupon, they were killed.
Little Emma made her escape from the Indians several years afterwards, when a trader from Pittsburgh, who occasionally made trips
to the Seneca country in Northwestern Pennsylvania, found her

among the Indians, secreted her among some furs in his boat, and brought her to Pittsburgh."

Attack on Walthour's Station—The Lame Indian

Some time in April, 1782, the Indians invaded the Brush Creek settlement and attacked the stockade of Christopher Walthour, about a mile and a half east of Irwin, Westmoreland County. On this occasion six men were working in a field near the stockade, among them being Walthour's son-in-law, named Willard. The Indians killed Willard, and captured his daughter, aged sixteen, who was carrying water for the men at work. An Indian rushed forward to scalp Willard; but just as he was in the act, a bullet fired from the stockade wounded him in the leg. Uttering a howl of pain, he ran away into the thicket, leaving his gun behind him.

As soon as possible, a body of frontiersmen started in pursuit of the Indians. They followed their trail to the Allegheny River, but were unable to pursue them farther. About two months afterwards, some hunters found the body of Willard's daughter not far from Negley's Run. She had been tomahawked and scalped.

On the evening of the thirty-eighth day after the attack on Walthour's Station, a lame Indian limped into the village of Pittsburgh, almost starved, a living skeleton in appearance. Feebly asking a young woman for a drink, she gave him a cup of milk and other nourishment; and, after he had eaten ravenously, he told her that he had received the wound on his leg in a quarrel with a Mingo Indian on the Beaver River. The Indian was then taken to the fort, where he was recognized as Davy, a Delaware sub-chief. The surgeon of the fort upon examining Davy's wound, found that it was an old one; and the officers therefore entirely discredited his story about the quarrel with a Mingo. Later, Davy confessed to the officers at Fort Pitt that he was the Indian who had killed Willard, and had been wounded when he was in the act of scalping him. He said that, owing to the bone in his leg having been broken by the bullet from the stockade, he was unable to keep up with his companions; that he had lived on nothing but berries and roots for more than five weeks; that, crawling toward the Allegheny River, he lay for several days on a hill above a small stockade on Turtle Creek, meditating surrender, but finding that the garrison of this stockade were militiamen, and not regulars, he knew that surrender meant death.

Davy was confined in the guard house at Fort Pitt and presently the news of his capture reached the settlement of Brush Creek. Then Mrs. Mary Willard, wife of the man whom Davy had killed, came to Fort Pitt and asked General Irvine to give up the prisoner into the hands of the Brush Creek settlers. At that time, Mrs. Willard was not aware that her daughter had been killed. Mrs. Willard was finally persuaded to let Davy remain at Fort Pitt, in the hope that an arrangement might be made for trading him for her daughter. Shortly after Mrs. Willard's visit, the body of the daughter was found; and then a mass meeting was held of the Brush Creek settlement, and a committee composed of Joseph Studebaker, Jacob Byerly, Francis Byerly, Jack Rutdorf, Henry Willard, and Frederick Willard were chosen to go to Fort Pitt and ask for the surrender of Davy. On July 21st, General Irvine delivered Davy to this committee, enjoining them that they were not to punish him without first giving him a trial by two Justices of the Peace and reputable citizens.

The committee forthwith took Davy back to the Brush Creek settlement and made preparations for burning him at the stake on the very spot where he had killed Willard. Word was sent throughout the settlements for the assembling of the magistrates. Davy was confined in a log block house for several days. On the night before he was to be burned, the young men who were guarding the block-house, fell asleep, and when they awoke in the morning, found that Davy had made his escape by crawling through the narrow space between the roof and the top of the wall. For two days the angry settlers searched for the Indian. On the third day, a boy who had gone into the forest after some horses, ran breathless to Walthour's stockade and said that he had seen a crippled Indian mount a horse from a large log, and beating it with a stick, dash off in the direction of the Allegheny River. The settlers at once took up the pursuit, following the trail with considerable difficulty, as the Indian had ridden the horse along the bed of streams, so as not to leave a track. Finally, when they reached a point near the mouth of the Kiskiminetas River, they found the horse covered with foam eating grass near the water's edge. Although the river bank was searched for miles, Davy was never found. Possibly he had drowned while endeavoring to swim the river, or had died of starvation in the wilderness.

Attack on Rice's Fort

On September 13th, 1782, a band of about seventy Indians attacked the block house of Abraham Rice, on Buffalo Creek, in what is now Donegal Township, Washington County. The attack continued from two o'clock in the afternoon until two o'clock the following morning. Although the little fort was defended by only six men, yet the Indians were not able to capture it. One of the defenders, George Felebaum, was shot through the brain while peering through a loop-hole, and four of the Indians were killed. As the Indian band was returning to the Ohio River, they met two settlers who were on their way to the relief of Rice's stockade, and killed them. The attack on Rice's fort was the last invasion of Western Pennsylvania by a large body of Indians.

End of the Revolutionary War

Cornwallis surrendered his army of more than eight thousand men to Washington at Yorktown, on October 19th, 1781. However, as we have seen, warfare continued on the frontier throughout the following year. Finally, on April 19th, 1783, exactly eight years after the battle of Lexington, Washington proclaimed that the war was at an end, and discharged the patriot army. The Angel of Peace then descended on the war-scarred, desolated country to plume her ruffled pinions, and to bring the blessings of Heaven in her train.

CHAPTER XXXIII.

Last of Indian Outrages
in Pennsylvania

UPON the close of the Revolutionary War, enterprising men turned their attention to the settlement of the vast and fertile region west of the Alleghenies; and Congress, in 1787, formed the Northwest Territory out of which the states of Ohio, Indiana, Illinois, Michigan, and Wisconsin have been formed. General Arthur St. Clair was appointed governor of the Northwest Territory, and, early in 1789, held a treaty at Fort Harmar, at the mouth of the Muskingum River, with representatives of the Six Nations, Wyandots, Delawares, Ottawas and other Western Indians, by the terms of which they ceded large tracts of land to the United States. However, the great majority of these Indians refused to acknowledge the validity of the treaty, and shortly thereafter, instigated by British traders, went on the warpath, sending many of their war parties into the valleys of the Ohio and Allegheny.

General Harmar's Defeat

General Harmar was then sent with an army against these western tribes, leaving Fort Washington, (Cincinnati, Ohio), on September 30th, 1790. His force consisted of about fourteen hundred militia and regulars. After a march of seventeen days, he came within striking distance of the enemy, and on October 21st, his army went down to inglorious and overwhelming defeat. The Miami chief, Little Turtle, and the Seneca chief, Blue Jacket, commanded the Indian forces.

Attack on the Home of James Kirkpatrick and
Capture of John and Nancy Sloan

Following the defeat of General Harmar, many bloody incursions were made upon the Western Pennsylvania frontier. One of these was the attack on the fortified home of James Kirkpatrick, in South Bend Township, Armstrong County, on April 28th, 1791. Mr. Kirkpatrick's family had just completed morning worship, when George Miller, who was at the home at that time, went to the

door and found three savages with their rifles cocked and tomahawks ready for attack. They rushed forward to enter the house,
but Miller succeeded in closing it before them. The Indians then
fired through the door and wounded Mr. Miller in the wrist, and
killed Kirkpatrick's child lying in its cradle. Mr. Kirkpatrick
then went to the loft, made an incision in the wall, and began to
fire on the Indians, killing one of them on the spot. In the meantime, Mrs. Kirkpatrick remained below busily employed in making
bullets, while her husband and his companion were defending the
house.

The above is the account given by most historians; but attention is called to the fact that, on Page 555 of Volume Four of the
Second Series of the Pennsylvania Archives, William Findley, in
a letter written to A. Dallas, Secretary of the Commonwealth, on
April 29th, 1791, states that there were six militia in Kirkpatrick's
house at the time of the attack. Also Andrew Gregg, in a letter
written to Colonel Samuel Bryson, and recorded in the same
volume of the Pennsylvania Archives, Page 559, states that two
men were killed in this attack and one wounded, in addition to the
killing of the babe. Smith, in his "History of Armstrong
County", describes this attack and the capture of John and Nancy
Sloan, about the same time, as follows:

"The early settlers were subject to the attacks of the Indians.
A blockhouse was built on the land then owned by William Clark,
but which is now (1883) owned by S. E. Jones. There was another house with port holes—not built, perhaps, expressly for a
blockhouse, but used as a place of refuge and defense from those
attacks—on the road now leading from Elderton to the old
Crooked Creek salt works, on the farm heretofore known as the
Down's farm. It was attacked one morning by the Indians.
George Miller and James Kirkpatrick were then in charge of it;
the Indians fired upon them, killed a child in the cradle, and
wounded an adult person in the building. The women made
bullets while the men were defending them and their children. One
Indian, while putting a charge of powder in his gun, was shot
through the hand and body, and was killed, and some of the other
Indians were wounded. George Miller escaped from the rear of
the building, mounted a horse and started for Clark's blockhouse.
In his absence the Indians fled, carrying with them the dead and
wounded.

"Two children, John Sloan and his sister Nancy, were captured about the time of that affair on the farm near the present

Lutheran and Reformed church, formerly in Plum Creek, but now in South Bend Township [Armstrong County], and about sixty rods northwest from the present residence of William Heintzelman. They were working in the cornfield at the time. Having been retained by the Indians several years, they were exchanged near Cincinnati or Sandusky, Ohio. They returned home the same year that Samuel Sloan, still living (1883), was born. Their relatives and some other settlers soon after their capture, followed the trail of the Indians to the point where they crossed the Allegheny River above Kittanning. The writer's informant, Ex-Sheriff Joseph Clark, also said he had seen bullet holes in the door of the above mentioned house on the Down's farm, and that his aunt, Mrs. Joseph Clark, had told him that she used to stand with rifle in hand, and guard her husband while at work on the farm now occupied by William T. Clark in Plum Creek Township."

Murder of Mrs. Mitchell

The Mitchell family lived in Derry Township, Westmoreland County, on the Loyalhanna, about two miles east of Latrobe. In 1791 the family consisted of the mother and two children, Charles, aged seventeen, and Susan, aged fifteen, the father having died a few years before. During this year, four Indians approachd the home while Charles and Susan were in the stable attending to the work of feeding the stock. Charles tried to escape by running towards the Loyalhanna, but was captured. Susan hid under a trough for feeding horses, and the Indians were unable to discover her. They then captured the mother, and started north with her and Charles. They soon found that Mrs. Mitchell was too old to travel. Then two Indians pushed on ahead with Charles, while the other two loitered behind with Mrs. Mitchell. After a while those conducting Charles stopped to build a fire, when the two who had charge of Mrs. Mitchell joined them with her bleeding scalp. They stretched and dried it in the presence of her son. The band then crossed the Kiskiminetas into Armstrong County where they came upon the tracks of two white men, which Charles recognized as those of Captain John Sloan and Harry Hill. There was snow on the ground, and Captain Sloan's exceedingly large feet made such large marks as to astonish the Indians. One of them took the ramrod of his rifle and measured Sloan's tracks. Charles told him that Sloan was a well-known Indian fighter; whereupon the Indians decided not to follow Sloan and Hill, and immediately pushed on northward, taking Charles to the Senecas on the headwaters of the Allegheny River. Here he escaped three years later, and returned to the Ligonier Valley.

Captain John Sloan was a prominent figure in the early history of Westmoreland County. In 1795, he and his nephew, John Wallace, and two neighbors named Hunt and Knott left Derry Township, Westmoreland County, for a trip to the valley of the Big Maumee. Here they were attacked by Indians. Knott was killed, Sloan wounded, and Hunt captured, never to be heard of again. Sloan and Wallace then went to Fort Hamilton, which had been erected four years before by General St. Clair. In an attack upon this fort by the Indians the day after Sloan and Wallace arrived there, Sloan killed and scalped an Indian. Returning to his home on the Loyalhanna, Sloan brought the Indian's scalp with him, and displayed it on a number of public occasions for many years thereafter. He was elected sheriff of Westmoreland County, serving from 1804 to 1807.

Capture of Jacob Nicely

One of the outrages committed by the Senecas was the capture of little Jacob Nicely, aged five years, the son of Adam Nicely, who lived on Four Mile Run, in Westmoreland County, about two miles from its junction with the Loyalhanna. Authorities differ as to the time of the capture, some stating that it was during the summer of 1790, and others during the summer of 1791.

Little Jacob and his brothers and sisters were picking blackberries. Jacob returned to the house where his mother, who was baking, gave him a cake and told him to rejoin his brothers and sisters. He then started to return to the other children, when a band of Senecas, who were concealed in the woods, captured him. The father with some companions followed the captors as far as the Kiskiminetas, where their trail was lost in the forest.

Years came and went, and no trace of the captured child was found. Finally, in 1828, a man from Westmoreland County, who was trading among the Senecas in Warren County, recognized Jacob, and brought back this information to the mother, who was then an old lady past seventy years of age. In the meantime the father had died. A brother then traveled on horseback to the Seneca reservation, and found the long-lost Jacob. The brothers recognized each other. Jacob had been adopted by the Indians, had a family, and considerable possessions. A tradition in the

Nicely family says that some time prior to 1828, Jacob had made a journey to Westmoreland County, in an effort to locate his relatives, but being unable to speak English and mispronouncing the family name, had returned to his Indian family without finding his mother, brothers, and sisters.

Jacob accompanied his brother part way on the latter's return to Westmoreland County, and presented him with a rifle and other implements. He promised to return the following summer to visit the aged mother. However, he did not return as he had promised, perhaps having died. It is said that the father was unable to converse on the subject of the capture of "Jakey" without shedding tears. The aged mother went to her grave with the vivid recollection of her child captured so many years before.

Attack on Mead's Settlement

In the spring of 1791 occurred the attack on Mead's settlement, where the town of Meadville, the county seat of Crawford County, now stands, thus described by Hon. William Reynolds in the "Centennial History of Crawford County":

"During 1789 the little colony known as "Mead's settlement" was reinforced by the arrival of the family of Darius Mead, Frederick Baum, and Robert Ritz Randolph and their families, Frederick Haymaker, William Gregg, Samuel Lord and John Wentworth. On April 1st, 1791, the settlers were warned by Flying Cloud—a son of the Chief Connedaughta—of threatened danger from the hostile western tribes, and on the same day eleven strange Indians were seen a few miles northwest of the settlement. The women and children of the colony were gathered within the Mead house and cellar and on the next day sent in canoes to Fort Franklin. The Indian chief, Half Town—who was a half-brother to Cornplanter—was encamped here at the time with twenty-seven of his braves. Twelve of these he sent to guard the canoe, six on each side of the creek, and with his remaining warriors he joined the settlers in a fruitless search for the hostiles seen by Gregg. On the following day all the men departed for Franklin with their horses, cattle and moveable effects.

"On May 3rd, Cornelius VanHorne, William Gregg and Thomas Ray returned to plant the spring crops. Stopping for the night at Gregg's cabin, they shelled a bag of corn, part of which they ground the next morning at the Mead house. Arriving at the corn field, VanHorne laid his gun on the bag of seed corn and ploughed while Gregg and Ray planted. At noon Gregg and Ray returned to the Mead house for dinner and fresh horses. While ploughing, VanHorne saw two Indians emerge from the woods. The one dropping his bow and the other his gun, they rushed to the attack with their tomahawks. VanHorne grasped the uplifted arm of the first savage and entered on a struggle for life. By his superior strength and agility he shielded himself from the attack of his more formidable foe with the body of his weaker antagonist, calling loudly for help. After a time the Indians promised his life on condition of surrender. Mounting the horses, VanHorne between them, they crossed the Cussewago, and entering a ravine on the hillside they met two other Indians. They tied the arms of their prisoner and three returned to the corn field. Van Horne and the Indian rode the horses to Conneaut Lake and crossed the outlet. Here they dismounted and VanHorne was tied by the ends of the rope which secured his arms to a tree while his captors left in search of game. With a knife he had secreted he succeeded in cutting the rope and made his escape to the settlement where by good fortune he found thirty soldiers under Ensign Jeffers, on their return from Erie to Fort Franklin.

"Gregg and Ray returning with the horses discovered the three Indians and fled, crossing the Cussewago near its mouth. Gregg, after reaching the opposite bank, was wounded, and seating himself on a log he was shot by his pursuers through the head with his own gun. Ray was captured and carried to Detroit, then occupied by a British garrison. Here he was recognized by an old school-fellow of his boyhood in Scotland, Captain White, who purchased him from his captors for two gallons of whiskey, furnished him money and sent him on a vessel to Buffalo, from whence he was piloted to Franklin by Stripe Neck—an old Mohawk chief, who lived after the early settlement on the west side of French Creek near the site of the present tannery in Kerrtown. Ray made his settlement and ended his days in the northwest corner of Mead Township.

"In the summer of the same year Darius Mead, the father of David and John, was captured near Franklin. His body was found side by side with that of one of his captors, Captain Bull, a Delaware chief. The duel had been to the death and they were buried side by side where found, near the Shenango Creek in Mercer County."

General St. Clair's Defeat

President Washington chose General Arthur St. Clair to lead an army against the Western Indians. "Beware of a surprise," said Washington, as St. Clair left Philadelphia to take charge of the army. With eighteen hundred men, he marched from Fort Washington, in October, 1791, and proceeded against the Miami villages. As he advanced into the Indian country, his force became weakened by desertions and mutiny. On November 4th, his forces were ambushed on a branch of the Wabash, and defeated with great slaughter. Nearly half of their number lay dead or wounded on the field, while the remainder fled precipitately through the forest. Among the slain was General Richard Butler, second in command, for whom Butler County is named.

This was one of the most crushing and disastrous defeats in the Indian annals of America. The country was shocked, humiliated, and disheartened; and the Indians were much emboldened. Washington was extremely agitated on hearing of St. Clair's misfortune, and gave way to passionate invective, but recovering himself said: "General St. Clair shall have justice. I will receive him without displeasure; I will hear him without prejudice; he shall have full justice." His investigation into St. Clair's conduct resulted in the General's honorable acquittal.

St. Clair had fought courageously against the Indian hordes led by Blue Jacket, Little Turtle, and Simon Girty, the renegade; but he never rose again in public estimation. Upon his removal as Governor of the Northwest Territory, in 1802, he retired to his mansion, which in the days of his affluence, he had built about two miles northwest of Ligonier, in the Ligonier Valley. Financial reverses soon came upon him, and his beautiful home and all his other property were sold. He then removed to a log house on the summit of the Chestnut Ridge, where his son had purchased a small farm for him. Here the old soldier spent the remainder of his days in poverty, eking out a miserable existence by keeping tavern and selling supplies to teamsters. He made frequent appeals to the Legislature of Pennsylvania and to Congress for aid in his declining years. His claim against the Government was based upon the fact that he personally stood good for the supplying of much provisions and equipment for the army which he led against the Ohio Indians, on the promise of the Secretary of the Treasury to reimburse him. In 1813 Pennsylvania gave him an annuity of four hundred dollars; and shortly before his death, Congress voted him the sum of two thousand dollars in settlement of his claims against the Government, and a pension of sixty dollars per month, dated back one year. Not a dollar of the settlement gave any relief to the aged man, as it was all seized by his creditors.

On August 30th, 1918, while driving down the Chestnut Ridge with a pony hitched to an old wagon, he fell from the jolting vehicle upon the rough road, where Susan Steinbarger found him lying unconscious as she was going out to gather berries. The pony was standing nearby. The General was then taken to his humble home, but never regained consciousness, dying the next day at the great age of eighty-four years. He is buried in the old Presbyterian cemetery at Greensburg, where the Masons have erected a monument at his grave containing the statement that it is "erected to supply the place of a nobler one due from his country."

Capture of Massa Harbison

Massa Harbison, whose terrible sufferings at the hands of the Indians have been given wide publicity in Western Pennsylvania, was born in Amwell Township, Somerset County, New Jersey, March 18th, 1770, the daughter of Edward White, a soldier in the Revolutionary War. As a child she witnessed the battles of Long Island, Trenton, and Monmouth. In 1773 her father settled in Brownsville, Fayette County, where she married John Harbison, in 1787.

Her husband was a soldier in St. Clair's army. Being wounded at the defeat of St. Clair, he was given lighter duty as a scout, serving along the Allegheny frontier. On March 18th, 1792, Indians attacked the home of Thomas Dick below the mouth of Deer Creek, Allegheny County, and captured the entire family. On the 22nd of March of the same year, seven Indians attacked the house of Abraham Roose, about two miles above the mouth of Bull Creek in the same county, and massacred his entire family. The news of these massacres alarmed Mrs. Harbison, and with a small child in her arms and another tied on the horse behind her, she traveled seven miles from her home to James Paul's at Pine Run, at which place about seventy women and children were collected and from there taken to a place on the east side of the Allegheny River, called Reed's block house, or Reed's station, about two miles below the mouth of the Kiskiminetas.

Here Mrs. Harbison was captured within gunshot of the block house on May 22nd, 1792, by a band of Munsees and other

Indians, the account of which is thus related in Smith's authoritative "History of Armstrong County":

"John Harbison was a soldier in St. Clair's army. Having been wounded, he was, after his recovery, employed as a spy to watch the movements of the savages. In the spring of 1792, his family resided in a house near Reed's station. While he was absent on duty, his house, about 200 yards distant from the block house, was entered by Indians on the morning of May 22nd, and his wife and children were captured. Before proceeding with the account of their capture, the reader's attention is directed to what William Findley wrote to A. J. Dallas, Secretary of the Commonwealth, June 1: 'I was but a few days at home until the Indians broke into the settlement by Reed's station. It was garrisoned by rangers under Cooper. They had never scouted any. They had been drinking and were surprised, in want of ammunition, and the officer was absent from the station. However, the Indans fired only a few rounds upon the blockhouse, with which they killed one man and wounded another, and went away without any exertions being made by the rangers. They then killed and took Harbison's family in sight of the station. Harbison was one of the spies, and was reported as having relaxed a little in his duty. Indeed, the duties of the spies in this county is (are) too hard, and they are not assisted by the troops as was designed at laying the plan. The alarm was quickly spread; indeed, they themselves (the Indians) promoted the news of their coming by burning some of the first houses they came to. This occasioned the country to fly before them with the greatest rapidity, and being about forty in number took the country before them, keeping nearly the course of the Kiskiminetas, going in small parties from five to seven, as far as has been observed.'

"Two spies, Davis and Sutton, having lodged at Harbison's house, left the next morning, Sunday, May 22nd, when the horn at the blockhouse was blown, leaving the door open. Several Indians soon afterward entered, and drew Mrs. Massey (corrupted from Mera) Harbison and her two eldest children by their feet from their beds, the third or youngest one, about a year old, being in bed with her. While these dusky burglars were rummaging the house and scrambling to secure whatever each one could of her clothing and other articles, she went outdoors and hallooed to the men in the blockhouse. One Indian then ran up and stopped her mouth; another rushed toward her with his raised tomahawk, which a third one seized, calling her his squaw and claiming her as

his own. Fifteen Indians then advanced toward and fired upon both
the blockhouse and the storehouse, killing one and wounding another of the soldiers, one of whom, by the name of Wolf, was returning from the spring and the other either coming or looking out
of the storehouse. When Mrs. Harbison told the Indians who remained with her that there were forty men in the blockhouse, each
having two guns, those who were firing were brought back. Then
they began to drive her and the children away. Because one of
her boys, three years old, was unwilling to leave and was crying,
they seized him by his feet, dashed his brains out against the
threshold of the door, and then stabbed and scalped him. Her
heart rent with agony, almost bereft of sight and all her other
senses, still keeping her infant in her arms, she gave a terrific
scream, and for that one of her savage captors dealt a heavy blow
on her head and face, which restored her to consciousness.

"She and her two surviving children were then taken to the
top of a hill, where they all stopped, and while the Indians were
tying up their booty, she counted them, their number being thirty-
two, among whom were two white men painted like Indians.
Those were probably the 'treacherous persons among us' mentioned in another part of Findley's letter to Secretary Dallas. Several
of those Indians could speak English. Mrs. Harbison knew three
or four of them very well; two were Senecas and two were Munsees, whose guns her husband had repaired almost two years before. Two Indians were detailed to guard her, and the rest then
went toward Puckety. When she, her children and their guards
had advanced about 200 yards, the latter caught two of her uncle
John Currie's horses, and then placing her and the youngest child
on one and one of the guards and the remaining child on the other,
proceeded toward the Kiskiminetas to a point opposite the upper
end of Todd's island, where in descending the steep river hill, the
Indian's horse fell and rolled more than once. The boy fell over
the horse's back, receiving a slight injury, and was taken up by one
of the Indians. On reaching the shore the horses could not be
made to swim, so the Indians took the captives across to the head
of that island in bark canoes. [The Island in the Allegheny,
opposite Freeport, Armstrong County.]

"After landing, the elder boy, five years old, complaining of
the injury he had received from his fall and still lamenting the
death of his brother, one of the guards tomahawked and then scalped him, the other guard having first ordered the mother to move on
ahead of them, actuated, perhaps, by a slight assertion of human-

ity, to save her the pain of witnessing the murder of another of her children.   When she beheld that second massacre of her offspring, she fell senseless to the ground with her infant in her arms beneath her with its little hands about her head.   She knew not how long she remained in that insensible condition.   The first thing she remembered on recovering her consciousness, was raising her head from the ground and being overcome by an extreme, uncontrollable drowsiness, and beholding as she looked around, the bloody scalp of her boy in the hand of one of these savages.   She then involuntarily sank again to the earth upon her infant.   The first thing which she remembered after that, was the severe castigation that her cruel guards were inflicting upon her, after which they aided her in rising and supported her when on her feet.   Why they did not massacre her she attributed to the interposition of Divine Providence in her behalf.   There must have still been a little streak of humanity lingering in their ferocious breasts, for they concealed the scalp of her boy from her sight.   Having restored her dormant senses by leading her knee-deep into the river, all proceeded to a shoal near the head of the island, between it and the mainland or 'Indian side of the country,' where her guards forced her before them into and through the water breast deep, she holding her child above the surface, and by their assistance she with her child safely reached the opposite shore.

"They all moved thence as fast as they could across the forks to the Big Buffalo, which, being a very rapid stream, her guards were obliged to aid her in crossing.   Thence they took a straight course 'to the Connoquenessing Creek, the very place where Butler now stands.'   (The narrator probably wrote or the compositor printed 'to' for 'toward'.)   Thence they advanced along the Indian trail, heretofore mentioned, to the Little Buffalo, which they crossed at the very place where B. Sarver's mill stood when her narrative was written, and there ascended the hill.   Having become weary of life, she fully determined to make these savages kill her, to end her fatigue and the prospective miseries and cruelties which she conceived awaited her.   They were then moving in single file, one guard before and the other behind her.   She stopped, withdrew from her shoulder a large powderhorn which, besides her child, they compelled her to carry, and threw it to the ground, closing her eyes momentarily expecting to feel their deadly tomahawks.   But, contrary to her expectations, they replaced it on her shoulder.   She threw it off a second time, expecting death. But they, indignant and frightful, again replaced it.   She threw it down a third time as far as she could over the rocks.   While the one that had been engaged in that little contest was recovering it, the other one who had claimed her as his squaw and who had witnessed the affair, approached and said: 'Well done; you did right and are a good squaw, and he is a lazy son of a b—h; he may carry it himself.'   That would-be husband of hers had evidently a penchant for at least some of the polite language which he had heard some of the white men use.   The guards having changed their positions, the latter taking the rear probably to prevent the other from injuring her, they proceeded until they reached, shortly before dark, without refreshment during the day, the Salt Lick on the Connoquenessing, nearly two miles above the present site of Butler, where there was an Indian camp made of stakes driven into the ground sloping, covered with chestnut bark, long enough for fifty men, appeared to have been occupied for some time, was very much beaten, and from which large beaten paths extended in different directions.

"Mrs. Harbison was taken that night from that camp into a large dark bottom, about 300 rods up a run, where they cut away the brush in a thicket, placed a blanket on the ground and permitted her to sit down with her child, which it was difficult for her to manage, as they had pinioned her arms so that she had but slight freedom of their use.   There, without refreshment, thus pinioned, with those two savages who had that day massacred in her presence two of her boys, one of those guards on each side of her, she passed the first night of her captivity.

"The next morning one of the guards left to watch the trail they had traveled, and ascertain whether any of the white people were in pursuit.   During his absence the other, being the one who claimed her as his squaw, and who had that day killed her second boy, remained with her and took from his bosom the scalp which he had so humanely concealed from her sight on the island, and stretched it upon a hoop.   She then meditated revenge, attempting to take the tomahawk which hung by his side, and deal a fatal blow, but was, alas! detected.   Her dusky wooer turned, cursed her, and called her a Yankee, thus intimating that he understood her intention, and to prevent a repetition of her attempt, faced her.   The feigned reason that she gave for handling his tomahawk was, that her child wanted to play with its handle.   The guard that had been out, returned from his lookout about noon, and reported that he had not discovered any pursuers, and remained on guard while the other went out for the same purpose.   The one then guarding her, after questioning her respecting the whites, the strength of their armies, and boasting of the achievements of the Indians in St. Clair's defeat, examined the plunder which he had brought from her house, among which he found her pocketbook, containing $10 in silver and a half-guinea in gold. All the food that she received from her guards on that Sunday and Monday was a piece of dried venison, about the size of an egg, each day, for herself and her child, but by reason of the blows which they had inflicted upon her jaws she could not eat any of it, and broke it up and gave it to her child. The guard who had been on the lookout in the afternoon returned about dark. Having been removed to another station in the valley of that run, that evening, she was again pinioned, guarded, and kept without either fire or refreshment, the second night of her captivity, just as she had been during the first one. She, however, fell asleep occasionally and dreamed several times of her arrival at Pittsburgh.

"Her ears were regaled the next morning by the singing of a flock of mocking-birds and robins that hovered over her irksome camp. To her imagination they seemed to sing, 'Get up and go off!' One of the guards having left at daybreak to watch the trail, the remaining one appeared to be sleeping, on observing which, she began to snore and feigned to be asleep. When she was satisfied that he had really fallen asleep, she concluded it was her time to escape. She would then have slain or disabled him, but for the crying of her child when out of her arms, which would of course awaken him and jeopardize her own life. She, therefore, was content to take a short gown, handkerchief, and child's frock from the pillow case containing the articles which the Indians had brought from her house, and escape, about half an hour after sunrise. Guided by those birds, and wisely taking a direction from instead of toward her home, in order to mislead her captors she passed over the hill, reached the Connoquenessing, about two miles from the point at which she and they had crossed it, and descended it through thorns and briers, and over rocks and precipices, with bare feet and legs. Having discovered by the sun and the course of the stream that she was advancing too far in her course from her home, she changed it, ascended the hill, sat down till sunset, determined her direction for the morrow by the evening star, gathered leaves for her bed, without food, her feet painful from the thorns that were in them, reclined and slept.

"About daybreak the next morning, she was awakened by that flock of birds which seemed to her to be attending and guiding her through the wilderness.   When light enough to find her way, she started on her fourth days' trial of hunger and fatigue, advancing, according to her knowledge of courses and distances, toward the Allegheny River.   Nothing unusual occurred during the day.   It having commenced raining moderately about sunset, she prepared to make her bed of leaves, but was prevented by the crying of her child when she set him down.   Listening she distinctly heard the footsteps of a man following her.   Such was the condition of the soil that her footprints might be discerned.   Fearing that she was thus exposed to a second captivity, she looked for a place of concealment and providentially discovered a large fallen tree, into whose thick foliage she crept with her child in her arms, where, aided by the darkness, she avoided detection by the Indian, whose footsteps she had heard.   He having heard the child's cry, came to the spot whence the sound proceeded, halted, put down his gun, and was then so near to her that she distinctly heard the wiping-stick strike against his gun.   Fortunately the child, pressed to her bosom, became warm and lay quiet during the continuance of their imminent peril.   That Indian in the meantime, amidst that unbroken stillness, stood for nearly two hours with listening ears to again catch the sound of the child's cry; and so profound was that stillness that the beating of her own heart was all she heard, and which seemed to her to be so loud that she feared her dusky pursuer would hear it.   Finally, answering the sound of a bell and a cry like a night-owl's, signals which his companions had given, and giving a horrid, soul-harrowing yell, he departed.

"Deeming it imprudent to remain there until morning, lest her tracks might be discovered in daylight, she endeavored, but found it difficult, by reason of her exhaustion, to remove; but compelled by a stern necessity and her love of life, she threw her coat around the child, with one end between her teeth, thus carrying the child with her teeth and one arm; with the other, she groped her way among the trees a mile or two, and there sat in the damp, cold air till morning.

"At daylight the next morning, wet, hungry, exhausted, wretched, she advanced across the headwaters of Pine Creek, not knowing what they were, and became alarmed by two freshly indented moccasin tracks of men traveling in the same direction that she was.   As they were ahead of her, she concluded that she could see them as soon as they could see her.   So she proceeded about three miles to a hunter's camp at the confluence of another branch of the creek, at which those who preceded her had kindled a fire, breakfasted, and leaving the fire burning, had departed. She afterward learned that they were spies, viz: James Anderson and John Thompson. Having become still more alarmed, she left that path, ascended a hill, struck another path, and while meditating there what to do, saw three deer advancing toward her at full speed. They turned to look and she, too, looked intently at their pursuers, and saw the flash and heard the instantaneous report of a gun. Seeing some dogs start after the deer, she crouched behind a large log for shelter, but fortunately not close to it; for, as she placed her hand on the ground to raise herself up, that she might see the hunters, she saw a large mass of rattlesnakes, her face being very near the top one, which lay coiled ready to strike its deadly fangs into her. With a supreme effort she left that dangerous spot, bearing to the left, reached the headwaters of Squaw Run, which through rain, she followed the rest of the day, her limbs so cold and shivering that she could not help giving an occasional involuntary groan. Though her jaws had sufficiently recovered from the pain caused by the blows inflicted upon her by the Indians, she suffered from hunger, procuring grapevines whenever she could and chewing them for what little sustenance they afforded. Having arrived at eveningtide within a mile of the Allegheny River, though she did not know it, at the root of a tree, holding her child in her lap and her head against the tree to shelter him from that night's drenching rain, she lodged that fifth night since her capture.

"She was unable for a considerable time the next morning to raise herself from the ground. Having, with a hard struggle, gained her feet, with nature so nearly exhausted and her spirits so completely depressed as they were, her progress was very slow and discouraging. After proceeding a short distance, she struck a path over which cattle had passed, following which for about a mile, she reached an uninhabited cabin on the river bottom. Not knowing where she was, and overcome with despair, she went to its threshold, having resolved to enter it and then lie down and die. But the thought of the suffering to be endured in that event, nerved her to another desperate effort to live. Hearing the sound of a cowbell, which awakened a gleam of hope in her extreme despondency, she followed that sound until she reached a point opposite the fort at Six-Mile Island, where, with feelings which can be more readily imagined than expressed, she beheld three men on the left bank of the river. They appeared to be unwilling to come for her when she called to them, and requested her to inform them who she was. When she told them that she was the one who had been taken prisoner up the Allegheny on the morning of the 22nd—in the narrative, it is Tuesday morning—and had escaped, they requested her to walk up the bank of the river for awhile, that they might see whether or not the Indians were making a decoy of her. When she told them her feet were so sore that she could not walk, James Closier came over for her in a canoe, while the other two stood on the river bank with cocked rifles, ready to fire in case she proved to be a decoy. When Closier approached the shore and saw her haggard and dejected appearance, he exclaimed: 'Who in the name of God, are you?' So great was the change wrought by her six days' sufferings that he, one of her nearest neighbors, did not recognize either her face or voice.

"When she arrived on the other side of the river, she was unable to move or to help herself in any way. The people at the fort ran to see her. Some of them took her child and others took her from the canoe to Mr. Carter's house. Then, all danger being passed, she enjoyed for the first time since her capture, the relief which comes from a copious flow of tears. Coming too suddenly to the fire and the smell of the victuals, she fainted. Those hospitable people might have killed her with their exuberant kindness, had not Maj. McCulley, who then commanded the line along the Allegheny River, fortunately arrived. When he saw her situation and the bountiful provision those good people were making for her, he immediately ordered her out of the house, away from the heat of the fire and the smell of the victuals which were being cooked, and prohibited her from taking anything but the whey of buttermilk, in very small quantities, which he himself administered. By that judicious treatment, she was gradually restored to health and strength of mind and body. Sarah Carter and Mary Ann Crozier—whether single or married is not stated—then began to extract the thorns from her feet and legs, to the number of 150, as counted by Felix Negley, who watched the operation, and who afterward resided at the mouth of Bull Creek (Tarentum). Many more were extracted the next evening. Some of the thorns went through and came out on the top of her feet. The skin and flesh were excruciatingly mangled, and hung in shreds to her feet and legs. So much exposure of her naked body to rain by night and heat of the sun by day, and carrying her child so long in her arms without relief, caused so much of her skin to come off that nearly her whole body was raw, and for two weeks her feet were not sufficiently healed to enable her to put them to the ground to walk.

"The news of her escape spread rapidly in various directions, reaching Pittsburgh the same evening of her arrival at the fort at Six-Mile Island. Two spies proceeded that evening to Coe's—now Tarentum—and the next morning to Reed's station, bearing the intelligence to her husband. A young man employed by the magistrates at Pittsburgh came for her to go thither for the purpose of making before one of them her affidavit of the facts connected with her captivity and escape, as was customary in early times, for publication. Being unable either to walk or ride on horseback, she was carried by some of the men into a canoe. After arriving at Pittsburgh she was borne in their arms to the office of John Wilkins, a justice of the peace and a son of the late Judge Wilkins of the United States Court, before whom she made her affidavit, May 28, 1792. The facts which she thus stated being circulated, caused a lively sensation in and for twenty miles around Pittsburgh. Her husband arrived there that evening, and the next morning she was conveyed to Coe's station. That evening she gave to those about her an account of the murder of her boy on Todd's Island, whither a scout went the next morning, found and buried the corpse, which had lain there unburied nine days.

"From her above-mentioned affidavit and her subsequent and more elaborate narrative, prepared from her statement by John Winter, the writer has condensed the foregoing facts, credited by the early settlers who were her neighbors, and which were made during those six terrible days of her life.

"She resided during several subsequent years at Salt Lick, a mile and a half north of Butler, on the Connoquenessing, at or near the site of the Indian camp mentioned in her affidavit and narrative. The last years of her life were passed in a cabin on the lot on the northeastern corner of Fourth Street and Mulberry Alley, Freeport, opposite the Methodist Episcopal Church, being the same lot now occupied by William Murphy, where she died on Saturday, December 9th, 1837."

Concerning her husband, John Harbison, Smith's "History of Armstrong County" relates the following incident:

"On a certain occasion Craig [Captain John Craig, commander of the blockhouse at Freeport], ordered a scouting party to make a tour of observation as far up the country as the mouth of Red Bank. They went, and on their return reported that they had not discovered any Indians. One of them, however, while on his death-bed, many years afterward, sent for Craig and confessed to him that, while on that tour, he and his comrades had captured an Indian, and after obtaining all the information possible from him, and not wishing to have the trouble of taking him as a prisoner to the blockhouse, they concluded to keep his capture a secret, and to dispatch him by tying him to a tree and each one shooting him, so that, all being equally guilty, there would be no danger of anyone disclosing their dread secret.   Others of that scouting party, having been questioned about that affair, acknowledged to finding the Indian, but averred that John Harbison, who had just cause for a deadly hate toward all Indians, tomahawked him while he was conversing with another one of the party who understood the Indian language, and that they all agreed to keep that deed secret on Harbison's account."

Massa, however, in her narrative says that the killing of this Indian occurred on Puckety Creek, Westmoreland County.

The capture of Massa Harbison was the most memorable of any on the Allegheny frontier; yet no tablet has been erected on the site of the home from which she and her children were dragged by the ruthless savages, and on whose threshold her little son was killed.   Her dust with that of many others of the pioneers, was removed to the new cemetery at Freeport some years ago, where a marble monument has been erected at her grave, bearing the following inscription:

Massa, Wife of John Harbison,
1770—1837
Captured By Indians May 22,
and Escaped May 27, 1792.

Murder on Fort Run Near Kittanning

In 1791 or 1792, an outrage occurred on Fort Run, near Kittanning, thus described in Smith's "History of Armstrong County":

"George Cook, who was born about 1764, was a soldier, a scout, and resided in the Manor [Manor Township] from either his boyhood or his early manhood until he was nearly four score, used to narrate to his neighbors, among whom was William McKellog, of 'Glentworth Park,' from whom the writer obtained a statement of these tragical facts: While Cook was a member of a scouting party who occupied a fort or blockhouse near Fort Run, so called from Fort Armstrong, some Indians made a small cord from the inner bark of a linden tree, with which they anchored a duck in a hole or pool in that run, formed by the action of the water about the roots of a sugar maple tree on its brink. Three of the scouting party, while out on a tour of duty, noticed the duck which must have appeared to them to be floating on the water. They set their guns up against a buttonwood tree, which with the sugar maple tree, was cut down after that land came into the possession of Richard Bailey. While they were stooping to catch the duck, as it was presumed they did, they were shot by Indians, probably three, because three reports of guns were heard. They fell dead into the run, whose water was colored with their blood. Hence that stream also bears the name of Bloody Run. The bodies of those three men were buried on a knoll opposite where they were shot, eight or ten rods higher up the river. The Indians were probably concealed among the weeds, which were then quite rank and abundant."

"Several of the men who were in the fort or blockhouse, on hearing the gun shots, came out, saw what had occurred, and discovered the Indians' trail, which, on that or the next day, they followed to the mouth of Pine Creek, and were about to give up the pursuit, when, looking up the hill, they saw a smoke on its face. After dark, they crossed the mouth of the creek, and ascertained the exact position in which the Indians were. The next morning they crawled as carefully and quickly as possible through the weeds and willows, until they thought they were within sure gunshot of the murderers of their comrades. They saw one of them mending his moccasin. The other two were, they thought, cooking meat for breakfast. They shot and killed two of the Indians, and captured the other. Having brought him past the mouth of that creek, on their return, and having reached 'an open grove,' they told him that they would give him a start of some distance ahead of them, and if he would beat them in running a race, he should be released. He accepted the offer, started, but was overtaken, fatally shot, and his body was left where he fell."

The Attack on the Party of Captain Sharp

In May, 1794, the Indians again made their appearance on the Allegheny and attacked a canoe going up the river to Franklin, killing John Carter and wounding William Cousins and Peter Kinner. They were unable to get any scalps on this occasion, as the other occupants paddled it out of their reach.

Major Denny mentions the above attack in his journal under June 1, 1794, stating that this band of Indians then "crossed to the Kiskiminetas and unfortunately fell in with a Kentucky boat full of women and children, with but four men, lying to, feeding their cattle." This was the attack on Captain Sharp, which is thus described in Smith's "History of Armstrong County":

"Among the pioneers in the Plum Creek region was Captain Andrew Sharp, who had been an officer in the Revolutionary service, under Washington. He, with his wife and infant child, emigrated to this region in 1784, and purchased, settled upon, and improved the tract of land, consisting of several hundred acres, on which are Shelocta and the United Presbyterian Church, near the county line.

"Captain Sharp, after residing about ten years on his farm, revisited his kindred in Cumberland County, procured a supply of school books and Bibles for his children, and returned to his home in the wilderness. Determined that his children should have facilities for education which did not exist there, he traded his farm there for one in Kentucky. In the spring of 1794, he removed with his family to Black Lick Creek, where he either built or purchased a flatboat, in which he, his wife and six children, a Mr. Connor, wife and five children, a Mr. Taylor, wife and one child, and Messrs. McCoy and Connor, single men, twenty in all, with their baggage and household effects, embarked on the proposed passage down the Kiskiminetas and Allegheny rivers to Pittsburgh, and thence on to Kentucky. Low water in the Black Lick rendered their descent down it difficult. They glided down the Conemaugh and Kiskiminetas to a point two miles below the falls of the latter, at the mouth of Two Mile Run, below the present site of Apollo. Capt. Sharp tied the boat there, and went back for the canoe which had been detached while crossing the falls. When he returned the children were gathering berries and playing on the bank; the women were preparing supper, and the men who led the horses had arrived. It was about an hour and a half before sunset. A man then came along and reported that the Indians were near. The women and children were called into the boat, and the men having charge of the horses tied them on shore.

"It was then thought best that the party should go to the home of David Hall, who was the father of David Hall, of North Buffalo Township, this county, and the grandfather of Rev. David Hall D. D., the present (1883) pastor of the Presbyterian Church at Indiana, Pennsylvania, to spend the night. While the men were tying the horses, seven Indians concealed behind a large fallen tree, on the other side of which the children had been playing half-an-hour before, fired on the party in the boat. Capt. Sharp's right eyebrow was shot off by the first firing. Taylor is said to have mounted one of his horses and fled to the woods, leaving his wife and child to the care and protection of others. While Capt. Sharp was cutting one end of the boat loose, he received a bullet wound in his left side, and, while cutting the other end loose, received another wound in his right side. Nevertheless, he succeeded in removing the boat from its fastenings before the Indians could enter it, and, discovering an Indian in the woods, and calling for his gun, which his wife handed to him, shot and killed the Indian. While the boat was in the whirlpool, it whirled around for two and a half hours. When the open side of the boat, that is, the side on which the baggage was not piled up for a breastwork, was toward the land, the Indians fired into it. They followed it twelve miles down the river, and bade those in it to disembark, else they would fire into them again. Mrs. Connor and her eldest son—a young man—wished to land. The latter requested the Indians to come to the boat, informing them that all the men had been shot. Capt. Sharp ordered him to desist, saying that he would shoot him, if he did not. Just then young Connor was shot by one of the Indians, and fell dead across Mrs. Sharp's feet. McCoy was killed. All the women and children escaped injury. Mr. Connor was severely wounded. After the Indians ceased following, Capt. Sharp became so much exhausted by his exertions and loss of blood, that his wife was obliged to manage the boat all night. At daylight the next morning they were within nine miles of Pittsburgh. Some men on shore, having been signaled, came to their assistance. One of them preceded the party in a canoe, so that when they reached Pittsburgh, a physician was ready to attend upon them. Other preparations had been made for their comfort and hospitable reception, by the good people of that place.

"Capt. Sharp, having suffered severely from his wounds, died July 8, 1794, forty days after he was wounded, with the roar of cannon, so to speak, reverberating in his ears, which he had heard celebrating the eighteenth anniversary of our national independence, which he, under Washington, had helped achieve. Two of his daughters were the only members of his family that could follow his remains to the grave. He was buried with the honors of war, in the presence of a large concourse of people. His youngest child was then only eleven days old. As soon as his widow had sufficiently recovered, she was conducted by her eldest daughter, Hannah, to his grave.

"Col. Charles Campbell, in his letter to Gov. Mifflin, June 5th, 1794, respecting the stopping of the draft of the support of the Presque Isle station, stated: 'The Indians, on the evening of May 30th, fired on a boat that left my place to go to Kentucky, about two miles below the Falls of the Kiskiminetas, killed three persons and wounded one, who were all the men in the boat, which drifted down to about twelve miles above Pittsburgh, whence they were aided by some persons on their way to Pittsburgh.'

"Mrs. Sharp—her maiden name was Ann Wood—and her children were removed to their kindred in Cumberland County, Pennsylvania. Having remained there three years, they returned to the farm near Crooked Creek, of which they had been repossessed, where the family remained together for a long time.

"Mrs. Sharp's death occurred fifteen years after her husband's. Their daughter Agnes is said to have been the first white child born this side, or west, of Crooked Creek, in this section of Pennsylvania. She was born on that farm February 21, 1785; married to David Ralston in 1803, and, after his death, to James Mitchell in 1810, and died August 2, 1862, and was buried in the Crooked Creek cemetery."

The attack on Capt. Sharp and his party was the last Indian outrage in Pennsylvania, except the murder of the Wigton family, in Butler County, June 30th, 1843, by Samuel Mohawk, while returning to his home on the upper Allegheny, from Pittsburgh, to which place he had assisted in floating a raft of lumber down the Allegheny. This outrage, however, does not belong to the period of Indian occupation.

CHAPTER XXXIV.

Wayne's Victory and Final Peace

HE uprising of the Western Indians and the raids upon the Western Pennsylvania frontier continuing, as we have seen, the country, burning under the disgrace of Harmar's and St. Clair's defeats, called loudly for a third expedition. Then President Washington chose General Wayne, "Mad Anthony", the hero of Stony Point, to lead the expedition. He was a strict disciplinarian, and determined to avoid the faults which brought overwhelming and inglorious defeat upon his predecessors. He arrived in Pittsburgh in June, 1792, having been furnished with instructions from Washington in which it was stated "that another defeat would be irredeemably ruinous to the reputation of the Government." His force was to consist of five thousand men, carefully drilled, and to be called "The Legion of the United States."

In December, 1792, his legion was taken to the beautiful plain overlooking the Ohio, about twenty miles below Pittsburgh, where sham battles were fought and daily drills held. The place of this winter camp is known as Legionville to this day. While here, he was visited by the old Indian chiefs, Guyasuta and Cornplanter, then friends of the United States.

Breaking camp on April 13th, 1793, Wayne led his forces to Cincinnati, where they were reinforced by regulars and mounted militia from Kentucky. It was so late in the season before all his forces were collected and supplies procured, that the offensive movement was delayed until the next spring. During the winter, Wayne remained at a fort which he had built on a western fork of the Little Miami, swept the country between this place and the Miami villages, and took possession of the ground upon which St. Clair was defeated, erecting a fort there which he called Fort Recovery. His force now consisted of thirty-six hundred troops.

In the meantime, in the spring of 1793, commissioners representing the United States met the western tribes in council, and proposed that, in consideration of the lands ceded by the treaty at Fort Harmar, the United States should pay the Indians "a large sum of money, or goods, besides a full yearly supply of such articles as they needed." The chiefs replied that money was of no value to them. Said they: "You talk to us about concessions. It appears strange that you should expect any from us, who have only been defending our just rights against your invasions. We want peace. Restore to us our country, and we shall be enemies no longer."

In the summer of 1794, Wayne was joined by General Charles Scott, with sixteen hundred mounted volunteers from Kentucky. He then moved forward, skirmishing with bands of lurking Indians as he advanced. Arriving at the site of the present village of Defiance, Ohio, Wayne erected Fort Defiance, and made proposals of peace with the Indians. These were rejected contrary to the advice of Little Turtle, and in accordance with the advice of Blue Jacket. Said Little Turtle: "We have beaten the enemy twice under separate commanders. We cannot expect the same good fortune always to attend us. The Americans are now led by a chief who never sleeps. The night and the day are alike to him, and during all the time that he has been marching upon our villages, notwithstanding the watchfulness of our young men, we have never been able to surprise him." Indeed, so stealthy had been Wayne's advance that the Indians nicknamed him "the Blacksnake".

On the morning of August 20th, Wayne advanced and had proceeded about five miles, when his advance guard was fired upon heavily by Indians in concealment, and fell back. He then formed his men in two lines where a tornado had blown down a number of trees in the woods—a circumstance which gave the engagement the name of the "Battle of the Fallen Timbers." The fallen trees made cavalry operations difficult, and afforded a shelter for the two thousand Indians and Canadians who were posted among them in three lines. Wayne's militia charged impetuously with the bayonet, leaping over the logs and delivering a well-directed fire, while General Scott with his mounted volunteers, turned the right flank of the enemy by a circuitous movement, and Colonel Campbell, with his legionary cavalry, turned the enemy's left flank. The Indians were driven for more than two miles through the forest, and decisively beaten. Nine of their chiefs lay dead on the field.

The Indians were driven under the guns of the British fort in the neighborhood, and so strong was the resentment of Wayne's men against the English, that it was with difficulty that they could be restrained from storming the fort. Indeed, many of the Kentucky troops advanced within gunshot of the fort and hurled a volley of curses against the garrison. Captain Campbell, the British commandant, sent a message to Wayne, complaining of this insult and demanding by what authority Wayne's troops trespassed upon the precincts of the British garrison. Mad Anthony replied in terms little less polite than those of the Kentucky troops, informing Captain Campbell that his only chance of safety was silence and civility. Then Wayne's troops destroyed the Indian cornfields, orchards, trading-houses, and stores. In addition to breaking forever the power of the western tribes, one of the results of the battle of the Fallen Timbers was the surrender to the United States of Niagara, Detroit, Mackinac, Miami, and other posts hitherto held by the British, from which bases they had assisted and encouraged the Indians in their hostility against the Americans.

Finally, on August 3rd, 1795, the conquered tribes signed the Treaty of Greenville, Darke County, Ohio, by the terms of which they ceded to the United States 25,000 square miles of territory north of the Ohio River, about two-thirds of the present state of Ohio. That part of Pennsylvania west of the Allegheny River and hitherto known as "the Indian country", henceforth was free from Indian raids. Settlers rapidly took up their abode in the fertile region, felling the forest, cultivating the virgin soil, and laying the foundation of the material prosperity which there abounds today. Meanwhile the Indian continued his march toward the untrodden West before the great tide of white immigration that was pressing him away from the lands he and his forefathers considered their own, as the gift of the Great Spirit, Who had stocked the forests with game and the streams with fish for His Red Children.

CONCLUSION

The first overt act of war committed by the Indians of Pennsylvania against the Province was the attack on the German settlers on Penn's Creek, October 16th, 1755. Less than forty years elapsed between that event and the Treaty of Greenville. Before this latter event took place, all the Indians of Pennsylvania had removed from her borders, except the few hundred Senecas on Cornplanter's Reservation in Warren County, and a few families here and there who fondly lingered on choice hunting grounds in the western counties. The recital of the terrible atrocities committed by the Pennsylvania Indians, during these forty years, is a shocking and appalling story; but over against these, must be placed the atrocities committed upon the untutored Indian by the anointed children of education and civilization—the massacre of the Conestogas by the "Paxton Boys", the murder of ten Indians by Frederick Stump, the murder of the family of Logan, chief of the Mingoes, the murder of Cornstalk and his son, the murder of the friendly old Delaware, Joseph Wipey, the murder of the Delaware, Dr. John, and his family, and the butchering of the Moravian Indians by the settlers of Washington County.

There were many frontiersmen who, actuated by unrelenting hatred for the whole Indian race, made no distinction between good Indians and bad Indians. They were simply Indian hunters and killers at all times, whether in peace or in war, and without regard to age or sex. A good example of these was Tom Quick, "the Indian killer", who is said to have claimed on his death bed, in 1795, that he had killed ninety-nine Indians, and begged that an old Indian who lived near might be brought to him, in order that he might kill him, and thus bring his record to an even hundred.

Nor should we lose sight of the fact that hundreds of atrocities perpetrated by the Indians on the settlers of Pennsylvania, during the Revolutionary War, were committed at the instigation of the British and British agents, who paid the Indians substantial rewards for American scalps. Furthermore, we should remember, as pointed out in former chapters, that Pennsylvania gave rewards for Indian scalps, not exempting Indian boys and girls over the age of ten years. Think of offering a reward for the scalp of a ten year old Indian girl!

In weighing the conduct and estimating the character of the Pennsylvania Indians, we must not lose sight of degradation of character wrought among them by the abuses of the rum traffic. Rum was the curse of the Red Man, and their leading chiefs recognized it as such. Hence, from the very beginning of this traffic among them, we find a series of protests by their chiefs to the Pennsylvania Authorities. The great Shikellamy, it will be remembered, shortly after taking up his residence on the Susquehanna, notified the Colonial Authorities that, if the soul destroying traffic were not better regulated, friendly relations between the Six Nations and the Province would cease. "The rum ruins us", said Scarouady at the Carlisle Conference of October, 1753. And Conrad Weiser, than whom no one was better qualified to speak, in writing to the Provincial Council, November 28th, 1747, characterized the havoc wrought among the Indians by the rum traffic as "an abomination before God and man."

Unhappily, too, the Pennsylvania Indians came into direct and frequent contact with the worst element among the whites—

the English traders, who, taking advantage of the Indians' inordinate appetite for rum, cheated them out of their skins and furs, and debauched their women. The Pennsylvania Assembly, in a message to Governor Hamilton, February 27th, 1754, characterized the traders as "the vilest of our own inhabitants and convicts imported from Great Britain and Ireland." The traders of the other colonies, many of whom entered Pennsylvania, were no better. Said Governor Dinwiddie of Virginia, in a letter to Governor Hamilton of Pennsylvania, May 21st, 1753: "The Indian traders, in general, appear to me to be a set of abandoned wretches." In a word, the English traders, with few exceptions, were a vile and infamous horde, who, instead of contributing to the betterment of the Indian, corrupted and debauched him.

And what shall we say of the land frauds, especially the Walking Purchase of 1737 and the Albany Purchase of 1754? The least that we can say is that they had much to do with alienating the Delawares and Shawnees and causing them to bring upon Pennsylvania the bloodiest Indian invasion in American history.

Furthermore, the settling of the whites on lands not purchased from the Indians, especially in the valleys of the Juniata, Monongahela, and Youghiogheny, greatly aggravated the Red Man. The white man's inordinate greed for land aroused the wild passions of the children of the forest.

The Pennsylvania Indians loved the hills, the mountains, the valleys, and the streams of this great state. They exulted in the fact that they were the first owners of this vast region which they were fighting and dying to protect. They were proud spirits who were born free, and loved freedom more than life itself. They were a proud race that abhorred the thought of extinction. Now that they have yielded their pleasant land to the stronger hand of the white man, and live only in the songs and chronicles of the race that pressed them away from their loved hunting grounds, may these chronicles be faithful to their rude virtues as men. They were children of nature. They had no background of centuries of Christian civilization—no knowledge of the God of Revelation. Down the perspective of history comes the impartial verdict that the fate forced upon them by a more highly favored race was galling and unjust. And it shall be more tolerable for them, in the Judgment than their conquerors, the children of the God of Revelation.

THE END

Chronological Table of Some Leading Events in the Indian History of Pennsylvania

—•◄❃II❃►•—

INDEX

BUTCHER

By
Reid Matthias

ISBN - paperback: 978-0-6450472-0-2
            ebook: 978-0-6450472-1-9

This edition first published by A 13 in December 2020

Typesetting by Ben Morton

Publication assistance from Immortalise

Cover art from Unsplash

To my parents, Vic and Diane, and the small town of
Rake, Iowa which they call home.

Acknowledgements

Butcher is a work of fiction, which will become increasingly clear as one turns the pages. Some of the place names are real, drawn from the state of Iowa, but Amicable is not. Although its geography and layout may seem to be familiar (almost all Iowan towns seem to have the same configurations), Amicable is situated nowhere near the Boondocks and not even close to Gravity. All characters are figments of my own imagination and any bearing even a passing resemblance to any readers is unintentional, although welcomed.

A special thanks to Christine, my wife and editor, who rejoiced and suffered with the characters while reminding me constantly that consistency is very important. Elsa, Josephine and Greta, thank you for finding laughter in the pages of the small town, which is, embedded invisibly in your DNA. Anji Neil, a proofreader non pareil; thank you for your own self-diagnosed OCD.

Prologue

Dearest Reader,

In your hands you hold both page and word, spine and cover, the meandering verbal paintings that create another life not so different than this, except that it will appear only in your mind. The images you conjure will be nothing like the colors and shapes in my mind or of anyone else. For that, be thankful. In your ability to create a mental picture from printed word, you are the author of this story as much as I.

Now, as you sit in your favorite reading chair, or lie in your glorious bed, maybe you have taken this book on your summer (or winter) vacation and are looking forward to a few hours, or days, of uninterrupted creation, you are ready for a story. I hope you haven't chosen this book in hopes that it would be the memoirs of a sociopath reminiscing about his various diabolical conquests, blood and gore splattered across the pages. This is not that kind of book. I hope you forgive me, for the title that may be somewhat misleading. This story is not one of murderer and victim, viscera and blood, (well, not intentionally) but of a wonderful man named Leopold Jensen who just happens to be a butcher. You know, the kind that works in a meat locker.

Leopold will be a different character than many you will ever encounter, not just because this is a different book and a different story, but that very few call him by his given name.

They simply know him as Butcher.

My dearest reader, I hope that you enter Leopold's town with sympathetic heart and empathetic eyes to see that in the midst of life, there is something immensely beautiful about living life together. When we share our sorrows and joys, we recognize that the only true disease is loneliness.

Those who are sick can find healing in the embrace of a spouse.
Those who are sad can find comfort in the whisper of shared sorrow between brothers.

1

Butcher

Those who are joyful can find completion in sharing the raucous laughter of a neighbor.
Those who are terrified can stand behind the hero.

To be inoculated against loneliness is to live life as it was meant to be lived.

Chapter 1.

Penny Reynolds' footwear - comfortable and practical, white tennis shoes with blue laces, just a hint of color, very much like her life - made no noise as she purposefully strode down First Street East. As she passed by the shops, she did her very best not to let her gaze be drawn by her moving reflection, but the mirrored glass allowed her to take advantage of what she believed to be a very attractive middle-aged woman reflected in the shop windows. Penny knew that with each shop she passed, whether hardware, bakery, bank or grocery store, she would be noticed if she were to stare at her appearance. The patrons inside the stores would smirk at the townswoman in a floral print blouse and blue jeans (ubiquitous uniform among the denizens of the town) and think to themselves, *That's a bit vain for Penny to be staring at her reflection in the glass.* Which is exactly why Penny kept up her brisk pace. She did not want anyone to judge her as guilty of the venial sin of vanity.

She was faster than most of the residents of the town of Amicable, not that that was saying much. The town's slowest resident, George Hendriks, who also happened to be its oldest citizen, topped out at one or two miles per hour. That was walking or driving. George had steadfastly refused to give up his driver's license even when Louise Nelson, the town police officer, requested with Amicable politeness that he cede his plastic identification card. No one was going to tell the nonagenarian when and where he could go with his 1981 Dodge Omni, burnt orange with ribbed Naugahyde seat cushions. No sirree, George would be taking his good, sweet time making his way to the post office to pick up his mail, even if it took the entire morning for him to drive there. Other residents of Amicable would smile patronizingly at the old man as he puttered up the street hunched over the steering wheel, grimly staring at the road through thick bifocaled glasses.

Penny greeted other pedestrians with a cheery good morning, because that's how it happens in Amicable, Iowa. The town itself, population 1,056 (largely dependent on how long George kept kicking) was a carbon copy of many of the other small towns in the Midwest. Amicable's Main Street, three blocks long, a true thoroughfare with neither stop sign nor stop light to impede the progress of Mr. Hendriks or any other motorist regardless of speed, was lined with not-so-thriving businesses. These included the aforementioned bakery, cafe and grocery or the Hogard's Shoe House. The Traveler's Choice Restaurant and Wilson's Body Shop, owned and operated by Liam Wilson, an oil stained mechanic who seemed to have a perpetual five o'clock shadow and a chronic disdain for anything urban or foreign, were stationed like blood valves on the aorta of Amicable – Highway 10. These businesses brought modest amounts of business from surrounding agrarian communities.

Niceness seemed to be in the DNA of all small towns in the Midwest. The gene, passed on from generations of farmers known for piety and piquancy, a true irony, was carried by anyone who had lived in Amicable for more than twenty years. The locals would have said this was the determinative number of years one must live in the town before one could take on the term 'local,' although many 'foreigners' from other states would have said that one would need generations of relatives to gain acceptance as a 'local.'

Amicable was known for its niceness, or at least that of the external kind. The streets lined with elms, maples and oak trees laden with acorns squished underfoot, were straight and true. Blue sky seemed to infuse the town with a perpetual sense of comfortable niceness, except in the winter when the stubborn winter clouds hurled endless amounts of frozen precipitation on the town causing Amicableans *(Am-ih-CAH-blee-ans: stress the third syllable, thank you very much)* to grumble under their breaths at the thought of hefting one more shovelful from their driveways. Swearing was limited to true hardship (or card playing for some) not for casual conversation. For those who were unable to control their tongues, they were met with frowns of disfavor and tsk tsks of disappointment in their uncouth-ness. The profaners were left dispirited with a sense of *I need to try better. That would be the nicer thing to do.*

Amicable's public school was a nice, big, blocky edifice at the heart of the town, which pumped out nice, educated children who could read, write and excel at good sportsmanship while suffering through decades of losing seasons in every conceivable arena of athletics. Although the number of children in Amicable had gradually been diminishing in the last two or three decades due mainly to the lack of career opportunities afforded in Amicable for young families, it didn't seem to bother Amicableans that much. Sooner or later, the young people would all come back with nice young families, not like these immigrant families who were so different than everyone else. This was the predominant thought for many of the upper crust elites of the Amicable township. Immigration is what had begun to unravel the niceness of the community. These people who came from different countries, not even different states! Bringing their non-Amicable cultures and traditions. Some of them didn't even go to church!

How could they not see that the citizenry of Amicable were friendly and open hearted as long as the foreigners worked hard for a living and spoke English?

Penny turned right at the corner of Second Avenue and almost ran into Donna Humphries, a similarly clad matron who was meandering too close to the center of the sidewalk.

"Oh," Penny said, perturbed but far too nice to show it, "I'm so sorry, Donna."

Donna's face registered similar irritation momentarily, but she was quick to hide it. "Penny, heavens! You must be in a hurry."

Penny held up her hands to squelch that kind of urban talk. "No, no no, Donna, just out for a brisk walk to pick up my pork chops this morning. On sale."

"Sure, sure. Good idea." Unsure of how long to continue the meaningless conversation, Donna put her hands on her hips giving the impression of permanence and patience allowing Penny to make the first move away. A moment of awkward silence ensued before Donna looked up at the sky and started down the conversational highway that all nice Amicableans would travel. "It's a beautiful day today, isn't it?"

Penny followed Donna's eyes to the sky, not needing to, but it was proper to give one's own meteorological assessment of the day. "Yes, a nice day, although we may get some rain next week."

Donna frowned.

"Okay, then, Donna, I'm going to get going. You have a good day, now."

Donna nodded and unhitched her hands from her hips signaling her intent to keep moving also. Penny turned and Donna watched her retreating form, her blue jeans devoid of wrinkles and her floral print flashing in the sun. Somewhat jealous of Penny's appropriately colored hair, the same hue as a copper cent coin, Donna frowned momentarily and then turned to go her own way down First Street East.

Something had been niggling in the back of Penny's mind, a small worm of discontent pushing through the coral-like membranes of her brain. Everything should have been fine: a beautiful late summer day, sun shining, blue sky glinting, birds singing. It was as if Amicable was humming its own tune, but Penny was fixated on something her daughter Naida had said the night before. Something disquieting, like a dripping tap at night. Naida, named after Penny's great grandmother Diana but with letters rearranged, (and a source of consternation to Amicableans who were used to 'normal' names like Jane, Joy and Jenny) had dropped in for a visit. Unannounced, Naida had dropped by and after a brief 'hello' had moved to the kitchen and reached into the cupboard for a sachet of tea. (It was inappropriate to have a beer on a weeknight. That would have been frowned upon by even the most liberal of Amicableans.) Naida proceeded to wreak havoc on Penny's contentedness. Naida and her husband (a very respectably named James) were having 'difficulties,' which Naida metaphorically captured by using her fingers as faux quotation marks. When Penny pressed her about what 'difficulties' meant, mirroring the same use of fingers, Naida sighed deeply and said they were having a failure to communicate.

"You need to figure that out."

Naida put her chin on her hands, which were resting on the table staring morosely at the untouched steaming cup of tea in front of her eyes. "I know, Mom, I don't need a lecture." A tear formed in the corner of her left eye, a gentle pool of emotion that rarely appeared. "But it's really hard. I think he wants a…"

Naida could not bring herself to speak of the 'D' word, which in Amicable was as damaging as death. Divorce meant death of a relationship, whereas death was, in the minds of the gentle people of Amicable, an inevitability where nice Amicablean lives passed on to the pleasant confines of heaven which, in the imagination of the populace, would be almost identical to the earthly town of Amicable replete with bakery, cafe and grocery store. Divorce was not nice. Divorce had no place in Amicable.

As Penny journeyed to the butcher's shop, she noticed an incredibly tall man standing in front of the door of the bowling alley looking at a piece of paper in his hands. Glancing up and down, as if making dreadfully sure that this was the right place and knowing that it wasn't, but looking dreadfully out of place because no one ever got lost in Amicable, the man turned to his left to see Penny approaching. A warm smile, gentle and broad, welcomed her close to him, and almost instantaneously, Penny was drawn to ask him the inevitable Amicable question.

"Can I help you?" Whenever an Amicablean produced these words, there was a surety, a heartfelt *knowing*, that the receiver of the question would respond *No, thank you. I'll be fine.*

But the man crushed the paper up in his large hand (Penny had noticed this already) and put it in his pocket. "Yes. Could you?"

Taken aback by the positive response, but feeling slightly warmed by the opportunity to actually help someone in need, (thankfully not an immigrant) Penny stood next to the tall man. Looking up into his brown eyes, deep, intense pools of concentration and, Penny noticed with a slight hiccup of breath, kindness, Penny smiled back at him. "Certainly."

"I'm looking for Peterson's Butcher Shop. Is this it?" He was staring at the address on the wall which had seemed to match the one on the recently crumpled piece of paper. "13 First Avenue, Amicable?"

Penny shook her head. "You've got the right number, but wrong road. This is First Street. First Avenue is just around the corner. Fortunately for you (good Amicableans would never have registered their fate to luck - only fortune) I'm going there too. Would you like me to take you?"

"That would be wonderful," the man responded. He waited for Penny to make the next move.

Aware now of the slight conundrum that had presented itself, that of walking the streets of Amicable with a strange man, who was not her husband, Penny had a decision to make. Penny's husband, Tony, was what Amicableans would call an 'old fashioned' man. His instincts for matrimonial protection were not about jealousy but how things would look. What would Tony say if he saw her walking with this tall man? What would Amicableans say? Shrugging her shoulders slightly, Penny decided she was happy to be helping him and if people around town wanted to talk, let them talk. Amicable needed shaking up every once in a while.

Walking together in silence, Penny felt an excitement, not physical, but a *stirring*, a new feeling of something different occurring. Amicable didn't get many strangers, and this man with his certain *tallness*, would stand out as a stranger even if he was just going to pick up discounted pork chops from Peterson's.

Breaking the silence, the man stopped and turned towards Penny. "My name is Leopold. Leopold Jensen." He stuck his hand out and down to her.

Penny looked down at his hand and studied it before shaking. Small tufts of blond hair sprouted from the skin between his knuckles. She was surprised to see a variety of cuts, some scabbed others already morphed into white scars. Taking his hand in hers and shaking it firmly (that's how it was done in Amicable - two shakes and drop, especially between men and women), Penny introduced herself.

"Mrs. Penny Reynolds." It was proper for her to give her marital status so as not to give any ideas. His hand was warm. She was surprised when he reached up with his other hand for the somewhat inappropriate two-handed shake reserved for close friends, or Reverend Deakins on Sunday mornings, as he stood appropriately spaced apart from his flock in his white alb at the back of the church. Penny had forgotten what it felt like to be pleased and uncomfortable at the same time.

"Nice to meet you, Mrs. Reynolds."

After his admission of her marital status, it was perfectly acceptable to drop pretenses. "Penny, please."

"Okay, then. You can call me Leo."

They began walking again. His long strides outpaced hers. He slowed to accommodate her steps. She noticed. "Where are you from, Leo?"

Leo shrugged. "Here and there. I've been on the road for a while looking for work." He didn't seem embarrassed to be without a job. This would have been a rarity in Amicable.

Penny's heart raced at this interesting morsel of information. She flicked her hair over her shoulder consciously aware that she was living in the tension of opposing forces: she was hoping that no one was watching her walk with the strange man, and yet she was secretly desiring everyone in Amicable to notice her. As much as gossip was outwardly frowned upon, it was the gasoline which kept the engine of the town running. If they didn't talk about each other, nothing exciting would ever happen.

Penny had forgotten what it was like to flirt. Her heart raced as she walked with the stranger. Inwardly, she knew that there was assuredly no chance of anything transpiring from this interaction, but imaginations could be strong. A little sliver can become infected quickly.

Stranger danger. Briefly, Penny's thoughts were drawn to Tony and his limited movement from the lounge chair towards the kitchen, but she squashed them. Nothing wrong with a little bit of dangerous liaising. "You're not so talkative, are you?"

"What would you like to talk about?"

Unfortunately, they were within thirty footsteps of Peterson's Locker. Penny slowed slightly, shortening her steps even further to stretch the time out, but she knew it would be short lived.

"I don't know. I guess we most often talk about the weather."

Leo's face turned slightly to her. "Okay. The weather is nice. Next topic."

Well, that was kind of rude, Penny thought. *We should be discussing the threat of rain, or the speed of the wind, perhaps the cloud cover before we get into deeper topics like car types, farming or (gulp) politics.* "Right," she said slowly, "We could talk about why you're here in Amicable." Her voice formed the statement into a sentence as if asking permission first.

"Ah," Leo said looking up at the white and blue striped awning with the name Peterson's Locker stenciled across the front in large, block blue letters. "Here it is - Peterson's. Thank you very much, Penny, for bringing me here safely." Looking up at the brown stone building built almost one hundred years ago, birthed at very much the same time as George Hendriks and almost identical to all the other edifices in Amicable, Leo smiled as he stopped just short of the two steps up.

Penny looked into his brown eyes while ignoring the posters proclaiming the pork chop sale and the stenciled lettering on the window pointing to "This week's specials – Hamburger: ONLY FIVE DOLLARS PER POUND! YOU WANT PORK CHOPS? WE GOT 'EM. IOWA CHOPS. SO GOOD FOR GRILLING!"

"You're very welcome, Leo," she said somewhat disappointedly.

The tall man ascended the cement stairs freshly swept of dirt and loose stone and opened the door. A small bell suspended above the door tinkled as he opened it. With a smile he looked back towards Penny who followed him upwards.

As he held the door open, Penny nodded in thanks for his consideration and then moved through the carnage of recently slaughtered farm animals to select from raw cuts of loin, chop and shoulder, all the while keeping an ear open for the conversation, which she knew was going to occur behind her.

Leopold glanced around the butchery. Like most other butcheries, Peterson's was long, narrow and white. Display cases holding cuts of beef, pork and chicken were decorated with links of sausage and rashers of bacon. The tiled floor sparkled from the polishing given earlier that morning. A saw buzzed in the background. All noises echoed, resonating back and forth through the front of the shop. As Leopold approached the weary looking butcher, a young man in his twenties who was stifling his seventeenth yawn for the day, he was aware of the dismal sense of drudgery that filled the room. This young man had a sense of hopelessness about him, a future that was so clear, but so unenviable, it was written all over his face.

Leo cleared his throat and the young man looked up. "Can I help you?"

Nodding, Leo moved towards the display case and leaned on it. "I'm looking for Nash Peterson."

The young man, Derek, as was written in gold stenciling on his blood-stained apron, looked back over his shoulder. "Nash!" he shouted just as the saw started up again. Waiting for the sound to stop, Derek smiled and shrugged. Leo returned the smile and waited with him. When the saw quit, Derek repeated his shout.

"Nash!"

"What!" The voice called from the back.

"You've got a visitor."

"Who is it?" Obviously, Nash was busy with other things, but it was uncommon for a shop owner to neglect a patron. That wasn't nice.

"What's your name?" Derek asked quietly.

"Leopold. Leopold Jensen."

"LEOPOLD JENSEN!" Leo smirked at the exchange.

"Who is that?" Nash called out.

"I don't know, Nash. Maybe you should COME OUT HERE AND FIND OUT!" Derek shrugged apologizing with his hands.

As the newborn silence reigned, Derek moved away from Leo and towards Penny. "Is there anything I can get for you, Mrs. Reynolds?"

"Yes, Derek, but give me a few more moments. I haven't decided what I'm going to take home with me." Penny's hands were pushed into the back pockets of her blue jeans as she stared into the glass display.

"Okay, Mrs. Reynolds."

At that moment, Nash Peterson walked around the corner. Wiping his hands on his apron, he approached the counter and lifted the bench which folded up and over. Nash Peterson was Derek Peterson's identical twin. As Derek smiled, Leo was disconcerted by the *sameness* of the two butchers. Nash extended his hand and Leo's first response, because of the gore, was to refrain, but he was used to the accoutrements of the abattoir. Shaking his hand, Leo reintroduced himself.

"Ah, yes," Nash crossed his arms and leaned back slightly. The young butcher had a full head of dark hair, sparkling white teeth and milky brown eyes. He exuded both a sense of restlessness and confidence, a comfort in his own skin somewhat dissimilar to his identical twin brother. "You're the one who applied for the job."

Penny's ears perked up. So, this could be a new resident of Amicable? How exciting!

"Yes, I read about the opening on your website. Is the position still available?"

Nash nodded. "We're looking to add one more set of hands to cut meat. Do you want to come back to the office to talk?"

Leo shook his head. "Whatever is on the paper is just words. I can show you what I can do, if you'd like. That might be better than any resume, right?"

Nash and Derek both laughed at the same time. Leo smiled.

"Sure, sure. Why don't you come on behind the counter, we'll get you an apron and break this side of pork."

Leo moved past Nash and walked over to the wall smelling familiarly of blood and lard. The cool air of the butchery bought instantaneous goosebumps to his arms. For the first time, he noticed the sound of a radio playing in the background. Throwback music to the 1980's. The music seemed to be the rage around the Midwest, or maybe it had never not been the rage. Madonna was singing about all the possessions that she would like her man to give her. Putting his head through the apron strap, Leo then tied it behind his back.

"Do you want a mesh glove?" Nash asked.

"No thank you," Leo said.

"Suit yourself. Knife?"

Leo laughed. "It's harder to cut with my teeth, but if that's what you want…" Nash smiled broadly, already liking this man.

"So, how would you like this?" Leo asked.

"How about you cut it up and tell me what you're doing." Nash crossed his arms wondering how the 'interview' would play out, but then, just seconds later, he watched with awe as Leo's knife flashed with a speed he had never seen.

"Loin cuts, roasts and chops, Mr. Peterson." Within minutes, Leo had trimmed the meat out and set the cuts into piles. Derek, who had left his post as salesman, watched mouth open also. It seemed as if Leo had not even broken a sweat. Not only did it appear as if he had not broken a sweat, Nash wasn't sure if he even had his eyes open.

"Impressive," Nash said and turned towards his brother who shrugged and smirked. "But please don't call me Mr. Peterson."

"Yeah," Derek called from his position in the doorway. "I'm Mr. Peterson."

Nash rolled his eyes. "You can call me Nash. This is our father's shop; he and our mom are on vacation for the next few months."

"How old are you two?" Leo asked.

Nash tilted his head back, laughed and looked at his brother before answering. "I'll be asking the questions here, Mr. Jensen."

Leopold grinned, but waited for an answer.

"We're twenty-one years old. How about yourself?"

The tall man paused before answering and then clasped his hands in front of him. "I'm old enough to be your… uncle, at least."

"And are you married?"

"Is it a prerequisite?"

Penny's ears were straining to hear the answer to the last question. She was disappointed that the stranger had not answered it. Why the mystery?

"Just curious. If you're going to work in Amicable, you'll recognize that everyone has… what's the right phrase, Derek?"

Derek scratched his wavy head of hair. "Guarded inquisitiveness."

Nash's gaze returned to Leopold. "Yeah, that's a good way to put it. People want to know your business without actually wanting to know you."

"What do you mean?"

Nash shrugged. "It's like any other kind of information - there's power in it. If I know your data, your statistics, if you're married, have kids, for instance, then I can formulate some patterns and ideas about how you operate."

"And then what?" Leopold smirked and raised an eyebrow.

"Then what *what*?"

"What happens when you get to know the person rather than just their information? It would seem that eventually by asking questions, one might start to… what's the phrase I'm looking for?"

Derek was ready to fill in. "You might adhere to them?"

Leo nodded. "I like that. That's good - adhere to them."

"Nah," Nash responded crossing his arms. "People don't stick here in Amicable. We're kind of like a big town made out of Teflon. Everything just slides on and off."

Penny, silent and listening, wanted to disagree and interject, but she couldn't. Spending time in the eaves listening to the droppings of conversation was not considered a nice way to interact socially. Amicableans, though, were incredibly good at *finding out* the details of their neighbor's lives.

"Sounds lonely."

All three butchers shrugged simultaneously. Penny, Derek and Nash were unconcerned with the loneliness factor as long as the people of Amicable had no dirt. Trust was the most precious commodity in the town and very few people attempted to mine for it. The outer crust, years of detritus packed by pressure and circumstances, apathy and fear, broke the bits of friendship causing the small town to simply float into the future. The bedrock of trust was left largely untouched because prospecting for it would be far too emotionally expensive and painful.

Penny tugged at her shirt pulling the tuck out from her jeans just a little further to unconsciously cover her middle, but the core of her existence was to protect herself. If pressed, she would say that she trusted Tony, although that would probably be an exaggeration. Verbally she would express her confidence in Naida, but if she was honest with herself, she would recognize how little of her own mind and heart she shared with her daughter because of her fear that Naida's willingness to share with others in the community would have negative consequences in Penny's life.

"No," Nash said, "It's just the reality of where we live."

"So, what you're saying is," Leopold said, "If I want to have a job without relational attachments, Amicable is the place to be?"

"Exactly," the twins responded at the same time.

"And if I want relational attachments?"

"There's always online dating." Derek thought this incredibly witty and began to slap the glass in front of him.

Leopold sighed. "Okay."

"Okay, what?" Nash responded.

"I'll take the job."

"I haven't offered it to you yet."

"So...?"

Nash looked at his brother who shrugged and raised his eyes. "Do we have the authority to hire someone when Dad isn't here?"

Derek's face flashed dark for a moment. Something deeper stung inside of him, a memory, or a pain of the past. "It's Dad's fault if a great butcher shows up and wants a job. I say, welcome to Peterson's butchery, Mr. Jensen."

"Agreed." Nash stuck out his hand over the counter, extending the greeting. "Do you want to sign the papers now?"

Leo shook his head. "No, I'll come back tomorrow. I'd like to spend some time today finding a place to live."

"Suit yourself," Nash said. "We'll see you tomorrow at 7:30 a.m. How does that sound?"

Leo nodded. "I'll see you then."

The tall man left and moments after the doorbell tinkled signaling his departure, Nash, Derek and Penny looked at each other. "That was interesting," Derek said.

"Interesting indeed," Nash responded. "Now, Mrs. Reynolds. Have you decided yet?"

Penny's thoughts were still trailing at a polite distance behind the stranger walking down the street. She shook her head and fixed her eyes back on Nash. "Honestly, I don't remember. But, as long as I'm here, I'll get some steaks."

"Good choice, Mrs. Reynolds. Good choice."

Chapter 2.

Liam Wilson heard the phone ring, but, after a full day of working, he felt that he was unavailable for interruptions at, he checked his watch, 8:47 p.m. It was traditional, if not considerate, to never call after eight o'clock p.m. and only then if an emergency. If such a moment arose, the caller must first apologize for the lateness of the hour and then, with as much haste as possible, state one's business and get on with it. Liam was hoping this was not an emergency, and it usually wasn't. Almost always, when someone called at this time of night, they were stuck on County Road 72, out of gas, a blown tire, or maybe even a radiator that was screaming. Tonight, though, Liam was ready to put his feet up and not worry one bit about the rest of the automotive world outside of Amicable.

It had been a normal day of oil changes, disc repair and a few tire alignments. Sometimes he wished someone would really blow a gasket, or at the very least, drop the transmission. Those kinds of things rarely happened in Amicable as the residents were prompt about their oil changes, lube jobs and engine services. A blown engine was about as likely as the moon to fall out of the sky into Lake Ikmakota. Though Liam lived in perpetual hope, if someone really messed up their car, they were much more likely to take it into Clancy imagining that a big city mechanic would know so much better with his big city computer and big city tools.

Rolling his eyes, Liam leaned over the arm rest of his chair to where his cell phone was dancing on the lamp stand. Because there was no illuminated name, this usually meant an emergency. Sighing deeply, Liam pushed the green button and spoke into the phone.

"Yup. Liam Wilson here."

A low voice greeted him through the speaker. "Good evening."

"Yes, I said 'hello.' How can I help you?"

"Mr. Wilson, I read the ad in the paper that you have a room to rent."

No apology for the late hour? Strange. "Yes," Liam responded slowly. "My name is Liam. No 'Mr.' is necessary. And yes, I do have a room for rent. Actually, it's an entire house. Who's speaking?"

"My name is Jensen. Leopold Jensen. I just moved to Amicable and I'm looking for accommodation."

Looking for accommodation? Who talks like that in Amicable? "Is this a prank call? Ethan, is that you?" Ethan Ellsworth worked at the Amicable Elevator as a grain intake man. Ethan and Liam had been friends since elementary school. Now that they were adults, though neither married, they still spent a great deal of time together. Often, pulling pranks on each other.

"No, Mis... Liam. I've just been hired by Peterson's butchery and I need to find a place to stay. There are no available rooms anywhere in Amicable."

"No kidding," Liam mumbled, his eyes finally opening, it was then, and not for the first time, that Liam Wilson noticed that the ceiling fan needed to be cleaned. Dust bunnies hung from the end of every blade and mold, black and speckled, dotted the latticed blades. "I guess you shouldn't be that surprised. I suppose you could head up the road to Clancy - that's about fifteen miles away. I think there is a Motel 6 or 8 or whatever the number is. I would guess..."

"I don't mean to be rude, Liam, but there is a reason I chose your rental in the advertisements. I actually want to rent your room, or house. Would that be possible?"

Liam checked his watch. "It's awfully late. We'd have to get the paperwork ready, and finding the keys might be a task right now."

Silence on the other end of the phone. All of Liam's excuses seemed to be swallowed in a silent exasperation. "I would really appreciate it," Leopold said with as much patience as possible.

"Oh, I suppose." Grunting, Liam pressured the foot of the reclining chair and it snapped shut with a creak and groan. Planting his bare feet on the carpet, Liam padded across the brown shag carpet so full of dust and forgotten food it seemed to almost crunch like bare earth. "Give me a few minutes. After I find the keys, I'll meet you at the house. Do you know where it is?"

"Yes, 184 Peppertree Lane."

"Yeah, okay, but do you know how to get there."

"I'm sure that I can find it."

"Don't bet on it," Liam mumbled again acknowledging the sketchiness of cell phone reception in and around Amicable city limits. "I'll see in you in about fifteen minutes, okay?"

"Good." Jensen disconnected the phone without so much as a goodbye, which, from Liam Wilson's perspective, was completely out of touch with proper manners, but he let it go. Now that he was up and around the house, even though late, there seemed to be a chance he would make some money. All funds would go well into his investment for traveling south this winter. Last year he went to Texas, maybe this year the roads would lead to Florida, or maybe even Arizona. Anything to get out of the snow.

It was a warm summer's night, so Liam didn't take his coat. As he exited the house, he looked up at the wide expanse of stars and planets above Amicable. Mars glittered like a ruby in the inky black sky, while Venus thrust her pulsing eerie light towards her male counterpart. Not much one for astronomy, Liam could put names to a few constellations, certainly Orion's belt and maybe Cassiopeia, but other than that, they were just Litebrites into heaven. That's what he thought when he was little.

Six minutes later, keys in hand, Liam killed the ignition of his car. Not seeing another vehicle in the vicinity, Liam waited for a few minutes. Then, with growing frustration, thinking that Ethan had really messed with him, he was about to turn the ignition when a form appeared at the driver's side and tapped on the window.

Liam jumped. "Holy crap!" He exclaimed. Rolling down his window, the old knob of his pride and joy, a 1976 Ford Mustang, pine green, creaked. Liam was shouting at the man before the window was halfway down.

"What in the heck are you doing?"

"Did I frighten you?" The man asked.

"Of course, you did, you maniac! Jeepers Pete, what are you doing wandering out here in the dark?"

"I was waiting for you."

For the first time, Liam noticed the man, not so much his physical appearance, but his physical presence. He was wide at the shoulder, strong, probably; it seemed like his jacket could barely contain his chest. He was tall, must be well over six feet, maybe even six-five. He was wearing dark clothing, jeans and a button-down shirt, which was weird because male Amicableans only wore t-shirts depicting the state university team logo, the local high school mascot or any form of car racing emblem.

"Where's your car? Why didn't you park in front of the house?"

The man took a step back from the Mustang allowing Liam to swing open the door. When he did, Liam was astounded to see that the man was even taller than he thought.

"I didn't drive."

"What do you mean you didn't drive? How did you get here?"

The man was silent for a moment. After pondering the questions, he folded his hands in front of his waist. Instantly, Liam thought that he was gay. Inwardly, Liam was already making generalizations about the stranger, but to let it taint the business transaction would have been rude. Still, Liam was immediately on his guard. *The stranger would probably make a pass at him. That's what gay people do.*

"I don't have a car. I… I had a friend drop me off in town."

Liam looked down at the suitcase beside him. "Is that all the stuff you have?" He nodded. "Well, all right then." The mechanic extended his hand, which the stranger took in his and Liam was surprised at how strong his handshake was. Liam was quite sure gay people weren't supposed to be strong. "I'm Liam Wilson. I own the autobody shop on the edge of town. I live right next door to it. It's not very far from here, but I don't like to walk that much."

"Nice to meet you," the stranger said. "Leopold Jensen."

"Okay, well, I'll take you to the house and you can see if it's something you want to live in. I don't know how long a lease you want to sign, but we usually go month by month in Amicable. There aren't many people that want to rent. Only a few people who get divorced and one of them gets kicked out, or maybe some immigrants who want to live twelve people in a house…" Liam's voice trailed off.

"Month by month will be fine. I'll take it."

"You haven't even seen the inside yet." There had to be something wrong with this guy. He hadn't even told him the price yet.

"I trust that everything will be in order. Do you want first month's rent and a down payment?"

Liam swallowed. *Is this guy going to have gay parties in there?* "Yeah, that would be good. I've brought the paperwork. That will be four hundred dollars per month." Liam was sure the exorbitant price would send the stranger away, but he pulled out his wallet from his back pocket, and proceeded to count out eight one hundred-dollar bills. Liam's eyes widened - he'd never seen that much cash before.

He's not only gay, but he's a drug dealer too. Great. A gay drug dealer. There's going to be AIDS all over the place.

Accepting the bills with his fingertips, Liam made a mental note that he would need to wash the AIDS off them when he got back to his own apartment. Liam walked down the front sidewalk aware that grass and dandelions were winning a war of attrition against the cracks in the cement. Ascending the four steps, he took the keys from his pocket. Three tries and the key worked into the hole. The screen door swung outwards and after another triumvirate of attempts at the wooden door, it pushed inwards. Greeted by the smell of long deceased dust motes and too-old carpet, Liam took a deep breath. Flicking on the switch to the front living room, Liam was welcomed by the sight of his old house, dusty carpet, dusty walls and dusty memories.

"It's not much, but it's a roof over your head."

"It's very nice," Leopold said. "I'm sure it will be fine."

Liam gave him the tour of the house, through the living room with its wood paneled walls and brown carpet, which bore more than a passing resemblance to the carpet in Liam's apartment, and into the kitchen, a true throwback to the eighties with pistachio colored wall paper and yellow linoleum covering the floor. A small table with three chairs created an island in the middle of the room. A butcher's block stuck out from the counter like a culinary isthmus.

"There are a few dishes in the cupboards," Liam opened them to show Leo where they were. "And some silverware in the drawers. I'm sure you'll want to purchase your own things eventually, but this should get you through." Jensen nodded.

They moved down a corridor where two bedrooms branched from it. In each, there was a solitary bed and a cheap antique dresser. As they walked down the hallway, Liam pointed to the ceiling above them where the 'master' bedroom was located. 'Master' was in quotation marks because the 'master' bedroom lacked a 'master' bathroom. In these bedrooms, Liam mentioned the beautiful handmade quilts covering the beds. Unfortunately, these quilts seemed to have been part of a gastronomic cuisine for moths. Leo noticed that apart from the living room with its solitary sofa, a worn out recliner and a kitchen table and chairs, the house was bereft of an interior decorator's touch.

"I'm sorry there isn't more for you to sit on, but the place doesn't get used much. It seems kind of silly to furnish it." He shrugged and moved back out to the living room. "If you want a TV, I can round one up for you somewhere."

"No, that will be fine. I don't watch TV."

Liam stared up into his eyes for a few seconds aware of the oddity of his statement. *This guy must be an alien - from a different planet. A gay alien who deals drugs. Who doesn't watch TV? In Amicable, that's like saying you're a vegetarian!* "Okay..." Liam said slowly. "Is there anything I can get you? Something to eat, maybe?"

"That's very nice of you," Jensen responded, "But I'll be just fine. I had dinner at the restaurant on Highway 10 a little bit earlier. I can't remember the name of it."

"That'll be The Traveler's Choice. People around here call it The Traveler's Choke because there was this one time that Josh Aalgard choked on some kind of chicken and they had to do the Hindlick maneuver on him."

Leo smirked, but did not correct the mechanic. He knew that Midwesterners sometimes mispronounced words – exchanging 'prostrate' and 'prostate' being the most unfortunate. "Good to know, Liam."

"Okay, then, Leopold. Folks in this town don't appreciate parties, loud noises, this includes shouting, pounding, music, etcetera, etcetera, etcetera," he motioned with his hand as if it were the most boring thing in the world. He stopped. It seemed like kind of a gay thing to do. "No smoking, pets, if you have them or if you get them, will require that I keep your deposit for cleaning at the end."

"I don't have any pets."

"If you had them," Liam responded, "They probably wouldn't be that happy living in your suitcase."

Leo Jensen chuckled. It was a low grumble, three quick exhalations, *ha he he*, which in Liam's expert opinion sounded strangely like a 1995 Cavalier starting up.

"I'm going to get going now, but you have my phone number if you need it." Liam tapped his pocket. "Feel free to call me day or night as long as it's day and not night." Leopold smiled again unsure if the mechanic was serious or not.

"Thank you, Liam."

Liam walked to the front door and swung it shut behind him. "You don't really have to worry about locking up at night. Your neighbor's next door, the Walton's, are pretty good about keeping an eye on things and they certainly aren't shy about calling the cops, or in Amicable's case, the cop, Louise Nelson. Unfortunately, if you or they call her, it will take at least twenty minutes to get here."

"Does she live a long way away?"

"No," Liam responded without explaining. "I'll see you whenever. Stop by sometime if you need a car. I could have something for you if you need it."

"I appreciate it."

Liam opened the screen door and looked back towards Jensen who was standing motionless in the middle of the dusty living room. Closing the door behind him, Liam shook his head.

I bet he was staring at my butt. That's what gay people do.

Chapter 3.

Rhonda Redman opened The Traveler's Choice at six o'clock every morning. It was her regular routine to open the doors, turn on the coffee makers, open the blinds and start the air conditioning, all in that order. Now that it was five twenty-seven, she knew the farmers would be waiting outside to come in. Usually it was David Kellog first, or sometimes Joseph Bartman. Both kept fastidiously to their regular routines even during the long, dark hours of the winter. Bottomless cups of coffee were the fuel of the community. Rhonda knew that in cities people would buy singular cups of coffee, which were placed into semi-heat resistant paper cups. The city folks would then walk around in the morning looking important and busy while sipping their coffee and carrying on unnecessarily loud conversations with other similarly important and busy city folks. City folks didn't do well around Amicable, though, and no Amicablean in his or her right mind would dare carry one of those paper cups around town. It was best to load up at The Traveler's Choice, drink as much coffee as possible in thirty minutes and then spend the rest of the morning running back and forth from the bathroom.

As she wiped down the tables, a figure passed by the front windows. Too quick for her to catch who it was, Rhonda assumed it was Dean Swenson and continued to prepare for the morning onslaught of Amicableans needing coffee, breakfasts of bacon and eggs and orders of toast with strawberry jam on the side. Once, many years ago, she tried to buy blueberry jam, but the outcry was so loud, she donated the jar to the trashcan a few hours later.

The front door opened and she was surprised to see that it was neither Dave nor Joe nor Dean, but a stranger. A very tall stranger. Rhonda thought she knew almost everyone in the tri-county area, and especially someone of this size, but then it hit her - this was the man that Penny was talking about yesterday afternoon. Penny Reynolds and her exercise group, six other ladies, all middle aged, all seeking social opportunities, normally stopped in on exercise afternoons to have a glass of water and a muffin. Rhonda was unsure if they actually worked off the calories for a muffin, but she didn't care.

Penny had been speaking loudly enough about her encounter for the entire patronage of the restaurant to hear her. "He was so mysterious. It was like he was a spy or something."

Linda Harmsen, still wearing her exercise outfit, a billowy t-shirt, appliqued flowers and an American flag, and sweatpants, leaned forward chin melting into the cupped palm of her hand. Her incredibly large breasts rested on the table. "I love a mystery. There's nothing mysterious about Richard. He's like a billboard. Everything advertised, nothing hidden."

The others laughed.

Leslie Tielman took a nervous sip of her coffee. "Tell us more about him. Was he good looking?" For most of the women, the definition of good looking was a lack of love handles and a general sense of hygiene.

"He was," Penny said gravely, enjoying the attention of the not-so-desperate wives. "He was incredibly tall - freakishly, maybe about six foot six." The tallest husband of the five women was Ed Simpson, Leona's husband, who was a shade over six foot one. He had played on Amicable's basketball team way back in the 80's and was considered something of a local legend. Leona was always quick to bring up her husband's athletic exploits even if they had been moldering for more than thirty years. "He also had incredibly intense eyes."

"What color were they?" Jeannie Dolling asked.

Penny thought for a moment. "I don't know. I was too taken by his…" Her pause caused all the other women to lean in, anxious to hear Penny's recollection of the strange new man. Hoping beyond hope that she wouldn't speak of his personality. They all wanted to hear her talk about his…

"Muscles."

The women tittered, some blushing, some reddening at the thought of a man actually having muscles that were not hidden behind sedimentary adipose tissue.

"So, he had big..." Leslie could barely speak. Taking herself to the place of imagining the muscles of another man would be a big no-no in Reverend Deakins' book. At least one, if not two, commandments would be broken if continuing down that path.

"Yes," Penny said quietly, "his sleeves were straining at the biceps." She looked around at the others who were in states of metaphorical fanning.

"I think I'm going to check this man out," Jeannie proclaimed guiltily and then looked around at the rest of the diner to see if anyone actually heard her exclamation.

"Shhhh," Linda pushed a finger to her lips, even though no one else in the room was paying attention to their conversation.

"What else can you tell us about him?" Jeannie questioned.

"Not much. He's beginning a job at Peterson's, quite a wizard with the knife, I'll say. He didn't have a place to stay so he was going out looking for a room after the interview."

"What's his name?" Linda asked.

A strange look came over Penny's face as if she'd chewed on an eggshell and it was still crunching between her teeth. To hide her embarrassment, she took another sip of her coffee, but she couldn't remember his name. Penny shrugged. "Does it matter?"

"Does it matter! Are you kidding, Penny?" Leona was exasperated. "Of course it matters. How else will we know how to address him?"

Penny frowned. "I'm sorry. I don't remember," she said. "We might as well call him 'Butcher.'"

"How vulgar," Linda rolled her eyes. "You can't call him by his career. That's stupid."

"Why not?" Penny responded with more intensity than necessary, but something was stirring in her. "We call doctors, 'Dr.' and pastors, 'Reverend,' why not butchers?"

The group pondered the logic and then nodded in unison. "Okay," Leona said, "We'll call him 'Butcher.'"

Rhonda watched as Butcher approached the front counter, his blue jeans seemed just a little bit short for his frame. Penny was right; he must be close to six foot eight. Muscular, taut, as if he was pulled and stretched to the very limits of thinness, this man seemed angular and muscular at the same time. Rhonda wiped her hands and moved towards the front desk where a sign proclaimed in movable type that visitors should refrain from seating themselves.

Rhonda looked up into his eyes. They seemed like a mile away. She was captivated by the large brown orbs. "Table for one?" Rhonda's voice squeaked. She cleared her throat and berated herself. He was just a stranger after all, but goodness, a handsome one. A smirk had magically appeared on his face. He looked like a male version of the Mona Lisa.

The Mona Louis.

"Yes," his deep, resonant voice seemed to echo in the vacant room. "I'll take a table for one, coffee for starters and then a menu would be great."

Rhonda nodded and showed him to the corner window table. No one else had entered the restaurant so she would give him the best of the tables. *Was it to curry favor with him?* Leading him to the table, Rhonda was aware of her ever so slight extra sway of her hips; a small movement of her wrist like a ballerina focusing her charms and even her hair how it danced behind her head in a beautiful ponytail. Although Rhonda was tall, she seemed dwarfed by the giant behind her.

"Here you go," she welcomed him to the corner table with her hand. Feeling silly about the hand movements, she reached into her apron pocket and extracted a green order slip. As he sat down, she filled his coffee mug to the brim and motioned towards a menu stuck resolutely into the stainless-steel stand in front of the window. "Just signal when you know what you want." For a moment, she did not realize the double entendre of her statement, but when she did, she blushed and turned away from him. Fortunately, he was already busying himself with the menu.

"I'll have the pancakes," he spoke to her leaving form before she took half a dozen steps from him. Turning around, she noticed that the sun was reflecting in the window behind his head causing his hair to glow.

"Good choice," she said.

"Thanks," he smiled at her and turned to look out the window at the not-quite-busy highway outside. Most Amicableans believed a traffic jam was occurring if a tractor held up traffic for five minutes. Although this was an annoyance, none of them would grumble, and certainly no one would honk their horns. Beeping was never used in frustration. That would not be nice. Honking occurred only with joy when the football team won, or a short tap was given when you recognized someone on the street.

Rhonda took the order back to the cook who was leaning lazily against the aluminum kitchen bench flitting through his social media account. Rodrigo, a naturalized American citizen from Mexico, one of the foreigners who were derided for 'taking the jobs of real Americans,' smiled at his phone. Rodrigo was not the Amicablean stereotype of a Mexican. He learned English quickly and blended into the community, or as much as his darker skin would allow him. Rodrigo was quite certain that the job that he had 'taken' wasn't highly sought after by any other Amicablean.

"Drigo," Rhonda and Rodrigo enjoyed working together. He was quiet and friendly and she had never seen him sink to anger. "Order in."

Rodrigo quickly turned off his phone, adjusted his hairnet and smiled. "Bueno, señorita."

Rhonda looked back towards the front window where the stranger sat, still transfixed by the slowly moving pickups beginning to move into town. Rhonda was sure that almost every citizen of Amicable owned at least one pickup truck, if not two, and all would be of a domestic make. Derision followed David Phelps when he bought a Nissan, once. Phelps sold the taboo object two weeks later and bought a Ford. A big one.

Ten minutes later, Rodrigo interrupted Rhonda's pensive staring with a bell. "Order up, Rhonda." He pronounced her name, 'Rohwnda,' which always made her smile.

Taking the plate from him, she gathered a glass jug of maple syrup, and made her way across the well-aged brown carpet (that used to be maroon) worn thin with foot traffic. Placing the light, fluffy pancakes in front of the stranger, she stepped back, hands on her hips and stared down at him.

"So, you're the new guy in town. The butcher."

He looked up sharply, wondering how news had travelled so quickly. "How did you know?"

"I hear all sorts of things at the Chok…" she almost pronounced it 'Choke' but caught herself. "The Traveler's Choice."

He shrugged.

"So, you're going to be staying a while?" Rhonda knew that her question could be considered nosy, especially around the Midwest.

"I hope so," he responded as he began to pour a lake of syrup around his pancakes.

"Do you mind if I ask you a question?"

Smiling, but not looking at her, he nodded and then proceeded to cut a forkful of pancake and stuff it into his open mouth.

"Where are you from?"

Leo finished swallowing, then took his napkin and wiped his mouth before answering. "Did you want to sit down?" He pointed to the seat opposite him.

"I really shouldn't," Rhonda's eyes went to the empty chair.

"I don't think the rest of the clientele will care." They both looked around at the empty restaurant, the early morning light filtered through half open blinds.

"Okay," she said quickly, pulling out a chair. "But only for a little bit."

"Only for a little bit." He took a sip of coffee and leaned back in his chair. "I'm thirty-nine years old."

"That's not the question I asked."

30

Leopold stared into her green eyes positioned behind heavily made up lids bordered by black mascara. He cleared his throat and moved forward. "Why does everyone want to know where I'm from."

She laughed. "You do realize that you're in the Midwest, don't you? People can make a living finding out where other people come from."

"What about you? Is that how you make a living?"

"No," she said slowly, "but I'm pretty sure I know where every human being in this town is from, and probably their parents and grandparents too. See, it's just..." Rhonda paused to find the right words. "If you know where someone is from, you're likely to know how they'll act and react in different situations."

"For instance...?"

"Let's say you were from a big city like Omaha, or even bigger, like Minneapolis," Leopold smiled at her 'big' city choices, "The odds are you'd get frustrated quickly. You'd be impatient and pushy. You wouldn't last very long."

"I'm not from either of those places. What about if I was from Missouri?"

Rhonda's eyes glinted. "I know you're not from Missouri because of your accent."

"Where do you think I'm from?" Leo took another bite of his pancakes and smirked at his dining partner.

Appraising his hair, his clothes and his demeanor, Rhonda scratched her head. "Well, you don't come across as a big city person, which rules out Kansas City and Chicago." She shivered with a memory. "Your accent places you probably somewhere in the Midwest south of North Dakota and north of Missouri. My guess is that if you've come to Amicable, you're probably small-town Iowa."

"Huh." He didn't look at her, but took another sip of coffee. "Interesting."

"Am I right?"

He shrugged and waggled a hand. "Kind of..."

"What does that mean?"

Leopold stopped for a moment and looked out the window again where the slow-moving forms of Gordon and Anne Johnson, (married sixty-three years in May) who both required walking aids, were struggling across the gravel parking lot which once again had been destroyed by the winter snows. Gordon and Anne were faithful patrons every morning at The Traveler's Choice. Gordon's ability to drive was as suspect as George Hendriks' even though he was a full ten years younger. *A spring chicken*, George would say.

Leo spoke to the window. His voice bounced off the glass towards Rhonda. "I didn't come from a big city, but I have lived in them before; I didn't grow up in a small town, but I do enjoy them… for the most part."

Rhonda's eyes narrowed and she too followed the glacial movement of the Johnsons as they made their way to the front door. "You don't really want to tell me anything about yourself, do you?"

Leopold smirked. "What about you? Where are you from?"

Rhonda pushed herself back from the table. "Here, where else? You don't think just anybody would qualify for this job." Standing up, she began to make her way to the front door where Gordon and Anne would be entering momentarily.

"Are you coming back?" Leo asked.

"Do you want me to?"

He nodded.

"Give me a few minutes to get these two situated. I can't promise I'll be able to sit down, though." Something warm surged inside her, a tide of intrigue, like she had taken a large sip of hot chocolate on a winter night and it was heating her up from the inside out.

The front door opened slowly and even slower still, the elderly couple managed to allow Rhonda to push past them so that they could finagle their walkers under her arched arm. Gordon, who used to be almost six feet tall, barely reached five seven now. As the tall waitress held the door for him, he thanked her. Anne, on the other hand, tried to swat Rhonda out of the way. Grumpy by nature, Anne seemed to be in a perpetual state of irritation. She did not like growing old. She did not like other people patronizing her. She did not like it at all.

Placing them at a table as far away from the butcher as possible, she took their orders - scrambled eggs and bacon for him, and an omelet with tabasco sauce for her (Rhonda was never surprised), poured them some coffee and then gave Rodrigo his next orders.

Keeping busy for ten minutes while Rodrigo prepared, Rhonda looked over at the butcher who seemed not to be in a hurry whatsoever. *He must be from Iowa. Maybe Nebraska, if you pushed it.* After Rodrigo signaled the order ready with the bell, she hurriedly brought the food to the octogenarians.

"Thank you," Gordon said and patted her hip. Anne noticed where his hand was and gave him, and her, a dirty look. He smiled congenially at his wife who began to shake large doses of tabasco sauce on top of her omelet.

"Is there anything else I can get for you, Mr. and Mrs. Johnson?"

Simultaneously they shook their heads. Rhonda made her way across the room to where the butcher was waiting for her. Without asking, she decided to slide into the seat again.

"Thanks for coming back to me, Rhonda." He had finished his pancakes and had refilled his coffee mug at least once while waiting for her.

"My pleasure."

"So, you're from here," the butcher continued the conversation asking a question in the form of a statement.

Rhonda crossed her arms. "I'll be asking the questions around here," her voice quivered slightly as she laughed at her joke. "I'd like to know what you think you can guess about my past just from first blush." It was first blush because she looked down as the red rose to her cheeks. She waited as the butcher's eyes took in her appearance, sliding from her eyes, to her lips, down her neck, to her name tag and apron.

"My guess," he said slowly, both hands cupping the coffee mug in front of him, "is that not only have you lived here your entire life, but you haven't really had a choice." Rhonda looked up sharply, a nerve had

33

already been touched. "One of your parents has needed your help, probably financial as much as anything else, and you stayed because, my guess is, they made you feel guilty." Rhonda swallowed. "You took the job in this restaurant because the owners would hire someone like you."

"What do you mean by that?"

Leopold's eyes fastened on hers. "You had promise in high school, the homecoming queen, or at least an athlete of note with the height of yours." She had been both. "You were set to go to college, not a large one, maybe even a community college, on a scholarship, athletic, probably. But your parents – no, mother - didn't want you to go, so you didn't and now that you've stayed in Amicable, every day you wonder what could have been."

Rhonda's mouth dropped open. "How did you know that? Who have you been talking to?"

It was Leo's turn to look down. "I've been to a lot of places. I know how to read people."

The front door opened again, and Rhonda was frustrated that she would have to get up to serve them. This mysterious man in front of her had somehow gleaned her life from her appearance.

"Will you wait a little. I just have to…"

Leo reached out his hand. "I can't. I've got to get to work. Can I have my check, please?"

Distractedly she nodded and reached into her apron pocket extracting the green order pad. Ripping it off, she handed it to him.

He smiled. She didn't.

It was a very weird start to the day.

Chapter 4.

Nash Peterson watched the form of their new employee walking across the street. It was only seven o'clock in the morning, but he had been at the butchery since 6:30 prepping the tables, knives and anything else for the day ahead. Derek did not have the same gumption as Nash did, and Nash was quite sure that his brother was just getting out of bed, probably checking his social media. If he was lucky, Derek would arrive by 7:40 for an 8:00 opening, but he didn't really mind that much. The two brothers were best friends and if Derek had a shortcoming about being prompt, he could forgive him. Nash wasn't all that good with other things, so they evened each other out.

Nash watched Leopold Jensen cross the road and was amused to see other Amicableans behind him stare at the stranger. Staring was generally considered rude in Amicable, but for outsiders, it was allowed. This new guy was definitely an outsider. *Look at the way he walks! And how tall is he? Six ten? Where did he get his clothes? Do I need to show him the barber shop?* All these questions passed quickly through the young man's brain and out again.

Leopold approached the door and after looking left and right, he pushed on the door. It was locked, so he put two hands to the glass and peered through. When he saw Nash, he waved. Nash, still behind the counter, pointed up at the clock and mouthed the words *You're early,* to which Leopold nodded and opened his hands. *Probably a brown-noser,* Nash thought. Making a good impression, at least. No sense showing up after Derek.

Lifting the folded part of the bench, Nash moved towards the door. Leopold had backed away and was looking up and down the street at the townspeople who were not-so-surreptitiously avoiding his sight now. He smiled. Nash opened the door and the fresh morning air greeted him. Although he'd been outside briefly, the sun had brought different scents to the air: freshly mown grass from Winslow Park five

35

blocks away. The smell of growing things and black earth wafted from the oceans of fields surrounding the town. In the recipe for early morning goodness was the aroma of baking bread from Goldman's Bakery, *2nd best bagels in the Midwest!*; and the scent of early morning exhaust fumes from the steady flow of domestic pickups parading slowly down the street, some heading to The Traveler's Choice, the others stopping at the grocery store for early morning shopping.

"Come on in, Leo," Nash said, holding the door open for the waiting giant. "You're a little bit early."

"I know, but I was ready to get started."

"You know you don't get paid by the hour," Nash started. "You're on salary, just like Derek and me. If you show up early, that's your volunteer hours."

"Gotcha, boss." The tall man was already waiting at the folded counter door for Nash who was closing the front door and locking it.

"We don't start until eight o'clock, so if you want to make yourself useful, you can start taking the plastic wrap off the front meat trays."

Leo nodded. "And after that?"

Nash looked around. "We have pork trimmings left over from last night. Are you any good at making sausages? Bratwursts?"

"Not a problem." For the next half hour (it was forty-two minutes exactly before Derek showed up, his hair sticking up at odd angles, and one of his buttons was missing) Leo did exactly as he was told. His efficiency was so great, though, that after the short tour and groundwork of workplace health and safety, Leo had linked six dozen sausages into hog casings ready for sale.

Nash watched him out of the corner of his eye and then, when Leo was about to ask the next logistical question, he spoke first. "You're pretty quick."

"Yes," Leo said simply.

"You can slow down. Maybe even match Derek's pace or you might work us out of a job." Nash laughed at his semi-serious attempt at humor.

"I know I can slow down," Leo said as he stood with his hands folded in front of him, "but I choose not to."

Nash looked around at the freshly prepped meat display with twenty minutes to spare. He could see Derek behind Leo's shoulder moving towards the cafe to buy their morning caffeine.

"What do you like to do, Butcher?" Nash was pleased with his nickname of the new employee. His father would never allow him to call Leo that, but he couldn't let his dad control everything.

"I like to walk. I play a little bit of music. You know, just normal things."

"I don't like walking or playing music," Nash responded.

"I know," Leo said.

Nash frowned. "How could you know that?"

"I could tell."

"Please," Nash said, spreading his hands. "Impress me."

For many years, Leopold Jensen had known he had a gift. It wasn't one of those gifts that one unpacked, or unwrapped; it was not bound by ribbons and paper. He wasn't even sure how he got hold of the gift other than the fact that it came in very handy when he was travelling from town to town. Other times, when he just wanted his mind to be quiet, it wasn't quite as enjoyable. Leopold Jensen could read people the way some read books. The front cover was just the outer presentation, and certainly, many could intuit the difficulties of people's lives, the overview of the story from their appearance. But Leo read everything - the littlest pieces of language, phrases that might have held other meanings, the smaller non-verbal signals, vocal or visual. By looking at their hands, it was almost as if he could read the sentences of their life in the lines of their palms. Leo had at times, attempted to hide his ability. It frightened some people. Strangely, more often than not, his gift allowed him to almost, foresee the future.

Almost.

Leo knew already that Nash was the favorite twin, just by the way he held himself and the way that Derek had yelled for him the day before. The simple fact that Derek was late for work signaled a message inside Leo's brain that Nash found his value in his father's approval.

Nash was a relic of the past, a hard worker destined for community recognition in philanthropy as he donated some of his hard-earned cash to help young Amicableans. Nash said that he didn't like playing music, but he did like music as shown by the radio playing overhead, but none of the new stuff - no rap, techno, dance or the like. Listening to the 80's was not just a preference but a philosophical statement.

For Amicableans, the past was preferable to both present and future.

Leo was hesitant about sharing his gift with others too soon, although he had given Rhonda, at the restaurant, a small taste. He pondered why he had done it – to impress her? To prove superiority? He could have been much more specific including her past interactions with men, but she might have become suspicious.

"Well, your taste in music is probably limited to the last century, roughly the 1960s onward which would have been your father's music."

Nash smiled. "That's pretty good, but not all that impressive as the radio is tuned to the 'oldies' pretty much every minute of the day. That doesn't bother you, does it, Butcher?"

It was the second time that Nash had called him that, and although Leo guessed that Nash meant it as a term of superiority, he took it as a friendly exchange. "None whatsoever."

"What else?"

"How far do you want me to go?" Leo asked.

"Don't hurt me," Nash needled.

Leo smirked. "You're an identical twin which means that the two of you have shared experiences that only one in four hundred have. I've done a little reading about it after interacting with identical twins earlier in my life."

"Where was that?" Nash asked.

Leo ignored the question and raised an eyebrow. "Due to increased use of IV fertilization, especially in the last twenty years, I'd say that the odds are your parents couldn't conceive naturally which would lead me to believe that you two are test tube miracles."

Nash's eyebrows arched. "Holy sh..."

At that moment, Derek's key turned in the front door, and as he entered, his whistling echoed in the cold shop. Looking up, Derek noticed Nash's expression. "What's going on?"

"Derek, you've got to listen to this guy. He's like Sherlock Holmes or something." Nash's mouth was still slightly agape.

"What are you talking about?" Derek walked past his brother and the tall man and entered the butchers' sanctuary behind the folding door.

"He can... I don't know, see inside our souls, or something like that."

Derek scrunched up his face.

"Really! It's like he's known us all along." Nash looked at Leo. "Keep going, Butcher."

Leo looked between the two brothers. "I don't know."

As Derek put his butcher's apron over his head, he looked at Leo. "Show me what you got."

Leo took a deep breath. "So, my assumption is that you are IV babies which means your parents have treated you a little *differently* than other kids. Special. You probably weren't allowed to play football which frustrated you immensely. Well, maybe Derek was allowed to, but Nash wasn't."

Derek's jaw dropped to almost his collar. "What the heck."

"Nash you were allowed one sport, probably swimming, or some other non-contact sport. Considering that we're in the Midwest, it won't be swimming because the nearest indoor swimming pool might be three hours away. Cross country?"

Nash slapped his hand on the counter. "Holy Biscuit. You are a freak of nature. And you say you can just figure that out?"

Butcher nodded. "It doesn't take that much to figure out."

Derek's eyes opened. "Oh yes, it does. Holy crap, people don't just do that." He paused, his eyes glinting before asking the next question. "And you're saying that you can do this with anyone?"

"Yes."

Derek rubbed his hands together. "This is going to be an awesome day."

Butcher looked back and forth between the brothers. "What do you mean?"

Nash followed his brother's line of thinking. "Every person that comes into the store, we'll probably know. We want you to…" He looked at his brother to finish the sentence.

"We want you to read them, just like you did to us."

Butcher held up his hands. "No, I don't think that's such a great idea. I mean, I came here to be a butcher, to cut up meat."

"You can do that too," Nash said, "but this will add a little spice to the day."

"Still a little hesitant…"

"How about this," Derek said as he put his thumbs behind his apron straps pulling them away from his chest. "Every fifth person that walks into the store, you read them. If you get it right, we buy you a… what do you like to drink?"

Unsure of what to say, Butcher held out his hands in question. "You mean like an alcoholic drink?"

Derek rolled his eyes. "No, a quart of milk, Dipstick. Yes, of course! An alcoholic drink. You do drink booze, don't you?"

"Yes. How about some wine?"

Derek stared at him then rolled his eyes. "This is the Midwest, Butcher. Wine tastes like chicken urine."

Nash laughed at his brother. "Do chickens even piss?"

"I don't know," Derek responded, "but if they did, I'm sure it would taste like Midwestern wine."

"So what do you suggest?" Butcher asked.

"Beer, dude. Beer." Nash and Derek were of one mind on this. Derek gave his preference. "Busch Light or maybe Bud Light."

"Or, if you're really adventurous," Nash said, "you could drink Old Mud. Old Milwaukee. That stuff will set your anus on fire for days."

Derek thought this was the funniest suggestion in the world. "So, just to set the terms of this agreement: you read people, we buy you beer. Good?"

Not wanting to put off his new workmates, Butcher agreed.

"But if you get it wrong, you buy us beer. Deal?" Derek stuck out his hand to the tall man. Butcher's eyes moved back and forth between the twins. With only a slight hesitation, he reached out and shook their hands.

"I'm not really that keen on getting drunk."

Nash shook his hand and slapped him on the back. "Better get them all right then, Butcher. Problem is, there's some pretty weird people around Amicable."

Leo looked out the window and shook his head. *Don't bet your beer on it.*

Exactly eighteen minutes later, Nash unlocked the front door. Both Derek and Butcher were behind the counter preparing meat cuts. Derek, accustomed to *easing* into the work day, spent as much time sipping his coffee, now lukewarm, as he did working on the meat, but he was in awe of how quickly Butcher could cut up a quarter of beef. Butcher's knife blade seemed to be a scalpel, or a scimitar, slicing and dicing through prime muscle cuts, sinew, bone and cartilage, faster than Derek had ever seen. Setting the prime cuts to the side, Butcher did not sense the passing of time; he simply whistled unconsciously away with the 80's tunes playing on the speakers mounted above him on the walls. Whether Simon and Garfunkel, Michael Jackson or Tina Turner, Butcher's vast memory of music astounded Derek.

At precisely 8:04, the first customer of the day walked through the door and both Nash and Derek looked towards Butcher who hadn't noticed that a human had entered the shop.

"Butcher," Derek whispered. "It's time to shine."

41

"It's not the fifth customer," Butcher protested.

"We start on the first one, then the sixth, eleventh, and so forth." Derek's hands were still cradling the cup of coffee behind the counter.

Routine broken, Butcher looked up from the back of the shop, wiped his hands on his apron and carried a mittful of beef to the front counter. Various cuts of blade, rib and flank steak were draped over his large hands, but they seemed to weigh nothing.

A woman stood at the front counter peering through the glass at sausages, chops and chickens. She was roughly fifty years of age; her glasses bespoke of another generation - large rims, thick lenses, and her hair was coiffed into a ball around her head. Her makeup, which seemed to have been replicated since the mid-1970s, was tinted with blues, greens and pinks, rouged cheeks and thick eyelashes crusty with mascara. Lipstick was attached to both lip and (unfortunately) teeth. Her jeans were tight and riding high (mom jeans as he had heard from teenagers) and her blouse, a floral number, flowing around her, deemphasized her voluminous breasts, which were held firmly in place by a cross-your-heart bra.

"Hello, Mrs. Harmsen," Nash said. "What can we get you this morning?"

"Well, I don't know. What are your specials…?" Linda Harmsen pretended to *only just now* notice the tall man in the back. "Oh, Nash. You have a new employee?"

"Let me introduce you, Mrs. Harmsen. This is Butcher. Butcher, Linda Harmsen."

Butcher strode forward, long legs carrying him slowly to the display case. Linda watched him glide towards her and unconsciously adjusted her hair. "How are you?" His low voice seemed to echo deeply inside of her.

"I'm… I'm… doing just fine. That's a strange first name you have." Linda pushed a hand through the back of her hair.

"My name is…"

"His name is 'Butcher,'" Derek interjected, "although his mother gave him a different name, we like to call him 'Butcher.'"

"How could you possibly know what to call him?" Linda asked. "He's been working here all of, what, one day? Isn't that right Mr...?"

Leo smiled. "You can call me Butcher, ma'am."

"Oooh, that's funny. He called me 'ma'am'." Linda Harmsen wasn't sure whether to be offended or highly stimulated.

"Now, 'ma'am,'" Derek said leaning on the display case. "Have you made a decision yet?"

"Is there a hurry today, Derek?"

Derek fidgeted. "No, Mrs. Harmsen, just want to make sure that you don't waste a good portion of your Thursday looking at fresh meat."

Nash sniggered at the double entendre. Butcher frowned at his workmates.

"I think I'll take some pork chops, a whole chicken and, what are those?" She leaned forward allowing her blouse to drop open slightly onto the case. This ploy had worked with two generations of boys and men. Displaying her ample cleavage had been a source of true joy for many young male Amicableans.

"Those are called T-bone steaks, Mrs. Harmsen," Nash said. "You can tell because the bone seems to make a 'T' in the middle."

"How silly of me."

Nash took her order and began to wrap it up in white butcher paper. After weighing them on a scale, he ripped off a sticky price tag and sealed the paper with it. "That will be twenty-four dollars, Mrs. Harmsen."

Opening her small leather handbag, Linda rummaged through Kleenexes (no Amicablean woman would be without them) a tube of lip balm, her keys, spare change and then found her wallet from which she withdrew twenty-five dollars. Nash received the money, punched the numbers into the cash register and handed the change back.

"Are you going to be here for long?" Linda asked Butcher.

"I hope so, Mrs. Harmsen."

"Please," she said holding her blouse to her chest with a hand, drawing his attention back to her chest, "call me Linda."

"Okay, Linda."

Taking her order from Nash, Linda turned on her heel and walked out of the shop. Before the door had shut completely, the twins had both turned towards the taller man with arms crossed. "Soooooo?"

Butcher leaned back against the far counter. "Are you sure you want to do this?"

"Yup."

"Okay," Butcher said hesitantly, but he knew that his reading would endear himself to his new workmates. Both Nash and Derek had crossed their arms. To Butcher, they looked like the twin sphinxes of Egypt except for the broad grins and lack of bosoms.

"Linda Harmsen is not a local."

"How can you tell?" Derek asked, attempting to hide his astonishment.

"She has a different lilt in her voice than you guys, or even Penny, and this lady, Rhonda, I met at The Traveler's Choice this morning."

A look passed between the twins, a language without words, but full of meaning. They both knew who Rhonda was; she was the golden child of Amicable, winning athletic awards and always looking good in her uniforms. Although she was quite a bit older than the twins, that didn't stop them from dreaming.

"Yeah, okay." Derek's voice was sprinkled with mirth. "What else?"

Butcher had known immediately from seeing Linda as she walked through the door a fakeness about her happiness. Her forced smile, he supposed it could have been nervousness, but he doubted it. She carried the characteristics of a woman who had been objectified her whole life, not because she was particularly beautiful, but because she was well-endowed. Linda Harmsen, he surmised as she had leaned forward to allow a view of her cleavage, had used her 'assets' to attract attention, lookin' for love in all the wrong places, as some of the locals would say.

Butcher also surmised that Linda sought the sexual approval of men that stemmed from her father's over-attentiveness. When Linda looked at him, he wanted to apologize on behalf of all men everywhere.

Understanding this, Butcher glanced at the two young men not willing to share the entirety of Linda's reading which could be a dangerous thing in a town like this. Linda had probably kept the secret her entire life, even from her husbands, and ultimately, it may have been the very reason her marriages didn't last.

"Tell me if I'm wrong, but I would guess that Linda would know quite a bit of the local gossip, probably shares quite a bit of it too."

"That's nothing special. Every woman in town is like that," Derek said, his cultural misogyny rearing its ugly head.

Butcher shrugged. "Hair stylists probably are the hub of all gossip in any town."

Nash nodded. "Nice try. You probably saw her store as you were walking yesterday or today - Harmsen's Hair and Beauty."

Nodding, Butcher moved back towards the counter. "Yes, I did."

Nash popped his gum. "See, I can read people too."

"Absolutely," Butcher said, "But when you get really good at it, you'll know that someone like Linda Harmsen can damage your image pretty quickly."

Derek started bouncing up and down. "Ohhh! How did he do that?" Twisting his hat sideways, like a rural gangster, Derek crossed his arms in front of him. "Damn, boy, you good."

"That's like a superpower, Butcher," Nash said, pretending to punch him in the arm. "You got a cape or something to go with that?"

Butcher smiled wryly. "It's not a superpower; I'm just a student of human nature."

"Where did you learn how to do it?" The twins were so impressed that they hadn't noticed the front door opening. Leslie Tielman had shouldered her way through the door. She was dressed casually, as most people of Amicable were wont to do on weekdays, her crisp, light blue jeans with a neat and colorful t-shirt tucked tightly inside the waist. Leslie's value and sense of identity was imbued with following rules (and making certain everyone else did as well). Some would have said that Leslie was wound tight as a spring; others would have said that was understating the obvious. Leslie, though, was thrilled and excited at the news of a new arrival in Amicable.

As Leslie walked to the glass display case, Derek stood across from her behind the counter. Trying not to look towards the new butcher, Leslie's foot missed a step as she tripped over one of the tiles. After falling against the display, her head came up and she saw Derek standing on the other side, his baseball hat askew.

As he was moving towards the cutting room, Butcher wiped his hands on his apron and spoke over his shoulder. "You owe me a beer," Butcher said. "Both of you."

"Get back to work, Butcher," Nash shouted gleefully.

The twins laughed, but Leslie frowned. *An alcoholic*, she thought. *I'll have to speak with Reverend Deakins about that.*

"Good morning, Ms. Tielman. How are we today?" Derek asked.

"Fine, fine." She pretended to be studying the cuts of meat closely, but all three men in the room knew that she was attempting to check out Butcher. The twins, at least, knew which women's gathering she was part of:

Penny Reynolds
Linda Harmsen
Leona Simpson
Jeannie Dolling

It was the Fearsome Fivesome, a cartel of estrogen bottled so tightly that few other women came close to the circle of connection. The women spread gossip faster than an Ebola-laced sneeze.

"It's a beautiful morning isn't it? A great day for a stroll. Out meeting people today, Ms. Tielman?" Derek's smirk was barely contained behind an upraised hand.

"No, no, just out shopping. Need to stop at the grocery store for some lemons, maybe I'll get my hair done today…"

"Mrs. Harmsen was just in before you. She might not be ready for patients yet."

"Clients, Derek. Clients." Leslie's frown appeared again as she looked up over her small, tight glasses that had fallen down on her nose. She pushed them up with her index finger.

"Sorry Ms. Tielman."

Leslie's lips pressed together. "I think I'll get some bacon today, Derek. Six rashers - not too much fat on the back, please." Derek reached into the case with a plastic bag and grabbed the bacon and slid it into the bag. "Anything else?"

Leslie looked up and pretended to suddenly notice the hulking new employee of Peterson's butchery. Butcher, at this point, was busily arranging a side of beef on the table and prepping the saw. His hands were quick and steady, but the table was low for his height; his stoop looked uncomfortable. "So, this is the new butcher, Derek?" she said softly.

"Yes, Ms. Tielman, he started *today*." Derek spoke slowly insinuating that Butcher was already the source of gossip throughout town. He knew where the info had come from - Penny Reynolds. "How did you hear about him?"

Voice lowered, Leslie leaned towards the counter. "I have my sources."

"You're like a secret agent, Ms. Tielman." Derek's eyes glowed with good humor. Leslie showed outward displeasure but secretly loved the idea of being a secret agent.

"You behave, young man," she said.

"Ms. Tielman, you're only like fifteen years older than I am."

"Well," she said tightly, "I'm old enough to be your... aunt, or at least Godparent. It takes a village to raise kids these days and I'm just trying to help you boys gr..."

Derek interrupted her. "Hey, Butcher!" He yelled over his shoulder. "Come meet one of the prominent members of the community, Ms. Tielman. She's a good friend of Mrs. Harmsen who was in here not ten minutes ago. That's quite a coincidence, isn't it, Ms. Tielman?"

Leslie's frown deepened and she blushed. "That won't be necessary. I've just come for my bacon." But it was too late; Butcher was already standing next to Derek behind the glass display case.

"Ms. Tielman, let me introduce you to Butcher. Butcher, Ms. Tielman." Butcher reached out his hand across the glass display case but forgot that he hadn't taken off his rubber gloves; then quickly, apologetically, he removed his right one. Leslie looked at his hand with distaste and did not accept the greeting.

"How do you do, Ma'am?" Butcher pulled back his hand.

"I'm not a 'ma'am,' I'm a 'Ms.' thank you very much. I'm well." She gave him the once over, then twice; his height arrested her gaze, his boyish good lucks, wavy head of hair and slight smile caused her breath to hitch, but she didn't let it show.

"That's not your real name is it, Mr. Butcher?"

Butcher shrugged. "It will do. It's just a name."

"Where are you from?" Leslie's words held a twinge that Butcher had heard many times before. She was not asking him for her own sake, or to get to know him, but to control him.

Derek looked up at the tall man next to him wondering if he'd reply. Butcher smiled. "I like my secrets, Ms. Tielman."

"Well," Leslie blustered. "I'm just trying to be friendly."

"You're doing a great job, Ms. Tielman. I can tell that you are a very amicable person." Nash snorted from the back room; Leslie's face reddened at the alternative, yet somehow derogatory, meaning of the new butcher's words. Snatching at the plastic bag full of bacon, Leslie marched to the cash register where Derek had moved. Butcher retreated to the cutting room again and within seconds the saw began squealing.

"That will be three dollars, Ms. Tielman," Derek smiled broadly at the young woman. Quickly, she opened her handbag and pulled out a coin purse from which she pulled ten dollars-worth of change including fifteen pennies that she meticulously counted out. Derek waited patiently for the coins - it was how she always paid and secretly he wondered where she gathered all the spare change. Just as she was about to leave the store, the bone and gristle passed through the saw, grinding and cutting, the noise, irritating and grating to the eardrums, was almost painful.

"Thank you," she said.

"What?" Derek said loudly.

"I said, 'Thank you, Derek,'" this time shouting. Derek nodded and watched her walk out the door unsurprised to see the form of Leona Simpson appearing regally in front of the butchery. Sharing a look, Leona and Leslie passed each other without speaking.

Derek looked behind him at his brother who must have felt Derek's eyes on him. Derek motioned with his head towards the doorway where Leona was already ascending. Nash looked over at Butcher whose safety glasses were distorting his eyes.

Butcher was going to be *very* good for business.

Nash never would have imagined what kind of business it would be.

Butcher

Chapter 5.

Reverend John Thomas Deakins was on his third home visit of the day, and to be quite honest, he was wearied by conversation and fare. Deakins, named after his parents' two favorite disciples, the mystic and the doubter, had always known his calling in life. Though not necessarily a spiritual man by nature, he certainly was religious by practice. The ritual and pageantry of the pastoral calling had appealed to him from a young age; the texture of the worship service, the longing by old people to talk about old things, the coarse cover of his grandfather's Bible as it had been handed on to him after two generations of use – these were things that stirred positive emotions. Often during his home visits, the elderly women of the congregation would shower him with sweets and cookies. This endless routine, a cycle of neediness – his and theirs – created a comfortable life, but an uncomfortable subconscious reality: John Thomas Deakins was very lonely.

Reverend Deakins had never thought much about his sexual identity; he wasn't gay, but he just wasn't interested in the energy and demand that a relationship would entail. He was sure that when the time came, the right woman would happen along, strolling through Amicable into church one day, interested in a *finely aged* wine like him. Because he didn't actively seek out intimate relationships with women, he also did not care that his thirty-six-year-old physique slid relentlessly southwards, like a gravity-induced adipose glacier scraping youthful muscles into caverns of inactivity. Although he was aware that he, as a man of the cloth, could sustain an intimate relationship, he preferred not to hide, or even fold the cloth. In fact, he celebrated the raiment of his profession and was never seen in public without, as some of the young kids called it behind his back, his dog collar. On Sundays, without exception, he wore his white robe with appropriate stole colored with the appropriate season of the ecclesiastical calendar. Now, late summer, he still wore the green of Pentecost season.

Pentecost - season of change. Sometimes Reverend Deakins desperately desired change, but he was also aware that this desire would never occur as long as he was called to Amicable. Change, to the residents of St. Clements Methodist Church, was about as likely as Jesus returning: it was going to happen, but the odds were it wasn't going to be soon.

The people of Amicable had always been very hospitable to him. Seven years before, when he first moved into the parsonage across the street from the solid red brick building, the congregation members helped carry his furniture and personal effects in. He was quite certain that many of the members were assisting that day just to see what kind of worldly things this man of the cloth owned. Although it had taken almost eighteen months for his parishioners to speak in confidence to him, he now felt that he was part of the furniture.

Reverend Deakins' closest confidant, Leslie Tielman, was an invaluable source of information and could be counted on to let him know the background of almost every single person in Amicable. When they met, they always met on the porch and *never* entered inside together so as not to arouse suspicions of any Amicablean who might be watching out of their blinded windows. In Amicable, arousal of any sort was not necessarily a positive thing. Reverend Deakins and Leslie held their summer discussions with sweating glasses of iced tea in hand, although once, Deakins had proposed that they share a glass of wine together. Leslie conjured a frown and Reverend Deakins made a hasty retreat into the house for an appropriate sweating glass of tea.

Leslie always called ahead of time so that there would be no suggestion of impropriety. Today he was happy that she had called him at Nola Bradshaw's house as they were plowing through lemon meringue pie and coffee. Deakins had already heard Nola's list of medications twice (she was entering the onramp of the superhighway of dementia, he was sure) and he was delightedly pleased to announce to Nola that there was an emergency to which he need attend. Of course, this piqued Nola's interest. Nola was quite sure that ministers never really had emergencies. It's not as if they had to rush off to perform a double bypass baptism or put out a four-alarm heresy fire.

Reverend Deakins bade Mrs. Bradshaw a hasty goodbye, moved out the door and down the steps into the bright morning sun. He turned around, knowing Nola would want and expect a departing wave. Her face was close enough to be seen, but the rest of her body hidden in the dark recesses of the room. A spasm of guilt squeezed Deakins' heart; old age was difficult for the young to understand, and often the young patronizingly patted the hands of the elderly, wishing them well but unaware of the constant toll of declining health took on them. Reverend Deakins asked God for forgiveness and strode quickly to his car feeling the coffee and sweets swirling nauseatingly in his stomach.

It had been quite a while since Leslie had called to meet him outside of their normal Tuesday afternoon session. Leslie had not detailed what she wanted to talk about, but she sounded insistent, strained. Although he was used to her peculiarly *tight* nature, this request was out of the ordinary. He sincerely hoped that she was okay.

After driving two blocks north on First Street East, he turned left on Second Avenue South. Above the skyline of Amicable, with only two manmade buildings taller (the elevator and the water tower) St. Clements stood resolutely as a monument to the past. Pointing to the heavens, seeming to scrape the clouds from lofty nests, St. Clements' steeple reminded him of the permanence of faith. There was something incredibly comforting about seeing the building rise from the earth, puncturing the firmament like an immense theological water balloon bringing down God's blessings upon the humble people of Amicable.

Already parked in front of the parsonage was Leslie's tiny green Peugeot. Leslie, as was her habit, remained inside the car. Reverend Deakins pulled into the driveway behind her and turned off the ignition. Grunting as he teased his bulk from the car, Deakins was aware of the effect that his anti-diet diet was having on his girth. It wouldn't be many more months before he'd have to adjust his collar and black suit. Reverend Deakins walked over the crunching gravel and rapped on Leslie's window. "Leslie. Are you okay?"

Leslie was sitting in the driver's seat, hands on the steering wheel staring out the windshield. Startled, she looked up at him.

"It's got to be eighty-five degrees inside that car already. Come out." He opened the door for her.

"Hello, Reverend Deakins," she said coolly adjusting her t-shirt, smoothing it against her thin stomach.

"Is something wrong?"

For the first time, Leslie Tielman's face registered an emotion other than frustration or hardness. For an instant, her bottom lip quivered. Deakins' eyes widened - *Sadness? Sorrow? Pain?* "Please, Leslie, let's go to the porch where we can talk."

Without answering, Leslie emerged from her car and walked beside the black suited clergyman to the front porch of the parsonage. Slowly and deliberately they approached the front steps. Reverend Deakins waited for her to climb the steps in front of him, and then, without intention or thinking, his eyes fell on her backside. Apologizing to her inside of his head, he looked away and followed her up the stairs, but his brain stumbled on why his eyes had gone to that place. *John, what are you thinking?*

"Would you like an iced tea?"

"No thank you, Reverend."

Deakins sat down in his own matching wicker chair and pulled it slightly closer to her. "What is it, Leslie? Has something happened? A death?" Guiltily, Deakins thought that someone's death might break up the monotony of his days; nothing like a good funeral to bring the people of Amicable back to church. It had been so long since they had been together - Easter, at least, and even then, the service attendance was dropping.

"I've been to Peterson's..."

Reverend Deakins frowned. "I don't understand. Why would this cause you...?"

"There's a new butcher in town."

"And...?"

Leslie looked sharply at the pastor. "You don't understand. The new butcher wouldn't even tell me where he was from."

Reverend Deakins sucked in a surprised breath and then held up his hands. "Wait. Back up. How did you hear about this new butcher?"

"Penny Reynolds."

Of course, John thought. "But what has got you so upset, Leslie?"

Impatiently, she tapped her legs in front of her. They were closed very tightly. "Listen to me, Reverend. I went in to buy some bacon this morning, which is still in the car. I need to get going soon, and then stop at Linda's to have my hair done. It's been so long, almost two weeks..."

Deakins interrupted her. "Leslie, focus."

"He's an *outsider*, Reverend. We don't know where he's from, where he's been, what he's been doing. We don't know if he's married or if he has children." She lowered her voice. "We don't know his politics. He might be..." she lowered her voice. "A Democrat."

Deakins gasped. There weren't many Democrats in Amicable, although some rebellious youths were beginning to spout left-wing rhetoric regarding human sexuality, gender identity, immigration and welfare policies. A young seventeen-year-old high school student, Tracey Thomas, had even, without her parents' knowledge, put a bumper sticker on her car which read: *Dairy Is Scary. Go Vegan!* Needless to say, Tracey's father, definitely not a Democrat, had ripped the sticker off and rightly grounded Tracey for ten days.

"We need to have a plan, Reverend. It's people like this who can ruin an entire town."

John Thomas Deakins was well aware of the danger, in a general sense, of jumping to conclusions. The problem was jumping to conclusions was an Olympic event in Amicable. Worse yet, it was a team sport. Now that Leslie had set the bar for the leap, Deakins was quick to respond.

"We'll need to gather more information, Leslie, much more. We need to have spies on every corner, in every shop." He ran his hand through his thick, dark hair. "I might even have to go native..."

It was Leslie's turn to gasp. "You don't mean it, Reverend. What will the people say?"

"For the good of the town, I'll take off my clerical collar, Leslie."

"I suppose it must be God's will then that this foreigner would come like an evil spirit to settle in our midst." Leslie's hand was shaking with fear and excitement. "We'll call the prayer team together."

"Good idea. Then call your friends to see if they can find out any more information about this man, his history and anything that might help the cause." Reaching out to Leslie, Reverend Deakins extended his hand. Leslie's face, awash with excitement, smiled broadly and she unfolded her hands to grasp the clergyman's in her own. When their skin met, a tingle of excitement coursed through her body. For that moment, a surge of electricity jump-started something inside of her, a dormant electrode which had been corroded by years of anxiety and insecurity. It seemed that Deakins, too, felt the same shock, but he was controlled enough not to say anything. Nothing could corrupt this mission.

"Thank you for bringing this to my attention, Leslie. Please contact me when the groundwork has been laid."

Leslie nodded, and moved with purpose to her Peugeot where, after opening the driver's side door, she noticed that a pigeon had dropped three large splats of guano on her windshield.

On this exciting day, it didn't bother her.

Chapter 6.

It would be far too easy to blame bludgeoned stereotypes of a repressed clergyman and a spinster-to-be for wanting to suppress the winds of change in a small, idyllic town like Amicable. The intense reaction to change, to establish buttresses on walls built on tradition, is one that occurs over decades. Each successive generation lays its own sediment of convictions on top of the last, and so on and so forth, until the bedrock of communal health is buried so deeply underneath the detritus of fear that life just seems to flow over it like the mighty Mississippi River to its delta.

But the winds of change rarely manifest in turbulent, tornadic activity uprooting the trees and the foundation of civic beliefs; no, it is usually a gentler breeze, full of scents from a faraway spring, of earth and water and growing things, whispering to the tiniest hairs of the ears that haven't been frozen by winter's harsh breath. That gentle breeze coming from the east stirs up a dust particle, which buries itself in the coppery nose hair of a gardener, who sneezes mightily into her sleeve, who wipes her nose and eyes with the back of her gloved hand. She wonders if the change of season will bring on hay fever or rose blossoms, and then as quickly as she can look past the sinking sun, she sees that which she hasn't seen since the end of the last summer.

Fireflies. Lightning bugs - whatever they are called in Amicable. And she smiles at the thought that these little insects are on the prowl for mates, and she wishes, just for a brief instant, that her husband's backside would glow like the fireflies once again. This makes her laugh, but her laughter pushes the breeze towards a leaf, which attracts the attention of a bird, and the movement of the bird snares the gaze of a fancy feline residing on the warm stoop of her neighbor's house. And that cat stretches its black and white paws. *Bootsie*, his owner calls him, and it releases the most delicious yawn a tabby has ever yawned.

And when he is done yawning, he looks back at the bird, that lovely little morsel sitting just out of reach on the lowest branch of the maple tree. Bootsie stops on the sidewalk letting the bird know that if it flies any lower, it will be missing a few drumsticks, and then begins to lick one of his paws, slow and sure, up and down.

But then, as Bootsie pauses on the sidewalk, watching the bird which is staring at the fluttering leaf blown by the gardener, Jim the Mailman turns the corner down the sidewalk. While he is staring at the small bits of bills and junk mail in his hand (it is the 21st century, of course, when snail mail is as useful as horses are to agriculture), he frowns into the pieces of paper because he is not quite sure if the mail…

And then Jim the Mailman trips on Bootsie the Cat, causing Bootsie no end of irritation, but Jim the Mailman is much the worse for wear as his calamitous tripping throws his mailbag up into the same breeze that lifted the small bit of dust into the gardener's nose. As gravity does its thing, the gardener's neighbor's mail is blown gently out into the street where it is snatched right out of the winds of change by one large fist belonging to a very tall man.

"Nice catch," Nash said to Butcher as he moved towards the flustered mailman who had taken careful aim with his boot at Bootsie the Cat. Fortunately, for Bootsie, he had at least four more lives to unleash on his owner, and he skedaddled across the grass to find a more suitable place to watch the birds.

Jim the Mailman accepted the envelope that the man had plucked from the air and looked up at the tall man. "Thank you… uh…"

"His name is 'Butcher,'" Derek said while smiling at the befuddled Jim the Mailman. "He's our new employee at the shop."

"Oh, say, that's good," Jim said and paused as all good Amicableans do no matter their relative level of busyness. Jim pushed his hat back on his head and put his hands on his hips.

"Where are you from?"

Butcher's face betrayed no expression, but he was, at that very point, quite sure that he would be asked that question by every single one of the one thousand and fifty-six residents of Amicable. "Out of town."

"Oh, you don't say." Jim was far too nice to pry any further. "Where are you boys going?"

Derek leaned across Butcher. "We're going to the BA."

"That's sounds like fun, Nash."

"It's Derek, Mr. Johnson."

Jim the Mailman's face turned a shade of lovely red. "I'm so sorry, Derek. I can never tell you boys apart."

"Don't worry about it."

Nash's face popped in next to his brothers. If they got any closer, they could have been Siamese twins. "We haven't been to the Bowling Alley in a while, but we thought we'd show Butcher, here, a good night out on the town."

Jim nodded with understanding. "Nothing like tossing down a few beers at the BA on league night. I remember when I was younger I was part of a team. We used to really clean up the pins." A faraway look stretched across his face; the same look that almost every other Amicablean got when they thought about something that occurred in the 80's.

"I bet that was really fun, Mr. Johnson," Derek's voice dripped sarcastically.

"It sure was," the mailman responded missing the droplets. Butcher, at this point, almost knocked their heads together, but chose to refrain as the mailman was still lost somewhere back in 1980 when bowling was still considered a sport and bowlers were considered 'athletes'.

"Okay, we're going to get going, but stop over at the BA after your route if you want to toss down a few suds."

Jim the Mailman shook his head, and like an Etch-A-Sketch, he reset his vision on the boys in the present. "That sounds like a good idea. I will definitely think about it."

Butcher could tell from the mailman's eyes that he had already thought about it... and he had already weighed the consequences of missing out on his nightly episode of Family Feud. Jim would not be journeying to the Bowling Alley.

Jim nodded and, with a smile and a wave, walked away.

Derek and Nash laughed and positioned their knuckles together to bump them. Butcher frowned.

"Ah, Butcher, don't be like that. We were just having a little fun."

Butcher's eyes wandered back and forth between the two. There was no malice between them, only a youthful vibrancy immune to the rest of the town suffering from a severe case of nostalgia.

As they walked down the street, Butcher glanced at his watch. It was 5:05 in the evening. The cleanup had been quicker than ever before, or so it seemed, because Derek and Nash were on a mission to buy four beers apiece for Butcher. He had miraculously described perfect strangers.

"Hey, Butcher," Derek said as the sauntered down First Street West, "how do you do it? I get that you can pick up a few weird things about people, tics and personality spasms, but not the real deep grimy stuff. Like, how could you possibly know all that about Jeannie Dolling?"

Butcher had answered that same question in many variations for the last thirty years. He wasn't sure when the 'gift' had been given, or even that he actually enjoyed having it. He could remember when his mother (not his father who had streaked for freedom early in Leo's life) would describe visitors and friends coming by the house and Leo's uncanny ability would allow him to instantaneously know who they were and what they were like. In some ways, Lenore had taken advantage of Leo's gift by taking him to the stores for big ticket items. One of Leo's favorite memories occurred when he was seven years old and his mother needed a new car.

Leo and Lenore took the bus to the used car lot (not 'pre-owned' or 'pre-loved' as they were stupidly called now), Lenore stood gazing at the mind-numbing number of cars stretched as far as the eye could see, all looking at her despairingly like multicolored puppies at the dog pound wanting to be 'newly-owned' or 'newly-

loved.' Overwhelmed by choice, Lenore looked down at her son who was quite tall for his age, and patted him on the head.

"Do your thing, Spud." He loved it when his mom called him that.

For a few minutes, they walked between green sedans and red station wagons. A VW Beetle appeared from almost nowhere, but Lenore was not interested. She wanted style and value. A Dodge Dart glinted in the sun; it seemed to smile at her and Lenore was sure that it would pant if it could.

"Is this the one you want, Mom?" She nodded. "Okay," Leo responded rubbing his hands together. It wasn't often that his mother actively encouraged the gift. Most times it frightened her, but when she really needed it, he was ready.

A salesman had been watching them from the fishbowl office, windows shouting, "SALE! SALE! ALL OLD STOCK MUST GO!" What the average moron knew was that it was all old stock - that's why it was a used car lot. Like a shark, the salesman exited the office, blowing warm air onto his hands as if it was remotely cold, which it wasn't; he smoothed his hair and his moustache. The salesman knew that this was the best kind of sale: single woman, single child, threadbare clothes, arrived on bus. My lucky day. She was most likely a waitress (which she wasn't) and of low intelligence (also incorrect).

"Well, good morning, Ma'am and Little Pardner." The smarmy salesman doffed an invisible cowboy hat to them and put on a thousand dollar smile. "How are we all doin' today?"

"Fine, thank you," Lenore responded as she gripped her handbag closer to her chest.

"What are we looking for today?" The salesman's eyes were not so surreptitiously driving a circuitous route around the curves of Lenore's body.

"We're looking for a sedan," Leo said moving in front of his mother and taking captive the salesman's wandering eyes.

The salesman seemed surprised. The boy's eyes, both youthful and aged, were intensely brown. "Well, little Buckaroo, that will be..."

"My name is Leo. Stop patronizing us."

The salesman's eyes narrowed. Even though he didn't know what the word 'patronizing' meant, he was pretty sure that it wasn't positive. "Okay, Leo," he said slowly, "What would you like to see today, sir."

61

Leo needed the man to actually let down his guard. Go ahead, Punk. Are you feeling lucky? Leo thought, Make my day.

"I'd like to know about this Dart." *Leo motioned to the shining mustard brown automobile next to them, but he never took his eyes off the salesman.*

"That's a fine car," *the salesman said.* "My name is Dirk."

"We don't care what your name is," *Leo said,* "just tell us about the car." *Lenore stifled a laugh behind her son.*

Dirk's face turned red. "There's no reason to be rude. I was just trying to help."

"So, help!" *Leo lifted his eyebrows with exasperation.*

The salesman took a deep breath and looked over his shoulder. His manager was bemusedly watching from the front of the fishbowl, one arm folded across his ample belly, the other cupping his chin. "It's a 1973 Dodge Dart sedan, leather seats and it even has power steering."

Leo moved to the car and looked through the window past the sticker proclaiming the price to be $1199. What a rip-off. "Those are not leather seats," *Leo said as he pressed his face into the window."*

"Sure they are," *Dirk's face turned red.* "That's what it says on the sticker." *He moved toward the car and underlined the 'leather seats' with his hand.*

"You'd have to be a grade A moron not to be able to tell the difference between fake leather and real leather. Come on, Dirk, I can tell the difference, why can't you?"

Dirk huffed. "Listen, son…"

Leo whipped around. "Don't call me that again." *Something in the boy's face made the salesman take a large step back. Lenore placed a hand on his shoulder.*

"I'm sorry," *she said.* "We've had a … difficult time lately." *Her words were apologetic, but her voice betrayed her frustration.* "Look, we've come to buy a car; we like the look of this one. You're a salesman, sell it to us, but don't try to rip us off. He can tell." *She placed a hand on Leo's shoulder.*

Raising his hands in surrender, Dirk shook his head. The commission on just one car was apt to put food on the table for him for a month. "I… I… I just go by what the sticker says. Okay? I'll have it changed."

"How much are you going to take off the price for lying to us?" *Leo asked.*

Dirk glanced again behind him. This is not going to end well. "How would you feel about one hundred dollars? Does that sound fair?"

Leo slowly shook his seven-year-old head. "Nope. Not even close. Three hundred to start."

Dirk began to calculate the figures of his decreasing commission. Much lower, and he'd barely have his salary paid for. "Two-fifty."

"That's a start," Leo said. "But I'm warning you, I really can tell when you are lying."

"Sure," Dirk agreed.

"I already know your name isn't Dirk." The salesman's eyes widened slightly. "Something close, isn't it."

"Please," Dirk began to plead, "Let's just work on the sale." He was beginning to feel a sense of panicky fear.

"Dominick?" Nothing.

"Douglas?" Leo watched his face. "It's Doug, isn't it?"

The man previously known as Dirk paled. "How did you do that?"

Leo smugly crossed his arms. "You are very easy to read, Doug. Now, how about selling us this car?"

Doug sold the 1973 Dodge Dart to them for $875. Lenore was happy.

Because Butcher could read almost everything about a person in seconds, and from that information formulate an amazingly detailed and accurate understanding of how people predictably would react to stimuli and situations, he seemed to be able to read the future. And from this ability came the heartache of *knowing*. Not all knowledge was good – sometimes it was a forbidden fruit. There was a reason God told Adam and Even not to touch *that* tree. For Butcher, to see a past and a future was a true curse sometimes.

Before he could answer Derek's question, a honking horn brought him back to reality. A 2014 Green Toyota Camry pulled up beside the walking trio. Because there were no other cars on the street, and even if there were, they would have waited patiently for the conversation to close, the Camry stopped beside them and a woman stuck her head out the window. The young woman, perhaps in her mid to late twenties, levered her elbow out the window and smiled to the threesome. Her eyes, greenish with gold flecks, glinted in the lowering sunlight; she appeared good-humored, but immediately, Butcher knew that something was troubling this girl.

"Hey-ya boys," she intoned out the window. "You guys going on a date?"

Nash moved over to the car and leaned over to talk to the young woman. Butcher looked at Derek who had crossed his arms and was frowning.

"What's the problem?" Butcher mumbled.

Derek shook his head. "That girl is bad news," he said. "Nash should just leave her alone."

"Who is she?"

"Come on," Derek said as he pulled on Butcher's arm towards the sidewalk. "We'll keep walking. Maybe that will hurry Nash up." Derek looked back at his brother. "That's Naida Thompson. She and Nash have always had kind of a thing for each other." He swallowed hard and rubbed his forehead with the back of his hand. "Only bad things can come from this. C'mon. Let's go inside and I'll tell you more."

Derek looked back over his shoulder at his brother who now had his arm on top of the roof of the young woman's car. She had reclined back in her seat as almost in invitation for Nash to view her curves.

Derek shook his head and opened the first of two doors, and allowed Butcher to enter. Already, the sounds of bowling balls being dropped, pins crunching, jukebox playing and people laughing, reached their ears. It wasn't until the second door was breached that the full extent of the noise hit them. It was like a tidal wave of sound and smell. Along with the typical echoes was the scent of decades old cigarette smoke suspended in the updrafts of the lanes.

Senses assaulted, Butcher stopped and Derek pushed him from behind. "Come on, Butcher, you'll be fine. There's nothing in here that is going to kill you. In fact, you'd be hard pressed to find anything in here that would actually stimulate your imagination enough to want to stay." Butcher stumbled forward and Derek clapped him on the back. "Let's head over to the bar area. If you want to bowl, we can do that after a few of the beers we owe you. Who knows? You might even want to share them with us."

Butcher began walking. To his left was the front desk where a bored looking teenager was snapping her gum, sitting on a stool and scrolling through her phone searching for anything to escape. A wall of bowling shoes of differing sizes stood behind her. The young girl looked up momentarily, but when she caught Butcher's eyes, she shyly smiled and dropped her gaze again.

To his right were twelve highly oiled wooden lanes. Ball return machines connected subterraneously to the yawning maws of pins at the end of the lane, hunched morosely near the 'athletes', vomited out their cannon balls before they were hurled strategically, or more often, randomly, towards the pins. Butcher was content to move towards the bar area, a room behind the lanes, which was vacant except for half a dozen or so regulars eating deep fried food and watching the television above the bar. In the dim lighting of the Greedy Pecker bar, the lonely souls seemed to be caught in a strange kind of rutted-road-purgatory.

Derek led Butcher through the door-less entrance and they perched themselves on the chrome swivel stools covered by fake leather. Derek smiled at the bartender who was mixing a drink for another patron.

"Evening, Shania."

"Derek," she nodded. "Give me a second and I'll be back to pour your beers." Situating the mixed drink on a black plastic tray with cork bottom, she exited the bar station and carried the drink to the end of the bar to one of the locals who, after receiving the drink, looked appreciatively at the waitress as she disappeared. Shania was used to it, but it still bothered her. For some reason, people who purchased drinks always believed they were purchasing the right to ogle her also. She was a beautiful woman with a beautiful body, but she did not dress to attract attention

Making her way back behind the bar, Shania began to pour a Busch Light beer into a frozen glass. "What will you have?" She asked Butcher.

Derek interrupted. "This is our new coworker, Butcher. Butcher, Shania."

"How do you do?" Butcher asked.

Shania raised her eyebrows. "Well, aren't we Mr. Formal? I'm doing well, and you on this fine evening, Mr. Butcher?"

He laughed. "Fine, thank you."

"He'll have an Old Milwaukee, Shania." Derek was smiling and punched Butcher lightly on the arm.

Shania poured him the drink. "That will be four dollars."

"We're going to start a tab. Nash should be in in a sec." Shania's eyes lit up for a moment, and then she moved away from them.

Butcher turned to Derek. "So, Naida Thompson?"

Derek knew what he was asking, but he paused to take a sip of his beer before he answered. "Yeah, Naida."

"Who is she?"

Derek hunched over his drink. "She's married to James Thompson, a local guy, went to school at Amicable High. He drives trucks for farmers. Nice enough guy, just not that interested in Naida."

"So, now she's taken an interest in Nash, is that what's happened?" Derek had seen enough in a day with Butcher to recognize that he would have known this already. He nodded.

Butcher took a sip of his beer and winced. There was no way he was going to stomach a whole pint of this much less multiple ones. "How do you drink this?"

Derek laughed. "Straight down the gullet like the rest of them. After a while, it starts to taste like water."

Butcher shook his head, tried again with the same result. "Better than urine, I guess. Are you sure the wine's not any better?"

"Positive."

A form crossed in front of the doorframe and Nash smiled as he pulled up a stool next to his brother. "I see you started without me."

He signaled and Shania immediately poured him a Bud Light. Shania smiled and rang it up on the tab and moved back to wash some dishes.

"So, what did I miss?" Nash asked. "Did you read anyone else?"

Butcher looked at the young man. It was obvious that he was smitten, but the enamoration was probably more about Naida's restrictive relationships - a challenge - than it was about actually falling for the girl. Although she was pretty, there were already lines around her eyes; a wariness with humanity that only came when experience dredged too many tears from one's eyes.

"No, Nash. I'm not here to read people."

He smiled. "But you can't help it, can you?"

Butcher paused. "No. Not really." There were many times in Butcher's life when he wished there were a toggle switch for his gift. Even when he shut his eyes, people could not hide things from him.

"So how do you deal with it?" The twins were looking at him with curiosity.

"Well," Butcher sighed deeply, "I don't really deal with it. I mostly ignore close relationships with people. When I get to know too much about them and their predictability, I simply move on."

"So, you're not planning on sticking around here very long then, is that right?" Nash had chugged half of his beer and was raising it to his lips once again.

Butcher shrugged and motioned for Shania. "Can I have a different drink? Maybe a scotch on the rocks?"

Shania nodded. "How many rocks? How many fingers?"

"One of each, please." Within seconds she had placed one finger of scotch on top of one ice cube into an angular snifter and placed it in front of the tall man. He thanked her, and then looked back at the twins.

"No, I've never stayed anywhere that long."

"Where did you come from? How long did you stay there?"

Butcher read the interest in their faces, no guile or malice, simply a need for connection. As twins, the Petersons probably had different ways of encountering new friendships and their formulations for making those friends was always weighed against the difficulties of communicating nonverbally. Nash and Derek never really had to speak to each other; they knew intrinsically what each other was thinking, and words sometimes got in the way.

"If you don't mind, we'll save that discussion for another time, but I want you to know that I've always had the desire to put down roots. I'm not allergic to it. There have always been reasons to leave or reasons I have been asked to leave." The cryptic statement hung in the air and the twins peered at each other wanting to ask that next question but knowing that it wouldn't be answered.

"Okay," Derek said. "Here's to the mysterious Butcher." They toasted each other, clinked their glass containers together and drank.

It was then that Butcher's eye fell on the next patron at the door.

Surprised, Butcher almost choked on the warm liquid and both Derek's and Nash's eyes were drawn to the entry.

Rhonda Redman.

Derek's mug was frozen an inch from his mouth as he watched Butcher's reaction to the woman. Rhonda had changed from her waitressing clothes and now wore a summery dress, which showed off her beautiful, long, suntanned legs. Because she was so tall, Rhonda almost always, wore flat sandals which were not necessarily good for her feet (especially because she was on them all day long).

"Butcher," Derek whispered, "Your mouth is open and you're drooling."

Snapping from his stare, Butcher closed his mouth and frowned at Derek. "Whatever," he muttered, but when Rhonda entered the room, she noticed Butcher and shyly avoided his gaze, but then returned to it and lifted a hand in greeting.

"Wait a minute," Nash said. "You know each other?"

"I told you, we met this morning at The Traveler's Choice. She was my waitress."

"What did she serve you?" Derek sarcastically asked. "A fresh serving of badabing badaboom?"

Butcher glared at the young man.

Rhonda walked closer to the trio of men. Casually, she tossed her hair off her neck, which drew attention to it and the soft skin beneath her chin. Summer freckles dotted her collarbone and the curves of her shoulders bespoke youthful vibrancy.

"Hi," she said simply to Butcher.

Nash swung towards his brother on the swivel chair. "Oh, look. There's, um… another person we need to talk to." Nash grabbed his brother's arm.

"Come on, Nash, I want to watch. This could be the most awkward moment in history."

"It will be if you sit here, Derek," Nash whispered. "And I'm pretty sure you don't want to be one of Butcher's readings tomorrow, Derek." They pushed off towards an empty table leaving Butcher and Rhonda alone. Rhonda stood awkwardly for a moment, before Butcher realized that she was waiting for an invitation.

"Do you want to sit down?" He pointed to the recently vacated stool. She smiled, sat down and placed her handbag on the bar.

"Thank you."

"Fancy meeting you here." Butcher was not always out of sorts with women, but there was something about Rhonda that reminded him of someone else, someone he couldn't put his finger on. He looked into her green eyes. Even in the dim light, he could sense a natural intelligence and a kindness that wasn't present in other places. He tried to shut off his internal reading light, but it was already illuminating some things about this young woman. Fortunately, they were good. "Can I buy you a drink?"

"That would be very nice," Rhonda responded not taking her eyes off Butcher. "I'll have a glass of Coke."

Butcher ordered it. "Not a drinker?"

"Well, sometimes," she said, "but it's a weeknight and I come here for the stimulating social engagement." She motioned sarcastically at the half a dozen people around the bar area. Butcher followed her graceful hand noticing its contours until it passed the Peterson twins who quickly looked away. They were doing a poor job of pretending not to be watching.

Butcher laughed. "So why do you come down here, if it's not for the social engagement?"

"I was being kind of serious," she said, "but I like the sound - the bowling alley, the laughter, the juke box and..." her face turned red.

"What?"

"I like to play the old arcade games."

"You're kidding! What do you like?" Butcher was smiling broadly. He hadn't read that from her!

"You'll make fun of me."

"No, I won't."

Her eyes strayed outside the door to the video games. There was a pinball machine, a console Frogger machine and game with a gun attached to it, which allowed the player to hunt down digital deer and moose while avoiding humans. "I'm not much of an online gamer, or even PlayStation or anything like that, but I love pinball and Frogger and even that Big Game Hunter out there." She looked down. "You probably think that's sophomoric."

"Absolutely," Butcher said. "But I think it's the best thing ever!" Rhonda smiled and her whole face lit up which caused something warm and different to begin brewing inside Butcher. It had been a long time since...

"Do you want to play?" She asked quietly. "We could play pinball. That's my favorite. Something so simple about it, a ball, two flippers, lights and sounds. Gosh, it just makes me happy." Her eyes lit up with happiness.

"I would love to play. Can we take our drinks out there?"

Rhonda nodded. "Come on," she said, a lilt of excitement in her voice. "I challenge you to a game of pinball." Another smile, another hiccup in Butcher's heart.

Rhonda led him out of the Greedy Pecker and into the arcade. Butcher looked over his shoulder where the twins were grinning maniacally at him. Derek gave him the thumbs up. Butcher lifted up a fist.

The pinball machine was themed. The frowning face of Harrison Ford as Indiana Jones was lit up on the back of the machine. Beside him was Sean Connery and the other man named Sallah, who Butcher couldn't remember his name. The Indiana Jones theme music was playing, the game lights flashed intermittently drawing attention to the game. Where normal pinball machines had a plunger, this one had a handgun and trigger to push the ball into play.

"This is pretty cool," Butcher said.

Rhonda nodded and unclipped her handbag. Retrieving a roll of quarters, she reddened again. She knew what this must look like. Total nerd. She looked up shyly at him and held out a quarter.

"Do you want to go first?"

Butcher shook his head. "No, I want to watch you do it first."

She giggled. *What's wrong with me? I don't giggle!*

Inserting the coin into the slot, the game came to life and Harrison Ford's voice let her know that the Grail Quest was about to begin. Lights flashing, sound pinging, Rhonda grinned at the handsome stranger standing beside her. She pulled the trigger and the ball bounded up the chute and down between the bumpers. As it jumped back and forth between rope bridges, airplanes, sidecars and dirigibles, she pushed the flippers. While she was playing, Butcher looked peripherally at her. Rhonda was tall, of course not as tall as he, but certainly close to six feet tall; her arms, used to carrying trays of food, were taut and muscular and as much as he wanted to refrain, he snuck a peek at her long legs which were dancing back and forth, calf muscles roped tight in delicious game time agitation. The game pinged away and for over two minutes, Rhonda continued to move and sway. As the ball pushed down towards the middle between the flippers, she moved her body slightly, not enough to tilt the game, but just enough to move the ball, which then shot from one flipper to the next up into the dirigible where more and more points were racked up.

"I'm impressed," Butcher said.

"These games are about my only vice. Normally I have to take care of…" She paused, and her guard was let down which caused the ball to carom recklessly out of play down the left-hand side of the machine. She pounded on the glass lightly, perturbed.

She couldn't have possibly known Butcher had already gleaned the truth from her.

Rhonda was in her mid-thirties; her accent betrayed the fact that she was a lifelong resident of Amicable. This would explain why her only vice was pinball and antique video games. It wasn't as if she didn't want to travel, she had to take care of a parent, probably her mother, and her escape through video games was more enjoyable than her escape to work early every morning. Her mother must have some kind of disease, maybe even something as devastating as dementia, and Rhonda must be the primary, probably only, carer. Not an easy life.

"Your turn to play," she said handing a quarter to him. He smiled and took it from her, trading places behind the gun. His hulking form bent almost in half over the machine designed for young players, generally kids. He noticed the high scores on the glass and the initials next to them.

"RCR. I take it that's you?" Butcher pointed to the scoreboard.

She nodded. "I've been playing a while."

"Rhonda what?"

"Rhonda Redman."

"And the middle name?"

"I don't give that out on first dates." Immediately she regretted her choice of words, but Butcher didn't react because he was already in the midst of the game.

Butcher was not very good at pinball; his reaction time was slow and his inability to guess the angles caused him to hit the buttons too early allowing the ball to go under the flippers. He looked at her and grimaced. "Sorry for wasting your quarter."

"Just getting warmed up." Rhonda pushed him out of the way. Inserting another quarter, she began the next round. "So, what do you think of the Peterson twins?"

Butcher looked back at the twins who were surrounded by second and third beer glasses. Nash was scrolling through his phone while Derek was watching the television screen above the bar.

"Harmless," he said. "Very nice young men."

"Mmm," she grunted.

"You don't like them?"

"No, they're okay," she said pushing her shoulders to the side and flipping the ball back up into Kate Capshaw's face. "Just immature."

"That's a good descriptor."

"So today was your first day at Peterson's?"

Butcher nodded. "Yes."

Silence. The ball wandered into a Nazi submarine where it was held for five seconds racking up points. Rhonda took her hands off the buttons and blew on them. "You know, I don't know your real name."

He smiled. "It's Leo. Leo Jensen."

"Nice to meet you," she moved back into the game as the ball torpedoed out of the submarine.

A commotion made Butcher look behind his back. The front door of the bowling alley opened and a group of ten or so high school youth entered. The young woman at the front counter smiled and greeted them all; the group responded, but none of them looked up from their phones. All ten of them were staring at the screen in front of them. Mindlessly walking to the sitting area, they took up seats around a semicircular formation of chairs, like a ring atoll, focused on the bowling area, and proceeded to laugh at whatever video that popped up on their screens. Then, tapping their neighbor on the shoulder, they pushed their screen in front of them and laughed together. The sound of failure emanated from the pinball machine and Rhonda looked around Butcher at the group of kids.

"Millennial herd."

"Excuse me?"

She pointed with her finger as she laid a hand on his shoulder. "It's a herd of millennials - you can always hear them coming, and you have to watch out or you'll fall under their stampede."

"I've never heard them called that before."

"I made it up," she said. "When they come into the restaurant, they move like a giant blob towards a table, and without even looking up - you'd think they had active sonar or something - they situate themselves around a table and order drinks with money that their parents give them. They laugh at videos or text someone. I have never heard them have a meaningful conversation."

"I feel sorry for them," Butcher watched the young people slouch in their chairs and stare hopelessly into the three-inch screens oblivious to all else around them.

Rhonda put another quarter in the pinball machine and watched Harrison Ford's face light up. "They've got everything they want - clothes, food, entertainment, no responsibility, no work. How can they not be happy?" Rhonda was projecting all of her frustration onto the young people and Butcher could sense in her movements her annoyance that they had what she desired.

"But they don't have the two things that they desperately want and don't even think about."

"What's that? A new car?"

"Nope," Butcher said. "They don't have hope and they don't have peace."

Rhonda looked over at him. "What are you, the Dalai Lama?"

He laughed. "Not yet. Look, see that one over there, the girl with the really tiny shorts and the white tank top?" Rhonda glanced quickly and nodded. "You can tell she's faking it. She doesn't really want to be staring at her phone. She really wants to engage with people."

"How can you tell that?" Rhonda's score was doubling up as she hit one of the bonus points

"She's not showing anyone what's on her phone, and there, look at that." He pointed. "Her eyes wistfully wander up to the bowling lanes. I think she actually wants to play."

"Why don't you go ask her to play?" Rhonda's voice sounded perturbed that he was paying more attention to the high school girl than to her.

"What, and have a police investigation hand delivered to the Amicable stranger who asks a teenage girl to play a game of bowling? Yeah, right. I couldn't get within four steps and two words from her and they'd all turn their phones on, record my picture and post it on their Twitter accounts that a pedophile is stalking the children of Amicable."

"Oh, come on, it's not that bad, is it?" Rhonda hit the flipper hard and the ball sailed back into the beginning shoot, which caused her to hoot with glee. "Yes!"

Butcher took a sip of his drink, which was now so watered down, he wasn't sure what he was drinking. "You wouldn't know. You're a woman."

Rhonda made a gagging noise. "Oh please, now we're supposed to put on the sob story for guys after all these years of suppression."

Butcher rose to the challenge. "For the ninety-nine percent of men who have not approached pedophile status, I'm sure that we can certainly rue the effect of the contemporary media on unfair portrayal."

Rhonda's demeanor was becoming more agitated. "Men! That's such bullshit! You all think you're innocent, but you're not!"

Her face swung to him; the sudden vitriol had flushed her cheeks and she dropped her hands from the video game. "You don't know the first thing about it!"

It was then that Butcher realized his mistake and he quickly (and unconsciously) read Rhonda's history. Somewhere in her past, her father, uncle, or some other close male had done or said something unmentionable. Rhonda's soul was pinched somewhere between horror and rage, and it just so happened that he became an illogical projection place for both. Butcher became the bullseye through which to send her arrow of anger. Even though she stood roughly half a foot shorter, she put a finger right into his face. After exhausting her feelings through a vitriolic tirade, she realized that the bowling alley had fallen quiet. No balls were being rolled; the patrons of the bar had ceased talking and the only sounds were from the television above the bar. Even the video game bleeping seemed to stop. A few of the Millennial Herd were talking excitedly into their phones as they recorded the showdown between the very tall people by the Indiana Jones pinball machine.

"Agh!" Rhonda cried in frustration and stomped away from the still figure of Butcher.

Butcher turned around to watch her go and cringed at the phalanx recording this moment in his history. Only one phone had not recorded the moment - the girl with the tank top. She looked empathetic.

Butcher remained motionless for a moment and then, with head down, abashedly walked towards the front door, past the bowling balls, past the phone-addicted teenagers, past the front desk teenager staring with mouth agape. He pushed open the doors and moved out into the warm and lonely night air.

There would be plenty of rumors tomorrow on the streets of Amicable.

Chapter 7.

James Thompson sat disconsolately at a red light. The engine of his tractor-trailer grumbled, rumbling underneath him like an impatient rhino ready to charge. As the semi idled, he looked down out of the driver's window at the passenger seat of the car beside him. From his vantage point, all James could see were the young, toned legs of the passenger with her feet up on the dash, and for a moment he thought that he would like to know what the rest of the girl looked like, not just her calves and thighs. He was only twenty-five years old – young enough to imagine certain things, but in reality, the ring that encircled his finger was a game-breaker. James stared at the small, gold handcuff around the fourth finger of his left hand and wondered (not for the first or last time) if Tolkein's talisman spoke more truth than just the fairy tale. One ring to rule his whole life.

The inglorious defeat of his bachelorhood had come for multiple reasons, the first – their immaturity. Both James and Naida had unrealistic expectations of marriage. With visions of happily ever after trimmed with the vows of 'til death parts us, they had no true understanding of the work necessary for a solid relationship. The second, and probably larger reason, was that both of them teetered precariously on the edge of alcoholism. Sometimes he would find himself off balance, arms swinging, falling towards the gaping maw, the abyss, and he would catch himself just in time. Naida, on the other hand, was adept at falling in and climbing back out of the steep chasm to dance on the lip of respectability.

It seemed like a natural progression to ask Naida to marry him. Even though he was twenty-one and she, nineteen, in their own minds, they felt ready to tie the knot. Unfortunately, they had no idea how difficult it was to keep that knot from fraying; it only took two years before James' time on the road began to interfere with the depth of the relationship. What once was a red-hot interaction between two teenagers had gradually simmered into a lukewarm cohabitation. Romance was as abundant as eighty-degree temperatures in February - it happened once in a while, but it was more luck than anything else. Sometimes, James would stumble across a card or, while pausing at a truck stop, see a trinket or gift. It seemed like a good substitute for the real thing. Romance was untaught, and the more they were left to their own devices (phone, internet or otherwise) the more they believed that sex and romance were synonymous. Naida had her own mind of what she wanted James to say and do; and James, certainly, had different ideas.

And thus, slowly, like continental drifts sometimes separating and other times pushing into each other, building mountains between them, the two young lovers heard the crack in their relationship. Sadly, they felt as if the inevitable unseen forces drawing them apart were too strong to fight against.

But it was a different day.

James yawned loudly as the light turned green. The small car next to him containing the young legs took off with a squeal of tires. James rolled his eyes and unconsciously recognized that this was a metaphor for his life: everybody else raced off into the future while he plodded along pulling a heavy trailer named Naida. Sighing, he switched through the gears and, after picking up speed, motored down the road towards Amicable. He had already dumped his load at Depot Junction, and now, at the end of the day, he was ready to be home, feet up with a beer in hand and six or seven more waiting for him in the fridge. This thought made him happy; beer and the chance to watch a football game. Leaning back in his seat, he patted his ever-enlarging gut. Although he enjoyed truck driving, it was a far cry from his more mobile days in high school when he was the starting defensive end on the football team.

Twenty minutes later he checked his watch. 6:12. He slowed as he approached Amicable's town limits. Although he knew that he shouldn't use his engine brakes, he did anyway just to release some pent up aggression. It's not like there were any cops around (Louise Nelson did not really count) to pull him over and ticket him for noise pollution. One of the local residents shook their head at him as he drove by; James shook his head. Old people just don't remember what it's like to make noise.

He was passing streets like Third Street East, Main Street and First Street West (the names of the streets were as exciting as watching the corn turn brown in the fall). He turned to peer down the street towards The Greedy Pecker and his heart stopped for a moment. He could have sworn that he saw Naida's car paused in the street, and there was a guy leaning over her window. It all happened so quickly, but immediately James' brain went into overdrive. Who was it? When he found out, he was going to pound the living daylights out of him. Rage reared inside James and he almost jammed on the brakes to make a turn and pull up behind the bastard. *That's my wife your flirting with!* For the next minute, James pre-played the scene of him stepping out of his truck next to Naida's car; the boy, frightened out of his wits, would back up, pleading with James. Adulterers needed to be taught a lesson. As James pummeled the adulterer in his mind, he began to feel better immediately.

Spirits lightened, James drove towards his garage where he parked the rig and turned off the engine. Shutting the garage door behind him, he opened his pickup door and began to drive home. His thoughts of revenge were interrupted by the image of the six pack of beers in the fridge. Excitement - he could have a few of them down before Naida returned home and then he could confront her.

That sounded like fun.

Naida suddenly looked at the glowing dashboard clock of her car radio. *Shoot,* she whispered and looked up at Nash who was indolently looking out over the street, unconsciously flexing his abdominal muscles, which made Naida smile. Nash was a really nice boy. He was easy to talk to; he took an interest in her opinions, and seemed quite content to simply flirt.

"I've got to go," Naida said and started the car. She knew that she had to get home. The thought of what awaited her - James sitting with his feet up on the coffee table scooping leftovers into his mouth, plate under his face, a six pack of beer sweating on the lamp stand next to him while the TV was tuned into ESPN to pick up the day's scores that he had missed - caused her stomach to cramp. The set routine, a rut, hardened washboard on the gravel road of her life, was not conducive to marital bliss when married couples tolerated each other at night, ignored each other in the morning and were blessedly separated by their workplaces during the day. Every once in a while, James would get it into his head to take her out to eat. Unfortunately, he would only choose establishments which had ESPN on the television.

Now that they had been married for a while, the seven-year itch had turned into a full-blown case of the four-year hives. The lackluster nature of their physical and emotional connection left them restlessly numb. It was no surprise that Naida spent many of her afternoons after work driving around the streets of Amicable looking for someone - anyone at all - to talk to. Nash happened to be willing and available.

Nash was two years younger than she; not quite as big as James, especially around the middle. Naida blushed thinking about Nash's middle and the wiry strength in his arms. Chiding herself for breaking a commandment, or at least skating dangerously close to the edges of number six, Naida tapped her steering wheel.

"I'll see you later, Nash."

He rapped on the roof of the car and backed away. She could tell he was disappointed but she was not. That someone would want to spend time building a relationship with her was wonderful; she wished that the Amicablean culture allowed heterosexual friendships without gossamer gossiping strings attached, but tautologically speaking, it was what it was.

After honking her horn, she drove towards home. Minutes later she pulled into the driveway, stomach churning, heart sinking into the pit of her stomach. Briefly, she was aware that this was not the way she should feel about seeing her husband after a long day, but the guilt was short lived. Naida took a deep breath and released it. Pursing her lips and checking her expression in the rearview mirror, she ashamedly hoped James was three beers into his melancholy, which would allow her to sink into the cushy chair in her bedroom with a glass of rum and coke and a book.

Naida pulled her car in behind James' pickup, turned the car off and opened the door. Dragging herself to the front door, she was aware of an assortment of late-summer sensory stimulants: the sinking sun silhouetting the oak leaves on the branches arching over their driveway, birds still singing, the sky turned an azure ocean blue. It would have been a beautiful evening for a walk. Maybe she could find a way to eat and disappear without James noticing.

The front door groaned as she opened it. She winced at the sound which would announce her arrival. The door's locking mechanism had been sticking for a few months, but James was too 'busy' to fix it. Even though Naida was capable of fixing it herself, the door gave her a sufficient reason to denigrate him inside her head. Naida was unconscious of the ways that she was fertilizing negative thoughts about her husband. The seeds of their thoughts were producing enough poisonous fruit to kill the marriage.

Naida entered the house and threw her keys into the bowl near the front door. She saw that the catch all container was overflowing with various odds and ends of their communal, but uncommitted, relationship: fingernail clippers, throat lozenges, toothpicks and even a few buttons that had come off coats and shirts.

James, as she presupposed, was exactly where she knew he would be. His evening meal was already eaten and the dirty plate was on the table. One cold beer was clamped in his meaty hand while five others were sweating onto the lamp stand. James did not glance up when she walked through the living room, and without a word she entered the kitchen and began to prepare herself a supper. Bending over, she reached into the cupboard for the cast iron frying pan to sauté some onions and peppers. When she straightened, she was surprised to find that James was standing behind her.

"Ooh! You scared me, James!" Her hand was pressed to her chest and she almost dropped the skillet.

"I bet." He was still holding the beer in his right hand while his left thumb was tucked into his belt.

Naida ignored him, pushed past and busied herself with turning the stove on. As she moved back to the stovetop, she placed the pan over the gas flame. Turning to the cutting board she began to slice the onion and red pepper.

"What were you doing this afternoon?" Like the knife in her hand, James' voice had a sharp edge to it. Chop. Chop.

"Just driving around."

A pause. "I saw you."

"Saw me what...?" Naida's heart raced.

"I saw you with him."

Naida turned slightly. "With who?"

"Don't pretend, Naida." He spit out her name.

Frustration gripped Naida's voice. "Don't start, James. Okay?"

"Who was it?" James gripped her arm and turned her towards him. Both were aware of the knife's edge that was separating them, the very real physical knife in Naida's hand and the symbolic edge on which they were walking.

"Oh, please, James, you don't even really care. I was talking with lots of people and you probably just happened to see me with..." she stopped herself and twisted her arm from his grip. "It doesn't matter."

"So, there is another guy." James could feel the blood rush to his face. Anger suffused his chest.

"No, James," Naida said exasperatedly and turned back to the stove to push the vegetables into the pan where they began to sizzle loudly. "There is *no one*. That includes you. If we had a healthy relationship, we wouldn't even be having this discussion. It's so old, and I'm sick of it."

"What do you mean we don't have a healthy relationship. It's always been this way."

Now Naida felt the anger and she dropped the knife on the counter for fear that she'd use it in a way that wouldn't benefit anyone. "That's right, James! It's always been this way! You go to work. I go to work. You drink and watch television. I drink and read books. Sometimes we go out, maybe to a movie where we don't have to talk to each other, or to a restaurant where you stare over my head and we don't have to talk to each other." She thrust her hands into his face. "We never, ever talk to each other!"

"We talk..." James began to pout, but then realized the pleading tone in his voice. He took another drink of his beer.

"No, we don't. Never. That's why I enjoy *talking* to Nash. He..."

"Peterson? Nash! You've got to be kidding. What is he, eighteen years old?"

Naida, surprisingly defensive about Nash, turned her back on her husband. "That's rich, James. You who look online for 'friendships'" she made quotation marks with her fingers without looking at him, "with 'barely eighteen-year-old' girls who are ready to *do whatever you like*." The sarcasm was biting, but they had crossed the threshold, which could lead into the chasm of conflict.

James' face reddened.

"Stop trying to change the subject. This is about *you*."

"No, James. You don't get it: this is about us. I'm this close," she made an indication with her fingers, "to walking out."

"So you can go be with him? Is that it? You already have this figured out. You'll blame me, the distant husband who works hard, but doesn't know how to romance his wife. Priceless." James backed out of the kitchen.

"Just like always, James, first one to run away," she muttered under her breath above the sound of sizzling onions, and then punctuated it with one word that she knew would infuriate him, but at this point, she couldn't help it. "Coward."

Like a bull he turned and charged, overshadowing her small form. He didn't strike, but he spluttered and blustered his complaints ranging from her work habits to her inabilities to do 'womanly' jobs. Her ironing was awful; the dishes were never done; the laundry would pile up. Neither one realized that the partnership had deteriorated because of the small things, not the big ones. Communication simply had ceased, and they were left with an empty, silent relationship that was eroding in the storm of their discontent.

While James unleashed his outrage, Naida ignored him by imagining something, anything else. Her mind flashed to the sunset, the oak trees and their blanket of sky. The birds and their singing. Her mother - how was she going to take this latest episode? - and finally to Nash. Guiltily, she was aware that this relationship was the only thing she enjoyed in her life right now.

Finally, the verbal onslaught began to subside and Naida looked down at her sautéed vegetables. Charred to a crisp. Smoke rose from the pan and almost casually, she dumped the contents into the sink. James returned to his chair, arms crossed and then turned the volume up on the television. As the steam rose from the sink, Naida looked out the kitchen window into the serenity of their neighbor's front yard. She wondered how the Lawsons did it; after forty years of marriage, they seemed perfectly content to enjoy life together. A happy couple.

Naida wondered if she and James would make it to five.

At this point, she hoped not.

Chapter 8.

Rhonda was embarrassed.

Eight o'clock on a Thursday night and she was home from the bowling alley. When she had seen Butcher sitting with the Peterson boys, she had been intrigued. How the conversation had devolved so quickly into her petulant tantrum, she wasn't quite sure. Replaying the night back in her mind, Rhonda's pulse quickened at the thought of how well he could read her emotions. And yet, he had clumsily unpacked the worst of her baggage. There was no way he could have possibly known about her father. When she was twelve years old, he had pulled up stakes and left Rhonda and her mother to fend for themselves. Rhonda knew all too well the difficulties her mother had, but what he had done was unconscionable. For him, life was far too short to have to put up with Connie's antics, her depression, anxiety and social awkwardness. He wanted to run free, live life in the fast lane, sow his oats, and so, with barely a wave of the hand, he walked out the door. On that April morning eight days after Easter, Davis Redman took the family car and went on a permanent vacation from reality. On that cold spring morning, her father thumbed his nose at their familial future leaving a pubescent Rhonda to assimilate the pieces of her rapidly approaching adulthood.

And, she had to take care of her mother and all of her difficulties.

In Amicable, people weren't 'diagnosed' with depression and anxiety, but there were whispers when someone was struggling. In this current world of social media, her mother thrived on the attention she received because of her posts. Connie's struggles put a strain on almost all of Rhonda's friendships also. If people wanted to talk to Rhonda, they would have to move in close proximity to Connie. When people talked to Rhonda's mother it was like swimming in a shallow pool filled with sharp rocks. Eventually, no one wanted to swim anywhere near either one of them.

Rhonda and Connie lived together. As Rhonda slid through her twenties and into her thirties, her resentment had grown exponentially. It wasn't that Rhonda didn't have compassion for her mother, but whenever Rhonda would get close to anyone, male or female, Connie would find a way to push them away. There was only a small amount of personal space in Connie's world, and the only silhouette that fit into it belonged to Rhonda.

As Rhonda busied herself in the living room, she looked out the window at the last rays of sunshine spilling in from the west. It was the most beautiful time of year, much better than the frigid early evenings of winter, even if she did enjoy Christmas. Lightning bugs were beginning their nightly dance, a sultry samba, flitting and floating from current to draft, seeking intimacy. Rhonda's thoughts went back to the tall butcher, Leo Jensen. For a moment she wanted to call him; she probably would have if he had given her his number, but the reality was, she knew it was best that she and Butcher simply remain ships passing in the night and day.

"Rhonda?" Connie's voice called out from the dark hallway. Rhonda's mother had been secreting herself away in the bedroom presumably sewing, crocheting or conniving future ways to make Rhonda's life more miserable.

"Yes, Mother. I'm home."

Connie appeared at the intersection of the hallway and the living room. Not stepping quite into the light, Connie held her hands out to touch the walls, steadying herself. Often, she pretended to be feeble. Although she had visited the doctor in Clancy, the doctor had said that Connie was simply not eating the right foods - more protein, or something ridiculous like that. But Rhonda knew that her mother's problems had nothing to do with a protein deficiency. It was her outlook on life. Most people knew Connie well enough to realize that Connie didn't need physical help, she needed therapy.

So they went to therapy, both of them. Connie thrilled at the thought of one dedicated person paid to listen to her complaints.

"Were you at the bowling alley?"

"Yes, Mother."

"That's a vile place, Rhonda. You shouldn't be going there, a woman of your age."

Rhonda rolled her eyes. She'd heard it all before. "Thank you for your advice, Mother."

"No need to get smart with me, young lady."

Rhonda hated it when her mother treated her like a child. "I'm thirty-three years old and have, in fact, held down a job for more than half of them, unlike you." The barb slipped out. As soon as she said it, she wanted to take it back, not because it wasn't true, but she knew her mother would enjoy the process of making her feel guilty.

Connie's face fell. "That's not fair, Rhonda. For all these years I've taken care of you. I've supported you, fed you and clothed you."

"You're so right, Mother. How could I ever have been able to live on my own?"

Connie looked at her daughter's back. Rhonda's hair was catching the last rays of sunlight, golden strands sparkling. Without realizing it, Connie was jealous of almost everything about her daughter: her looks, her height (which she'd received from her father's side, *curse his name*) and even her youth. There were many days that Connie regretted almost every facet of her life.

"You're awfully testy tonight. What happened at that *place*?"

"You wouldn't understand."

Connie moved into the room a little farther. "Try me."

"No, Mother. It will only end up in another argument."

"We don't argue. We just…" she tried to find the right synonym for how she treated her daughter. "We just have differences of opinion."

"Whatever." Rhonda finished rinsing the dishes that her mother had left from her dinner and placed them into the dishwasher.

"Do you want to go for a walk?" Connie asked.

Rhonda looked at her mother, who was already in her dressing gown, and rolled her eyes.

"I could get dressed again."

"No. You just go back to what you were doing and I'll finish cleaning up around here." Rhonda moved past her mother and began to tidy the living area littered with magazines projecting happy, idealized people, faces shining with happiness and all the answers in the world.

"That's another way of saying that I don't do anything around here, isn't it?" Rhonda could hear the whine in her mother's voice and she desperately wanted to nod, to tell her mother exactly how her neediness made her feel, but it would only bring on another round of pathetic-ness.

"No, that's not another way of saying it."

Connie cinched the belt of her robe tighter around her and walked around to Rhonda, arms crossed. "Tell me what happened at the bowling alley tonight."

Rhonda sighed deeply as she adjusted the coffee table, put down the footrest of the recliner and tossed a few used tissues into the garbage can. "I met a man tonight."

Connie's jaw tightened. She'd been through this before. Rhonda would find a boy, they would get to know each other and then, without fail, they would take off – just like her ex-husband. That's what men do. If only she'd introduce the boys to her, Connie was sure she could get a good read on them. She and Rhonda could have a mother/daughter talk about how best to move forward in the relationship.

"What's his name?"

"You wouldn't know him."

"I bet I would."

Rhonda stood up straight towering over her cross-armed mother. "I bet you all the money in the world you wouldn't know him." Connie backed down but raised an eyebrow. "He moved into town yesterday. He's working for the butchers, you know, the Peterson boys."

"Oh yes, I know them, or I've heard of their... exploits." Connie said this as if she had intimate knowledge of every person in town. Inwardly, though, Connie wasn't sure she could pick out the Peterson boys from a lineup.

Rhonda's eyes rolled again, and her frown deepened. "His name is Leo Jensen, but it seems like everyone calls him Butcher."

"What's he like?"

For a moment, Rhonda's face flushed and she was aware that her mother, if she could have been a normal mother, would have picked up on the coloring.

"He's tall."

"How tall?"

"I'd guess about six foot six."

"Oh, that tall."

"He's got brown eyes and brown hair. He's clean shaven and he's got a nice voice."

Connie smirked at her daughter. "Sounds like you're smitten with the boy."

That was another thing that irritated Rhonda: when she called the men she was interested in 'boys.' If Connie could debase them in Rhonda's mind, that she was too old for them, too beautiful, too tall, too anything, Rhonda would come to her senses, snap out of it and recognize that she was far too *everything* for these *boys*. The right one would come along, Connie was quite sure, but only after Rhonda grew up and got an adult job.

And Connie vetted them.

"This is why I don't talk about these kinds of things with you. You patronize me."

"I don't patronize you," Connie said defensively.

"The *man* is thirty-nine years old. He's not a boy."

"That old... He's almost past child-rearing age."

"Oh, for God's sake!" Rhonda threw a pillow onto the sofa and began to stomp down towards the hallway.

"Don't you take the Lord's name in vain!" Connie said. "We won't be having any of that!"

Rhonda whipped around and stood over her mother. "I sincerely think that God would be much more interested in your selfishness than in my actual use of his name."

"My selfishness? MY SELFISHNESS!" Connie's voice began to rise; hysteria coming from both right and left field creating a whirlwind of egocentrism that was sucking both of them to the bottom of their familial frustration. "I sit here at home worrying about you every day and night, praying for your immortal soul, and all that you can think of is blasting me with your anger. It's a good thing I am a patient woman. I might have to…"

"What are you going to do, Mom! What? Are you going to spank me? Ground me? Take away my toys? What is it that *you* can think of to punish your middle-aged spinster daughter taking care of her past middle-aged divorcee mother who sits high in her castle waiting for either Prince Charming or Rumpelstiltskin to ride by to rescue her, taking her to his castle so she can suck the life out of him also?" Suddenly, Rhonda knew that she had taken one step too far.

Connie's eyes flashed, hurt. "I see," she said quietly. "I'm sucking the life out of you." Academy Award guilt.

"I'm sorry, Mother. Truly, I am. But I've had a rough day."

"As have I." Connie began to walk quietly back to her room.

Rhonda was highly doubtful that her mother had a rough day, but it wasn't worth pursuing at this moment. "I'm going outside." Rhonda watched her mother's shoulders sag as she trudged down the hallway swallowed by the darkness that would manifest itself into something different by the morning, what kind of beast that might be, she didn't know. Rhonda shook her head and sighed deeply. After her mother's door snapped shut, Rhonda let herself out of the house.

George Hendriks was sitting on his front patio sipping a glass of beer. It was an astonishment to most of the citizenry of Amicable that he was still living at home by himself. Most people assumed that he would have moved to Clancy, to the nursing home, to be with people his own age. George would say, 'You can shove that idea up your wazoo.' George would be quite secure and content living in his small house until the day that he died. When he did, he was hoping that the first person to find him would notice how well he kept his house at the over-ripe age of ninety-seven. Although much of the furniture was mid-20th century vintage, George believed that if it wasn't broken, it didn't need to be replaced. Most of the people who agreed with him were already dead, including his dear wife Mabel. He thought about her every morning, day and evening wishing that he could hear her voice just one more time. Twenty-four years was a long time to be alone.

Generally, his favorite voice was that of his next-door neighbor Rhonda Redman. Often when she came home from work, he would beckon her to his front porch where she would smile and gratefully climb the four stairs onto his wooden deck. George would point a gnarled finger through the front door to the kitchen. Rhonda would nod and smile and walk through the open door to the fridge and grab a cold can of Budweiser. There were times when Rhonda had stayed up with him talking about random things, odd things, things that only best friends talked about. She asked questions about the past and future and he was glad to do the same. George felt sorry for Rhonda. He knew Connie's struggles. But, families take care of families. George's children had both preceded him in death; Lois, unmarried, died of cancer; Ronald from a car accident in his thirties. Both tragedies had taken their toll on him and Mabel. It was only the strength of the small town that had brought them through to the other side.

In the twilight, George saw the Redmans' door open and Rhonda step out. Even from this distance, he could tell that Rhonda was not in a good frame of mind. They'd spent enough time together that he could read her body language like he could read a book.

"Need some company, Homey?" George yelled across the property divide towards Rhonda.

"Nah, just some fresh air tonight, George."

"Anything I can help with?" Rhonda stared into the street avoiding his gaze rather than to the west, towards George's house, where the shimmering sunset was finally pouring its last rays out into the ever-darkening sky.

Rhonda was quiet for a moment and then her head dropped. "Yes, I guess I wouldn't mind a little pleasant company." There was a subtle implication that the company inside her own house was decidedly unpleasant.

"Come and get yourself a cold one."

Rhonda descended her steps, turned right and walked down the pebble encrusted sidewalk. The winters had been harsh to the cement; ice and snow cracked them like granite skin. Then, the summers baked them. Like hardened arteries, these footpaths connected the people of Amicable, but time puts a strain on all things. Rhonda smiled as she looked up at her aged friend reclining in his Adirondack chair. Shaking her head and smiling, she climbed the steps and moved past him, placing her hand on his shoulder, and moving into the house. After grabbing two cold beers, one for each of them, she went back out to the porch where her chair was permanently positioned. Both of them faced the west, and after tapping him again on the shoulder with the sweating beer, she took her seat next to him.

"Are you trying to liquor me up to take advantage of me?" George's smile, wide and toothy (he still had a few of his originals), was flanked by grizzled cheeks, covered with stalks of sharp white whiskers and wrinkles of ages past.

Rhonda snorted. "If you were sixty years younger, George, I might take a run at you."

They both chuckled.

"The lightning bugs are out tonight," he pointed with his gnarled, arthritic index finger. "I love them. I hope there are a whole bunch of 'em in heaven."

George didn't often talk about death, but when he did, it was never with fear, only a kind of longing, like a caterpillar ready to shed its skin and fly away. "They are beautiful," she agreed.

"What's on your mind, Rhodie?"

Rhonda took a deep swig of beer. "It's complicated, Georgie."

George waited for her in silence.

Chapter 8.

"I met a guy this morning," she began slowly. Rhonda dented the can in her hand and it made a slight popping sound.

"That sounds good."

She nodded. "He came to the Choke, a new guy in town."

"Well, that's interesting. New people don't come to Amicable unless they're stopping for gas."

"I know, but this guy is staying. He's taken a job at Peterson's."

"Butcher, huh?"

"That's right." The moon had begun to make an appearance behind them in the east. A crescent. "He's got very kind eyes and a gentle voice."

"A great beginning. You can always tell by the eyes." Even though she wasn't looking at him, Rhonda knew that he was pointing to his eyes.

"His name is Jensen. Leo Jensen. We talked for a while this morning and it was the weirdest thing. It was like he knew everything about me. I didn't really say anything. He just looked at me; he knew things - even about my life, like about my mom."

"Did you tell him about your dad?"

Rhonda shook her head. "No."

"You didn't tell him about…"

"No," Rhonda cut in. "Absolutely not." There were parts of Rhonda's past that needed to stay parked there. Nothing good could come of revealing that.

"That's good. Don't want to scare him off. Your dad and that guy were assholes."

Rhonda laughed. "Sometimes my mother seems just as bad. She's driving me crazy."

Silence. Fireflies captured their attention. Like floating Christmas lights, the insects flew in sparkling parabolas, each floating on the breeze waiting and hoping for the right moment to attract another firefly. In a dance, they were alight then dim. Light, then dim. "So, this guy, the butcher, we bumped into each other tonight at the Greedy Pecker. Everything was going really well until I let my anger get the best

93

of me." She sighed, closed her eyes and she stretched her neck to both sides. "I blew it."

"Keep going."

"Because of, well, you know, what happened to me all those years ago..." They both fell into silence. The memory of her past was not something Rhonda wanted to dwell on, but invariably and unfortunately, the *idea* of *him* wormed its way, like a mind bore, into her thoughts almost every day.

"It's okay, Rhodie," he said sympathetically. "You don't have to talk about it." George shook his head and threw his empty beer can across the porch and opened the next one. "I'm going to pay for this in the morning."

"Probably," Rhonda said.

George looked at the can. "I'm glad you accepted my proposal for a drink tonight. I was feeling a little bit lonely."

"Sorry, George."

"Aach, tonight isn't about me. Tell me about this butcher, Rhodie."

Rhonda wasn't sure how much she could tell him, but she related what had happened in the bowling alley until the moment she argued with her mother. George didn't say anything; he didn't need to say anything. His presence counted more than words.

"What do you think I should do, Georgie?"

George turned his legs around to face her. In the dim light of the stirring streetlights, she could see the contours of his face. Sparse hair, long since cared for, stuck out at odd angles behind his ears and around the crown of his head. Holding the can in both hands, he rested them on his thin stomach. His breath caught once, and then he spoke, softly, as if unwilling to disturb the peace of the late summer's eve. "Not for me to say, but I think you already know the answer. You just have to be willing to face your fears in order to do it. If it were me, I'd take a leap. You're old enough to do whatever you want. Be a woman, Rhodie."

Rhonda looked at her aged neighbor and inwardly thanked him. The world needed more George Hendrikses.

"I'm going to go to bed while I can still walk. I know it's early, but I'm going to the cemetery tomorrow. Thanks for stopping by, Rhonda. Stay as long as you want." He rose slowly; she could hear his joints screaming at him. Then, stopping next to her, he placed a hand on her shoulder. She leaned her face into his hand, an intimate gesture of friendship rarely seen in the twenty-first century.

"Thanks for your companionship, Neighbor." Rhonda said and finished off her beer. She stood and helped George back into the house where he had various handholds set up. After a hug, she left the house and sat outside on her own deck waiting for as long as possible hoping that her mother had gone to sleep.

Butcher

96

Chapter 9.

Tracey Thomas watched from her bedroom window as the willowy brunette passed by her house. The woman seemed dejected, as if someone had let the air out of her tires. Hands tucked deep into her front pockets, she walked slowly, staring at something, yet nothing in particular, hoping the cement cracks would widen and draw her into the void.

Tracey knew this young woman - Naida something-or-other. She had graduated from high school before Tracey had started. It wasn't small news that she had married one of the local boys, although for the life of her, Tracey couldn't remember what the boy's name was. Not that it mattered much. Local boys were all the same; big fish in a very small toilet bowl.

That's the way Tracey felt on this exact evening as she watched Naida pass by her house. Unknown to Tracey, further down the street, an old man and his next-door neighbor were discussing the perplexities of life – why the pieces didn't seem to have the right pictures on them, and the edges of the puzzle were round, not flat. It seemed as if almost everyone was pondering the difficulties of life on this warm, late summer evening. Tracey's own mind was spinning. More than anything, she wanted to escape this ever-present hamster wheel that seemed to be her life. It wasn't that she didn't like high school or even the small town; it was the fact that it didn't seem like there was any future *anywhere* for any of them.

Apathy just seemed to be a way of life for her because she was so damn tired. So tired of everything.

All the adults in her life (and out of her life - she could always hear them whispering) seemed to denigrate anyone under the age of twenty. *They've got it so easy. Why, when I was a kid... Look at those spoiled brats playing on their gadgets and telephones. Pretty soon they'll have them growing out of their ears. Why, when I was a kid... Why can't these kids just sit still?*

They've got to rock in their chairs, jiggle back and forth on their feet, their hands always have to be active. They used to call us hyperactive, ants in our pants. Now they've got to label it with a fancy medical name and dose them up on drugs. Now, when I was a kid...

Nobody wants to know what it was like when you were a kid, because it DOESN'T MATTER ANYMORE! YOU'RE NOT A KID!

Tracey understood her parents' protectiveness; she was an only child and their bright and shiny star. Tracey wished that they'd loosen the apron strings so she could actually enjoy her childhood. Every weekend was filled with frivolous offerings of dance and ballet, creative writing classes, piano lessons, the list went on and on. These were all things Tracey's parents would rhapsodize about, "We always wanted to do these things when we were younger, but we never had the time..." Tracey never really seemed to have a moment to sit and be quiet; her parents always said that they wanted her to experience everything, but what they wanted was to experience everything through Tracey's life.

Usually, she was afraid to talk to her parents about her fear of the future and her difficulties with understanding life as a teenager in the 21st century. If she could simply insert herself into the time her parents were growing up, she was sure that life would have been a hell of a lot easier.

Opening up her computer, Tracey was tempted to call one of her friends, Alyssa, but Tracey knew that she probably wouldn't even be home from the bowling alley yet. Even though Tracey had to leave at eight o'clock (because of the stupid grounding thing for putting a bumper sticker on her car), the rest of her friends stayed. Instead of calling, she decided to do homework before she went to bed. Got to keep up the good habits to get into a good college... Her one hope of escape.

Tracey's parents were downstairs, her father doing the bookkeeping and her mother working on the shopping list for the weekend. They never seemed to stop and in the midst of all of their domestic duties, they found time to 'visit.' This was one of Tracey's least favorite words. 'Visiting' meant that she would be dragged around to the houses of her parents' friends where they would *chat* and *small talk* and sit around a fire pit drinking coffee while she was left to entertain the little brats of the aforementioned friends. Tracey wasn't sure if her parents were afraid that if they sat still, they would, like she felt, begin to decay a little bit more every day.

Butcher

Chapter 10.

Leo Jensen stared at his face in the mirror of his new bathroom. As the glowing light of the fluorescent bulb hummed above his head, Butcher stared at his face, the face of a convenient stranger. He noticed the puckering around the corners of his eyes, the silvering of his hair and the imperfections in his skin. Other than the sound of the running water and the scratching, *scrish, scrish, scrish* of the toothbrush, the house was quiet. Unnervingly quiet. Except for his thoughts, which were shouting loudly into the cavernous reality of what just happened. Butcher felt like a butcher, and he cringed multiple times as he brushed his teeth, recollecting the events of the night.

There was no doubt he was attracted to Rhonda. As always, though, Butcher had to be careful about making connections. For the last years of his life, he had done his share of building some walls and tearing down others. Adeptly, Butcher could see behind the darkness of others' lives, deeply into the crevices of the closets where people stored their secrets. Whether he wanted to or not, Butcher pulled skeletons into the sunshine. Sometimes this made him a popular man, other times decidedly not.

Before arriving in Amicable, Butcher had spent just over a year in Colorado working in a large grocery store chain. During the summer, the hikers would come with their hair tied up in man buns, their flannel shirts wrapped around their waists while their partners wore short shorts, woolen socks, hiking boots and exposed, unshaven legs. Butcher wasn't quite sure where they were going hiking as most of the trails in Colorado were immaculately groomed, many of them available for wheelchair access. These people would come in for their beef jerky, turkey jerky, hurkey jerky - it didn't matter - and stuff it by the fistful into their large green Katmandu backpacks, bursting at the seams with a thousand dollars worth of camping gear, as if they were trekking into the vast expanses of the Himalayas.

Butcher

The winter season was far worse; the rich and beautiful would show up on the threshold of the Rocky Mountains in their metal behemoths, Leviathan automobiles, designed by the military to carry troops, but in Colorado held husband and wife (usually of the second or third variety - money tends to ruin first marriages) and a mittful of stepchildren, none of whom took in the scenery around them because their parents had individual movie screens for each child. As they pulled up to Breckenridge just after Christmas, the husband and wife would stand shoulder to shoulder breathing in the 'freedom' of the mountains, reveling in the Christmas lights and music, thinking that there could be no greater wonderland (at, and for, their disposal) in the entire world. Surrounded by like-minded rich and beautiful people, they would exchange pleasantries while at the same time covet everything whether spouse, children, vehicle, toys or accommodation. Butcher could watch out the front window as they arrived, preening and prancing, and he wondered if there could be anything more fake than these people.

It was an unintended consequence of his gift; even though Butcher did not want to judge people, he couldn't help it. Especially people like these. Often, he would ponder whether this sense of judgmentalism was due to jealousy. He shivered at the thought. As the travelers would enter the grocery store stocking up with enough food for an entire winter, not just a week vacation, rarely would they attempt a conversation with Butcher. Usually, they would glance at their Rolex watches tapping their feet in half time wanting him to 'hurry, hurry, hurry, the slopes are calling.' As Butcher watched them, he read in them, like a skipping record, variations of the same thing: vacuous lives filled with air and space. Their eyes betrayed nothing but greed and envy; happiness was as far from them as the sun from the moon. Butcher remembered one such interaction with a man from Chicago.

His name was Kyle Sturm and his third wife's name was Kelsey. Kyle would have been at least fifteen years older than Kelsey. Their courtship, Butcher was quite certain, had commenced at an office party in a Chicago restaurant where Kyle had ogled her ceaselessly while she served his table. Kelsey had been wearing something that emphasized her top, a tight t-shirt and a dangling necklace lost between her

102

breasts. Kyle had probably dropped his phone number onto the credit card receipt, which would have made Kelsey giggle and not-so-surreptitiously lick her lips signaling to the businessman that she was open for transactions, even though the last transaction, his second wife, Tonya, had not been wiped from the books.

"Hi, there. Can I get four cuts of your best steak, and when I mean best, I *really mean the best.*" Kyle actually leaned over the counter towards Butcher who was cutting up chicken. He was wearing expensive outdoor gear.

"Yes," Butcher responded simply, somehow refraining from rolling his eyes.

"But I need you to hurry. The slopes are calling." Butcher wanted to gag.

Straightening up to his full height made Kyle step back slightly. "What are they saying to you?"

"Excuse me?"

"You just said the slopes are calling to you. What are they saying?" Butcher didn't look at the man as he opened the glass display case and grabbed four of the worst pieces of steak that he had. Butcher was pretty sure that this man had as much a chance of telling a good piece of meat from a bad one as he did from ascertaining his prospective mates.

"Ah, yes. It's just a phrase we say."

"Hmmm."

Kyle took his phone out of his pocket and thumbed impatiently through his messages. "Any chance of this moving a little quicker?"

At this point, Butcher looked at the smaller man with beady, darting eyes and pinched mouth with bleached white teeth. "There's a chance," Butcher said with a smile.

The man began to frown. A woman who looked young enough to be his daughter bounded up behind him and drummed on his shoulders. She was wearing a bright blue ski coat and a stocking cap made of the finest llama fur. The dangling blue balls made Butcher smirk.

"Come on, Kyle, hurry up," she said, grabbing onto his arm and leaning her head on his shoulder. "I want to get into the hot tub."

"As soon as this man gets us our meat, we'll be on our way, Kelsey." Kyle jabbed a finger at Butcher. Okay, pal, you asked for it.

"Will that be all?" He wrapped up the meat and began to put a sticker on it. "Or, did you need something for your girlfriend?"

"Excuse me? This isn't my girlfriend, this is my wife."

Butcher nodded. "I know that. Probably your third or fourth wife judging by her clinginess."

"How dare you!" Kyle's face reddened in outrage.

"Your girlfriend is probably waiting for you on the slopes tapping her own watch wondering if you're going to show up."

Both Kelsey and Kyle's mouths dropped, neither one could quite comprehend what was happening. "I saw you checking your phone, that little smile on your face - she probably said something dirty - that was when you told me to hurry up. You already know that Kelsey is going to sit in the hot tub all day, so why not slide down someone else's slope for a while." Butcher pointed out the window. "How many kids you got in the car? Two - that would be my guess - and they want nothing to do with you because they don't like their new mother."

Kelsey looked at Kyle whose mouth was opening and closing like a fish out of its element gasping for water but finding nothing.

"Is that true?" Kelsey asked pulling away from her husband.

"Of course not!" He spluttered. "You're my wife and this... this... butcher," he spit the word out, "is obviously having a bad day. Give me my meat and we'll be going!"

"Have a nice day, Kyle and Kelsey. I hope you enjoy the slopes and giving your meat to someone else."

Kelsey gasped. "Kyle, we need to talk to the manager!"

Kyle's face reddened. "Let's just go!"

"You're not going to stick up for me! My reputation is on the line!"

Kyle grabbed Kelsey by the elbow. "Let's go."

The ensuing commotion as the couple stomped out of the store caught the attention of Gerald, the store manager, who walked towards the deli where Leo was standing smugly behind the glass. Gerald looked towards the couple at the checkout lane where the woman stood, arms crossed, anger etched into every fiber of her being. The man handed a credit card to the checkout lady.

Gerald looked up into the eyes of his employee. "What did you do, Butcher?"

"I served the customers, boss."

"Butcher, how many times have I told you, just keep your mouth shut?"

"I think we're up to eighteen, boss."

"Well," Gerald said with an exasperated sigh, *"I think it was the seventh time where I said I'd have to let you go if you couldn't keep silent. If you weren't so good at your job, I'd have let you go months ago."*

"Thanks, boss."

Gerald's face reddened. "That's not a compliment, Butcher."

"Did you want me to pack up my things, boss?"

Gerald shook his head. "It's the beginning of the ski season - I can't afford to lose you, but can I beg - do I need to get down on my knees - will you just... keep... your... thoughts... to... yourself?"

Butcher was silent.

"Well, are you going to say anything?"

"You just told me to keep my thoughts to myself, boss."

Gerald threw his hands up in the air. "I give up! Get back to work, Butcher!"

The memory gave Butcher pause as his reflection in the mirror convicted him. After spitting into the sink, he rinsed out his mouth and dried it. Turning away from the mirror, he turned off the light and walked into the living room continuing his self-castigation.

How did I miss it? How could I not have seen that she had problems with a male in her past? Who was it? The thought that he had missed something, or even misread her, both thrilled and frightened Leo at the same time. It had been a long time since that had happened, maybe not since his teenage years.

Just as he was about to sit down in his chair, there was a knock at the door. For a moment, his heart raced and he hoped that it was Rhonda. Walking to the front door, he saw a face peering in and disappointedly, he saw that it was Liam Wilson.

Leo opened the door; Liam was grinning. "To what do I owe this pleasure? Am I having a house inspection on my second night in Amicable?"

Liam laughed. "Heck, no. I just thought I'd stop by to see how you're doing. Maybe share a beer."

Leo shook his head. "I haven't been to the store and I don't have any beer."

"That's all right," Liam responded. "I've brought some." Butcher watched the broad form of the mechanic stroll slowly back to his pickup and reach through the open window into the back seat. Liam's pants sagged and his crack appeared like a rising crescent moon. Pulling out a six-pack of beer, he returned to the front door in the glow of the street light.

"Does everyone carry beer around in the back of their truck?"

Liam smiled. "Just for emergency medicinal purposes." He waited at the front step until Butcher stepped out of the way to let him in. Sighing, Butcher noticed that it was already almost nine o'clock, and just as Liam stepped in, Butcher noticed the woman from the car in the street, *what was her name?* – Naida – strolling slowly on the sidewalk. Butcher shrugged and closed the door behind him.

Liam had already situated himself in the reclining chair - his reclining chair - and pushed the footrest up. Having taken off his shoes, Liam displayed prominent toe holes in his socks. "Have you figured out what Amicable is like yet?"

Butcher walked around to the brown sofa near the wall opposite the recliner. Sinking into the sofa it seemed as if his knees were higher than his head. "I've only been in the town for one day."

"That's all it should take," Liam responded, popping the beer in his hands. Freed from the confines of the can, the beer began to explode from the can like a hops flavored volcano. Liam covered the hole with his mouth and sucked the foam in. Once the tide had been stemmed, he smiled guiltily at Butcher and belched. Noticing that some of the contents of the beer had flowed onto his shirt, he cleaned it with his hand and wiped it on the chair. "Sorry about that."

"It's your house."

"I suppose it is."

"What do you mean it should only take one day to figure out the town?"

Butcher was aware that they were supposed to be drinking beer together, but he was not at all displeased that Liam had not offered him one. He wasn't sure how cold they were anyway.

"Well," Liam said, as he pushed his Wilson Garage hat back farther onto his head. "Amicable is about as exciting as watching a grasshopper eat leaves and spit tobacco."

"That is exciting."

"I suppose it is if you're an alien and never seen a grasshopper before." Another sip. "Anyway, the people of Amicable are predictable, which is a good and bad thing. If you make it through a year without getting sucked into the tractor beam of boredom, you'll be a Jedi." He made another sucking noise with his mouth.

"I'll try to use the force."

"Atta boy."

"So, what should I look out for?" Butcher asked.

"For starters, you should watch out for the ladies. If they're over forty years of age, they're going to gossip – that's a guarantee, and when that happens, look out." Butcher pretended to be taking notes and writing them down on his hand.

"Check. Watch out for women."

The sarcasm floated right over Wilson's head. "Then, make sure that you're nice and friendly to people, especially the old ones."

"What does that mean?"

"It's the Amicable way, my friend. If they ask you a question, smile and make them feel like they are the smartest person on the planet even if you think they are an imbecile."

"What if it's a stupid question?"

Liam gave him a sharp look and ignored the question. "That's a stupid question. Anyway, try not to give away too much info. It's the easiest way to get attacked. If you feel threatened, talk about the weather, or the basketball team - anything that steers people away from learning about you personally. That's a slick, dark road. You can end up in the ditch real quick by getting personal." He lifted his beer to Butcher. "At least for the first ten years or so."

Butcher didn't respond.

"And even then, you won't be a local, but at least you might be able to talk about politics or maybe national news or somethin'. But people *really* have to trust you first." Liam finished the beer, crushed it and opened another one.

"Why would anyone move to Amicable then?" Butcher scratched his head and looked at his fingers.

"They don't, Butcher. Nobody moves here, they only leave."

"Maybe that's because people aren't that welcoming."

"Maybe, but that kind of language will get you a first class ticket out of here on the Amicable Express." Liam spread his hands. "Look, you just have to be *nice*. People in Amicable think this is the friendliest town in America; we even put it on our sign - *We're Amicable - the Friendliest Town this side of the Mississippi.*"

"What are the criteria?"

"The cri... cripes, what?"

"Criteria. You know, how do they decide that they are friendlier than other communities?"

Liam rolled his eyes. "It's just a saying, Butcher. It doesn't have to be true."

"Okay," Leo sighed deeply. "I really appreciate you coming by, Liam, but I've got an early start tomorrow morning..." Butcher let the sentence trail off, hoping that Liam would get the hint.

He didn't.

"Oh, I forgot to give you a beer." Reaching down between his legs, Liam grabbed a beer and tossed it to Leo who fumbled with it. "Better not drink that yet. It'll probably explode because you kind of dropped it there."

"I'll let it age a while," Butcher noticed that the beer had taken on an oddly human 98.6 degrees after its incubation between the mechanic's thighs.

Liam pursed his lips and put down the footrest. "Listen, Butcher, there are some people in town I need to warn you about in case you can't read people very well." Butcher coughed into his hand. "I guess warn might be the wrong word, and it sounds bad because the first person is Reverend Deakins. He can be a little…" Wilson see-sawed his hand. "Overwhelming. He likes things a certain way. Control is kind of his thing. If you don't go to church, better start thinking about it."

"Sounds wonderful."

"Everybody does it. Social gathering, Sundays at ten o'clock. Early enough to get the casserole in the oven, but late enough for us young folks to get our sleep in. About a year ago," Liam adjusted himself in the chair causing it to creak, "Clancy set up a Sunday morning soccer league. You would have thought Armageddon occurred. Reverend Deakins put up billboards on Highway 10 that said stuff like *Stop the Soccer! It's Satan's pitfall!* Bunch of hooey if you ask me; just a game, but Deakins, he likes the tradition of Sunday mornings in Amicable and he usually gets what he wants."

"Did the soccer league go ahead?"

Liam nodded. "Yeah, and it was pretty funny because Clancy's soccer team is called 'The Demons.' But Amicable didn't put in a team. I guess they're all going to hell for playing soccer while we all go to heaven for playing church."

"Anyone else I should know about?"

Liam thought for a minute. "Yeah, a really good person to avoid is George Hendriks. He's a town relic, fought in World War II, I think. He's ninety-seven and can be a little crotchety. He lives next to the Redmans and the Sternbergs."

Butcher's ears perked up for the first time. *Rhonda Redman?* "Who are they?" His pulse quickened slightly.

"The Sternbergs are an older retired couple, farmers, who moved to town about five years ago. They travel south in the winter to Arizona, or something like that. And the Redmans, well, you should know something about them too. Connie is a divorcee, kind of a recluse - doesn't come into the light. Might be a vampire for all I know." Wilson laughed at his own joke. "And she lives with her daughter, Rhonda, who works at the Choke. Nice looking lady but…"

"But what?"

Liam lowered his voice. "Damaged goods."

"What does that mean?"

"I don't want to be a gossip or nothing but, well, there's a story going around that she... I shouldn't say any more; that wouldn't be the Christian thing to do."

Butcher, frustrated, stood up. "Okay, Liam, thanks for stopping by and I appreciate the..." he looked at the can, "Schlitz Premium, but I need to get to bed so I can go to work in the morning."

"Oh, sure, sure," Liam responded and pushed his bulk forward once, and then a second time, before the chair released him. "I should let you do that." He stood up and held the other three beers contained in their plastic tab to Butcher. "Here, you keep these as a housewarming gift."

Butcher looked disdainfully at the three cans of beer. "No, no, that's all right. You keep them."

"No, I insist," Liam said and tossed them into the now empty, but warm, recliner. "That way, when I come back sometime, you've got some beer to share with me."

Butcher nodded. "That would be really nice."

"That's Amicable," the mechanic said as he walked to the door and belched. "We're nice."

Chapter 11.

When Rhonda arrived at The Traveler's Choice, the clock in her car read 5:55 a.m. but strangely, there were cars already waiting in the parking lot. Exiting her car, Rhonda locked it (unlike most Amicableans, their fear of theft negligible) and strolled past the patiently waiting early morning coffee drinkers. Even though she couldn't see into their windshields, she knew by their cars who was waiting. Rhonda sighed as the Fearsome Fivesome, Penny and her Posse, were all watching as she walked towards the front door. Last night's episode at the bowling alley would surely cause some clucking in the henhouse. Gordon and Anne were already opening their respective doors; Joe and David were right behind them. Rhonda glanced around for one other person, but he was not there. Rhonda wasn't sure if she hoped that Butcher would show up.

Unlocking the door, she was not surprised to find Rodrigo already inside. Whistling a Hispanic tune, Rodrigo waved to his colleague.

"Buenos Días, amiga."

"Buenos Días, amigo," she returned. At the front desk, she turned on the cash register and logged in. Grabbing her order pad, she walked to the front door to see the nine people standing outside talking with each other in the cool morning. Rhonda opened the door and the sound of their talking filled the entryway of the restaurant.

"Good morning," Gordon rasped while Anne pushed her stroller past without greeting.

"Good morning, Gordon."

As each person passed by, Rhonda felt like Reverend Deakins on Sunday mornings greeting the congregants.

"David, Joe, Linda, Penny, Jeannie, Leona, Leslie." Leslie's mouth was pursed as always.

Each member, just like they did on Sundays at church, took their traditional seats – Gordon and Anne near the front window, David and Joe near the salad bar and the Fearsome Fivesome in the center of the

111

room where they could be seen and overheard. For the next ten minutes, Rhonda took orders and entered them into the computer.

The front bell tinkled behind her and Rhonda turned quickly, expectantly, hoping to see Butcher, but it was Reverend Deakins. *What a surprise!* The Reverend was rarely out of bed before eight o'clock, or at least that was the rumor she heard. Arising that late would be a source of shame for almost anyone else, but Reverend Deakins often claimed that he stayed up all hours of the night praying for his community. Deakins, even more surprisingly, entered in his civilian clothes, his clerical collar jettisoned for a more secular setting. Not stooping quite to overalls, the pastor wore blue jeans and a button-down shirt with dazzlingly white New Balance tennis shoes. He seemed uncomfortable to be seen out of his uniform, like a recently shorn sheep. He waved uncomfortably to the Johnsons and the farmers before stopping at the table of women. Standing behind Leslie Tielman, he helloed everyone but for the first time, Rhonda noticed that his hand was dangerously close to Leslie's back. *Was there something going on with those two? Talk about gossip!*

"Good morning, Ladies, how are we all this morning?" His thumb was twitching near Leslie's shoulder.

"Oh, Reverend Deakins," Jeannie said, "You look so different in your casual clothes."

He frowned. "Yes, it's a change for me, but I thought I'd try something different this week."

"What are you doing here this morning?" Linda asked, leaning forward and resting her breasts on her arms.

"I've come for a cup of coffee and some exercise. I walked from the church this morning."

They gasped. "That's almost... what, ten blocks?" Penny said.

"Twelve, I counted. Took me almost an hour." He was sweating profusely.

"Why don't you sit down with us before you expire." Leona smiled up at him.

Deakins let the jibe pass over his head. "Thank you very much." The women made room for him at their table shifting their place settings. He grabbed a chair from an adjacent table and sat on it backwards, his arms resting on the top of the backrest. Jeannie giggled. *He's trying so hard to be normal.*

Penny leaned in and spoke quietly. "Did you hear what happened last night at the bowling alley?"

Linda nodded, enjoying the delight of their sanctimonious gossip. "I heard that there were some fireworks." She looked over at Rhonda who was busy with the Johnsons. "According to Gabby, whose daughter, Jessica, was there last night, Rhonda and the new butcher had a little spat. Supposedly the kids recorded it all on their phones."

"I heard that too," Penny said. "But from what I understand, it was more than a spat..." She left the information hanging.

"What did you hear?" Deakins asked, moving closer into the circle of confidence. His left leg touched Leslie's, and she withdrew it quickly as if she'd been shocked. Deakins looked at her, but she did not make eye contact.

Penny leaned into the table, but pulled back again when Rhonda made her way through the islands of tables to the Fearsome Fivesome plus one. They all looked down guiltily; Leslie put her hands in her lap.

Rhonda knew what they were talking about. Standing with her hands on her hips, she smiled at Reverend Deakins. "Good morning, Reverend. What can I get for you?"

All eyes turned toward the pastor whose frightened eyes looked around at the table. It was one thing to gossip but it was another thing to be caught doing it. "I'll... have black coffee... maybe some pancakes?" His stammer and red face gave credence to Rhonda's suspicions.

"Coming right up." Rhonda turned away, but then thought about it and rotated back to the group. "By the way, I just met the man yesterday. He came in for a cup of coffee." Eyes down again. "Last night we ran into each other at the bowling alley; he said something that didn't sit well and, after a long day of serving, I lost my cool. You can keep talking about it if you like. Dissect away." Rhonda went to the kitchen and placed the order on the rotating serving tray for Rodrigo who was smiling at her.

Leslie replaced her hands on the table and tapped them three times. "Why, I never…"

Reverend Deakins patted Leslie's hand. "There, there, Leslie." The other eyes at the table looked around at each other. They knew that Deakins and Leslie worked together, and quite often they could be seen publicly discussing various churchy things, but it was another thing to see the pastor touch the woman on the hand. Leslie, sensing a faux pas, pulled her hand back.

"What I mean, ladies, is that we don't have to be outraged by Ms. Redman's outburst. She has a difficult job but she's good at what she does." This mollified the women, or at least postponed the awkward gossip that might be shared when Leslie and Deakins had left. But Reverend Deakins surprisingly felt a strange warmth in standing up for the tall waitress. It had been quite a while since he had delivered a spontaneous compliment.

"I guess that makes sense, Reverend Deakins." Penny nodded, vigorously glancing around at the others to see if they shared the same opinion.

Ten minutes later, Rhonda began delivering orders to all corners of the room. As she placed Leslie's order in front of her, the front door opened once again and somehow Rhonda knew immediately that Butcher had entered the room, not by any sense of ESP, but merely the fact that all sound in the room had been sucked into a vacuum of space. As all eyes turned towards the front door, they quickly settled back on the waitress, who then put her head down onto her chest. "Please," she pleaded, "please don't say anything to him."

Turning around, Rhonda saw Butcher standing in the entrance. His face betrayed very little, but his stance was contrite, apologetic. Rhonda looked away from him and walked back to the kitchen where Rodrigo, too, was staring at the stranger. Although he had seen him yesterday morning, Rodrigo was as shocked as anyone else after hearing what had happened the night before. "You okay, Rhownda?"

She nodded and turned taking the Johnsons their orders. As she walked by Butcher, she didn't look at him but spoke softly. "Just find a table and I'll be with you shortly."

Butcher looked out over the room and noticed that when his eyes caught those of the other patrons, gazes were quickly averted. Moving slowly across the room, he situated himself in the corner facing inwards, his back reflecting in the window behind him. Patiently, he crossed his arms and stuck his long legs out under the table.

Two minutes later, Rhonda approached him, notebook in hand. "What can I get for you this morning?"

Butcher looked up at the beautiful woman, her sandy brown hair pulled back in a ponytail behind her head.

"I would assume that they have all been talking about us already?"

"What can I get you, sir?" Rhonda stood stiffly, pen in hand.

Butcher looked beyond her. "I'll have a black coffee and waffles, thank you."

"I'll have them to you in a couple of minutes." She turned on her heel and walked the gauntlet of small-town stares, voices muted. Linda broke the uncomfortable, coffee-table silence.

"So, how is Naida?"

"She's fine," Penny said predictably. The response would have been the same even if Naida had been doing poorly.

Butcher watched the action from the corner. There was a man sitting at the table with five women; most of the women he'd already met before, in fact all of them had been into the butchery at some point the day before. But the man... there was something about him that was recognizable, not his face, but his demeanor. And then it hit him: this must be the Reverend Deakins that Liam had warned him about. Deakins was doing his best to ignore Butcher, but failing miserably. Finally, when Reverend Deakins' eyes lingered for a split second too long, Butcher smiled and waved. His eyes widened and he looked away quickly. But when he looked back, Butcher beckoned him over to his table.

115

The Reverend swallowed and began to stand.

"Where are you going?" Penny asked.

"I'm going to talk to the new guy. Perhaps a new member of the flock?"

A low murmur rumbled through the group of women, but none would contradict a man of the cloth. All eyes in the restaurant followed Deakins as he straightened his starched shirt and walked erectly to the back table. David and Joe sipped their coffee from mugs that hung in suspended animation in front of their lips. All conversation was frozen as the reverend faked a smile and extended his hand to the man relaxing at the table, like a lonely present-day Jesus preparing not for a last supper, but for a first breakfast.

"John Deakins." A titter from the women's section. They'd never heard the reverend introduce himself without his title.

"Leo Jensen." They shook hands, Butcher's immense paw enveloping the fragile, smooth hand of the pastor. "My friends call me Butcher."

"Okay, Butcher," Deakins stood awkwardly unsure what to do with his hand.

"Do you want to sit down?"

Deakins almost looked over his shoulder at the women, but he stopped himself. "No, no, that's okay. I just wanted to come over and introduce myself."

"Suit yourself."

Conversation began again in the background. "Where are you from, Butcher?"

"Colorado."

Suddenly, all eyes turned. Other people had asked the question already, but this is the first time he had given any information.

"Are you married?"

"Nope."

All ears were straining. Deakins was beaming that the man was being so forthright with him. It must be his winsome demeanor as a pastor.

"Are you married?" Butcher asked.

Deakins' ears turned red and his neck radiated heat. "No, I am not."

"What do you do for a living, John?"

"I'm a pastor."

"Fascinating," Butcher said still leaning back in his chair. "What denomination?"

"Methodist. So, you are a believer then?"

Butcher shrugged. "I do believe in many things."

"That's not much of an answer."

"So, you're a believer then?" Butcher asked.

Deakins frowned. "I just told you I was a pastor."

"For some, those two things aren't necessarily compatible." A snicker from David caused the crimson in Deakins' neck to glow brighter.

"I can assure you, I believe *deeply*." Deakins' voice dropped and slowed on the last word.

"That's a relief," Butcher said.

"Well," Deakins said curtly, "it's nice to meet you. I hope that we'll see you at church on Sunday mornings, ten o'clock."

"Yes, nice to meet you," Butcher responded noncommittally. Deakins wheeled, turning back toward the women who were watching the pastor's face.

Within seconds, Rhonda returned to Butcher's table, coffee and waffles in hand. "How did that go?" She asked quietly.

"He's... interesting," Butcher responded in the same conspiratorial tone.

"Tell me about it."

"I'd like to," Butcher said leaning forward. "Look, Rhonda, I wanted to apologize for last night. I didn't mean..."

Rhonda's face silenced him. "Apology accepted."

"Would it be possible to make it up to you? Can I offer you a game of Pacman or Pinball?" Finally, the tension on Rhonda's face eased and Butcher knew that he had broken the shell.

Rhonda wrote on her pad. "No," she said, "I don't think that's such a good idea." She ripped off the pad. "Here is your bill when you are finished eating. Please pay at the counter." She placed it on the table face down beside him. "Thank you for coming to The Traveler's Choice."

Rhonda moved to check on the Johnsons who were the only ones uninterested in the drama of the room.

Leo looked at the piece of paper and a practiced look of dejection spread across his face. He hoped that his acting abilities were good enough, because the paper she handed him read:

Yes, we can meet, but let's go to Clancy. No prying eyes. Meet me at The Creek Restaurant. 8:00. Tonight.

Butcher looked around at the other patrons. Some of them met him haughtily as if he had been caught trying to pick one of the town's flowers; others showed pity, but none of them were willing to say anything. Reverend Deakins' sneer was smeared across his face; he did not try to hide it. Taking his checkbook out of his pocket, Butcher wrote on the top check, ripped it out and then put the checkbook back in his pocket. Then, picking up his knife and fork he ate his breakfast while the rest of the restaurant conversed in low tones. Rodrigo had turned the stereo on and a local radio station blared dismal country tunes. Though his heart pounded, he kept his cool. When he had finished his meal, he wiped his mouth on the white paper napkin drawn from the dispenser in the center of the table. Pulling himself up to his full height, he navigated between the tables, reefs of social trouble.

"It was nice seeing all of you again today," Butcher said as he passed the center table. Jeannie had to restrain from fanning herself; she had a *slight* crush on the stranger. The other ladies were impressed that Butcher could remain amicable in spite of the circumstances. Butcher pretended to tip his cap to the pastor. "I hope I didn't offend you, pastor. It wasn't my intention."

Deakins, offended by the thought that he might be offended, smiled civilly at Butcher.

Butcher continued to the counter where Rhonda was waiting for him.

"All set then?"

"Yes, thank you for the waffles. Please thank the chef for me." Rhonda looked over her shoulder at Rodrigo who was goofily smiling at them. He waved.

"*De nada*," Rodrigo said.

Butcher reached into his wallet and withdrew the check from it, along with ten dollars, and handed it to Rhonda. "Thank you," he said and exited the building. "Keep the change."

Rhonda looked down at the money in her hand.

The check had a message:

I accept with pleasure, but I don't have a car. Pick me up at 7:30 if you would please. I'll look forward to it. Peppertree Lane. Liam Wilson's rental.

The waitress blushed as Butcher left. She looked once more at the note and her eyes, along with all the other customers' eyes, followed him out the door.

Butcher

Chapter 12.

For the first time in a year, Derek was on time for work. Early, actually. After the excitement last night at the bowling alley, he wanted to be at the butchery as Butcher showed up. Nash, who arrived at almost the same time, looked shocked that his brother was waiting. Derek handed the cup of coffee to Nash and they both took a sip at the same time, simultaneously burning their top lips.

Derek sucked air in through his mouth. "He's not here yet?"

"No," Nash responded rubbing his lip. "He should be here any minute." Nash looked at his watch.

Derek mirrored the rubbing. "I wonder what happened last night."

Nash shrugged. "He got in an argument."

"How can he get in an argument the second day in town? And with Rhonda. She's like the nicest girl in town."

Nash snorted. "Yeah right."

"She is. Local sports hero, takes care of her mother. I mean, she's like a saint or something."

"You don't remember what happened?"

Derek's eyes opened. "What? What are you talking about?"

At that moment, Butcher rounded the corner strolling casually down the street towards them. Whistling happily, tunelessly, he looked down at the twins who were sipping coffee in front of the shop.

"What are you doing here so early, Derek?" Butcher asked.

Derek looked back and forth between the two of them. "What do you mean? How do you know that about me already?" Derek watched Butcher's eyes. "I mean, don't you talk to me like that."

Butcher smirked. "I didn't say anything."

"No, but your eyes just looked at me as if you assaulted my soul."

Nash almost spit out his coffee.

Butcher lifted his hands apologetically. "I'm sorry you feel that way."

"Whatever. We'd better get to work."

Nash looked at Butcher who raised an eyebrow. This was completely unlike Derek to spring lightly up the steps into work. With the three of them on time, they would easily have everything prepared by the eight o'clock opening.

As Nash opened the door, the smell of sanitizers mixed with the odor of raw meat wafted through the air. Nash moved to the bank of lights and flipped the switches. Overhead fluorescent tubes flickered twice, blinked out and then buzzed as they came to life. Nash pointed to the radio where Derek brought the music to life - Hall and Oates. Meanwhile, Butcher lifted the server's counter and moved to the cold room where he knew whole sides of beef awaited the saw. Opening the door, he flipped the light switch and felt the cold blast of air as it hit him in the face. The smell of raw beef forced its way into his olfactory organs. After putting on his work apron, Butcher took a meat hook and stuck it under a rib pulling the side of beef across the railing. Closing the door with his foot, he dropped the side of beef on the table and immediately began to work the saw.

In the front of the shop, the twins nonchalantly prepared the displays stopping every so often to drink coffee and chat. When they returned to the back, they found that Butcher had not only cut up the first side of beef, but the saw was cutting through the second.

"Holy crap, Nash," Derek said as he watched the stack of meat grow quickly. "What is he, a lumberjack? You know those guys that climb up the trees and saw through..."

"I know what a lumberjack is, dipstick," Nash responded. "Butcher, you know you don't have to do the entire day's work before the day actually starts?"

Butcher nodded. "Yeah, but you never know what's going to happen during the day. Might as well get it done while I can."

Derek rolled his eyes unwilling to agree with Butcher's assessment of work.

Butcher smiled but didn't look up. When the shop opened, Butcher had already sawn through the day's beef as well as the pork. Derek and Nash sat at the front table, feet up on the windowsill drinking coffee. A few early morning shoppers were walking the streets, people the boys knew, and they waved, small-town friendliness exuding. Promptly at 8:00, Nash walked to the front door and unlocked it. Various townspeople began to enter. Fridays were always like this.

First, Donna Humphries. Derek and Nash looked back at Butcher who shook his head. *No way, boys.* Disappointed, the boys served customers filling orders while Butcher kept sawing in the back. A stream of customers continued for the first two hours.

Cleaned chickens, breasts and thighs, went in and out faster and faster, and yet Butcher kept up. Gradually, the tide stemmed. Butcher took a breath while the Peterson twins schmoozed with the customers. They couldn't remember a better and easier day in the butchery. Just as the clock turned 11:23, a slow-moving customer mounted the stairs of the shop. One step at a time, hand firmly grasping the railing, the other gripping his cane, the old man gained purchase on the uppermost step like a soldier reaching the crest of a conquered hill. Breathing deeply, the old man opened the door and looked up over the smeared lenses of his trifocal glasses.

"Good morning, boys."

Nash smiled and crossed his arms. "Morning, Mr. Hendriks."

At the name, Butcher looked up. Even from this distance, there was an aura about the old man, someone who had known immeasurable glory and pain, love and anguish. Butcher almost staggered as he read the man. He moved out from behind the table and approached the counter.

"Can I have a twenty-minute break, boss?" He posed the question to Nash who, only fourteen minutes older than his brother, seemed to be in charge.

"You can have an hour, Butcher, as much work as you've done today."

Butcher lifted the gate and approached the old man. At his age, George Hendriks was almost a foot shorter than the butcher, but it was Leo who felt dwarfed by the hero standing beside him.

"Good morning, sir."

"Good morning to you. What are you, a giant?" George looked up at the tall man, his neck almost hurting from peering up into the butcher's eyes.

"No, sir. Just unnaturally tall."

"I'll say."

"Can I ask you a question, sir?"

"You can if you stop calling me 'sir.' My name is Hendriks. George Hendriks."

"It's an honor to meet you, George."

George frowned. "Are you yankin' my chain?"

"No sir, uh, George. But I am always awed by men who have served, especially one as well as you."

"What do you know about it?"

Butcher looked over at the twins who were inching closer to the conversation. "I know a war hero when I see one."

"Bah. I'm no hero."

"That's what all heroes say."

George laughed. "All right, then. I'm a hero."

Butcher joined him in laughter. "I know you are. I can see it."

"I don't read you," George said.

"No, but I read you. Do you mind if we sit down?" Butcher asked.

"It sure as hell would be easier on my neck than staring up at your head like a skyscraper." George was enjoying the attention even though it was a conversation he never spoke about with anyone else. He, like most of the veterans, was reticent to talk about his war experiences.

Butcher followed George to the table and sat down across from him. George had put his cane on the table. Butcher had never seen these kinds of lines around the eyes before, battle scars. True battle scars from a lifetime past. Scenes of dancing and destruction, love and desecration; the immensity of it was like a blow to Butcher's heart.

"Where did you get your scars?" Butcher asked. "The visible ones."

George's jaw clenched. "I don't speak about it."

"Do you mind if I try to guess? I'm good at it."

Hendriks leaned back in his chair putting his arms on the rests. "Be my guest."

Butcher didn't know where to start, but at the beginning. "If I'm right, you'll let me purchase all of your meat for you today."

"And if you don't get it right?"

"I'll buy you a beer or two."

"Sounds like I win either way."

Butcher nodded. "Please don't be frightened."

"Either do your thing or shut up. I'm on a tight schedule." George looked at his watch, but Butcher knew that George's schedule was neither tight nor full.

"You got married right before going off to war. She was younger than you, but she's been gone a while, hasn't she?"

Hendriks looked up sharply. "Who have you been talking to?"

Soldiering on, Butcher continued. "You weren't in the army. I've known a lot of army veterans and you neither hold yourself like an army man, nor do you talk like one. Air force, I would guess."

"Holy shit…" Hendriks mumbled under his breath.

"Your plane was shot down somewhere over Europe. Most runs were over Germany, but I would guess over France for you. Just a guess, though." It wasn't. He could tell by Hendriks' reaction that he had read it right.

"Parachuted out?" George shook his head slowly, not in negation, but in amazement.

"How much time did you spend in a concentration camp?"

George looked up at the tall man across from him and then at the boys behind him. A tear had shaped in the corner of his right eye, a dewdrop of emotion. "How can you possibly know all this…?" He whispered. The tear trekked across the valleys of George Hendriks' wrinkles. They were deep chasms of loss and grief, and as Butcher furrowed into them unearthing the pain of the past, Hendriks attempted to rise, but his weakness kept him seated.

"You are a true gem in Amicable's crown," Butcher responded with his own great emotion, "and your life is a treasure for all people."

"Stop," George whispered. "You have to stop. I can't go back there."

"Of course, sir." Butcher said and held up his hands. "I'm sorry if I have offended you, but I thank you for the opportunity to even sit with you. Can I get you a cup of coffee, or anything else?"

George nodded and motioned with his hand.

"Black coffee, Derek, if you would. I'll buy." Butcher reached into his back pocket and pulled out a twenty-dollar bill.

"Are you sure he wants black coffee? Milk or sugar?"

"He was in World War II, Derek. All soldiers drank real black coffee when they got back. The ersatz stuff they had overseas used to drive them crazy."

Derek took the money and headed for the door. "I don't even know what 'ersatz' means."

"I'll tell you when you get back. On second thought," Derek paused at the door, "buy us all a round of coffee."

"You got it, Butcher." Derek's face lit up and he ran out the door at the prospect of another cup of coffee. Nash came out from behind the counter and turned the *Open* sign to *Back in Five Minutes*. Even though they were sitting in the window, Nash knew that they needed to give George Hendriks some time to recover.

"Are you okay, Mr. Hendriks?" Nash asked as he took the seat next to George.

"Fine. Yes, just give me a minute. I haven't thought about those memories in years." George was sucking in big gasps of air.

"You're not having a heart attack are you, Mr. Hendriks?" Nash couldn't remember his CPR compressions to blows, and he wondered if he tried George would literally break in half.

126

The question hardened George and he sat up straighter. "Shut up, Peterson. I'm stronger than I ever have been. I just want to know how your butcher here knew all that stuff."

They both looked at Butcher who raised his eyebrows and sighed. "It's a gift or a curse however you want to look at it," he leaned forward placing his elbows and forearms on the table. "Ever since I was little, I have been able to notice insanely small details about people which gives me a pretty good educated guess about them. The littlest twitches in facial muscles, tics, vocal patterns or stress. Sometimes I don't even realize I'm doing it, but I can't turn it off."

"That's insane," Nash said.

"I've often thought I was crazy, Nash. But as you saw yesterday, I can do it to anyone."

"How did you know all that stuff about me?" George said, staring at the tall man across from him.

"Short or long version?"

"Short," George said. "I don't know how soon before I die."

Butcher laughed. "That's going to be a while if left to natural causes. You've got great circulation." Nash looked at Butcher and he shrugged. "Anyway, I can see you wear a wedding ring and it's been worn down to a small circle - you've never taken it off, not even in wartime, which means you might have married your high school sweetheart."

"Her name was Mabel."

"What a beautiful name."

"There were many of us who left for the war who got married before leaving because they wanted the chance to experience a wedding as well as…" Butcher coughed into his hand.

George smiled. "We were all virgins back then. The lot of us. Yeah, Mabel was a hottie."

Nash laughed at the thought of this ninety-seven-year-old man having sex.

"Laugh it up, boy. When you get to be my age, we'll see how you like it when young whippersnappers laugh at you."

"Sorry, sir."

"Keep going, Butcher," George encouraged. "You're doing pretty good."

"Turret gunner is the hardest of the tasks on a bomber as you protect the aircraft during the bombing runs. A long time ago, I talked to another turret gunner, and he had the same burn as you did down your right arm. Flak broke the shell around the turret and the gun jammed. He had to manually turn it; he was wearing gloves, but the gun, hot as hell, burned him on the arm."

"You're just guessing, now."

"That was the hardest one, George, but I'll go backwards now. You spent some time in a concentration camp because I see that you've spent money having the numbered tattoo removed from your left arm. I would guess you didn't spend too much time there because you're still alive. Well, and your age suggests it was near the end of the war when you entered it."

"So far so good, kid."

"You got to the concentration camp because you had to parachute out of the plane. On the landing, I would guess that you broke your leg, which is why you still have a noticeable limp. Normally, the Germans would have shot airmen right away, but since it was near the end of the war, I would guess they needed you as collateral for return. So, they stuck you in a concentration camp. Which one was it?"

"You tell me."

Butcher stared into the eyes of the old man. Memories seemed to float in front of his eyes, visions of smoke and war and destruction; the sounds of wailing and the absence of sound as human lives collapsed into the arms of death. George looked down at the scar on his arm; Butcher followed his gaze. "Struthof, wasn't it?" Butcher said.

"You're a carnie!" George exclaimed and rapped the table with his knuckles. "How did you guess?"

"Many of the surviving pilots were shot down over France and the only French concentration camp built after the war began was Natzweiler-Struthof."

"They could have transported me somewhere else?" George was testing him.

"They did, didn't they, George?" Hendriks was silent. "Near the end of the war as the Allies were approaching, the Germans emptied Struthof and transported all the internees to... Dachau."

George looked as if he'd been slapped. Dachau. It was a name that made him cringe even after seventy years. He pinched his eyes shut in an attempt to eradicate the sights, sounds and screams.

"That's where you got your numbered tattoo, wasn't it?" With his eyes still pinched closed, he nodded. "The things you experienced must have been hell on earth."

"I think we can stop now," George said softly.

At that moment, Derek hit the front door expecting it to be open, but it was locked. Amazingly, only one of the coffee cups exploded against the window and splashed against Derek. The insiders turned quickly at the sound and they could read Derek's lips. It wasn't pretty. The coffee had burned his arm but he had somehow managed to refrain from dropping the cardboard cup carrier.

"Open the fricking door!" He shouted. Nash was laughing very hard by this point. He walked slowly to let his brother in. After unlocking it and opening it, Derek entered.

"Nice job, Buttmunch. I've got third degree burns on my arm."

"You'll be fine, Derek."

Derek blustered inside and set the coffee cups on the table. Butcher took the now half-filled one and took a sip. "Thanks for the coffee, Derek."

"Don't mention it. Now, what did I miss?" He looked back and forth between the other three men, a secret had been exposed. "Don't tell me you're already done!"

"Don't worry, Derek. With Mr. Hendriks' permission, I'll tell you later."

George looked at the twins and nodded. "But please keep it between yourselves."

Butcher assured the old man. "They will not even mention that there is a Congressional Medal of Honor winner sitting beside them."

Derek's eyes widened. "What in the wide world of cheese just happened?"

George leaned forward. "Now it's my turn, Butcher."

Butcher grinned. "Your turn for what?"

"My turn to read the future: if you hurt Rhonda, I'm going to kick your ass."

It was Butcher's turn to sit with mouth agape.

Chapter 13.

The Reverend John Thomas Deakins was incensed at the way that he had been treated in the restaurant. Although he had put on a tough face, inwardly he was roiling. Unused to anyone treating him, a man of God, in that way, Deakins was contemplating means in which he could avenge his honor in a completely pious way. For him, this would be conversations with other people, usually women in his congregation, who would take his side, and, if his expression was pained enough, they would supply enough pity for him to fight whoever it was that offended him. It wouldn't be the first time that he had pulled the trick; when the soccer-billboard fiasco occurred, there was a member of another congregation in Clancy who wrote a stern letter about 'taking God's name in vain and using it to condemn or shame others to hell.'

After their interaction this morning, Deakins was quite sure that he had met one of the great heathens of all time in this... this... butcher. Deakins' mind spit the word onto the curb of his disdain. *How dare he.*

After arriving back home, Deakins stomped up the front porch, through the front door and up the stairs to his bedroom. Ripping off his civilian shirt, he threw it on the bed. With authority, he flung wide the closet doors where hung his rainbow of clerical shirts, at least two for each season. With the events of the morning, he grabbed one of the blacks. Moving to the front of the bedside mirror, he noticed his slightly bulging stomach (*I must fast a little bit more*, he thought) and put on the long-sleeved black top over his undershirt. Heaving a deep sigh of relief, he actually felt as if his nakedness was covered. It had been such a long time since Deakins had been out in public without the trappings of his calling. He pushed the white tabbed collar in place.

Righteous anger rose from his heart and into his throat. As he pondered the visceral reaction of changing his clothes, something in Deakins' consciousness snagged, like a fingernail on a sock. What was it?

What did the stranger say that scratched him so deeply? Was there some kind of truth embedded in his disrespect? Deakins shook his head. There was no room for that kind of thought. He needed to take charge, to take...

Are you a believer, Reverend? As he looked in the mirror, Deakins tightened his shirt cuffs then put on his grey pants.

For some people, those two things aren't necessarily compatible. The reverend tucked his shirt tightly into his pants and snugly cinched his belt around his waist.

Is he questioning my faith? Am I questioning my faith?

A spasm of fear shook John Thomas Deakins. Strengthening himself with his best prayerful voice he asked God to look after him in the battle ahead.

Armageddon in Amicable.

From the lower level, Deakins heard a knock at the door. Checking his watch, which was resting on his Bible, he saw that it was just after eight o'clock in the morning. Wondering who could *possibly* need anything at this hour of the day, he checked himself in the mirror one more time and then retraced his steps down the stairs to the front door. Because of the beveled glass, the image was distorted. Unlocking the deadbolt, Deakins pulled open the door and to his surprise, a trembling Leslie Tielman stood on his porch. She was holding her arms across her chest as if in protection.

"Leslie," the pastor said breathlessly. The exercise of climbing and descending the stairs had worn him out. "Are you okay?"

"Yes, Reverend Deakins. I'm just... just..."

"What is it?"

Leslie looked around. "Would it be all right if I stepped inside for a few moments?"

Deakins' heart raced, but prudence, or caution, took over. "I... don't know if that would be... appropriate," he stammered.

A look of desperation crossed her face. "Please," she begged. "I need to talk to you."

Deakins nodded. "Of course, Leslie. Of course. Please, come in."

What was in Leslie Tielman's heart was completely unexpected, a seed that had been growing for months now. Because the thought had taken root, a fruit, whether good or bad, had grown. As she stepped across the threshold, she felt as if a line had been crossed in her personal life, for it had only been in these past few months that she had fully begun to realize her feelings for the delicate clergyman. When she had seen him maligned this morning by that - interloper - Leslie's heart cried out for John Thomas. In her mind she had called him that a few times, and each time she did, it sent a delicious thrill coursing through her veins. Leslie Tielman had never been in love before; she wasn't sure if this was love, yet, but whatever it was, it felt good. Most Amicableans, she was sure, thought she was an ice queen, or tight, or any other word that described someone who tied a tourniquet around their emotions. Deep down, though, Leslie was a delicate flower trembling in the warmth of the morning sun. And that morning sun had a name.

John Thomas Deakins.

When he had opened the door, the cellar door of her heart popped open and for the first time in her life, she almost - almost - gave in to her emotions. With years of practice, she fastidiously slammed that cellar door shut and stepped into the reverend's house. *But in his clergywear, he looks so damn sexy.* Leslie chided herself for consciously swearing inside her head and quickly changed the word to 'dang' but there he was, flesh and blood, the object of her affection staring down at her slim and trembling form in his living room. She had never been inside the parsonage before; she was surprised at how dark it was. The wood paneled walls and oak floors seemed highly polished. Because of the lack of carpet, she was afraid that he would be able to hear the hammering of her heart on the same kind of polished surface of her chest. On the walls were framed doilies and cross-stitched pictures of cats and rainbows and cuddly things. Black and white photos of his family, mother and father, two sisters, sat stiffly on the wooden cabinets. One entire wall was stacked floor to ceiling with books, mostly theological in nature. She inspected them quickly. There were a few romantic novels which surprised her. *Could he be a romantic at heart?*

"Would you like to take a seat, Leslie? Some coffee or tea?"

"No, thank you." She looked deeply into his eyes, dark and luminous; his black hair was parted to the side and his double chin seemed to hide the white tab at his throat.

"How can I help y…?"

Before he could finish the sentence, though, Leslie could control her passion no longer. The dam had cracked when he opened the door; it was as if he had broken down the door to her heart, destroyed the barricading bar, and now a tidal wave of desire could no longer be contained. Leslie crossed the distance and grabbed the man by the sides of his head pulling his face fiercely towards hers. As they kissed, Deakins' shock was so great that he did not have the strength to pull away. For a few forbidden seconds, the heat of long buried desire passed between them. The Reverend John Thomas Deakins had no words in his large, theological vocabulary to describe what was happening inside of him, only that he knew that he had to stop it, no matter how much his body wanted to encourage it.

He pulled away from her and a small moan escaped her lips. "Leslie!" He said breathlessly. "What…what… has come over you?"

Leslie touched her lips, the moisture still present and then moved to her cheek where she felt the flush of desire still evident. "I don't know, John. I think I've been wanting to do that for a very long time."

Deakins could not ascertain whether he was more shocked at the informal way she addressed him or the mere fact that this hot-blooded woman seemed to desire him - even in his clerical outfit. "I'm… shocked."

Leslie's face blushed an even deeper shade of crimson. A tear began to form in her eye. "You're disappointed."

He reached out for her, but then stopped. The distance, just a few inches, seemed like a Grand Canyon of separation and he dropped his hands quickly to his sides. They seemed to tingle. "That's not it."

Deakins' words were jumbled in the quick memory of her embrace. He couldn't remember the last time that he'd kissed anyone. High school? "That's not it at all."

Leslie's grey eyes searched his seeking understanding. "What do you mean?"

"I...I...don't know how to say this, but I have..."

"Yes?"

"The right word is escaping me." John couldn't hold her eyes and looked away.

"They're called feelings. I should know," Leslie answered. "I'm really good at not expressing them."

"But... we've worked together for so long. How...?" John found her eyes again. He wanted to reach out to her, to grab her hands, to touch her face.

For a moment, Leslie was tempted to cross the canyon, but she held back. Something in his eyes made her refrain. "When that butcher was testing you this morning, I felt like a lioness and I felt that I needed to protect you. But the rest of the women..." Her voice trailed out.

Deakins adjusted his shirt. Conflicting emotions, angels and imps, healthy intimacy and concupiscence, warred inside of him. For most of his life he had shut off the tap of his masculinity and drive to mate, but when Leslie had kissed him... Now, as he looked at the tiny woman seeking reassurance, love, maybe, he felt the broiling fear of ecclesial turmoil. *If the congregation found out that he was dallying with Leslie, there was a chance he would be asked to leave. Then what would he do?*

He stood up straighter. The plastic of his clerical collar bit under his chin. "As much as I have... feelings... for you, this can't happen." His hands pointed from her to him.

Leslie's lip trembled. "But what about those feelings? What do we do with them?"

Deakins swallowed. "We'll have to do the best we can in setting them aside."

Crossing her arms again, Leslie lowered her head. "I don't know if I can do that."

"You must."

Leslie's heart began to close; a steel trap snapped shut around her love, defensive walls erected in seconds. "As you wish, Reverend Deakins." Spinning on her heel, she turned towards the front door and pulled it open. For one long, aching moment she paused. If she turned, she would have seen that Deakins was allowing the angel of intimacy to win the battle. But she didn't turn. With jaws clenched, she re-crossed the threshold into the infernal world of Life-As-Normal.

Deakins opened the drapes of his living room window and watched her walk quickly down the footpath. Being careful to look both directions before crossing the road, Leslie Tielman stomped tightly into the sunny Amicablean day. Deakins despondently let the curtains drop. The room was enveloped in darkness once again. As his eyes adjusted to the dimness, a true sense of loss covered him like a heavy blanket and for not the last time, he recognized that he had made this lonely bed. He would continue to lie down in it.

Deakins had completely forgotten about the butcher.

Butcher's eyes widened. The old man's threat seemed to punch him in the face. Even as his two colleagues snickered into their hands, George Hendriks' clenched jaw seemed ready to back up his threat.

"How did you know...?"

"What, do you think that you're the only one that knows stuff?" George said. "This is Amicable. Everyone knows everyone's business, even if it's none of their business."

"What did you hear?"

Nash interrupted. "Mr. Hendriks and Rhonda are next door neighbors."

Understanding washed over Butcher. "She told you what happened."

George nodded.

"Do you talk a lot."

He nodded again.

"What did she say?"

George leaned forward, his hand on the cane resting on the table. "Let's just say she was a bit upset when she got home last night. There were words exchanged, probably some on both sides, that were... regrettable."

It was Butcher's turn to nod.

"She's a sweet kid, Butcher. She deserves the very best, because she's seen the very worst."

Butcher looked at the three men, two identical faces and one old. Grim. "People keep alluding to her past. I can't believe I didn't see it."

"Maybe you didn't want to see it." The old man rubbed a finger under his nose. It made a scratching sound against his whiskers.

"What do you mean?"

George took a deep breath and exhaled blowing his cheeks out. "You've got a gift, boy, an odd and scary one, but maybe in Rhonda's case, you didn't want to see where she's been. Because if you had, you may not like to go there with her, and that, my young seer, is the conundrum."

"But I've only known her for two days!"

The old man waved a hand at him deflecting his exclamation. "Two days, two hundred. When you know, you know. It took Mabel and me about two minutes."

Derek looked at Nash and made a gagging sign. Butcher threw him a sharp look.

"I guess you're right, George."

"Of course I'm right. Now, you've got a choice young man. You can either swim in the pool, or you can take your towel and go home. Up to you."

"But what is it? What's in her past?"

George's mouth closed slowly as if sewn shut by a tailor. Silence reigned. "You're going to have to talk to her yourself. That's not my business to be sharing. If she trusts you, she will. If not, don't force it. I promise you, it will go south faster than you can say 'Snowbird.'"

A rap at the front door broke the moment. Three women stood pressing their faces against the glass looking forlornly beyond the 'back in five minutes' sign. Linda, Leona and Jeannie. Nash looked towards Derek who read the expression: it was time to get back to work.

"Come on," Nash said. "There's meat to be slaughtered and money to be made." Derek grunted and pushed himself out of the chair and moved towards the door to let the trio inside. Butcher leaned forward to the nonagenarian.

"I won't betray your trust."

"You better not," George answered as he grabbed his cane from the table and put both hands on the crook to push himself up.

"Trust me."

George smiled as he finished the slow process of standing. "Good. Now about you buying my meat today…"

Butcher smiled and proceeded to lead the old man to the counter where he picked out the supplies he would eat for the week.

At the same time, the female threesome entered the door positively atwitter and nervous at the same time. Each wore the traditional dress of most of the women of Amicable: a variation of the three 'f's'. These would be t-shirts with pressed or embroidered pictures of flags, flora or fauna. To cover all bases, each one of the women wore one of these 'f's'. Linda's t-shirt sported a whipping American flag with the slogan, *If this offends you, let me help you pack.* Leona's floral ensemble with a collage of Midwestern flowers seemed to accentuate her very unnaturally colored platinum hair. Bringing up the rear, was Jeannie Dolling's large stag, a twelve-point buck if any man dared count the tines. Each woman sported washed out blue jeans riding high on the hips and white tennis shoes with white laces.

"Good morning, ladies," Derek schmoozed. "How can we help you today?"

The women, like Midwestern middle-aged Charlie's angels, stood back to back.

"Later, Derek. We need to talk to the new butcher here."

All eyes focused on Butcher who looked up from his sales pitch with George. Shrugging, he motioned Nash towards Mr. Hendriks and faced the onslaught of the triumvirate. "How can I help you?"

"We'd like to speak to you in private," Linda said, crossing her arms under her American flag.

"Uh, there's not much privacy in the butchery."

Leona pointed to the table from where the men had just arisen. "That will be fine."

Butcher nodded and moved out from the counter again. "Do you mind, boss?" He asked Nash who grinned and shook his head. *Enjoy.*

Butcher sat with his back to the window while the other three formed a formidable offensive wall around him. With his size, Butcher looked like a giant sitting with a group of elves. He waited for them to break the silence.

"We wanted to talk with you personally, Mr. Butcher," Linda started, "because, frankly, we were slightly peeved by your discussion with Reverend Deakins this morning."

"Yes, sure, peeved," Jeannie said.

"And we wanted to just clear the air," Linda made a motion with her hand as if erasing a whiteboard, "to make sure there won't be a repeat. He was highly upset."

Butcher raised an eyebrow but remained silent.

"Reverend Deakins is a good man, highly respected in the community and you, Mr. Butcher, haven't yet reached that status. As of now, you've been in Amicable two days and you've already made a mess of things."

Butcher pursed his lips together.

"We just want to know what your intentions are here in Amicable." Leona Simpson's eyebrows were furrowed as she spoke. "Do you intend to cause trouble? We know that last night, our good friend Rhonda Redman was in distress at the bowling alley because of you." Derek coughed loudly, hiding a laugh. "And now this morning your words caused serious harm to a man of the cloth. To me, that speaks of someone not interested in fitting in."

Still, Butcher said nothing. Like a sacrificial lamb before the slaughter.

"Now, we three," Leona indicated to herself and the other two women, "we can be your advocates in the community if you'll just let us know a couple of things…" she marked them off on her fingers. "One: How long are you intending on staying? Two: Are you an atheist, and if so, are you going to stir up trouble with our children? And three: Are you planning advances on any other women in Amicable? If so, it would be wise to tell us first so we can help you choose." Leona spoke with such honesty and openness, as if she truly wanted to help the 'new guy' instead of sabotage him, that it was hard for Butcher to feel negativity. "Does that make sense?"

Butcher nodded.

"Do you speak much?" Linda asked.

He waggled his hand, which seemed to frustrate all three of them.

"Will you let us know of your intentions?"

Leaning back in his chair, Butcher put his hands behind his head and smiled.

"We'll take that as a 'yes'."

"That's a big 'yes'," Jeannie said.

"It's been great talking to you," Leona said and rose from her seat extending her hand towards Butcher. Slowly, Butcher leaned forward and shook her hand. The other women followed suit, first Linda and then Jeannie. When Jeannie shook Butcher's hand, she giggled like a completely smitten adolescent.

The three women, a saccharine version of the Three Fates, Clotho, Lachesis and Atropos, Linda, Leona and Jeannie, turned as one towards the door. Already, it seemed as if Linda had spun the fate of the butcher, Leona had stretched the string to a length as far as it could go and Jeannie, giggling, held the trembling scissors of existence around

Butcher's life in Amicable. As they walked to the door as one mob, Nash called out behind them.

"Did you want to purchase anything today?"

Linda turned and the other two almost ran into her back. "We got what we needed, thank you." With a flourish, the ladies exited the store in a denim and cotton whirlwind.

Butcher, still reclining in the seat, looked up at the twins. "That was very interesting."

"Welcome to Amicable," Nash said. "Now, get back to work."

Butcher

Chapter 14.

Naida Thompson twirled her wedding ring on her finger. In the last days she'd come to think of the band as constricting her life; especially her future. If she continued down this path with James, would she live out the rest of her days in constant irritation, annoyed that she'd chosen to marry a local redneck? Or, would they somehow reconcile and get back to the First Days, as she called them, when the two of them were inseparable? For many troubled couples, somewhere ahead was a better boat on calmer waters. Abandon ship and swim for it.

Walking toward the locker, Naida could feel her heart race with excitement. She knew her trip to the butchery might cause tongues and chins to wag; rumors of her infatuation with Nash had reached the wrong ears, her mother's included. Nash was the only source of enjoyable distraction in her life right now, and, like any addiction, she couldn't stop thinking about him. Pulled in two directions - she could continue home and wait for James, or walk the path to see Nash - Naida felt her pulse quicken and she knew before she moved that her addiction to him would take precedence.

Turning left on First Avenue, she saw the white and blue striped awning for Peterson's Butchery. In front of the store a few Amicablean citizens loitered, arms crossed, chatting in the warm afternoon sun. The friendliness was one of the things she did enjoy about the small town; people would still stop to talk, to catch up, to ask about families, and not always for the sake of gossip. Stridently, Naida walked past the villagers who, bedecked in seed corn hats, threadbare blue jeans and worn out tennis shoes, were catching up on the news of the late summer storm that would be arriving sometime in the next week. The men barely glanced at her as she moved past the farmer huddle. Naida looked up into the window to see Nash standing behind the counter, hands on hips serving a customer. Not for the first time she wondered why she didn't find Nash first. Passing through the shade of the awning, she climbed the two steps and entered the shop.

As the doorbell rang merrily, the butchers simultaneously turned their eyes to her. Butcher and Derek looked at Nash who was handing change back to a little old woman (in Amicable, transactions were still done in hard currency rather than plastic). As the little old woman shuffled by Naida (ignoring her completely), Nash's eyes shifted to Naida.

"Good morning, Mrs. Thompson. How are you on this fine day?"

Naida's eyes darkened. Through clenched teeth she spoke. "Don't call me that."

Nash's face imploded and he looked back at his brother who was attempting to ignore the proceedings by wiping down an already clean glass as they were preparing to close up shop. "My apologies. Is there something I can get for you?"

Naida moved in closer, leaned on the display case and lowered her voice. "I'm sorry I snapped. James and I have been fighting and I'm in a sour mood. I just wanted to hear your voice."

Nash glanced toward the other two who pretended to ignore what was happening. Reaching behind him, he turned up the volume on the radio, adjusting the music to cover their discussion. Taking off his plastic gloves and wiping his hands on his apron, Nash announced his intentions. "I'm going to sit with Naida for a few minutes at the table."

Butcher didn't look up. He didn't need to *see* what was going on to *know* what was going on. How many times had this same scenario played out in front of him? A dozen? A hundred? A million? Love was difficult enough in understanding how life works, but throw in the contemporary roadblocks of social media, disposable relationships and Western Culture's addiction to the *Great Fairy Tale*, finding a life-long till-death-parts-us mate was almost impossible.

Butcher could hear in Naida's voice the plaintive call of an abandoned woman. He could hear from the way she sat down, a faint shuffle of her feet that she was prepared and willing to stay a while.

Butcher knew that this was a woman in danger - in danger of letting go of a trapeze under which there was no safety net.

"What's going on, Naida?"

"I don't know, Nash. Last night, James and I had it out. He saw us talking outside the bowling alley."

"Crap," Nash said as he leaned back in his chair and ran a hand through his hair.

Naida nodded. "I know, but it's not like we're doing anything wrong, right?" She searched his eyes, the question directed towards hearing his words of encouragement or intimacy.

"Of course," he said and smiled lightly. "We're just two friends hanging out enjoying each other's company."

Naida could tell that there was something else behind his words, a longing, maybe, of something that could never happen, like when humans watched birds fly. Both of them, it seemed, wanted that current to take them to a different place, but probably for much different reasons.

As Naida was about to speak again, a shadow covered the table. It was Butcher.

"Mind if I sit with the two of you for a little bit?"

Annoyance passed across Nash's face but before he could respond negatively, Butcher had pulled out a chair separating the two of them, Nash on his right and Naida on his left.

"Butcher, you should get back to work."

Butcher leaned forward and rested his forearms on the table. "I thought maybe I could help."

Naida looked at Nash. "Is this the new butcher?" Nash nodded and Naida gazed into the tall man's brown eyes. "My mother was talking about you today. You had a run in with Reverend Deakins?"

Butcher's head dropped and he chuckled.

"Couple that with your interaction with Rhonda last night at the bowling alley and I'd say you're on strike two."

"I might foul off a few more balls before hitting one out of the ballpark," Butcher responded.

"That's not the way it normally happens in Amicable," Naida said.

"So I've been told at least half a dozen times in my first two days."

Butcher's gaze stopped outside the shop on the trio of farmers who were still talking. They had put their hands in their pockets, a symbol of solidarity and inertia. Butcher looked at Nash, a burgeoning adult, but still molting.

Then he shifted his gaze to the young woman, and within seconds he knew. She was a young wife, spoiled for years by her mother, but bored with life. The stimulation of her youth had been erased by the maturation process, but she still held tightly to the umbilical cord. She had married young, necessitating a leave from her mother's presence while at the same time hoping she could be rescued like a damsel without distress. Her husband, enticed by her cuteness and her ability to flirt, had embraced the thought of capturing and controlling her. In the process, though, he had steamrolled the very things that had attracted her to him in the first place. She was hoping that Nash could be the one who pulled her from the boat of boredom into the pond of spontaneity to swim in her childhood dreams of princessdom again.

"How can you help?" Naida asked. "You're just a butcher." She paused. "No offense, Nash."

"None taken." Nash's arms were crossed. "Are you reading her, Butcher?"

Butcher didn't take his eyes off Naida.

"What does that mean?" Naida asked.

"He *knows* things just by looking at people. He can already tell you your story, if you want."

"Oh, please," Naida responded. "I've seen that kind of stuff on TV. It's all phooey."

"Do you want to know what I think?" Butcher asked.

"Enlighten me." Naida opened her arms and smiled mockingly.

"I have to tell you," Butcher began, "that this will be disconcerting for you, and I'm not necessarily doing it for your sake but for Nash's sake. You both have to realize where this road will take you if you continue on it."

"Are you saying that you can tell the future?" Naida, taking the posture of a petulant child, leaned back, crossed her arms and snapped her gum in her teeth.

"Look, Naida, I can tell with a high degree of certainty, that if you continue to flirt with Nash, both of you will be in for a large amount of pain. Emotional and physical."

"Are you saying that Nash is going to beat me up?" Naida's mouth dropped open and anger rouged her cheeks.

"No," he said quietly, "but your husband will, and not just you. He will pound Nash into a bloody pulp."

"Hey!" Nash exclaimed. "I can take care of..."

"I would guess that you both have been emotionally shut off since the first year of your marriage." Naida's face burned with shame while Nash's eyes opened wide. Butcher's eyes were on his own fidgeting hands. This was the hardest part - telling people the ignored truth. "What he needs is not sex, but love."

"What the hell does that mean?" Naida's eyes moved from Butcher to Nash, but Nash had already looked away.

"It's one of the great lies of our world that we can live without intimacy."

"You just said he didn't need sex, now you're saying that's what he needs?" Naida was close to walking out, but she was astounded that the man could see so much.

"I said intimacy, not sex."

"What are you, a sexual therapist?"

Butcher sighed. "No. Just a butcher."

"So what is this 'intimacy' then?" She used her fingers to quote the word.

"It's the subtlety of falling and remaining in love. For instance, when you think of your husband, what are the first adjectives out of your mouth?"

Nash began to feel uncomfortable. He rose and moved away from the table. "I think I'll start closing up." Naida watched him go.

"He's a pig."

"Intimacy would be difficult with a pig, wouldn't it?"

Naida ground her teeth. "It would indeed."

"Two more adjectives."

"Lazy and inconsiderate."

Butcher shifted his seat to face her. "We could add another thirty words or phrases, but these three will start us off well. Now," he tapped his leg, "you have drawn a picture in your mind of your husband James. In it, he is no longer the person that you married, but someone who is now a barnyard animal. Not only is he fat, lazy, smelly and dirty, but he doesn't look after your needs at all. I don't know if this is an accurate representation, but this is why you look to Nash to draw the new picture of happiness."

"Did you take classes in psychology?" Naida asked still not quite on board with what was going on.

"Didn't need to." Butcher smiled kindly. "Back to the subject at hand; the picture you've drawn in your mind is simply unlovable and the more you repeat to yourself that he is a pig and lazy and inconsiderate, the more you can give in to your own selfish nature, which, I would guess, looks like a princess."

Now her feathers were in full ruffle. "That's kind of rude."

"Kindness sometimes requires directness in order to see the truth. I could skirt around the issue of your egocentrism, but that wouldn't really help." Her eyes were half-lidded now, but he pressed on. "You're an only child; your mother has doted on you all the days of your life and you talk with her every day. And that's okay, to a point. My guess is that somewhere in your growing up years you got tired of your mother's constant attention and overwhelming expectations. This caused you to search for someone else who would untie you from your mother's apron strings and when that happened, you were willing to do whatever it took to please that young man; in this case, James."

Butcher paused a moment. "See, I've given him a name, which is what you should start doing too."

"How…"

"Now, I've come to the hardest part, Naida." He lowered his voice. "When you had the pregnancy scare in high school, how long before James asked you to marry him?"

Naida's face turned white and she held a hand to her mouth. Nash, watching from behind the glass. "Who have you been talking to? James and I are the only ones who knew about that…"

"When Nash said I have a gift, he meant it. Sometimes, it's a curse." Naida's ashen appearance worried Butcher, so he let her breathe for a few moments.

"I didn't even tell my mother."

"That's the real issue in your life, Naida. You have to figure out who you can trust. And as much as you like Nash, he's not the one."

"How can you say that? I thought you said he was your friend!"

"Listen to me, Naida," Butcher said quietly, "I'm saying this for all three of you. You can't trust a person who is willing to step into someone else's marriage, even with good intentions. He's a great guy and if you were single, unmarried, or whatever, I'd say go for it, but the minute he becomes the wedge in a relationship, he will always be that wedge. James wouldn't blame you for the break up, he would blame Nash and that, Naida, is where everyone would get hurt."

"So, what should I do?" Naida covered her mouth with her hand afraid to inhale.

Butcher smiled. "Naida, I can see an enormous reservoir of strength in you, deeper than many I've encountered in Amicable so far. You're much more than a pretty face. You don't have to please others to be happy. Love them, but love yourself first. Find ways to do things that bring you joy for its own sake rather than for someone else."

For the first time in a very long time, Naida felt a seed of hope growing inside of her. She had forgotten all the things that she loved doing including painting. James used to tell her that he really enjoyed her realism (because he was a realist); maybe it was time to start that again.

And what would happen if she went home tonight and cooked dinner for James? What would happen if they sat on the porch and talked about the present and the future? Naida looked into Butcher's eyes and saw an immense well of kindness and goodwill.

"Thank you, Butcher."

"What are you going to do?"

She shrugged. "I'm going to go home, I guess. Do you think that I could get some pork chops to throw on the grill?"

Butcher finally laughed. "You've come to the right place." He held out his hand and when she placed her small hand in his, he enveloped it. "I hope you find some peace tonight."

"Me too."

Standing up, Naida walked to the display case and pointed to two chops, which Butcher took out, wrapped up and then paid for himself. Handing them to Naida, he winked at her. "Go love life, Kid."

Naida smiled and without looking at Nash, walked out the door.

Nash was livid. "What in the world do you think you're doing? Naida and I are just friends. What, do we have to stop seeing each other now?"

Butcher stared down at Nash. "You can lie to yourself, Nash, but you can't lie to me. You would have landed on a planet of hurt."

"That's my call, not yours!"

Spreading his hands, Butcher smiled. "You're welcome."

Nash threw up his hands. "Asshole," he said under his breath and then wheeled around again. "Get out of here, Butcher. I've seen enough of you today."

Removing his apron, Butcher bowed like a solemn butler. "As you wish, Master Peterson." Derek tried not to laugh, but it didn't work.

"What are you laughing at, Butthead?"

"He's right, Nash," Derek said. "This is the best way."

Nash looked back at Butcher and pushed in one barb. "Are you going to the Greedy Pecker tonight, Butcher? Play some video games?"

It was Butcher's turn to be embarrassed, but the thought of his date with Rhonda helped him to overcome it. "Nope, just a lonely night at home. Watch some baseball, maybe, and then turn in for the night. I'll be going for a hike tomorrow. Any good places?"

"In Amicable?" Derek questioned. "Yeah right."

"Okay," Butcher said slowly, "I guess I'll figure something else out."

"Well, whatever you do, we'll see you at the bowling alley tomorrow night. It's league night and we're down a team member. You know how to bowl, right?"

Butcher had no idea. "Of course."

"See you then."

Butcher

Chapter 15.

Rhonda couldn't remember the last time she was so nervous. Certainly, before important basketball games in high school she would have butterflies cavorting in her stomach, and then, of course, in her time with...

Tonight was not the night to bring him into the picture. Rhonda glanced into the mirror one last time. From head to toe, she looked the picture of health and confidence. Her long sandy brown hair had been brushed into a shine, her makeup had been seductively balanced, emphasizing her luminous green eyes and sharp cheekbones and her hint of perfume was alluring. The blouse she had chosen, a white, long-sleeved top, accentuated her figure, hugging close to her curves while her blue jeans clung tightly to her lower limbs.

She turned sideways to peruse her long shapely legs from behind and was pleased. Although she was thirty-three years old, many people still believed she could pass for a woman in her twenties. Men found her attractive. Unfortunately, the only available men her age were middle-aged divorcees or drug dealers, neither of which inspired her to date again.

Then, Butcher showed up.

The image of this tall, broad shouldered man flashed in her consciousness and she blushed momentarily.

Rhonda checked her watch. She had half an hour to spare, but she didn't want to show up early: that might seem desperate; showing up late, though, would be disrespectful.

Rhonda left her room and attempted to close her door quietly, but it wasn't quiet enough. Her mother seemed to have another sense when it came to Rhonda's arrivals and departures, and within milliseconds of stepping outside of her room, Connie showed up in the doorframe of her room in her dressing gown and slippers. Although she wouldn't go to bed for another four or five hours, she enjoyed this domestic uniform which, at the same time, made her unfit for other domestic duties such as doing the dishes, the laundry and the vacuuming.

"Well don't you look nice?"

Rhonda's heart dropped.

"Where are you going tonight? Do you have a date? It's been a long time since you had one of those, not that I blame you. It's not that Butcher, is it…?"

"Thanks for the commentary, Mom."

"I remember when I used to go on dates, all the parties, the disco balls, the laughter." Her voice trailed off into the corridor and seemed to affix itself to the framed memories from the late seventies and eighties when she believed she was happiest.

"Please, Mother, you didn't like dates. You used to say it yourself - 'endless hours of putting yourself on a platter.'"

"No need to get snooty," Connie sniffed. "I'm just wondering where you're going."

"Out."

Connie placed a hand on the wall and changed tactics. "Remember when we used to talk about things, girl things, like doing our hair and baking cookies?"

"No, I don't. It must have been when I was four or five."

"I was sure it was just a few years ago," Connie responded, her wistful voice trailing behind her like a kite.

"Look, Mom, I've got to get going. I'll be home late. Do you think you can take care of yourself for the night?"

Her mother's jaw tightened. "I've taken care of myself for over fifty years, missy. I think I can last one night without you."

"Let's hope so," Rhonda said as she pulled a light jacket around her shoulders.

"Just call me if you need anything," her mother said already on her way back down the hallway to her room.

"I won't," Rhonda whispered under her breath and opened the front door. A cool late summer breeze replete with scents of pine trees, freshly cut grass, earth - goodness of rural life - greeted her nose.

Lightning bugs were flitting in the air flashing on and off, on and off, signaling to their mates their readiness for attention. *This life was far too short to be turned off for so long.* Pulling the door shut behind her, Rhonda walked out onto the deck and closed her eyes enjoying the freedom from her mother and towards adventure.

A voice spoke in the semi-dark. George. "You're looking sexy."

"I'm surprised you can even see me, old man," she laughed looking over at her neighbor.

"Even old men can appreciate a beautiful woman. You smell nice. You got a date?"

Stepping from her deck and alighting on the ground, she walked down the sidewalk, opened the gate, and went next door to George's deck.

"Yes," she said simply, looking over his railing, "I do."

"With the butcher." His terse response suggested he was worried.

"How did you know?"

"I just guessed. Are you feeling okay about it? After…" His thin voice floated into the branches of the trees and the vision of *him* came back to her, but she swallowed her pain.

"Yes, George, it's been almost fifteen years. I think I've gotten over it."

George looked to the west where the sunlight used to be; the memory still warming him. "Some things we never get over."

"What are you worried about, George?"

Placing both of his hands on the cane in front of him, George pulled himself erect and walked over to the other side of the porch, opposite the railing across from his beautiful neighbor. "There is something different about him, unnerving." Rhonda nodded - the exact same trait that was actually pulling her towards him. "I went to the locker this morning, Rhodie."

"Ah, George, you didn't."

"Yes. I needed to make sure that this guy was fit to be looking at you."

"You're not my father, George."

"Thank God for that. But I can be a father to you, and at this point in your life, I think I can be a source of wisdom for you."

"What's your wisdom?" A firefly landed on Rhonda's forearm. It tickled the hair.

Without hesitation, George spoke. "Be careful with that guy. Very careful. He knows things."

Rhonda immediately knew what he meant. "What did he say to you?"

"There were things that he knew that I hadn't told anyone - ever. Not you, not even Mabel, things about my past in the war. He said he could *read* it in me. That's craziness, right?"

"Yeah, I guess. How do you think he does it?" Rhonda was hoping he had the answer.

"No idea, Rhodie, but if he can pick me that fast, you have no chance of any secrets from this guy, and I mean *no secrets*."

A flaming arrow of fear pierced Rhonda's heart. *He can't ever know about THAT.* "Thank you for the warning, Georgie. I appreciate it. I'll be careful."

"You better be, or I'll kick your ass." It was the second time that day that the ninety-seven-year-old man threatened to punt a derriere.

Rhonda laughed and waved to George. "I'll see you tomorrow, neighbor."

"Just call me if you get in any trouble."

With deep affection she turned back to him. "You'd be the only one I'd call, George Hendriks. You're the only one I trust."

She drove slowly towards Peppertree Lane past the immense silos standing as silent sentries over Amicable. In the farming community, the elevator was king and everything else, including the bank, the grocery store, even the school, took secondary importance. In two months, the town would become a hive of tractors and trailers, dust and corn, noise and commotion as the farmers reaped the harvest from the soil and dumped it from the drying bins into the grates outside the elevator. When the bushels had been weighed and tested, hundreds of thousands - millions - of dollars passed from bank account to bank account.

Three blocks past the elevator she turned right. Slowly she pulled the car to a stop across the street from Butcher's rental and cut the ignition. The porch light of his house was on; the tall man sat in the glow underneath swatting at mosquitos and moths drawn to the light. Rhonda smiled. Opening the door of her Ford, she put a foot on the road, a step in the right direction, she hoped. Butcher stood, unravelling his body; Rhonda was consistently amazed by how tall he was - certainly there had been a handful of men taller in Amicable, but it would have been rare. She stopped at the edge of his walk; pausing five feet from him.

"You look beautiful," he said.

"You can't even see me," she responded, unconsciously touching her face.

"Not true. I can see you."

That's what worries me, she thought. "Well, not good enough."

"Correct. Shall we move into the light?" Awkwardly he approached her and leaned in to kiss her cheek. She turned away from it.

He blushed in the dark. "I'm sorry. Maybe that was presumptuous."

"Yes, probably," Rhonda responded. "Let's go."

The drive to Clancy was filled with silence, forced dialogue and unanswered questions about Iowa. As well as she could, Rhonda told him about the history of this part of the Midwest, but for the most part she wondered if she had made a mistake in meeting him tonight. Twenty minutes later, they reached the parking lot of The Creek Restaurant situated on the banks of the slow moving Kisahani River. The Creek Restaurant was known for its fish, but for the adventurous, they served local specialties such as bullfrog legs, duck eggs and fried eel. The decor of the restaurant was the typical understatement of all Midwestern establishments: ostentatiousness was something frowned upon whether in personal residences or businesses. The Creek contained thirty odd tables, some of them thirty or forty years old with wooden chairs padded with black cushions and corroded tacks, and black metal napkin dispensers in the middle. Plastic salt and pepper shakers bookended the napkins while stained menus poked up from the middle of the table.

The waitress, a young woman named Chelsea, sauntered over and led them to a table near the window overlooking a large waterwheel which thumped. The slow-moving stream pushed water up and over the side into a pond behind the berm. Even though it was a Friday night, there were only two other couples in the restaurant. A handful of locals were stationed around the bar gazing up at a television screen behind the bartender's head where a high school football game was being televised. Clancy was the largest town in the county - about six thousand citizens - and was known to be somewhat arrogant in its small-town big city way believing that it was a much better place to live than, say, a little backwater swamp like Amicable.

When they were seated, Rhonda filled their glasses with water and took a drink. Butcher smiled at her in the dim lighting as the waterwheel moved incessantly. "You don't have to serve tonight."

She smiled nervously and covered her mouth. "Sorry, just a habit."

"Is it hard to go out to a restaurant when you have to work in one every day?"

Rhonda shrugged. "It's better than eating at home."

"You don't like to cook?"

Rhonda could tell that he was playing dumb. "Look, Butcher, you already know about my mother and our... strained relationship. I do like to cook; it's one of my favorite things, but I don't like it to be critiqued by my mother for every meal."

"I understand."

Chelsea returned moments later with a pen and her pad of paper. "What can I getcha?"

Butcher motioned for Rhonda to go first. She wasn't sure she should have alcohol on their first *date*. Having a clear head would be helpful. Butcher read the thoughts going through her mind.

"Do you like wine?" He asked.

158

"It's okay."

"What kind of wine do you have?"

Chelsea scratched her head with her pencil. Her nasally voice squeaked and she snapped her gum. "Nobody has ever asked me that before. In fact, I can't remember a time when anyone ordered anything but beer or Black Velvet. I'll get back to you, okay?" Chelsea wheeled, ponytail bouncing and went to talk with the bartender. A few moments later, she returned and read from the list on her pad of paper.

"There's Chardonnay," she pronounced it with a hard 'ch' sound, like in 'chisel' which made Butcher smile. "And a," she inspected her notes, "A merlot," also intoned like 'harlot', "and something called a... a... cabernet... um... that's a really hard word, but do you know what I'm talking about?" Chelsea looked for help.

"Cabernet Sauvignon."

"That's it." Chelsea giggled, snapped her gum and pointed to her pad of paper. "You say that really nice. Do you speak Spanish?"

Rhonda bit her lip to keep from laughing out loud. "No, no we don't speak Spanish. But we'll take a bottle of the 'cab sav,' that's the easier way to say it."

Chelsea's eyes lit up. "So, like, you want a whole bottle? Will you be all right to drive after that?"

"I think we'll be okay," Rhonda responded.

Chelsea mouthed the words and wrote 'cab sav' on her pad, and went back to the bar where she read out the order. The bartender, an overweight, stubbly-cheeked local dressed in a t-shirt and baseball cap, grabbed two dusty glasses from overhead and opened a cabinet under the bar. Butcher was pretty sure that the bartender did not know if a cabernet sauvignon was a red or white wine, and his hunting for it meant that they had been in the dark under the bar for a while (which was probably a good thing). Exultantly, he stood up and examined the bottle, blowing the dust from it. Washing the glasses and wiping the bottle, he gave them to Chelsea who struggled with how to carry the glasses. Butcher, watching the proceedings, got up and walked over to Chelsea to help her carry the drinks. Once reaching her, he showed her the correct way to hold the glasses upside down between her fingers.

"Do you have a corkscrew?" Butcher asked the bartender. He patted his pockets and then dug through one of the drawers exhuming a corkscrew like an archaeologist digging up priceless treasure.

"Do you know how to work one of these?" The bartender asked Butcher.

. Butcher smiled. "I've wielded one once or twice."

"Go for it," the bartender said and handed the corkscrew to Butcher. Following Chelsea to the table, Butcher noticed Rhonda's amused look. Then, with a flourish, Butcher took the wine and presented the label to Rhonda.

"Is it any good?"

"But of course," Butcher said in a French accent. "It has hints of blueberry and chocolate that play games on the palate, while the bouquet remains bringing ecstasy to those who dare drink it." Deftly he uncorked the bottle and poured a splash inside Rhonda's glass. "You see, Chelsea," he continued the accent, "first the lovely lady swirls the wine in the glass and holds it against the light checking its color and contrasts. Does it cling to the sides of the glass? Does it long to remain there forever?" Chelsea giggled. "Then, the *cherie* holds the glass under her elegant nose tasting it with her nostrils, testing for the fruits which will bring joy. Yes! Joy!" Now, Rhonda was smiling. "At long last, the connection will be made and the lady lifts the trembling glass to her lips and tastes - sips the nectar which has been produced by the gods. If she closes her eyes," his voice dropped to a whisper, "she can taste the beginning of time."

Chelsea clapped her hands. "Whatever, man. It's like a twenty-dollar bottle of wine, and it's, like, old. 2009. I thought these things were supposed to go off."

After sipping the wine, Rhonda's eyes popped open. She had to admit that the wine was incredible. There was something deep and mysterious about it; she was quite sure that Butcher already knew this when he got his hands on it.

"Thank you, Chelsea, we'll take it, and the odds are, we'll take a couple more for the road, won't we, *mon cherie?*" Rhonda could only nod as she held out her glass for a full amount.

"Now, Chelsea, don't pour too much in. You must leave space at the top, room for the wine to breathe. It always must have space. Everything must have space to live, especially mysteries." Butcher's eyes fixed on Rhonda.

"Okay…" Chelsea poured the wine into both glasses and then began to leave.

"Chelsea," Butcher called after her, "when the customers buy the bottle, the bottle is left on the table."

Chelsea looked at her hands and then made a 'duh' slap against her forehead. "Sorry about that."

"Don't worry about it. When you get off your shift, come back and we'll let you try it." He looked down at the label. "Maybe."

After the waitress had walked off, Rhonda picked up her glass and swirled it again. "How did you know that was a good bottle of wine?"

Butcher leaned back in his chair throwing his legs out to the side. The Kisahani moved silently behind them giving the room a constant sense of motion. "I've moved around a lot. Seen many things, tasted others."

"Is there anything you haven't done?" She noticed that his collar was undone, an extra button revealing the top of two strong pectoral muscles. She hoped he hadn't noticed her wandering eyes.

"I haven't settled down before."

"Why is that?"

Butcher leaned forward suddenly and took a drink of the wine. Memories, by the thousands, came flooding over him. "It's a long story."

"I don't have a bedtime," Rhonda said.

One more sip. A trip back in time.

Butcher

Leo and Lenore Jensen sat across from each other in the dark confines of a small apartment. Outside, the snow was falling, light, delicate flakes, the kind that Christmas dreams are made of. The edges of the windowpanes were fogged over; in some cases the frost agitated the glass, to pucker it against the frigid temperatures on the other side of the window. A single candle, cranberry, sat squat and resolute between the mother and son each leaning back in their chairs with a glass of wine in hand.

Leo was sixteen, but vastly older than that in his maturity. For all of his life he had been called different, or odd; his particular favorite was 'special' designating him below average intelligence or a social outcast. Either way he recognized his peculiar abilities and embraced them, or abused them, depending on his and his mother's location. As she sat across from him, Lenore, a strikingly tall woman, dark haired, dark-eyed and dark-souled, now in her forties, stared into her son's eyes and smiled sadly. He was a lonely boy prone to fits of melancholy. His gift, as much as he tried to hide it, was a burden too great, and often she prayed to God that it would be taken from him so that he could remove the 'special' tag and simply be a 'normal' boy. For too long, he had been a Pinocchio…

By the time Leo was fifteen, they had moved thirty times - every six months, it seemed. Lenore knew that in the early days, Leo was not able to control his abilities and, to her discredit, she had too often encouraged him to take advantage of others for their own benefit. Time and time again this left him bereft of a conscience, and often when people flew into a rage, he couldn't understand why they didn't want to know the truth. When the heat from the fire became too hot, they picked up their meager belongings, a few suitcases, a couple of books and a handbag of cash, and took whatever mode of transportation they could to the next state. For Lenore, it was a life of grandeur living out of a suitcase, seeing the world, bilking the unsuspecting rich out of their easy earned cash. She felt like a mother/son pair of Robin of the Hoods. Except that they never gave to the poor - they were poor enough.

The Dodge Dart had broken down years before; Lenore had washed her hands of it. Leo never had a car to learn how to drive. Now, at sixteen years of age, a string bean of a young man, six feet five inches tall and perhaps a few more to go, he was 'special' in the fact that he could not drive himself anywhere. When exposed, this was another source of ridicule in whichever school he might be attending. Young people learned not to make fun of him, though.

Chapter 15.

That Christmas, Lenore had promised to try to remain in one place long enough for Leo to attend the same high school to graduate. But as she raised her glass to him, a Christmas toast, he already knew what was about to occur.

He sighed. "Where are we going this time?"

Lenore's eyes flashed to the map on the board behind his head. Pins had been pushed in thirty of the continental United States, in towns they had loitered for a while. If asked where her favorite place had been, Lenore would have scratched her head and scrunched up her face. They all seemed to blend together: maybe Utah? Alabama? Of course, Massachusetts was nice... As of Christmas in 1988, they were living in the coldest place they had ever been - Wisconsin. The people had been friendly-ish, but not overly so. The summer had been wonderful, but now that the Yule had arrived, Lenore felt in her bones that the wintery winds were blowing them elsewhere.

She would never chintz on moving days - the wine would be of top quality from somewhere exotic like South Africa or Italy - nothing domestic. She knew enough about wine to know that the U.S. developed a lot of good things, but vino was not one of them. The bottle sitting between them, an Australian shiraz, was superb. She wanted to relish the 1988 Christmas season because she knew, somewhere deep inside of her, that she didn't have many more to go.

"I was thinking maybe a little farther south. What do you think? We haven't been to Arkansas yet."

"Whatever you say, Mom."

"No, really, I want to know what you think."

A strange look came over Leo's face, a blend of frustration and defeat. "You already know what I think, Mom. I want to stay put. I promise I'll try to fit in."

Lenore's face contorted. "I don't want you just to 'fit in,' Leo, I want you to roar."

"That's not going to happen, Mother, and you know it."

Lenore did know it. "Let's just enjoy this Christmas - just you and me."

Leo did not need to tell her that it was the same 'just you and me' every Christmas, but he wanted other relationships. Something new and adventurous - something lasting. A best friend or at least someone else he could talk to.

"Yes, Mother."

"You're such a good boy," Lenore said. "I bet all mothers are jealous to have such a handsome man growing up in their house."

"I'm sure."

"So, it's Christmas," Lenore intoned after having sipped some of the wine, an incredible vintage from somewhere in South Australia, "Ask me any question you want and I'll answer truthfully."

Leo rolled his eyes. "As if I couldn't tell if you were lying."

"Come on," she laughed, "It'll be fun. Ask me."

Leo took a sip of wine and set the glass in front of him. "Why can't I read you?"

"But you can, Leo! You always have. Ever since you were a baby, you knew my emotions. I would come home from work and if I had a good day, you could sense it. You'd laugh your beautiful little head off, but if the customers were crazy, or someone had mistreated me, you could pick it up off of me no matter how hard I tried to hide it."

"I know, Mom. I can tell if you're lying or what mood you're in. Any idiot can do that. But why can't I read you?"

Lenore stared at the crimson liquid in her glass. As she rolled it around the edges watching it cling to the sides, it seemed like blood, not in its thickness, but in its ability to sustain life. "I don't know, Leo."

"You're lying."

Lenore looked up sharply knowing that anything that passed between them now would change their relationship. He was old enough to know the truth.

"Yes, I'm lying."

"So you do know why you can hide your past when no one else can."

"Yes."

"That's my Christmas question, then. Why can't I read you?"

Lenore reached to the middle of the table and filled her glass half-full - never too full, the wine needed space to move. Freedom, even for non-living objects, was important.

"Cheers, Leo." She raised her glass.

"Cheers, Mom." For one of the first times in his life he felt fear.

Lenore began her tale.

"My mother told me that day something that shocked me, and I wasn't used to being shocked."

"What was it?" Rhonda asked completely wrapped up in the tale.

Butcher's eyes noticed the movement beyond Rhonda's left shoulder. Chelsea was returning to take their orders.

"Have you decided what you want to eat?"

Butcher raised an eyebrow towards Rhonda. "Have you?"

"I haven't really looked at it, but how about we get the special. What's the special?"

Butcher smiled at the irony of the word 'special.'

"Um, our special tonight is roasted frog legs."

Rhonda's face wrinkled with distaste.

"We'll take those," Butcher said as he smiled at Chelsea.

"That's disgusting, Butcher," Rhonda said.

"Where's your sense of adventure? You said you wanted something different, right?"

Rhonda had said no such thing, but she was quite aware that Butcher could probably read that from her. "We'll try them, but if you even suggest we're getting a doggy bag for the way home, you'll be greatly disappointed."

He laughed.

"Now, getting back to your story. What was your mother's secret?"

"Are we in a hurry now?" Butcher's teasing put Rhonda at ease, but she was also aware that her glass was empty. Reaching forward, she poured more of the wine for them.

For the next twenty minutes, Butcher enjoyed the conversation beside the Kisahani River and the whumping sound of the endless turning waterwheel. He described his mother on that night, the surroundings and his deep, intensive longing for Christmas and his love of snow and lights. Because Iowa had no shortage of either snow or cold, he was already looking forward to the long winter that could start anywhere between early October and late December. Butcher was unused to talking so much, but the release seemed free and easy. And as he talked, he knew that a transformation had started in both of them. He knew that she had been prepped about his unusual abilities - almost always, people thought they were being judged.

Before long, Rhonda had completely forgotten about Butcher's mother and was intent on understanding the ins and outs of Butcher's abilities. Before he could continue, though, Chelsea brought their dinner. A full tray, ten pairs of bullfrog legs buttered and broiled, was set between them.

They both laughed at the sight. Rhonda was having more fun than she ever imagined. The man across from her was attractive, witty, respectful, responsive and able to carry on a conversation. He was fascinating; not only had he *been* places, he had *done* things, which was the complete antithesis of ninety-seven percent of the males who had grown up in Amicable. Both reached for the frogs legs at the same time and their hands met. It wasn't electricity, but connection that neither had felt for a long time. Butcher had connected with a woman, truly connected, only once when he was in his twenties. They had met in a butchery in New England. Butcher had hoped he would be able to forego his reading, but it was almost immediate. On the other side of the table, Rhonda was in no mood to contemplate her last connection with a man, and as soon as she realized that she was going to that place, she reached forward to finish off the bottle.

An hour later, frog legs consumed, the sides of potatoes and salad eaten, and after a dessert of chocolate mousse to top off the gastronomic delight, Butcher ordered another bottle of the same wine from the bar.

Chelsea came over at 10:30 p.m. The bar was shutting down at eleven and she wondered if they would need another bottle of wine.

"No, Chelsea, I think that will be enough. I can't believe that you shut at 11:00 on a Friday night." Rhonda smiled up at Chelsea.

"I know, it's early." The waitress popped her gum between her back teeth. "Everybody younger than forty knows it's early, but the old folks eat at five o'clock and then go home half an hour later to watch the news. At the bar," she motioned in the direction, "the regulars drink beer until the game is finished and, if they feel frisky, they might have a game of pool or darts, but mostly, they just go home to drink. It's cheaper." She took off her apron. "I don't mind, though. At least I get out of here at a good time. That way I can have a little time off before I start work tomorrow afternoon."

"You did a great job tonight, Chelsea," Rhonda said reaching out for her hand. "I should know. I'm a waitress too."

"What? You? You're way too beautiful to be a waitress. You should be a model or something. As tall as you are, with a body like that…" Chelsea blushed. "I'm sorry, I hope I didn't embarrass you."

Rhonda laughed. "Are you kidding? A woman your age calling me 'hot?' I should give you a larger tip."

"Well," Chelsea said giggling, "You haven't paid the bill yet."

Butcher smiled and pulled out his wallet. "Can you add one more bottle of the Australian wine for the road and then add fifty dollars to whatever the bill is for your tip."

"Holy cow!" Chelsea exclaimed. "I've never had a tip that large before."

"You deserve it, *mon cherie*." Butcher said with his French accent.

Rhonda's eyes were raised. "That's a pretty big tip. You didn't give me one like that."

Butcher leaned forward. "Well, Rhonda, my hope is that this won't be the last time we come to The Creek Restaurant, and I'm happy to buy your meal any time you want to come out."

"But you're only a butcher. Where do you get your money?"

Butcher placed a finger alongside his nose. "Buried treasure, my dear. Buried treasure."

Chelsea brought back another bottle of wine. Butcher opened his wallet and extracted three fifty-dollar bills. "Do you still want to try the wine, Chelsea?"

As her eyes lit up with interest, Chelsea returned with the receipt and the bottle of wine. There was still a swirl left in the last bottle, so he poured her a sip, which she held to the light, twirled in the glass and smelled before tasting. Her eyes, similar to Rhonda's, widened with pleasure.

"So, this is why people drink wine."

"That it is, Chelsea. That is why people drink wine."

On the way home, the mood was ebullient. Rhonda looked over at Butcher who was leaning back in his seat (a necessity due to his height) and he had a pleased, satisfied look on his face. The music on the radio was jubilant, a raucous run of 80's pop; nothing deep, only dancing on the ceiling, which made no sense at all. Most of the night did not seem to make sense.

But it didn't matter.

Although tipsy, not inebriated enough that she couldn't drive, Rhonda replayed the date in her mind, when suddenly, she remembered that Butcher hadn't told the entire story about the Christmas night with his mother. He hadn't explained why he couldn't read her.

"You never finished your story," she said loudly over the music.

"What?"

"About your mom. Why can't you read her?"

Butcher opened his eyes and looked over at the beautiful woman driving him home. At that moment, he wanted to erase the gift, but he couldn't. He immediately knew that his senses were downloading her history and he attempted to stop it.

"Maybe next time. It's probably best that I just go home."

"But the night is still young. It's only 11:30. You don't have to work tomorrow, do you?"

"No. But Rhonda, there's something I need to tell you."

She looked at him.

I know your secret.

He looked away. It was bad.

Chapter 16.

Three separate, and very distinct, conversations took place at roughly the same time Butcher and Rhonda were sharing a sip of wine with a pert young waitress named Chelsea. All were in different locations with different mindsets and emotions; the people involved each were in desperate attempts to control their lives and the lives around them. This, in and of itself, was a full-time job for most humans, but when threatened, control is the last Holy Grail. The Holy Grail, just like human control, is a myth.

A young couple sat on their porch staring out into the distance of their yard sipping their coffee. They had spent the night in a miraculous wonder; the young woman had prepared a meal and decorated the table with candles and small trinkets, memories of their relatively short history together. The man, full of sweat and stink, had clumped up the front steps at six o'clock in the evening, his boots trudging toward the door where he believed a new storm would be brewing. But when he opened the door, the smell of a beef roast, onions, carrots and potatoes greeted him. At first, he thought he might have entered the wrong house; he paused to look above the door at the house number; it was indeed his house.

When he had called out, she greeted him in an apron covering a beautiful dress. She had done her hair and makeup and the young man wondered what in the heck was going on. Instead of a cone of silence, music was playing in the background. Her smile spoke a billion words, phrases and sentences that he hadn't heard for months. She looked lovely and he looked down at his work clothes. The young woman told him to *take a shower, change clothes, and hurry up!* because they were going to have dinner together. He asked what the celebration was; she approached him and for the first time in what seemed like a lifetime, she touched his face and kissed him on the lips. Inwardly, the man was thinking *I am going to get lucky,* for this is what most men think, but he had no idea how lucky he was going to get that night, or how lucky he truly was to be married to such a wonderful young woman.

As they sat on the porch afterwards, coffee in hand, the husband draped his arm around his wife and they reminisced about the good old days. The wife put her hand on his muscular thigh and reminded him that the 'best of new days' was coming. Once said, she laid her head on his shoulder. And, strangely, they truly felt like they were in love.

On the other side of town, three women sat around a quilting rack each eyeing the different patterns on the fabric as part of their own handiwork. One woman was pulling out thread, while the one sitting next to her was measuring it out in lengths. The last was giggling as she snipped the threads. There was something essential about what they were doing, and as the quilt took shape, the image came into focus.

The conversation centered around one topic, that of a very tall man who had positioned himself at the nexus of almost all of the oddness that Amicable was encountering. Although he had only been in the town for two days, now (as the middle one looked her watch and exclaimed 'Goodness, it's almost midnight' although it wasn't much past ten o'clock) almost three days, it seemed as if he had established himself in disruption. Each one of them added more information while speaking through pursed lips clutching needle or thread. As for the factuality of their statements, it didn't matter. Close to the truth was close enough. The facts would presumably be filled in later. It didn't matter if they were right, as long as they were first.

As they talked and nattered and twittered around the quilt, they were quite certain that they had to do something about this man. What their action or activity was they didn't know yet, but pull, measure and snip away they did on this fine night approaching the end of August.

Halfway between the couple and the trio, a very disturbed clergyman stared at his feet that were stuck out in front of him. Sitting in his reclining chair, which he'd reclaimed from Goodwill (a testament to his anti-materialism ways) he pondered that which had alluded him all of his life: a true sense of adventure with the opposite sex. Surely, the woman who had kissed him, (and not just a peck either), was a powerful woman and the sheer magnitude of her will frightened him greatly. But it was not his fear that was keeping his vision on his feet, it was his wonderment. How could a beautiful woman think that he was a beautiful man and worthy of being sought after?

As the night deepened, Deakins, with shuddering breath and trembling hands, made the decision to pick up the handset on his turn-of-the-millennium telephone.

He was tempted to make a phone call to the beautiful woman he had spurned not twelve hours before. She had professed a sincere interest in him, and his response had been one of shock and rejection. What if she spurned his delayed amorous intentions? What if he had blown the one chance he had?

His pounding heart thudded in his chest. As his hand reached for the telephone, a weight pulled it back to his hip. In that moment, he wondered if Jesus had ever felt a transcendent fear like that, but then the reverend shook his head and felt silly.

The man, instead of putting his hand back on the phone, stood and walked to the front door of his house. Putting on his house shoes, rather than his outdoors shoes, the man exited his house and descended his steps to walk down the street in his slippers, his pajamas and nightshirt. It didn't strike him that his dress was inappropriate until he had already rung her doorbell. As he saw her shadow moving in front of the light in the house, he thought he would faint. He smoothed his shirt, flattening unseen wrinkles in the fabric. Perhaps he was ironing the unseen wrinkles in his soul hoping that she wouldn't notice his flaws and imperfection. When she opened the door, the only thing that he could think was, *God has sent me an angel.*

Her arms were crossed tightly across her chest as she beheld the strangely dressed visitor in his nightclothes and slippers. Obviously, he had walked six blocks, nine-hundred and seventy-four steps (she had counted them many times) to forlornly stand quivering on her front porch. She frowned, unsure of why he had come. Her feelings were still raw from his rejection, but she was hopeful - always hopeful - because that's what faithful people feel: hopeful that he had come to say that he had made a mistake.

For some reason, the man was unable to speak. Like the biblical Zechariah, struck dumb by the glory of the Lord, the man could only stand and motion from his heart to her heart. But she understood. And after looking from left to right, prying eyes would not be praying hands, she took the dumbstruck clergyman by the hand and pulled him into her house.

The sterility of her abode, the surroundings spartan, tasteful, utilitarian, did not surprise the man. The woman made him a cup of tea, honey with a squeeze of lemon, which thawed his vocal cords and within moments, he was looking into her eyes to tell her that somehow, somewhen, somewhere, he had fallen in love with her.

Questioning his intentions, but thrilled by the implications, she wondered with him about the morning, as he described his fear of rejection and failure and, in large part, the considerations of the congregation.

In no uncertain terms the woman was quite sure the town could go and... well... do something to itself. She couldn't bring herself to say it out loud, but both of them thought it at the same time and with wide eyes, they began to laugh hysterically. Of course, this is what people in love do, they laugh together. The mundane becomes comical and the profane becomes ridiculous.

The conversation quickly shifted from them and their soon-to-be courtship, to the way that they must rid the town of its new butcher. The tall man had to go and they must work together to do it.

The woman moved to the man and sat on his lap. It all felt strangely exciting and wonderful and mysterious and sinful, but she kissed him long and hard and promised that they would keep it a secret until the butcher had left.

Soon. It had to be soon.

172

When the man left, his slippers padded on the sidewalk creating very little sound. Unfortunately for him, and for the woman watching him inside, two peeping eyes from across the street, young eyes, high school eyes, saw him leave the woman's house. Accustomed to putting two and two together, she made a not quite accurate summation that the reverend was having a late-night dalliance with a parishioner.

Fortunately for them, she would hold on to that information until a much later date.

Chapter 17.

Tracey didn't sleep much. This fact was normal for a Friday night. Since she'd been pseudo-grounded, forced to stay home on *this* Friday night, she was frustrated beyond the margins of her consciousness. The now infamous bumper sticker proclaiming her preference for vegetables over barbecued flesh had been her demise. The term of her domestic incarceration was three weeks, and this was the last night of imprisonment; her parents always used the word 'discipline' instead of 'punishment' because *discipline was good for you*. Although her teenage sensibilities did not agree with the reason for discipline, she knew that her parents truly were right that discipline was necessary.

But she would never tell them that - or at least not until she was old, like, thirty.

Last night, though, from her Rapunzelesque perch in her upstairs bedroom, she espied Reverend John Thomas Deakins, clad only in what looked like his nightgown and slippers, slink to the maid Tielman's house; after gaining ingress, he left thirty minutes later twirling the cord of his bathrobe and whistling down the street.

When that happened in the movies, somebody just got lucky.

But Reverend Deakins? Tracey shuddered with revulsion. *Ewww.* He was nice enough and all, but a tryst with the tightest woman in town, Leslie Tielman? Tracey never in a million years would have guessed it or seen it coming. As her mind tripped over and over on this nugget, she mulled over what she was going to do with it, if anything at all. Was it any of her business? Did they do anything? And even if they did, who cares? They were consenting adults.

Tracey decided to hold on to the information, even just for a while.

Butcher

Chapter 18.

Saturday night bowling. Tracey stared morosely at Ethan Matthews and his girlfriend, LaDonna Frances, who were high-fiving each other after LaDonna had mowed down four pins. Tracey was sure that this was LaDonna's highest score of the night. As she giggled her way back to her seat, Ethan was already staring determinedly down to the end of the racked lane, his elbow cocked into his side, hand covered by a bowling glove and his brown shirt tucked tightly into his brown pants.

Now that the imposition of her grounding was finished, Tracey made a quick departure to go to the bowling alley and stay until late, to meet with friends and let off some steam. The bowling alley was the only social gathering place in town open after seven, so this is where people would gather. In recent years, even the Lanes had lost business. At first, the loss was due to more channels on TV, then the digitization of phones and now, the proliferation of home theaters and, strangely, a consistent fear of gatherings. The fact of the matter was that residents were choosing quiet nights in front of the TV to noisy nights with friends.

As Tracey looked around, she saw Keely yawning at the front desk. Four other people were stationed on lane six; two were bowling while their partners were scrolling through social media. All in all, the sound of the alley was underwhelming - no human voices, only the hum of electricity from the lights, the lanes, the background music and the thump and whump of bowling balls sliding down the wooden lanes.

Tracey assumed that most of her friends wouldn't arrive for a while, but she had been ready to get out of the house, to clear her mind and separate herself from her parents. Purposely avoiding her phone and its incessant buzzing from texts, social media messages and alerts, she noticed how edgy she was from the constant stimulation. She was jumpy. As her phone continued to goad her like a cattle prod, she was also aware of the anxiety she was feeling by not answering it. *What if someone really needed her?*

Just as she was about to reach into her back pocket and give in to the desires of her phone, the front door of the bowling alley opened and an odd couple walked in. Rhonda Redman and George Hendriks. The old man, leaning lightly on a cane, opened the door for the tall woman. Slowly, they made their way behind the chairs, in front of the racks of multicolored marble bowling balls and into the Greedy Pecker. George said something to Rhonda who leaned down to him, then straightened up again and laughed. As they entered the bar, the door opened again and Tracey turned to see the Peterson twins push their way in. Immediately after them, like a father duck, holding the door open above their heads, was the new butcher. Tracey did not know his name, but she had been sitting with her friends a few nights ago when his difficulty with Rhonda had occurred. It seemed strange that they would follow so quickly.

A few minutes later, after the trio had entered the Greedy Pecker, an odd collection of women opened the door and entered. It was surprising to see Mrs. Simpson, Mrs. Harmsen and Ms. Dolling in the bowling alley. They seemed uncomfortable, like zebras in Tibet, but they casually walked towards the bar checking their surroundings for predators.

Amazingly, about three minutes later, Ms. Tielman herself attempted to squeeze through the door unnoticed. If she could have located a jacket of invisibility, Tracey was quite sure she would have paid any amount for it. The milieu was certainly not hers. If Reverend Deakins would have walked in the door, Tracey's mind would explode, but the next time the door opened, it was the strange young woman, Naida Thompson and her husband, James. They were holding hands. Tracey smiled at the couple. She wished she could have a relationship like that.

All of the recently arrived people moved into the bar except for the last couple, Naida and James. As the arrivals settled into their places, Tracey waited for her friends to show up.

For the next half an hour, Tracey and her friends did what they always did: passed around funny videos. While her friends were surfing, Tracey kept an eye out for what was happening in the bar. Her vigilance paid off. Around 8:30, George, Rhonda and the tall butcher walked out from the Greedy Pecker, beers in hand. The butcher held two of them while Rhonda led the way. Stopping at a table, the three of them sat down together. As soon as they came out, Naida and James bounced up to the table and pulled up a few more chairs. The butcher stood slightly to reach out and shake Naida's husband's hand and the husband smiled handsomely at the butcher as if he was truly honored to meet him.

That's weird.

Tracey could see the way that Rhonda was looking at the butcher that there was something going on there - something resolved from the other night, and yet the butcher had an edginess about him, as if he was waiting for a shoe to drop. She could think of no other word than *cringy*.

Tracey excused herself from her friends, stood up and wandered surreptitiously to the video games where she pretended to watch how the pinball machine worked. From this vantage point she could see what was happening inside the bar and hear what was happening at the large gathering behind her.

Through the bar window, she saw the four ladies sipping cold wine coolers and leaning their heads in towards each other. Every once in a while they whispered to each other and looked out towards the conglomeration behind Tracey. It was as if there were two entities, Axis and Allies, battle lines, or so it seemed. The people at the table were not as quiet as the ladies; they were boisterous, raucous with laughter. George seemed to be telling stories of long ago while the rest of them leaned in to hear.

At another table in the bar, the Peterson twins sat looking up at the television. One of them (Tracey could never tell them apart) seemed to be staring forlornly at the table outside while the other kept punching him to look at the TV.

Snatches of conversation continued to prod her ears until finally, she turned around. The butcher was staring at her. At first Tracey felt slightly creeped out, but she smiled shyly and was about to turn away. Then, he signaled with his hand for her to come over. At first, she didn't think he was motioning to her, but he smiled and nodded, pointing at her.

Tracey swallowed and walked to the table where she stood behind Rhonda who seemed to be the safest of any of them.

"Hi," the butcher said. "My name is Leo, most people call me Butcher."

"I'm Tracey."

"I know you, don't I?" Naida said sitting up.

Tracey nodded. "Yes, I think you were graduating when I was in junior high or maybe just starting high school."

"I can't believe I'm that old," Naida said and pretended to be embarrassed.

George rolled his eyes. "You should probably shut your mouth." The table erupted again. "I'm George," he said and extended his hand for her to shake. "It's nice to meet you, young lady."

Tracey had never been invited into a group like this before. Usually adults avoided teenagers like the plague and vice versa.

Naida patted her husband's leg. "This is James and I think you might know Rhonda from the Choke… I mean, The Traveler's Choice." This time she did blush.

"Did you want to sit down?" Butcher asked.

Tracey looked at her friends who were staring at her with mouths agape. A few of them were recording the moment on their phones. "I should really get back to my friends."

Butcher's eyes narrowed but he still smiled. "You don't have to. I can tell you don't really want to, that's why you came over to play pinball. We'd be happy to have you sit with us. Invite your friends over if you want." Tracey stared at the butcher not sure if he was making fun of her. Feeling buoyant and brave, she pulled up another chair and sat down.

"What would you like to drink, Lacey," George asked.

"It's Tracey," she said, "but I'll be all right."

"Nonsense," George responded. "I'm loaded. Do you drink Pepsi?"

Tracey smiled. "Well, if you're sure. I'd rather have Dr. Pepper, please."

"One Dr. Pepper coming up." George rose stiffly from his seat and Tracey was about to say that she'd go get it, but the old man frowned and motioned for her to sit back down. He wanted to serve her.

"So, Tracey," Butcher said, "What grade are you in?"

"I'm a senior."

"What do you like to do?"

Unused to the adult attention, Tracey wanted to keep her answers short, but they seemed actively engaged, willing and wanting to hear about her. She leaned into the table and put her forearms down. "I'm not very good at sports, but I really like art. Drawing is my thing." Naida looked over at James who smiled.

"Naida's good at art, too," James said.

"What don't you like to do?" Butcher asked.

Tracey looked over at her friends. "I don't know."

Butcher smiled. "Not one for YouTube videos, are you?"

"How did you know that?"

Rhonda, Naida and James all stared at him, the former two knowing all too well Butcher's abilities. He shrugged. "Just get the sense that you'd rather be talking than watching."

"Yeah, you're right." George came back followed by Shania who brought an ice-cold Dr. Pepper and set it in front of Tracey.

"What did I miss?" George asked.

"Not much," Butcher responded, "But since James and Naida have a game of bowling waiting, why don't we all suit up and have a little tournament?"

Rhonda held up her hands. "I draw the line at Pinball."

George raised his hand. "Count me in." Five sets of eyes moved towards the old man and he grinned. "What? You don't think an old man can wipe the floor with you? I used to be quite the bowler back in the 1940's."

"Okay, I'll play," Tracey said.

Rhonda put her head down on her hands and laughed. "Whatever. Sign me up." Butcher watched the woman closely; he was happy that she was smiling.

The odd cadre of bowlers made their way to the front desk to rent bowling shoes and balls. James maneuvered his way to the rental lockers. He returned with his own shoes and ball.

"You're a regular player?" Butcher asked pointing to James' things.

"Yes. Every Monday and Thursday. Monday is men's night and Thursday is mixed league."

"I suppose it's a good way to interact. You know, chucking the marble up and down the polished lanes."

James' eyebrows furrowed. "It's not marble."

"What?"

"For the novice, the bowling balls look like marble, but they're actually made of a plastic or polyurethane. Some of them are resin. As you can see, they don't all have marbled patterns."

"Huh. Who would have thought?"

"I know a lot about bowling. By the way, the lane is oiled, not polished ," he rolled his eyes at the missing bowling acumen of the tall man, "and it's done in different patterns on the wood – long, or short, or…"

Butcher laughed. "You sound like Forrest Gump's friend – Bubba. You know when he says, 'Shrimp gumbo, cajon shrimp, shrimp scampi…"

James' face reddened. "I'm sorry. I really get into it."

"I didn't mean to offend you," Butcher responded as he held up his rental shoes and smiled. "This is all new to me and the facts are really good." Butcher put his hand on a yellow ball.

"You're not going to want that one."

"Why not?"

"It's six pounds. The lightest one."

"How do you know that?"

"Because it's yellow. They're color coded."

"Jeez, you do know a lot. So, which one am I supposed to throw." He hefted a blue ball.

Rookie, James thought and shook his head at Butcher. "Most adult *men* choose something that is ten percent of their weight."

"So, I've got to find a twenty-one pound ball?"

James looked Butcher up and down noticing his muscular frame. *210? Who would have thunk it?* "No, the biggest is sixteen pounds. One of the black ones."

"Pick one for me, will you?" Butcher smiled down at James.

Searching meticulously for an unblemished ball, James pointed to one on the third rack from the top. "That one will do."

Butcher hefted the ball and felt the significant weight. Thanking James, the two wended their way to the lane where the others had regathered.

When George Hendriks picked up his yellow bowling ball (Butcher noticed the color and touched his nose to James who smiled) and caned his way down the lane, the entire bowling alley stopped to watch. After he knocked down five pins on his first attempt, spontaneous applause erupted. George lifted a hand like a victorious Caesar and told them all to go back to what they were doing.

Meanwhile, conversation in the bar had turned from curiosity to ugliness. Leslie had taken the opportunity to jump to various conclusions about the odd sextet now bowling.

"Don't you think it's strange that this Butcher shows up and magically relationships start appearing? I mean, it's obvious that he and Rhonda are messing around already."

Linda hushed her. "Leslie, keep your voice down."

"You do know about her… her history, don't you?" Leslie's eyes looked from woman to woman.

"No," Jeannie said, "What is it?"

Leslie put a hand on her chest. "I don't like to gossip, but…" It was obvious from the way that she said it that the opposite was true. For the next five minutes, she emphatically told the story, embellishing where the facts weren't juicy enough and enjoying the gasps from her friends.

"Are you sure it's true?"

Leslie nodded solemnly. "I heard it from a very trusted source."

Leona's eyes widened. "From Reverend Deakins?"

Leslie's face blushed. Even though it wasn't from John Thomas - it wasn't from anyone, just bits and pieces of the story she'd heard somewhere else, she didn't deny it. More credibility. "I can't reveal my sources."

"Oh my goodness," Jeannie said.

"Do you think we need to protect Rhonda?" Linda asked the other three.

Leslie waited for them to make up their minds, and when they hesitated, she played her trump card. "For the sake of Rhonda and that young girl out there - who knows who this man is - we should probably find a way for this butcher to exit Amicable stage right."

"Ooooh, this is exciting," Jeannie cooed.

They hadn't had this much fun in years.

For the next two hours, more and more patrons entered the bowling alley to find a horde of bowlers with varying degrees of skill, laughing at the sights and sounds of the game. Tracey's friends put down their phones, the Peterson twins entered the fray. The only people who did not join in were the four ladies in the Greedy Pecker who, ignoring the proceedings on the lanes, left around 9:30 p.m.

Later, the group of thirty decided to mix it up and draw names for partners; people who had never interacted before soon were bumping knuckles, giving advice and laughing uproariously at five-foot gutter balls. Wrists and forearms tired, and Butcher stood above it all. As he looked around at the congregation, he wondered if this was what it was like to truly be accepted. Rhonda looked at him and smiled; he removed a hand from his hip, he waved. It had been a good night.

It was apparent that the last games were being played, but the good humor remained. Rallying cries, 'Alleluias' and psalms of victory were sung while teammates laughed and hugged at the skill, or luck, of the bowlers. Rhonda bumped Butcher's arm with her elbow at one point in the night and spoke into his ear.

"Excuse me, Mr. Butcher."

Butcher's eyes moved to the young man standing behind him on the step, almost the same height as Butcher with the boost.

"I just wanted to thank you for an awesome night. We," he pointed to the group of high schoolers behind him who were removing their shoes after hours of sliding up and down the wooden boards, "can't remember the last time we laughed so much."

Butcher turned and extended his hand. "You're very welcome. Hopefully we can do it again."

The boy shook Butcher's hand and turned away; as he walked to his herd, he fare-welled the entirety of the adults who were now finishing up their games.

Looking at his watch, Butcher raised his eyebrows. "It's not even eleven. Why is everyone leaving?"

A knowing grin spread across Rhonda's face. "Church tomorrow."

"What?"

"Everyone goes to church," she said simply. "Will I see you there?"

Butcher shrugged. "Is it a prerequisite for living in Amicable."

"Pretty much."

"I guess I'll be there." He paused. "But I thought we could maybe have a drink or a talk again tonight."

Rhonda's eyes fell. "I need to get George home and, to be honest we probably have to be careful about appearances."

"That's ridiculous."

"That's Amicable."

Butcher

Chapter 19.

Butcher couldn't remember the last time he had attended church. It wasn't that he was allergic, or averse, to spirituality or God, his own belief system in the supreme being and salvation had been shown to him when he was quite young. Butcher, though, hadn't encountered many (if any) churches which incorporated a purpose beyond survival of the institution. The last few he had attended in Colorado, attended sparsely by Baby Boomers and a few of their parents were so institutionally driven that he wondered why they gathered. People would show up five minutes before the service started, find their seats in the back, keep a low profile, and certainly no eye-contact, so that they could exit quickly once the service was finished. Butcher smiled at the best metaphor he could think of which was a yearly trip to a doctor's office for a perpetual inoculation against sin. No one really wanted to be there, the doctor was a paid professional who was supposed to know what was good for them, and no one lingered in the doctor's office afterwards to speak with other sick people.

Of course, there were some good things about religious institutions; they tried hard to take care of the infirm and poor, provide a service for newborns and those going out the other direction; but it seemed like the church had entered a kind of permanent paralysis where its cells were gradually petrifying and dying as time clicked by.

Part of the issue with the churches in Colorado was Butcher's reading of people. Although he knew that the church professed that all people were welcome, he had become increasingly aware that only certain types of sins were more socially acceptable. Greed, egocentrism, pride and apathy were overlooked (even subtly encouraged) as long as greed led to larger offerings, egocentrism led to better music programs and apathy kept their vision unfocused with regards to the true mission of the Church - to bring God's hope into a less than hopeful world.

Butcher looked at his reflection in the mirror and straightened his hair. Butcher assumed that most of the people (like most congregations) would be more concerned about his appearance rather than his attendance. After putting on his nicest shirt, a collared red flannel number, and dark blue jeans, he spritzed his hand with cologne and dabbed it on his neck.

Butcher checked his watch and noticed that there was still half an hour before the service started. One last peek into the mirror and he exited his domicile whistling happily and nervously about what he thought would happen in the next few hours.

The morning had a bite to it, as if Old Man Winter were putting in his false teeth and doing a practice chomp. Autumn was right around the corner and Butcher almost turned around again to enter the house to grab a jacket, but as he looked towards the east, he saw that the sun was high enough to warm his walk.

It only took three blocks until he was loosening another button on his shirt to allow the heat to escape up his neck.

While he walked the blocks, Butcher reflected on the woman who had jumped headlong into his life. At The Creek Restaurant the other night, Butcher had been unable to refrain from reading Rhonda's history. It had made him uneasy, not because she was a bad person, but...

Butcher shook his head and switched memories to the festive feeling of the bowling alley the night before. Although he was acutely aware of the stares emanating from the women at the bar, he hadn't let it bother him.

As Butcher was about to cross Highway 10, he looked up at the grain elevator which had momentarily blocked the sun causing him to shiver. The eight immense cement silos holding millions of bushels of grain seemed like town guardians, a true metaphorical representation of the power of agriculture in this small village. The elevator was the only edifice larger than St. Clements.

Butcher looked both directions in order to cross the highway. Once crossing, he continued on down Main Street past the bank (another institution that Butcher had reservations about), past the hardware store, the grocery store and salon and then turned left at X-Er-Cise. One block away, Butcher noticed the two other pillars of the community, both metaphorical and figurative, the Amicable school (all thirteen year levels in the same complex) and across from it, St. Clements Methodist Church. After turning the corner, Butcher slowed his walk and put his hands in his pockets. Now ten minutes before the worship service, cars and pickups were streaming towards the church. Almost late, these people would fret that they wouldn't get 'their' seats.

As the vehicles passed, Butcher noticed that most people waved. The driver raised his index finger from the steering wheel, the passenger, usually a wife, would cautiously lift her right hand quickly and then reestablish its position back in her lap while simultaneously turning towards her husband asking the question, "Who was that?"

There was a greeter at the front door of the church. His nametag on the lapel of his suit coat stated that his name was Bob. As Butcher extended his hand, Bob reached out and mumbled 'Welcome to church,' before shaking his hand firmly, twice, and then pulling Butcher past him into the narthex. A few other people were milling about; some were young parents straightening their children's hair or finding them a children's bulletin with which to amuse themselves during the usually-too-long-sermon. The narthex had twelve steps up to the sanctuary. Another usher, at the bottom of the holy stairs, gave him an odd look and a bulletin. Butcher looked down at the usher, an older gentleman in a grey suit, thanked him and ascended the stairs. He didn't need to look behind him to know that almost everyone waiting in the narthex was staring at him, not only his height but the fact that he was the only one wearing blue jeans.

Another set of greeters, these a younger couple similarly unwilling to speak to Butcher, opened the doors of the sanctuary for him and allowed him to pass. Walking into the sanctuary his vision was first drawn to the immensity of the space. For such a small community, Amicable's one church could easily seat almost six or seven hundred people. Optimistic in Amicable.

Twelve stained-glass windows, tall thin arches of blended color and light, showed the twelve disciples in their various poses of piety. All twelve of them seemed to be aged Caucasian men, unsmiling and unwelcoming, intent on reminding people that to follow Christ is to suffer. As he walked forward, he had already counted twenty-four pews in each of the three sections of the church and in each of the back seven or eight pews roughly half a dozen families were interspersed between them. As always, families did not abut; there was always a space, the size of an adult human, that separated them. The altar area, as Butcher gazed at it, was festooned with deep maroon colors, flowers of all shapes and sizes, and two flags, one the American and the other the Christian flag posted on opposite sides. The imposing altar itself featuring gigantic wood carved crosses, lambs and lions, seemed to be larger than life. Sacrifice was the most important message of the altar. On one side were the elements of Holy Communion, Christ's sacrifice, while on the other, offering baskets – human sacrifice.

Butcher wasn't quite sure where to sit and as he looked around the nave for Rhonda, George, or any friendly face for that fact, he noticed that people were pointing towards him and whispering. Finally, on the right side, half way to the front, Tracey Thomas caught his eye and waved Butcher towards her family. Patting the seat beside her, Butcher was relieved that at least one person was happy to have him in attendance. As he traversed the church, he looked to his right where the quartet of women, the Fates, and their families sat reverently and piously focused on the altar.

Sitting next to Tracey, he smiled at her and extended his hand to her parents. Tracey explained who Butcher was and how much fun she, and many Amicableans, had the night before. Tracey's parents greeted him quizzically, asked a few questions about who he was and where he was from, oh, and *What do you think of the weather?*

Then, somewhat theatrically, Reverend John Thomas Deakins appeared from the sacristy. Deakins was covered from neck to toe in a white robe trimmed with lace. Around his neck and trailing down his sizeable front was a green stole adorned with symbols of grain and grapes, a cross, all the symbols of Christianity. A thick rope held it all down and in. Across his heart, dangling from a gold chain, was an enormous, hand sized, bejeweled cross giving him, it seemed, authority over everyone in attendance. Not meaning to, but entirely unable to help it, Deakins strutted from the sacristy to the front of the pulpit like a proud rooster. Folding his hands in front of himself, he welcomed the congregation with practiced intonement.

"Good morning."

The communal response was a low rumble. Excitement was anathema in church.

"It is the fifteenth Sunday after Pentecost today, and it is a good morning to worship." For the next five minutes, Reverend Deakins updated the church on the congregational calendar including the women's Bible study, after school youth meetings, a bake sale and, of course, the quilting bazaar later in the year to fundraise for the new carpet in the dining area underneath the sanctuary.

With a flourish, Deakins raised his hand from his sleeved arm. "We begin this service in the name of the Father, and of the Son, and of the Holy Spirit."

Launching into the first hymn, which was displayed by a number on the front board above the lectern, the organist played with gusto. The congregation rose in one motion to sing; Tracey handed Butcher a hymnal and pointed towards the number and within seconds, Butcher was listening to a group of people singing songs that they had sung for a thousand years. It was a beautiful thing, something that didn't happen anywhere else in society, except, maybe, at a school karaoke night. Butcher's own voice, although not confident, was a rich baritone; he was pleased he knew the tune.

It was a numbingly comfortable service for the Amicableans; each of them knew the tempo and rhythm of the worship service by heart. All of them were content never to be pulled from their traditional norms, corporate confession and forgiveness, Bible readings, more songs. During the confession and forgiveness, Butcher opened his eyes to look around, and after reading a few less-than-contrite body postures, his eyes fell on the Peterson twins who were waving at him from the other side of the church. He grinned.

As Deakins rose for the sermon, supposedly the high point of the service for many people (but the low point for those with short attention spans) he adjusted his robes and stepped up into the large pulpit. For the next fifteen minutes, he launched into an exegetical diatribe about the failings of sin and the virtues of hard work and bootstrap pulling. Purity, chastity and honesty should be striven for, while change in all its subtle and various forms should be challenged. Cling to the gospel. Cling to doctrine. Cling to the Bible, no matter your interpretation, and salvation is yours.

The not-so-subtle message missed by most of the congregation was this: Be very wary of anything that disrupts the way things have always been done. That's the way it has to be, cause that's the way God likes it, uh huh, uh huh, he likes it.

Butcher looked around again. Finally, and at long last, he noticed that Rhonda, George and another woman who was fidgeting madly, were soaking in the Reverend's words. Well, at least Rhonda was - George was sleeping and the other woman, who Butcher assumed was Rhonda's mother, was chewing her fingernails and, with wild eyes, looking around the sanctuary. Rhonda waved at him surreptitiously with a hand under her arm.

Looking up into the balcony where the organ was housed, he saw that the organist was none other than Jim the Mailman who was following the written manuscript of the sermon closely; because it was being read to the congregation word for word, Jim probably knew that he had about two minutes before he was back on tap.

Turning the last page of his manuscript, Reverend Deakins' voice rose with practiced passion. "And so, God calls us all to turn our back on the things of this world and hold fast to the traditions he set aside for us. Be faithful and God will be faithful."

Butcher, hearing the blatant irregularity in the gospel message, hiccupped a laugh, which he attempted to cover with his hand, but the noise attracted the attention of almost everyone. Things like this never happened, and when children made a noise, they were certainly reprimanded when they got home. Reverend Deakins glared malevolently at Butcher who raised his hand in apology.

"And all of God's people said 'Amen.'"

The congregation mumbled their 'Amen' and Deakins descended his dais with gravitas. Jim the Mailman launched into the hymn 'Faith of Our Fathers' which was sung gustily. Reverend Deakins looked out over his flock and the tall man taking up residence by the Thomas family. Fuming, the reverend was unused to people interrupting his sermons. After the hymn, the offering was taken up, an eyebrow or two was raised when Butcher passed the basket without putting anything in it. Then, Holy Communion occurred. A few tongues started wagging when Butcher did not walk to the front to receive the consecrated elements; Reverend Deakins smugly believed that Butcher was a seeker rather than a 'real Christian.' After Communion, as the service was winding to a close, the Communion baskets were placed neatly back on the altar opposite the offerings, the last hymn was sung. Reverend Deakins once again descended to the first level of the sanctuary, not quite on the lowest where his flock was sitting or standing, but close, and theatrically raised his hand to bless the congregation. As he did, Butcher's eyes widened when he realized where Deakins was looking.

Leslie Tielman.

Everything came into focus. Deakins' life was laid bare for Butcher's perusal. And for the first time, Butcher felt pity for him. Loneliness, abandonment, difficulties with perfectionism, issues with self-esteem; Butcher sighed.

With a collective breath, the congregation breathed in the blessing from the broken man who was doing everything that he could to hold his life together. And yet, there was an ember glowing in his eyes; Butcher was happy to see that it was a person, not a doctrine. Then, with years of practice, as the service finished, the congregation members turned back to their seats to retrieve their belongings. They began moving towards the door as quickly as possible, interacting with as few as possible, so that they could get home to their roast beef or chicken in the crockpot.

"Okay, Butcher, service is over. Come on." Tracey laughed and pushed Butcher towards the aisle. As she did so, he turned around to see various people looking in his direction and then quickly glance away. Just as he was about to enter the aisle, like a car merging into traffic, Naida and James pushed across the middle pews and into his path.

Naida was breathless as she had pulled James recklessly by the hand. "Butcher! I'm so glad you are here today! We just wanted to tell you that we had such a great time last night."

"And, Butcher, we both wanted to thank you for the advice the other day at Peterson's. I think your honest and kind words may have saved our marriage." James, without saying anything, reached out his hand for Butcher to shake, which he did.

"My pleasure," Butcher said.

"I just want you to know," Naida said guiltily, "that I've told a few others about your... ability to listen and you might have some more people come talk to you."

Butcher swallowed. *Uh oh.*

"But it shouldn't be a big deal."

That's the way it always starts.

The Thompsons took their leave entering the flow of traffic out the back doors. Butcher pushed into the aisle and was carried along to the back by other people sitting towards the front, late comers sitting in the pews of shame (the front five rows in any section). They didn't introduce themselves, even though they noticed the stranger, but kept their collective distance both physical and emotional. Three pews from the back of the church, Rhonda, her mother and George were waiting for him. George, now fully awake after his Sunday morning nap, smiled broadly at Butcher. Pulling into the pew in front of the trio so that he wouldn't block the flow of traffic, Butcher loomed over them.

"Good morning, Ms. Redman," Butcher said.

Both Rhonda and her mother responded at the same time. With the greatest of charm, Butcher extended his hand to the nervous woman. "Hello, I'm Leo Jensen."

Connie looked at his hand briefly, as if he were offering her a snake, but then shook it quickly before releasing it. "I'm her mother, yes."

"Nice to meet you."

"Hmm."

"I had a great time last night, Butcher," George said. "I can't remember when I've had fun like that - maybe 1974?"

"So, what do we do now?" Butcher asked.

"Well," Rhonda said, "some go downstairs for a cup of coffee and then home for the rest of the day. Sometime people go visiting."

"Do people ever... linger?"

"No, not really. If we do, we usually talk about the weather, or the Vikings or Chiefs; if we're feeling really adventurous, maybe a question about the sermon, but that won't happen today. People will want to get home to talk about..."

"What?"

"You."

"Me, why me?"

She laughed. "Because you're new; you don't know the traditions and the words to say. Because you're refreshing whether they know it or not."

"Not everyone thinks that."

Rhonda raised her eyes as, in quick succession, the Harmsen, Simpson, Reynolds, Tielman and Dolling troops quickly passed Butcher. The Thomas family floated behind them, having been caught up talking to David Kellogg. As Tracey passed, George reached across for a high five, which she returned with a laugh and a *Have you gone crazy?* expression from her parents.

Just as they were about to continue the conversation, Butcher felt a presence behind his right shoulder. He turned.

The Reverend John Thomas Deakins had paused in the aisle waiting somewhat impatiently for Butcher to finish.

"Hello, Reverend Deakins," Butcher said noticing his professional armor, the black suit, black shirt and clerical collar.

"Good morning, Butcher."

"Thank you for the service this morning."

"Hmm. Yes. Well, I was wondering if you'd like to discuss it for a little bit."

"Ooooh," Rhonda said with a smile. "It's like going to the principal's office."

Deakins frowned, unappreciative of the humor, but he was wise enough to not let it show too much. "No, no," Deakins said raising his hands, "We only were able to speak briefly the other day at The Traveler's Choice. I thought we could get to know each other a little bit better."

"Great, John. Where would you like to meet?"

Rhonda smirked at Butcher's use of his common name. "My house is right behind the church. How does that sound?"

Like walking right into the lion's den. "I would like that."

"Give me a little time; I like to meet the parishioners, have a cup of coffee and chat. Would you like to come downstairs for that?"

"No, that's all right, Reverend. I'll stay up here and enjoy the view." He looked around at the sanctuary, but that isn't what he meant at all. His thoughts were on Rhonda.

While the regulars traipsed downstairs to the basement, Rhonda and Butcher sat and talked inside the sanctuary, the saints and their images beatifying the proceedings of discussion. Although there was something beautiful growing between them, it was also a shimmering mirage.

"I had a great time last night," Rhonda said after her mother and George left for coffee.

"Me too."

"How did you know that people would enjoy that kind of night - you know, mixing different ages up."

Butcher squinted at her. "What do you mean? That's the way it's always been, hasn't it?"

"Uh uh, no way. People sift by generations - young people get together and pretend that they're older; middle aged people get together and pretend that they're younger; old people get together and don't pretend at all. Believe me, they don't mix."

"But why not?"

Rhonda rolled her shoulders. "I don't know. That's the way it's always been."

"Now you sound like John Deakins."

Rhonda laughed. "That was pretty funny when you snorted at the end of his sermon."

"I didn't mean to."

"But you did. And it was fantastic. What were you laughing about, anyway?"

Butcher swallowed and turned his body around as far as possible resting his arm on the pew back. The wood underneath his backside was causing numbness, but they still had some time left until his meeting/showdown with Reverend Deakins.

"I just thought the last part of his sermon was about control. It seems to me that God is really looking for transformation, not business-as-usual. Don't you think it's a little stale? A little… safe in Amicable?"

"Do you have something against tradition?"

Butcher thought about that a moment. "Not necessarily, but think about what goes on in this church on Sunday mornings: you sing the same songs, you have the same readings, you hear the same message, blessing and confession every week. Your pastor," he pointed towards the front, "wears archaic outfits that don't mean anything to anyone, except for that little black number with the white choker - if he was living in the city, he might think twice about what that means."

"You think too much, Butcher. They're just clothes."

Butcher leaned a little closer to her and reached out with his left hand almost, but not quite, touching her leg. "That's the problem isn't it? I think too much."

Rhonda back-pedaled quickly. "And I don't think enough."

"No, Ms. Redman, I believe that your thought processes are quite well crafted. Now," he said softly, "we both have to learn something new."

"What is it?"

Butcher's eyes caught on hers and just as he was about to speak, a black form appeared behind her in the pew. Deakins.

"Have I arrived at an importune time?" Butcher couldn't remember the last time anyone used the word 'importune' in a sentence.

"No," Rhonda said, for the first time grateful for the Reverend's presence. "We were just talking about the service and the... um... tradition of it."

Deakins smiled and opened his hands magnanimously. "What would you like to know?"

Butcher shrugged. "What do you believe your sermon was about today?"

Pontifically, he nodded and steepled his hands together under his chin. "The gospel, of course."

"Which is...?"

The reverend frowned. "You mean you don't know?"

"Well, not necessarily from your sermon."

Deakins' eyes flashed. "I'm interested to hear your take." Translation: *What could you possibly know, Sinner?*

"Maybe we should wait until we go to your house, Reverend Deakins. I'm sure Ms. Redman here would be bored by our musings."

"No, no, I think it's good. Always good to hear the opinions of the *laity*." He emphasized the last word as if the common man had no grasp of the gospel.

"Okay. Here's what I heard." The two of them went back and forth trading salvos, blows of theology in theory and practice. Rhonda was amazed at Butcher's grasp (as was Deakins, but he would never say it). As two prize fighters trading blow after blow, Deakins finally leaned back in his pew, impressed, but not awed, surprisingly thankful for the discussion.

"Well, it's good to know that there are people in the congregation who think deeply about the scriptures even if…their assumptions might be skewed." Deakins said.

The final jibe was like a child taking his bat from the playground after losing. Butcher would not lose any sleep over it.

"Well, we may not even need to go to your house now, Reverend."

"Please, I insist. I want to hear about your life and stories."

Butcher's eyes narrowed. "Then, I accept."

Rhonda looked back and forth between the two. "Can I come?"

Deakins, holding Butcher's gaze, responded to her. "I think not this time. Maybe next time." He pointed to the exit. "Shall we go?"

Butcher looked at Rhonda. "I'll see you later, okay?"

"Have fun," she responded.

There was going to be a lot of chin wagging around town this week.

Butcher followed two steps behind the clergyman like a dutifully reprimanded school boy. The stroll, only a short walk from sanctuary to parsonage, was strangely ominous. It was not yet noon; the sun had not reached its zenith, but the summer flowers still soaked in the warmth in preparation for the long winter that was about to arrive. Deakins had taken off his black suit coat and slung it over his shoulder revealing a decidedly inglorious paunch, which was pushing out both pants and shirt. His black clerical shirt, stretched to its limitation, revealed a white shirt underneath where the buttons were straining to hold the fabric. His belt, already loosened two notches in the last year, still seemed tight, but Deakins did not want to lose the battle of the bulge, so he kept the belt tightened which he hoped would curb his appetite.

So far, no good.

"Well," Deakins said pointing to the large two-story grey house in front of him, permanently fixed green shutters decorated each of the upstairs windows, "my humble abode."

199

"If you want to see humble," Butcher said to the back of his head, "you should come to my house."

Deakins wasn't quite sure if this was a jab or an actual invitation. He hadn't really been able to read the butcher yet, but he was sure after this discussion he would have a better understanding. He needed to learn the enemy's weaknesses in order to coordinate the plan of attack - or, as he wanted to think of it, plan of defense. The quintet of women had met with him during coffee hour and, while heads were pressed towards the middle of the table, plans had been made.

Linda was of the opinion that spinning a tale of truth and, if necessary, threat, would be the best avenue.

Leona's idea was to stretch Butcher to his breaking point, to find out where his weaknesses were (there had to be plenty) and exploiting them.

Jeannie was happy to cut the cord on Butcher's stay in town immediately. Anything to keep Amicable as it had always been.

After they said a prayer, Deakins encouraged each of the ladies, including Leslie, who couldn't meet his eyes, and Penny Reynolds who was slightly cautious after hearing the miraculous turnaround of her daughter's relationship with her husband, to continue exploring various actions. Deakins, for a moment, felt guilty about manipulating both God and women, but it was for a noble cause.

Deakins unlocked his front door, opened it and allowed Butcher to enter first. "Please, make yourself comfortable."

It took about thirty seconds for his eyes to adjust from sunlight to darkness, but when they did, he was not surprised at the kinds of artifacts that graced the walls, floors and ceilings of the clerical palace. Butcher already knew that Deakins enjoyed living in the past where all of his best memories lay safely entombed. There were antiques of every kind: mostly wooden furniture, but also a lamp stand with a glass shade and vases from different eras that held dried flowers. Butcher wondered whether living in this house would be like living in a mausoleum; he shivered at the prospect of spending an extended amount of time in this house. Walking to the window, he threw open the shade allowing light to spill into the room like a tidal wave of mercy, but it also illuminated the dust motes gliding gleefully on the breeze.

"I guess you will make yourself comfortable," Deakins said with a cautious laugh.

"I'm not a big fan of dark places."

"Afraid of the dark?"

"No, just love the light."

"How very Christian of you," Deakins said. "Tell me about yourself, Mr. Jensen."

"What do you want to know?"

"Whatever you want to tell me. That's how people get to know each other."

Butcher knew that the pastor was sizing him up.

"Ask away."

"Why are you here?" Deakins' eyes bore into the older man who had yet to be offered a seat in the pastor's house.

"Are you asking from an existential or temporal perspective?" Deakins smiled, but was not amused. "I'll take that as a temporal - why am I in Amicable? How much time do you have?" He attempted a grin but it was not returned.

"How much time do you need?"

"Ten minutes? I know you've probably got a busy afternoon." Deakins spread his hands, neither agreeing nor disagreeing with Butcher's assessment of his social calendar.

"I was born in the United States, somewhere – I'm not sure; my mother remained single most of her life after my father left her." Butcher could see Deakins snagging that small bit of information – judging her. "When I was very young, we hit the road and I spent a lot of time in different schools."

"What did your mother do for a living?"

"Irrelevant at this point." Butcher attempted to control his irritation. "As we moved through the country - I've spent time in almost all of the states - I knew that I had a special... gift." Deakins waited for him to fill in the blank.

"Is this a Spiritual gift or otherwise?"

Butcher held the pastor's stare. "I'm not sure. You would have a better grasp of what it is."

Deakins moved closer to Butcher and spread his hands again. They were very soft and manicured. "Tell me about it."

Butcher sighed. "John, I can read people."

Deakins' smile hid his thoughts. "I don't know what you mean."

"I have a hypersensitivity to people and their signals."

"So you… read their… auras, or whatever that New Age junk is." Deakins' patronizing set Butcher's teeth on edge.

"No," Butcher said slowly, "but I am attuned to everything about people. I know when people are lying; I can read their past, and many times, I can predict how people will react in certain circumstances."

"That's ridiculous - like a circus trick, or one of those spiritualists on TV that speak about vague…"

Butcher tried to pull back from the edge. "Look, I'm sorry Reverend John, I moved to Amicable to start a new life and I hope that one day I can just fit in."

"I'll tell you what's wrong with you," Deakins said suddenly sure of himself, "you're possessed. You've got a demon inside you. That's the problem with dabbling with New Age mysticism. Certainly there are medications that can be taken, and I know a good psychologist…"

Butcher decided not to hold back. "Reverend Deakins, if this really were a demon, do you think they'd be controlled by Prozac? This is neither a psychological problem nor a spiritual one; my issue is physiological - I sense everything."

"Preposterous."

You asked for it, John Thomas Deakins.

"I know that you are in love with someone."

Deakins' eyes opened wide. "What…?"

"And I know that she has feelings for you also."

"This is ridiculous. I don't know where you're getting this foolish noti…"

"I know that it's Leslie Tielman." Butcher cringed as Deakins' face infused with blood.

"Are you accusing me of impropriety?" He shouted the word out and spittle landed on Butcher's shirt. "With one of my own congregation members?" Butcher knew that he was right. Everything about the Reverend's demeanor spoke of saving face, lying, false outrage, shame...

"I'm not accusing you of anything, Reverend. She seems like a really nice lady. And there's nothing improper about it. You're both single, she's...."

"Get out! Get out! And take your demons with you!"

"Please, John, calm down."

Deakins grabbed Butcher's arm and began pulling him towards the front door. "You will call me Reverend Deakins."

"Reverend Deakins, I told you that I have a terrible gift and I truly wish that I didn't."

Deakins opened the door and shoved Butcher out, and as his large frame stumbled down the steps, the man in black positioned himself in obdurate outraged on the top step his hands on his hips. "And if this conversation ever gets out, I'll make sure you regret every second of your stay in Amicable."

Deakins slammed the door.

Butcher stared at it briefly and then turned away. *Boy, he's fallen really hard.*

Butcher

Chapter 20.

The sound of the door slamming had not even finished echoing in the house before John Deakins began working his way towards the telephone hanging on the wall near the kitchen. Surprisingly, Deakins already had Leslie's phone number memorized and then realized how he had grown far closer to Leslie than he had imagined.

"Leslie speaking."

Deakins' heart beat faster.

"Leslie, John here."

"Hello, Reverend, how are…"

Deakins cut her off. "Did you tell him?"

"What? Reverend, I don't understand? Tell who, what?"

"The butcher. Did you tell him about us?"

Leslie gasped. "No! No! Of course not. We made the decision to be discreet."

"I know!" Deakins moaned. "But he knows! He was here not five minutes ago in my living room telling me that he could 'read' me and that he has some kind of extrasensory perception, or in his words, his 'hyper sensory perception,' which allows him to read in my facial patterns, or some bullcrap, that I have a crush on you."

Leslie was quiet a moment. "So, do you?"

"Leslie! Get a hold of yourself. This is serious! If this gets out, there could be severe consequences!"

"Reverend Deakins, I'm going to have to insist that you get a hold of yourself. You're talking crazy. Now, do you want me to come over so that we can talk about it?"

Every cell in his being cried out for a *Yes!* except for one little cell in his cerebral cortex that seemed to be larger than the rest - his proprietary brain cell. "Oh, Leslie, don't you see what a bad idea that would be?"

"I don't, Reverend," she said softly. Every fiber of her being thought it was a good idea, and there was nothing in her cerebral cortex that wanted to listen to any kind of external societal expectations.

"Let me play it out for you. Let's say you come over here and he's watching, or anyone else is watching and he's told someone already. People put four and four together, rumors begin; you know how much I would loathe to be in Amicablean rumors."

Leslie spoke softly into the receiver. "Why do you care what other people say?"

"Leslie!" Deakins' voice sounded shocked. "What's gotten into you? We just had a discussion in the basement of the church, the six of us, all around a pot of coffee, we prayed about it. Now, it's like you've turned one hundred and eighty degrees and suddenly, what… what's happened?"

"Reverend Deakins, I think you should walk casually to my house and we'll sit on the porch and have a nice cup of iced tea. After we decide what's best for us, then you'll walk home to the parsonage and I will continue to drink my tea on my porch. From that vantage point, we can certainly see if there is anyone who is watching us and reporting back to the butcher. If there is, well, we'll fix it when we come to that. How does that sound?"

Deakins was aware of how much he wanted to see her. "Okay, I'll be there in fifteen minutes."

"Don't change out of your clerical wear. It will seem like a professional call."

"But it is a professional call."

"Of course it is, Reverend Deakins." She hung up the phone and prepared herself for what was about to come.

Chapter 21.

Rodrigo Hermanoso leaned casually against the red brick of Carley's X-Er-Size studio. He was not a smoker - that was entirely frowned upon in Amicable unless you had a motorcycle, but he did enjoy the feel of rolling a toothpick around in his mouth. Rodrigo was of average height, a shade under six feet tall, had thick black hair and dark eyes. His skin, the color of chocolate was, ironically the shade all Caucasians tended to attempt when tanning.

In Amicable, Rodrigo found that the majority of the people were friendly and accepting of him. He worked hard; he was punctual and he kept his nose clean. They also were quite happy that he wasn't trying to 'mix with any of their girls,' which was offensive on many levels, but this, too, flowed off his back and into the big pond of xenophobia. Overall, people like Rhonda and George, the Johnsons and most of the early morning patrons of The Traveler's Choice would greet him if they saw him on the street. Usually a nod, or a 'good morning, Rodrigo,' and then walk away. But Rodrigo always noticed the almost unobservable step away from him, or what he called the 'White Man Flinch,' which happened when a couple was passing him by.

As Rodrigo leaned against the building, he watched from a distance as the big butcher exited Reverend Deakins' house. As the tall man stared back towards the stolid residence, Rodrigo noticed the butcher shake his head as if he was either frustrated or disappointed.

Although the Mexican-American man had not, as of yet, had a conversation with the newest resident of Amicable, Rodrigo knew that there was something different about him, and it wasn't just his height. There was something shimmery about him; he was like a human mirage - you could look at him, but you were not quite sure if the image was real. From what Rhonda had said about the man, this quality was what attracted him to her. Of course, Rhonda had not spoken about the butcher personally with him, but even a blind idiot could see that there was a spark between them.

The butcher saw Rodrigo and waved to him. Rodrigo looked around to make sure that Butcher was waving at him before shyly returning the gesture.

"Hello," Butcher said congenially.

"Hello."

Butcher extended his hand. "My name is Leo. Most people are calling me Butcher, though."

"Okay, Butcher. My name is Rodrigo, but people call me Drigo."

"By people, you mean Rhonda."

"Sí." Rodrigo could see in Butcher's eyes his feelings for Rhonda. "You like her?"

Butcher smiled. "Sí." They were two peas in the pod of outcasts. "You like her?"

"She is a good woman, a good friend."

There was an awkward pause. "What do you think of Amicable, Rodrigo?"

He shrugged. Rodrigo was not one to disparage anyone or anything. "The people are very nice; I like my job. I get to work with good people and meet good people. It is a beautiful place here in the country."

Butcher nodded.

Rodrigo smiled. "You like it here?"

"The people are nice; I like my job..." He copied Rodrigo's words.

"Why did you come to Amicable, Butcher?"

Butcher pondered the young man and made a decision. "Do you want to walk with me, Drigo? Maybe go get a cup of coffee, anywhere but The Traveler's Choice?"

Rodrigo laughed. "Not open today anyway. The only place is the gas station, and even then, who knows how old the coffee is?"

"Well, let's find the gas station then. If the coffee smells, we'll grab a Pepsi."

"Bien." Rodrigo pulled himself away from the wall and they began to walk. Both men moved with hands securely tucked in their pockets; strolling side by side, they looked like polar opposites. Butcher didn't look at Rodrigo when he spoke; he stared directly into the distance to the western horizon, over oceanic cornfields and into infinite blue skies.

"I came to Amicable by chance, really," Butcher said, feeling the sun's heat directly on top of his head. He couldn't imagine how Rodrigo, with his black hair, could deal effectively with the heat. "I was living in Colorado near the ski slopes and I kind of just put my finger on a map and it rested on Amicable."

"You're joking."

Butcher shook his head. "I figured it was fate that I was to land in such a friendly town."

Rodrigo covered his mouth and his eyes flashed with humor. "That's very funny, Butcher. You are a funny man."

Butcher joined him in laughter. "It seems that way now, Drigo, but I can see beyond the horizon, I think. Something better."

Drigo shook his head. "I think you'd better get some glasses, Butcher. As much as I think the people are nice, they are not too friendly."

Butcher shrugged. "In my wanderings, I always wondered what Utopia would look like; what characteristics would appear."

"I do not know that word 'Utopia.'"

"Um, like a perfect place - heaven, or something like it, on earth."

"I don't know, Amigo, it sounds like a nice place, but I'm not sure you're going to find it here." Rodrigo waved his hand over the town.

"That's the inevitable problem with the world, Rodrigo. We always tend to look at the negative, but we don't see the potential. Do you know what I mean?"

Rodrigo frowned. "No idea."

"I've been in so many places looking for perfection, but what I inevitably see are flaws. My idea of perfection is probably from

209

Hollywood: a place where people take care of each other, the lawns are mowed and the kids are all smart and happy."

"Maybe you want to try Clancy?" Rodrigo's face was grinning.

"That's the thing. I don't want to go anywhere looking for something else."

"Well, Amigo, you definitely picked a place like nowhere else on earth." The horizon of corn still seemed miles away, but their footsteps seemed to bring them closer.

Butcher pulled up short and Rodrigo turned around to face him. "Qué pasa?"

"That's where you're wrong, Rodrigo. This place is like everywhere else on earth, full of imperfect people with imperfect ideas and imperfect buildings, all flawed because of my expectations. People think that the *place* is the problem, but it's usually the *person* that's the problem." He gestured adamantly. "What I'm beginning to understand is that I'm part of the problem because my expectations are flawed. I want white picket fences, a high paying job and a gorgeous wife who wants to make babies with me."

"Nothing flawed about that, Butcher."

"Except that's someone else's dream. That's the dream that gets sold to every person who has lived in the United States since World War II, that they'll be happy if they have this big white house, a flawless picket fence protecting a great big green yard, and the job - something that gives me some disposable cash, not just to live on and feed my children, but more than enough to fly around the world and pretend I'm somebody I'm not. The life I've been sold is so... so... what's the word... unrealistic with who would be best for me, that I'm seeking somebody else's wife and kids?" Butcher's line of reasoning had fallen, suffered because of his gift. How could he be a good father and husband? He'd be able to tell instantaneously when they were lying, or where they'd been or...

"Amigo, you think too much." Rodrigo put his hands back in his pockets and wheeled back towards the horizon where he started walking. "*Vamanos.* Let's get some coffee."

Butcher stood rooted in his position, stuck, but at long last he lengthened his strides and caught up to the young Hispanic man and journeyed with him.

"Sorry about the rambling. You're right, I just think too much sometimes."

"What do you want, then?" Rodrigo pointed to the left where they turned. The gas station, with its neon colors and bold images on its sign, was tucked on the corner.

"I... I... don't know, really."

Rodrigo's ESP went off and was clanging loudly. "Pardon me, my friend, but I think you know exactly what you want. I can tell." He tapped his temple with a finger.

Butcher wasn't used to being read. "How can you tell?"

Rodrigo smiled. "A magician never tells his secrets."

Rolling his eyes, Butcher said, "I stumbled over my words - inflection raised, I probably looked down - guilty."

Suspicion aroused, Rodrigo slowed. "You know about it?"

"You have no idea."

"So then tell me what you really want, and I can tell if you are lying."

Amazed by Rodrigo's candor, Butcher searched his feelings to see if he could trust him, and surprisingly, he could. "I want something different than what is advertised. I want stability, roots, routine, friends, love, romance, a front porch with two Adirondack chairs and a table between them with two icy cold beers. I want to look over at my lovely, average wife whom I'm crazy about and she's smitten with me. I want neighbors to walk by my house and stop. I don't want them to be daunted by a picket fence because there is no white picket fence. There is only a small front yard overgrown with weeds and dandelions and thistles, and I won't care because the neighbor kid is minutes away from mowing my lawn for ten dollars while I watch him, or her, I don't care. I'll just drink beer with my amazingly average wife. And then, when the fireflies come out at night, I want to watch them sink and swim in the drafts of air moving through my very average oak trees, and if it comes to it, my own children will capture them for a few precious moments inside glass jars to stare at a true miracle of nature. And when it is all said and done," Butcher held up a finger, his face alight, "I want to die where I've lived, because in that dream, I truly have lived."

"That sounds like a good dream, Amigo."

"I probably sounded a little crazy, there." Butcher said apologetically.

"Don't apologize for your dreams. You just have to wake up to experience them though."

"Says the man who is too afraid to start his own restaurant."

It was Rodrigo's turn to pull up short. "Who told you that? Did Rhonda tell you? I told her to tell no one."

Butcher felt as if he'd really stepped in it. "No, Drigo, she didn't say anything. I…"

"You what?" Rodrigo's suspicion was on high alert.

"I can do what you do, but even more."

"I don't understand."

"Okay." Butcher sighed deeply. "Can we get our drinks and walk some more? I'll explain everything then."

After buying their sodas at the gas station, they walked in silence to Winslow Park. As they approached the Plastic Playground, Rodrigo pulled Butcher from his introspection. "Okay, we're here. Tell me what you know."

Butcher pointed to a park bench alongside the walking path.

"I just want you to know, Rodrigo, that at any point, you can tell me to stop and I will."

Rodrigo had crossed his arms and clenched his teeth together.

"You asked me what my dream was, and I told you, but I can see what yours is. Just like you could tell I was lying, well I can go way beyond that. I know where you've come from, what you've been through, and if I don't say anything, I could tell where you are going."

Rodrigo crossed his arms. "You are full of …, well, you know what I'm going to say."

"Everyone says that. Are you ready?"

Rodrigo spread his hands. "Be my guest."

"Rodrigo Hermanoso, eldest son of Mexican parents who lived in Texas for most of your life, probably on the west side of Texas - you don't sound like you're from Dallas or Houston, more like Amarillo. Your father died suddenly when he was young, and your mother did the best that she could, but the odds are she was treated terribly by the locals. Although everyone spoke Spanish, she forced herself and her children to learn English which made you angry, I think."

"Holy..." Rodrigo's eyes opened wide.

"You moved to Amicable less than five years ago, probably because your mother heard that they were hiring people in the Midwest to work on farms. Your skills are far beyond taking care of cattle or driving a tractor. Your mother taught you how to cook, and she did it well, but judging from the scar on your right arm, I would guess a hot oil burn, your mother told you that you shouldn't be cooking. You took this poorly and regret it to this day because not many years ago after you burned your arm, you left your mother without telling her and moved north to the Midwest. Judging by the way your jaw is twitching, I've touched a nerve which means that she probably has passed away while you have been here - suddenly - and you weren't able to make it back for the funeral."

"I...I...please... who are you?" Rodrigo was not sure whether to be appalled or frightened, but he wanted to see if Butcher would get it all right.

Butcher closed his eyes. "You live with guilt, and you think it's your fault that both your mother and father died, which isn't true at all, but your siblings make you think that way, which is why you still don't go back to them. Now that you live in Amicable, you have created a space for yourself that is entirely your own, far away from everything that you grew up with. At the same time you desperately yearn for connection, any connection, with your culture, your history, your parentage - just like everyone else." Butcher took a deep breath. "So now you want to begin your own restaurant, a Mexican restaurant, here in Amicable, so that your parents, especially your mother, can be proud of you."

Rodrigo stared at the man sitting next to him on a park bench. Butcher's eyes were closed, his face had lost some of its color. The sun glinted off the sweat on his skin, as if the reading itself had been an immense task; Rodrigo wondered if the external manifestation of this man was indeed a mirage. Butcher seemed to be shifting, changing shape, a contortion of emotions, joy and rage, pity and fear, all swirling in a ball inside of him.

"I say that God has given you a mighty gift, Amigo," he whispered.

Butcher opened his eyes. "And I say that God has cursed me."

Rodrigo smiled and leaned into the other foreigner in Amicable. "It was debatable whether the Virgin Mary was favored or cursed by the course of her actions, but that was for God to decide."

Smiling, Butcher took a drink of his Pepsi. "Thanks, Drigo. I was right, wasn't I?"

"Down to the last fact. I cannot believe it."

"So, what are you thinking about your Mexican restaurant in Amicable? I think it's a great idea."

Rodrigo beamed. "It's my dream. I know that I am a good cook - chef; Rhonda tells me all the time. She thinks that I should take my talents far from Amicable and make a good living, but I, like you, kind of enjoy this small town and its nice people. I want to make a difference here, to change minds and maybe the culture, even just a little bit."

"Now you're talking," Butcher said.

"There is a property on Highway 10 not far from here," he pointed to the southwest, "about two miles up the road. Right now, it's an old farmhouse with some barns and a fantastic acre of green lawn in front. I would love to buy it, renovate the house, decorate it to look modernly Spanish. I'd love to dig a pond in the lawn and build a gazebo. Maybe we could have wedding parties or dances - fiestas!" Rodrigo's eyes were shining, but then he looked around and lowered his voice. "I would call it *Nuestra Casa*. Our house."

Butcher was impressed. "I like that a lot."

"My dream is to have a community restaurant, a place where we can gather, to eat and to drink, to dance and to laugh, to watch the sunset cleanse us of long days. The Casa would hire only local high school youth - we'll keep the money in the town - and then, someday, we can raise our own crops. Only the best maize, peppers and tomatoes. Think of it, Butcher! Together!"

Rodrigo's enthusiasm overwhelmed Butcher. "I promise you, Rodrigo, when the chance arises, we will make this happen. I will wholeheartedly support you, financially and otherwise."

Rodrigo leaned back. "But why? You barely know me."

Butcher smirked. "You forget, Amigo. I know everything about you."

Butcher

216

Chapter 22.

After Rodrigo left, Butcher sighed and looked out over the western aspects of Amicable. Knowing what he would be going 'home' to, Butcher decided that it was better for his mental health to keep walking. Starting at Winslow Park, he began to walk north, past the nursing home, then the athletic fields of the high school. Butcher enjoyed the beautifully manicured grass of the football field cut horizontally from west to east; every ten yards the blade dropped to an inch high where, on Friday afternoons the school groundskeepers would paint the stripes. Ringing the football field was the track. Eight permanent lanes were painted on the rubbery, absorbent surface.

Then, for ten blocks, he walked east where he would see the same houses, the same yards, the same trees: two story houses of various colors, most of them white or grey. As he walked, there were children playing in driveways shooting baskets, or throwing footballs on the grass. A few were playing tag in and around the streets.

As he reached the municipal swimming pool on the east side of Amicable, a few brave souls were treading water in the increasingly cool afternoons. Through the chain link fence, he noticed that there were a few elementary school children in the pool splashing and enjoying the feel of their limber limbs in the water. A few junior high youth were standing along the edges of the water, the safety of the wall a security blanket. Some high school youth on their lofty perches in the deck chairs, girls sun bathing and boys standing behind them pretending not to flex. Finally, in the small wading pool, half a dozen toddlers were oblivious to everything but the sensation of water splashing and cascading over their chubby, cherubic bodies. Their mothers sat on the edge of the wading pool, feet dangling in the water, heads tilted back to the last summer rays. How good life was when the warmth of sunshine caressed one's face.

All things have a graduation day, but not all are marked by ceremonies of pomp and circumstance. No one pays attention, really, to the moment the toddler believes he or she is ready for the shallows of the 'big' pool, and then as they grow, is released from the edges into the deep. These graduations are really gradations; the older one becomes, the deeper they are allowed to swim. After a certain age, depth ceases to become exotic and exciting and moves to that frightening fear of the unknown. It can be paralyzing, no matter the age.

Butcher recognized that he and Rhonda had skipped the shallows and wading pool and dove head first into the deep end. No gradual gradation into the depths of their relationship. Time didn't seem to allow it.

Resurfacing from his pensive deliberations, Butcher found that he had already circumnavigated Amicable. Now that the sun was sinking into the western sky, the shadows of the silos seemed to dominate the entire east side of town. Those dark, looming representations, real but untouchable, threatened the village with a foreboding sense of doom. Butcher looked both ways, crossed Highway 10 and continued past the grain elevator. Within minutes, he approached the front of his house, but there, sitting on the front step, framed nicely by the shimmering leaves of his front yard trees, was a figure that made him smile.

Rhonda.

The western light played with her hair; as he drew near, Butcher saw that she was staring at her hands, both front and back, flipping them over staring at lines and creases, the rawness of physical labor both domestic and professional.

"Hey, stranger," Butcher said as he strolled up the walk.

Rhonda started, looked up apprehensively, but recovered quickly. "Hey," she said naturally and rose to her full height just under six feet tall, still so much shorter than he. Taking no steps toward him, she waited for him to approach.

"Are you looking for me, or is this a robbery?"

A hint of a smile played across her lips. "The former."

"Good. I've been thinking about you, too."

Butcher desired to lean down to the beautiful woman and gently kiss the lovely cheek, to feel the warm skin on his lips and drink deeply of the pungent smell of her hair. Rhonda would have received a hug. A million unspoken words expressed in an embrace. Neither could quite trust enough to make the first move, to test the bridge between them, to touch the other. Rhonda looked up at Butcher, her green eyes sparkling, a thousand scintillating slivers sharpened by the marine sky. *I am so afraid.*

Butcher read her thoughts and stopped short. *This poor woman...*

"Do you want to keep walking?" Rhonda asked.

Butcher stood with his hands in his pockets and paused looking back to the west.

"If you don't want to, it's okay."

"No, it's not that. I... I... don't know why I hesitated."

Simultaneously both of them thought, *Yes, we do.*

"So?"

He nodded and they once again walked down the sidewalk towards the street. They walked towards the slowly lowering sun.

A car was parked three blocks east towards the elevator, out of sight of the strolling couple. Inside the car, three women breathed a sigh of relief. The couple had walked west and not in their direction. Linda Harmsen tittered nervously as she yanked down the binoculars from her eyes and let them rest on her chest.

"Well, there it is. They're having an affair."

Leona rubbed her hands together and smiled. "It's been a long time since we've had such a juicy side story in Amicable. I wonder if they'll get it on when they get back."

Linda pretended to take a swipe at her friend. "Oh behave, Leona," she said playfully. "I'm sure they'll be discreet in Amicable."

"I hope not," Leona responded. "I hope they flaunt it."

"Me too," Jeannie piped up, "But not for the sake of gossip."

Leona put a hand to her chest, morally aghast. "You think this is about gossip? Jeannie," she replied condescendingly. "This is about decency and the protection of the innocent. That poor girl," she pointed in the direction of Rhonda, "has been through so much. It's only right that we should offer our assistance to rid Amicable of this... this..."

Linda filled in the word. "Interloper."

"I don't know what that means," Jeannie whispered after a beat.

"An outsider," Linda responded. "Someone who is infected, a carrier of a virus of discontent, or like a parasite that wants to feed on our Amicablean goodness and turn it into something else."

"I have a question," Jeannie spoke as she pulled her eyes away from the couple walking to the west. "Why do we really care? I mean, they're consenting adults, both, I guess..." Her voice trailed off waiting for acceptance from her friends, or their rebuke.

Leona turned to the back seat where Jeannie was opining. "The word 'consenting' is just a 21st century word for people who want to engage in sexual sin but can't figure out a way to justify it."

"Oh."

"No, what we really want," Linda said as she lifted the binoculars back to her eyes, "is for Amicable to retain the values it always has had - God, America and family."

"Yes, I get that, but what does that have to do with Butcher and Rhonda? I mean, what does that have to do with us?"

Leona rolled her eyes. "Don't you see, Jeannie. When sin is brought into the city, all people are affected. It's biblical. I'm sure of it."

"Sodom and Gomorrah, baby. Sodom and Gomorrah." Linda stated as she put the binoculars back to her eyes.

Butcher and Rhonda were out of sight.

The couple walked northwards crossing Highway 10. Butcher smiled as he was about to make a second lap of Amicable on this late Sunday afternoon. He still hadn't changed out of his 'church' clothes. To his left, Rhonda strolled comfortably, her hands swinging gently by her sides. As they walked in and out of sunlight, branches shadowing and disappearing, Butcher became aware that his insides were starting to quiver. This kind of reaction hadn't occurred in years, not since his mid-twenties when his last girlfriend had steamrolled him. Butcher had learned multiple things from that relationship, not the least of which was to guard his heart more closely. Certainly, in the guarding of his heart, he now consciously recognized that he had built impenetrable walls.

"I'm glad you came to Amicable." Rhonda said looking up at Butcher. The sun sparkled in the silver strands of his temples.

"I've been here less than a week."

"Surprising, isn't it? It seems like a lot longer. So many things are different already."

"What do you mean?" Butcher already knew - it happened every time, but he wanted to hear Rhonda enumerate them.

She marked them off on her fingers. "The bowling alley. I've never seen anything like what happened on Saturday night." Butcher smiled. "You've ruffled the feathers of a whole lot of big chickens in this town. Reverend Deakins, Linda Harmsen, Leslie Tielman..." at those names, Butcher flashed a glance at her, but she kept on with the names, "... even George. He hasn't stopped talking about you."

"Is that a good thing?"

"It certainly isn't a bad thing."

"Any other ways I've disrupted the community?" He smiled wryly.

"The Peterson twins - I've never seen them, how do I put this... so mature; what about Naida and James? I could keep going."

"Nah, you don't have to. You can just..." Butcher stopped his words short.

"I can just what?"

The peppery sun illuminated his blushing face. "You can just say that you are glad that I'm here."

It was Rhonda's turn to blush. "Okay. I can say that. I'm glad you're here." For the first time, the spark between them broke into flame; she reached out to him and linked her hand in his arm. It was an old-fashioned gesture, and yet it felt cosmopolitan and new. Butcher's skin seemed electrified by her fingers.

Butcher, in his years of quotidian life, furiously butchering from town to city, hadn't seen it coming.

And yet even as the tidal wave of his emotion threatened to overtake him, Butcher was aware of his berms of reservation. He had read her past. How could he possibly continue forward? How could he be sure she wouldn't do it to him?

For the moment, Butcher set aside his thoughts and simply enjoyed the moment with a beautiful woman strolling beside him. Better yet, she was glad he was with her.

"I'm glad I'm here too."

Rhonda laughed as they walked. "You might be the first outsider to ever say that about Amicable."

Butcher negotiated the troubled waters of this sentiment before speaking. "Why is that, do you think? Why do people seem to shy away from small towns?"

The warmth of the sun, the color of the sky, the sounds of the village and the smell of fresh cut lawn seemed to be an ironic contrast to the words that came from Rhonda's mouth. "Outsiders tend to view small towns as black holes in the country. They know that they exist, but they've never seen one, and believe that if you are sucked into one, you'll never escape." She laughed at her analogy. "You know," she gestured with her free left hand, "instead of smelling the fresh air and the flowers, they get a whiff of fertilizer from somewhere, roll up their noses and think, 'boy this is a real shithole,' without ever realizing that this 'shithole' is the only reason they are fed at any given point of the day. I think some of them believe that their food is actually grown in the grocery stores." Butcher grunted. He was fully aware of the people who considered themselves vegetarians, but then had no qualms about eating fish or chicken, as if somehow they turned into vegetables when they reached the supermarket. "Then, there's always the stereotyping of small-town people as being small minded."

"I see your point."

"No, the point is, that people don't want to come to small towns because they're afraid that there is something in them that may keep them, a gravitational pull – Death Star stuff - that won't let them escape."

"Like…?"

Rhonda paused before answering, unsure how it would come across to a world traveler. "Like true contentedness, peacefulness, I don't know, love?" She blushed. "But then the fear sets in and they wonder if they'd be missing out on some great kind of big city culture, big city social scene and big city anonymity, which, if I'm honest with myself, sounds kind of good sometimes."

Butcher nodded. "It would be nice to be walking down the street and not be acutely aware that the citizenry of Amicable was filling the corners of their eyes with the sight of us together."

Rhonda laughed at the imagery. "I know what you mean." They turned into Winslow Park and began to stroll down the mile-long walking track encircling it. "But if you live here long enough, there is something *magical* about Amicable. I don't know if it's the oasis-like feel of a small town nestled comfortably in tens of thousands of acres of growing things, or if it's the spirit of it, like a warm blanket on a chilly night. Whatever it is, it works for me."

"So, you never want to leave?"

They were moving into dangerous territory and Butcher could feel it. But he had to know.

"Yes," she said quietly, "there was a time when I wanted to leave - I did leave, in fact."

"What happened?" The question was like a nuclear blast; the heat wave pushed out and then up, the fireball sucking everything towards it. Here was the literal moment of truth. If she told him exactly what had happened, who knows where they could go, but if she lied to him (he would know it) everything between them might become radioactive.

"Butcher…" her voice almost broke. "I can't tell you yet. I hope there is a time when we can talk about it, but we've only just met, really, and…" She was at a loss for words. Something shattered inside of him, like the crashing of a plate glass window. He felt her desperate hand as it clung to his arm and the imploring look on her face for patience. His being was so overwhelmed by this tsunami of emotion, that he pulled her hand into his. This strange, intimate enclosure seemed to be an unbreakable bond, a fusion between two humans that was meant to be.

"It's okay, Rhonda, I'm not going anywhere." The veracity of the statement would come out in the wash, but in that moment, he meant it. It was a sentence of power, a life sentence in the best sense of the phrase, a commitment to an attempt of claiming life from chaos.

For the next half hour, they circled Winslow Park asking questions of less importance while the largest question still echoed behind them; then they turned back onto Sixth Street West and walked southwards, crossing Highway 10 and eastward onto Peppertree. At the end of the sidewalk they stopped. Rhonda looked up into his face. She could see the elevator looming behind him – large and imposing monoliths, her life and her love. Desperately she wanted to kiss him, and she was sure that Butcher desired the same, but the invisible fence between them stopped the connection. Instead, she smiled and tapped him on the chest.

Butcher wanted to destroy the barrier, but he couldn't and as she tapped him, he stood frozen to the spot unable to move. As she turned to leave, he wanted to shout out, 'Do you want to come inside?' He watched her walk away from him, her shape never seeming to shrink. If his eyes would have raised slightly, they would have caught three figures diving down into the seats of a parked car two blocks away.

They had been waiting quite a while.

Jeannie giggled in the back seat. "I feel like a private eye or a detective on a stakeout." She was lying on her back knees thrust to the side. Her blue jeans stretched at the hips threatening to dislocate her t-shirt.

"Yes, me too," Leona whispered barely suppressing the laughter that was bubbling up inside of her. Leona and Linda had almost bonked heads as they collapsed into the front seat of the 1984 Plymouth LTD.

"The good news," Linda added, "is that they didn't see us." She paused. "Do you think Rhonda has cleared us by now?"

"That's a roger, Linda," Jeannie said from the backseat her laughter now getting the best of her and she almost whimpered through her mirth. "Subject has passed us on Third Street West, copy. Or, Over. Heck, I don't know what I'm supposed to say."

The three women began to laugh uproariously at the situation and the car began to shake. Leona, who was trying to push herself up from the console slipped and bumped her chin on the plastic. This caught Linda square on the funny bone. If anyone, at that moment, had walked by, they would have thought there was some funny business going on in the backseat of the brown Plymouth LTD.

"Got your copy, over," Leona said once she had extricated her necklace from between the armrest and the chair, but her words sent them all into fresh paroxysms of laughter. "I'll just Xerox it over to the captain and we'll go bust the perp."

Linda took a deep breath which was copied by the other two with a loud exhaling *oh, heavens, ooh, my goodness* and *that's precious.* "Seriously, ladies, now back to the moment. I think we can safely conclude that the butcher and Rhonda are doing a little..." she waggled her eyebrows and said something like *hubba hubba.*

Jeannie was still smiling, but her thoughts were going in different directions. "Do we really need to say anything? I mean, they're kind of cute together."

Linda looked into the rearview mirror at her diminutive friend in the back seat. "There is nothing more dangerous to a town's wholesomeness than a couple of middle-aged yahoos doing a little horizontal mambo behind everyone's back. That would be horrible modelling for the young of our community. Just isn't right."

"I don't think they'd be the first. Remember..."

Linda shushed. "Jeannie, who's side are you on?"

Jeannie didn't really think this was about sides.

"Just remember," Linda said as she started the car, "this information could be the key to Amicable's future. One way or the other, Butcher is about to go down."

"Roger that," Leona said and put on her sunglasses.

Linda started laughing as they drove away.

Chapter 23.

Butcher was up bright and early on Monday morning.

At 6:15, he opened the door of his rental house to find a letter in his mailbox. Because no one outside of Amicable knew that he was here, he found it strange, and when he pulled the note from the box, it was even more curious that there was no postage stamp and no return address. The front of the envelope simply said 'Bucher'.

Walking down his front path, he opened the envelope ripping it with his finger.

Three sentences.

```
You don't belong here.
The woman you are medeling with is a black widow
- she will eat you alive if you keep going.
It would be good for your helth to move along.
```

Angrily, he folded the note back into shape and inserted it into the ripped envelope. Stuffing it in his pocket, he realized he needed to see Rhonda.

A short while later, he opened the door to the Choke. Rhonda was on the other side of the restaurant serving coffee to some early morning farmers. As Butcher walked across the restaurant, Rodrigo hailed him, but he ignored it.

Pulling up behind Rhonda, he spoke. "Do you have a minute to talk?"

Rhonda stood rigidly. "I'm working, Butcher."

"We need to talk."

She moved away from him, but the restaurant quieted as all eyes followed the two tall people. "It's not the right time, Butcher." She smiled fakely at David Kellogg who was holding out his coffee cup to her.

"I understand that." As he turned, all eyes seemed to skitter away like disturbed cockroaches. Suddenly, the diners were strangely absorbed with whatever was in front of them, a fork, a watch, even the ceiling. Striding back across The Traveler's Choice, avoiding both tables and humans, he made his way to the front door. Seconds after he shut it behind him, he heard the door tinkle open. It was Rhonda.

"You got one too, didn't you?"

"A letter? Yes."

"My mother found it in the letter box this morning, and needless to say she was quite upset." Rhonda's hand went to her mouth and tears formed in her eyes. Butcher wished that he could go to her, but he knew that the townspeople had control over this relationship. He did move closer, though.

"What does yours say?" Butcher asked.

She reached into her pocket. "I was going to stop by the butchery this afternoon after work." He opened it.

```
Connie,
I'm sorry to have to be the one to tell you this,
but your daughter is a hore. Yesterday afternoon,
I  encountered  her  with  that  new  bucher  and
needless  to  say,  her  activities  seem  to  be  less
than  pure.  I  suggest  that  you  have  a  talk  with
her about her sinfulness.
Sinserly,
A Concerned Sitisen.
```

"Shit."

Rhonda nodded and the tears traced down her cheeks. She looked through the windows back into the restaurant and saw that most of the patrons were staring at them. Grinding her teeth, Rhonda turned back to Butcher. "My mother started ranting and raving about how this affected her standing in the community. This made me angry and I said a few things that I shouldn't have, and before push came to shove, she was talking about 'whoring about like a common prostitute.'

228

"What did you tell her?" Butcher asked.

"I told her not to believe everything she reads." Rhonda wiped her eyes and Butcher noticed that her cheeks were already red and blotchy. "Damn it, Butcher. Why can't everybody mind their own business? Why?"

"Because people need to look at other people's problems to take the focus off themselves, that's why."

Butcher pulled his own letter from his back pocket and handed it to her.

Tears began in earnest and as she covered her mouth, a cry escaped her lips. "The bastards," she whispered. "What right do they have?"

"What does it mean?" He asked quietly.

Rhonda looked up at the sky pleading with God to change either the past or the present so that the future would turn out differently than what she was already expecting.

"Please, Leo, please give me a little time." Her eyes landed on the words *black widow* before she ripped the page in half and handed it back to him. Pulling her apron up to her eyes, she wiped them and then turned back towards the restaurant.

"Do you want to get something to eat tonight?" Butcher asked.

She shook her head. "No, not tonight. I'll stop by to see you this afternoon after I get off, okay?" Her voice was still trembling.

Butcher didn't respond as Rhonda opened the door and reentered. What a great way to start a day.

Twenty minutes later, Butcher stood outside the butchery and knocked on the door. Both Nash and Derek were inside preparing their stations, the display case was shining and emblazoned with the day's specials in neon on the glass. Butcher knocked on the door and Nash came from behind the counter with a smile to open the door. The bell rang as Butcher entered.

"Good morning, Butc..." Nash's greeting was cut short. "Hey, what's the matter?"

Butcher didn't answer but climbed the stairs and made his way behind the counter to the meat cutting area. After putting on his apron, he grabbed a knife and looked for the first side of beef to dissect. Nash looked at his brother whose eyes widened.

Following Butcher to the rear, Nash watched silently as the vein in Butcher's neck jumped. He plopped a quarter of beef onto the table sending a great crash echoing into the silence of the butchery. Nash cleared his throat.

Butcher did not look up. He made quick work of sinew and bone, sawing and slicing. Dismantling the beef into different cuts, he threw them to the side to be wrapped.

"Hey, Butcher," Nash said, "It's already dead. You don't need to murder it anymore." Butcher's jaw twitched, and even though he heard Nash, he didn't stop. "Okay, Butcher, if you want to be quiet, that's your business, but we're here for you." Turning around, the young man went back to the front of the shop and finished prepping for the day. When the clock clicked 8:00, there were already people waiting outside for the locker to open. It was a Monday, of course, and many citizens were out early, but not usually this many. Of course, Nash knew that many of the Amicableans were here to see the new butcher, but he was willing to take advantage of the foot traffic.

"Welcome, everyone!" He shouted joyfully. "Come on in! Buy everything - put our new butcher to the test. He's the fastest knife in the Midwest."

As Nash turned to look back at Butcher, he saw that he was already through his second quarter of beef, loins, ribs and shoulders all partitioned and put onto piles. Derek was standing beside him attempting to keep up with the wrapping, but was losing the battle and smiling about it.

One of the first people through was Penny Reynolds. She found herself staring over the display cases toward the hard-working butcher dressed in his white shirt, white apron (now smeared with gore) and blue jeans. Butcher wiped the sweat from his brow and turned to heft another side of beef onto the table.

"Good morning, Butcher," Penny called over the cases, leaning one elbow on the top. "Do you think I might have a word with you?" She looked at Nash. "Would that be okay?"

Nash shrugged. "Fine with me. My guess is that he has already almost surpassed his quota for the day." Then, Nash leaned forward and whispered. "He's not in a great mood today, so be careful." Penny nodded conspiratorially and crossed her heart.

"Butcher," Nash yelled, "Mrs. Reynolds would like a word with you."

Sighing heavily, Butcher leaned on the table in front of him. Then, after a moment, he wiped his hands again on the front of the apron and moved towards Penny.

"What can I do for you, Mrs. Reynolds?"

"Is there somewhere we could talk?"

"Not really."

"How about at that table over there?" She pointed to the nook where George and he had conversed.

Butcher shrugged and ground his teeth. He really wasn't in the mood for this; already he could sense that Penny Reynolds was in need of relationship advice, and in the current state of his own relationship, he wasn't sure that he wanted to help her. Nodding once, he followed her to the table where she took the chair farthest into the window while Butcher sat across from her. Folding her hands primly on the table in front, Penny sat up and leaned in. Her carefully permed hair framed her face well. Penny cleared her throat and looked around.

"I have some questions."

"I can't hear you," Butcher said.

Embarrassedly, she peered at the other customers, but Butcher sensed that she desired a privacy that the butchery could not provide.

Butcher spoke over his shoulder. "Derek, can you turn the radio up please?"

Derek nodded and turned up the music. "Is that better?" Butcher asked.

"Yes, thank you." Penny cleared her throat again. "As I was saying, I have a few questions about what you did for Naida and James."

"I didn't do anything."

Penny smiled and nodded, but disagreed in a very agreeable way. A nice way. "That's not what Naida told me. She said that you talked to her and gave her some... advice."

Butcher spread his hands. "Okay," he said slowly. "Is that what you want?"

"Yes, please."

"What seems to be the problem?" Butcher already knew the problem, but he wanted Penny to say it. "I... I... don't know what to do with my husband. He doesn't really seem to acknowledge my existence."

Butcher leaned forward. "Easy, throw the TV out the window and wear something revealing. It works every time." He stood up as if ending the conversation.

"But... but... that doesn't solve any of the problems. I can't just get rid of the TV and I don't really..." she made a signal at her body, as if to say, 'I don't really have the body for lingerie.'

Butcher looked at the woman sitting down in front of him, and for the first time for that day, his compassion kicked him in the guts. Penny's eyes pleaded with him. So desperate was she for the same kind of 'magical healing' that Naida had received, she had been willing to sit in an open space with a butcher and open her soul.

"I'm sorry, Penny. I've been rude. I've had a rough morning." He sat back down. "Look, I know things seem difficult with your husband, what's his name?"

"Tony."

"You're at the stage of life where you're on the cusp of menopause, but you haven't yet realized that Tony is on the edge of man-o-pause. In his mind, he is still a twenty-year-old young man. Every woman wants him, he thinks, and he has his choice of any woman in the world. If he never looked in the mirror, he would still feel that way about himself. But, now Tony sees himself and he thinks, *Good Lord, I'm a fifty-four-year-old man whose pants don't fit anymore. My six-pack is down to one large pack of fat, and I'm bored with life. And the worst part of it is that my wife doesn't find me attractive anymore.* He's right. You don't find him attractive."

"Of course I do," Penny responded looking away.

"You can try to lie about this, but it won't help." Penny nodded. "You don't find his appearance attractive because you don't find his personality attractive. To you, he seems like a lazy, lounge chair filler who does nothing. You complain about him to your friends which, by the way, doesn't do you any good, because they say the same things about their husbands."

"But…"

"Please don't interrupt, Mrs. Reynolds, because you asked for my advice and I'm giving it to you." She was taken aback by his audacity, but at the same time appreciative of it. "Both of you think you can 'go back to the way it was' but you both haven't stopped to think how much better 'the way it could be' could be. Have you personally thought about these wonderful years coming up? What happens when he retires? What happens when you have grandkids? What happens when you are married for forty years?"

"I haven't thought that far ahead."

"Well, you should start now, because the future really is a great place. Now, I know that you and Tony have had difficulties in the past - Tony's eyes have strayed, perhaps his heart at one point or another." Penny's eyes widened.

"How did you know that?"

"It doesn't matter, Mrs. Reynolds, but from this day forward, everything can change."

"How?"

Butcher ran his hand through his hair, leaned in to her and looked around before lowering his voice. "My suggestion is that the minute you get home today, change the furniture around. Move the TV to a different room, a smaller room. My guess is that you've never changed the furniture before, so this will be a signal to him." Penny's mouth dropped open, but then snapped back shut. "Cook his favorite meal and then, as he walks through the door, smile and tell him how much you love him. When he says, 'All right, what's going on?' - and he will - you say, 'I think we're ready for a change in life.'"

"Then what?" Penny's smile was growing.

"Then, approach him, pull his head toward you and give him the biggest kiss you've given him in years. It doesn't matter that he smells like diesel, or that his clothes are dirty. Take his hands and…" Butcher's voice went even quieter, "put them on your body."

Penny blushed an intense shade of red. "We haven't done…"

"I know. It's been a long time. Years."

Penny gasped. "I… How…? Are you…?"

For the first time of the day, Butcher smiled and laughed, the letter in his pocket forgotten. "I have a gift, Mrs. Reynolds."

"I'll say." If Penny had a fan, she would have been furiously waving it in front of her face. "And what do we do after…? You know." She waggled her eyebrows and blushed again.

"You eat your dinner then take him to the living room and you plan a vacation for the two of you, somewhere exotic."

"Ooh, I know just the place. We went there…"

Butcher interrupted. "Branson, Missouri is not an exotic place, Mrs. Reynolds."

"Holy crap, you're a mind reader!"

"No, Penny, I'm not. Just very aware of human nature."

"So where should we go then, Butcher?"

"Tony doesn't fly, so driving it is. I would suggest, at this time of year, or even next month, something like New Orleans. Neither of you have been there before."

Penny's jaw dropped by his ability, but she steadied herself making mental notes of all the things that Butcher was saying. "Anything else?"

"The most important thing, Mrs. Reynolds, is to continue to speak to and about your husband in a positive manner. Words change people and situations. If you want a future, you have to change your words."

Penny leaned forward and pushed her hand halfway across the table. "Thank you so much, Butcher. I really appreciate it."

"He will appreciate it, too. But, you're welcome."

Penny looked at the clock above Butcher's head. Already, half an hour had passed and a few of the patrons had left and others had come in, but a few others were waiting by the side. Penny stood up and shook Butcher's hand and then went to the counter to buy her meat for the week.

Butcher turned back to the counter, but three people were staring at him: Farmer Joe Bartman, Shania Zellner, who was the bartender from the bowling alley, and Louise Nelson, Amicable's police officer.

"What can I do for you all?"

The three looked back and forth between each other, but Louise spoke first. "I have a few questions I'd like to ask you."

"Is there something wrong, officer?"

"No, no," Louise said holding up her hands. "These are of a... personal... nature."

Butcher looked over the heads of the three people who were all looking down at the same time. Nash was smiling behind them giving Butcher a thumbs up.

They were all here because of his gift.

Tony Reynolds yawned as he approached the stairs of his house. His hands smelled of diesel and his clothes were grimy. All that he wanted to do was grab a beer and plop down in front of the TV.

As he opened the door, multiple sensory opportunities assailed him. Firstly, the smell from the kitchen was incredible; secondly, his recliner was not in its place; thirdly, the stereo was playing their favorite music from the 1970s and lastly, his wife was standing almost entirely naked except for an apron that said, 'Take it or leave it.'"

235

Tony shut the door hastily behind him, but his eyes remained on Penny. "All right, what's going on here?"

Penny smiled knowingly. "I think we're ready for a change in life."

She approached him and kissed him deeply, then she put his hands on her.

Tony hadn't forgotten what to do next.

Chapter 24.

At 3:37, the mid-afternoon sun was streaming just beyond the awning of Peterson's butchery. Pedestrians had wandered past the store all day, and as Derek and Nash were beginning to think about closing up for the afternoon (still an hour and twenty-three minutes until closing time), they were amazed at the amount of business that had come through the shop. More than one hundred customers had pushed money over the counter and into the till. A dozen of them had come just to talk to Butcher. Nash wasn't quite ready to text his father about what was happening in the shop, but he was pretty sure that his dad would be pleased with the business even if it was a little... unorthodox. Because Butcher could work so quickly, he could move out when someone wanted to 'ask a few questions.'

Because the day had flown by, the twins were singing to the music. Sometimes the shop seemed like a treadmill, but not today. Nash had an idea for the next day, though he hadn't shared it with Butcher. He was sure that Butcher wouldn't care.

Or, kind of sure.

At 3:38, another figure darkened the threshold, opened the door and sent the bell ringing. It was Rhonda Redman and it didn't appear as if she had had the same kind of easy day that Peterson Butchery had enjoyed.

"Hello, Rhonda," Nash said. "What can we do for you?"

"Is Butcher here?"

He nodded. "Next one here, Butcher," he yelled over his shoulder.

"What does that mean?" Rhonda asked.

Nash smiled and turned away from her. "I would guess that Butcher will tell you everything."

Seconds later, a smiling Butcher rounded the corner of the back room. His apron still speckled with gore. It seemed to be a suit of honor.

When his eyes met Rhonda's, his smile fell a little bit, but not because he wasn't glad to see her.

"Hi."

"How are you?" She asked.

"I'm okay. How about you?"

"Fine." Butcher could tell she was anything but fine. "Can we go somewhere else to talk? Maybe for a walk or something. I know it's still your work time, but..." The question lingered in the air for a moment.

Nash lifted a hand to her. "That's great, Rhonda. Get him out of here. He hasn't done much work today. We'll expect more from him tomorrow."

"Thanks boss."

A couple of minutes later, sans apron but with freshly washed hands, Butcher reappeared and lifted the counter to let himself out. Following Rhonda down the stairs and out the door, they walked past the last customers who, after seeing Butcher leave, had second thoughts about stepping into the store and turned around.

"What was Nash talking about in there?"

Butcher put his hands in his pockets and shrugged. "It's been an odd day to say the least." Relating the events, the counselling sessions with at least a dozen citizens including the town police officer, the mailman and a retired farmer, not to mention Shania's revelation which was not surprising and needed to be processed later, Butcher talked for fifteen straight minutes which was almost a record. As they walked, Butcher continued to share about helping the people of Amicable. Never before had his gift been used in this way, but he liked it. He only wished he could share it with Rhonda.

"Wow," she said half-heartedly. "It sounds like you had a great day."

"What happened with yours?"

"After you left, the Fearsome Foursome – for some reason, Penny Reynolds left early - feigned caring for me. Linda Harmsen even touched me on the arm, *oh you poor dear*, she said so condescendingly. I wanted to smack the smile from her face."

"I'm sorry."

"Then, at the end of the day, the owner of The Traveler's Choice, Dean Taylor, sits down at the back table and beckons for me to come over, which of course, I do. After I sit down, he says, 'I just want you to know, Rhonda," she mimicked his voice, "that I think you do a great job here, but I've heard some rumors about impropriety and I can't have that kind of negative publicity. As if the Choke has any positive publicity other than Rodrigo's cooking. But it was like this veiled threat, that somehow my personal life has anything to do with my professional."

"What are you going to do?"

"I don't know. That kind of stuff makes me want to quit, but where else am I going to get a job in Amicable? The elevator?" She laughed derisively.

"Why do you have to stay in Amicable?" He asked quietly.

Rhonda's face fell. "I don't think you fully understand my mother."

"Tell me about her." From reading Rhonda, he had a background of her mother already, but because he hadn't really met her, he wasn't quite sure.

"My mother is... needy." Rhonda kicked at a pebble on the ground, which rolled ten feet in front of them. As they came upon the same pebble again, she was keenly aware that she was about to kick the same stone. Without totally understanding why, Rhonda felt like the pebble. Whenever she got settled, someone would kick her. "She's not really that old, but she acts like it; she's not an invalid, nor does she have a physical disease. She's just... I really don't know how to put it. She's just completely consumed with the idea of guilt, which she places on me. Nothing is ever about gratitude or complimenting. When I was in high school playing basketball, we'd win the game, but she'd find some statistic to complain about - and it didn't even need to be about me, it could have been the coach of the other team, or a referee, or a teammate. Gradually, I learned to dislike basketball because my mother made me dislike the game and other people. When I decided I was going to attend college, she told me how smart I was, but probably not smart enough. It was a better idea to stick around Amicable - the safe thing. Then, when I got the job at the Choke, she was pleased because the money I would be bringing in would support both of us. But always, and I mean always, she makes it known that if I got a real job, we could move out of the house and into something bigger. But the true irony is, she doesn't want to move out of our house - she never leaves it. She spends every day, except for the occasional Sunday, indoors, doing God knows what and complaining about God knows everything. I'm just so sick of it." She kicked the pebble into the street and frustratedly threw her hands in the air.

Butcher remained silent knowing that anything he said right now would add annoyance to her. As they walked, without thinking, he sidled closer to her and slid his left hand into her right. The touch, unexpected and intimate, gentle, exactly what Rhonda needed in that moment, surprised her. Without thinking she grasped his hand as if it was a life preserver and pulled herself close to his side. In this, the earliest part of the relationship, they experienced true connection by the intertwining of hands. In some ways, holding hands was more intimate than a kiss.

Their steps slowed and Butcher could feel her shoulders shake slightly as she began to cry. All the years of frustration were being pulled from her by the strength of Butcher's hand. When they reached Fourth Avenue, they stopped at the corner of the school's playground and sat down on a park bench. Butcher's silence allowed Rhonda to work through her emotions rather than focusing on his words. She wiped the tears from her face and smiled at Butcher who was looking out over the empty playground on that Monday afternoon. The children had left over an hour ago, but for some reason, the echoes of their shouting and laughter still remained. The innocence of the playground, mixed with their wistful need for something different, almost brought Butcher to tears. He remembered the last time he wept.

It had not been a pretty sight.

On that horrific day, Butcher had returned from work, his hands and clothes still smelling of meat. After unlocking the door, he sensed that something was wrong. At twenty-four years of age Leopold Jensen knew that he wanted to live apart from his mother, but as she was incapable of looking after herself, it was incumbent upon him to provide for her as she had provided for him all of his early years.

"Hello, Mom?" His voice echoed through the small house. As he stepped through the doorway, he noticed that things were not in their normal places. In fact, it looked as if someone had raced through the house and adjusted everything, as if an earthquake had sent a seismic shock through their domicile. Picture frames were askew, furniture tilted, the coffee table upended, and the magazines and books were strewn across the floor. The television was on, muted, but the screen was facing towards the right. All the videos were pushed off the shelf and onto the floor. Worried, he called out again.

"Mom?"

At this point, he could hear water running. Dropping his keys on the counter, he walked down the hallway, and the sight that greeted him would haunt him for the rest of his life. As he turned into the bathroom, his mother was lying over the edge of the tub. The water was still running from the shower head, and her naked body was limp. Heart wedged deeply into his throat, Leo moved quickly to her side and pulled her head and body up from the edge of the tub. The water from the shower washed over him, but he didn't notice anything except the shade of purple that his mother's face had turned from the pooled blood. Her eyes were open, but the right side of her face sagged and Butcher immediately knew that his mother had suffered a stroke. Suddenly, she gasped and with intense fear, her left eye moved slightly towards Butcher.

"Mom! Mom! You're going to be okay!" Unfortunately, Butcher knew that he was lying to himself.

Lenore moaned and attempted to speak, but as her breaths came in gasps, Butcher knew that she was suffocating.

"Oh, Mom, I'm so sorry." His mother, her left hand, spasming, now grasping his arm, attempted to speak, but only a gurgle issued from her mouth: the death rattle. Within moments, he knew that Lenore Jensen had left her mortal body for somewhere hopefully very different and better. Unfortunately, Butcher was left behind holding his naked and contorted mother in a house that had been theirs for only five months. Falling back into the tub, water pouring over them, Butcher's tears flowed mixing with the drenching shower from above. All the memories of his mother and her care over the years poured over him, a baptism of pain and loss. His grief,

vocalized above the sound of the water, was horrific. Butcher wasn't sure how long he laid entombed in the bathtub with his mother, but when he finally pulled himself up, he turned off the water and covered her with a large bath towel. As if moving through molasses, he slowly walked to the TV and turned it off. The house, silent as a morgue, enveloped him in confusion. For some reason, it had seemed important to him to turn off the TV before calling the ambulance, but later, when the police interviewed him, he couldn't remember why he had done that.

Weeks later, the two reports, the coroner's and the police, were similar but with very different details. It was apparent to the coroner, even without seeing the scene of death, that Lenore Jensen had died of a massive stroke. But the police, noticing the disarray of the house, had another answer for what had happened. When they spoke to Butcher, they gave him the full details of the coroner's thoughts.

"She did die of a stroke, Mr. Jensen, but there were some extenuating circumstances." The police officer cleared his throat. "I'm sorry to tell you, Mr. Jensen, but your mother's stroke was brought on by a mixture of drugs."

"What?"

"She died of a drug overdose."

"That's impossible. My mother didn't take drugs."

"I know this is hard for you, Mr. Jensen, but even the condition of the house..." The officer's voice trailed off.

"So, she was hiding drugs in the house and forgot where she put them?" Butcher could read the police officer and what he saw made him furious. The officer, perpetually numb to the realities of the contemporary illegal pharmaceutical world, was looking at Butcher with anything but compassion, almost accusation. "So you think I'm faking this reaction? Is that what you're doing?"

"Mr. Jensen, I realize this is hard, but if you'd please take a deep breath." The officer held up his hands.

"Wow, condescension, nice work officer..." he read his name tag, "Collins. Is that your normal MO? I bet that works well at home for you."

"Okay, Mr. Jensen, you're going to have to..."

"Like your job a little too much? Maybe been neglecting the wife and kids at home," Butcher smiled malevolently, "couple of brats, huh?"

The officer's jaw constricted, his muscles jumping. "You're walking very close to the edge, Mr. Jensen."

Butcher couldn't help himself. The rage of his mother's death coursed through his veins, his anger flooding him with adrenaline. "It's too bad that your wife is cheating on you. That's what happens when you avoid your domestic responsibilities."

Officer Collins, now himself enraged, moved from the room towards the front door, but Butcher did not let him leave. The police officer was the metaphorical punching bag that he needed at that moment, and as the policeman passed him, he pulled on his shoulder. "Better get home…"

In that moment, both men knew that a distinct line of propriety had been crossed. Butcher should not have touched the policeman. The policeman, goaded into a fierce anger, projected his domestic issues onto the young man. Before he knew it, Butcher had been thrown to the floor and Officer Collins was pulling his hands behind his back to be put into cuffs.

An hour later, as he was being processed at the city jail, Butcher was perfectly aware of why he reacted the way that he did. The question he had asked himself for years: Why can't I read you, Mother? *resonated within the walls of his mind, but the answer could only be hypothesized. After his incarceration, a thick layer of guilt lay heavily on him. If only he would have had the ability to read his mother, he could have seen that she was a drug addict. Why didn't she display any addictive tendencies? How could he have missed it? Why had his gift, when he needed it most, abandoned him?*

Butcher, thrust back into the present, looked at the beautiful woman sitting next to him.

Rhonda rubbed her thumb across his as they held hands. "I'm feeling better now. Thank you, Butcher."

"You're welcome."

"Can you walk me home?" There was a pleading look in her eyes combined with a fear that if, and when, Butcher encountered her mother (and he read her), he would have an easy decision on whether or not to stay.

He swallowed and nodded. As they pulled themselves from the bench, they were unaware of a pair of eyes that watched them from the other side of the playground. These eyes, though, were bereft of compassion. Leslie Tielman was disgusted that the tawdry couple was openly displaying their sin.

This could end in no other way than their ultimate ejection from the Garden of Eden.

Chapter 25.

John Deakins sat in his armchair staring through the bay window into the street. As the workday wound down, many Amicableans were either walking or driving past his house. At various times, Deakins was happy that his house was on a main thoroughfare so that he could keep an eye on the town, but sometimes he wished that he lived out in the middle of the country surrounded by nothing more than cornfields and grasshoppers. To sit on the porch, western wind whispering across the deck, the scent of growing things sitting on the breeze - this would have been a dream. He loved his job and almost all that it entailed and he did it with joy.

But in the last week, his thoughts were evolving. For the first time, he stared at the walls surrounding him and recognized them as barriers to a fuller life; they were oddly empty even though filled with visions of his past. Now, it seemed that he desired something else to fill the space, noise and laughter, a smile (or even a frown). Just some assortment of life that would overcome his newly recognized feeling that he was almost assuredly going to be alone for the rest of his life. His parents had warned him about this when he first accepted the call to ministry, but while young, he assumed that he would find people who would look past his profession and enjoy time with him. This was true, in some ways, but his interaction with them was mostly superficial and one-sided. Deakins was called upon to listen to the ills of their worlds, but there was not one person with whom he was willing to share his own opinions.

That is, until this weekend.

When Leslie Tielman kissed him, his entire world had exploded. Nothing could have prepared him for the emotions, and now that he sat in his parsonage, on a Monday morning, he could not stop thinking about her.

Incredibly, just as he was thinking this, Leslie's form appeared at the end of his sidewalk. She was dressed in blue jeans and a t-shirt, but now, he realized something he missed before: there was something sensual about the normalcy of her appearance. Deakins wasn't sure why his consciousness was piqued, perhaps it had to do with the strangeness, or even taboo-ness, of the situation. Leslie checked both directions before turning onto the sidewalk and then primly and tightly, walked up the steps to his door. Wanting to meet her quickly, Deakins groaned and pulled himself upwards (on the second attempt he succeeded). Walking across the room, he saw her reach out for the doorbell, and just as she rang, he opened the door.

He smiled broadly. "Leslie."

"May I come in?" she asked properly.

"Of course, of course," he responded standing aside. Leslie did not look at him as she entered, but Deakins checked both directions outside before closing the door behind her.

Leslie had moved into the living room where she stood with her back to him. Deakins seemed not to be able to control his eyes and his gaze lingered over her slim form as he moved closer towards her. As if sensing the weight of his eyes, she shivered and turned. Unsmiling, she closed herself off to him.

"Reverend Deakins, I have some information for you that I think will come in handy."

"Please, Leslie, come in and have a seat." He motioned to the sofa where she sat on the left edge tucked into the corner. He took the opposite side and they turned towards each other. "What is it?"

"Two things," Leslie responded folding her hands in her lap. "Well, actually three."

He laughed. "You've been busy."

A frown. "I'm only doing what you asked us to do." He motioned for her to go on. "This morning, around 8:00, people started entering the butcher's shop." Deakins raised his eyebrows. "But they weren't buying meat."

"What were they doing?"

"You're not going to believe this, John, but they were going in there for help."

"What kind of help?"

"The psychological kind. That butcher must think he's some kind of amateur counsellor. People kept coming - first it was Penny Reynold's, then…"

"Wait a minute," Deakins said. "He was doing this in the shop?"

"Right at the table in the front window, and they were lined up behind him just waiting."

"But that's insane. What could a butcher possibly know about the inner workings of mankind? He cuts up meat, for God's sake." For a moment, Deakins' memory hiccupped back to his own interaction with the butcher. He erased the thought quickly from his mind.

"I guess he is directing the psychological saw also." For a millisecond, Leslie's gaze dropped to the reverend's throat. It was obvious that he hadn't shaved that morning as his four o'clock shadow was dark. She liked a rugged man.

Deakins caught the glance, and unconsciously dropped his own eyes to her slender and smooth throat, but his gaze lingered a brief instant longer, and he wondered what it would be like to run his fingers over the nape of her neck, to press his lips to the quickening pulse.

"Reverend Deakins," Leslie interrupted his thoughts. "Did you hear what I said?"

"I'm sorry, Leslie, what was that?"

She swallowed and her hand touched her face and moved down her neck; his eyes followed her slender fingers as they seemed to move in a slow, tantalizing slide.

"I was mentioning that I saw them together this afternoon, near the park. She had been crying."

Deakins cleared his throat and shook his head, attempting to focus. "Which park, Winslow?"

Shaking her head, Leslie's hand finished its path down her throat and moved down her chest to her heart. Deakins was aware that this

247

stopping point was inappropriate for his eyes to alight, but his libido was doing calisthenics.

"No, Reverend, the playground at the school. On the north side, you know where that park bench is overlooking the jungle gym?"

"Mmmm."

"They were holding hands and then she leaned into him. I think she was putting her breasts on his arm." Leslie's cheeks flushed, and something deep inside her stirred at the thought of a woman snuggling in to a man and placing her breasts, whether consciously or otherwise, on his arm. For a moment, Leslie thought about that very thing. More blood infused her face.

"Can you show me how they were sitting.... I just want to get an understanding to see if it was... appropriate." Deakins was straying far into unchartered territory with Leslie, but this feeling inside of him was like a snowball rolling downhill.

Leslie's eyes latched on to his. "Only if you think it will help determine if their behavior was sinful or not." Slowly moving across the sofa, Leslie moved her hips next to Deakins' and then incredibly slowly, she reached her hand out to intertwine it with his. "They were sitting like this." Her words came out quickly, but the electricity filling the room seemed to alter the sound, as if the air was charged with electrons waiting to zap. Fingers intertwined, Deakins could feel a pressure inside his chest; his heart was beating hard - very hard.

His voice, husky with desire, broke the silence. "So, then what did she do next?"

Leslie's eyes ceased to question. She trusted the reverend with every ounce of her being, and because she'd already told him how she felt, this seemed like a natural progression even if there was a chance of sinfulness. "She... she... pressed her..." she didn't want to say the word *breasts* as if somehow it was a dirty word, and it probably was for her, but there was something so pure about what they were doing. Pressing her small breasts into his arm, she heard him gasp.

"Anything else?" Deakins could not tear his gaze away from the woman.

"I think she took her right hand and… and… did this." Leslie's hand moved across the sofa and touched Deakins' left knee and began to move up his thigh. He groaned.

"Leslie…"

"Yes, John?" Her voice was thick as if speaking through a dense blanket.

"We… we… shouldn't…"

Leslie's hand went farther. "What shouldn't we do?" She whispered.

John Thomas Deakins could control himself no longer. Turning to Leslie Tielman, he brought her face to his with his right hand and kissed her deeply. Still holding hands, the two kissed passionately, drinking of a love that had been denied them by both culture and their own understanding of sinfulness. For what seemed a lifetime, they embraced, but then breathlessly broke apart.

"What is it?" Deakins asked.

"I've wanted to do that for so long." Leslie's face, inches away from John's, radiated heat.

"How long?"

"For a few years at least." Leslie moved back in to kiss him again, and after a few more stolen moments, they separated. Deakins eyes fell on her neck again. He wanted to kiss the small concave place just above her left shoulder. It was her turn to moan, and with intensity, their hands began to move to other places, long unexplored places. As if discovering a previously unconquered world and planting their individual flags claiming territory for themselves, they broke apart both wanting to take a next step.

But it was a very long, precipitous step.

"Leslie…"

"Yes?"

"Do you think this is wrong?"

Leslie's face dropped slightly. "What do you mean? What's wrong about it?"

Deakins pulled back from her. "I feel like I'm breaking one of the Commandments."

At the word Commandments the clock struck midnight. "Which one?" She said coolly pushing back from him and letting go of his hand.

"Adultery."

"John, John, John," she whispered. "I wish you could see your religion through the spectacles of something bigger."

"But... we were just play acting what the butcher and Rhonda were doing, and that..."

"Is that what we were doing?" Leslie's eyes flashed angrily. "Play acting? I..." She put a hand to her mouth and her lips began to tremble.

"Oh, I've made such a mess out of this. But I have to think about the congregation. If they knew that I was dallying..."

"John Thomas Deakins, how dare you! Do you think I came over here to seduce you? What, do you imagine me, some kind of 21st century Eve enticed by the serpent? Is my fruit too much for you? Good God, John, do you think God hates us so much that he doesn't actually want us to love each other, only him?"

"That's not what I meant, Leslie. I really enjoyed it."

Leslie pulled back to the other side of the sofa. "Wow, John, I feel so much better that you enjoyed kissing me when you're thinking about how inappropriate it was."

"Please, Leslie, I... I... You have to understand."

"No, you got it right the first time, Reverend Deakins - I... I... it's all about you." She pulled herself up from the sofa. Leslie wasn't sure of her own feelings, whether she was jealous of Rhonda and the butcher, or if she really was furious with the befuddled and stammering pastor trying to pull himself up after her.

"I'm new at this, Leslie. I have to think about my standing in the community. I have to be a shepherd to these people, a pure man."

"Oh, good heavens, John! This congregation doesn't need a holy man, they need a good man. And you are one," she added plaintively. "You are the best. That's why I'm attracted to you. Don't you understand?" Her voice was wistful as if pleading for him to see the reality of the situation.

"What is there to see?"

"Oh, John, I'm crazy about you in spite of the fact that you love your religion more than you love people."

"What's that supposed to mean?" Deakins was now getting frustrated with her.

She crossed her arms as he stood in front of her. "Your first thought as we were expressing our affection for each other was to think that we were in some kind of adulterous tryst. And worse yet, that we were breaking one of the Ten Commandments."

"We were, weren't we?"

"Adultery? Have you even read the biblical definition of adultery? It's about married men and married women and even when Jesus talks about it, he cautions about lustful men lusting after women they can't have. In case I haven't made it clear enough, you can have me!"

"I don't think I need a sermon from you, Leslie."

"YES YOU DO!" The vein in Leslie's forehead jumped as she shouted at the pastor, something she would have never believed possible. "You just can't get it through your thick skull that the Commandments were about keeping relationships safe - between God and humans, and humans and themselves. The intent was not to curb love, but to encourage it in healthy ways. Good Lord, I can't believe I have to tell you this."

Deakins was quiet for a moment knowing deep inside of himself that this woman, this perfectly imperfect woman was perfect for him, but he couldn't figure out what to do.

"John," she said calmly and approached him putting a hand on his forearm. "Don't you remember in the beginning, God made male and female, partners for the journey together. That's what we can be."

"I don't know how to do that."

"Let me show you."

Deakins, like a dog with a chew toy, just couldn't let it go. "But the congregation. What will…"

Leslie stopped him. "I'm going to give you a onetime offer, Reverend John Thomas Deakins. I am willing to stall this relationship to do two things: One, if you really need to go through with this thing of ruining the butcher and his girlfriend, I will help you do it, although I can now see that what they are doing is the exact same thing that I want to do. It would be hypocritical to think otherwise."

"But he could destroy the community. What if his ability to tell the future is from a demon? I mean, he knew immediately about us."

"Then let him know! I want everyone to know, but only in your right time. I'm willing to wait for you."

"What's the second?"

"I want to take you out on a date."

"A date? But..."

She shushed him again. "Like I said, one time offer. You will take me to The Creek Restaurant in Clancy on Friday night – pick me up at 6:45."

"But what if there are people from Amicable there?"

Leslie looked down at her hand on his arm and then pulled it away. "What is the greater risk for you, John - to lose face in the congregation, or to lose me?"

With that, Leslie Tielman, a woman known for her dogged persistence, turned away from the deliberating clergyman and walked out the front door.

Chapter 26.

Butcher could tell that Rhonda was slowing down. She had never brought him to her home and he knew why; her mother was unstable and a true source of worry in her life. If Connie walked out in her bathrobe, or worse, in a fiercely embarrassing mood, Rhonda would regret it.

Deeply.

Turning on Fourth Avenue, Butcher and Rhonda both noticed the figure on the front porch. George Hendriks saw the two of them together and his eyes widened, but he held up his hand and smiled.

"Afternoon, Sir and Madam. How are we this fine day?"

Butcher turned to Rhonda who was still holding his hand and then pulled her towards the old man. "Doing well, George, and how about yourself?"

"Fine. How about you Rhonda?"

Rhonda could not lie to him. "It hasn't been a great day, George." She reached into her back pocket and withdrew the letter. "This was in the mailbox this morning - no signature, no return address."

"What does it say?"

She told him. George's jaw twitched with anger. "Some people in this community are just plain jackasses. It's none of their damn business." He rolled his neck. "For what it's worth, I think you two are great together."

Rhonda blushed and let go of Butcher's hand. Already it had felt natural, like two pieces of a puzzle that were made to fit together. "Thank you, George."

"Don't mention it, Rhodie. If I catch who wrote that letter, I'm going to pee in their cereal."

This elicited laughter from Rhonda and Butcher. "Butcher got a letter too."

George swore under his breath. "Well, I wish there was something that I could do, but there's not, so my best advice is just to enjoy the ride. Not everyone gets to experience what you two are. I did, and it was wonderful..." George's voice trailed off as his mind chased a memory.

A sound came from the house next door - Rhonda's. As the front door opened, a figure stepped out, a tall woman, not quite as tall as Rhonda, but similar in build. Although they shared a common genetic code, there was a wildness about this woman, a squeezed look around her eyes as if something was wringing her mind like a wet towel. This woman, Rhonda's mother, had a shock of brown hair standing on end, and her hazel eyes blazed underneath thick eyebrows. Her Roman nose, long and aquiline, seemed in line with what Rhonda had said about her personality - sharp and determined.

Connie wore a white summer dress with prints of flowers around the skirt and up one side. She was barefoot and she held a glass of wine in her hand.

"Rhonda. I'm glad you are home."

In that instant, Rhonda was glad that she had dropped Butcher's hand. There was no telling what her mother would have said if she would have seen their physical connection. "Hello, Mother."

"Who's your friend?"

"Hello, Connie," George called from his seated position. His voice was anything but amicable.

Connie ignored him and repeated the question. "Who's your friend?"

"This is Leo Jensen, you met him at church yesterday."

Connie's eyes narrowed like a hawk sensing her prey's movement from a soaring distance. Butcher read her and what he saw gave him pause, even alarm. Here was a woman who was not completely sane, but whole enough to do damage.

"How are you?" It was all that he could think of to say, not because he really wanted to know - he already knew. She was bent, like a crowbar. Crazy was not quite right. *Something else...*

254

Chapter 26.

"I've heard about you already, Mr. Butcher. Causing some grief in Amicable?"

"I don't think I'd put it in those terms, Mrs. Redman."

"Don't call me that!" She hissed. "I'm not a 'Mrs.' I'm not married!"

"Mother, how could he possibly know that?"

Connie's eyes narrowed as she moved slowly to the edge of her deck. "He knows, Rhonda. You can see it. He knows."

"I'm so sorry, Butcher," Rhonda said under her breath, "She's not…"

"I know, dear," Connie said alighting on the ground. "I'm such an embarrassment to you. But I'm just looking out for your best interests. There can't be anything good that comes from engaging with a man of his nature."

"Mother!"

"Or any man in general. Pigs! All of them! Pigs!" She made a grunting noise and pushed her nose up like a sow. Butcher took a step back.

"Oh, Butcher, you should go. I'm so sorry." Rhonda's face was aghast.

As Butcher turned to leave, Connie began to chase him in her bare feet, wine glass sloshing dangerously in one hand, alternating between pig noises and shouting misanthropic epithets at his quickly retreating form. Rhonda caught her mother at the end of George's sidewalk. Tears were flowing down her cheeks and her embarrassment was palpable. It had happened exactly as she had feared.

"How could you, Mother? This man is so completely different than any other that I've met. Why? Why?"

Connie turned to her daughter and her face lost its glazed fury – sanity returned, but it did not bring an apology. "I'm just trying to protect you from them - from him," she pointed into the distance at Butcher's head, which hung low as he walked away. "Don't you remember? Don't you know what they are like? All of them?"

Rhonda pulled away from her mother. "Not this one, Mom. Not this one. I won't be seeing much of him again, I think."

Connie's smile, more grimace than an expression of happiness, was destructive. "Well, that's good then, Sweetheart. Don't worry, I'll be here with you. I'll be here to protect you..."

"That's enough, Mother," Rhonda said as she rushed back to her porch, opened the door and slammed it behind her.

Connie, still standing by the fence between the households, looked up at George who, instead of backing down, frowned at her.

Slowly, Connie sneered at her neighbor and raised the middle finger on her right hand. "Have a great night, George."

George turned away.

Chapter 27.

Traditionally, on Monday evenings, five women would gather at Linda's house because she had the nicest home with the nicest kitchen and nicest things. But on this particular Monday, only three would turn up. There was no possible way they could have known that Leslie had seduced Reverend John Thomas Deakins, and in the process nearly caused him to almost lose his mind; nor could they have known that Penny Reynolds was safely ensconced on the other side of the sexual spectrum, bedding her husband for the first time in ages and quite happy about it.

Sitting around the kitchen table, not a husband in sight, the remaining three stirred the cauldron of gossip.

"Well, anything interesting happen today?" Linda asked.

Jeannie smiled. "You know, after the episode at The Traveler's Choice, Rhonda left work early, I think."

"Yes, what happened?"

Leona raised an eyebrow. "You saw it, girls. Someone wrote a letter. She took it out of her pocket." Looking back and forth between her friends, Leona smiled. "Which one of you did it? Come on, out with it."

"Not me," Linda said.

"Me either," Jeannie repeated.

"Well, I certainly didn't do it," Leona retorted. "But that leaves only two people. It was either Penny or Leslie, and if I'm going to guess, I'd say it was Leslie. She's been acting awfully strange lately. You don't think…"

"What? What don't we think?"

Leona leaned in closer and put her arms on the table. "You don't think she's messing around with the butcher, do you? Maybe she's got a thing for him and wants to throw Rhonda out of the picture."

Leaning back and chortling, Linda shook her head. "That's ridiculous. Leslie isn't that kind of woman. I'm not even sure if she has ever... been with a man before."

The other two gasped. "Really?"

Linda nodded. "I think she might be waiting for Mr. Right. I'm not sure he has an address in Amicable. And she'll never leave Amicable. Can you imagine *her* in the outside world? In a city?"

Leona folded her arms on her chest and shook her head. "Not at all."

"Well, if it wasn't Leslie..." Jeannie's eyes were shining.

"I'm not saying it wasn't Leslie," Linda responded, "but it wouldn't be for that reason."

"Then I guess it might be Penny."

They pondered that thought thread until Linda moved them in another direction. "It doesn't really matter who wrote the note as long as we are moving towards the goal of ridding the butcher from the town. This is exactly what Reverend Deakins wants, and I think he's correct. There is nothing good that can come from this kind of change."

Jeannie continued to grin, but the question surfaced before she could pull it back. "What kind of change is it that we're supposed to be objecting to?"

Linda rolled her eyes. "It isn't the *kind* of change that's the problem - *any* change is not necessarily good for Amicable; things need to be studied and talked about; we need a committee for change, like we have at church."

"But we haven't changed anything in years at church," Jeannie's forehead was bunched up, wrinkled at the thoughts that were coursing through her mind.

"Exactly," Linda said.

Jeannie wasn't *exactly* sure what Linda was being *exact* about, but they all were becoming more and more aware that change was the enemy of rightness - or righteousness. And if there wasn't a good reason for change, all the more reason to curl up with the traditions that had worked for generations.

258

"So, what are we going to do?"

Linda turned in her chair and reached up onto the kitchen bench for a notebook. "I've been brainstorming some ideas since our meeting with Reverend Deakins yesterday, and I think these are the best courses of action: Leona, I think it best if you make the rounds of the local businesses and speak the truth to them about the dangers of having someone come in and change the economics of the town. I know that the grocery store is already reeling from a loss in meat sales. That's due in large course to the new butcher's arrival."

"What do you want me to say?"

"If it were me…? I'd probably talk about how outside influences can seriously undermine the trustful interactions between businesses. If the grocery store needs to cut prices, that affects the farmers and the price of meat; and if the farmers are disenfranchised, they won't be happy. This might cause them to seek alternative arrangements for all sorts of trading; they might even stop eating at The Traveler's Choice!"

A gasp. "And if The Traveler's Choice closed up, where would we be able to get a good cup of coffee?"

Jeannie raised her hand. "What about at the cafe?"

Linda shook her head. "You're not getting the point here, Jeannie. Because the butcher is trying to change things, he's affecting the foundational businesses and people in town."

"But I still don't understand what he is trying to change."

"Leona, explain it to her." Linda crossed her arms and looked away.

Like a fish pulled from the water, Leona's mouth opened and closed. "It's… I suppose it's not just about changing things, it's just that he's from somewhere else and if he has certain ideas about what's good for this town like… like…." She looked at Linda.

"Like getting people to bowl together at the bowling alley on a Saturday night. You see? You see?" Linda raised a finger in the air to punctuate her point.

Jeannie whined. "I don't. I don't."

Leona figured it out. "If all the young kids are staying out bowling with all the old people, they may miss church on Sunday mornings, offerings could go down, morals would be in decline, families would break up - Armageddon! Armageddon! The fight is real!"

The excessively large jump to the particularly false conclusion was astounding, a leap past all imagination, but there was a thread of truth that stretched well. If they could bring this conclusion to reality and allow the townspeople to recognize that this change, or any change at all, could be detrimental to morals, economics, education or the country, the fight would be over before it began.

"Ah, I see," Jeannie said, but clearly it had gone at least three feet over her head.

"So, Leona, you're going to visit businesses, Jeannie you're going to the school to chat with the guidance counsellor to plant seeds of doubt in his mind which will bear fruit in his interactions with young people. As soon as we've cut this butcher off from his source of influence with young and old alike, he'll have nowhere to go but back where he came from."

"And you, Linda, what are you going to do?" Leslie asked.

"I've got a plan for something a little more radical."

"What is it?"

"You'll know when it happens."

"But..." Jeannie whined.

"I'm going to spin a web of misinformation that will catch the fly in mid-flight. And when I do," Linda said with a twinkle in her eye. "I'm going to suck the lifeblood out of him."

Butcher felt... off, queasy, as if he'd been dipped in some kind of oil. Despite all attempts to wipe it off, or walk it off, nothing helped. As they had walked to Rhonda's house, he had known what a meeting with Rhonda's mother might do to him. As he had heard Rhonda's description of Connie, he had steeled himself for the moment when they would interact, but nothing could have prepared him for Connie's display.

Connie's life had not been easy - even before the divorce. From the brief time he read her, Butcher noticed distinctive traits, quirks that were common to people in Connie's situation. Butcher was sure that Connie had come from a large family; she was probably one of the middle children. Butcher's best guess was that there were six children - five girls - and her brother who was the treasured one; this was a source of great frustration for all the girls, especially Connie. As they had grown up, her brother had mercilessly teased his sisters and then, to top it all off, had strutted around like some kind of modern-day Joseph without any color of dream coat.

Connie had tried to ingratiate herself with her brother, but he spurned all attempts. As the youngest child, he had the opportunity to learn from his sisters' mistakes, but he had also learned how to goad them. This, in turn, created five mother hens attempting to tame him. As it would happen, the Larson sisters all married men whom they could control. In Connie's case, it was a mirage. From the beginning, they both had treated each other abysmally, and unsurprisingly, the marriage had not lasted.

For the last fifteen or so years, Connie had been consumed by self-pity and self-loathing. She questioned herself at all times: what did I do wrong? What's wrong with me? How could he do this to me? And then, after her questioning, she grew angry. Her designated fury lashed out at anyone nearby. Unfortunately, Rhonda always took the brunt of her anger because Connie had alienated herself from all other friendships. Even Amicableans had difficulties in faking their niceness towards her; eventually they learned to shun the house next to George Hendriks' on Fourth Avenue. This isolation, tempered with her own feelings of inadequacy, left Connie in a constant sense of confusion and pain.

Connie's reaction to Butcher, though, was strange. Where did that come from? Was her misanthropy uncontrollable, or was she really teetering on the edge of insanity?

261

The last few blocks to Peppertree passed quickly, and as he approached the porch, he was not surprised to see someone sitting on his front stoop. Strangely, this seemed to be something Amicableans did all the time: show up at someone's house and wait for them. Butcher tried to remember if people dropped by in Colorado, but he was pretty sure if they did, the police would be called.

Except this time, the police didn't need to be called.

It was the police. She raised her hand.

"Hello, Butcher."

"Hello, Louise. Are you okay?"

"Yes," she said looking sideways, to the right, at the setting sun, which was beginning to lick the top of the trees in the west. "I just had a few more questions for you. I've been thinking about our conversation this morning - a lot, actually - and wondering if we could continue the conversation."

"Of course." Butcher was awkwardly standing in front of her.

"I want to learn how to do what you do."

Butcher raised an eyebrow.

"I know, it's probably not something that's easy to teach, but I think it would really come in handy for my line of work." She smirked. "Any leg up for a police officer is a good thing, right?"

Butcher waggled his head and pursed his lips. "I suppose, for a police officer it's a good thing, but for a human being - a wife, or sister or mother…" He let the sentence trail off.

"What's the difference?"

"Do you mind if I sit down?" Butcher asked, pointing to the space on his own front step next to Louise.

"Sorry," she said, "This is your house, I probably shouldn't be trespassing."

"I won't call the cops."

"Now, you were saying?"

"There are certain things that I am gifted with and certain things that I'm cursed with." He looked out over the front sidewalk and watched the world pass by, his thoughts of Rhonda and her mother put on hold for the moment. "I'm not sure how it came to me, but I have a sensory acuity that most people don't have; I also have a mind that can instantaneously put fragmentary pieces together. Bingo, a gift or a curse depending on perspective." She frowned, not quite understanding.

"Okay, I'll put it this way. It's a great thing for me to be able to see when people are telling the truth or lying. I think most people would say they'd like to have that ability. What happens, though, is that you never get to have the blessed feeling of ignorance. Thus, a curse."

"So," Louise put her hand out to interrupt him, "you're telling me that you are like a human polygraph - every truth or lie is revealed immediately to you. You don't need baseline questions, just...?"

He nodded. "I can see in people's skin different changes of moisture level, or the briefest quickening of pulse. Most people don't know what their eyes do when they lie, and they certainly can't control what their voice does."

Louise clapped her hands. "That's awesome."

"You would think so, but what happens when someone close to you is lying and you don't even know why?" His thoughts went immediately to Rhonda who, technically, was not lying to him, only attempting to conceal the past. Then, just as quickly, his memory jumped to his mother's sallow, stroke ravaged face. He shook his head.

"But think how helpful it would be for a police officer! People would never try to get away with anything."

Butcher looked down at his hands. "Yes, they still would. Humans have an innate need to push the boundaries to test how far they can step over the line. He pointed to her. "Which is why you will always have a job."

"Teach me, master," she egged him.

Silence ensued before Butcher spoke. "Louise, you have to understand something. If we do this, you're going to find out a lot about yourself and other people that won't be particularly positive."

"I know. I know." Louise was not sure of her Daniel Webster status, but she felt that she was not making a deal with the devil. "Show me."

Butcher's mouth twitched, he scratched his head and sighed deeply. "All right. Let's start with this. You're going to tell me a story about something that happened in your life, but you're going to change a few facts. It's up to you when and where that will happen, but I'll tell you when you are lying."

Louise smiled. "Do you need to be looking at me?"

"For the most part, but I could probably tell just by listening to your voice."

"Okay, here goes." Louise paused for a few seconds and then started. "In 1987..."

"You're lying."

She laughed. "But I haven't even started yet."

"Your voice betrayed you. You were going to start with a lie to test me. I could hear it. The year was wrong already."

"Holy shipwreck."

"Start again."

"In 1986..."

Butcher made a loud buzzer noise. "All right, now start with a truth."

Louise's eyes widened. "Okay... when I was about eight years old, maybe nine, I can't remember exactly, my family and I were traveling to South Dakota to visit Custer National Park and go to Mt. Rushmore. My dad, his name was..."

"Don't lie. It's too easy to pick up on names."

"Walt. His name was Walt. He drove our old station wagon..." she paused to see if Butcher would stop her, but he didn't. *Wow, he is amazing.* "...across the entire state. Just after the Badlands and before we reached Custer National Park, out of nowhere this deer jumped in front of the car and nailed us head on. Boom. It sounded like a cannon shot. We got out of the car and I still remember the radiator steaming and clicking and making this weird noise, and then I saw the deer lying on its side in the ditch. One of its antlers was broken and I thought 'oh, the poor thing.'"

Louise looked at Butcher whose eyes reflected the sorrow in the woman's story. "It's okay, Louise. It wasn't your fault."

"You didn't stop me at the lie."

"I didn't need to. This is a lie you tell yourself all the time - so often, that it might have become true in your own head."

Louise's pupils dilated. "What do you mean?"

Butcher took a deep breath and sighed. "My guess is you were distracting your dad while he was driving - singing, maybe - and as he looked in the rearview mirror at his precious daughter, the greatest treasure on earth, he didn't see the stop sign and certainly not the motorcyclist that was rushing at the crossroads. It was too late, your father hit the brakes, but not quickly enough and the motorcyclist was crushed by the car throwing him into the ditch. Your father, shaken to his core, jumped out of the car and ran to the motorcyclist whose helmet was cracked and one of his arms was severely broken. That's just my guess dependent on how you've described the deer. Your father didn't know that you'd jumped out of the car behind him and you were scared out of your wits. Sometime later, as your father was attending to the broken man, another car pulled up. After ascertaining the situation, they called the state police and ambulance. When the police arrived, whether you know it or not, you saw your future because the police officer who took control of the situation did not reprimand your dad. He was kind, compassionate and helpful, especially to you. Which is why you always wanted to be a police officer. Now that you have achieved the goal, you enjoy your profession even if it is in Amicable."

Louise's face drained of color. Her voice was soft. "I can see why you think your gift is a curse."

Butcher put his head in his hands and Louise put a hand on his back. "I'm sorry."

He smiled down at the sidewalk now darkened by the sun's shipwreck on the reef of the horizon. "For all these years, I've spent many days wondering why I could do what so many people can't."

"So you can read everyone like you did me?"

"Yes," he said, *except for one.*

"Teach me to do what you do."

Butcher shook his head. "I'd really like to Louise, but I've never met anyone who was actually able to do it. Some are good at reading the signs of lying, but it's not the same."

"Well, that's a good start, just the lying part. Can you come down to the police station tomorrow and help me out? There are three 'felons,'" she used her fingers for quotations marks, "who all have different stories for how some graffiti ended up on the Amicable water tower."

"I hadn't even noticed."

"Most people never look up. Tomorrow, when you do, you'll see the word Amicable, of course, but then a giant 'SUCKS' behind it. Nobody seems to have seen exactly what happened, but these three hooligans know something."

"Sounds like fun."

"Do you think if I picked you up around two o'clock, you'd be able to come to the station and help me figure it out?"

"I'd have to talk to the bosses."

Louise stood up. "I'll compensate them for their lost work. My guess is, though, that you'll have all of yours done in the first couple of hours." Butcher smiled. "So, I'll see you tomorrow then?" She stuck out her hand for a shake.

"It's a deal. Just don't cuff me, okay? I have a hard enough time with rumors already."

"Okay, sure then. I'll see you at 1:55 tomorrow at Peterson's. Good night." Louse stepped off the stoop, fixed her police cap on top of her head and strutted down the sidewalk. When she reached her car, she noticed some locals gawking at her. *Strange*, she thought, *why would Linda Harmsen's car be parked there?* The thought was fleeting. Officer Nelson entered her car and returned home for the night.

Linda Harmsen, though, enjoyed the malevolent thread of thought that plowed through her mind.

Chapter 28

Butcher's dreams were replete with smoky visions of the past, memories not quite fully formed but disintegrating in front of his eyes. It had been quite a while since he had thought about his mother's ultimate demise. The memory struck a deep blow to his psyche. His mother, Lenore, had been raised in a blue collar, middle class family. She was fairly well adapted to the world in which she was immersed: suburban Detroit early 1950's. The automobile boom was in full bloom. Her father, an industrial welder, had plenty of work and even though they lived in a modest house, everything was paid for. Her father doted on her older brother Charles and when he needed to, Lenore. Because Charles was an all-around athlete, scholar and musician, he received a great deal of attention from the family and community, while Lenore, a middling golfer, C+ student and average singer, was largely overlooked.

His first memories of his mother were murky, but he remembered her voice, husky as if she'd been a three-pack-a-day smoker. Plaid was her favorite 'color,' she used to say, with white patent leather boots. Her hair, piled high on her head, always seemed to be a mountain of activity. A beehive, she called it, without the bees.

As he grew, his mother experienced his ability firsthand. She was disconcerted when she would tell him she was 'going out for some fresh air,' which meant she was going to have a smoke and he would yell out from wherever he was sitting, usually playing with Lincoln Logs or Tinker Toys, 'No you're not, Mother. You're having a Cigray.' That's what he called cigarettes. To this day, although he didn't smoke, Butcher still appreciated the aroma of Lucky Strikes as they brought back memories of his mother.

Eventually, his mother stopped trying to lie to him; she knew it was futile. For him, this was not necessarily a positive outcome. Because she told him who she was going out with and what she was going to be doing (which sometimes ended with sexual congress), Butcher learned not to ask questions. At the end, though, he felt guilty that he had not asked more. His guilt was less about interrogating her as wondering when his ability to read her had finished. Why had it happened? What was different about his mother?

On Saturdays, she would take him to the country markets. Wandering through lanes of fresh produce, farmers, each with greens or tomatoes or watermelons (his favorite) would push their goods on them. His mother would test the goodness of each and somehow the young boy could wheedle down the price to an acceptable level. Lenore would pretend to be embarrassed, but inwardly, she was proud and awed by his abilities. Hand in hand they would smell, pinch and taste. She seemed like a good mother.

Somewhere in his mid-teens, half way between a move and a stay, his mother's eyes turned glassy. He thought this was the strain of providing for him. Sometimes he thought he was the cause of her stress. She drank more than she used to, but she still talked to him and often, as they pondered the mysteries of the world, she would sit beside him smoking her cigrays and drinking her brandy, calling him into a depth of understanding that he hadn't previously considered. She connected dots for him - people had histories, which were mysteries, mysterious and entirely predictable. Birth order, culture, class, race, creed, religion or lack thereof all played a part in reading people and although she herself wasn't good at it, she was a good teacher. Like many great maestros, she knew the music but did not play.

His mother never brought anyone home – neither did he. So, the two of them lived a reclusive life together, mostly on the road, pausing only to make a few dollars and then packing up again.

Lenore Jensen was the best of mothers and Leo Jensen still missed her, but his dreams of her were rarely pleasant. The nightmare of her last breaths was tattooed into his memory. To cope, he ran away. Life was still an endless escape from the pain. It had been a difficult road, one fraught with distrust and difficulty. Now that he had lived in Amicable for all of one week, he was wondering why, suddenly, his mother's memory was reappearing.

After a night of tossing and turning, Butcher awakened to the sound of the robins announcing the arrival of the newly birthed sun. After rubbing his eyes and tussling his hair, Butcher tossed back the covers and padded into the bathroom to relieve himself. The cold wooden floor caused his toes to curl. Tiptoeing back to his room, he dressed and moved to the kitchen to prepare a cup of coffee and a bowl of cereal.

The steaming cup wisped steam upwards towards the ceiling. He inhaled deeply while moving into the living room to stand on the carpet rather than the cold kitchen linoleum. Entering the living room, he turned on the lights. When he looked out the bay window, he was startled to see that someone had drawn in large white letters on the glass a phrase that he wasn't expecting.

Go away, Bucher.
You are a menase.
Or else...

Butcher almost dropped his cup of coffee, but fortunately he managed to set it on the lamp stand while nearing the window to investigate. Although the message startled him, he wasn't particularly frightened by a graffitist who flunked spelling; he took his time surveying the 'crime scene.' The message, read from the inside, was backwards. Thankfully, the graffitist could not gain egress. Butcher's instinct was to go outside and look for clues. Although he liked Louise, he wasn't certain she was a paragon of sleuthing.

Butcher walked back into his bedroom and grabbed his tennis shoes and coat. After covering himself, he walked outside. Stepping down the front stairs, he looked around hoping to find the author somewhere nearby, perhaps at a neighbor's house penning another note, worthy of Shakespeare. Although there was no suspect, clues had been left. Criminals in the Amicable township usually had little to worry about, so leaving footprints in the mud was probably not the first thing on his or her mind. But there they were - decent sized shoe prints below the window. They were definitely not his. A few branches from the bush had been broken off and were lying on the ground. Butcher reached up to the window and noticed that the writing was high but not intensely so. This person must have been about eight inches shorter, which would put them around five foot nine or ten. Because there were only a few twigs knocked down, the person must have been slender. The writing was not that of a villain - just a nice, normal townsperson who had found a bee or two buzzing around inside their bonnet.

Butcher touched the writing - it wasn't paint, it was something else. He smelled it and rolled his eyes.

Marshmallow spread.

Only in Amicable would a felon incriminate himself with a bucket full of marshmallow paste and some kind of painting tool. Butcher guessed it was his finger, but it could have been the end of a brush. Either way, the message did not quite seem dangerous, nor did the threat seem quite... threatening. It was like challenging a bear with a particularly large bottle of ketchup.

Butcher shook his head and stepped back out from underneath the window. He was careful not to disturb the footprints in the dirt. Taking off his tennis shoes at the front door, he went to the kitchen, washed his hands and ate his breakfast while at the same time pondered the gall of this modern-day Andy Warhol. As his brain wandered the town of Amicable, there weren't many suspects who could fall into the category of felon armed with marshmallow fluff.

Wiping his mouth, Butcher went to get dressed. Ten minutes later, he was out of his house walking east towards the Choke. He glanced back at the bay window and shook his head.

It was a Tuesday morning, only a little over a week into his sojourn into the township of Amicable. Butcher was not surprised that he already had a good knowledge of quite a few names of the townspeople who had gathered outside the Choke. Incredibly, it seemed as if the early morning breakfast crew was growing. Butcher was not sure if this was because they were thronging to eat Rodrigo's fare or they wanted to see if the new butcher would show up to speak with his 'supposed' girlfriend. Either way, they would not be disappointed on this day.

As he began his walk and the morning light began to rise, Butcher looked up at the water tower.

Amicable SUCKS.

A few minutes later, Butcher entered the restaurant. Both warmth and aroma greeted him as well as a friendly voice.

"Hello, Butcher," George called out.

"Morning, George. Early start for you?"

"I couldn't sleep much last night after," George glanced at the gossipers table. "… our discussion."

Butcher shrugged. "Well, you'll sleep better tonight."

"Anything new for you?"

Butcher thought about telling George about the message on the window, but then thought better of it. He looked towards the front counter and caught a glimpse of Rhonda who was inputting orders. Her long, lean limbs stirred something in him and he looked back to George who was smirking. "No, just another night in the Garden of Eden."

George cackled, a high and throaty old man laugh that caused many of the group to turn and look. James and Naida waved to George and Butcher as did Penny and Tony.

Taking his seat next to George, Butcher was aware of the oddness of the room. Like a surreal Last Supper, or Last Breakfast in this case, twelve plus four people sat in different areas of the room. George, uncaring of the thoughts of the other disciples, waited for Rhonda to come around to gather their orders. He looked through the menu, pointed to one thing and mumbled something to Butcher who nodded.

Meanwhile, Leona Simpson leaned in towards the middle of the table. "Any juicy details from last night?"

Linda, with a self-satisfied smirk, crossed her arms and licked her lips. "Officer Nelson stopped by his house last night."

Gasps. Linda nodded. "Yes, I have it on good authority that Louise and him were plotting something."

"What were they talking about?"

Linda rolled her eyes. "What do you think?"

Jeannie whispered. "Is he cheating on Rhonda already?"

Leona touched Jeannie's arm. "No, silly. She was probably prepping him for his arrest."

"Oh, for Pete's sake," Leslie muttered.

Linda's eyes turned towards Leslie. "What's wrong, Leslie?"

"Don't you ever get tired of gossip?"

"We're not gossiping, Leslie. We're just exchanging information." Leona's mouth tightened as she spoke.

"Really? Both you and Linda have just verbalized unsubstantiated rumors that have absolutely no basis in reality. For all we know, Louise could have been checking to see how the new butcher is doing in town. Remember the anonymous note that both he and Rhonda received yesterday?"

Linda's eyes narrowed. "That's hypocritical coming from you, Leslie. You're one of his biggest opponents - something about pulling apart the moral fiber of Amicable, remember?"

Leslie's gaze fell to her hands. "I said no such thing."

"Sure, sure. You and Reverend Deakins have been plotting - we all have, don't you remember? As of yesterday, the two of you were wanting to 'reinforce' his willingness to leave."

"Well, I don't know…"

Jeannie jumped in. "Yes, yes, you were there. Maybe it was you who wrote the notes."

Her face turning red, Leslie pushed back her chair from the table. "We don't even know what was in the notes. But, thank you for accusing me."

Linda shrugged and lifted her hands palms up. "You're not denying it."

For the first time ever, the scales fell from Leslie's eyes and the truth of what she had been mired in was visible. Leslie looked around at her friends and she could see the darkness inside of them, a demon of discomfort; at that moment, she was frightened of them. What if they obtained the information that she and Reverend Deakins were dabbling in some non-marital relations? What if they were to do exactly what they were doing to Rhonda and the butcher? How would she feel?

"Linda," Leslie said calmly, "Just think about what we're doing here. It's a Tuesday morning and the four of us are around a table gossiping about..."

"Sharing information," Leona interrupted by raising a finger.

Frustrated, Leslie pushed on. "...talking about two people, one who has been in Amicable her whole life and yes, she has a checkered past. Think deeply: are there things about your life that you wouldn't want shared?"

"Yes, of course," Linda retorted, "But we don't go around flaunting it."

Leslie crossed her arms. "How, exactly, is Rhonda flaunting it?"

"Because she's doing the same thing. We're just looking out for..." Linda's words trailed off.

"Looking out for... the butcher?" They looked over in his direction. He was casually glancing at them, but their conversation had been quiet enough not to be overheard. "That's ridiculous. How can you be looking out for him and trying to get rid of him at the same time?"

Linda, Leona and Jeannie all leaned back in their chairs to look at Leslie. "Be careful," Linda said.

Leslie's mouth dropped open. "Are you threatening me?"

Linda shook her head, but her eyes said something else. "I'm just saying that self-righteousness is a dangerous river to be swimming in."

Unable to respond, Leslie blinked twice and then glanced toward the butcher one last time before standing to leave the restaurant. On the way out, Rhonda, as she was carrying four meals on a brown platter, said something unheard and Leslie shook her head. Making her way to the table, Rhonda perused the faces of the silent women who were studiously rearranging napkins, forks and shakers. Something had happened, something momentous. As Rhonda placed the meals in front of them, she cast a quick glance over at Butcher, whose eyes widened.

Meanwhile, Penny, who had been watching her friends in the middle of the restaurant, watched Leslie exit the Choke. Penny noticed that Tony was eating a heaping forkful of scrambled eggs with glee. The last two days had been nothing short of miraculous. Penny had forgotten how much communication, and romance, could heal some of the ills that had plagued their relationship for years. Naida and James seemed to be as positively affected by Butcher's advice as she and Tony.

Penny saw that Butcher was now sitting with George, Liam and Ethan. Butcher was quiet; something was going on and Penny wondered what it was. Tony bumped her arm and asked her to pass the salt.

Butcher's mind was on autopilot. Not only was he pondering the marshmallow-penned note on his window and the author of it, he was also wondering what was happening on the margins of Rhonda's thoughts. He could read her body language, facial expressions and everything else. He knew she was troubled, but he wanted to hear her voice; he wanted to touch her arm and her face; he wanted to look into her eyes and tell her that everything was going to be fine, even if the future was cloudy.

Rhonda finally made it to his table. The Tuesday morning fishbowl was driving her crazy, but this was her job and if she wanted to keep it, or so the boss said, she'd better not cause problems. If she lost her waitressing job, there weren't many other opportunities in town. Although she wanted to leave the town, to instigate her own Exodus, to get away from Amicable and her mother, there was a mysterious gravity keeping her here.

"Can I get you anything else?"

"I would like to talk to you," Butcher said.

Through closed teeth, she smiled and then, like a ventriloquist, said, "I can't do that right now."

"I got another message today."

Rhonda glanced at him sharply while George finally looked up from his fork. Attention alternating between Butcher and Rhonda, George paused waiting for one of them to fill the silence. Liam and Ethan took no notice.

"Can we talk about this later?" Rhonda finally said.

Butcher faked his smile also and spoke through his own lips. "Yes, what time would be good for you?"

"I'll come around later this afternoon. Right before closing time."

"I'll see you then," he said. Rhonda ripped off tickets and placed them on the table in front of the men. George took his and Butcher's, while both Liam and Ethan stared at their own, waiting hopefully for the other to pick up the tab. They were left unrewarded. Ethan pointed at Liam who reluctantly picked up the check. While they were arguing over the bill, Butcher watched Rhonda's retreating form from the table.

"What was that about another message?" George asked.

Butcher pulled his eyes away from Rhonda. "Two days in a row someone has left a note for me at the house."

"What, you mean like the nasty note in the mail box?"

Butcher smirked. "The one today was a little different. I didn't find it in my mailbox."

"Where was it?"

"It was written on my window. In marshmallow."

"What?" George asked incredulously.

"I'm serious. Someone wrote a message on my front bay window in the sticky medium of melted marshmallow."

Liam looked over, now interested. "On the front window of the rental?" He was holding the check out in front of him, like a droopy leaf of spinach.

"It's still there if you want to look at it."

Liam pushed his chair back. "You bet I do. Come on, Ethan."

"Oh yeah! This is going to be awesome!"

Within seconds, the two of them were pushing each other out of the way to get to the counter. Rhonda, raising an eyebrow, tallied the bill in an ancient plastic cash register. Liam handed over a ten spot and told her to keep the change, which, unfortunately for her sake, amounted to thirty-two cents.

"Gee, thanks you guys." It was too late for them to hear; they were already out the door.

Back at the table, Butcher told George what the message said.

"And this is the second day in a row."

"Somebody wants me out of Amicable, I guess."

George shook his head and pushed himself up from the table. "You got to stay strong, Butcher. She's going to need you."

Butcher looked over at Rhonda again. "I know, George. I know."

Fifteen minutes later, Butcher was walking north on Main Street. There was a crowd gathered outside Peterson's Butchery, and a message written in the window.

He wasn't sure that he liked this one any better.

Chapter 29

John Deakins found that his tiredness was a direct result of a quivering soul. It was a flickering of danger, excitement, fear and something else, something he couldn't quite put his finger on. If he could have scratched just an inch deeper, he would have encountered an artesian well of faith in his soul, like the small piece of earth that caps an underground spring.

John Deakins' struggle with the transcendental was a mirrored reflection of Amicable's temporal struggle with change. Although most Amicableans would outwardly frown at change, a vast majority of them desperately wanted something different to happen, a real and powerful subterranean shift in the bedrock of their Midwestern culture. Change had always been considered one of those 'Big City' ideas that would indelibly scar the small town; the most alluring ideas of fashion, music, art and literature were kept at arm's length.

In Amicable's history, there had been a few attempts by resident Amicableans to stray, to exchange the norm for the transcendent. There was just too much to lose, though, by risking the safe, values-driven society by reaching for the darkly mysterious *something* beyond the invisible walls of the town. It was a true fear, taught from ages past, from George Hendriks' generation right down to Ally Fenimore's (Amicable's most recently born citizen, pushed into the world twenty-seven days earlier in the Clancy Municipal Hospital) that there was no other wholesome life than the one represented in Amicable.

Most Amicableans had no idea that the same fears that seemed to threaten their existence were identical to those of any other town, small or large. In their endless push for 'progress,' those who lived in cities had casually (and not always gently) laid aside everything that smacked of authority, usually spiritual in nature; faith no longer was an operating system; the Commandments and all things helpful for ordering society, became a hobbling rope for progress. Once the metropolitan horse was unreined, small town folk stood back and watched with folded arms as the culture crumbled beneath them: gun violence, gang warfare, sexual practices justified as 'normal impulses,' the biblical versions of perversions where humans exchanged their natural attractions and love for each other for unmentionable things including the pornification of children. Small town people, although not entirely innocent of these curses or devoid of blame, frowned and tsk tsked because their big city brothers and sisters were unable to cope with the world they had created. The cities were so intent on staying the same - progressive - that they had neither identity nor direction.

Thus, John Thomas Deakins was torn in two. Weekly, daily, hourly, he struggled with wanting to bring Amicable closer to a recognizable idea of a God of the universe that desired humans not to obey out of fear, but because obeying the natural laws and the spiritual laws brought harmony. If they could only agree on what those laws were, life would be so much easier.

Now that this wrench had been thrown into the very guts of the machinery of his life, Deakins laid awake staring up at his bedroom ceiling. He noticed a few new cracks tracking from southeast to northwest (he would have to remind the property committee about that) and that the light was clawing over the top edge of the curtains. Because of Leslie's revelation and argument with him yesterday, John had slept badly and awoken even worse. He grumbled as he tossed his bare feet over the edge of the bed and stepped into his house shoes while noticing that his bedside clock was blaring the time.

6:42 a.m.

"Tuesdays," he mumbled and walked to the bathroom.

As he looked at his reflection in the mirror, he rubbed his face. Something was troubling him about yesterday's talk with Leslie. In fact, there were many things, not the least of which were his responses to her kiss, her questions and her anger. Why couldn't he be strong? Why couldn't he address his fears? What was it about this woman that stirred him up like no other? She was beautiful, yes, but there was a deeper intensity to her that he had never seen before. All life before seemed bland.

Bland, that is, until that butcher had shown up not even two weeks ago. On Sunday, they had exchanged pleasantries and, ultimately, barbs and accusations. There was something sincerely odd and frightening about the man that Deakins couldn't put his finger on. There was no way he should (or could) have known the things that he did.

After showering and shaving, Reverend Deakins put on his clerical wear, tightened his collar and checked his appearance. His dark, wavy hair, not one follicle misplaced, was parted to the left; his brown eyes radiated calmness in spite of the bubbling disturbance underneath, but dark circles ringing them gave off a certain aura of overworkedness. He liked this. His congregation members would comment and ask him about his health and, he hoped, they would recommend that he take some time off to which he would object, a pious saint toiling for his sheep.

With a shock, Reverend Deakins shook his head. He had to erase any of those thoughts until the current crisis was neutralized.

And then he felt it: loneliness. His call to the congregation in Amicable had become the millstone around his neck, and his faith no longer was keeping him afloat.

He needed to talk to the butcher, and that annoyed the heck out of him.

"What in the world…" Butcher muttered as he stared at the new lettering on the large pane of glass. Of the three panes of glass, eight feet tall and five feet wide, one of them, the one on the right, had been completely blacked out. Where the chair and tables normally were positioned was nothing but black paper. Written on the outer glass were the daily specials, cuts of beef, pork and *Whole Chickens for Ten Dollars!* But above them was a new sign - a new stenciling that proclaimed:

PETERSON BUTCHERY AND COUNSELING SERVICES!
ADVICE IS FREE, BUT THE MEAT ISN'T.

Butcher pushed his way through the small crowd waiting outside Peterson's. A few were looking at the tall man as he moved through them; one person, Tooky Barlowe, a retired medical practitioner, wanted to have a discussion with him, but Butcher pushed him aside and moved up the steps and into the locker. Seeing Derek standing behind the counter, hands on hips, grinning like a monkey caught with his hand in the banana bunch, made Butcher grind his teeth. Derek waved and pointed at Butcher. That was when he saw Nash in the back room approaching the flip bench holding his hands out to his sides and mouthing the words, *What do you think?*

"Open the door, Nash."

Nash walked slowly towards the door and opened the locks.

"Morning, Butcher. I hope you slept…"

"What the hell is that?" Butcher pointed to the sign on the window.

"Tsk tsk, Butcher. It's not polite to swear in Amicable."

"Shut up, Nash. Just tell me what's going on."

Nash backed up into the front of the butchery; Butcher pushed in behind him. Then, moving towards the darkened-out section of the window, Butcher noticed for the first time that a cubicle had been set up. "Do you like it?"

"How can I like it if I don't know what it is. What's going on?"

Derek came out to stand beside his brother adding moral support, or something like it. Derek's smile had not ceased. "It was easy, Butcher. We've decided that your gifts lend greatly to diversifying the locker's products. Profits have been up about fifty percent since you started, even if that's just one week. It's no surprise, though, that people are coming not just for the quality of the meat, but also for…"

Nash interjected his thoughts. "…For the psychological help. So, we decided that we'd partition off a little segment of the butchery for

280

you to do your magic while we 'slave away' in the back." His inverted commas irked Butcher even more than the sign on the window.

"Did you ever ponder whether I'd want to do this?"

"Ah, Butcher, don't be sore about it. You're so good at it. Haven't you ever thought about using your powers for good?" Nash had taken a step back from the big man.

"Haven't you ever thought about the common courtesy of asking before acting?" Butcher pointed outside. "All those people, are they here to have a chat, or are they here for the sales?"

"Who cares?" Derek said exasperatedly. "Look, we can see you're upset, but we're willing to give you a raise in salary - heck, we'll even raise it by fifty percent, almost to what we're making."

"How magnanimous," Butcher said sarcastically.

"All you have to do is cut up some meat in the morning, and we'll throw out the sign that basically says 'The Doctor Is In.'"

"Nash! I'm not a doctor! I'm not a psychiatrist, psychologist or even a counsellor. I have no training whatsoever."

"Do you think those people out there care what kind of degree you have?" Nash pointed to the half a dozen people milling outside at 7:30 on a Tuesday morning, "You're a butcher who knows stuff and they like that."

Butcher looked out at the people who were exchanging pleasantries about the chill of the morning, the chance of rain, or even clouds, by three o'clock in the afternoon. A few of them might have delved into deeper topics of Labor Day plans or recapping summer vacations, but for the most part they stood with crossed arms attempting not to look at each other or into the butchery. "I don't know…" Butcher said hesitantly.

"Come on, Butcher. Try it for one day. See what you think. You might really like it."

"Yeah, and I could get arrested, too, for practicing without a license."

"Well, at least we'd sell some steaks before that happened." Nash laughed. "You'll be fine, Butcher. I promise."

"Why do I feel as if you're toying with me?"

A Cheshire like grin spread identically across both boys' faces and they spoke at the same time.

"Meow."

This caused an outburst of laughter between the twins who gave each other high fives. They turned towards Butcher for one also, but they were left hanging. All three moved behind the counter and into the saw room where, for the next thirty minutes, they cut, sawed and wrapped the fare of the day. At 8:00, Nash went out to open the front door where there was now a crowd of fifteen people.

"Welcome, everyone! Come on in. If you need your orders placed, just let us know, but if you want to talk to Butcher, you'll have to schedule a time with the receptionist." Nash pointed at Derek who was waving.

"Hi!' He said brightly.

Nash continued his spiel. "The Butcher will be taking clients starting at 8:30. These visits, due to high demand, must be limited to fifteen minutes. Well, that and Butcher has to be a butcher also." The people in the crowd laughed and pushed in through the open doors. Moving like a tidal wave towards Derek, they ordered their meats and then signed up for times with Butcher.

Within twenty minutes, Butcher's counselling day was full, as was Wednesday's, Thursday's and Friday's. People were signing up not only their own names, but also family members and friends. Derek laughed as he wrote down names on one pad, and cuts of meat on another.

At 8:15, a surprising figure entered the doorway. Dark in garb and demeanor, Reverend John Thomas Deakins frowned as he encountered the sign on the window. For much of his pastoral career, Deakins had espoused his qualifications as a counsellor, but very few took advantage of his ears or advice. Yet here in the local meat market was an unqualified butcher giving Amicableans the idea that he was some kind of therapist. Deakins would certainly have to call the Better Business Bureau about this one, or more importantly, the mayor. This sign, at best, was false advertising; at worst, Deakins was sure that Butcher could do some harm to psychologically sensitive Amicableans.

"Good morning, Reverend Deakins," Nash said loudly. "It's a beautiful September morning. What can we do for you? Meat or mentoring?" Nash laughed but Deakins did not.

"I have not come for counselling, but I do need to have a conversation with the butcher."

"Sorry, Pastor, but Butcher is booked for the rest of the week, but if you'd like to make an appointment for next week…"

"Nash! Don't patronize me." Deakins' cutting whisper shredded Nash's smile.

"Sorry, Reverend Deakins. I'll see if Butcher can speak with you right now." Checking his watch, Nash noticed it was 8:20. "If you could keep it to ten minu…"

"Nash," Deakins warned.

Nash held his hands up in surrender. "Butcher, Reverend Deakins wants to see you." Butcher looked out from the back, wiped his hands and made his way forward. "But try to make it quick," he whispered. "You've got a full schedule today."

Butcher frowned at Nash, but moved towards Deakins and extended his hand. "Good morning, Reverend." Butcher knew immediately that something was disturbing the clergyman - Leslie. Something had happened between them, something… odd. "What can I do for you?"

"Is there somewhere we could speak privately? Maybe outside?"

"I don't think it would be private," Butcher said as he glanced at the milling crowd of onlookers, but if you want, we can go sit in the little cubicle. I haven't been in there yet, and frankly, I'm not really that pleased with the idea. This was," he pointed towards the area, "not my idea at all."

For some reason, Deakins was relieved. "Okay, we'll sit for a little bit."

At 8:21, Reverend Deakins and Butcher pulled aside the curtain to enter the booth that the boys had made. Butcher cringed, both inwardly and outwardly, at the tacky little room behind the curtain. There were four 'walls' made of hinged plywood covered with black cloth. Pinned to the black curtain were pithy positive quotes from famous people. Butcher gagged at the syrupy sayings. As he quickly scanned the words, he already hated a few, especially the one by Oprah which actually made no sense whatsoever: *If you look at what you'll have in life, you'll always have more.*

Butcher apologized. "Sorry about this little 'room.'"

The boys had replaced the hard chairs with two small cushioned ones. The table had been thrown out and a small bookshelf had been pushed against the corner. Once again, Butcher rolled his eyes at their choices. Norman Vincent Peale, Dale Carnegie, Zig Ziglar and his personal loathsome non-favorite: Joel Osteen.

"Does it bother you to be doing this? It seems kind of corny." Deakins settled into the groaning chair.

"It bothers me quite a lot."

"Then why are you doing it?"

Butcher shrugged. "Because as I was standing outside getting frustrated, someone tapped me on the shoulder and I knew immediately that there was something that they wanted to talk about. It doesn't have to be me, but as I'm starting to appreciate, Amicableans aren't particularly good about sharing with others."

"So why would they share with you?" Deakins opened his hands and then tepeed them in front of his lips as if he was doing the questioning.

"Because I'm a stranger and in this day and age, sometimes that feels safer."

"How did you come to that idea?"

Butcher looked over at another quote. *Clouds come floating into my life no longer to carry rain but to add color to my sunset sky.* He had never heard of Rabindranath Tagore and certainly with a quote like that, he wouldn't be running to the library to check out his (or her - he wasn't quite sure with a name like Rabindranath) book.

"Do you ever notice how many people are drawn to on-line chat groups? Look, Reverend Deakins, I could continue to tell you about my philosophy for life, but really, you invited me in here. Can you give me an idea of what you want to talk about?"

"I thought that you'd already know. Supposedly your powers of observation would give you that knowledge."

Butcher sighed deeply. "Is that how you want this to go down? Or, would you like to tell me exactly what you want me to know?"

"I want you to give me advice. That's what the sign says." Deakins' smugness was an attempt to unsettle the butcher, but Butcher suppressed his annoyance.

"The last time we talked, we had a discussion about a specific person." Deakins' face reddened slightly. "You made it quite clear to me that this information would stay confidential even though you denied it, but your response confirmed that you had... feelings for this person."

"These are not being recorded in any way, are they?" Deakins looked around.

"No, or as far as I know, they are not. Unless the boys have planted some bugs in one of the books, we should be fine."

"Good. That's good. Thank you for your decency."

"Reverend Deakins, it's now 8:30 and the boys have told me that I have to meet with almost twenty people today. If you could let me know how I could help, that would be prudent."

Deakins looked at his hands, opening and shutting them, flexing the strain from the fingers. "This person we talked about," he said quietly, "has been on my mind greatly in the last week – much more since you've arrived. It seems that your appearance in Amicable has stirred many things, emotions that have been... dormant for a long time."

"You've fallen in love with her."

"I...I... don't... It's hard to say," Deakins stammered, "But there are many other considerations to take into account."

"Such as?"

"Such as my role in the congregation, my standing in Amicable. There are areas of influence, that you couldn't possibly understand, where I have a large role. If I were to be seen as a…"

"As a what?"

"As a negative moral influence, I believe that my time would be cut short here."

"So, you're worried about your job."

Deakins' voice rose. "It's a calling, sir. I have been called by God to be a shepherd in this community. Why…"

Butcher waited for the reverend to calm down.

"I'm sorry," Deakins said. "That was uncalled for and overly sanctimonious. God calls all of us to different areas."

"I agree. But John - you told me to call you that - is your fear of losing your calling worth the tradeoff of one God-blessed shot at happiness? At love? Maybe at marriage and a family?"

Deakins looked at his watch. The time had leaked out over the 8:30 time slot. "I'm not sure you understand the intricacies."

Butcher shook his head. "I understand, and I have a decent grasp on the Bible, too. My guess is that you are a great fan of the Apostle Paul and his ideas of celibacy. Perhaps you think you can be a better pastor if you don't have the 'distraction' of a family or a romantic relationship, but you forget that he also says it's better to be married than burn with passion."

"That's a generalized assessment of Paul's writings. I think it is better for clergy to…"

"Look, Reverend, we can debate hermeneutics or we can get to the heart of your matter."

"You know the word 'hermeneutics?' I'm impressed."

Jeez, this man needs to loosen up. "You want to figure out what to do with Leslie, right?" Deakins nodded.

A voice came over the speaker system. It was Nash. "Dr. Butcher," snickering could be heard throughout the butchery. "Your 8:30 patient is here."

"Good Lord." Butcher got up and stuck his head out of the curtain. "Look, Nash," he said as he found the young man behind the counter holding the microphone. "My patience is going to run out really quickly if you do that."

"I'm just letting you know that your next client, Gladys, is here."

Butcher looked at Gladys, smiled and then cast his gaze back towards the smirking young butcher in a gore encrusted apron holding an old-fashioned microphone. "They're not clients, they're not patients, and I'm not a doctor. If they have to wait, they have to wait."

"But…" Nash started.

Butcher held up a warning finger. "Don't test me, Nash." Butcher pulled his head back through the curtain.

"Okay, Reverend. I can tell by your body language that she's already asked you out on a date and it's probably sometime soon."

Deakins' jaw dropped again.

"You can ask me again how I know, and I'll tell you the same story - a gift or a curse, depending on perspective. Let me lay out the future ramifications of each. If you choose to accept," he touched his right index finger to his left, "the course directed could take you down the long, exhausting, excruciatingly beautiful path of getting to know someone on an incredibly deep and wonderfully painful level. You'll find the very limits of your trust and your inability to be vulnerable will be tested pretty much every morning."

"How…?"

"Don't stop me now."

"But…"

"I don't have much time – I saw that Gladys is getting antsy."

"Is that Gladys Turnbull? Why I haven't…"

Butcher held up the same finger in the same way that he had towards Nash. "If you choose love, you will get hurt, but you will also live a better and more wonderful life than you ever could have imagined. But if you decide not to accept the invitation," he touched a second finger, "you will be safe… and tortured. Leslie will not come to your church anymore, but you can rest assured that your congregation will not know any differently. They will be distressed that a valued member of the church is gone, but your piety will remain respectfully intact. You could, and probably would, live out your days in Amicable as a gentle bachelor who slips faithfully, and full of loneliness, into old age."

Reverend Deakins knew better than to interrupt now. "So, what you're saying is that both options have pros and cons?"

"Doesn't every choice we make have consequences? You get up in the morning and you decide to come to the butchery to talk to me instead of to the Choke to talk to three women who are bordering quite near to the scandalous cusp of slander."

"What have they said?"

Or, what have they written, Butcher thought. "They have said nothing publicly to me, but as you know, I don't necessarily need to hear them."

"Oh my."

"That's neither here nor there. I know this is not of your doing." Butcher was somewhat convinced of the opposite, but he didn't say that.

"What would you do if you were me?" Deakins leaned forward on his comfy seat, his belt digging uncomfortably into his waist.

Butcher mirrored the gesture. "That, Reverend John, is a question best left unanswered."

Deakins took a deep breath and exhaled to the floor. "Thank you, Butcher. Shall we pray?"

Butcher looked over his shoulder at the crack in the curtain. "Yes, of course, John, but you can pray on my behalf as you leave. If we take any more time, Gladys might pass the kidney stone that is causing her so much trouble."

The stout pastor, a likened resemblance to the mythical Friar Tuck, stood and adjusted his black suit coat. They shook hands and he opened the curtain.

"Oh, Reverend, as you've already made up your mind, make sure that you go in your civvies." Butcher smiled and Deakins' eyes widened. He left without speaking another word. As he left, Nash stuck his head into the chamber.

288

"Are you ready, Doc?"

"Nash, I'm warning you. If you don't knock it off, I'm going to kick your ass."

Nash's face beamed. "Now, now, that's no way for a doctor to speak." He pulled his head out and within seconds, Gladys Turnbull entered.

"Oh, Mr. Butcher. It's so nice to meet you. I think this is just lovely what you're doing. I've heard so much about you already and I have so many things I want to get off my chest." She paused and looked at the black wall. "Oh, and I just loooove Oprah."

It was all Butcher could do to refrain from rolling his eyes.

Butcher looked at his watch. It was 3:00 and according to his 'secretary,' his list of appointments still ran for another hour before closing down the shop. Standing, Butcher's neck cracked as he rolled it. He was unsure how many years it had been since he had sat this much in one day. Oddly, he was more exhausted by listening to six hours of conversation than doing his normal butchering. He poked his head out the door, but to his surprise, the face that he encountered was not Louise Nelson but Rhonda Redman. She looked very tired.

"Can I talk to you?" She asked quietly.

He nodded and opened the drape.

"Do we have to meet here?"

"What, you don't like my new office?" His attempted joke fell flat. "We could go for a walk, but I'm not sure we'd have any more privacy, and I'm supposed to meet with a few more people today."

Rhonda moved closer to the tall man. "What are you doing?"

"I'm using my listening skills."

"Then you do understand how ridiculous this whole thing is." She waved her hand around at the people who were sitting on chairs that Derek had put out. Nash had fetched some magazines and crossword puzzles at lunchtime. Before long, Butcher was pretty sure they were going to get a coffee machine and maybe hang a TV on the wall.

289

"I do. They didn't ask me."

"Then why are you doing it?"

"Reverend Deakins asked me the same question."

"Deakins has been here?"

Butcher smirked. "I can't reveal any confidential client information."

For the first time, Rhonda half-smiled and took a swipe at him. "Please, come into my office and lie down on my sofa." Rhonda ducked to move through the curtain and took one look around before shaking her head.

"Holy crap, this is a travesty."

"Tell me about it," Butcher responded as he plopped down in a chair and removed his shoes. The slightly personal gesture made Rhonda sigh.

"Now," he said. "Tell me about your mother."

This time, she did not smile. "Time for serious, Butcher. Okay?" He nodded. "I got a message last night too."

Butcher sat upright. "What did it say?"

"Before I get to that, you said that you got a message last night. Show it to me. I want to match the handwriting."

Butcher shook his head. "I can't."

"Why not?"

"Because it was written on my window this morning." He chuckled.

"You think this is funny?"

"A little. I mean, someone came to my house in the middle of the night with a jar full of marshmallow glue and a penchant for bad spelling. What do you do with that? I can laugh about it, or I can obsess about it and let it drive me crazy because one person in Amicable has it out for me."

"But it's not just you," Rhonda's voice was tinged with worry. "It's me also." She unfolded a note and handed it to Butcher. "This was in my mailbox this morning. My name was on it and my mother found it again. She was distraught."

I bet she was. Butcher hadn't quite forgotten Connie chasing him down the path grunting like a pig. He took the letter from her hand.

You are acting like a prostitute.
Amicable doesn't need hores.
Ether get rid of him or we'll get rid of you.

"Fascinating. Same bad speller also."

"It sounds like your message was tame compared to this one." Tears had welled up in her eyes. "I don't know if I can do this, Butcher. I mean, I really like you but this..." she tapped the letter with her hand.

"Look, Rhonda, let's get out of Dodge again, maybe go back to Clancy. That was a really good little restaurant."

"I don't know."

"Pick me up again on Friday. We'll eat, drink and be merry and pretend that there is nothing wrong in the friendly town of Amicable."

Rhonda was quiet for a moment before nodding. "Okay. Okay, but..."

At that moment, Nash stuck his head through the door. "Good. You guys aren't making out." Butcher gave him the evil eye. "Anyway, Louise is out here. She's looking for you."

"Oh, yeah." Butcher looked back at Rhonda. "We've got lots to talk about. Your story and mine."

"Yes, but what are you doing with Louise?"

Butcher shrugged and exited the 'office' with Rhonda close behind him. Louise approached Butcher and nodded to Rhonda.

"Are you ready?" She asked.

"Yes, officer," he said.

"What's this about?" Nash asked. "He's got more people he needs to see."

"I'm sorry, Nash, but this is police business."

Rhonda looked at Butcher who smiled. "I'm sorry our meeting was cut short. I'll talk to you later, okay? We can talk about..." he motioned with his head towards the booth.

Completely puzzled, Rhonda nodded and Louise took Butcher by the arm and led him from Peterson's Butchery. Unfortunately, every person inside and outside the locker watched Butcher being ushered to the police car by a uniformed officer, Louise Nelson.

This included a triumvirate of particularly proficient gossipers.

Linda, Leona and Jeannie stared with mouths agape. Their most beautiful gossiping dreams were coming true.

Chapter 30.

Louise Nelson slammed the car door shut behind her. Butcher was already positioned in the front passenger seat, his long legs poking straight out in front of him.

"You can adjust the seat back if you want."

Butcher shook his head. "I assume we're not going far."

"Won't even need to turn the siren on." Louise started the engine; as they drove off, Butcher looked up into the window of the butchery where Rhonda, Nash, Derek and four other 'clients' were staring morosely as he and Officer Nelson drove off.

"Thanks for your discretion," Louise said. "It's kind of embarrassing that I need to call in help to interrogate suspects."

"There's nothing embarrassing about it, Louise," Butcher said. "It just takes practice and knowing what to look for. I can give you some tips, but the hard work is up to you."

Louise turned to her right to look at Butcher. "Thank you for helping. It's very kind of you."

"Don't mention it."

"I won't," she said and laughed.

Two minutes later, they arrived at the Amicable police station and jail, a small building of four rooms - a large central area which served a double role as office and holding area, a bathroom, a cell and, what Louise called, 'the discussion area,' which was a typical interrogation room with a mono-directional glass. No one ever sat behind it, but the threat of it seemed to loosen a few tongues. She could remember a time when a teenage boy had 'borrowed' a car from the local dealership but was unwilling to include any details. While she was asking him questions with his parents in the room, she kept looking over her shoulder into the mirror as if 'making sure that those behind the glass were hearing.' The boy had sung like a canary. With more difficult people, the tactic didn't seem to work as well.

"Okay," Louise said as she parked the car and turned off the ignition. "Here's how I'd like it to work. I'm going to let you into the room and then I'm going to bring in the graffitists one by one and ask them a few questions. I'll have a radio earpiece in and after I ask the questions, you can tell me if they're lying or not."

"Okay. Sounds simple."

"I hope so." Louise led Butcher around to the back. Leading him to the room behind the glass, she opened the door for him. "Do you want a cup of coffee or something?"

"You're supposed to offer me cigarettes and a steak, aren't you?" Butcher smiled far down at the diminutive police officer.

"Get in there." She followed Butcher into the room. Opening a cupboard door, Louise extracted a microphone and earpieces. "Okay," she said, "This is the one I place in my ear and this is the one in your ear. You'll be holding the microphone so whenever you have information for me, just speak into it and we'll both hear it."

"Gotcha."

They tested the equipment and adjusted volume levels before Louise went to get the first 'criminal,' a young man of about sixteen years of age who was in an advanced stage of rebellion against his parents. Louise brought him into the discussion room and offered him a seat. The boy sat down, splayed his legs out in front of himself and scowled at the mirror.

"Okay, Dylan, I just want to go over your answers again."

"Whatever. I told you, I didn't do it."

Louise paused waiting for Butcher who was studying the young man. For a moment, Butcher remembered what it was like to be sixteen, full of hormones and hunger. The body changed every second of every day, and with that change, pain. This young man, Dylan, who slouched in the chair on the other side of the glass seemed to be the prototypical version of a teenage boy encountered in countless coming of age movies - the bad boy and the good girl.

"He's telling the truth. He didn't write on the water tower."

Louise touched her earpiece. "Are you sure?"

"Who are you talking to?" Dylan asked.

"A specialist. A friend of mine who I called in."

"Why isn't he in here? Is he chicken?"

"How do you know it's a he?"

Dylan shrugged and scowled.

"Yes, I'm sure, but he's not entirely innocent. My guess is he was an accomplice at the very least. Look at him, pouting. He's actually quite proud that he was part of it, but he still doesn't want his parents to know."

"What can you tell me?" Louise still had her finger to her ear.

"Spoiled all his life; he's recently got a car, some kind of old beater, nothing nice. You can tell by the key marks in the pocket of his pants. Old cars had bigger keys that didn't fold over. But he takes good care of it."

Louise smiled. "How's your car doing, Dylan?"

He looked up at her. "How did you know about that?"

She tapped a file in front of her. "Just some notes around town. I keep an eye on things pretty well." There was nothing in the folder. "It's a pretty old car. Got a few miles on it?"

He shrugged. "About one sixty. But I take good care of it."

"I bet you do."

Butcher looked closely through the glass. "Ask him about his drinking problem."

Louise cleared her throat. "Tell me about your drinking." Her hand still rested on the file folder.

"I don't know what you're talking about."

"It's okay, Dylan, I'm not going to do anything about that. I'm just asking."

"Are my parents behind that wall, because if they are," he leaned forward, "I'm never coming home! Ever!" His anger was misplaced, false, a bravado that didn't match him. He was on the verge of crying.

Butcher held the microphone in front of his face. "Comfort him. Tell him that you just want to find out the truth so we can stop it from happening again. Tell him that you believe him and that you know he didn't do it, but if he could just help point the way to who did, they could help repaint the water tower."

Louise repeated what Butcher said.

"I ain't no snitch," he said.

"Ah, but he is," Butcher responded. "Louise, bring the other two into the room and leave. Come in here and see what happens. My guess is that they will tell us without us even asking any questions."

"Okay." Louise told Dylan what she was going to do, and a minute later, two other boys, Chad and Robbie, were brought in and situated around the table.

"I'm going to get a cup of coffee," she said and left the room. After she had left, Dylan's first look was at Robbie and then he nodded towards the glass window. Robbie nodded.

In a moment, Louise entered Wonderland. "What do we do now?"

"I'll show you how to read them," he said. "Robbie is the gang leader, Dylan is the escape car driver and young Chad," he pointed at the pimply boy on the left wearing studded bracelets and ripped jeans, "is our Da Vinci."

"How do you know?"

"See how Chad sits? He's more erect than the other two, and if you watch closely, he keeps checking his fingernails to see if there is any paint on them. Robbie, on the other hand, is trying so hard to be cool, that he's not allowing his blood pressure to actually normalize. If you go in there and ask them any question, it doesn't even matter what it is, Robbie is going to blow up. Don't be afraid, it's all bluster. Dylan will be afraid and probably start to cry; Chad, on the other hand, will notice his two compadres and the distress that they are in, and, because he is, at heart, a really nice kid with just an enormously large chip on his shoulder, he will admit to doing the spray painting as long as you 'let the other guys go.' Which sounds ludicrously Hollywood-esque, but it will work."

"What question am I supposed to ask?" Louise asked.

Butcher leaned in. "It doesn't matter at all." He said slowly. "You could ask them about the weather, about the chances of the Royals winning the World Series. You could ask them if they know what your middle name is - it literally makes no difference. Just ask a question."

Louise looked skeptical. "Any question?"

"Any question."

"Okay." Louise stood up again and opened the door.

"By the way, Louise. You'll need to get a cup of coffee even if you don't want to drink it." She held up a finger in remembering. One minute later she opened the door with a steaming cup of coffee in her hand.

"So," she said to the boys, "What do you think about the chances of Amicable winning a football game this year?"

Robbie exploded out his chair. "What does that have to do with anything? You've got us locked up down here like a couple of criminals, and you know we didn't do anything! You know it! We're innocent, and when my parents find out that we've been detained by some two-bit town cop, they're going to rip you to shreds. Do you hear me?" Robbie blustered around the room and Louise's eyes widened.

Dylan, hearing his friend's outburst began to cry. He hated to see Robbie like this and it had kind of been his idea, but before he could admit to anything, Chad raised his hand and placed it on the table. "Robbie, relax. It wasn't you - we all know it. Officer Nelson, it was me. I climbed the ladder this weekend, took my spray paint up while Robbie did the look out. Dylan just drove the car," he rubbed his hair ruefully. "He's got a car and neither of us do."

Louise's mouth dropped open. *Exactly as he said it would happen! Amazing!* "Okay, go on," she said.

"We wanted to write it up there because, well, because we're tired of Amicable and all of its stifling rules and regulations. There's nowhere for us to hang out, to, you know, let our hair down. Look at Winslow Park - a toddler hang out, and the high school," he blew air out between his lips buzzing them, "what a joke. And then, and then!" He pointed up with his index finger, "Where are we going to get jobs? What are we going to do for a living?"

As much as she was frustrated by their graffiti, she understood the frustration of youth and the inability to comprehend a murky future. "You could always be a painter."

For a moment, the boys were silent. Then, Robbie looked at her and he laughed. "That's very funny, Officer."

Louise took a sip of her coffee. "Look, guys, I understand that Amicable doesn't seem to have a lot to offer you young men, but defacing public property does no good whatsoever."

Chad raised his hand again. "This was all my idea. Just let the other two go. I made them do it."

Louise smirked at the final piece being played. "I had an idea you'd say that," she said. "How about this..." She made a step towards them. "How about we four, all of us," she circled herself in with them, "we repaint that section of the water tower and then we four," she emphasized their togetherness again, "come up with some plans to make the town a little more young adult friendly. How does that sound?"

Dylan wiped his eyes. "Are you joking? What are you going to tell our parents?"

Waggling her head, she pursed her lips. "I'm not going to tell them anything, but you are, because when you do, you'll be free. When you tell them the truth, the locks are off and you can begin to trust each other again. There might be a few consequences, but..."

The boys looked down shamefacedly. "Okay, we agree."

Louise looked toward Wonderland and gave a thumbs up, but Butcher wasn't watching. Something deep down inside of him had exploded and his conscious mind was hanging by a thread. In that brief moment, all the pieces fell into place and Butcher, for the first time in his life, realized a foundational shift.

I know why I could never read my mother.
And it's beautiful.

Chapter 31.

"Leo. Leo. Wake up." The insistent voice pushed through the membranes of his sleep; Leo was not happy about it. He'd been having such a wonderful dream; a wooded countryside, a creek in which to play, three friends and a puppy to run with. The sun had been shining and the smell of fresh and growing things hung in the air to be plucked like ripe fruit. Leo had been running through the field, his Labrador retriever nipping playfully at his heels and there were shouts of laughter as his friends chased him. They were going to the creek to their special cave where all of their treasures were stored. If he could just get his hands on...

"Leo, Honey. Get up. We've got to get moving."

Leo groaned and rolled over. Through squinting eyes staring up towards the bright light of his bedroom, he saw his mother's silhouette eclipse the light. Her face, angelic, was smiling, but he could tell there was something wrong.

"That's a good boy," she said and pushed his clothes onto his recently sleeping form. *"You have to get dressed. I've already packed so you can help me carry the bags down to the curb."*

"Where are we going?" Leo's voice was still gravelly.

"I've got tickets," her forced smile said everything. *"Bus tickets to Wyoming!"*

"But I like Arkansas." Leo pulled the covers up over his head. *"Why can't we stay here?"* His voice was muffled by the blankets.

Lenore sat down on the bed beside her son and rubbed his back. She knew what a stress this was on him and how much he desperately wanted to put down roots, but there were problems in her life from which running was the only potion.

"I know, Sweetheart. If there was any other way, I'd gladly try to make it work, but..."

Leo forcefully moved and his mother pulled her hand from his back and stood up. *"Look, you've got ten minutes, my little lion. Ten minutes and then we'll eat and move on to the next adventure."*

Leo could think of nothing worse than to have another adventure.

Thirteen minutes later (it was Leo's small act of protest as an eleven-year-old) Leo stumbled out of his bedroom fully dressed, but his hair was sticking up at odd ends from his head. Stumbling into the kitchen, he rubbed his eyes, grabbed a bowl of cereal and ate while his mother busied herself with their predictable last-minute checklist. She was unnaturally edgy; her usual calm demeanor had been swallowed by this fidgety woman whose eyes were darting back and forth between door, window and room. She mumbled under her breath, talking to herself. Leo had rarely seen her do this.

Leo took another mouthful of cereal, chewed and swallowed, then looked up at this mother. "What's the matter, Mom?" He knew she was in some kind of trouble; any moron would be able to read that. In the past there were always financial issues, but this was something different. Something that was fuzzy around the edges. He couldn't quite make it out, but it had to do with a man. And not a nice one.

Lenore stopped moving and placed her hands on her hips. "My little lion," she intoned with great love. "You always know - everything. The gift you have…. Well, I wish I had that gift. It would make my life a whole lot easier."

Leo shook his head. He did not believe that his gift was in fact, a gift, or one that she would excel at using.

"I know, I know - you think it's a curse because you don't have as many friends who see how amazing you are and how beautiful you are." She moved in closer to rub his head while he ate his cereal. "But here is the deal…"

Lenore sat down next to her son. Like a young girl she pulled a leg up underneath her; took a hesitant and trembling breath. "If I had your gift, I'd be able to tell who the bad people and the good people are."

Leo stopped chewing so that he could hear his mother correctly. As if in a thought bubble, he could read his mother's inner dialogue and the pictures that were forming. He knew that she was debating, wrestling over whether to tell him exactly what was going on or tell him the partial truth because he was a child. This frustrated him because she already knew he knew and yet she still attempted to pull wool over his eyes.

Then, suddenly, his mother's attitude changed and the thought bubble popped. In shock, Leo's eyes widened and he dropped his spoon in the bowl.

"What just happened?" He asked.

Chapter 31.

Tears started to form in his mother's eyes and she wiped them away with a trembling hand. "You know, Leo," she said softly, "You are the one good and perfect thing in my life. I've been trying to protect you from my problems ever since you were born. Even though I knew you were different," she pretended to reach out and touch his nose, "I tried to make us a 'normal' family - whatever that is." Lenore looked down at her trembling hands and closed them in a fist.

"But now I'm going to tell you the truth, the whole truth and nothing but the truth, so help me God."

Butcher stared at his mother. She was starting to shimmer. This had never happened to him before.

"Leo…"

For the next thirty minutes, Lenore started from the beginning, her high school years and the endless procession of boys and men in her life who found her appealing. They used her and she enjoyed the attention; some of them told her that they loved her, but when they had taken what she had given freely, they found a desperate and love-starved woman who needed companionship far more than she needed physical intimacy. This scared them because they were not nice people, not nice at all, no sirree. There were a few of the men who physically intimidated her, dark, malignant men who enjoyed power, but they seemed so nice at first and she was so sure that she could change them, to make them feel good about themselves. Then, there were those men who seemed mysterious and distant, always leading her to a place where she would give but receive nothing in return. Why couldn't she see this? Why couldn't she read it in their faces? Then there was Leo's father who had been the nicest of them all, but there was something wrong with her, wasn't there? There had to be, because none of these men could see that she was desirable for so much more than her outward appearance.

As Leo listened and watched his mother spill her story out like a tipped rain bucket, the glow around her and the shimmer that had blurred her edges began to fade. At the end of her story, when she talked about their endless running from state to state, house to house, worry to worry, his mother had ceased to be readable. Leo now knew everything about her from her dark past, her dull present and her presumably difficult future. They were leaving to go to Wyoming because there was a man looking for her, someone from whom she had borrowed money and was expecting

301

her to 'work it off.' Leo did not know what this meant, what kind of work she was supposed to be doing, but he was beyond caring.

Something had fundamentally changed in their relationship as she told her story. Finally, just finally, she had trusted him enough to tell him the whole story, and in that trust, he no longer had to 'read' her. He trusted that she was telling the truth.

Standing up from his chair, Leo pulled his long, lanky limbs into order and crossed the chasm between them to his sobbing mother who felt guilty, ashamed, lonely and lost. Wrapping his arms around his mother, he pressed his face into her hair and told her that everything would be fine. Wyoming would be a wonderful place and maybe, just maybe, they could find a new way of life.

"If you want to, Mom, you can parade these guys in front of me and I'll give you a thumbs up or down."

Lenore laughed into her son's shoulder. "You're such a good boy, Leo. Such a good boy." She pulled him back away from him, her tear stained face a mess but still beautiful. "It's going to be different. I promise."

It already is, Leo thought. I can't read you anymore.

Leo smiled broadly.

Butcher wasn't sure the last time that he had yawned so widely. Leaning back in the chair, he stretched and groaned. After checking his watch and noticing that it was 4:30, he wondered if he could keep up the pace. As it was now Friday, he was ready to be done for the week. His schedule showed that he had seen thirty people in the three preceding days, and each one seemed to suck more energy out of him. Although he was enjoying helping others, he would have to do something about the utter exhaustion settling in his bones. Butcher stood and pulled back the curtain thankful that the twins had allowed him to decorate more to his tastes.

Butcher walked out of the booth.

"We've got to talk, fellas."

Nash was wiping down the counters while Derek was closing the till. The last of the customers had exited fifteen minutes ago and the butchery was officially closed. "You're doing a great job, Butcher," Nash said.

"Be that as it may, this is a pace that I am unwilling and unable to keep."

"But Butcher," Derek said as he thumbed through a stack of twenty-dollar bills and marked it against the receipts, "you're helping people. They love you."

"I didn't apply for a job to be a therapist, Derek."

"Well, you should have," he responded and laughed.

Butcher yawned into his fist. "Look, I'm willing to keep up this charade for a little longer, but I would like one hour on and one hour off. It's too much to listen for eight straight hours."

"Technically," Nash said, "the longest you have to do is the four hours in the morning. You get a lunch break, remember."

"Gee, thanks boss. A whole half an hour to wolf down a sandwich while the next people are staring at me."

"You're just a popular man." Nash smiled and whistled as he pushed the remnants into his hand and dumped them into the wastebasket.

"Not as popular as you are."

Nash stopped. Uh oh. "Butcher, don't say anything…"

Derek looked over at his brother. "You haven't been dawdling with Naida again, have you?"

Raising his hands, Nash shook his head. "No way, man. That ship has sailed into the sunset."

Butcher raised an eyebrow and smiled.

"Don't do it, Butcher. Don't do it."

There were times when Butcher's gift was a gift, and this was one of those times. Butcher had recently read something different in Nash's body language. On the first night that they had taken him to the bowling alley, Nash had been blind to it, but Butcher had seen it immediately. Shania had blatantly ogled Nash. To Butcher, the attraction was a neon light. Because Nash had snagged on an already married woman, he wouldn't have noticed, but in the last week, as he was drowning his misery, Nash had gone to the Pecker to hang out with Shania who was an active listener.

"I'll tell you what, Nash. You agree to cutting my counselling hours and I won't say anything."

"That's counsellor/client confidentiality. You couldn't say anything anyway."

"Nash," Butcher said shaking his head, "as much as you wouldn't like to admit it, I'm not a counsellor, or a licensed therapist, only an active listener and each person who comes into the Booth knows that. Remember?" He pointed to the outside wall of the Booth and the disclaimer that was posted on it.

"Please, Butcher, I'm not ready."

"What's going on!" Derek was beside himself itching to be let in on the secret.

"What do you think, Nash?"

"Okay, okay! You win! Start at nine and alternate hours. Odd hours. I don't care."

"Thank you," Butcher said as he walked behind the counter and entered his hours in the book. "And I still expect that my wages will remain the same."

"Fricking shipwreck, Butcher," Nash mumbled, "You're a fricking pirate."

Butcher said goodbye to the twins and exited the butchery. He wanted to get home and get cleaned up before his night with Rhonda. On his walk home, he noticed two extraordinary signs which made him smile and almost (but not quite completely) forget the fact that he'd received messages at his home. He was tempted to put up a camera, but he'd have to ask Liam about it first and, frankly, he didn't want that kind of exposure in town. Although most of the town seemed pleased by his advent, especially those who had taken advantage of fifteen-minute tune-ups at the butchery, there was still an undercurrent, low and subsonic, a wariness about this outsider 'coming in to change our way of life.'

Chapter 31.

The two signs that Butcher saw were patently visible to anyone, no gift needed to read them. The first, underneath the glowing light of the Greedy Pecker, was a sentence that Butcher had not seen coming.

Welcome Teens!
Every Sat. night FREE BOWLING under 18's
Must bowl with a non-parent adult!

The other sign had been erased. As he crossed Highway 10, he looked up at the water tower where four people were finishing the white washing of the word 'Sucks' from beside the town name. Even from this distance, Butcher could make out the slight form of Louise Nelson who was, like the other four, clipped into the railing. Even from that distance, he could make out that they were laughing and enjoying themselves. The angry boy what was his name? Chad? Robbie? - was painting with gusto while Louise was wiping her hands on a towel. The two other boys were leaning against the railing staring out over the little town that seemed so parochial from the ground, but gorgeous from a birds-eye perspective. Butcher smiled.

As he approached the house, he checked to see if there were any other oddities, any clues that might have been left. This morning when he had risen at 5:00, he had opened the door to find a paper bag of cat feces with a note attached.

I think you are crap.
Stay away from her, Bucher
And go away, now.

This person obviously had a sense of humor. A haiku? *Talk about random.* Butcher had taken the bag of feces and chucked it into the industrial bin across the street. Rolling up the piece of message, he took it back inside and placed it with the others. Although he hadn't kept the marshmallow message on the window, he took a picture of it and printed

305

it out at work. Rhonda had kept hers also, but she had given them to Butcher to hopefully use his magic to figure out who the mysterious agitator was. *The Illiterate Bandit,* as they were now calling him.

After showering, Butcher grabbed a beer from the fridge, one of Liam's crappy beers, and settled onto the front steps to watch the sun set. Rhonda would be by to pick him up in twenty minutes - just enough time to relax for a moment. As he plopped himself down, he stretched out his legs and reclined against the step. He was far too tall to sit on the steps comfortably which made him realize that sooner or later he would have to invest in some outdoor furniture, a comfy chair or maybe even a picnic table. The corollary would mean staying put for a while in Amicable, which when he thought about it, especially in light of his dream last night, was a welcome idea. It was rare that he found a comfort so quickly. Though there was a malevolent undercurrent, something else was pulling at him to stay, and it wasn't just Rhonda.

For the next fifteen minutes, post-supper walkers strolled in the beauty of the late summer, or Indian summer as it was called. Those who were out walking on a Friday seemed at ease - the weekend had come again and with it a sense of relaxing work. Saturday would be time for chores and domestic duties, the weekly cleaning, lawn mowing, or in the case of the farmers, increased preparation for the upcoming harvest. Soy beans were already starting to wither and brown, their seeds preparing for another usefulness, while the corn leaves began to wrinkle in their late life stage. Now, husbands and wives, parents and children, neighbors and friends walked across the town of Amicable content to talk or be silent depending on both fitness level and relationship.

Butcher finished his beer and belched into his hand. As he set the can to his side, a familiar car, an 80's Buick Century model, pulled up across the street. Rhonda waved at him from the window of her car. Checking his watch, 7:20, he stood and moved towards her. His heart was pounding. Butcher was aware that something was going to change this night, for better or for worse, and he was hoping for the former.

Something had to change.

Chapter 31.

Walking around to the passenger side of the car, he opened the creaking door and inserted himself.

"Good evening, Madam," he said and reached over to touch her hand. She recoiled slightly, ever aware that there could be people watching.

"Hi, Butcher." Her voice was curt. They began to drive the miles to Clancy in silence.

Butcher

Chapter 32.

Penny drove the car while Tony sat on the passenger side absentmindedly fiddling with his seat belt. He had dressed up for the occasion, which meant wearing his church clothes outside of church. Tony was not particularly comfortable in his dress slacks and a button-down shirt, but tonight seemed like a big deal for them. It had been far too long since nights had been big deals to them.

As the miles slid by, the headlights beamed in front of them catching the white and yellow lines whizzing and snapping underneath the car; Tony glanced at Penny whose appearance had been transformed. Tony smiled.

Penny looked into the back seat where another couple sat, but much closer than the divided space in the front. Like two high school kids, James and Naida were almost sitting on top of each other, their hands were intertwined and Naida's head lay against his shoulder. As they snuggled, James looked out the front window knowing full well that his in-laws were watching. It didn't matter. The parents and children had decided that this was a great weekend to drive to Clancy, The Creek Restaurant, where James and Naida had celebrated their wedding reception. They were looking forward to a great meal, some good conversation and if all developed well, maybe some live music and dancing also.

Penny checked the glowing clock on the dashboard. 7:25. They were all hungry, but it was a healthy practice to wait.

John Deakins checked his watch – 7:15.

He had picked Leslie up at her house half an hour before and driven the dozen miles to Clancy in approaching darkness. Both were so nervous that they had difficulties conversing. Leslie, though, dealt with her nervousness in a completely different way than John. She talked incessantly. At one point, John looked over and spoke a word of calming, even though he was as anxious as she. He was not sure how many years it had been since he'd been on a date - fifteen?

After being ushered to their table in The Creek Restaurant, the last rays of the sun glinted above the western horizon illuminating dust motes circling over their place settings. The light from under the shade was eclipsed to create an effect where their faces were half-illuminated. Jaws and lips, noses shone in the light, but eyes were kept in the dark, not in a sinister way, but shrouded in mystery. Now that John and Leslie were sitting at the table, menus in front of them, John looked over the top of the black folder uncaring of the appetizers and entrees, pastas and mains, and looked up into Leslie's shadowed eyes.

"I just wanted to tell you, Leslie, that you look stunning tonight." Leslie blushed and unconsciously touched her hair. Her hands strayed to her collar where a string of pearls delicately clung to her collarbone. Leslie's makeup accentuated her eyes. He was pleased that he could make her blush.

"Thank you, John," she said looking down at her menu. "You look very nice too."

Alternatively, John had chosen (after much deliberation) to dress up in a suit and tie which, ironically, made him feel naked. Because he wasn't wearing his clerical collar, his first impulse was to feel like imposter. Now that they were anonymously sitting in the restaurant, he could relax and be himself. Leaning forward, Deakins took a drink of his water and chewed a small bit of ice.

"Would you like to get a bottle of wine?" John asked.

"Oh, I don't know. I'm not much of a drinker." Leslie thought that alcohol was not so much 'of the devil,' but alcohol could certainly help you find him quicker.

"Oh, okay."

"But you go ahead."

"Well, I would prefer not to have a glass of wine alone."

Leslie looked up at him. "Well, I suppose we could have a glass - if I don't finish mine, you can." She smiled, but it was more of a warning rather than an invitation. *As much as I want you to try to make a move, I can't have alcohol open the door. You have to open it.*

Deakins motioned for the waitress, a young woman whose name tag read 'Chelsea,' who emerged from the dim recesses of the front desk snapping her gum between her teeth.

"Hi, what can I get for ya?"

John pointed to the menu. "We'll each have a glass of white wine to start with."

"What kind of white wine?"

He looked at Leslie who shrugged. "What would you suggest?"

"Well," Chelsea said, "I don't really drink wine, but I have heard a few other people say that you choose a wine that goes with your meal. Maybe if you choose what you're going to eat, I'll Google it."

"Do you know what you want, Leslie?"

She nodded. "I'll have the chicken cordon bleu." Chelsea nodded and wrote it down on her pad.

"And you, sir?"

John smiled. There weren't many people that called him that. "I'll have the small T-bone steak."

"Very good, sir." Chelsea wrote it down and then began to walk back to the kitchen when Deakins stopped her.

"Excuse me, Chelsea?" She looked back. "If I have some left over, are there boxes for take home?"

"Of course, sir," Chelsea's gum popped. "This is a first-class Iowa restaurant; no food will go to waste."

"Thank you."

"So, do you want me to look up what kind of wine you want?" Chelsea's pen was paused over her notepad. Her eyes expressed a boredom that her face tried to fake.

"That would be very nice." Deakins smiled at the young woman. He then smiled at Leslie nervously. "Thank you for inviting me out tonight." Anxiously, he looked around the almost empty restaurant.

"You're welcome, John," Leslie said. The background music was a cornucopia of Country. "Have you been thinking about me this week?"

John put his elbow on the table in front of him and cupped his chin in his hand. *Yes, Leslie, you're all that I could think about. Every part of you from your hair to your graceful neck. I couldn't stop thinking about your voice and the way your eyes light up when you are excited; the way you touch your throat when you are uncomfortable. The way you smile when you mean to frown and the other way around.*

"Well, yes, Leslie, even though I was pretty busy this week." Inwardly, John bemoaned his cowardice. Did he really think she was interested in him justifying his job?

"Oh," her voice sounded disappointed.

"But…" he stammered, "If you were to ask me what I did this week, I probably couldn't tell you other than the fact that I went in to my office. This week has gone so slowly because I've been constantly thinking about this night. Equal portions fear and excitement."

"What do you mean?"

Chelsea interrupted them; the sound of her gum preceded her and cracked the mood between them. "Well, it looks like red wine goes with the steak and white wine goes with the chicken. How does that sound?"

"Good, that's fine," John said.

"It was really interesting," Chelsea continued, "supposedly you choose wine that… accompanies…" she stumbled over the word, "the color of the flesh you want. So, you…"

"Thank you, Chelsea. We trust you did your homework well." John's interruption seemed to not register with the young woman.

"But you didn't choose the kind of red wine. Do you want a cabernet or a merlot," She said their names slowly remembering with fondness Butcher's caution to not pronounce them phonetically, 'cabernette,' and 'merlaht.'

"I don't really care, Chelsea. We trust you to choose."

"All right," Chelsea replied slowly, her voice rising as if distrusting their decision to trust her. "But if you get some kind of negative reaction to the food because you didn't choose the right one, it's not my fault."

"Yes, yes, Chelsea," John's voice was tinged with frustration. Chelsea left to give the order to the bartender.

"Now, you were saying?"

Unfortunately, John's mind had stuck on the words that Chelsea had said: *the color of the flesh you want*. Like a scratched record, his mind repeated these words over and over, and his eyes connected with the flesh of her arms, her neck and her cheeks. *The color of flesh I want*.

"John," Leslie's voice pushed the needle forward. "You were saying...?"

"Ah," his cheeks flushed and he readjusted to the moment. "When you asked me to accompany you here to The Creek Restaurant, I have to admit, my first response was fear. All the questions of my pastoral calling came crashing down on me like a tidal wave: What will the congregation think if they find out? The Bible says it is better to be un-hitched, so what happens if I become... crazy about her? Will I lose focus? Will I be able to continue as a pastor?"

Leslie's eyes fell and her mouth pinched with disappointment.

"But then," he said, "I thought about you, and only you, and how brave it was for you to ask me out, to push me beyond my stupidity and arrogance, and I was excited because..."

"Yes?"

"Because..."

Chelsea barged in again carrying two glasses of wine, one red and one white. After setting them in front of the respective drinkers, she paused asked, "Is there anything else I can get for you while you wait?"

"No." John said impatiently.

"Because we have some delicious rolls. Don, the cook..."

"No!" They both said at the same time.

Chelsea's eyes widened and for a moment; she looked like a rabbit spotted by a predator. Then, finally sensing her un-neededness, she twirled to move back to the bar wondering exactly why the people at table fourteen were so rude.

"Because...?" Leslie's eyes were beginning to look frantic.

"I... I... can't believe how much..."

The front door opened and Deakins' jaw dropped, his face drained and in one quick motion, he reached forward, grabbed their glasses of wine and put them on the table next to them.

"What are you doing?" Leslie whispered. "Are you crazy?"

John's eyes fell on the people coming through the front door. Butcher and Rhonda.

Damnit.

Butcher spotted Reverend Deakins immediately and he smiled which Deakins read as smug and self-congratulatory. Noticing that Leslie was across from him, he spoke softly to Rhonda and pointed casually to the pair. Rhonda smiled also which Deakins also misinterpreted. What had started out as a night to remember was now turning into a nightmare to remember. Butcher and Rhonda walked across the restaurant towards Leslie and Reverend Deakins. When Chelsea spotted them, she clapped her hands and came over.

"Hi!" She shouted across. "Hi, there!"

Rhonda greeted Chelsea with a hug, which caused Leslie to raise an eyebrow. Leslie was not happy, not happy at all, at the turn of events. She had been hoping for an uninterrupted evening with John; they would finally talk without outside influences, maybe even kiss each other again, but now her dream, like the Colossus of Rhodes, was crumbling into the ocean due to an unforeseen earthquake.

"It's so good to have you back," Chelsea said. "Can I get you a table near the window?"

Butcher shook her hand. "Give us a sec, Chelsea. We're just going to talk to these fine people for a moment."

Chelsea was not so sure about his assessment of the tight people at the table, but she noticed their wine glasses had been moved. "How did these end up here? Did you want…"

Deakins raised his hand. "Thank you, miss, but those aren't ours…"

"What?" Chelsea was very confused.

"They must have belonged to someone else."

"Do you want me to leave them here?"

314

"That's fine, thank you."

Deakins looked up at Butcher. He was dressed smartly, Sunday clothes, John guessed; Rhonda looked strikingly beautiful and content. "Well, this is certainly a surprise," Deakins said. "We didn't expect to see you here? Were you following us?"

Butcher laughed. "Nothing so stalkingly extraordinary. No, we came here last week and loved the atmosphere and thought we'd come back. It's hard for us to be seen together in Amicable."

"Tell me about it," Leslie mumbled under her breath.

"But it's weird," Butcher continued, "you drive fifteen miles down the road and it's like a new world, like you've escaped a prison. You can talk, eat, drink, be merry - you know what I mean?"

Deakins stared up at him without responding.

"So..." Butcher stammered uncomfortably, "You're here on a..."

Deakins interjected. "We're here to discuss the... um... church budget. It's that time of year where we're starting to think about the next." He quickly glanced at Leslie who was turning a brilliant shade of crimson.

"That's... that's wonderful to be so... preplanned." Butcher wasn't quite sure what to say to the man's obvious lie.

Leslie pushed back her chair. "Excuse me. I need to use the restroom." Her voice quivered. Emotion was sitting shotgun in the runaway car of her control. Dropping her napkin on the chair, she smoothed the creases in her dress and moved quickly towards the bathroom.

Butcher and Rhonda shared a look. "I need to use the bathroom too." Rhonda said. "Why don't you..." she wasn't sure how to finish the sentence, so she just waved her hand around the setting and followed Leslie across the restaurant.

A brief moment of awkwardness passed between the two men. Deakins, not to be intimidated, stood up and back from Butcher who towered over him. "Why are you here?"

315

"We're on a date?" Butcher responded. "Why are you covering up yours?" The dark suit, starched shirt and blue tie were tight on the pastor.

"I'm not covering up anything, and this," he motioned to the table, "Is not a date. It's a... a..."

"You can go on denying it, Reverend Deakins, but you already know that I can spot a lie from ten thousand miles away. Why don't you just embrace it? Why don't you enjoy the fact that a beautiful woman has said 'yes' to spending time with you? Gosh, you're out of Amicable, just the two of you. That's great!"

Deakins' face reddened. "You couldn't possibly understand the nuances of my life. First," he held his index finger, "there are the congregational implications. Secondly, the spiritual ramifications. Thirdly..."

"Your excuses should have started with, one, I'm afraid; Two, I don't like rejection; Three, what if I behave like a moron? Seems like you're on a pretty good roll now."

John's eyes strayed towards the bathroom. "Okay. Okay, I get it. You can psychoanalyze me all you want, but you still don't know what it's like?"

Butcher rolled his eyes. "Just enjoy the night. Remember what it's like to be a man."

"How dare you! I know what it's like..."

"I don't mean that you're feminine, but just let your..." Butcher pursed his lips and pounded his chest. "...hormones roil around inside you. Embrace the nervousness. Enjoy the fear of interacting with a woman. Pull out her chair and drink wine with her." Butcher's eyes strayed towards the glasses at the next table.

"Those aren't..." Deakins stopped short.

"Come on, John, let it go - for one night, for your sake and for Leslie's. She's crumbling before your eyes because your courage is faltering and you're unable to stand up for her, for you both, for your relationship. Don't you see? This is the fulcrum of your relationship."

"What, are you a marriage counsellor now?"

Butcher shook his head. "Sarcasm won't help."

Deakins looked down at his hands. Everything that Butcher had said was correct. He was afraid of all sorts of things, but he was more afraid of never having someone to belong to, he just hadn't accepted it yet. What would happen if he rejected Leslie tonight, and in ten years, he looked back, lonely and discontented, but still 'theologically' pure. His hands shook slightly.

"But what if..." His voice faltered.

"Screw 'what if.'" Butcher said and placed a hand on John's shoulder. "Embrace 'now then.'"

"So, what should I do?" Deakins' eyes implored the butcher to make the decision for him. "Should we make public the thing that we fear most?"

"And what is that fear?"

The clergyman blew air out of his mouth. "That the town of Amicable will judge us to be unworthy..."

"And what is the worst thing that could happen?"

Deakins was about to speak, but no words came to the surface. He snapped his mouth shut as he saw movement behind Butcher's back.

Oh, for Pete's sake.

This night could not get much worse.

Leslie cradled her head in her hands crying softly in front of the mirror. She had invested so much of her emotion, time and energy into Reverend John Deakins that she was reeling. He was such a fearful man - always afraid of what things look like, or what other people might think. He was always second guessing himself. After his sermons, he'd take the slightest bit of critique as biting criticism of him personally. Afraid of the power of public opinion, he rarely confronted people about their words or habits and would often do whatever it took to mollify people in hopes that an awkward peace could abound. And he desperately wanted them to like him.

But tonight, she had hoped his shell would crack. It almost had, but when Butcher and Rhonda arrived, his entire being was hermetically sealed back up into its container of fear. She could see it in his eyes; she could sense it in his posture. Just as he was about to reveal the great joy and excitement which could come from their relationship, Butcher and Rhonda walked through the door. The symbolism of moving the wine glasses to the next table destroyed everything she had hoped for and now, Leslie was uncertain as to how she could possibly finish the rest of the night with him.

The bathroom door opened behind her and Leslie started. It was Rhonda.

"Leslie?"

"Go away, Rhonda."

"Are you okay?"

"I said, go away. I don't want to talk about it." Their voices were echoing in the small room.

Silence. Then, Leslie felt a hand on her shoulder. "Leslie, I know what it's like."

Leslie's eyes flashed. "How could you possibly know what it's like? To constantly be wanting something, or someone, and never knowing if it's going to come to fruition. How could you possibly know? You're a…"

Rhonda's cheeks crimsoned and she took her hand away.

Whore. There was no way that Leslie would have spoken the word, but there was a sense that Leslie did not really know what had happened in Rhonda's life, only bubbling rumors that had seemed to boil to the surface. Leslie looked at Rhonda in the mirror and finally saw not a whore but a woman seeking the same thing she was.

"I'm a what…? What were you going to say?"

Leslie wiped her eyes. "You're a… fine one to talk. This Butcher waltzes into town, tall and handsome like a movie set cowboy with his big shoulders and brown eyes, a smile that melts your heart, and you go with the flow. Do what you feel like regardless of the consequences."

"I know what the consequences are," Rhonda said softly.

"Oh, Rhonda." Leslie's vitriol was exhausted. "I feel like a teenage girl wanting to push a note across the desk to a cute boy hoping that he'll check the box that says 'yes, I like you too.'"

Rhonda looked around the bathroom and felt an odd sense of déjà vu. Surely, women like them had gathered in bathrooms for generations commiserating the fact that boys just didn't 'get' them.

"Maybe tonight will be different." Rhonda returned her hand to Leslie's shoulder who then, without conscious will, turned towards her. Rhonda enfolded the much shorter woman in a friendly embrace. Leslie did not return the hug keeping her arms in front of her, but she did melt slightly. The human touch, one of sympathy, seemed to comfort her.

The bathroom door opened behind them. Penny and Naida walked in apologizing for the intrusion, but then gaped at the two women they encountered who were hugging in front of the mirror.

Leslie's mind erupted as if hit by a torpedo.

Oh, no.

Deakins and Butcher watched Tony and James draw closer to them. Like most men, they were oblivious to the strangeness of situations. From their perspective, it was good to see some other Amicableans in Clancy, and even though they had come for a double date, the common bond was comfortable.

"Hello, Butcher. Reverend." James extended his hand to Butcher and then to Reverend Deakins. "This is my father-in-law, Tony Reynolds." Butcher shook his hand while Deakins smiled his greeting, unable to speak. "Fancy seeing you guys here."

"Yes, we've decided to get the heck out of Amicable tonight and enjoy the food and fare here." Butcher could feel the turmoil in Reverend Deakins' silence.

"So, did you come by yourselves, or did someone else come with you? Is Rhonda here?"

"We…" Butcher wasn't sure what to say, but the situation called for some massaging of the facts. "Yes, Rhonda and I decided to take

319

Reverend Deakins out to dinner and Rhonda thought it would be a good idea to invite Leslie - you know Leslie, right?" Deakins looked sideways at Butcher, shocked.

"Of course we know Leslie. She's one of my mother's good friends."

They stood awkwardly for a moment and then Butcher cleared his throat. "Do you guys want a drink?"

Tony blew out his breath. "Thank God, yes." He said quickly and looked at Deakins. "Sorry, preacher. I didn't mean anything by that."

Deakins attempted to smile and held up his hands. "It's okay."

Tony walked to the bar. "Would anyone else like something?"

James raised his hand. "Get me a beer, would you Tony? Butcher, would you like a beer?"

"No, I'm thinking about getting a bottle of champagne. Anyone want to share with me?" Both James and Tony made a face, almost an identical gesture, like sucking on a lemon.

"I could get some champagne glasses and we could pour the beer into them." James smiled and walked to Tony to help him carry the drinks. "I'm sure Penny and Naida will share some with you though. Reverend Deakins?"

John Thomas Deakins paused and for one of the few times in his life, he was blatantly aware of a choice that had to be made which could alter the course of his destiny. If he refused, he somehow knew that, even though this refusal would be more proper, his relationship with Leslie would come crashing down around his ears. The ride home would be so incredibly uncomfortable, that he would probably not sleep through the night. On the other hand, if he accepted a drink (or even if he picked up the one he'd already ordered), he might find the courage to do and say some things that would allow for a different life, one that he was both excited about and afraid of.

Deakins looked over at Butcher. "What do you think?" He asked softly knowing that Butcher had already seen the future options before he had.

320

Butcher took a deep breath. "This is a decision that you'll have to make on your own."

John Deakins swallowed hard and looked towards James who was waiting patiently. "I'll have a beer, please."

James nodded and turned back to the bar to retrieve the beers and the champagne. James didn't react; he didn't say anything. It was as if Deakins was a normal person, a friend out on the town for the night. John turned towards Butcher who was smiling.

"Atta boy, John."

A great weight had fallen from his shoulders at the realization and relief that there was no judgement lurking, like a snarling, drooling beast, around every corner. "Thank you, Leo."

"Rhonda. Leslie?" Penny's voice expressed confusion as she and Naida plugged the doorway.

Rhonda released the smaller woman and turned towards the incoming duo. "Hello Penny and Naida."

"Is everything all right?"

Leslie looked up at Rhonda. She nodded. "It's okay. I'm okay."

"But... you're crying."

Leslie shrugged. "Sometimes it happens."

Penny was very certain that she had never seen Leslie cry before, not even at funerals. To see her like this, Penny was frightened. "Is there anything that we can do?"

Naida pushed her mother in the back. "We could move a little farther into the bathroom so we don't have to give a live viewing to the entire restaurant what is going on in the women's restroom."

Penny moved forward and approached Leslie's left side while Rhonda remained on her right. "I wasn't expecting to see you here tonight."

"Nor I, you."

"Did you come with Reverend Deakins?"

Leslie knew that she was at a crossroads in her life and she instantaneously computed the two outcomes by which her future would be changed. She could speak the truth and be at the mercy of Penny, or she could lie and bury everything that was happening between them.

Before she could answer, Rhonda interjected. "Butcher and I brought them." Leslie looked up quickly at Rhonda. "Butcher wanted to get to know the Reverend better and I thought it would be a good idea to bring Leslie along as a member of the church so that Reverend Deakins did not seem like a third wheel."

Penny's eyes narrowed. There were quite a few things in that statement that didn't quite add up, but did it really matter? "That's wonderful," she replied cautiously.

"I think it's great, too," Naida said, "but do you mind if I go the bathroom. I really have to pee."

The other three women looked at the youngest of the group who was smiling impatiently and apologetically; they moved out of the way.

Rhonda looked at Penny who was looking at Leslie who was looking at Rhonda.

This was going to get really interesting.

With Chelsea's help, the men joined three tables so that they could all eat together. John asked Chelsea if she could put their order on hold while everyone else ordered. Then, he waited uneasily for the women to emerge from the bathroom. The men, still standing with drinks in hand, chatted about the weather, sports and so as not to preclude Reverend Deakins from the conversation, (because they assumed that he had no interest in sports) they spoke briefly and quickly about politics. Thankfully, the topic was interrupted by the four women exiting the bathroom.

Naida lead the group. James' eyes sparkled at her young form, a knee length green dress showing off her firm calves. Then, Penny, wearing blue slacks and a pleated cream-colored blouse with a string of pearls accentuating it. Tony's eyes were pulled from his daughter to his wife and he was happy she was smiling. Leslie, next, her eyes puffy from crying. Neither James nor Tony would have noticed this. She was surprised to see the new setting of tables. She searched Reverend Deakins' eyes for any confusion, but she was taken aback by his broad smile. Lastly, Rhonda, the tallest of the group, caught Butcher's eyes and her own widened. What was going on? Although she was disappointed that she and Butcher were not going to be able to speak privately about their messages, or even more importantly about their thoughts regarding the future, she was keenly interested in what was going to happen next.

"We've decided to have a celebration meal together, like a first supper." Butcher was amused at his own joke, thankful Deakins did not seem to think that it was too irreverent.

"What are we celebrating?" Naida asked.

"New relationships." Butcher's eyes moved back and forth between the other diners. Each person looked at their partner.

"Well," Leslie said, "What, um, why are we celebrating? Naida and James? Penny and Tony? You've both been married for a while - how are yours new?"

Penny spoke for the four of them. "We've kind of got a new lease on our lives. A change, a new wind blowing, or something like it. We found that even after a long time together, we can remember what love is like." Both she and Tony blushed, but Tony coughed into his hand to hide his embarrassment.

Butcher picked up the champagne bottle and offered it to the women. "Would any of you care to share a toast with us men?"

"I will," Naida said enthusiastically. "I'd love some." Rhonda and Penny grabbed a glass while Leslie looked at John who was holding a beer.

"I will too," she said softly.

Naida filled the glasses, handed one to each of the women and gave the toast. "Here's to different lives!" They all repeated it. Everyone took a sip except Naida who downed her entire glass of champagne and reached out for more. The others, seeing that Naida was ebullient and full of cheer, mirrored the gesture, except for Leslie, who smiled primly and sipped her champagne.

Chelsea appeared magically behind the women; a table of eight automatically meant a fifteen percent gratuity, which on a slow night like this, would be a real blessing. On top of that, the tall man, who, last week, had dropped quite a bit of extra cash onto the bill, was part of the group. "So, what can I get everyone on this festive night?"

The other six, after looking at the menu, ordered their meals and they settled into polite conversation. As they worked through the bottle of champagne and bottles of domestic beer, their moods rose, all except for the smallest woman who continually looked over at Reverend Deakins and wondered what was going on in his mind. They were supposed to be talking about the future. She wasn't sure whether to behave like a sinner or judge like a saint.

Twenty minutes later, Chelsea arrived with the battery of food. The Creek Restaurant served not just frog legs and eels but enticing freshwater fish species, delectable beef steaks and pork loin chops that would melt in the mouth. As they hoed into the food laughing raucously at jokes that would previously be considered bad taste, they all felt as if they had entered a sanctuary where, like Superman's Fortress of Solitude, they could commune in a Bastion of Togetherness. Without speaking of it, they presumed that whatever was said or done that night would remain between the eight of them. John Deakins found, maybe for the first time since he was a child, that life and faith, mirth and reverence could coexist simultaneously. As he chatted vociferously with Tony Reynolds, he noticed something wonderful: the stories and thoughts of others, their daily lives and daily desires, were amazingly similar to his own. People needed and desired love and respect, community and opportunities to share wisdom and idiocy, a heart full of trust to share life on the journey. He looked over at Leslie who was smiling politely at Naida. It seemed she had yet to embrace the sanctity of the First Supper and was reserved. He wished that he could help her lighten up.

Butcher, on the other hand, lifted his glass to Rhonda and toasted her while smiling broadly at this beautiful intrusion into their lives. Although he knew a very difficult discussion had to happen very soon, he was content to enjoy that moment, in that place, in that mood. He watched Rhonda's eyes as they sparkled. Her cheeks glowed; she radiated health and happiness. It had been a long time since she, too, had been part of a congregation of people who wandered the trails of life together. In fact, all eight of them there with their different backgrounds and stories and struggles and temptations - this was something new and oddly profound in a culture that prided itself on niceness, neighborliness and purity.

"I'd like to make another toast," Naida said as she struggled to her feet and raised her glass. A chorus of laughter, someone shouted 'Only one toast per person per night!' which brought another gale of happy roaring.

"Seriously," Naida said as she raised her hand, "I'd like to make a toast to Butcher. His descent upon our little town of Amicable has been something quite..." she waved her free hand around. "Can we each fill in the blank?" Somewhat tipsily she looked around at the others whose glasses were already raised. Silence ensued; no one was willing to take the first step out onto the narrow limb.

John Deakins cleared his throat and stood with Naida. "Miraculous," he said humbly. "I was wrong about you, Leo. Very, very wrong, and I'm sorry."

The gathering collectively gasped and looked around at each other. Leslie covered her heart as if protecting it from the apology. She'd never heard the reverend publicly apologize for anything.

"Stunning," Rhonda said quietly but audibly.

"Refreshing," Penny stated while looking at Tony.

"That's enough, everyone," Butcher held up his hands. "Enough. This isn't about me; this is about you and your ability to adapt and change."

"Those are dirty words in Amicable," Naida said which brought another guffaw.

John Deakins interrupted by standing up with his half-finished glass of beer. The table quieted, unsure of what the clergyman was going to say, but his effusive mood seemed to lend itself to a hopeful and expansive toast. "Well," he said with a whoosh of breath, "I never would have expected to be here tonight with you all, not that I've minded whatsoever." Polite smiles. "When I left the house tonight, I picked up Leslie to bring her to The Creek Restaurant to get out of Amicable. It is a nice town, but I think we can all agree, it can be slightly constricting for a social life."

"Amen to that," James proclaimed. More grins.

"It was not my intention to spend the night with you, but solely with Leslie." Confused looks around the circle, which ended up on Leslie whose face was ribboning with color.

"I thought you came with Butcher?" James asked.

"That's what Butcher said; he was trying to cover for me, because... I am a coward."

Eyes widened. Jaws dropped. Expressions given over to surprise.

"You see, my cowardice comes from the fact that I often hide behind my clerical garb, my collar, the black of my wardrobe, even my calling, to avoid deep interactions and investments with people. Because I have been taught to believe that the life of a pastor is to be sacred and removed, I have not allowed people into my life. If I rearranged the letters of the word 'sacred' to form 'scared,' you know what's wrong with me. I'm scared." He wanted to take a drink, but he had to finish.

"I think I'm ready to move beyond scared. I'm ready to move into relationships that can be frightening for me. Does that make sense?"

Rhonda nodded. "All of us do that on a daily basis. That's the only thing in life that brings meaning. Sometimes you get hurt, sometimes you find the extraordinary."

"That sounds like something Jesus would have said." Deakins' face was alight with realization that he had missed out on a large segment of life. "So, tonight I allowed Butcher to cover for me, and my guess is that Rhonda did the same for Leslie because..."

Leslie broke her silence. "No, Reverend, you don't..."

"Yes, yes, I do, Leslie, and I think you can call me John."

Surprised looks around the circle.

"But…"

"I've decided," Deakins said, "that I'd like to trust you with my… openness… about my feelings for Leslie." All eyes shifted back and forth between the smartly dressed pastor, black suit clinging to his curves, and the tiny woman sitting across the table from him, head bowed. Penny, especially, seemed shocked beyond words.

"What in the world…?" Naida's question hung in the air.

"For the last few weeks, well, really since Butcher's arrival, I've been experiencing a strange awakening regarding this amazing woman." Rhonda looked at Butcher who was smiling. Deakins continued. "So, as part of my transformation into a true human being, I've apologized to all of you, I've publicly shared drinks with you," he raised his beer again and smiled, "I've proclaimed my admiration for a beautiful woman, and now I want you all to call me John - even in public." More gasps from around the table. He looked over at Leslie whose head was still looking down into her lap.

Momentary silence, then Leslie pushed back her chair and looked up. Eyes full of tears she began to move away from the table as if leaving them, but she stopped, her shoulders shaking slightly. A war had been raging inside of her, a battle that had no clear winner. Her terror at being a Mary Magdalene to her congregation. Throughout the night, she had attempted to process the entirety of what was transpiring - this very public and vocal discussion about life and the joys contained therein. Beyond the fear was a frightening hope that this very thing that was occurring before her eyes, and her heart, would be real. Her tears, unshown for years, had appeared unsummoned and unannounced. But as she sat at the table listening to the Reverend John Deakins, the object of her affection, she saw the fulcrum of her life appearing and the weight of her future balancing on the decision. Turning around she looked at no one but John Thomas Deakins. Slowly, she moved towards the suited man who stood still. Deakins' face began to fall. Leslie was not smiling; in fact, there was no expression whatsoever, just a determined walk towards him.

"Leslie…" he started.

She shook her head and moved the last few steps very quickly to stand in front of him. Then, with tremendous gravity, she put her hands to his cheeks and pulled his face towards hers where she kissed him full on the lips. His eyes as wide as dish saucers betrayed his immense surprise. As the onlookers looked on, he noticed that Leslie was beginning to laugh through her tears and her kiss.

"You big buffoon," she said softly. "You could have told me you were going to do that first."

The ensemble erupted into cheering and laughter. Congratulations were passed between those who had been seated and were now arising and the freshly minted couple standing awkwardly in the middle. Whatever drinks were left were quickly consumed and one last round was ordered with a shout towards the bar. Chelsea appeared from her hiding spot and nodded.

As the noise continued, Leslie shot a glance at Penny who was smiling quizzically at her, the unexpectedness of the revelation seemed akin only to the second coming of Christ the Lord. Leslie shrugged and smiled and Penny raised her glass to her. *Good for you, Leslie. Good for you.*

Chelsea brought the drinks as the company stood in a circle. Deakins, holding Leslie's small, delicate hand in his own, a trembling new feeling for him, held up his glass. He could feel the sweat begin to stand out on his forehead. "My last toast, not only for this beautiful woman beside me, but a boon to ask." They waited patiently for him to wipe his brow with the back of his drink hand and smile again. "If there is any way that you could keep this information to yourselves for a little while so that we, Leslie and I, can sort out how we want to move forward, I think I," he stopped himself, "We, would really appreciate it."

James lifted his glass first. "What happens in Clancy stays in Clancy."

If only that would have remained true.

On the way home, Penny's conscience felt as if there was an itch that needed to be scratched. She looked over at Tony who was driving, a seemingly permanent smile plastered on his face. He looked over at her and reached a hand out to place on her leg. Although they were in an expansive mood, dulled slightly by the alcohol, they were content. The four couples, they could think of themselves in that way now, were a secret group, and those did not happen easily in Amicable.

Secrets, that is.

When alliances were cemented, especially when they broke old ties, things tended to get heated and messy, and Penny knew that a battle would be stirring. Although she was happy for Leslie, a woman who had been controlled by her control for most of her life, the need to share the information with her friends was overwhelming. Penny, like the rest of them, loved to be the first one to share a juicy morsel of gossip. To be first, to see the look on her friends' faces, was addictive and priceless. Deep down inside, Penny knew that she should keep the information to herself, but she justified her willingness to tell her friends by the fact that she thought that they would not tell anyone or do anything about it. She *hoped* that they wouldn't tell anyone else.

"So," Tony said to the entirety of the car, "that was a totally unexpected night, wasn't it?"

"Holy crap, Dad," Naida said as she leaned forward from the back seat. "You aren't kidding. Who would have ever thought that Reverend Deakins…"

"You're supposed to call him 'John,'" James said from behind Naida.

"Pardon me. Who would have ever thought that John would have girded up his loins to go into battle for love?"

James laughed. "Not me. But it is kind of cool that he could find love at his age."

"What do you mean by that? 'Love at his age…' He's probably only in his thirties." Tony spoke while looking into the mirror.

"Well, I think that's still pretty late," Naida said.

"It just takes some people a little longer to find love," Tony said as he looked at his wife who was staring distractedly out the passenger side window. "Right Pen?"

"Hmmm?"

Tony frowned. "Never mind. "

"So, we can't tell anyone, right?" Naida asked.

"John asked us not to, so I'd guess we'd better hold ourselves to it."

Penny heard what Tony said; she registered that Naida was attempting to give heed to Reverend Deakins' plea, but her need, her desperate need, to tell her friends was winning the war.

When she got home, she would have to make a decision.

"Oh, John, I'm so nervous." Leslie's hands were shaking as they drove from Clancy back to Amicable in the Stygian darkness. "There are so many things that have to go right for us for this relationship to succeed."

"I assume that you are already attempting to work out all possible permutations of the future with me."

She smiled and looked at the clock. 10:39 p.m. "I have this immense fear that in an hour and twenty-one minutes, the fairy godmother is going to arrive and she's going to be angry."

John laughed. "What?"

Clearing her throat, Leslie glanced at the man she had come to adore. "For all my years in Amicable, I've been admiring from afar, like Cinderella and Prince Charming; I've felt plain and restricted, my clothes might as well be covered with cinders. And, if I'm honest, I've been spending a lot of time with the squeaking mice - my friends." She fell quiet.

"And now," he filled in the silence, "you feel like your mouse friends are going to make a lot of noise about this when they find out."

She nodded.

"What's the worst thing that can happen?"

Leslie checked them off on her fingers. "One: you could lose your call at the church. Two: you could lose your ministry. Three: We could spend time with each other for a while and you could end up hating me, or disliking my propensity for control. Four…"

Deakins chuckled. "Hold on, Leslie. Let's walk down the other path together. What is the best possible scenario?"

Even in the dark, Leslie could feel herself blushing. "We could fall in love, get married, have children, see them grow up - you know, the fairy tale without the godmother."

"I like that one better," John said.

"But…"

He interrupted her doubt. "How about tonight, just tonight, we pretend that we are a normal couple who just had a great night out together? How about we get back to your house, I escort you up to the front porch and then we sit still for a while enjoying the cool late summer evening breeze. Maybe we can have a glass of tea and then, when I'm ready to leave, I can give you a long, lingering kiss with tons of promise attached to it."

"I like the sound of *that* better," she responded quietly.

The rest of the drive was spent in expectant silence.

Rhonda and Butcher's drive home was not as joyful as their companions'. Butcher attempted to engage her in conversation. Although she had been joyful at the restaurant, Rhonda had fallen into a melancholic abyss that defied logic. He knew, though, what she was suffering from. As their own pivot to the future approached them, he read that she was not quite ready to turn with him or away from him.

Rhonda drove down Peppertree and shut off the car. The overhead light came on illuminating the two tall people whose heads were close to touching the ceiling. Shadows covered both of their eyes giving them a haunted look, but the haunting draped their hearts also.

Butcher looked over at his date, letting his gaze fall upon her face, which was staring into the darkness of the front windshield. "Can you come in for a little bit?"

She didn't turn towards him. "I don't know if that would be a good idea, Butcher."

"Why not?"

Her silence spoke much more than he wanted. "Because if I come inside with you, we would have to talk. We'd have to talk about what's going between us and around us. We'd have to talk about tonight; the messages that keep coming to us; my mother; my…" He waited for the next word. "…past."

"But that's good," he said putting a hand on her arm. She flinched and he drew it back. He pushed on. "We need to talk about these things. That's what people do. That's what couples do."

Rhonda turned towards him. "Are we a couple? I don't know if we are. I've been on this seesaw, up and down, up - this is the man I've been waiting for. Down - who is this guy? Where is he really from? What is he really after? How can he be so mysterious and beautiful at the same time?"

"Ask me any question you want. Any question at all."

"If we are going to do this, then we are going into your house because I'm not going to sit here in my car where anybody with a set of eyes can leap to conclusions."

"That's what I wanted to happen from the beginning," Butcher said.

"Butcher," Rhonda said desperately. "You just don't know anything about me. You think you do, but you don't. There's no way you could possibly know and when you do, you'll walk out, just like the others."

He shook his head. "I already know, Rhonda. I truly do."

She opened the car door and stood up. After shutting it behind her, she began to walk into the dark towards his house. Butcher could only see his reflection in the passenger side window. His appearance was skewed, warped by the concavity of the glass - he looked stretched, drawn to the surrealistic quarters of his subconscious mind and it was at that point he wondered if this night would end up like all the other nights, a neon arrow pointing to a quick departure to another state.

Chapter 32.

He opened the door and followed Rhonda into his house.

Tony opened the door for Penny who entered, took off her light jacket and hung it on a hook in the alcove. Yawning and following her, Tony tapped her on the bottom and moved past her into the living room. He didn't turn on any lights but moved towards the bedroom. By the time he had reached the bedroom, he had already taken off his shirt.

"I'm going to bed," he said with another yawn. For Tony, eleven o'clock was pushing the limit of his consciousness. Combined with alcohol and excitement, he would be asleep almost before inserting himself between the sheets.

"I'll be right there," she said.

Penny waited for the bedroom door to close and then opened her purse. Her phone was resting in the pouch. As she looked at her phone, it became like a ball of plutonium. She knew that if she touched it, she would do the very thing that she didn't want to do. Unfortunately, there was something so pleasurable about gossiping, even if the gossip was true and good. Aware of the damage that sending a text message to her friends could do, she shook her head. *They would never attempt anything untoward, would they? No, of course not.* They were nice Amicableans who happened to care for many different people. Linda, Jeannie and Leona were part of her circle of friends and this amazing information might be an opportunity for celebration. Maybe they would love the idea that Leslie had found someone, or the fact that Reverend Deakins was looking outwards into the 21st century where clergymen could (and should) find partners for their lives. Maybe they could help ease the community into sharing life with them?

It was this false thread of thought that Penny Reynolds, well-intentioned as she was, gave into her addiction, picked up her phone and sent a message.

It was an exciting night. Went out to eat with Tony, James and Naida, but you'll never guess who else was there.

Reverend John Deakins and Leslie.

And they shared a secret that I think you'll like.

She sent the clickbait message and waited for her friends to reply with variations of 'do tell.' Penny smiled and typed a response.

We can erase Reverend Deakins and Leslie Tielman from the eligible singles list.

Tracey Thomas always had trouble sleeping on Friday nights. The school's football game had gone predictably bad and Tracey, along with many of her friends, waited for some of the players to exit the locker room so that they could console them on their forty-one-point loss. Although she cared nothing about football, she was happy to be with her classmates as they waited.

Tracey arrived home around ten o'clock. As she was still attempting to return to her parents' good graces, she popped her head in the door and called out to her parents who were sitting in front of the TV. Her mother was reading a book and her father was watching the nightly news. Tracey went to the kitchen for a drink of water, then traipsed to her room where she turned on the bedside light and got ready for bed. Around a quarter to eleven, she turned off the light and stood by her window listening to the sounds of the small Midwestern town as they floated around the still streets. A few cars could be seen cruising the alleyways. For the most part, though, the streets were silent. Just as she was about to turn away from the window, she noticed movement across the street on Leslie Tielman's porch. Two figures were perched on the Adirondack chairs, the glow of a streetlamp illuminating their forms. They were sitting very close to each other, far closer than she had ever seen anyone else on her porch other than when Reverend Deakins had visited.

Could he be back again? Was there something going on between the two of them still?

Tracey was certain that it was someone else (she couldn't see their faces) - the larger figure was not wearing the traditional garb that Reverend Deakins normally would be wearing. This one was clad in a suit and he was sitting next to the smaller figure of Leslie. Tracey noticed that their hands seemed to be interlocked. She rubbed her eyes and drew closer to the glass. Holding her breath so as not to fog up the window, she strained her eyes to see what was happening. Sure enough, just a few moments later, Leslie leaned over and kissed the man. Like a cat snuggling into its owner, Leslie nestled her head on the man's shoulder.

For five minutes, the couple sat in silence until the man tenderly leaned in and kissed Leslie once again. *If this was indeed Reverend Deakins, what would the parish say?*

The man stood and pulled Leslie to her feet and they embraced one last time. After the hug, the man turned from her, waved his hand over his head and stepped down into the street. It was then that the streetlight fully illuminated him: it was indeed the Right Reverend John Thomas Deakins. Without thinking, Tracey took out her phone, opened up the camera and zoomed in. Feeling like a detective on a stakeout, she took a few quick photographs. Then, as Reverend Deakins whistled his way softly down the path, he looked both directions before entering his car. A brief twinge of guilt racked Tracey, but unlike the last time this very event occurred, she felt oddly exuberant. She had to tell someone, but who could she talk to? Tracey went through her list of contacts until she found David, the one person with whom she felt most comfortable. Although he was not her best friend, that was Alyssa, David was a person who she thought she could trust.

Tapping on the photo, she entered David's phone number into the bar. If the photo was enlarged, the face of Reverend Deakins could be seen clearly.

David, you're not going to believe this. I took this picture tonight from my room across the street from Ms. Tielman's house. The mysterious man is... Reverend Deakins! I had to tell someone, but please! Please! Keep this a secret. I'll talk to you about it tomorrow. Okay? She attached a shocked emoticon as well as one with a finger over its lips for secrecy.

Ten minutes later, David Matthews encountered the picture. Not wasting any time, he had sent it to three people with almost the exact same message as Tracey's with the same plea for secrecy. Unfortunately,

335

gossip does indeed spread like a virus, and by the time both Reverend Deakins and Leslie Tielman woke up the next morning, two teenagers and four middle-aged women had changed the entire future of Amicable.

Butcher handed a cup of tea to Rhonda who had pulled her legs up under her in the sole reclining chair in the living room. A solitary light shone through an assortment of deceased bugs, which littered the white cover like the aftermath of a nuclear blast. Dust and mold seemed to permeate every corner of the room, but on this night it didn't seem to matter.

For a moment, they sat cupping the warm brews in their hands putting off the impending transition of their relationship. Whatever would occur in the next moments, whatever words spoken or retained, would determine the future for both of them whether together or apart. It was simply a matter of letting the lightning strike where it may.

"You said I could ask any question I wanted and you will answer truthfully, yes?"

Butcher nodded. "Whether I answer truthfully or not, you would be able to tell, but I will answer in the best way that I can."

"Okay," she said slowly, "Where do you really come from?"

"That's a difficult question." He cleared his throat. "The last place was Colorado. I was a butcher in Aspen. But if you are asking me what state I was born in, the honest answer is, I don't really know. I have never seen my birth certificate."

"How is that possible? Don't you need a birth certificate for certain documents?"

He shrugged. "I suppose, but by the time I needed the documents, my mother had already procured them for me including my passport. I don't have a driver's license. Since then, I've simply needed to renew it."

"What's your best guess?"

Butcher studied the woman across from him whose green eyes were latched onto his own. "Somewhere south of here, probably Kentucky or Tennessee."

"What makes you say that?"

Leaning back in his chair, he stretched his arms over his head and grunted the first words of his answer. "Sometimes I have dreams, visions of large hills, or small mountains shrouded in fog and mist. I hear a voice, a call through an echoing valley and a word, sorrowful, long and drawn out, like the hills were sighing. And then I see a figure stepping out from the mist and the fog. A woman. It's my mother and she is young, younger than I have ever seen her; she's wearing a long flowing skirt decorated with flowers and she has a ribbon in her hair. She is smiling and with her is a tall man - unbelievably tall - a man who has no face because it is shrouded in darkness. I think this man is my father, or at least that's my guess."

Butcher's eyes closed, remembering. "In my dream, the man speaks, just a few phrases but he has a southern accent. I have been around enough to know that this is a Smokey Mountains drawl, or at least in the relative vicinity."

Rhonda scratched her cheek. "I thought you said you never met your dad."

"I haven't, or at least I don't remember it, but, as you know, Rhonda, there's something a little different about the connections in my brain."

"So, you think that this image," her fingers bracketed the word 'image', "is an echo of your father?"

"I don't know, Rhonda, but I kind of hope so. I never knew my father, but I would have liked to."

"You aren't missing much."

Butcher had read this part of Rhonda's story; she had intimated some of it. "You didn't like your father much?"

"No," she said tapping her leg. "I didn't like him much at all. That's one thing we have in common - neither one of us grew up with a dad."

"Which is why you are frightened of a relationship?"

Rhonda froze. She hadn't wanted to get into this discussion yet, but the edge of the abyss was rapidly approaching. "We'll get to that soon. I have another question to ask. It's a repeat, really, from last weekend."

Butcher knew it was coming. He looked up at the light cover to notice a few more late summer bugs, which had been drawn to the light and their death. "You want to know about my mother?"

Nodding, Rhonda followed Butcher's eyes to the light.

"I had a breakthrough a few days ago. And I understood one of the deepest, most painful things in my life that has permanently changed me."

"What was it?" Rhonda leaned forward in her chair.

"It started with you, Rhonda, believe it or not, as I was pondering why I was having such difficulty trusting you." She stiffened. "It sounds harsh, but it's a reality, not because it's what I want, but it's the way that I am."

Butcher rose slowly from his seat and made his way towards Rhonda. After a few steps, he sank to the floor and sat cross-legged in front of her. Gazing up, he noticed the kitchen light behind her head made it difficult to see her eyes, but he already knew what she was thinking.

"I had a flashback to the way my mother died." Butcher watched Rhonda freeze; the words of Butcher's mother's death were not what she was expecting.

"I was twenty-six years old. My mother and I had lived together our whole lives. As we moved around, neither one of us ever grew close to anyone else, so it was just me and Mom, Mom and me. Any time Mom did something stupid, we'd pack up in the middle of the night, putting our measly belongings into a plastic bag and then we'd take the wad of cash that we'd accumulated, or, to be more to the point, what I'd amassed playing poker…"

Rhonda smiled. "That makes a lot of sense."

"It does. I never lost - not once, unless I needed to keep up a sense of fallibility or else no one would play cards with me. Anyway, my mother and I would pack all of our belongings and we'd take the bus to another state, any other state which we'd never been to before. Our last state together would be Rhode Island. On that fateful day, I came home from work reeking of ground beef and after entering the house, I found my mother, naked and lying halfway out of the bathtub. She was dead - a drug overdose."

"I'm so sorry, Butcher," Rhonda said. She reached out to him and he took her hands in one of his.

"This sounds bad, but it wasn't so much that my mother was addicted to drugs, but the fact that I had not read it in her. How could I, an undefeated poker champion, an idiot savant with regards to interpreting verbal and nonverbal signals and translating them into reading both past, present and future, not know! NOT READ! that my own mother was a drug addict and she had been for a very long time." The words spilled out quickly, but he was willing to let them fall where they may. "I could scam the car salesman out of a perfectly good car; I could get the local electronics dealer to take fifty percent off the price of a television. Heck, even the vacuum cleaner retailer almost gave me a free vacuum simply because he was afraid of me. But how, tell me, how could I not see that my mother was addicted to oxycodone?"

Rhonda rubbed Butcher's hand. "And the answer came to me the other night when you asked me that very question about why I couldn't read my mother. It was so simple, so easy; the truth finally set me free."

"What was the truth, Butcher?"

Their eyes connected before Butcher placed Rhonda's hands on his cheek. "Because I trusted her completely."

Rhonda frowned. "That doesn't make sense."

"I know. I know!" Butcher threw both of his hands above his head. "But there it was. My mother, throughout my youth, had told me the God's honest truth about anything and everything. Every question I ever wanted answered, I asked and she told me. Eventually, I must have subconsciously known that I didn't need to read her anymore because I trusted her. And when I stopped reading her, I stopped asking questions; when I stopped asking questions, we ceased communicating with each other. She didn't tell me because I didn't ask."

"So, what does that have to do with the present?"

Butcher's silence dragged on for an eternity. Then, he raised his head, his face trembled. "My mother was the last person I ever trusted, and from that point on, I've been reading people so that I would never, ever, have to feel the pain of what I felt on that day. I couldn't deal with the guilt, or the pain, of having someone else die on me. So I read them first and decided if they were worth my time. Until you, Rhonda, anytime I would get close to someone else, I knew everything about them and I would run because I knew - I just knew - that it would end badly. Their past had made them who they were, which, in time, would bring about a future that didn't include me. And thus, I ran away. Running. Running away. Running from. Running out of time. Running for my life."

"But then you came into my stratosphere, Rhonda, like a shooting star and I wanted to connect with you more than anyone I'd met since my mother. The problem was, Rhonda…" he paused and put his head down guiltily again. "…I read you."

The way he said it made Rhonda's skin crawl, as if he had taken out her personal diary and not only read it, but made notes and judgements about it.

"So?"

"I know about your past."

Rhonda pulled back from him. "You don't know that part of me! You might have heard rumors, but that's just gossip. No one knows the true story. Only me."

For many years, Rhonda knew that this fear had been a rampart, a wall and a moat around her heart, built by her hands alone. Her loneliness was a result of her own distrust of men, not because they were universal objects of distrust, but that they had been lumped together as a common species, who were unworthy and selfishly seeking only personal release and satisfaction.

"Tell me, Rhonda, tell me so that I can trust you."

She gasped. "How dare you presume that I would tell you. I don't know you well enough yet."

Butcher pulled himself to his knees, begging her to release him from his imposed exile on an island of his own making. "If you don't tell me, Rhonda, I will always read you - I won't be able to help it."

Rhonda was angry now. "You're trying to manipulate me into revealing my secret. You want to know so you can control me!"

Holding up his hands, Butcher leaned back on his heels. "No! No! That is not what I'm trying to do. You must believe me. In order for me to open up to you, you must trust me enough to tell me what happened. But believe me, I already know."

"You can't possibly know!"

"You've seen my gift in action. How can I know these things?"

"I don't know, but my case is different. If I tell you, there is no way you'll stay with me. No way at all!"

"I promise, Rhonda, that when you tell me, we'll work something out."

Rhonda had risen and was retreating to the front door, escaping from a past that she never wanted to confront again. Only her mother knew the real truth, what actually happened in Chicago all those years ago. The man, their time together, the end of the relationship. Butcher would not understand and if she told him, he could use it against her. Amicable was not big enough for both of them and their secrets.

"Don't go, Rhonda. Don't go!"

"I have to, Butcher. I've got to think about this. I like you, I really do, but you're asking the impossible of me." He looked imploringly at her. "Don't, Leo... I'll..." Tears began to stream down her face. "I'll find you tomorrow and we'll talk about something different, okay?" Rhonda fled to the front door and opened it quickly running out into the night.

Déjà vu set in while Butcher remained on his knees in a moment of despair.

It appeared as if he was going to have to move again.

Chapter 33.

Deep in the heart of the night, a figure walked the outskirts of Amicable. Shuffling, legs stepping gingerly, out of light and out of sight, the figure stayed in the shadows and walked down the far eastern edges of town. Although this was not the shortest route to the destination, it was the one out of view for much of the town. A crescent moon hung suspended by a celestial thread illuminating only a quarter of what was occurring in a typical Midwestern small town on a Friday evening in September. Somewhere, on the other side of Amicable, a party was occurring. Even a mile away, the thumping bass could be felt through the trees. Although Louise was sometimes called, she rarely broke up parties unless there was a danger of someone being hurt. For the most part it was easier for her to be a keeper of the peace rather than a punisher of the noisy.

The figure approached Highway 10 and checked both ways before crossing. It was an unbreakable habit. At two thirty-seven in the morning, no one would be driving, but it was always best to check anyway. The figure looked up at the silhouette of the grain elevator looming large over the town. Its moon shadow, a quarter of a mile long, seemed to cast darkness across a large segment of the town. The walker wondered if the agricultural temple wasn't part of the slow recession into the darkness of the past.

Thus it had been with Rhonda Redman. She had grown despondently uncomfortable with the thought of her village life and its parochial ways. Rhonda had told her mother about her plans to desert Amicable and move to the city - any city, really, but she chose Chicago, the heart of the United States. In Chicago she hoped to find adventure and meaning, while creating a life away from Amicable. She had hoped that the small town's grip on her would be released and she could be swept away from her omnipresent mother and the memory of her omni-absent father.

After taking the bus to Des Moines, stopping in Davenport for a brief rest, she arrived in Chicago with a heart full of desires and a mind full of expectations.

The first weeks had been gloriously different than life in Amicable. The city of Chicago came alive in late May - the baseball teams seesawed through their seasons, the river life was significantly busier and noisier; the pulse of Lake Michigan seemed to throb with promise. Even from her one-bedroom apartment in the western suburbs, there were times when she could feel the throb emanating from Navy Pier and the screams of delight as the Ferris wheel turned and turned taking locals and tourists alike to see the sights and sounds above the lakefront. Fatefully, she took the train into the city one early summer Saturday to see the vistas of the sun meandering down the western sky behind the skyscrapers creating a crenelated battlement to the city of Chicago.

When Rhonda had returned to Amicable two years later, shame and guilt written large over her face, the details given with adjectival orgy in the Chicago tabloids, her mother had drawn Rhonda back into her home unwilling to allow the big bad world to take her away again. Connie had, with matriarchal condescension, shaken her head and said "I told you so" ad nauseum. That statement had been Rhonda's most hated phrase.

Rhonda's shame had whipped across town like a wildfire; the gossip levelled the good will and niceness of Amicable. Even though a few had read the Chicago rag and passed it on to others, most took the word of the rumor mill as the grist of gospel. Though the prodigal daughter had returned, she was tainted beyond measure, an object of distrust.

The figure moved across Highway 10 aware that what was about to occur might rip the community apart, but for Amicable's sake it had to be done. Messages had been placed in or near the houses of both the butcher and his whore, but the town needed restoration. The sign in front of the bowling alley had changed - a distasteful place where the youth of Amicable were corrupted, surrounded by alcoholics, gamblers and men of ill-repute alike. These young people, the last remnants of a vibrant town, the detritus of a glorious agricultural past, were being sucked into the vortex of sin. It would take an act of God to turn them around, to bring repentance, and if it had to happen, someone had to be the sacrificial lamb.

Head shaking briefly to clear the last thought, the figure checked the time. 2:51. It was a proven fact that the deepest sleep of the night was from three to four o'clock in the morning. Softly, the figure approached Peppertree Lane and turned right. Slinking farther in the shadows, the figure hugged the hedges and trees out of the spotlight until reaching the butcher's house. Knowing that there was no turning back, a glass jar was pulled from a pocket and placed at the end of the sidewalk. Inside was a message which could not be misinterpreted.

With a deep breath and silent steps, the figure moved to the front of the house, pulled out a wad of dryer lint, placed it with some kindling just inside the front screen door. Striking the flint of the cigarette lighter, the lint caught fire quickly and set the kindling ablaze. The arsonist then stood back and waited to make sure that the flame would continue. When it did, climbing higher against the wooden front door, scorching black marks onto the thin wood, pleasure came.

Just like Jesus. Turning over the sinners' tables, upsetting the plans of the evil one.

Butcher's door began to smoke and soon the fire spread to the frame and siding.

The figure hurried back down the sidewalk to return from where they came.

Either the butcher would meet his Maker or get the message. Either way, he would be gone.

Smoke wafted through the front door, across the living room and filled the kitchen. Upstairs, in the bedroom, something in Butcher's subconscious sleeping mind rattled like an alarm bell and he woke groggily. Checking the time - just before three o'clock - he looked around the room. Through the front window, he could see stars to the south, a clear night, but it seemed like a haze was rising from the ground in front of the window. It was then that the first wisping curls of smoke reached his olfactory organs and adrenaline began to course through his system. Immediately, he wondered if he was dreaming, because if he wasn't, the smoke detectors should be screaming.

Butcher's first need was to evacuate the house. Throwing back the sheets, he pulled on his clothes from the previous night (later he would remember that they were his Sunday clothes) and then he opened the door to the downstairs hallway. Smoke was leaking under the door and rising quickly to the top floor. Butcher wondered how long the fire had been burning and if he could safely exit. Closing the door, he moved to the front window and threw it open. As he looked down, he could see that the lower level of his house was radiating heat and light. The ground was fifteen feet below and he was not keen on jumping, but the alternative would be far worse. Fortunately, there was a gable underneath the bedroom window, a slight promontory by which he could at least lower himself six feet. Clambering out backwards through the window frame, Butcher dropped down onto the gable and then shimmying along the small peak, he turned around. Almost losing his balance, he looked out over the front sidewalk and noticed something sitting on the cement, but his attention was focused on the leap of faith. It would be much easier if he could have bent down to drop onto the front porch, just a three-foot drop, but there was no way he could maneuver his body to do so.

Butcher coughed as the fire began to grow and the smoke leapt in front of his face. *I guess it's now or never*, Butcher thought. On the descent, he recalled later thinking another thought: *This is really going to hurt.*

And it did. A lot.

Chapter 33.

Butcher caught the ground squarely with both of his feet and became immediately aware that his right leg had broken loudly and quickly. Within seconds he knew that the situation was far from over. As he rolled over, he saw that the house was now consumed with fire and in the distance, he could hear the town fire siren blaring into the air. The pain consumed him just as the fire consumed the house. Darkness pulled up a blanket over his vision from the bottom to the top. Butcher could hear voices - they seemed to be far away - and then a gentle tug pulling him away from the heat of the burning house. A fresh wave of exquisite, torturous pain washed over him. Just before he passed out, a strange thought entered Butcher's mind.

What was at the end of my sidewalk?

Butcher

Chapter 34.

Groggily, Butcher felt himself pulled from a muffled world of wool. His mouth and ears were stuffed with cotton balls and as soon as he felt himself surfacing towards consciousness, he knew beyond a shadow of a doubt that he was about to be sick. His stomach convulsed and the contents came up from beneath.

Fortunately, a nurse had been standing beside the hospital bed and as he vomited, she caught most of the mess with a look of numb disinterest. It was a daily event for her, even if not for the patient. When he had finished, she took the bowl from him and emptied the contents into the toilet. Flushing it, she came back into the room. Leopold Jensen was sitting slightly upright, his long legs, one inside a monstrous cast, stretched out in front of him. His eyes confusedly looked around the room trying to grasp what had happened. He had been brought by ambulance to the Clancy Regional Hospital, sirens blaring, just after 3:45 a.m. The nurse, Christine Goff, had been having a wonderfully easy night taking care of a stroke victim, two flu patients and a newborn with her mother, but when Mr. Jensen had been pushed into the hospital, she moved quickly to assist the doctor on call. A specialist surgeon had been roused from her sleep in Omaha and at 5:00 a.m. surgery began. After two hours, his tibia had a shiny rod inserted into it.

"Good morning, Mr. Jensen," Christine said to him. "Welcome back. I would guess you have plenty of questions, but I'm going to have to leave them for the doctor. Is there anyone you want me to call?"

Butcher simply stared at her. The words made some sense, but his brain wouldn't allow his voice to work. There were still too many cobwebs stretched across his left frontal lobe where speech was manufactured. He shook his head.

"The woman that came in yesterday, the tall one. Do you want me to call her?"

Butcher's confusion reigned supreme. *Rhonda?* It was obvious that he was in a hospital, but how he got here, he could not remember. His last memory was lying on the ground outside his house staring up at an inferno.

The effort to create words brought a fresh wave of nausea. Nurse Goff put a hand on his arm. "Relax. It will all come back. I'll bring you some ice chips and water and you can decide how much your stomach can handle." The nurse turned to leave the room.

Butcher found himself surrounded by the absence of sound; no people and no objects. Although he couldn't communicate with the nurse, he could read her still, and her body language said that there was nothing to fear. The pain, though deadened by narcotics, still throbbed. His thoughts moved from his pain to his property and the memory of the fire came back. Was his house completely destroyed? What had happened? He didn't remember leaving any appliances on. Of course, the house was old and perhaps the wiring was faulty, but instinctively he knew foul play was a real possibility.

There was a knock at the door and his head swiveled slowly towards it. Rhonda's tall, shapely form filled the doorway. She was dressed in her work clothes, black pants and white shirt. A coffee stain created the shape of Australia on her shirt. Her hair was in a state of disarray. Her eyes were concerned, but there was something else, something deeper than worry. Butcher knew that her coming was not solely about her anxiousness for his health, but also about the fire and about their future.

"Hi," she said as she stood transfixed in the doorway. "How are you?"

Butcher's voice was still buried in a tomb of pain and smoke inhalation. He waggled his left hand.

"Can I come in?" It took a few seconds before his head was able to affirm her request positively; Rhonda entered and pulled up a vinyl blue chair to sit beside him. "I brought you something." Rhonda handed over a book, *Your Best Life Now,* by Joel Osteen. The sight of it made him want to both laugh and vomit at the same time. He laughed in spite of the pain, and then winced.

"How bad is it?"

He shrugged.

"Do you know what happened? Do you remember?"

He shook his head.

Rhonda began to wring her hands. "The fire started around 3:00, or that's what the authorities say. I keep thinking about it, just a few hours after I left you. Imagine if I would have been there with you, maybe we could have escaped together."

Butcher's eyes widened and he shook his head again.

"I know, I know what you'd like to say, 'it's not your fault,' but I feel like I've let you down. And then this thought hit me: if I would have lost you, I'd never forgive myself." Butcher was trying to keep up with the speed of her words, but he was struggling. "So," she said slowly, "that was Friday and now it's Tuesday."

Four days, his eyes widened. He'd been out for four days. *So that's what Lazarus would have experienced...*

"I came after work to see if you were awake. I'm glad you are. We need to talk. The fire at your house wasn't an accident. Someone started it in your doorway. The fire marshal came yesterday and although the findings are supposed to be confidential - you know how confidential Amicable is." Rhonda rolled her eyes. "At the end of the sidewalk was a glass jar. Louise told me about it later knowing that I would be worried because the contents affect me too."

Butcher cleared his throat but still, he could not speak. "You don't have to try to talk, I can read you," she smiled wryly. "There was a note inside the jar and it was much more malevolent than the others which, coincidentally, we never had a chance to talk about. I've brought them all today, because it seems like a day of reckoning. After our talk Friday night, the air needs a definite clearing."

The tall man nodded.

Rhonda took a piece of paper from her jacket pocket and unfolded it. "These messages are all similar; I've brought my own, also, to match them. I can't stop thinking about them and about what they mean for us."

```
     I warned you. Every day I've been giving you the
                    oppotunity to leave.
            The hore needs to be left alone.
                     She is toxik.
                  But you are deadly.
       If you survive the blaze, it will give you a
          taste of what your afterlife will be like.
```

"Here is my message."

```
    We're all disapointed in you, bringing your
             horing ways back to Amicable.
                 Won't you ever learn?
                  Leave him or lose him.
```

"This was obviously premeditated, Butcher." He concurred. "The last line of mine has haunted me for three days." She shook the piece of paper in her hand and began to cry. "Oh, Butcher, I don't want to do either one of those things." The tears streamed down her face. "I don't want to leave you and certainly, I don't want this to happen again either. Whoever is writing this," the anger sputtered from her lips, "Needs to be put into jail. This is disgusting and completely unlike any respectable Amicablean."

"So, you're thinking, 'What are we going to do about it?'" She asked and he nodded, but the silence was deafening. "I have so much fear about telling you. You say you know, but you don't, not really." Butcher didn't disagree with her, but he could have. "Maybe it's best that you can't say anything right now. That will make this so much easier." Butcher's heart began to pound; it registered on the monitor beeping behind his head. Rhonda sniffed and wiped her tears with her hands.

After a deep, trembling breath, Rhonda Redman began to pull the covers off a past she had long wanted to leave asleep.

"The messages all have one connection word – *whore.* My mother would always dance around that word, describing what she would consider 'proper activity' for a lady, which, ironically, in my mother's opinion, meant dressing primly, courting openly and getting married. My mother's hypocrisy was immense: she was not primly dressed, her own courtship was hidden from her parents and her marriage fell miserably under the constant weight of her perpetual nagging criticism. I feel like I should get a lifetime achievement award just for living with her." Rhonda stopped to smile through her tears and then reached over to the bedstead to grab a tissue before blowing her nose.

"But the word never leaves. Whore. I've had to come to grips with it because I am a whore, but not in the traditional sense - I don't sleep around and I don't have sex for money, but the lines of sexual freedom and sexual inhibition are extraordinarily thin. The town of Amicable has a skewed perception of what happened to me in Chicago, which they've gathered from the newspaper, or plucked from the gossip tree. Sometimes I think that the fruit in the Garden of Eden was not physical, but a metaphorical rumor that humans could be just like God - omniscient."

She paused and glanced out the hospital window at the billowing trees and floating clouds. "I'm procrastinating." Butcher's eyes remained locked on the trembling woman and he wished that he had control over his nervous system. He wished that he could take her in his arms and tell her everything was going to be fine.

"I went to Chicago to search for a new life. On the first day, I took the train into the city and walked up and down Navy Pier. The sights and sounds of the city were overwhelming, like a sensory tidal wave. The Pier juts out into Lake Michigan and is lined with shops, restaurants, rides and the smell of fresh air. The breeze is like nothing you've ever felt and as you look east over Lake Michigan, you think it's an ocean but without the salt. On that night, I was overcome with passion for the new direction my life was taking, but I hadn't prepared myself for meeting Gus the next day."

Butcher's heart raced. *She was doing it!*

"He was standing by The Bean, this enormous metallic sculpture along the Riverwalk made of seamless stainless steel; although there were dozens of people milling around taking pictures of their reflected views, I saw behind me this tall, handsome, bearded man who looked as if he'd stepped right out of the great Northwoods. He was wearing a flannel shirt and khaki pants and I swore that I'd never seen anyone as beautiful as he. In the reflection of The Bean, he was upside down and strangely, that's how I came to know him." Rhonda's hand trembled in Butcher's. "That was the first night of getting to know each other, and much to my surprise and chagrin, I went home with him. I'd never had a one-night stand, or any other stand, mind you, but the environment was so exotic and new, I let myself be swept away by him."

"For the rest of the summer, we spent most nights together enjoying the town, seeing the sights, having a great time, but then, at the end of the summer, he invited me to his cabin in Wisconsin. I'd never been there before and so I thought, 'Okay, this should be fun.' What I didn't realize was that his cabin was farther out into the woods than I felt comfortable with. As the headlights bored a hole in the darkness, I began to have second thoughts. How well did I really know him? Was this really a safe environment?"

Butcher could tell that she was coming to the most sensitive part of the story; he attempted to say something, but still found himself mute.

"The cabin was like a cave when we arrived, and as he opened the front screen door, it seemed to screech like in a horror movie. I had this weird premonition that something was off, but I thought I was just nervous. Gus pulled the covers off all the chairs; the dust was thrown up into the air, the lights were dangling by power cords and I stood in the doorway unsure of whether to enter or run."

"'What are you waiting for?' He asked. But I wasn't sure. I liked Gus a lot, maybe too much. But I was naïve. Very naïve. We had dinner that night but he kept looking at me strangely, like a dog drooling over a piece of meat. Then, just as we were about to go to bed, he caught me by the fireplace and he started saying these awful things to me, things I can't tell you, Butcher. I tried to relax and just go with the flow. I kissed him and that seemed to make it better, but then he started to get rough." Butcher could feel the vibration of Rhonda's pulse in his hand.

"I ripped myself away from him and ran from the house. I went to a neighbor's house, knocked on the door and wanted to call for a ride, but the neighbor insisted that I wait with her for the night. I didn't tell her what had happened, but she seemed to instinctively understand another woman's distress. The next day, the woman took it upon herself to drive me all the way back to Chicago."

Butcher waited for the last piece of the story, the most difficult part that he knew should be coming, but it didn't, and terror raced through him. *She didn't trust him,* or at least not enough to finish the story.

"And...?" He croaked. Finally, he could speak.

She looked down. She couldn't tell him. "And what? That's the end of the story. I came back to Amicable in disgrace; the community had found out about my failings. It was in the newspaper." Rhonda's false sense of victimization made Butcher feel nauseous again.

"I'm so sorry, Rhonda," Butcher croaked. She couldn't understand at this point that he was talking about the end of their relationship, not about his empathy for what had happened. She seemed to breathe a little deeper as if feeling that she had put one past him and that he really couldn't read her.

"Now that I've told you, do you trust me?"

Butcher removed his hand from hers. It was symbolic enough.

Rhonda began to cry. "I knew that if you heard the story, that you wouldn't trust me afterwards." With a false sense of righteous indignation, she rose from her seat and began to walk towards the door. "It was my greatest fear and now, just like every other man, you've decided to take rather than give." She walked out the door and closed it behind her.

Why couldn't you have just told me the truth, Rhonda? Why?

Time ceased to have no meaning and when Butcher awoke, he was startled to see another figure in the room. Reverend Deakins. He was reading the Bible, a chapter somewhere towards the back. John was wearing blue jeans and a plain blue t-shirt and he seemed incredibly relaxed - beatified, in a way, as if there was nothing in the world that was troubling him. Butcher sniffed and the pastor looked up from his reading, smiled and closed the book.

"Hello, Leo."

"John," he croaked.

"I'm glad to see that you are okay."

Butcher swallowed. "Yes, I'm on the mend." He looked down at his leg, which was throbbing considerably.

"You've been missed."

Butcher pushed himself up in the bed a little higher and winced. "I bet."

"No really, you have, or at least by a significant segment of the town. You've made a real difference, Leo."

Rubbing a hand over his scratchy jaw, Butcher looked up to the ceiling. "No, John, that difference is because of you."

He laughed. "Think of all the people you've affected - Rhonda, Naida, James, Penny, Tony, George, Leslie... me.... Should I go on?"

"You can if you want to."

"We're blessed to have you in Amicable," John said softly.

"Well, it will be short lived. I don't have a home, belongings - nothing. I don't even have my health."

"You've got us. We'll help you rebuild. Maybe you can buy your own house."

"I don't think that's going to happen."

"Why not?"

Turning towards John, Butcher finally looked into his eyes. "Why are you here, John?"

Deakins smiled. "It's my job. Shamefully, I don't remember the last time I visited such a young person in the hospital. Besides the fact that I consider you a part of my congregation, I wanted to update you on some happenings in Amicable." John shuffled the chair closer. "To start with, the bowling alley had a record night the other night. Their promotion went off amazingly well. Young people came en masse to enjoy free bowling and oddly, a whole group of adults journeyed in at the same time. It was well past midnight that Saturday night when they started to journey home. Needless to say, one would have thought that services on Sunday would have been pretty tame and tired."

"But that's not the case, is it?"

"You always know, Butcher. No, the word got out somehow. I think it was the young girl, Tracey, who lives across the street from Leslie who snapped a picture of me leaving Leslie's house that night. She passed it on to one of her friends, a young man, I think, with the directive of 'don't tell anyone else!' Unfortunately, these words are the largest red flag in front of a digital bull. He passed it on to a few other friends, so on and so forth, and what had been a wonderfully ebullient, romantic night turned into a wonderfully ebullient romantic nightmare. Leslie called me before church as she had received three phone calls all at 7:00 a.m., the perfect time of day for an Amicablean: respectful enough to allow the person to sleep in, but not too late as to find out about the gossip the night before."

"How is she doing?"

"She didn't go to church that morning - it would have been too much for her. After she called me, I soldiered in to the worship service knowing the storm that was about to ensue. Incredibly, the church was packed - fuller than I'd ever seen it. People who hadn't sat in the pews for years had heard about my 'escapade,' as Linda Harmsen had called it, and they wanted to know if it was true."

"How did you respond?"

John smiled. "I knew immediately why they had all come and it certainly wasn't because of my prepared sermon about the difficulties of Joseph. One of the incredible statements that Joseph speaks at the end of his trial was, 'What you intended for evil, God used for good.' So, I shrugged my shoulders, brought a chair to the front and we had a conversation even before the service started."

Butcher smiled.

"I told them that I had feelings for Leslie, but it was a new thing and I was feeling particularly sensitive for her because she had received phone calls already that morning looking for gossip. I knew who it was - Linda, Leona and Jeannie."

He paused before beginning again. His voice was hesitant, catching on his emotion. "I have a confession to make, Butcher. I tried to use those women to get rid of you - before I knew you." John chortled. "How strange does that sound? But it looks like it has come back to bite me, not you. The women had a campaign to force my removal from the congregation on the grounds of 'moral failings,' but I think they might find that the log in their own collective eye blinds them from anything else."

"I'm having trouble keeping up."

"Sorry. I realize you might still groggy, but I wanted to apologize to you for my gross negligence."

"Apology accepted." It was at that point that Butcher felt something brush across his soul - he'd only felt it once before, and even then, he couldn't quite put his finger on what it was. Anyone else would have understood that it was a sense of trust for another human being. Somehow with John's confession and apology, Butcher had lost the ability and the need to read him. John was a blank slate and for Butcher, this was a beautiful miracle.

"The rest of the congregation took the news well. Because of my honesty, they were willing to look into the idea of a pastor having a relationship with a congregation member. If the leadership decides that it won't work, I promised them that I would leave the office gracefully." He winked at Butcher. "I didn't promise that I would leave Amicable, though."

"What happened next?"

"After the service, I put on my civvies and walked the blocks to Leslie's house. It was obvious that she'd been crying. More than once she had looked up at Tracey's window and scowled, but it's really not Tracey's fault. It's nothing that good, truthful, kind and gentle communication can't fix."

"Amen to that."

"So now we've come to you, Butcher. What are we going to do with you?"

Butcher looked back out the window at the gathering clouds, not threatening, but billowing masses of alternating warm and hot air pushing and pulling at the same time. "I don't know, John. I'm kind of at a loss for dreams."

"You're really thinking about leaving then?"

"Well, as soon as I can walk. I'm at the mercy and goodwill of others."

"Sounds like we're two peas in a pod." The two men looked at each other and understood the import of the words. "You could stay with me for a while. The parsonage has plenty of room and I'm not beyond sharing. It would be a first, but there are lots of firsts entering my life."

Butcher smiled. "Thanks for the offer, but I think I have to be by myself right now."

"I understand. But the offer remains open." John leaned back in his chair and crossed his arms. The expression on his face suggested amusement, as if something was funny.

"What's so humorous?"

"You. This." John waved his hand around the room like a brush, over the walls garnished with garish paintings and finally painting Butcher's broken body. "I mean, it's not funny ha ha, but humorous that you're trapped in Amicable - you can't run away even if you wanted to."

"Good thing we're not in Amicable," Butcher responded.

"My sentiments exactly." John leaned forward in his chair. "I'm going to have something to eat with Leslie and then go for a walk - sorry for rubbing it in. Is there anything that I can get for you? Any food?"

"No, thank you."

"I want you to stay, Leo. You're an asset to the community. We'll make it through together."

"Only if they catch the culprit."

Deakins' face darkened. "They will. The State Police have been called, but…" John made one more step back towards the bed, "Louise and her band of deputies already have a lead. Somebody saw something on that night; someone walking towards your house."

"Deputies?"

Deakins smiled. "Louise's boys - you know, the graffiti artists? They have been very helpful since their redecoration of the water tower. The whole town is talking about it. Amazing what second chances do."

Second chances. Does anyone deserve second chances? Butcher's thoughts strayed back to Rhonda.

"Anyway, this weekend, they are having an 80's theme night at the bowling alley and I'm going. Do you want to come if you're feeling better?"

Butcher looked at his leg. "I think you'll have to rustle up a miracle for that to happen."

John rose from his seat and turned towards the door. "Okay. I'll look for a miracle on the way home. You get better." He waved and exited.

It was going to take a lot more than a miracle. It was going to take a cataclysm.

Chapter 35.

Butcher continued receiving visitors and phone callers. For the most part, these interactions were limited to the Peterson twins making prank phone calls during work hours. Derek pretended to be the fire marshal and wanted to know how it was that they found a kilo of marijuana in Butcher's kitchen fridge. Nash wanted to know when Butcher was coming back because they were falling behind at the butchery and the Confessional was falling into disuse. A group of bowlers called on Thursday night wishing him a speedy recovery and a quick return to the lanes. As of yet, Rhonda had not made another attempt to connect with him.

Leslie called to check on his wellbeing. She sounded relaxed although there was a tinge of stress leaking from her vocal cords. Now that he was laid up in the Clancy hospital, her relationship with Reverend Deakins was about the only source of fresh gossip in town.

On Saturday afternoon, three weeks after the arson and subsequent surgery, the doctors proclaimed him fit enough to go home. The problem was that he didn't have a home. This fact was left unspoken in case they required that he stay in the hospital until he found a place to live. Butcher had had enough of hospital food, antiseptic odors and therapists who claimed 'to be doing what was best for him,' or his personal favorite, 'I'm doing this for your benefit, not mine,' as they sadistically pulled and stretched Butcher's leg to create flexibility where the ligaments and tendons were gradually settling into stasis.

When it was time for him to leave, he called Liam Wilson to come pick him up. Sitting in his wheelchair, he stared morosely at his broken leg, the toes sticking out of the cast.

He thanked the hospital staff for their work. After Nurse Goff had pushed him down the hallway to the front doors, she hugged him.

"Take it easy, Leo the Lion."

"I will. Be good to yourself. You deserve it." One more squeeze and she was gone.

Fifteen minutes later, a car pulled up in the semicircular drop off area. The window rolled down. It was Liam Wilson. "Hey Butcher! Get out of the chair. We're on a time crunch!"

Butcher made a gesture for Liam to roll down the window again and when he did, Butcher cupped his hands in front of his mouth. "I'm going to need your help, Liam."

Sheepishly, Liam put the car in park and hopped out. Running to Butcher, Liam moved behind him and pushed him quickly to the curb. The speed at which Liam moved him was a cause for concern. Butcher held onto the armrests for dear life. Once at the curb, Liam stood Butcher up, steadied him against the car and whisked the chair out from behind him. Liam opened the car door and carefully manhandled Butcher into the passenger seat. Bolts of pain shot through Butcher's nervous system; the activity caused him to breathe heavily. It had been a while since he had done anything that required lungs full of breath. After shoving the crutches into the trunk, Liam slammed Butcher's car door shut (which caused Butcher to almost yell out in pain) and then he raced around the front of the car.

A bead of sweat appeared on Butcher's brow. "What's the hurry, Liam?"

In a gesture of expectation, Liam rubbed his hands together. "You'll see."

"Come on, Liam, I can read you like an open book. You're taking me to the bowling alley, aren't you?"

An expression of faux shock ran across his face and he touched his chest. "*Moi?* Taking you somewhere?" Liam's fake French accent made Butcher smile in spite of his pain. Liam put the car into gear and squealed out of the pick up/drop off area causing Butcher to twist uncomfortably in his seat. Apologizing, Liam turned left out of the parking lot towards highway ten. The clock red 5:32.

"Thanks for coming to pick me up, Liam."

"Not a problem, Amigo. Happy to do it. I'm sorry about the smoke detector in the house. I should have had that looked at earlier."

"It's not your fault. How could you have possibly known that someone was going to start your house on fire?"

"Yeah, it's pretty freaky, isn't it? I mean, this is Amicable; not Omaha or Des Moines or Chicago where that stuff happens all the time."

Butcher shook his head and looked over at the young mechanic. "Do you really believe that?"

"What?"

"Do you believe that stuff like this only happens in big cities?"

"Well, yeah, I mean, it's never happened in Amicable before. Sure, people's houses have burned down, but an attempted murder?" he whispered the word with awe, "you only see that in the movies and it's almost always in a big city."

"It's not true, you know, that arson and murder and rape and drugs only happen in the cities."

Liam looked over at Butcher.

"Liam, life gets interrupted in Amicable just as much as it does in Chicago, Des Moines, Kansas City or Los Angeles. Murder might not happen daily but have you noticed that people's reputations are murdered overnight by gossip? What about the rape of our children's minds by setting them up in front of screens for ten hours a day? Arson - the intentional burning of institutions, including the church and the family farm – that's definitely a form of arson. And drugs? Don't get me started."

"Whoa, chill, Butcher. Sheesh. You want a Tic Tac? How about we just have a good time tonight? It's all you can eat chicken wings at the Greedy Pecker."

The thought of chicken wings made Butcher's stomach growl and he quickly remembered he had eaten nothing but hospital food for the last three weeks. Liam heard the growl and tossed over a half-eaten blueberry muffin. "I had half of it this morning for breakfast, but it's still good if you want to eat it." Butcher smelled the muffin, felt its rich softness and took a bite. He felt as if he had never eaten anything so wonderful in his whole life.

"Got it from the cafe this morning, but I got busy. Glad you like it."

The drive from Clancy to Amicable took less than the prescribed twelve minutes as Liam's lead foot buried itself in the bed of the car. About the eight-minute mark, Butcher questioned Liam about a place to stay for the night, but he shrugged noncommittally. "Something will come up tonight," he said. "I'd have you at my place, but I'm positive that will be a last resort. Plus, you'd have to battle the steps above the garage and, frankly, you're not in the greatest shape."

Something would come up. Someone would offer him a place for a few nights until he could heal and walk. Then he could get on the road, another state, another untold and unseen paradise awaited him.

Liam turned left on First Street and was shocked by the large number of cars. "Are all of these people here for the all-you-can-eat wings?" Butcher asked.

Grinning, Liam kept driving down First Street until he was almost to the high school. In his hurry, Liam parked the car on the curb, two wheels flattening on the cement, and opened the trunk to retrieve Butcher's crutches. Putting them onto the sidewalk, he then opened Butcher's door.

"Come on, let's go!"

"But the bowling alley is way back there. I can't walk that far!" Butcher's complaint fell on deaf ears.

"Boo hoo for Butcher. Come on, ya wuss. You have to get stronger; you might as well start now." Liam reached into the car to extricate Butcher.

"Take it easy!"

Liam stood up and reached into his pocket. "You want a tissue for your issue? Get a move on, big boy. Those wings be callin' me."

A little more gently, Liam pulled the butcher to his feet and handed him his crutches. Oblivious to the pain that Butcher was experiencing, Liam rubbed his hands again, a wide smile stretched across his face. Already breathing heavily, Butcher looked at the distance separating them from their evening meal. He was positive that there was no way he was going to make it in his condition.

"Relax, Butcher," Liam said. "I'll be right with you the entire way. We can take our time. It's still before six. The wings are going until eight, but we have to get there before all these bloomin' high school kids get their mitts on them. Bottomless pits."

Butcher rolled his eyes. "You don't have much room to talk, Liam. You're less than ten years removed from high school."

"Yeah, yeah, come on, wise guy."

As they walked, it seemed like every person in Amicable, both young and old, had driven their car and parked it along the streets. Strangely, they were still descending upon the bowling alley like ants drawn to a drop of honey. A few people noticed Butcher and called out to him.

As they approached the bowling alley, Liam pointed up to the Greedy Pecker sign. Because Butcher had been paying far more attention to the road in front of him, he hadn't noticed the words underneath the sign. Liam stood like a grinning idiot as he pointed up.

"Well, do you like it?"

"Like what?" Butcher said exhaustedly.

"The sign. Read it." He pointed up again.

Welcome home, Butcher. We've missed you. Glad you are okay. You get free bowling for the next month.

"Ha ha," Butcher said, pleased, even though the humor of the sign was somewhat insulting.

"What do you mean?" Liam asked innocently.

"What do you mean?" Butcher mimicked. He tapped his crutches. "How am I going to bowl with a broken leg?"

"Oh…" The realization hit Liam like a brick. "You think they were having a little joke at your expense?"

Butcher shook his head and laughed. "You're an idiot, Liam. Let's go inside."

The mechanic followed the butcher, smiling broadly. Liam loved being in on the joke and the mere fact that he had been the one to pick up Butcher and bring him to the party was a true honor. Liam moved around the slow-moving butcher and helped him up the three steps. Then, opening the door, he ushered the crippled man through. The noise from inside the bowling alley was almost deafening; at least one hundred people were standing in line for wings; another fifty high school students were waiting for bowling shoes (they'd actually run out, an historical first), and another fifty or so Amicableans stood at the bar window for drinks. Butcher looked out over the packed bowling lanes where forty youth were partnered up with twenty or so adults laughing uproariously at the deficiencies of their technique. Naida and James saw him first and waved, then bumped the people whom they were sitting next to, a couple of high school students with messy wing fingers. Soon, the entire assembly took notice of the mechanic and the butcher standing side by side in the entryway.

As one body, they turned simultaneously to the town's newest butcher and began to clap, cheer, whistle and shout encouragement. Shocked, Butcher looked back to Liam who was pounding his hands together and grinning maniacally.

"What's going on?" Butcher shouted over the din.

"Let him tell you." Liam pointed at a figure emerging from crowd. It was the oldest man in Amicable, George Hendriks. He was walking more confidently and taller than he had in ages. When he reached Butcher, he turned to the crowd and hushed them with his hands. People in the back near the bar were still making noise; someone hushed them with a loud 'Shut up!' which caused the congregation to murmur laughter.

"Hello, Butcher," George said, his voice strong, but reedy. "We're glad you're here."

"We can't hear you?" A voice yelled from the back.

Someone near the front bumped George's arm; they had pulled the microphone from the front desk. The microphone barely reached the old man. Someone showed him how to use it, but he smacked their hand away. "I was born fifty years before this thing was," he grumbled, but then looked out over the crowd and held the mic to his mouth. "It's been a long time coming since Amicable has had a celebration like this."

"But what are we...?" Butcher's question was decapitated by George's hand.

"We are here," George stressed, "because a grave injustice was done to you, my friend. Many of us here were outraged by the unconscionable act, and the mere fact that you survived with minor injuries," George raised an eyebrow which caused a chorus of mirth, "is a testament to your strength." George's words were slow but determined.

"It's hard to believe that you came to town only a couple months ago," George said, his voice beginning to shimmer with emotion and with intensity. "From the moment you asked Penny Reynolds where Peterson Butchery happened to be, things began to change - and change for the better, in my opinion." George, the senior statesman of Amicable, a World War II hero, a faithful husband and decent father, a good neighbor and excellent Amicablean, looked around at the people whose lives had been altered in the last weeks.

"You might think that the scope of your change was limited to a small group, but look around you now. All of them - and I'm not exaggerating - all of them are here because you allowed us to see something different in our small, Iowa town. Remember that first night you were here when Nash and Derek brought you to the bowling alley?
"You had a few drinks but then you came out and sat with us. We had a conversation about life and how quickly it passes. You were there to sit with us that night, and I remember talking about the young folks, the high school kids with their digital addictions beeping and flashing in their hands." For the first time, Butcher realized that no one in the bowling alley had a phone out. "And you wanted that to change, I think; you wanted serious connections between people of all ages, so you invited the kids to come bowling, but only if they bowled with someone who wasn't their parent."

"I don't think that was me," Butcher said.

"No, it was me, but you put the thought there." George smiled broadly. "All these people here tonight are here to go bowling, yes, and all of the people under eighteen are bowling for free. The first time we did it, I paid for it. I paid for one hundred and twenty-five games of bowling, and I was happy to do it. Then, last Friday night when you were out in Clancy, one hundred and fifty people showed up to go bowling with each other, but I was here waiting for them. And you know what I did?" Butcher shook his head. "I set a great big basket at the front and told each one of them, adult and child alike, that their bowling would be free if they'd put their phones in the basket until they were ready to leave." He giggled. "At first you would have thought I'd asked them to cut off their earlobes, but after the first game started, it didn't matter. I don't know how long the bowling went on; it must have been after midnight. A few people even forgot their phones."

"These people all came back tonight because they've been told that the idea to mix the generations was yours, and it has had a drastic impact on our community."

"I still don't understand."

George leaned as close to Butcher as the cord would allow. "The counselling, the relationship advice, your help with Louise and her deputies, these are things that don't normally happen in Amicable because we all believe that none of us need counselling, our relationships are already perfect and our youth will sort themselves out eventually. But it's not true." George sighed. "We're all in this together and you reminded us of that."

Butcher's arms were beginning to shake. "I'm honored to have been a small part of this quick transformation."

George waved his hand at the suggestion. "We know you're humble, too. The fact is, we wanted to celebrate your return and we want you to know that we want you to stay. Don't move on; don't run away. We'll catch the guy who did this to your house and then Amicable will be all right again."

Butcher was close to collapse, but he moved closer to George. "Don't fall into that trap, George. Any of you. The moment we start wanting to go back to the way things used to be is the moment that a town begins to seek control. By all means, plan for the future, but be adaptable, flexible, spontaneous and for God's sake, be generous with your time."

"Amen to that," a voice called out from the middle. It was John Deakins dressed in a chino work shirt and blue jeans.

"I offer exhibit A for change, your honor," George said as John Deakins walked to the front.

Deakins did not offer his hand for a shake, but a hug. Carefully, he wrapped his arm around Butcher's shoulder and tapped him lightly, then, taking the microphone, cleared his throat into it. It fed back slightly, but he pulled it away from his mouth to accommodate for his louder voice. "Butcher... Leo Jensen... we would all like to say thank you, and on behalf of I who have been changed as much as anyone else, and on behalf of my..." the crowd waited for his next word. "... congregation..."

Laughter, boos and hisses ensued. He raised his hands once again. "Okay, on behalf of my girlfriend, Leslie and I..." Now the shouts of joy carried into the rafters for a few moments until decorum was restored. "We'd like to express our gratitude." Leslie peaked her embarrassed face out from the middle of the revelers and waved timidly.

"Because tonight seems like a holiday, the church board and I have decided to call off worship services tomorrow morning so that we can celebrate life together, with God, in this place, tonight." More cheering, not just that worship on Sunday morning was postponed, but that their spiritual leader could entertain the thought of understanding that the congregation gathered outside of a church building was as pleasing to God as the rote recital of traditional liturgy inside the building once per week.

"Thank you, Leo," John said softly and handed the microphone back to George.

"Now," George said as loudly as he could, "Who thinks we can buy some wings for this fine gentleman in front of us!" Like the parting

369

of the Red Sea, the congregation broke and gave him a direct shot to the front of the line.

Butcher, smiling, waved at everyone, silently thanking them for their overwhelming generosity. But he leaned in closer to George's ear.

"I don't think I can make it there, George. My legs are trembling, my hands are shaking and I feel like I have to pee."

George smiled and nodded. "Welcome to my world, young man. Welcome to my world."

Like the ocean's tides, the night ebbed and flowed. At times the lanes were flooded with younger people; other times, Amicable's senior citizens took center stage showing the 'whippersnappers' a thing or two about tossing the polished marble down the oily lane. When ten bells chimed, someone turned on the jukebox and dancing broke out. No one expected it, but the first ones onto the floor were John Deakins and Leslie Tielman. The entire town seemed to be embracing the coming together of the couple. Because of it, both pastor and his chosen seemed to glow with joy.

All throughout the night, Butcher kept his eye open for the one person he most wanted to see - Rhonda Redman, but she was not to be found, not at ten o'clock, midnight, or even one o'clock when the last of the party hounds were leaving.

It was not to be.

George, to his credit, played the part of the host incredibly well, and as such, he was the last to leave. Helping the staff clean up afterwards (which most of the town did also), they left the premises around 1:30 a.m. George thanked the owners, who, in turn, thanked both George and Butcher for making the bowling alley and the Greedy Pecker a highly profitable and popular place.

Fortunately, George had his pick of the parking spots. His car was parked directly in front of the bowling alley, and as the ninety-seven-year-old man helped the much younger man down the steps, everything felt right in the world. As they situated themselves in the seats, George, his eyes looking dreadfully old and tired, made sure that his young friend was feeling comfortable. Butcher nodded, aware that every time he did so, his chin was less and less likely to make its way back north.

"Thank you, George. You've been very good to me," Butcher mumbled.

George started the car. "You've still got some barbeque sauce on your face, Butcher, but you're welcome."

It had been decided that the best place for Butcher to matriculate would be the Hendriks' house. After parking in the driveway, George was acutely aware that both of them were dangerously close to falling asleep in the car. Gently, he nudged Butcher. "Hey, it's time to go inside."

Ten minutes later, the duo made it to their respective bedrooms - George on the left and Butcher on the right - before falling blissfully asleep, a miraculous Saturday safely tucked into the past.

Butcher

Chapter 36.

Butcher didn't wake up until almost one o'clock in the afternoon. This was due to the fact of two pressing emergencies, the first, the sound of the lawn being mowed next door and the second, the uncomfortable feeling that his bladder was about to burst. When he first opened his eyes, Butcher had no idea where he was. His last sleeping memory was in a hospital bed and now, as he awoke, he saw that the room in which he was staying was lined with pennants of baseball teams, some now moved to other locations. No more Brooklyn Giants or Washington Senators or Milwaukee Braves. The dark cedar walls held photographs of smiling generations; Butcher had known that both of George's children and his wife had died before him. Butcher was aware that this room was the one in which Ronald had slept and the things of this room were memories of decades past.

Butcher attempted to move, but pain paralyzed him. Immediately he understood that he had overexerted himself the night before. It had been well worth it, though. He had never felt that kind of appreciation before; this small, seemingly inconsequential Iowa town was able to see far beyond his own personal idiosyncrasies.

Steeling himself for the inevitable pain, he breathed deeply and, like a man who was about to jump off the high dive, counted to three. Pulling himself upright, the unbelievable pain threatened to yank him backwards onto the mattress, but he persevered and overcame the twinkling lights of his consciousness. It took three attempts to attain full uprightness. Legs, weak from the exertion the night before, threatened to mutiny, but he held firm as captain of his own body. After opening the door to the bedroom, he poked his head into the hallway to find a wide-awake George Hendriks still in his pajamas and sitting happily in his living room reclining chair.

"Good morning, sleepyhead," he intoned. "The bathroom is two doors down the hallway on the left. Take your time."

"Don't worry, George. There is no other way to do it in my condition."

Fifteen minutes later, Butcher had returned from his morning, or in this case, afternoon, ablutions. Dressed in the only clothes that belonged to him, Butcher thumped down the hallway. George had just finished the newspaper and he pointed to the front page of the weekly Amicable Tribune where a picture of Butcher's abode was shown smoldering.

"It says here that the authorities are quite sure of arson, but they don't have a suspect yet."

"I thought Liam said that Louise and the boys were hot on the trail of the guy who did it?"

"Gossip. Just gossip."

"I thought we were moving beyond gossip, George. I thought that was the whole point of your speech last night."

"Baby steps, my friend."

George watched Butcher and set the paper in his lap. "What happened with you and Rhonda, by the way? It seemed like everything was going so well."

Butcher wasn't sure how much to tell him. "We ran into a snag, George."

"Can it be overcome?"

Butcher shrugged.

"Better make it so," George said. "There's many a man who wasted his entire life swimming in regret. I didn't do that. I knew what I wanted and held onto her for many years - more than fifty - and when she left, I regretted nothing."

"Have you talked to Rhonda?"

George shrugged. "She hasn't talked to anyone since that night. She's like a clam all snapped up on herself."

"Did she ever talk to you about... you know..."

"What? Chicago?" George blew out of his lips. "It's none of my business. It's none of anyone's business.

Butcher sighed.

374

"You want to know what I know?"

Butcher shook his head. "No, I already know. I could read it."

George pulled himself out of his chair and faced his guest. "And what do you think?" He asked.

Butcher took his time. He knew that Rhonda and George were an odd couple of best friends; but there was something extraordinary about their relationship that age did not threaten. "I think that Rhonda has had a rough time of life - her father's abandonment, her mother's..."

George filled in the blank. "Insanity."

Nodding, Butcher continued. "And her time in Chicago, but through it all, she's retained an incredible spirit and a loveliness that defies reality." George didn't disagree. "But if she could only trust me. Then, I think I could stay."

"Do you trust her?"

"Not until she trusts me first."

Shaking his head, George made his way into the bright kitchen. Reaching into the cupboard, George produced a can of instant coffee and put two teaspoons in two cups. "I know that it's already afternoon and coffee may be a foregone conclusion today, but my guess is that a little bit of caffeine might help your grogginess. Right?"

Butcher nodded.

A few minutes later, George had brewed two cups of ersatz coffee and begun to fix a couple of fried eggs. The smell made Butcher's mouth water; he sat down at the table to await the meal. When George had finally placed the fare in front of his boarder, he settled in across the table and watched the man eat. "How is it?"

"Good. Thank you."

"Do you trust me?" George asked.

Butcher's chewing slowed but he nodded.

"You might have to set aside your abilities in this case. Whatever you think about Rhonda is probably partially right and mostly wrong." He spread his hands. "She's been treated badly and the mere fact that you think you can make her say things, or act a certain way, only plays into her preconceived ideas about men. Are you hearing me?"

Nodding, Butcher took another bite of his eggs.

"If I were you, and I'm not, but if I were, I'd be taking a short walk out of this house and down the sidewalk, make a left and find the very same woman who sets my life on fire, the woman who is mowing the lawn. If I were you, that is." He punctuated the words with his finger. A tear filled George's right eye. "Angels might only come across your path once or twice in life, and my advice to you, Mr. Butcher, is to fly with 'em."

Butcher was astonished at the passion of the old man sitting across the table from him and he took a moment to reflect on George's words.

"But the thing she did…"

George's face went red. "Screw the things she did, or the thing you think she did. Do you love her?" Silence.

Unaware of how to answer, Butcher pushed his plate forward in front of him, the leftovers no longer edible. "How can you love someone you don't trust?"

Waiting for a moment, George scratched his head. "The real question you should ask yourself is this: how can you love someone completely by needing to control them?"

"You don't know what you're talking about." If Butcher could have walked out, he would have. George was hitting far too close to home.

"You think your gift of reading people is about helping them, but it's not. It's about controlling them. If you can read the truth about them, you have power over them. Yes, you know things, but you also have difficulty feeling things. It's not her lack of trust that is holding you back," he pushed his finger into Butcher's chest, "it's yours."

The thought drove a wedge into Butcher's soul. The revelation that he had not been able to trust a woman since his mother's death had awakened something deep and powerful inside him. George's alternate explanation, his difficulty keeping others at arm's length, was troubling to say the least.

"My God," Butcher whispered, "you're right."

"No shit, Sherlock. Old people are often right, just to let you know."

"So, I need to go to her?"

"There's not going to be a neon sign with an arrow pointing the way."

Butcher had grown accustomed to the thought of leaving. It was as if he had erased one of the chapters of the book of his life, and now that he was talking to George about that chapter, the rest of the book didn't make any sense without Rhonda. In the last months, he had experienced a closeness with her unlike any other in his life; he had shared things, connected with her on an emotional and spiritual level. Now that he was on the precipice of running away, he felt an incredible sense of unease.

"George," Butcher said, "I don't know what to say."

"Well then," George said as he threw his hands up in the air, "just shut up. Let her do the talking, and when she's done, find a way to ask for her forgiveness."

"But what have I done wrong? What do I need to apologize for?"

Turning away from Butcher, George sighed and scratched his nose. "If you need me to answer that, then you don't deserve her."

"George, please…"

"Go. Figure it out." The old man made his way to the sink. For the first time, he looked his age. As his hands rested on the aluminum sink, it seemed as if he was crying.

"George."

"She's the granddaughter I never had, Butcher. If she loses you, I might lose her."

Butcher took a deep breath and pulled himself up on his crutches. Steeling himself for the encounter that was about to occur, Butcher felt his cheeks and the four-day-old stubble that had sprung up from unshaven skin. He was aware that he had lost weight; his clothes were worn out and his hair was unkept. Now, he was about to walk out the door and talk to a woman he believed he loved but wasn't sure he could trust. Was this the way it was for normal people? Was this the kind of anxiety that non-readers had to fear when selecting a partner?

Butcher swallowed. These were questions previously unasked because they were unnecessary. He knew that he had access to trust, but it was dependent on the other person. Unfortunately, the onus was now on him. Shaking his head, he walked to the front door, and as he pulled it open, he was aware that he was stepping into an entirely new and frightening world.

As he exited into the sun, his senses came alive overwhelmed by the stimuli of the small town. This beautiful Sunday afternoon was blanketed with sunlight; the cloudless sky seemed to drip with an aquamarine blue; the sound of the lawnmower could not quite cover up the sounds of children playing across the street in the school playground, or George's neighbors who were standing in the backyard playing cornhole and combatively talking about which football team would have the better season - the Vikings, the Chiefs or the Packers. Good natured banter over a beer. Various smells floated back and forth like the shuttle on a loom - freshly mown grass, trees settling in for autumn, some already shedding their summer wardrobe of green to wrap themselves in the tinged orange of fall. Someone to the west was having a barbecue and he could smell the remnants of the last grill as they burnt off before the freshly marinated meat was placed on the sizzling metal. A breeze blew up softly and caressed his cheeks. He wondered, not for the first time, if all of this was a setup orchestrated by Amicable itself to make him reluctant to leave. Because this day, in its very essence, was a perfect reason to make a home in the small town.

Struggling through the door way and out onto the porch, he heard the lawnmower behind the Redman house which gave him some time to get down the stairs, out onto the sidewalk and towards the front gate of her fence. Gasping at the effort it took to reach the gate, Butcher sat on the ground leaning against the gate. Waiting for a few minutes, he took pleasure in the activity all around him and the ease at which people lived.

The lawnmower's motor cut and Butcher's heart began to beat harder. He pretended not to be aware of the footsteps coming quickly behind him, then slower until she finally stopped a few feet from him on the other side of the gate.

"Hi," his voice was aimed away from her, but his thoughts were completely wrapped up in her.

Nothing.

"I wanted to see you. I know our last moments together weren't exactly conducive to leaving a lasting, positive memory."

Silence.

"I wanted to say, my dearest Rhonda, that... I'm sorry. I'm sorry I didn't trust you, but you have to know this one thing, that I'm not sure I want to live life without you."

Still no response.

"I was talking to George about you. His words were, 'the granddaughter I never had' - but I'm not sure you know how much he desires that you find happiness in your life after... what you've been through." Butcher paused, thinking about his words. "You probably think I'm trying to manipulate you, but that's the last thing I want you to think."

The first sound. An intake of breath.

"I wish I didn't have this gift to see. I wish that I could be normal and appreciate relationships for what they are and not what I expect them to be. I wish that I could trust you - anyone - without reservation, with abandonment, throw my heart out on the water and see if it floats, but after my mother, I'm afraid of the pain."

Another sound, like the beginning of a sob.

"But I was wrong. There is no love without risk, and I'd like to take a risk with you, Rhonda Redman. I want to figure out what it's like to be so gloriously overwhelmed with someone as beautiful as you, that I can't breathe properly. I want to see what it's like to be frustrated beyond belief by someone who doesn't appreciate herself and has problems letting others do it also. I want to wake up every morning and see your face and thank God that I stumbled into this tiny little hole in the universe to uncover the most priceless, precious gem ever created. I'm ready to trust you even if you can't tell me…" His voice trailed off into the fearful abyss he had just opened.

"Butcher," Rhonda's voice finally came, so close, and yet the fence separated them; it seemed like a vast chasm of impossibility, a metaphor for what reality was like for them.

Silence. Butcher couldn't respond with words. He felt the shiver of worry that his outpouring had fallen on deaf ears, that Rhonda's own fear was incapacitating for her. The fence that stood between them was an insurmountable prison wall from which neither of them could escape nor enter.

Rhonda's voice was soft and anguished. "Please don't turn around. I can't bear to look at your face. This will hurt far more than I'm sure I ever expected, but I have to tell you so that you can make your own decision about me."

Butcher didn't respond.

Tears coursed down Rhonda's cheeks but she let them go. The dirt and grime which had accumulated from mowing was washed away in streaks; it left a dirty stain on the collar of her shirt. "His name was Gus, that much was true, and we did go to the cabin in Wisconsin, we had a glorious week together. He was generous and gentle, a truly beautiful human being. I was young and naive, yes, but I also knew what I was doing. Without Gus knowing, I used him to separate myself from Amicable. I used him and his niceness…" she sniffed through her tears causing her to splutter. "He would have fit in so well in Amicable. We made love four times during that week, but at the end of the week something twisted inside of me and I felt shame and guilt for what I was doing, not because the act was dirty, but because I was using him to get what I wanted. So, on the fifth night, I decided that I didn't want to sleep with him anymore and it frustrated him. He didn't harm me, really, but he got angry. As I left the house, a neighbor found me crying outside. She put two and two together and came up with five and…" Rhonda covered her mouth, her voice caught in her hand. Butcher desperately wanted to reach out to her, to take her in his good arm and squeeze out all the pain.

"I let her come up with the wrong sum. That's the way of the world now, and in that small town in Wisconsin, the police came and arrested Gus. To my great shame, I didn't speak to his innocence. I didn't want to look like a whore. I pretended that I couldn't speak, and in our world today, you are guilty until proven innocent."

Her hands reached the fence and she bent over letting her tears drip on the wood just a foot behind him. "The neighbor testified against Gus and I said nothing - I didn't want to upset anyone in Amicable or in that little town in Wisconsin, so I let Gus, an innocent man, be charged with sexual assault." Her breaths were coming in gasps. "No one except my mother knows the true story in Amicable - they all think that I was raped. Even those who have read the newspapers think they know the story; the mysterious message writer believes he knows me - knows that I am a whore. Gus' reputation was destroyed. He lost his job and his spark for life."

Rhonda began to wail. "Butcher, his last words to me in the courtroom were, 'Tell them the truth, Rhonda! Tell them!'"

"But I didn't, Butcher, I didn't. Oh my God, I'm evil!"

Butcher attempted to turn. He had read much of this in her, but not everything. It would be the first time he had ever had details hidden from him.

"Don't turn around! Not yet! I have to finish the story!"

The sound of Rhonda's form crumpling to the ground was almost too much for him to bear. Because of his incapacitation, he wouldn't be able to make it anyway. He froze like a statue allowing his own tears to enter the fray in the battle for his future.

"After the court's decision for Gus – two years in jail and a hefty fine - I came back home to Amicable in disgrace. My mother allowed me to live with her, but you saw her response when she met you for the first time. She believes it was all Gus' fault even though I dispelled any of his guilt. Because of her own dealings with men, she thinks they are all callous and predatory, and her precious daughter was assaulted in much the same way as she was. The truth of the matter is, Butcher - I was the predator."

Butcher did not know what to say.

"About three years after the incident, I received a letter in the mail with no return address, just my hand-written name. I have no idea how Gus got my address, but he did. And when I had read it, I almost went insane."

Wanting to ask, but afraid to do so, Butcher remained mute but wiped his eyes.

"I memorized it."

"*Rhonda,*

Over the last year I have reflected greatly on the circumstances of my demise, my loss of job, income, reputation, security - I had to move because people were writing obscene words on the walls of my house, and I was getting tired of painting over them. I was very angry for a long time, outraged, irate - I don't know how to write all the words other than to say I made you into a monster.

But one day, I got up from bed (somehow) and walked to the kitchen sink and I looked over the wreckage of my life and I could no longer be angry with you. I don't know the reasons for why you did what you did, and, I suppose, if you wanted to, you could take this letter to the authorities and I might be taken to jail again, but that would be no greater hell than the one I currently live in.

I just want you to know, Rhonda, that I still think you are beautiful, and that I don't hate you. But now I've learned to hate myself.

Thus, I've decided to end my life and cease whiting out the walls of my house.

Still, I forgive you.
I'll see you on the other side.
I hope.

Gus.

Rhonda moved into the corner of the fence behind Butcher and for a full minute she sobbed. Not strangely, life around them did not stop - the children kept playing, the beer and barbecue in the backyard did not cease and another lawnmower started up across town. But Rhonda, spending every last cent of her soul, lay curled up in a ball, her face in the grass tortured beyond imagination.

"Rhonda," Butcher said softly, but she didn't hear him. He finally turned and with great effort, got up and put weight on his healing leg. Although the doctor told him to stay off it for another few weeks, he found that he was willing to take the risk. His first torturous step wracked him with pain, but he saw the woman that he loved in greater misery than his. Opening the gate, he shuffled slowly and painfully to where she lay in the corner. Her crying had grown quiet, but her body still shook from what she had just endured. Standing above her, a pathetic authority figure, he recognized that this woman, like all humans, was guilty of something, but none of them had any right to judgement: that was best left to God. It was simply their responsibility to curl up in the corner of this little hole in the universe and cry together.

With his hand on the fence, Butcher lowered himself on his good knee and flopped to the ground behind her. Excruciating pain blistered his brain, but he stayed conscious long enough to move into place. Matching her curl with his own spoon, he rested his head against the back of her neck and cried with her.

"I just want you to know," Butcher whispered to Rhonda, "In spite of what you just told me or what you think about yourself, I intend to love you forever."

A wave of relief exploded from Rhonda and she rolled over to meet him face to face tears streaming again. Their foreheads touched, but nothing else. Mind to mind they connected, and as they laid in the freshly cut grass, the world quaked and shook around them; the earth trembled at the magnitude of a man and woman coming together despite all odds.

It was cataclysmic.

Leo Jensen and Rhonda Redman laid on the ground for what seemed like a lifetime. Four minutes into their shared grief, she reached out to touch his face. Five minutes, she kissed his cheeks. Seven minutes she kissed his lips and at ten minutes, Butcher told her he was about to pass out from pain and that there was no way that he was going to be able to pull himself up from the ground.

Rhonda began to laugh. It started as a giggle, but then it transformed into a full throated, belly-holding laughter. It had been years since she had expressed this - well before her time with Gus. After finishing, she wiped the tears of joy from her eyes and pulled herself up. George was sitting on his porch with a beer in his hand. She smiled at him.

"Do you think you could help me for a moment, Georgie?"

"Anything for you, Rhodie."

"Butcher is lying on the ground here and he's having difficulty getting up."

"What in the world is he doing that for?"

Shaking his head and smiling, George set his beer down on the table and walked down the steps and onto the sidewalk. He could tell that there was something different in her voice, as if a dam had broken and water was flowing rather than trickling. Rhonda seemed loosened, maybe 'released' was a better word. Pushing Butcher's crutches aside, he entered the open gate and found the tall, lanky man firmly implanted in the ground. Blades of grass clung to his hair and cheeks, and his face seemed to be a dark shade of red from holding his breath from the pain. Gently reaching under his head and body, George and Rhonda sat Butcher up and let him rest against the fence while George retrieved the crutches. For a couple of minutes, Butcher took deep breaths while Rhonda sat beside him smiling.

"How are you feeling now?" She asked.

Even though his vision was swirling, he was able to joke through it. "I feel like I've jumped out of a burning building and splatted against the ground."

"Very funny," she said.

"Do you think you're ready to move?"

He nodded.

With great effort, the oldest man in Amicable and his beautiful neighbor resurrected the newest butcher from his outdoor tomb behind Rhonda's fence. After getting him to stand, they walked him back to George's porch where he sprawled in one of the deck chairs. George went to retrieve a beer for Butcher, which George thought would do him more good than a glass of water, while Rhonda stared into his face and picked grass from his body.

"So," he said with his eyes closed, "what are you thinking?"

"I'm thinking we're both a little insane."

He smiled. "Yes, that would probably be a good assessment of the situation."

"Where do we go from here?" Rhonda asked rubbing his arm and wondering if the moment was too good to be true.

Butcher opened his eyes. "I guess this is where we simply let the wind take us where it will."

"What about the notes? He could still be around and loose. Maybe the next time we won't be so lucky." Rhonda's eyes searched the thinking face of her companion.

"Lucky," he mumbled while looking at his leg. Perspective was such a delicate and amazing thing. "I don't know, Rhonda, but we have to stay here for a little while at least. I can't really move, so I guess we'll have to be vigilant."

Without thinking, both Rhonda and Butcher turned to survey the comings and goings of Fourth Avenue in case the murderous note writer was walking up the street planning his next attack. The same children still played in the schoolyard, a few strollers enjoyed the late afternoon sun; among them, Linda, Leona and Jeannie were walking quickly in their brightly colored exercise outfits holding small weights in their hands as they pushed towards Carley's X-Er-Size studio. They were in deep conversation, Linda in the middle of the other two (as always), speaking like a tennis ball being struck back and forth over a net.

Looking to her left, Rhonda's heart dropped into her stomach as she saw the curtains of the kitchen window in her own house part and close quickly. Connie backed away from the window and into the darkness of the house. *I wish that she could just accept me for who I am now, not what happened to me in the past.* Inwardly, Rhonda knew that a significant moment had occurred when she had confessed to Butcher everything about her time with Gus - the pain and worry, the constant guilt and shame and the incessant turmoil that caused her to doubt all of her relationships, not just with males.

Rhonda glanced back at Butcher who was leaning back in his chair, his face soaking in the Sunday afternoon sun. "Did you really know my story before I told you?"

He didn't open his eyes. At first, she thought he was asleep, but he wasn't. "Does it matter?"

She frowned. "Well, a little. Am I going to have to constantly worry that you're reading me in the future?"

Butcher's left eye opened and squinted at her. "I can't read you anymore," he said with a sly smile. "I told you, when you trusted me enough to tell me what was deepest inside of you, my ability to read you would cease."

"How can that be true? I thought you couldn't control it."

Butcher closed his eye again. "Most of my gift, Rhonda, is being observant - probably too observant. I pick up on things that other people don't, but the greater issue was not only would I observe, but I would carry forward logical conclusions that usually turned out to be right."

"Usually?"

"Okay. As of yesterday, always."

"And now."

Butcher sighed contentedly. "I think I'll just stop thinking."

Rhonda reached over from her chair and touched his left hand, which he clasped in his own. "That's a great idea."

The door behind them opened and George emerged with three beer bottles in his hand. Passing them out to his friends, he pulled over the last chair dragging it across the deck scattering butterflies and dragonflies alike. Bugs began to float and lift from the chrysanthemums on the three steps leading down to the sidewalk. As they looked out, the first of the lightning bugs popped into motion. Life had stirred again. George held up his bottle to his mostly-adopted granddaughter and her strange, behemoth boyfriend and offered a toast.

"Here's to starting over."

They clinked beer bottles and drank deeply.

Butcher

Chapter 37.

Butcher was tired - exhausted - and ready to put his feet up. His leg ached badly. Even though he had arisen after noon, at ten o'clock he was ready for bed; his body still needed to rest so that he could recover from the traumatic experience.

At 10:30 after the baseball game had wrapped up, George grunted, pulled himself from his armchair and moved the beer bottles into the kitchen. They clinked as he put them on the table. Rhonda stood also and stretched her long, lithe arms above her head.

"Well, I suppose I better get going, Georgie."

Pausing, George took a deep breath and turned around. "You can stay the night if you like. I'm not so old-fashioned."

Rhonda laughed. "No offense, George, but I think you're a little too old for me."

George slapped the chair in front of him as he joined her in the joke. "Not me, you blockhead." He nodded towards the other bedroom and wiggled his eyes.

"I don't know. He's pretty sore."

"Yeah," George said, "And he's also a man. My guess is that he might appreciate just the company after a few years of loneliness, don't you think?"

A warm glow flushed through Rhonda - nervousness, worry, excitement, adrenaline - but she wasn't sure how to make the next step.

"Go," George urged. "Think of it as a sleepover. Talk the night away, mumble into the pillows, giggle like young lovers. I don't care. I can't hear you anyway."

"I don't have any pajamas."

"You can keep making excuses, Rhodie, or you can go tell him you love him. It's up to you. Frankly, I'd rather not hear your excuses."

Rhonda took a deep breath, paused and then nodded. With shaking hands and trembling heart, she stepped quietly down the hallway and stopped at the room that used to belong to George's son. She had only been in there once when George was giving her a tour all those years ago, but the echo was still the same. Echoes of the past, silenced voices about to be raised; expectations of life and love resurrected from an age long since buried.

Without knocking on the door, Rhonda opened it and peered into the bedroom. Butcher was lying on his left side facing away from her. He didn't roll over, but he sensed the presence in the doorway. "Did you need something, George?"

Without speaking, Rhonda entered the room and closed the door behind her. The silence and darkness were all consuming and it took a few moments before her eyes and ears started to adjust. "I need to be with you."

Butcher tried to move but his leg screamed out in pain. "What are you doing?"

Crossing to the other side of the bed, Rhonda stood silhouetted against the curtained window. Slowly, silhouetted, she started to take off her clothes, her shirt and then her pants.

Butcher's heart was beating incredibly hard, but there was nothing he could do. "Of all the times to be incapacitated." Rhonda, now down to her underwear, giggled nervously and pulled back the covers to slide in opposite him. The bed was firm and comfortable. Moving in as close as possible without nudging his leg, she reached out to touch his face. She stroked his hair and cheeks. Sighing, Butcher closed his eyes and enjoyed the feel of her hand on his skin, and even though his brain was caught like a scratching record on the last seconds of her undressing, he appreciated beyond belief that she was here with him tonight. It felt like home.

"I just wanted you to know, Leo, that I'm falling in love with you too."

He smiled. "Better hurry and catch up to me, because I finished falling earlier today."

Ten minutes later, Rhonda's hand on his left bicep, they fell asleep.

Butcher woke with a start. Something wasn't right. He could sense it. All of his sensory receptors were sending alarm bells into his head. Even though it was not the same as the night his house went up in flames, there was a malevolent spirit in the room.

He couldn't move but his eyes caught on the sinister shadow, a similar silhouette standing in front of the window. Adrenaline coursed through his body. At first, he thought it a demon, or some spiritual dark force, which had manifested in his bedroom.

"Who are you?" He whispered.

The figure moved forward. He could see the hair of a woman standing at odd ends from her head.

"Why did you stay?" The voice seemed to come from the pit of hell. "You are ruining her life."

Butcher recognized the voice.

Connie Redman.

Realization flooded over him. Because of his current state of immobility, he desperately desired to stand and throw the woman out of George's house, but he couldn't. And as he lay in the bed next to his sleeping girlfriend, his thoughts went quickly to protecting Rhonda.

"It was you. You were the one who wrote the notes. You were the one who burned down my house."

Connie cackled, the sound of her lunacy mixed with anger and resentment, rage and disappointment. Even though Butcher could not see her, he could read from her body language that she was bent to the point of snapping.

"I was merely helping you understand that your presence in Amicable is not needed. Rhonda and I get along just fine without you."

At her name, Rhonda stirred.

"Are you okay?" Rhonda whispered still unaware that her mother was in the room.

"Yes," Butcher said flatly.

"What's wrong?"

Then, Connie sucked a deep breath in and with a malice unheard of in Amicable ever, she screamed out the word that only she'd been writing.

"WHORE!"

Rhonda, startled and then mortified, rolled over quickly to turn on the bedside lamp. As the light flooded the room, both Rhonda and Butcher squinted towards the window where they were frightened to see Connie, hands hanging limply at her sides, completely naked. Not a stitch of clothing. Her skin, milky white because of her lack of exposure to the sun, stood in stark contrast to her hair. Her breasts, losing the battle to both gravity and motherhood, sagged to her stomach. As Butcher beheld Rhonda's mother standing there in eerie stillness, his thoughts flashed back to his own mother on her last night on earth. Butcher gasped. Could this happen again?

"Mom?" Rhonda began to weep again, sobbing, embarrassed and insulted, sucked back into the vortex of shame. Rhonda was paralyzed.

"After you got back from the big city," she spit the words out as if they were rancid pieces of meat, "I knew that you would need looking after, but I never got over my embarrassment that my daughter was a prostitute sleeping with every guy who comes crawling around like tomcats." Connie was sneering at her daughter, but she still remained motionless. Unabashedly, she seemed to have no shame standing in front of them naked.

"For a while you were a good girl, but as always, boys come round, sniffing and feeling, touching and tasting. Your nectar is just too good, I guess."

Butcher stared up at Connie and attempted to speak. This woman, so consumed by suffering, stood naked not just physically, but emotionally; he could read it all - everything. In that moment, Butcher felt nothing but pity. Connie Redman had suffered at the hands of men her whole life and when her own daughter fell into the trap, she lost her mind. Her maternal instinct wanted to protect Rhonda, but her instinct was to punish her daughter for her own imagined sins. She was naked not to shock them, but because she had to punish them.

"Mom," Rhonda said, "You don't have to do this! We can talk about this. He can help."

Connie's eyes turned on her daughter, a frightening mix of hatred and adoration. "He can't help anything. He's destroyed it all."

Crying, Rhonda turned away from her mother again curling up into an identical posture that she had in the yard yesterday afternoon.

"What are you going to do?" Butcher asked.

For the first time, Connie moved and started to walk around to Butcher's side of the bed. Almost comatose with shock and grief, Rhonda, incapacitated by her fear, could only listen. Similarly, Butcher could not follow her movements and as he felt Connie's naked presence behind him, his body began to seize in preparation for something untoward.

Connie leaned slowly over his form and he could feel her breath on his ear. "I want you to feel what I feel every day of my life since my innocence was taken away from me - and hers." Her voice was like the sound of fingernails on slate, scratching and cutting his soul.

Reaching out, Connie put her hand on Butcher's leg and began to push. The pain was intense and Butcher began to moan. He looked over at Rhonda who was covering her ears shutting out the nightmare that was occurring in reality in real time. Harder and harder she pushed. Butcher had no other recourse but to shout out in pain.

"Can you feel my pain now, Butcher?"

At that moment, the door opened and George walked in. "Connie?"

At the sound of her name, Connie straightened up and faced the old man. She made no move to cover herself and George instinctively took a step back.

"What are you doing?"

"I came to visit the whore and her boyfriend. In bed, just as I would have expected." She turned her head back to Butcher. "How much are you paying her?"

Butcher couldn't answer. His pain was too great.

Without thinking, George Hendriks moved towards Connie with his arms extended.

"What are you doing, old man?"

George kept coming and Connie did not defend herself. Although George was inches shorter than Connie, his force seemed bigger. She cringed, waiting for a blow, but it didn't come. Instead, the old man wrapped his arms around the naked woman and hugged her. "It's okay, Connie. It's okay. We'll be all right."

Connie, standing stiffly, felt a stirring of something she hadn't felt for a while. Something foreign.

Hope.

George's embrace was a symbol of forgiveness. As he held her, she did something she hadn't done in years.

Connie Redman began to cry.

George held her through the storm of her grief, the lost years of hopelessness and the difficulty of living life as an outsider. She sobbed into his arms still unable to hug him back. And yet, she allowed herself to be enfolded in the graceful gesture of a caring man who happened to be her geriatric neighbor. Great spasms of sorrow made her jerk as if she was convulsing, but George found a deep reservoir of strength inside his soul. Butcher overcoming his pain, was painfully aware that George Hendriks had, for at least the second time in his life, swooped in and heroically saved the day: the first during World War II, the second in his own house seventy years later.

Spent, Connie allowed herself to be led from the bedroom where George sat her on the living room sofa and wrapped her in a blanket. Then, at three o'clock on that Monday morning, he made a hot jug of water for some tea.

At the same time, Butcher did the only thing he could think of.

"Rhonda," he called out softly. "It's over. It's over. I love you."

After a moment, the waitress moved closer to the butcher.

394

Epilogue

Dearest Reader,

No story really ends happily ever after, although some get surprisingly close. If you don't care to know about what happened to some of the Amicableans, please feel free to take your finger out of this book, or turn off your e-reader or whatever, but I always think it's best to tidy up the place before you leave it.

Leopold and Rhonda were married almost one year to the day after they met. George Hendriks was the best man at the wedding as well as the stand-in father-of-the-bride. The wedding was held in the St. Clements Methodist Church of Amicable, Reverend John Thomas Deakins presiding. One year after their marriage, Rhonda and Butcher, with fear and trepidation, traveled to Wisconsin where they found a lonely tombstone marking the grave of a man who died tragically. Rhonda was inconsolable, but they continue to seek a way to honor a life that was ruined.

Two weeks after the episode at George's house, Officer Louise Nelson, with hat in hand, knocked on the door of the Redman house. Almost apologetically, she said that they had substantial evidence regarding the arson on Peppertree Lane. Louise asked if Connie had an alibi for the night in question, which George, Leo and Rhonda provided with a wink and a hug. The case went 'unsolved' and the insurance company reimbursed Liam Wilson three years later. After her new lease on life, Connie was often seen walking outside with some of her new friends - a trio of young high school boys who called their group 'the Deputies.' She became their second mother.

They even took her bowling.

Eventually, Rodrigo Hermanoso left The Traveler's Choice to purchase the land outside of Amicable to build his hacienda-like restaurant. With a sizeable loan from George Hendriks, Nuestro Casa is a thriving business for Amicable. Hiring only employees from the Amicable high school, Nuestro Casa soon became the most popular eating establishment in the county, even overshadowing The Creek Restaurant.

Peterson Butchery is still a thriving business, but Butcher no longer works there. He went to the local community college in Clancy to get a degree in counselling (as if he really needed the piece of paper). He bought the building next door to Peterson Butchery and has a thriving practice for people who want to talk. Butcher's office is called 'The Chop Shop.'

John and I married not long after Butcher and Rhonda. We remain fast friends.

So ends our tale.

Small towns are endless sources of fascination when people move beyond stereotypes. They are filled with magic and wonder, sound and lights even if the lights are not quite as bright and the sounds not quite as loud as those of the big city. Every once in a while, if you were to walk the twilight course of late summer in Amicable, you might feel the power and majesty of the small town and be drawn to its beauty. You simply need to sit on the front porch with a beer, a companion and delight to watch fireflies dance.

Find your small town.

Sincerely,

Leslie Deakins

Butcher sat back with his hands behind his head and his long legs stretched out in front. Sitting across from him was Raymond Balvance, a farmhand for one of the large agricultural corporations which owned much of the land around Amicable. Raymond had booked his appointment weeks before and Butcher had taken him on as a new client, not just because it was good business, but Raymond was actually a really nice guy. Although it was almost closing time and Butcher had heard more than his share of confessions, he attentively listened to Raymond's tales of woe even though most of them were self-induced by a chronic condition which Butcher called 'Apathetic Procrastination.' Butcher was well aware that his counselling degree did not allow him the ability to diagnose, but no one in Amicable came to The Chop Shop for diagnostics; most came to talk to Butcher and more than most asked for him to give them an idea of 'what might be coming around the corner.'

Stifling a yawn, Butcher leaned forward in his chair to give Raymond a hint that his time was just about up.

"As I was saying, Butcher, I really feel like I could do some good on the farm if…"

The intercom buzzed. "Butcher," Hossein's resonant voice projected oddly through the system, "There are two people who want now see you."

Butcher frowned. In the last three years, Amicable had become a place of refuge for many migrants from the Middle East including Hossein, his receptionist. As the war and strife increased in Syria, John Deakins had pressed the community to open houses for the refugees to stay. With that incredible act of hospitality, the town had been transformed.

"Whoever it is, let them know that I'm with someone. Tell them…"

The door opened and two heads poked around the corner, one on top of the other. Derek and Nash, now twenty-four years of age, had not lost any of their youthful exuberance, nor had they shed any of their mannerisms which could be somewhat… distracting.

"Psst, Butcher," Derek said, his face smiling above his brother's as they peered around the doorjamb.

"Derek," Butcher responded with frustration. "How many times have I told you that I can't have you interrupting me while…"

"Oh, Butcher, stop being such a stick in the mud. We've got something to show you." Nash's grinning face below his brother's seemed Cheshire-like.

Hossein stood in the open door. "I so sorry, Butcher. I try to keep them out, but they push by and then open door." Hossein's face, a bright shade of crimson, looked down at the twins who were still positioned in the doorway.

"It's all right, Hossein, it's not your fault. These two… young men have always had a streak of obstinance in them."

"I do not know the word… 'ostibance?'" Hossein's face screwed into a ball.

"It means," Derek said as he turned his face to the dark Syrian man above him, "that we have a tendency to do whatever we want, whenever we want." His voice dropped to a whisper. "We're a couple of dipsticks."

"That does not help me." Hossein looked back at his boss who was holding up his hands.

"I'll take care of this, Hossein. Thank you." Butcher's gaze turned back to the twins. "Look, this is highly inappropriate. You need to go."

"But Butcher," Derek whined and pulled himself under Hossein's arm to enter the room. "We have to show you something."

"What is it?"

Derek looked at Nash and grinned broadly. "It's our act for the community talent show."

Nash nodded. "It's going to be great."

Raymond smiled. "It's not a problem for me," he said and then looked at the twins. "Can I watch too?"

"Yes!" Derek slapped Nash's hand and then held his palm up for a high five from Hossein who was not inclined to rejoice with him. "Come on! The more the merrier!"

Butcher leaned over and clasped his hands almost in a posture of prayer. Gradually he grunted and pulled himself from the chair.

Minutes later, Butcher, Raymond, and a few other town members were drawn into Peterson's Butchery where the front had been transformed into a stage. Derek came out with tight black pants and a black shirt opened at the collar to his breastbone. For some reason, Derek had taped some hair (who knows where it had come from; it might have been cowhide for all anyone knew) onto his chest and combed his hair in such a way that it looked as if it had been intentionally fluffed in the wind. Derek's excited smile seemed to bring mirth to everyone in attendance.

Suddenly, the music began to play.

Butcher, unconsciously looked back and forth from the speaker to Derek's face, and he recognized the first line of the song. *Oh heavens, no!*

The song, from the movie Dirty Dancing, began. Nash came out from the back with a side of pork wrapped in a white dress. Nash, obviously, was playing the part of Baby, while Derek's Johnny, was motioning with his finger for the side of pig to come dancing with him.

The Peterson twins parodied the dance scene so closely, that soon, Butcher was doubled over in laughter. Derek and Nash, straight-faced, had the time of their lives, and when the big moment came, as the music sped up, the entire audience in Peterson's Butchery began clapping as Nash, with his side of pork, ran towards Derek so that 'Baby' could be lifted over his head. The entourage cheered loudly.

Just then, the door opened behind them.

It was Derek and Nash's father.

"What the...?"

Derek's focus wavered and he lost control of the meat where it landed on his chest and caused him to crash to the floor.

Nash looked over at his dad laughing uproariously and Derek giggled. "Hi, Dad!" They exclaimed.

"You two pieces of butt fuzz better get this cleaned up before I get back to work on Monday," Mr. Peterson shook his head as he walked back out the door.

Butcher grinned.

What a nice place to live.